AF531394

Flowers of Wisdom

FLOWERS OF WISDOM

Dr. P.C. Babu

M.B., B.S., D.A. (England), M.D.
Srinivasa Rao Thota
Guntur-522 004
Andhra Pradesh
(India)

Editor

Dr. Digumarti Bhaskara Rao

M.Sc., M.A., M.A., M.Ed., Ph.D.,
Secretary
Academy of Communication Culture
Education Science and Service
Guntur-522 006
Andhra Pradesh

2003

DISCOVERY PUBLISHING HOUSE

NEW DELHI-110002

First Published-2003

ISBN 81-7141-695-0

Published by

DISCOVERY PUBLISHING HOUSE
4831/24, Ansari Road, Prahlad Street,
Darya Ganj, New Delhi- 110002 (India)
Phone: 23279245 • Fax: 91-11-23253475
E-mail:dphtemp@ indiatimes.com

Printed at: Tarun Offset Printers.

Foreword

Wisdom is flowering from every nook and corner of the world and it is guiding the human race in progressing ahead with all successes.

The wisdom of Nagarjuna, Aarya, Confucius, Lao Tzu, Muhammad, Laotse, Zoroaster, Talmud, Solomon, Buddha, Basavanna, Guru Nanak, Thiru Kural, Sankaracharya, Sarvajna, Kabir, Vemana, Asia, Jainism, Mahabharata, etc., are explained in detail in this book.

This book on the wisdom of the whole world will make the mankind memorable.

Dr. Digumarti Bhaskara Rao

CONTENTS

Foreword

1. Suhrullekha-Aacharya Nagarjuna 1
2. Aarya - Sundara Pandya 2
3. Wisdom of Confucius 7
4. Wisdom of Lao Tzu 12
5. Wisdom of Asia 16
6. Prophet Muhammad and His Teachings (A.D. 570 – 633) 23
7. Wisdom of Laotse 33
8. Zen Interpretation of Laotsu 47
9. Zoroaster and the Good Religion 55
10. The Talmud and the Voice of Wisdom 63
11. Wisdom of Solomon 75
12. Words to Live By I 80
13. Jainism (Mahaveera, 599–527 B.C.) 86
14. Dharmapadam—Gowtama Buddha 95
15. The Spiritual Quest 107
16. Guru Nanak and His Message 121
17. Vachanas of Basavanna 128
18. Thirukural—Thiruvalluvar 145
19. Sri Sankaracharya and His Message 207
20. Yaksha Prasna 228
21. Sarvajna and His Message 243
22. Amaravāni 260
23. Kabir and his Message 294
24. Selected Proverbs from Nine Religions 310
25. Morals from Mahabharata 322
26. Yogi Vemana and his Message 366
27. Chāru Charya (Exemplary Conduct) 444

1

SUHRULLEKHA-AACHARYA NAGARJUNA

Suhrullekha literally means that it is a letter from a friend. Aacharya Nagarjuna wrote it to SATAKARNI (SATAVAHANA KING), explaining the teachings of GOUTAMA BHUDDHA.

1. *Eat moderately*: Eat to sustain health only. *Do not eat with relish or with distaste.* Do not eat to increase your strength, stamina or beauty. Treat food with the same care and caution, that you bestow on a health giving medicine.
2. *More wealth you gather, more cares and more worries for you. The only wayout is to reduce your desires (TRUSHNA).*
3. If you entertain thoughts such as "They scolded me they insulted me they stole my wealth, and they defeated me, such hostile thoughts will lead you to further quarrels and to enmity and finally rob your peace of mind.
   Do not entertain such hostile thoughts.
4. *Do not perform evil deeds even for the sake of* 1. *Wife* 2. *Children* 3. *Parents* 4. Guests 5. Servants 6. Beggars 7. Brahmanas and 8. Devatas.
   None of them will share the SIN (PAPAPHALAM) that accrues from evil deeds, though they may enjoy its benefit.
5. Human body ultimately disintegrates and its constituents disperse. By this knowledge *DEHASAKTI* (undue interest and attachment to ones body) is dispelled.
6. *None can bestow MOKSHA (LIBERATION) on you*: You have to get it by your own 1. *ADHYAYANA (STUDY)* 2. *DHYANA* (CONCENTRATION) and 3. *DHARMAVARTANA* (MORALITY).

Source

1. Telugu translation of Dr. Vavila Subba Rao, 1991, Amaravathi.

2

AARYA - SUNDARA PANDYA

Aarya was written in SANSKRIT by SUNDARA PANDYA prior to *7th century* in AARYA CHANDASSU.

1. As a man who seeks distinction and respectability wears precious diamonds, a Sajjana should cherish SUBHASITARATNAS (MORALS AND MAXIMS) in his heart.
2. A PANDITA should not criticize others openly in a public meeting and should avoid revealing of unpleasant facts.
3. A Pandita should avoid contradicting the following persons as far as possible. They are 1. A king 2. a rich man 3. a man of TAPAS 3. a learned men 4. *a crowd* 5. inbeciles 6. enemies 7. Gurus and 8. ones parents
4. A Pandita should avoid harsh speech.
5. If you want others to talk pleasantly with you, you must talk pleasantly with them first.
6. An intelligent man talks precisely and concisely. A fool talks and talks many meaningless words.
7. The words of a Pandita can be likened to a beautiful woman. Her clothes are made up of beautiful and meaningful words and TRUTH is her main ornament (SATYĀBHARANĀ).
8. The words uttered by a DURJANA (Evil person) can be compared to a poisonous snake. A SAJJANA bitten by such a snake can be cured only by a powerful medicine termed '*PATIENCE*'.
9. Anger can be compared to a fire. This fire arises from insults one met with in the past. The flames of this fire are boosted by foul speech. Sajjanas quench this fire with plenty of cold water termed '*JNANA*'.
10. Pleasant speech is preferred even to 1. Moonlight 2. cool shade 3. Water and 4. Sandalwood paste.
11. Harsh speech inflicts more pain than a 1. weapon 2. fire 3. poison 4. terrible disease and 5. an enemy.
12. Sajjana's words are more pleasant and cooler than moonlight and sandal paste.

13. Durjanas words are more unpleasant than, hot sun rays and the heat of a fire.
14. The friendship of a sajjana gradually increases in course of time, where as the friendship of a Durjana gradually decreases in course of time.
    The stalk of a cane sugar when eaten from the tip to the bottom tastes sweeter and sweeter. And when eaten from the bottom to the tip, its sweetish taste gradually decreases.
15. When one has to deal with imbeciles who will never listen to reason, it is better to pretend ignorance.
16. It is better not to have any type of contact with an imbecile.
17. The DHANA of a Durjana is of no use to Sajjanas. The fruits of a tree in the midst of a forest are eaten by insects and birds only.
18. The wealth guarded and hoarded by a miser will ultimately be spent by others, just like a girl who grows in the house, to be ultimately taken as a bride in to another house.
19. The Dhana of a man is of no use if he does not give Dana to the needy.
20. A man's life is useful, if he is the source of livelihood for many.
21. A Sajjana gives a DANA, respectfully, and secretly to the needy.
    A Durjana gives a DANA, rather reluctantly and with a lot of publicity, to the needy and that too with an ulterior purpose.
22. A man without DHANA, even if he has character, purity composure, kindness, gentleness and a noble lineage, is not respected.
23. A man without DHANA even if he has self-respect, pride knowledge, valour and extraordinary intelligence is not valued.
24. The words of a poor man even when they are appropriate and authoritative are not heeded.
    The words of a rich man even when they are indistinct and meaningless are listened to with respect.
25. PALARSA flower (MODUGA FLOWER) is very beautiful to look at but it has no scent. Similarly if a man has no good qualities, even though, he is of noble lineage, handsome, well dressed and a gifted orator, *he has no value.*
26. An elephant bathes in the river for many hours, yet as soon as it comes out of the river, it squirts dust and rubbish all over its body. By this act, hours of bathing is made futile. *It has given rise to the idiom 'GAJASNANA'.*
    Similarly a man who has no character, even if he has 1. VIDYA 2. SASTRABHYA-SAM 3. TAPAS 4. Wealth 5. FAME and 6. INFLUENCE, is considered to be futile.
27. A man of character needs no further decorations such as garland, perfumes etc.
28. A man of noble lineage must strive his best to maintain the noble traditions of this family. *For the sake of DHANA one should not sacrifice character.*
29. A BRAHMANA who has 1. Pride (Durabhimanam) 2. Ostentation (Dhambikam) 3. Paradroha Chinta 4. Slandering (Pisunaha) and 5. Vikatandanaha (Boasting) is to be considered as a NEECHA= (SVAPAAKA EVA = one who eats dog's flesh).
    Hence a BRAHMANA should strive to eradicate such evil traits from his character.

30. SAJJANAS Cherish SATYA (TRUTH) and ARJAVAM (Straight forward behaviour) in their hearts, and they sincerely believe that others also cherish the same traits. *They take the credibility of others for granted.*
31. A Duratma (EVIL PERSON) first approaches as a dear relative, then he changes in to a friend and finally he becomes an enemy.
32. A Neecha (Inferior person), as long as he has work with you, behaves as a SAJJANA (SUPERIOR PERSON). *As soon as his work is over, he changes in to an enemy.*
33. When one starts observing superficial formalities with a friend, it is a sign of beginning of the end of that relationship.
34. A Sajjana tolerates a hundred faults of a friend for the sake of one good act.
    A Durjana forgets a hundred good acts of a friend if by chance he does one fault.
35. The characteristic traits of a true friend are
    1. Similarity of preferences and tastes
    2. Straightforward behaviour
    3. Absence of cunning and hatred in his heart
    4. Generosity
    5. Steadfastness and
    6. He is Energetic and skilled.
36. One who has kept his senses (INDRIYAS) under control will enjoy peace and happiness here and hereafter.
37. A Sajjana's heart is full of patience
    A Durjanas heart is full of hatred.
38. An enmity and hatred of a Sajjana are temporary, like a writing on water.
    An enmity and hatred of a Durjana are permanent like (words) scratches made on stone.
39. If anybody criticizes you for a fault, and if it happens to be true, bear it patiently.
    If the criticism is not founded on truth, then also bear it patiently, as you are free from the fault attributed to you.
40. A Durjana gets a lot of pleasure in tormenting others. A Sajjana regrets any torment caused by his harshspeech.
41. *A superior person does his WORK (Karma) properly and he does not waste time in words,*
    A second rate person talks and does his work.
    An inferior person talks, talks and does not perform his work.
    A *Jack fruit tree* yields its fruits even without any flower.
    A *Mango tree* comes out in flowers first and then yields fruits.
    A *PAATALA Tree* displays plenty of flowers and it does not yield any fruits.
    The three types of men above mentioned can be compared to the above three types of trees respectively.
42. The following undesirable qualities are to be eschewed (avoided).
    1. Laziness 2. Fickleminded behaviour (Lowlyam) 3. Greed (Lobhaha) 4. Slander (Paraninda) 5. Anger and 6. Conceit (Atimānascha).

43. *One may, be very learned yet he may be ignorant about ordinary matters*
One may be very rich yet he may be a LOBHI (MISER)
One may be of a noble lineage, yet he may be poor
One may possess many good qualities, yet he may be an illiterate
The ways of Almighty are inscrutable (myterious)
44. *Fruits of wisdom are*
    1. when faced with a calamity, a wise man does not loose his composure
    2. when fortune smiles on him, a wise man does not loose his equanimity
45. It is better to acquire learning (VIDYA) than to strive for DHANA
Anybody can acquire DHANA, where as learning (VIDYA) is acquired with great effort only.
46. A man who has acquired DHANA, if he does not use it wisely, will be the loser in the long run. He will have to face, many troubles in earning it, and saving it, and finally he has to bear sorrow, when it disappears.
47. One who is committed to SATYA (TRUTH) and who is a GUNAVAKTA (Rutuvakta) (who speaks about good qualities) and a Hitavakta (who has your welfare at heart), is rare indeed.
48. One should be wary of an evil person even when he has received many benefits from you as his inherent evil nature does not change. A neem tree even when it is bathed in pure milk does not forgo its bitter taste.
49. Dhana (even when it is little) of a Sajjana is of benefit to all around him Dhana (even when it is of large amount) of a Durjana is of no benefit to all around him. Fresh water even from a small tank is preferred to brackish water of the sea.
50. A Sajjana only can recognise the good qualities of another, where as a Durjana fails to recognise the good qualities of another, even when is close by. A butterfly from a far away forest goes in search of a lotus in a distant pond, where as a frog living in the same pond, pays no attention to the lotus.
51. A benefit conferred on a Sajjana yields better results, where as a benefit conferred on a Durjana yields only evil.
A cow feeds on grass and yields milk.
A cobra drinks milk/and yields poison only.

ANUBANDHAHA

1. One who has the following qualities is called on ARYA
    1. He is free from deception (ASATHA HRUDAYAHA)
    2. He is grateful (KRUTAJANA HA)
    3. He has a merciful heart (SĀNU KRŌSAHA)
    4. He always walks in the path of Sajjanas
    5. He avoids finding faults in others
    6. *Any task he does is bound to be flawless* (SUCHIKARMARATAHA)
2. One should strive to achieve his task, undeterred by the likes and dislikes of the

people around him.

3. One is able to recognise the defects of others yet he fails to recognise his own faults. Eye is able to see the spots on the distant moon, yet it can not notice any ulcer on itself.
4. Even a precious thing is not valued if it is easily available. (KoopaSnanam) People in PRAYAGA prefer to bathe in well waters than in PRAYAGA waters (HOLY WATERS OF GANGA YAMUNA SANGAM).
5. One should never move out of his proper place. If one moves out of his place, his own friends will change to enemies.
   A lotus flower in water blooms in full sunshine, but it wilts down under the sunshine if it is out of water.
6. To acquire power is difficult and even when acquired, it wont stay for long in ones hands. Hence it should be used to benefit friends and relatives and to suppress enemies.
7. Thunder clouds of SARATKALA (SEASON) make lot of noise, but there is no rain where as clouds of rainy reason are silent yet they yield is plenty of rain
   Similarly a Neecha (an inferior person) talks and talks, but does not deliver the goods where as a SAJJANA (a superior person) does his work and keeps quite.
8. *One who is skilled in his work acquires wealth*
   One who is moderate in his diet has health
   One who has health has happiness
   One who studies earnestly acquires VIDYA
   VIDYA makes a man humble (VIDYĀM VINEETAHA)
   VIDYA paves the way for DHARMA, ARTHA and YASAS (Name and fame)

Sources

1. Telugu translation of Aarya by Sri Rallapalli Anantha Krishna Sarma, 1970.
2. *Telugu translation of Aarya* by Dr. Pullela Sreeramachandrulu, 1981.

3

WISDOM OF CONFUCIUS

CONFUCIUS (B. C. 551–479) is the greatest name in Chinese Philosophy. He was a great teacher but not a systematic thinker.

CONFUCIOUS, the man as people saw him.

"At fifteen I set my heart on learning. At thirty I knew where I stood. At forty I had no more doubts. At fifty I understood the decrees of Heaven. At sixty my ear was obedient to their call. At seventy I followed my hearts desire, for I did not overstep the boundaries of the right".

"The possession of high station without generosity the conduct of ritual without reverence, the discharge of mourning duties without grief, these are things I can not bear to see."

The Master's way is simply this, to be undeviating in his *reciprocity.*

"For a man to live he must be upright. If he is not upright and keeps alive, it is a stroke of luck in escaping death".

"I am *transmitter* and not a *creator.* I believe in and have a passion for the ancients....

In silence I get to know...

I keep on learning without being satiated

I go on teaching without being wearied what more is there to be said of me?...

"A biased mind, arbitrary judgements, obstinancy and self centredness" are the qualities one should eradicate"...

Tzu Lu asked the Master about *DEATH*

The MASTER replied "If you do not understand life, how can you understand death?

CONFUCIOUS AND THE INDIVIDUAL

"Rotten wood is no good for carving"...

"In the beginning I used to listen to what people said and trust them to act. *Now I both listen to what people say and observe what they do*"

"I have never seen anyone, who could see his own faults"...

"you can not rob the humblest man of his aims"

The Master said "*A wiseman does not get perplexed,* and a *courageous man does not get frightened*".

The master said "At birth all men are nearly alike but as they grow, they differ in their habits"

"It is only the wisest and the stupidest who do not change"

ON HUMAN HEARTEDNESS

"It is only the human hearted man, who is capable of really liking men and really disliking them"

"One who wants security for himself, makes others secure. One who wants to extend his sphere of influence, tries first to extend the sphere of influence of others."

"In public behave as you would in the presence of an honoured guest"

"The treatment you would not have for yourself do not hand out to other people and thus avoid resentment"

"To be cautious in what one says is difficult hence be cautious in your speech"

ON WEALTH AND HIGH STATION

"Wealth and high station are what all men would like to have but if they can not be obtained in conformity with principle (TAO), they must not be held. Poverty and low station, these are what men dislike, but if they can not be avoided without contravention of principle, they must be accepted."

"If the man of breeding be light minded, people will not look up to him, and what he learns will not stay by him. *The first thing is loyalty and keeping his word.* He will have no friends who do not come up to his standard and if he does wrong he will not shirk mending his ways."

The Master said: "A sage neither anticipates deceit nor suspects bad faith in others, *yet is prompt to detect them when they appear."*

ON GOOD AND EVIL

Someone asked: "*How do you regard the principle of returning good for evil?*

Master said "What then is to be the return for good? Rather should you *return justice for injutice and good for good."*

"A man of honour is not a mere tool"

"Amongst men of honour, there is nothing to cause selfish rivalry"

"A man of breeding sets his heart on spiritual power in himself; the man of no breeding sets his heart on land"

"The desire of a man of honour is to be slow in speech, and quick in action"

"Moral power does not exist alone. It is sure to have neighbours"

"Be trustworthy in every respect, be devoted to the acquisition of learning, *be steadfast for the good unto death. Do not enter any dangerous or risky areas.* Do not live in a place, where the people are in rebellion. If the way prevails among the states you can make yourself prominent, but if does not prevail, then keep in retirement"

"A man of honour has no self pity and no fears. When he examines his heart and finds no taint, what cause has he for self pity or for fear"?

"Men of true breeding are in harmony with people although they do not agree with them; but men of no breeding agree with people and yet are not in harmony with them"

"A man of true breeding is easy to serve, but hard to please; for if you try to please him by any other means than the way, he is not pleased".

"A man of no breeding is hard to serve, but easy to please; for you can please him by other means than the way. But when it is a matter of setting men tasks, he expects them to be ready for anything."

"Men of true breeding have dignity, but are not arrogant men of no breeding are arrogant, but have no dignity"

"Men of true breeding are ashamed for their words to go beyond their deeds"

"Men of true breeding bring their personality in to flower with a view to reverent action, and to bring peace to every family and clan"

"Men of true breeding can endure penury; men without breeding in such circumstances are immediately swept off their feet".

"The man of honour who uses the right as his raw material and ritual as the means for putting it in to effect, who modestly sets to work on what is right and faithfully carries it to completion, what a sense of honour he has!

"The man of honour makes demands on himself; the man without a sense of honour makes demands on others"

"Men of honour hate those who proclaim abroad other mens' evil. They hate those vulgar fellows who slander those, above them. They hate those who are bold in action, but have no idea of good form. They hate those who are presumptuous and obstructive.

Confucius on the Relationship Between Governor and Governed

"The confidence of the people, adequate stores of munitions and adequate supplies of food are necessary in governing a state"

"And if you unavoidably had to dispense with one of these, which would you forgo "TZU KUNG asked the Master.

'Munitions' said the Master.

"And of the remaining two, if he had to dispense with one, which would you forgo "TZU KUNG asked the Master

The Master replied "Food, for all down history, people died of famine, and yet society survives, *but if the people have no confidence in their rulers, a state can not be governed.*

"Sir! to rule is to straighten things out. If the Ruler should take the lead in straightening things out, who would dare to unstraighten them?

"Let your desires be good and the people will be good. The wind resembles the ruling class, and the grass resembles the working class. When the grass encounters the wind, it always bends"

"When a Ruler is right in himself, things will get done without his giving orders when he

is not right in himself, he may give orders, but they will not be obeyed"

"Do not hanker after quick results, nor seek petty profits If you hanker after quick results, you will not have any great influence."

"If you seek petty profits, the really important things will not get done."

"If you try to lead the people by means of regulations and to order their life by means of punishments, they will try to avoid them, without any conscience whatever. *If however you try to lead them by your own moral power and* order their life by means of rituals, their conscience will act, and *they will follow your lead*"

Confucius 'On Heaven'

"The man who sins against Heaven, has nowhere, where he can pray".

'On the Past'

"I have transmitted and do not create a new. I am faithful to the men of old and love them".

"In the old days men studied the past with a view to their self improvement. Now a days they study with an eye on other people (*i.e.*, to getting a reputation).

On Knowledge

"I am not one who was born with knowledge. I am one who loves the past and earnestly seeks to know it".

"There may be those who act without knowledge. I do not. Hearing much and selecting what is good in what I hear and following this"; seeing much and making note of it; this is the secondary kind of knowledge.

"If a man learns, but does not think, then he is nothing. If he thinks but does not learn, then he is in a dangerous state".

"I tell you what knowledge is; when you know a thing to recognize that you know it; and when you donot know a thing to recognize that you do not know it. That is knowledge".

"The man who reanimates the old, and so gets to know the new is fit to be a teacher".

Five Ethical Judgements

TZU KUNG asked the Master whether there was one word to guide a man in his whole life.

Master replied *'RECIPROCITY'* is the word to guide a man in his whole life. "What you do not wish done to yourself, do not do to others".

"While a man's father is alive, observe the bent of his mind. When his father dies, observe his actions. If during three years of mourning he makes no alterations in his father's way, he may be called a filial son".

"The life of a man consists in his honesty. If he is not honest, it is sheer luck that he keeps alive".

ON RITUAL

"To regard the dead as dead is inhuman and so indefensible. Yet to regard the dead as alive shows a lack of knowledge and so indefensible".

ON GRIEF

On the death of his mother, a man wept with the abandon of a child. Master watched the grief of the man and said "Grief! This indeed is grief. *The difficulty, is to keep on like this. Rituals and traditions exist to moderate wailing and weeping on such occasions*".

ON MOURNING RITES

"*To be reverent is the most important,* the feeling of grief is second to it and emaciation of the body is the least important of all.

Source

Chinese philosophy in classical times. Edited and translated by Dr. E.R. Hughes, 1942.

4

WISDOM OF LAO TZU

The Individualistic Philosophy of the TAO EXPERTS

TAO TE CHING – A text book on man's freedom in his natural environment – LAO TZU, late 4th century B.C.

This book is one of the most famous in China, inspite of its teaching running counter to Confucianist orthodoxy, appealing permanently to something very deep in Chinese hearts.

It is a very composite work containing old fragments embedded in much later contexts. *It is poetry in the fullest sense, mystic poetry at that, for all its common sense.*

TAO

"If the TAO could be comprised in words, it would not be the unchangeable TAO"...

"When he has achieved any success, he does not stay by it,
In this not staying by his success, he is unique. And this is why he is not deprived of it"...

"Let nothing desirable be visible; this will save the peoples minds from moral confusion"...

"Heaven and earth are not human hearted; for them all creatures are but straw dogs.

"It is better to hold fast to the mean (between too much and too little confidence in heaven and earth)"...

"A sage puts himself in the second place and then finds himself in the forefront.
Puts himself out side of things and events, yet survives in them.
Surely it is because he has no personal desires, that he is able to fulfil his desires"...
"The goodness of a house consists in it being on the ground,
The goodness of a man's mind consists in its being profound
The goodness of speech consists in its being reliable
The goodness of companionship consists in human heartedness
The goodness of government consists in bringing good order
The goodness of any business consists in its being efficiently done
The goodness of any movement consists in its being timely
Only in all this there must be no striving
For thus only can nothing go wrong"...

"To set out deliberately to be full to the brim (i.e., satisfy every desire) *is not so good as (to know when) to stop,*
If you are thorough in sharpening a sword, you cannot preserve its edge for long
If you fill your hall with gold and jade, there is no way by which you can guard it
If you are rich and of exalted station, you become proud and thus abandon yourself to Unavoidable ruin.
When everything goes well, put yourself in the background
That is the way Heaven acts."
"Are you able to love the people and rule a state without being known to men?
Are you able to have a right understanding of all creatures and never interfere"?
"Thirty spokes together make one wheel,
And they fit in to nothing at the centre,
Herein lies the usefulness of a carriage
The clay is moulded to make a pot
Herein lies the usefulness of the pot
Doors and windows are provided in the walls of a house
And they fit round nothing
Herein lies the usefulness of the house.
"Thus it is that while it must be taken to be advantageous to have something there
It must also be taken as useful to have nothing there"...
"If you adopt yourself, then you remain part of the whole
For if a thing is forced, it will get straight again
If the ground is low, it will be filled
If you are ruined, then you can start afresh
For if there is little in hand, there is the opportunity for acquiring
Whilst if there is much it leads one astray"...
"*The sage does not display himself*
Thus it is that he is brilliantly displayed
He does not count himself right
Thus it is that his rightness is made manifest
He does not fight his own cause
Thus it is that he is victorious
(He does not fight his own cause
Thus it is that he is victorious)
He does not boast of his achievements
Thus it is that he becomes a leader
He alone does not strive with men
And thus it is that all men are unable to strive with him
If you adapt yourself then you remain part of the whole
Reality in men is being part of the whole and so belonging to it".

"The men who set out to capture all under heaven and make it their own, according to my observation do not succeed...

Some like constructing and others like destroying. That is why the sage has nothing to do with the *excessive,* the *extravagant* or with being *exalted.*"

"But the real success must not be one of force
For the weakness of old age, accompanies the vigour of youth
The explanation is this; *force is not of the TAO*
And what is not of the TAO quickly perishes"...
"only by knowing when it is time to stop, can danger be avoided
TO TAO all under heaven will come
As streams, torrents and rivers flow into the sea".
"To know men is to be wise
To know one's self is to be illumined
To conquer men is to have strength
To conquer one's self is to be stronger still
And to know when you have enough is to be rich
For vigorous action may bring a man what he is determined to have
But to keep ones place is to endure
And to die and not be lost, this is the real blessing of a long life"

"The high exponent of power in personality is without power and this is why he has power in personality

The inferior exponent of power is set on not losing his power and this is why he has no real power in personality

The high exponent taking no action has no ulterior ends
whilst the inferior exponent has ulterior ends to his activity
The high exponent of human heartedness has no ulterior ends to his activity,
This is why the really grown man concentrates *on the core of things* and *not the husk.*
"Not to go out of the house is to know the world of men
Not to look out of the window is to know the ways of heavens
For the further a man travels
The less he knows".
"The firmly rooted can not be torn up
The firmly grasped can not slip out of your hand".
"We have three treasures; so keep hold of them and guard them
The first is *kindness,* the second *thrift* and *the third not presuming to be first* among men
Be kind and thus you can be brave
Be thrifty and thus you can be generous

Do not presume to be first and thus you can become the chief of all the appliances for governing"...

"A really expert advance guard does not intimidate
Really expert fighters do not display any rage
Really expert conquerors are victorious without joining battle
And really expert users of men, put themselves below them
"Only if you do not despise them, will they not despise you

This is why the sage knows himself and does not display himself
Has his self love but does not overvalue himself"
"The way of TAO is not to contend and yet to be able to conquer
Not to declare its will and yet to get a response
Not to summon but have things come spontaneously
To work very slowly with well-laid plans
Heaven's net is vast with wide meshes
yet nothing is lost
"A sage does not hoard
Having used what he has on behalf of other men
"He has the more in himself
Having given that away
He is all the richer
This is the way of Heaven
A profit which involves no loss
This is the way of a sage
His actions involve no quarrelling over what is his and what is other men's..."

5

WISDOM OF ASIA

1. It is fitting then for us not be ashamed to acknowledge truth and to assimilate it from whatever source it comes to us, even if it is brought to us by former generations, and foreign peoples.
   For him who seeks the truth, there is nothing of higher value than truth itself; it never cheapens nor abases him, who searches for it, but ennobles and honours him
   – *AL-KINDI*
2. The law of life requires: sincerity to GOD, severity to self, justice to all people, service to elders, kindness to the young, generosity to the poor, *good counsel to friends, forbearance with enemies, indifference to fools,* and *respect to the learned.*
   – S. ABDULLAH ANSARI
3. The brotherhood of TRUTH is one in all ages: it is the narrow men who create sects
   – THE KORAN
4. **PRECEPTS OF SHINTO**
   1. Do not transgress the will of GODS;
   2. Do not transgress the decrees of the STATE
   3. Do not forget that the world is one great family;
   4. Do not forget the limitations of your own person;
   5. Even though others become angry, do not become angry yourself;
   6. Do not be slothful in your business;
   7. Do not be carried away by foreign teachings;
   – *JAPAN*
5. Heaven arms with pity those whom it would not see destroyed
   – LAO TZU (CHINA)
6. A certain person in your eyes is like a *snake;* the same person in the eyes of some other, *is a picture of breatuy;* because in your mind there is the thought of his infidelity; and in the mind of his friend, there is the thought of his belief
   – *MASNAVI (PERSIA)*
7. **THE PRISONER**
   "I thought I could out do everybody in the world in *wealth* and *power* and I *amassed*"...

"Prisoner, tell me who was it that forged your unbreakable chains?
"It was I "said the prisoner" who forged this chain very carefully. Night and day, I worked at the chain with huge fires and cruel hard strokes. When at last the work was done, and the links were complete and unbreakable I found that I was a prisoner until DEATH"

– RABINDRANATH TAGORE (INDIA)

8. **PUNISHMENT**
Punishment alone governs all created beings, *punishment alone protects them, punishment watches over them, while they sleep; the wise declare punishment to be identical with the law. If punishment is properly inflicted after due consideration, it* makes all people happy; but inflicted without consideration, it destroys everything... *The whole world is kept in order by punishment, for a guiltless man is hard to find;* through fear of punishment, the whole world yields the enjoyment which it owes".

– MANU (INDIA)

9. "To gag the voice of the people is more dangerous than to dam the flow of a river. The wise engineer of the river deepens its basin, and facilitates its flow. *The wise ruler encourages men to speak out freely*

– MENCIUS (CHINA)

10. "The one is a man, a perfect man is three – himself, his wife and his son

– MANU (INDIA)

11. "A mother exceedeth a thousand fathers in the right to reverence"

– MANU (INDIA)

12. *Incription on a statue in the ancestral temple of LO*
"The ancients were guarded in their speech and like them we should avoid loquacity.
Many words invite many defeats.
Avoid also engaging in many businesses, for many businesses create many difficulties"

(CHINA)

13. *Equality in Friendship*
"In friendship there should be no pretension to superiority because of age or rank, or the position of one's relatives such as brothers. Friendship with a person is friendship with him for his virtue; there can not be any pretension to superiority

– MENCIUS (CHINA)

14. *"Children, if a man of weight associate with a worthless person he also will become base"*
"How is that Sir?
"If a heavy stone pillar is tied to a light raft, it will itself become light and float on the water. Know that it is so"
"Children, if one has acquired wealth, lay it up, neither enjoying it himself nor bestowing it on others, strangers will take possession of it"
"How is that Sir?"
"Hunters will drive away the bee that hoards honey in its nest without eating it or

giving it to others and appropriate the honey. Know that it is so"

– *PALA–POTHAM (INDIA)*

15. **NATURE OF MAN**

"What are the feelings of men? They are joy, anger sadness, fear, love, disliking and liking. These seven feelings belong to men, without their learning them...

Truthfulness in speech and the cultivation of harmony are advantageous to men. Quarrels, plunderings and murders are things disastrous to men.

Meat, drink and *sexual pleasure* are greatly desired by men, where as suffering, poverty, exile and death are greatly disliked by men"

– *SHIH CHING (CHINA)*

16. **HONOUR THY FOOD**

"Honour thy food, receive it thankfully eat it contentedly and joyfully, never hold it in contempt; avoid excess for gluttony is hateful, injures health and may lead to death"

– *MANU (INDIA)*

17. ON SANE LIVING

Do not let a day slip by without enjoyment...

Do not allow yourself to be tormented by the stupidity of others... *The world has never been free from fools.*

– *KAIBARA EKKEN (JAPAN)*

18. **THE EYE**

"No part of the body is more excellent than the eye

If the heart is upright, the eye is bright; if not then it is dull.

Hear what a man has to say and watch his eyes while he speaks – can he conceal his character from you?

– *MENCIUS (CHINA)*

19. **AVVAIAR'S MAXIMS**

Honour thy father and mother
Forget not the favours thou hast received
Seek the society of the good
Live in harmony with others
Remain in thy own place
Speak ill of none
The sweetest bread is that earned by labour
Knowledge is riches
what one learns in youth is engraven on stone
The wise is he, who knows himself
There is no tranquil sleep without a good conscience, nor any virtue without religion

– *AVVAIAR (INDIA)*

20. **UNITY**

Inscription in the HALL OF LIGHT (CHINA)

The union of many threads makes an unbreakable cord

21. **GOOD IN ALL RELIGIONS**

Like the bee gathering honey from different flowers, the wise man accepts the essence of different scriptures and sees only the good in all religions

– *SRIMAD BHAGAVATHAM (INDIA)*

22. **PROVERBS**

1. If you stumble you can pick yourself up; but if you utter an unwise word you will pay for it
2. When feeding animals, beware of their teeth
3. Beware of your daughter who pretends not to have lovers and beware of your mother who pretends to have no debts.
4. Take to yourself a woman whilst your heart is warm
5. All is palatable to him who is hungry; nothing is ugly to him who loves
6. If you wish to learn, realize you know nothing
7. To steal can bring profit; but to be caught will cost more
8. Do not disdain the tortuous road, nor follow only the straight one before you, but rather the one created by your forefathers.

– *CHINA*

23. **PROVERBS**

1. A man loves his own fault
2. A slap of the hand from an enemy will not hurt, but the angry touch even with a flower from a friend will wound
3. *The mother cries 'Daughter, daughter'. The daughter cries 'Husband and husband'*

(1, 2 and 3 Proverbs – *INDIA)*

4. *You can not catch one rabbit, if you chase two at once*

(KOREA)

5. *To judge a young girl, take a look at her mother*

(LAOS)

6. One must listen with one ear and hold the other one in reserve

(LAOS)

7. *Ten mouths relating are not worth seeing with your own eyes*

(LAOS)

8. *Friends for the table are easy to find, but rare are those when danger is near*

(LAOS)

9. The mouth too voluble dispels confidence, the feet too agile can fall from the tree

(LAOS)

10. *If you want to travel fast, keep to the old roads*

(BURMA)

11. *A mountain is climbed by degrees; property acquired by degrees; wisdom learned by degrees*

(BURMA)

12. *The more you know, the better your luck*

(BURMA)

24. **SCIENCE**

Hearsay and mere assertion have no authority in Science. It may be taken as an absolutely rigorous principle that any proposition, which is not supported by proofs, is nothing more than an assertion, which may be true or false. *It is only when a man brings proof of his assertion that we say your proposition is true*

– THE KORAN (ARABIC)

25. **ON THE ART OF HEALING**

"Make a careful diagnosis, discover the true cause of the disease, think out the proper remedy and apply it effectively.

Right treatment consists of four elements, the patient, the doctor, the remedy and the attendent

The man who stops just a little before he feels he has had enough retains the joy of eating; on the other hand, a glutton invites disease.

Much pain is saved if one learns to eat only what has been found to suit one's health, *and to say 'NO' (i.e.: if one exercises self restraint in respect of quality and quantity of food one eats)*

– THE TIRUKURAL (INDIA)

26. **TRAINING OF CHILDREN**

Parents are responsible for looking after their children properly. He may grow up to be an ideal citizen if he is educated well, or *he may grow up to be a harmful person if he is neglected or ill trained.*

A child imitates carefully whatever he watches. Teach him good behaviour, edify him and *keep him away from bad company. He must be accustomed to rough and hard life and not luxury.* He should not be encouraged to be fond of money or material things, as this is the first step toward useless quarrels.

– AL GHAZALI (ARABIC)

27. **TEXT BOOKS**

An excess of books written on a subject is an obstacle in the way of mastering the subject. A DIGEST is a very concise form of a subject or a science. These digests are harmful not only to style but to understanding, for the beginner suddenly finds himself confronted with the most advanced parts of the subject, for which he is mentally unprepared.

– IBN KHALDUN (ARABIC)

28. **TIME**

Never talk with any man or undertake any trifling employment merely to pass the time away; for everyday well spent may become a day of salvation, and the time rightly employed is an "acceptable time"

–JEREMY TAYLOR

29. **CONTENTMENT**

Great is their peace who know their ambitious minds, and have learnt to be contented with the appointments and bounds of Providence; and are not careful to be great, but being great are humble and do good...

– *WILLIAM PENN*

30. **SOLITUDE**

Meditate as much while on this journey, as if you were shut up in a hermitage or a cell; our body is our cell and the soul is the hermit who dwells in it, there to pray and meditate

– *ST. FRANCIS OF ASSISI*

31. **THE PRESENCE OF GOD**

Accustom yourself gradually to let your prayer spread over all your daily activities. *Speak, act, and work quietly as though you were praying,* as indeed you ought to be.

– *FENELON*

32. **THE DUTY OF JOY**

"Rejoice with them that do rejoice". Little thing as this seems, yet it requires true wisdom. For many weep with them that weep, but still do not rejoice with them that rejoice... So great is the tyranny of a grudging spirit

– *ST. CHRYSOSTOM*

33. **PATIENCE WITH SELF**

Bear charitably with self as with another. Know what needs correction with self as well as elsewhere. Strive heartily and vigorously to correct it. Set to work patiently, not exacting more than is practicable under present circumstances, and do not be disheartened, *because perfection is not attainable in a day*

– *FENELON*

34. **WISDOM**

Neither despise nor oppose, what you do not understand

– *WILLIAM PENN*

35. **A REASONABLE FAITH**

Look thoroughly in to everything and see what it really is... *Do what is just and say what is true...*

Heap one good act on another, so close that not a chink is left between

– *MARCUS AURELIUS*

36. **THE WISE PATIENCE**

The man of perfect knowledge should not unsettle the foolish whose knowledge is imperfect

– *BHAGAVAD GITA*

37. **THE PROSPECT OF DEATH IN OLD AGE**

Death becomes a very different and far more real matter, when you contemplate it in solitude and in old age. To give one's self up deliberately with a calm gaze on approaching death is a much greater struggle...

– *FENELON*

38. **THE GREAT ORDER**

Nature says "Depart out of this world, even as you came in to it. The same way you came from death to life, return without passion or amazement from life to death; your *death is but a piece of the world's order...*

– *MONTAIGNE*

39. **THE GATE OF LIFE**

Death is no less essential to us than to live or to be born
In flying death, thou flie it thyself; thy essence is equally parted in to these two, life and death...

– *SIR HENRY VANE*

40. **AT LAST**

For neither will many friends avail me, nor strong helpers bring me succour, nor wise counsellors give a useful answer, nor books of learned men console me, nor all precious substance set me free, nor any secret and pleasant place keep me safe, *if THOU THYSELF stand not by me, help not, strengthen, cheer, teach and keep me*

– *THOMAS A KEMPIS*

Sources

1. BALDOON DHINGRA, 1959.
2. A Little Book of Life and Death by Elizabeth Waterhouse, 1902.

6

PROPHET MUHAMMAD AND HIS TEACHINGS
(A.D. 570 – 633)

1. *Actions will be judged according to intentions*
2. No man is a true beliver unless he desires for his brother that which he desires for himself
3. That which is lawful is clear and that which is unlawful likewise, *but there are certain doubtful things between the two, from which it is well to abstain*
4. Kill not yourself with excess of eating and drinking
5. The nearest to me are the abstinent, whoever they are and wherever they are
6. The adultery of the eye is to look with desire on the wife of another; and the audltery of the tongue is to utter what is forbidden
7. Verily to honour an old man is to show respect to God
8. The best of alms is that which the right hand gives and the left hand knows not of
9. The most excellent of alms is that of a man of small property which he has earned by labour, and from which he gives as much as he is able
10. A man's first charity should be to his own family if poor
11. Fear GOD, in treating dumb animals, and ride them when they are fit to be ridden, and get off them when they are tired
12. Whoever has food for a day and night, it is prohibited for him to beg
13. Do not beg unless absolutely compelled, then only from the virtuous
14. There are two benefits of which the generality of men are losers and of which they do not know the value *health* and *leisure*
15. Every good act is charity
16. Doing justice between two people is charity;
    Assiting a man upon his beast is charity
    and lifting his baggage
    Pure and comforting words are charity
    Answering a questioner with mildness is charity
    Removing thorns, and stones etc. (inconveniences to way farers) is charity

17. your smiling in your brother's face is charity
your exhorting mankind to virtuous deeds is charity
your prohibiting the forbidden is charity
your showing the road to men in the land in which they lose it is charity
your assisting the blind is charity
18. Modesty and chastity are parts of the *FAITH*
19. Do not exceed bounds in praising me, as the Christians do in praising Jesus, the son of Mary by calling him God and the son of God;
I am only the LORD's servant; *then call me the servant of God and his messenger*
20. When the bier of anyone passes by you, whether Jew, Christian or Muslim, rise to thy feet
21. GOD is pure and loves purity and cleanliness.
22. *when anything pricks your conscience, forsake it.*
23. *Riches are not from abundance of wordly goods but from a contented mind*
24. when you see a person who has been given more than you in money and beauty, then look to those who have been given less.
25. The most excellent JIHAD (HOLYWAR) is that for the conquest of self
26. whoever has been given gentleness, has been given a good portion in this world and the next
27. That person is wise and sensible, who subdues his carnal desires and hopes for rewards from GOD; and he is an ignorant man who follows his lustful appetites, and with all this asks GOD's forgiveness.
28. "Do not be angry"
29. Humility and courtesy are acts of piety
30. No father has given his child anything better than good manners.
31. It is not right for a guest to stay so long as to incommode his host
32. *Respect people according to their eminence*
33. It is of my ways that a man shall come out with his guest, to the door of his house
34. Meekness and modesty are two branches of FAITH; and vain talking and embellishing are two branches of hypocrisy
35. *when three persons are together, two of them must not whisper to each other, when others are present, because it would hurt him*
36. of the dead: "you have passed on before us, and we are following you."
37. Do not speak ill of the dead
38. of DEATH: Wish not, nor supplicate for death before its time cometh; for verily when you die, hope is out and the ambition for reward;
39. Death is a bridge that unites friend with friend
40. *Sleep is the brother of DEATH.*
41. Who so has a thing where with to discharge a debt and refuses to do it, it is right to dishonour and punish him
42. *Deliberation in undertakings is pleasing to GOD*
43. A good disposition and deliberation in affairs and a moderation (medium) in all

things are one part of twenty four parts of the qualities of the prophets

44. He is the best of Muslims whose disposition is most liked by his own family
45. Mankind will not go astray after having found the right road, unless from disputation
46. The thing which is lawful but disliked by GOD is divorce
47. "To do unto all men as you would wish to have done unto you and to reject for others what you would reject for yourself."
48. When you speak, speak the truth; perform when you promise; discharge your trust; Commit not fornication; be chaste; have no impure desires; withhold your hands from striking, and from taking that which is unlawful or evil
49. Let him speak what is good or remain silent
50. Let him not injure his neighbours
51. Speak to men according to their mental capacities for if you speak all things to all men, some can not understand you, and so fall in to errors.
52. Verily your deeds will be brought back to you, as if you yourself were the creator of your own punishment
53. Feed the hungry and visit the sick and free the captive, if he be unjustly confined. Assist any person oppressed, whether Muslim or nonmuslim.
54. The six duties of Muslims to each other are
    1. when you meet a muslim, greet him
    2. when he inviteth you to dinner accept
    3. when he asks you for advice, give it to him
    4. when he sneezes and says "Praise be to God", do you say 'May God have mercy upon thee'
    5. when he is sick, visit him
    6. And he dies, follow his bier
55. Commandments are of three kinds;
    one commands an action, the reward of which is clear then do it;
    Another forbids an action which leads astray, abstain from it;
    And in another arise contradictions, resign that to God
56. The world is forbidden to those of the life to come, and the life to come is forbidden to those of this world
57. Do a good deed after every bad deed that it may blot out the latter
58. A true Muslim is thankful to God in prosperity and resigned to his will in adversity
59. That which is lawful is clear and that which is unlawful likewise; but there are certain doubtful things between the two from which it is well to abstain
60. He is true who protects his brethern both present and absent
61. Assist your brother Muslim, whether he be an oppressor or an oppressed
    "But how shall we do it when he is an oppressor?" enquired a companion.
    Muhammad replied *"Assisting an oppressor consists in forbidding and withholding him from oppression."*
62. The proof of a muslim's sincerity is that *he payeth no heed to that which is not his business.*
63. The faithful are those who perform their trust, and fail not in their word, and keep

their pledge

64. No man is a true believer unless he desires for his brother that which he desires for himself
65. It is unworthy of a muslim to injure people's reputations; and it is unworthy to curse anyone; and it is unworthy to abuse anyone; and it is unworthy to talk vainly.
66. It is better to sit alone than in company with the bad and it is better to sit with the good than to sit alone
    And it is better to speak words to a seeker of knowledge than to remain silent; and silence is better than bad words.
67. Guard yourselves from six things; They are
    1. When you speak, speak the truth
    2. Perform when you promise
    3. Discharge your trust
    4. Be chaste in thought and action
    5. Withhold your hand from striking and
    6. From taking that which is unlawful and bad
68. That person is not of us who inveiteth others to aid him in oppression;
    and he is not of us who fights for his tribe in injustice;
    and he is not of us, who dies in assisting his tribe in tyranny
69. He is not of us who is not affectionate to his little ones, and does not respect the feelings of the aged; and he is not of us who does not order that which is good and prohibit that which is evil
70. Fear not the obloquy (contradiction) of the detractor in showing God's religion
71. That person is not a perfect muslim, who eats his fill and leaves his neighbours hungry
72. If people do you good, do good to them and if they oppress you, do not oppress them
73. Desire not the world and GOD will love you, and
    desire not what men have and men will love you
74. In prayers all thoughts must be laid aside but those of God;
    In conversation no word is to be uttered which may afterwards be repented of;
    Do not covet from others or have any hopes from them
75. My GOD has commanded me nine things;
    1. To reverence GOD externally and internally
    2. To speak the truth, and with propriety in prosperity and adversity
    3. Moderation in affluence and poverty
    4. To benefit my relations and kindred, who do not benefit me
    5. To give alms to him who refuseth me
    6. To forgive him who injures me
    7. That my silence should be in attaining a knowledge of GOD
    8. That when I speak, I should mention him
    9. That when I look on God's creatures, it should be as an example for them; and

God has ordered me to direct in that which is lawful

76. A muslim who mixes with people and bears inconveniences is better than one who does not mix with them and bears no inconveniences.
77. *Keep yourself far from envy; because it eats up and takes away good actions, like as fire eats up and burns wood;*
78. He is not a perfect man of fortitude, who has not fallen in to misfortunes, and *there is no physician but the experienced*
79. Those who are patient in adversity and forgive wrongs are the doers of excellence
80. Forgive your servants seventy times a day
81. That person is nearest to God, who pardons, when he has in his power, him who would have injured him
82. Verily, God is fond of mildness, and He gives to the mild what he does not to the harsh
83. God loves gentleness and fortitude
84. "And who so seeks to approach ME *one span* (the maximum distance between the tips of the thumb and little finger = 9"), I seek to approach on *cubit* (approximately the length of the forearm)...
    And who so walks towards Me, I run towards him
85. O men... pray to GOD who hears and sees; and He is with you; and He to whom you pray is nearer to you than the neck of your camel
86. *Do you love your creator? then love your fellow-beings first*
87. Gods kindness towards His creatures is more than a mother's towards her babe
88. *Trust in GOD, but tie your camel*
89. GOD is not merciful to him, who is not so to mankind
90. *Be persistent in good actions*
91. When the heart is good, the whole body is good
    When the heart is bad, the whole body is bad
92. Goodness is a thing from which your heart finds firmness and rest, and badness is a thing which throws you in to doubt, although men may acquit you
93. Hell is veiled in delights and Heaven in hardships and miseries
94. *Heaven lies at the feet of mothers*
95. He will not enter hell who has faith equal to a mustard seed in his heart; and he will not enter paradise, who has a single grain of pride, equal to a mustard seed in his heart
96. Deal gently with the people and be not harsh; cheer them and condemn them not
97. The people entitled to heaven are three
    1. A just king, a doer of good to his people and endowed with virtue
    2. An affectionate man of a tender heart to relations and others
    3. A virtuous man

98. Honour your guest
99. It is not right for a guest to stay so long as to incommode his host
100. Humility and courtesy are acts of piety
101. I believe in GOD; after which I obey the commandments and abandon the things forbidden
102. Purity of speech and charity are Islam
103. The greatest enemies of GOD are those who do acts of infidelity and who without cause shed the blood of man
104. Every child is born with a disposition towards the natural religion. It is the parents who make it a Jew, Christian or a Magian (a member of priestly caste of Ancient Persia)
105. The following sap the foundations of Islam and ruin it
    1. The errors of the learned destroy it
    2. The disputations of the hypocrite
    3. The orders of the kings who have lost the road
106. What actions are most excellent?
    To gladden the heart of a human being, to feed the hungry to help the afflicted, to lighten the sorrow of the sorrowful and to remove the wrongs of the injured
107. Who is the most favoured of GOD?
    He from whom the greatest good comes to His creatures
108. To gladden the heart of the weary, to remove the suffering of the afflicted, has its own reward. In the day of trouble the memory of the action comes like a rush of the torrent and takes our burden away
109. He who is not kind to GOD's creatures, and to his own children GOD will not be kind to him.
110. Kindness is a mark of faith, whoever has not kindness has not faith
111. The Kuran consists of five heads;
    1. Things lawful 2. Things unlawful 3. Clear and positive precepts 4. Mysteries and 5. Examples
    Then consider that lawful which is there declared to be so and that which is forbidden as unlawful; obey the precepts; believe in the mysteries and take warning from the examples
112. The Kuran was sent down in seven dialects; and in every one of its sentences, there is an external and internal meaning.
113. "By what rule would you be guided, O MUAZ, in your administration of yeomen" said Muhammad
    "By the law of the Kuran"
    "But if you find no direction in the Kuran"?
    "Then I will act according to the example of the messenger of GOD"
    "But if that fails"?
    "Then I will exercise my reason and judgement."
114. He who neither works for himself nor for others, will not receive the reward of GOD.
115. Those who earn an honest living are the beloved of GOD

116. God is gracious to him that earns his living by his own labour, and not by begging
117. *Give the labourer his wage before his perspiration be dry*
118. *He dies not who gives life to learning*
119. Who so honours the learned, honours me
120. The worst of men is a bad learned man, and *a good learned man is the best.*
121. *An hour's contemplation is better than a year's adoration*
122. *Go in quest to knowledge even unto China* (i.e., even unto the edge of the earth)
123. *Seek knowledge from the cradle to the grave*
124. Whoever seeks knowledge and finds it will get two rewards; one of them, the reward for desiring it, and the other for attaining it; therefore even if he does not attain it, for him is one reward.
125. To spend more time in learning is better than spending more time in praying; the support of religion is abstinence
It is better to teach knowledge one hour in the night than to pray the whole night
126. *One learned man is harder on the devil than a thousand ignorant worshippers*
127. The pursuit of knowledge is a divine commandment for every muslim; and to waste knowledge on those who are unworthy of it is like putting pearls, jewels and gold on the necks of swine
128. The person who shall pursue the path of knowledge, GOD will direct him to the path of paradise;
and *verily the superiority of a learned man over an ignorant worshipper is like that of the full moon over all the stars*
129. *He who knows his own self, knows GOD*
130. To listen to the words of the learned, and to instill in to others, the lessons of science is better than religious exercises.
131. *The ink of the scholar is more holy than the blood of the martyr*
132. *He who leaves home in search of knowledge, walks in the path of GOD*
133. One hour's meditation on the work of the creator is better than seventy years of prayer
134. God has treasures beneath the throne, the keys where of are the tongues of poets
135. The acquisition of knowledge is a duty incumbent on every muslim male and female
136. Learn to know thyself
137. The calamity of knowledge is forgetfulness; and to waste knowledge is to speak of it, to the unworthy.
138. *Who are the learned? They who practice what they know*
139. *Acquire knowledge.* It enables its possessor to distinguish right from wrong; it is our friend in the desert, our society in solitude, our companion when friendless; it guides us to happiness; it sustaineth us in misery; it is an ornament amongst friends, and an armour against enemies.
140. With knowledge man rises to the heights of goodness and to a noble position, associates with sovereigns in this world, and attains to the perfection of happiness in the next.

141. As a man grows, and with him grow two things the love of wealth, and love of long life.
142. Who is the best man?
He is the best man, whose life is long end whose actions are good
Then who is the worst man?
He whose life is long and whose actions are bad
143. *Marriage is incumbent on all who possess the ability*
144. A woman may be married by four qualifications;
One on account of her money
Another on account of the nobility of her pedigree (SHIJRA)
Another on account of her beauty
The fourth on account of her virtue
Therefore look out for a woman that has virtue, but if
you do it from any other consideration, your hands be rubbed in dirt.
145. Shall I tell you the very worst among you?
Those who eat alone, whip the slaves and give to nobody
146. *Whatever mishap may be fall you; it is on account of something which you have done*
147. No misfortune or vexation be falls a servant of GOD,
small or great, but on account of his faults committed;
and most of these GOD forgives.
148. True modesty is the source of all virtues
149. Modesty and chastity are parts of the FAITH.
150. Meekness and modesty are two branches of IMĀN;
and vain talking and embellishing are two branches of hypocrisy
151. Monopoly is unlawful in ISLAM
152. The holder of a monopoly is a sinner and offender
153. Who so keeps back grain in order to sell at a higher rate is cursed
154. Heaven lies at the feet of mothers
155. "I am no more than man; when I order you
anything respecting religion, receive it, and
when I order you anything about the affairs,
then I am nothing more than man"—MUHAMMAD—The Prophet.
156. Convey to other persons, none of my words, except those you know of a surety (annul)
157. My sayings do not abrogate the word of GOD, but
the word of GOD can abrogate my sayings
158. Verily my heart is veiled with melancholy and
sadness for my followers, and verily
I ask pardon of GOD, one hundred times daily
159. Ambassadors of BANI AMIR said to MUHAMMAD "you are our master"
Muhammad replied "*GOD is your master*"
Then they said "you are most excellent of the highest degree"
Then Muhammad said "say so or less and do not exceed reasonable bounds in praise".
160. To the light I have attained and in the light I live.

161. "O messenger of GOD! curse the infidels" cried Muhammad's followers
Muhammad said "I am not sent for this; nor was I sent but as a mercy to mankind"
162. The best person in GOD's sight is the best amongst his friends; and the best of neighbours, and is the best person in his own neighbourhood
163. A muslim who mixes with people and puts up with their inconveniences is better than one who does not mix with them and bear with patience
164. *Do you love your creator? Love your fellow-beings first*
165. *Do not consult oracles or be influenced by omens like the ignorant– put your whole trust in GOD*
166. The best Muslim house is that in which is an orphan who is benefited;
And the worst muslim house is that in which is an orphan ill-treated.
167. He who wishes to enter paradise, must please his father and mother
A man is bound to do good to his parents, although they may have injured him.
168. Making peace between one another is a better act than fasting, alms giving and prayers;
Enmity and malice tear up heavenly rewards by the roots
169. "Know that everything is vanity save GOD" said LABID, the poet
170. O LORD! keep me alive a poorman, and let me die poor; and raise me amongst the poor
171. I seek for my satisfaction in that of the poor and needy
172. "If you are sincere, then prepare yourself for poverty;
for poverty reaches him who loves ME, quicker than a torrent reaches the sea
173. Say your prayers standing; but if you are not able
sitting; and if unable, on your sides
174. That person will not enter paradise, who has one atom of pride in his heart
175. GOD is Beauty and delights in the beautiful;
but pride is holding a man in contempt
176. *Everyone is divinely furthered in accordance with his character*
177. *It is your own conduct which will lead you reward or punishment, as if you had been destined there for*
178. Every human being has two inclinations – one prompting him to GOOD, and other impelling him to EVIL, but Divine assistance is nigh (near), and who asks the help of GOD in contending with the evil promptings of his own heart obtains it
179. The best of good acts is that which is constantly attended to although in a small degree
180. Those who have a true, pure and merciful heart will enter paradise.
181. GOD has not created anything better than *REASON* or anything more perfect or more beautiful than REASON; and the benefits which GOD gives are on its account; and understanding is by it; and GOD's wrath is caused by disregard of it
182. A good muslim is one whose disposition is most liked by his own family
183. The favour of GOD does not descend upon that family in which is one, who deserts his relations
184. The duty of a junior to a senior brother, is as that of a child to its father.
185. A man's first charity should be to his own family if poor
186. A sincere repenter of faults, is like him, who has committed none.

187. Riches are not from abundance of wordy goods, but from a contented mind.
188. It is difficult for a man laden with riches, to climb the steep path that leads to bliss
189. Wealth properly employed is a blessing; and a man may lawfully endeavour to increase it by honest means
190. To those of your servants who please you, give to eat what you eat yourself and clothe them as yourself; *but part with them who do not please you;* and punish not GOD's creatures
191. Feed the hungry and visit the sick and free the captive, if he be unjustly confined
Assist any person oppressed, whether Muslim or non-muslim
192. When you go to visit the sick, comfort his grief and say *"you will get well and live long" because although this saying will not prevent, what is predestined, it will solace his soul.*
193. Much silence and a good disposition are worthy of cultivation by all.
194. *A man of TRUTH is true in thought, word and deed*
195. *Strive always to excel in virtue and truth*
196. *Say what is true, although it may be bitter and displeasing to people*
197. One who speaks falsely, and who breaks his promises and who betrays his trust is not a muslim
198. The taker of *usury* (usury = giving loans on exorbitant rates of interest) and the giver of it and the writer of its papers and the witness to it, are equal in crime.
199. *Admonish your wife with kindness.*
A muslim must not hate his wife; and if he be displeased with one bad quality in her, then let him be pleased with another quality which is good
200. Give your wife good counsel; and if she has goodness in her she will soon take it; do not beat your wife and do not treat her (like a slave)
Leave off idle talking
201. *GOD enjoins you to treat women well for they are your mothers, daughters and aunts*
202. *Women are the twin halves of men*
203. The world and all things in it are valuable, but the most valuable thing in the world is a virtuous woman
204. A virtuous woman is most affectionate to infants and most careful of her husband's property
205. The love of the world is the root of all evil
206. This world is a prison for the Faithful but a paradise for unbelievers
Be in the world like a traveller, or like a passer on, and reckon yourself as of the dead.

Source

'The Sayings of Muhammed' by Allama Sir Abdullah Al-Mamun Al. Suhrawardy, 1941.

7

WISDOM OF LAOTSE

LAOTSE was born in KUHSIEN in *571 B.C.* He was a contemporary of CONFUCIUS, probably twenty years older. He came from an old cultured family. He was a keeper of the Imperial Archives, at the capital. He retired and disappear·d in middle life, and lived probably to a grand old age, possibly over ninety.

1. **The Character of TAO**
   The TAO that can be told of
   Is not the Absolute TAO...
2. **The Rise of Relative Opposites**
   Therefore the Sage
   Manages affairs without action
   Preaches the doctrine without words...
   He acts but does not appropriate
   Accomplishes but claims no credit
   It is because he lays claim to no credit
   That the credit can not be taken away from him
3. **Action Without Deeds**
   Exalt not the wise
   So that the people shall not scheme and contend
   Prize not rare objects
   So that the people shall not steal
   Shut out from sight, the things of desire
   So that the peoples heart shall not be disturbed
4. **The Character of TAO**
   TAO is a hollow vessel
   And its use is inexhaustible
5. **Nature**
   Nature is cruel (unkind)
   It treats the creation like sacrificial straw dogs

The sage is cruel
He treats the people like sacrificial straw dogs
By many words is wit exhausted
Rather therefore hold to the core

6. **The Spirit of the Valley**
The spirit of the valley never dies
It is called the mystic female
The door of the mystic female
Is the root of heaven and earth
Continuously it seems to remain
Draw upon it
And it serves you with ease.

7. **Living for Others**
The universe is everlasting
The reason the universe is evelasting
Is that it does not live forself
Therefore it can long endure
Therefore the Sage puts himself last
And finds himself in the foremost place
Regards his body as accidental
And his body is thereby preserved
Is it not because, he does not live for self
That his self is realized

8. **Water**
The best of men is like water
Water benefits all things
But does not compete with them
It dwells in the lowly places that all disdain
Where in it comes near to the TAO
In his dwelling the Sage loves the lowly earth
In his heart, he loves what is profound
In his relations with others, he loves kindness
In his words he loves sincerity
In government, he loves peace
In business affairs, he loves ability,
In his actions, he loves choosing the right time
It is because he does not contend
That he is without reproach

9. **The Danger of Overweening Success**
Stretch a bow to the very full
And you will wish, you had stoped in time
Temper a sword edge to its very sharpest

And the edge will not last long
When gold and jade fill your hall
You will not be able to keep them safe
To be proud with wealth and honour
Is to sow the seeds of one's own downfall
Retire when your work is done
Such is the Heavens way

10. **Embracing the One**

In embracing the one with your soul
Can you never forsake the TAO
In loving the people and governing the kingdom
Can you rule without interference...
In comprehending all knowledge
Can you renounce the mind?
To act without appropriation
To be chief among men without managing them
This is the mystic virtue

11. **The Utility of Not-being**

Thirty spokes unite around the nave (hub of a wheel)
From the loss of their individuality
Arises the utility of the wheel
From the clay vessles' hollow
Arises the utility of the vessel
Doors and windows in the house
Provide the empty spaces
From their empty spaces arise the utility of the house
Therefore by the existence of things we profit
And by the non-existence of things we are served

12. **The Senses**

The five colours blind the eyes of man
The five musical notes deafen the ears of man
The five flavours dull the taste of man
Chasing, hunting and horse-racing madden the minds of man
Gold, and diamonds keep their owners awake at night
Therefore the Sage
Provides for the Inner Self and not for the External Self...

13. **Praise and Blame**

Favour and disgrace cause one dismay
What we value and what we fear, are within our self...

14. **Prehistoric Origins**

...

15. **The Wise Ones of Old**
He who embraces this TAO
Guards against being overfull
Because he guards against being overfull
He is beyond wearing out...
16. **Knowing the Eternal Law**
He who knows the Eternal law is tolerant
Being tolerant he is impartial and in accord with Nature
Being in accord with nature, he is in accord with TAO...
17. **Rulers**
Of the best rulers
The people only know that they exist
The next best they love and praise
The next they fear
And the next they revile...
But of the best when their task is accomplished, their work done
All remark "we have done it ourselves"
18. **The Decline of TAO**
On the decline of the great TAO
The doctrines of humanity and justice arose
When knowledge and cleverness appeared
Hypocrisy followed in its wake.
19. **Realize the Simple Self**
Reveal they simple self
Embrace thy original nature
Check thy selfishness
Curtail thy desires.
20. **The world and I**
The valgar are clever and self assured...
I alone differ from the other people...
I draw sustenance from the mother nature
21. **Manifestations of TAO**
22. **Futility of Contention**
To yield is to be preserved whole
To be bent is to become straight
To be empty is to be filled
To have plenty is to be confused...
Sage does not reveal himself
He does not justify himself
And is therefore farfamed,
He does not boast of himself
And therefore people give him credit

It is because he does not contend
That none can contend against him
To yield is to be preserved whole
Thus he is preserved and the world does him homage...

23. **Identification with TAO**
He who is identified with TAO
TAO is also glad to welcome him...
He who has not enough faith
Will not be able to command faith from others

24. **The Dregs and Tumors of Virtue**
He who stands on tip toe does not stand firm
He who reveals himself is not luminous
He who justifies himself is not for famed
He who boasts of himself is not given credit...
Therefore, the man of TAO spurns them

25. **The Four Eternal Models**
Man models himself after the EARTH...
TAO models itself after Nature

26. **Heaviness and Lightness**
The Solid (Honesty, generosity, endurance) is the root of the light
The quiescent is the master of the hasty...
In the midst of honour and glory
He lives leisurely, undisturbed
In light frivolity, the centre is lost
In hasty action, self mastery is lost

27. **On Stealing the Light**
A good runner leaves no track
A good speech leaves no flaws for attack
A good recknoer makes use of no counters
A well-shut door makes use of no bolts
And yet can not be opened...
Therefore the good man is the teacher of bad
And the bad man is the lesson of the good
He who neither values his teacher
Nor loves the lesson
Is one gone far astray
Though he be learned
–Such is the subtle secret

28. **Keeping to the Female**
He who is familiar with honour and glory
But keeps to obscurity...
He has an eternal power which always suffices...

29. Warning Against Interference
The world is God's own vessel
It can not be made by human interference
He who make's it spoils it
He who holds it loses it...
Hence the Sage avoids excess
...avoids extravagance
(ESCHEWS) *avoids pride*

30. Warning Against Use of Force
He who by TAO purposes to help the ruler of men
Will oppose all conquest by force of arms
For such things are wont to rebound
Where armies are, thorns and brambles grow
The raising of a great host
Is followed by a year of famine
Therefore a good general effects his purpose and stops
He dares not rely upon the strength of arms
Effects his purpose and does not glory in it
Effects his purpose and does not boast of it
Effects his purpose and does not take pride in it
Effects his purpose as a regrettable necessity
Effects his purpose but does not love violence...
Violence would be against the TAO
And he who is against the TAO, perishes young

31. Weapons of Evil
Soldiers are weapons of evil
They are not the weapons of the gentleman
When the use of soldiers can not be helped
The best policy is calm restraint
He who delights in slaughter
Will not succeed in his ambition to rule the world

32. TAO is Like the Sea
He who knows where and when to stop
May be exempt from danger
TAO in the world
May be compared to rivers that run in to the sea

33. Knowing Oneself
He who knows others is learned
He who knows himself is wise
He who conqurs others has power of muscles
He who conquers himself is strong
He who is contented is rich
He who does not lose his centre endures...

34. **The Greet T.A.O. Flows Everywhere**
...Because to the end it does not claim greatness
Its greatness is achieved

35. **The Peace of TAO**
But TAO is mild to the taste
Looked at it can not be seen
Listened to, it can not be heard
Applied, its supply never fails

36. **The Rhythm of Life**
He who is to be made to dwindle in power
Must first be caused to expand
He who is to be weakened
Must first be made strong
He who is to be laid low
Must first be exalted to power
He who is to be taken way from
Must first be given...
Gentleness overcomes strength
Fish should be left in the deep pool
And sharp weapons of the state should be left
Where none can see them.

37. **World Peace**
The TAO never does
yet through it everything is done...

38. **Degeneration**
The man of superior character is not conscious of his character
Hence he has character
The man of inferior character is intent on not losing character
Hence he is devoid of character
The man of superior character never acts
Nor ever (does so) with an ulterior motive
The man of inferior character acts
And does so with an ulterior motive
The superior man dwells in the fruit
And not in mere expression (flower)
Therefore he rejects the flower and accepts the fruit...

39. **Unity Through Complements**
The nobility depend upon the common man for support
And *the exalted ones depend upon the lowly for their base*

40. **The Principle of Reversion**
Reversion is the action of TAO
Gentleness is the function of TAO
The things of this world come from Being

And being comes from Non-Being

41. Qualities of the TAOIST

When the highest type of men hear the TAO
They try hard to live in accordance with it
When the mediocre type hear the TAO
They seem to be aware and yet unaware of it
When the lowest type hear the TAO
They break in to loud laughter
If it were not laughed at, it would not be TAO
... Great character appears like insufficient
Solid character appears like infirmity
Great talent takes long to mature

42. The Violent Man

"The violent man shall die a violent death"

43. The Softest Substance

The softest substance of the world
Goes through the hardest

44. Be Content

Fame or one's own self which does one love more?
One's own self or material goods, which has more worth?
Loss of self or possession of goods, which is the greater evil?
Therefore: he who loves most spends most
He who hoards much loses much
The contented man meets no disgrace
He who knows when to stop runs into no danger
He can long endure

45. Calm Quietude

Who is calm and quiet becomes the guide for the universe

46. Racing Horses

When the world lives in accord with TAO
Racing horses are made to haul refuse carts...
There is no greater curse than the lack of contentment
No greater sin than the desire for possession
Therefore he who is contented with contentment shall be always content

47. Pursuit of Knowledge

Without stepping outside ones doors
One can know what is happening in the world
The farther one pursues knowledge
The less one knows
Therefore the sage knows without running about
Understands without seeing
Accomplishes without doing

48. **Conquering the World by inaction**
He who conquers the world often does so by doing nothing

49. **The People's Hearts**
The sage has no decided opinions and feelings
But regards the people's opinions and feelings as his own...
The sage dwells in the world *peacefully* and *harmoniously*
And the sage regards them all as his own children

50. **The Preserving of Life**
Out of life death enters
(Death is the beginning of life)...
(Soul once coming in to this world, it runs its course until it is exhausted. To be harassed by the wear and tear of life, and to be driven along without possibility of arresting ones course–is not this pitiful indeed? *To labour without cease all life and then without living to enjoy, the fruit, worn out with labour to depart, one knows not whither is not this a just cause for grief?*
Wise men of the past did not know what it was to love life or to hate death"–

51. **The Mystic Virtue**
TAO gives them birth
Makes them grow, develops them...
It gives them birth and does not own them
It helps and does not appropriate them
It is superior yet does not control them
This is the Mystic Virtue.

52. **Sleightying the Absolute**
He who can see the small is clear sighted
He who stays by gentility is strong...
This is to rest in the absolute

53. **Brigandage**
The main path is easy to walk on
I would avoid the by-paths
Yet people love the small by-paths...

54. **The Individual and the State**
Who is firmly established is not easily shaken
Who has a firm grasp does not easily let go...
According to the character of the individual, judge the individual,
According to the character of the family, judge the family
According to the character of the village, judge the village
According to the character of the state, judge the state
According to the character of the world, judge the world.
The nine tests of CONFUCIUS for judging men
"Mans mind is more treacherous than mountains and rivers and more difficult to know than the sky. *Man hides his character behind an inscrutable appearance.* There are those who appear tame and self-effacing, but canceal a terrible pride. There are

those who have some special ability, but appear to be stupid. There are those who are complaint and yielding, but always get their objective. Some are hard outside but soft inside, and some are slow without but impatient within. Some rush forward to the righteous thing as if they were craving for it and later drop it like something hot.

THE NINE TESTS

1. A gentleman sends a man to a distant mission to test his loyalty
2. He employs him near by in order to observe his manners.
3. He gives him a lot to do in order to judge his ability
4. He suddenly puts a question to him in order to test his knowledge
5. He makes a commitment with him under difficult circumstances to test his ability to live upto his word
6. He trusts him with money in order to test his heart
7. He announces to him the coming of a crisis to test his integrity
8. He makes him drunk in order to see the inside of his character
9. He puts him in female company to see his attitude towards women.

Submitted to these nine tests, a fool always reveals himself.

55. **The Character of the Child**
Who is rich in character
Is like a child
And he who is against TAO perishes young

56. **Beyond Honour and Disgrace**
He who knows does not speak
He who speaks does not know...
Honour and disgrace cannot affect him
Therefore he is the honoured one of the world

57. **The Art of Government**
The greater the number of statutes
The greater the number of thieves and brigands...

58. **Lazy Government**
The sage has firm principles but not sharp cornered
Has integrity but does not hurt others

59. **Be Sparing**
In managing human affairs, there is no better rule than to be sparing (*Never do too much*) *To be sparing is to fore stall*
To fore stall is to be prepared and strengthened
To be prepared and strengthened is to be ever victorious

60. **Ruling a Big Country**
Rule a big country as you would fry small fish
(Let alone or the fish will become paste by constant turning about)

61. **Big and Small Countries**
The female overcomes the male by quietude

And achieves the lowly position by quietude
Therefore if a big country places itself below a small country
It absorbs the small country
And if a small country places itself below a big country
It absorbs (merges with) the big country...

62. **The Goodman's Treasure**
TAO is the mysterious secret of the universe
The goodman's treasure
And the bad man's refuge...
Though there be bad people
Why reject them

63. **Difficult and Easy**
Requite the hatred with virtue
Deal with the difficult while yet it is easy...
The great problems of the world
Must be dealt with while they are yet easy and small
Therefore the sage by never dealing with great problems
Accomplishes greatness
He who lightly makes a promise
Will find it often hard to keep his faith
He who makes light of many things
Will encounter many difficulties
Hence even the sage regards things as difficult
And for that reason never meets with difficulties.

64. **Beginning and End**
Deal with a thing before it is there
Check disorder before it is rife
A tree with a full span's girth begins from a tiny sprout
A nine storied terrace begins with a clod of earth
A journey of a thousand miles begins with one step
He who acts spoils
He who grasps lets slip
Because the sage does not act, he does not spoil
Because he does not grasp, he does not let slip
The affairs of men are often spoiled with in an ace of completion
By being careful at the end as at the beginning
Failure is averted

65. **The Grand Harmony**
...

66. **The Lord of the Ravines**
In order to be foremost among the people
One must walk behind them

Thus it is that the sage stays above
And the people do not feel his weight...
Because he does not contend
No one in the world can contend against him
"A distinguished man who can act as other men's inferior is sure to obtain the following of men"

67. **The Three Treasures**
I have three treasures
Guard them and keep them safe
The first is *LOVE*
The second is *FRUGALITY* (Never too much)
The third is *never be the first in the world*
Through love one has no fear
Through not doing too much one has Reserve Power
Through not presuming to be the first in the world
One can develop one's talent and let it mature
IF one forsakes love and fearlessness
Forsakes restraint and reserve power
Forsakes following behind and rushes in front
For love is victorious in attack And invulnerable in defence
Heaven arms with love Those it would not see destroyed

68. **The Virtue of Not-contending**
The brave soldier is not violent
The good fighter does not lose his temper
The great conqueror does not fight on small issues
The good user of men places himself below others...

69. **Camouflage**
There is no greater catastrophe than to underestimate the enemy
To underestimate the enemy might entail the loss of my treasures
Therefore when two equally matched armies meet
It is the man who yields wins

70. **They Know Me Not**
My teachings are very easy to understand and very easy to practice
But no one can understand them and no one can practice them...

71. **Sick-Mindedness**
Who knows that he does not know is the highest
Who pretends to know what he does not know is sick-minded.

72. **On Punishment**
Despise not their dwellings
Dislike not their progeny
Because you do not dislike them
you will not be disliked yourself

Therefore the sage knows himself, but does not show himself
Loves himself, but does not exalt himself
Therefore the sage rejects force and accepts gentility

73. **On Punishment (2)**
Even if Heaven dislikes certain people
Who would know who are to be killed and why
Therefore even the sage regards it as a difficult question
TAO is good at conquest without strife
The heaven net is broad and wide
With big meshs, yet letting nothing slip through

74. **On Punishement (3)**
Often it happens that the executioner is killed
And to take the place of the executioner
Is like handling the hatchet for the master carpenter
He who handles the hatchet
Seldom escapes injury to his hands

75. **On Punishment (4)**
When people are hungry
It is because their rulers eat too much tax grain
Therefore the unruliness of hungry people
Is due to the interference of their rulers–...
It is those who interfere not with their living
That are wise in exalting life
On Valuing Life:
PRINCE MOV said to CHANTSE "I am living abroad at present, but my mind keeps thinking of my palace at WEI. What should I do *"Think of your life first"* replied chantse "for if *you value your life, then you put less weight on the luxuries of life.*"

76. **Hard And Soft**
When a man is born he is tender and weak
At death he is hard and stiff
Therefore hardness and stiffness are the companions of death
And softness and gentleness are the companions of life
Therefore when an army is head strong it will lose in battle
When a tree is hard it will be cut down
The big and strong belong underneath
The gentle and weak belong at the top

77. **Bending the Bow**
The way of Heaven
Is it not like the bending of a bow
The top end comes down and the bottom end goes up...
Therefore the sage acts, but does not possess

Accomplishes but lays claim to no credit
Because he has no wish to seem superior

78. **Nothing Weaker than Water**
There is nothing weaker than water
But none is superior to it in overcoming the hard
For which there is no substitute
That weakness overcomes strength
And gentleness overcomes rigidity...

79. **Peace Settlements**
Patching up a great hatred is sure to leave some hatred behind,
How can this be regarded as satisfactory...
The virtuous man is for patching up
The vicious is for fixing guilt
But the way of heaven is impartial
It sides only with the good man

80. **The Small Utopia**
Let there be a small country with a small population
Where the supply of goods are tenfold or hundred fold more than they can use
Let the people value their lives and not migrate far...
Let the people enjoy their food...
Let them be satisfied with their homes and delight in their customs
When the neighbouring settlements overlook one another
They can hear the banking of dogs and crowing of cocks of their neighbours
And the people till the end of their days shall never have been outside their country

81. **The Way of Heaven**
True words are not fine sounding
Fine sounding words are not true
A good man does not argue
He who argues is not a good man
The wise one does not know many things
He who knows many things in not wise
The sage lives for other people
And grows richer himself
He gives to other people
And has greater abundance
The TAO of Heaven
Blesses but does not harm
The way of the sge
Accomplishes, but does not contend.

Source

The Wisdom of Laotse, translated and edited by Lin Yatang, 1948.

8

ZEN INTERPRETATION OF LAOTSU

Zen is the essence of the oriental mind and it is a formless stream running through the whole of Asia. Its germ of thought is seen in Indian classics such as the VEDAS and UPANISHADS, its body of religion is formed by Mahayana Buddhism and Taoism in China, its flower of culture has blossomed in China and Japan and the application of its principles in daily life is flourishing in Japan even today.

The term ZEN comes from 'CHAN-NA' which is the Chinese transliteration of a SANSKRIT word *'DHYANA'*. It signifies the mystical experience in which man and God commune or in which subjectivity and objectivity merge. In general it is used to describe a special sect of BUDDHISM called ZEN BUDDHISM. *BODHI DHARMA,* an Indian monk who came to China about *A.D. 520 is regarded as the founder of the sect.* Bodhidharma's sect is known as SOSHIZEN, in distinction to Hinayana, Tathagata and Heretical ZEN sects.

ZEN INTERPRETATION OF LAOTSU

1. The TAO that can be defined is not the everlasting TAO.
   The unknown is the origin of heaven and earth, and the known is the mother of all things.
2. The sage preaches silence and rules the world by non action
   All things arise from TAO
   The sage lives in perfect accord with all
   He creates all things, but does not possess them
   He works for them but does not depend on them
   He completes the work but claims no credit for himself
   Because he does not claim credit, he is always given credit.
3. When talents are not esteemed men stop competing with each other
   When gold and precious stones are not treasured, people will not steal
   when valuable things are not on show, there is no opportunity for people to get confused or steal
4. The TAO is without content and it is the source of all things. Its utility can not be exhausted

5. *Heaven, Earth and the sage are not benevolent*
   They regard all things as sacrificial offerings (on the alter of nature) (insignificant things)
   Too much of talk leads to exhaustion, it is far better to observe the golden mean.
6. The valley spirit does not die. It is imperceptible yet its utility cannot be exhausted
7. *The sage puts himself last, yet others place him first. By being selfless, he completes his personality*
8. The sage overcomes all effortlessly, like water
   The Sage cherishes the things of TAO, which the multitude hates
   The sage associates with the virtuous and adapts himself to any environment
   The words of a sage inspire confidence, his actions are timely, his ability settles affairs and his rule brings order.
   He competes with none and hence none can compete with him.
9. If you place a valuable vase on show you are likely to lose it
   If you sharpen the edge of a sword too much, it will not last long
   A house in which there is a hoard of gold and precious stones is never secure
   when a man boasts about his honour or wealth he is sure to invite trouble for himself
   Heaven withdraws her support when success has been won.
10. The TAO forms and fosters all things without possessing them. It is called the Mysterious Virtue
11. The axle hole is essential to the usefulness of the wheel
    The hollow of a pot is essential to the use of a pot
    Doors and windows are essential to the usefulness of a house
    Forms are therefore useful because of their formlessness.
12. The five colours blind the eye
    Five tones deafen the ear
    Five flavours vitiate the palate
    Racing and hunting derange his mind
    Goods hard to obtain affect his conduct
    Therefore the sage is concerned with the belly and not with the eye
    He looks after the one and neglects the other
13. People prefer honour to disgrace, yet they are equally excited when they are honoured, and also when faced with disgrace
    This is because they are conscious of their bodies when they are not so conscious of their bodies, what disaster can bother them
14. *To trace the orign of the ancient rules is to understand the principles of TAO*
15. *In the ancient days to TAO, people moved cautiously acted hesitantly and behaved reverently with others.* They were simple, artless and adapted themselves to any event quickly. They were never satiated. *They did not undergo premature decay*
16. *All things go through the cycle of changes and finally return to their original state. Original state of a thing means that it has reached its appointed end*
    To understand this law is called Enlightenment. While to ignore it leads to wild

actions and evil results. One who follows TAO lasts long and escapes danger till the end of his days.

17. Under the best ruler, people are unaware of his existence
    With the next type of ruler, they feel intimate and praise him
    of the next type they are afraid of him
    And with the inferior type of ruler, people look down upon him with contempt
    One who has no confidence in himself fails to inspire confidence in others
18. When TAO is forgotten, benevolence righteousness and filial piety become fashionable, at the cost of harmony in life.
19. When wit and wisdom are discarded, people are benefited greatly
    when benevolence ceases and obligations are forgotten
    People become filial and kindly
    When the motive of profit is discarded, thieves and robbers disappear
    Let people be independent, be less selfish and have fewer desires. Let them cherish simplicity and honesty
20. *A man who renounces learning is free from trouble*
21. He form of the great virtue is vague and intangible like TAO. Yet there is a vital principle in it
22. *He whose desires are few achieves them and a man of many desires is bound to go astray*
    The sage is free from self-display and self-assertion and so his merit is acknowledged
    The sage never competes with any one and so none competes with him.
23. Violent wind does not last the whole morning nor sudden wind the whole day
    To be silent is to be natural
    Those who lack confidence in themselves are never trusted by others
24. *Rich clothing and a surplus of food cause envy in others, hence a man of TAO avoids them*
    One who stands on tiptoes cannot stand firmly
    One who takes long strides cannot walk for long
    Self asserters and self-complacent never acquire merit or superiority
25. TAO is all pervading without undermining anything. *TAO is the mother of universe*
26. Weight supports lightness, stillness overcomes movement.
    The sage if he marches with an army, never goes far from his baggage.
27. *Good words leave no room for criticism*
    Good actions leave no traces
    Good reckoners need no abacus (An oblong frame with Beads strung on wires used for calculations)
    A skilful closer needs no bolts or bars, yet no one can open what he has shut
    A skilful binder needs no cords yet none can release what he has bound
    The sage saves men and things skilfully and wastes nothing. This is called all embracing intelligence
28. Whoever is aware of his manly strength, yet is as tender as a new born baby and as

gentle as a woman, such a one is free from strain

29. *People in general are always changing.* They follow and then they lead; they are weak and then they are strong; they fall behind and then they rise.
The sage avoids excess, extravagance and superfluity
30. Briars and thorns grow where a large army is stationed and big battles are inevitably followed by years of famine. Therefore a good general stops the war after strinking a decisive blow, and never pursues for supremacy.
He is careful not to be proud of his success, not to boast of his victory; nor to live arrogantly. He is not aggressive to the defeated and he does not harm the weak.
When things have matured fully they become old
Those who oppose TAO, perish soon.
31. *The superior man uses weapons only as a last resort*
He esteems calm and repose, he avoids victory by force...
War is a cause for mourning as it involves killing of many people
32. *When a ruler remains simple in his rule, all spontaneously submit to his rule.*
33. *It is useful to know others but better to know oneself*
A man content with his lot is rich
A man develops a strong will, if he acts with energy
A man endures by staying in his own niche
A man becomes an immortal if his reputation survives his death
34. *All things arise from TAO and TAO claims no merit for what it does.*
35. TAO is nothing to look at and nothing to hear, but when used it can not be exhausted
36. *He who would take must first give*
What is to be weakened must first be strengthened
What is to be cutdown, must first be set up
What is to be shrunk, must first be stretched
The weak can overcome the strong
The soft can overcome the hard
Sharp weapons of the State should not be on display
Big fish should be left undisturbed in the sea
37. TAO is ever inactive, yet it leaves nothing undone
38. *The Superior man is not conscious of his virtue and hence he never looses it*
The Inferior man is always afraid of loosing his little virtue and hence he is likely to lose it
The Superior man does nothing with an ulterior purpose yet nothing is left undone by him.
The Inferior man does everything with an ulterior purpose and even though he is always actively employed, much is left undone by him
When benevolence is most highly esteemed people practice it for its own sake
When righteousness for its own good
When propriety because they are forced to do so
Propriety is caused by lack of sincerity and loyalty, and it denotes the beginning of disorder

Thus when TAO is lost, virtue is esteemed, when virtue is lost benevolence, and then in turn righteousness and finally propriety are esteemed.
Truly great men abide in what is real and deep
and they shun the ornamental and the shallows

39. *Verily the mighty grow from humble roots, and the high is supported by the low*
If one is concerned with self praise, then he is not worthy of it.
40. The quality of TAO is weakness, and the movement of TAO is returning.
41. A superior man hearing of the TAO, puts it into practice
A mediocre man takes it up one minute and loses it the next
An inferior man laughs at TAO. If such a man did not laugh at it, it would not be TAO
Who ever imagines beforehand that a task will be easy, is sure to face difficulties in the completion of it.
42. Things are increased by being diminished, and diminished by being increased
43. The softest thing overcomes the hardest
44. Which is more precious life or property
Which is more preferable gain or loss
A man who loves things greatly has to spend largely
A man who possesses much has to lose more
A man who is content with his lot will be free from disgrace
A man who knows when and where to stop will avoid danger and will enjoy a long and peaceful life.
45. What is straight may appear crooked, the most skilful seem clumsy and the most eloquent awkward calm overcomes unrest, heat banishes cold, and purity and stillness rectify the world.
46. There is no fault greater than the desire for gain
There is no disaster than the feeling of disappointment
Truly the contented man is always satisfied.
47. Without leaving the front door, one can guess all that goes on in the world. *For the further you move, the less you know*
Therefore the sage acquires wisdom without travelling
Understands without seeing and succeeds without undue effort
48. Learning consists in adding to ones stock of knowledge day by day, where as the practice of TAO consists in diminishing that stock daily
49. The sage has no opinions of his own, so he uses the opinions of the people. He treats the good and evil men alike because they are human beings
50. *Men are born to live and them die.* Of every ten men three are wedded to life, three to death, and three have already begun to decay. why? *Because they strive too hard*
51. TAO nourishes, matures and protects all things yet it does not possess them. This is called its mysterious way of working
52. *A man who is a slave to his senses and who tries to gratify all his desires, can not be saved*

A man who follows his inner light will avoid danger to the end of his days. This is called the preservation of insight

53. *The great TAO is easy to follow but people mistakenly wander down blind alleys*
54. The grip of a man who holds fast cannot be loosened easily
    A well established man cannot be displaced easily
    When a man practices the TAO, his conduct becomes sincere
    When a family practices the TAO its virtue increases
    When a village practices the TAO its influence spreads
    When a state practices the TAO it becomes strong
55. When things become strong they already begin to age
    Who ever and what ever is against TAO will soon perish
56. Those who know TAO do not speak about it; those who speak about it, do not know it
    A man who can not be moved by affection or estrangement, gain or loss, honour or disgrace, is the noblest creature under heaven.
57. *In a kingdom if there are more laws, there will be more thieves and robbers.*
58. Good and Evil are neighbours. There is no absolute right or wrong, for right may turn into wrong and good in to evil.
    Therefore the sage is strict without accusing and he is honest without hurting others and he is upright without condemning
59. *Moderation is the best way to rule men and serve heaven.*
60. *Governing a state is similar to frying fish.* More frequently you turn the fish, the more likely they are reduced to a paste. The best way to fry them is not to turn them frequently. Similarly in governing a state, *non interference is the best policy*
61. The female always overcomes the male with stillness. *Stillness and humility go together*
    Therefore by being humble, a large state may absorb a small state, and a small state by being humble, may be absorbed by a larger state. Thus in one case abasement brings adherence and in the other favour.
    The great state only wishes to unite with the little state and the little one wants to be accepted by the great one and serve it. Both will get what they want, but *the great one must learn first to be humble.*
62. Why then did men of old esteem the TAO so much? Because by it the needy obtain what is needed and the guilty escape accusation
63. Live without being conscious of living, work without being conscious of working, regard the small as the great and reward injury with kindness. *Deal with the difficult while it is easy and settle great affairs while they are still small, what is difficult now, was once easy and what is a serious matter now was once a simple matter.*
    A man who promises easily will face many difficulties to keep up his promises. Hence the sage does not promise easily and is free from such difficulties.
64. *Deal with events before they take place and put them in order before they get in to confusion*

A big tree grows from a tiny sapling, A nine storeyed building rises from a small heap of bricks. *A journey of a thousand miles begins with a single step. He who acts purposefully fails and he who grabs loses.*

People often fail at their work when they are within an ace of completing it. It they are as careful at the end as they were at the beginning, there will not be so many failures.

65. In the old days of TAO, people were encouraged to remain simple and ignorant and not become clever. *Clever people are difficult to manage.* He who tries to rule with knowledge will land in troubles and one who rules with wisdom brings good fortune to the state.
66. Therefore the sage wishing be above people should speak as though he is beneath them and *wishing to be infront should place himself behind others.* Only then people will not feel his weight (importance) and their feelings will not be hurt
67. I have three treasures which I prize and hold fast. *The first is compassion, the second fragality, and the third humility.*
    Compassion makes me brave, frugality liberal and humility enables me to assume power
    In attack compassion wins the day and in defence it guards one well.
    Heaven arms with compassion those it would save.
68. A good ruler of men is humble, a good fighter is not impatient, a good soldier is not aggressive and a *good winner is not quarrelsome.*
69. In a war, to underestimate the enemy is the greatest failure. One does so at the risk of losing one's treasure and life also.
70. TAO is very easy to understand and to practice yet no one tries to understand or practice it
71. To know without thinking is best
    To think and not to understand is a calamity
72. The sage knows his own worth and importance, yet does not show off. He rids himself of pride and is content.
73. In war a brave man looses his life and a coward escapes with his life. This is harmful to the brave and profitable to the coward. Even the sage finds it difficult to explain this.
74. It all the wrong doers are duly punished, who will dare to do wrong?
    An Execuioner of ten looses his life by violent means. A carpenter's apprentice who cuts wood, often cuts his own hand.
75. *The people starve because their rulers tax them too heavily. The government deteriorates because its officers are too busy with their own affairs*
76. *When one is alive, he is soft and at death he becomes rigid. The be soft is the way of life and to be rigid is the way of death*
77. When the top part of the bow is pulled down, the lower part is pulled up. Heaven takes from those who have too much and gives to those, who do not have enough. This is the way of heaven *whereas man robs the poor to serve the rich. This is the*

way of man.

The sage acts without a wish for return. He achieves his aim without claiming any credit

He is free from self-display

78. Nothing in the world is softer or weaker than water. Yet when it attacks things that are hard and strong, they crumble

All are aware that soft overcomes hard and the weak the strong. Yet no one puts this principle in to practice

79. *There can be reconciliation even after great hatred, yet some of the hatred remains.*

Therefore the sage, while keeping the bond does not reproach those who were responsible.

A superior person is concerned with his own obligations, where as the inferior person is always intent on blaming others

80. In a small state with few inhabitants, I would let the people not move far away to survive. I would like them to be satisfied with simple food, simple houses and their ancient customs. Neighbouring states would be insight of each other *I would teach them to eschew weapons and violence.*

81. Sincere words are not fine and fine words may not be sincere

The sage does not store up knowledge for himself but the more he gives to others, the wiser he becomes

The way of the sage is to serve and not to compete

The way of the heaven is to benefit and not to harm

Source

Zen Interpretation of Laotsu by Sohaku Ogata, 1959.

9

ZOROASTER AND THE GOOD RELIGION

Introduction

Zoroastrianism and its main tenets have come down to us in the so called *Pahlavi Books* (written in a dialect of Middle Persian) after the Muhammadan conquest of Persia, in the middle of *the 7th century.*

Zoroastrianism is the religion founded by ZOROASTER, the prophet of ancient Iran (*588 B.C.*). The surving sacred books of Zoroastrianism are known as *AVESTA.*

AVESTA contains three distinct parts: They are :

1. *GATHAS*: They are songs or odes which are generally and rightly ascribed to Zoroaster himself.
2. *YASHTS*: Sacrificial hymns addressed to various dieties.
3. VENDIDAD OR VIDEVDĀT– It is a treatise dealing mainly with ritual impurity

   All religions necessarily start with MAN and his relationship to the world. Zoroastrianism sets out to explain the relationship of man to GOD *(OHRMAZD)* and the DEVIL (*AHRIMAN*). Man is by origin a spiritual being created by GOD. *Man's soul is not eternally preexistent as in many Eastern religions.* Man's soul is created by God and to GOD alone it returns. Over against GOD stands the DEVIL (AHRIMAN) *Devil like GOD is a pure spirit.* God and the Devil are eternal antagonists, and sooner or later, a struggle between them becomes inevitable. GOD is all goodness and light and the Devil is all wickedness, darkness, deceit and death.

   Each individual is free to choose good or evil. The material world is the handiwork of GOD, a weapon fashioned by HIM, with which to destroy the DEVIL.

   Man's role in this world is to cooperate with nature on the natural plane, and to lead a virtuous life of good thoughts, good words and good deeds on the moral plane.

COUNSELS OF THE ANCIENT SAGES

1. My first duty on earth is to have faith in the GOOD Religion and to discriminate evil from good and profit from loss.

2. My second duty is to take a wife and raise a family.
3. My third duty is to cultivate and till the soil.
4. My fourth duty is to treat all livestock justly.
5. My fifth duty is to spend a third of days in attending the seminary and listening to the wisdom of holymen.
6. *There is only one religious way* – that of good thoughts, good words and good deeds.
7. All men are mortal. At the time of death, SOUL Leaves the body and the body itself disintegrates.
8. *Of thoughts, words and deeds, it is deeds only that are the criterion to judge a man, for thoughts are unfathomable and words or mere words.*
9. Parents must teach their children, the good religion before they reach their 15th year. *Parents are responsible for any sin committed by their children* (who have attained majority).
10. Be agreeable to good works. Do not be a party to any sin.
11. Be zealous in the performance of your duty
    Be grateful for good things in life
    Be patient in a adversity and in affliction
12. Overcome concupiscence (Sexual desire) with contentment.
    Overcome falsehood with TRUTH
    Overcome anger with serenity
    Overcome envy with benevolence
    Overcome want with vigilance
    Overcome strife (conflict) with peace.
13. *Do not pay respect to evil men so far as lies within your power. When you pay respect to EVIL, EVIL enters into your heart and the Good is driven out.*
14. Be deligent in the acquisition of learning for learning is the seed of knowledge and its fruit is wisdom.
15. Do not mock at anyone, for the man who mocks will himself be mocked at, and he will lose his dignity.
16. Seek everyday the company of good men to ask their advice and thus obtain a greater share of virtue and holiness.
17. Take great care never to vex your father and mother or your superior.
18. The human body is mortal, but the soul is immortal.
19. Do not abandon the care of the soul for the body's sake.
20. All the goods of this world must perish sooner or later hence do not run after anything that will bring punishment on your body and retribution on your soul.

THE GOOD ETHICS

Zoroastrianism is predominantly an ethical region, and its morality is based on 1. GOOD THOUGHTS 2. GOOD WORDS and 3. GOOD DEEDS, and the greatest of these *is GOOD DEEDS.*

THE COUNSELS OF ADHURBADH, SON OF MAHRASPAND

1. My SON, think upon virtue and never on sin, and always prefer the things of the spirit to that of matter.
2. Put out of your mind what is past, and do not fret and worry about what has not yet come to pass.
3. *Put not your trust and confidence in kings and princes.*
4. Do not do unto others, what would not be good for yourself.
5. Be single minded among rulers and friends.
6. *Do not deliver yourself up as a slave to any man.*
7. Stay far away from any man who approaches you in anger or in enmity.
8. *Make friends with such men as will profit you.*
9. *Tell no secret to a woman.*
10. *Listen to all that you hear, and do not repeat it at random.*
11. Do not let your wife and children out of your sight, except for reasons of good manners, lest care and grievous annoyance come upon you and you repent of it.
12. Do not give alms out of season.
13. Do not mock at anyone.
14. Do not share your secrets with a wrong headed man.
15. Do not make a choleric (irascible or angry) man, your travelling companion.
16. Do not take a frivolous man for your counsellor.
17. Do not make a rich man the companion of your table.
18. Do not make a drunkard your boon companion.
19. Do not borrow from a man of bad character or base lineage for you will pay heavily in interest and he will be for ever at your door or will always be sending messengers to your house, and great loss will you suffer thereby.
20. Do not summon an ill disposed person to help you.
21. Do not show your property to an envious man.
22. Do not put in to force a false judgement in the presence of rulers.
23. Do not listen to the words of liars and calumniators (slanderer).
24. Do not be over-zealous in punishing others.
25. Do not pick a quarrel at a feast.
26. Do not strike others.
27. *Do not strive for position.*
28. Consult men who are of gentlestock, experienced in affairs, clever and of good character; make these your friends.
29. Take great care that no heavy burden is laid on you in a conflict or battle.
30. Keep away from vengeful men in a position of power.
31. Do not come in to conflict with a scribe (a person who writes documents).
32. Do not tell your secrets to a babbler.
33. Listen to the opinion of a wiseman of exalted and esteemed position.
34. Do not tell a lie to anyone.
35. Do not accept the goods of anyman who is devoid of shame.

36. Do not consciously wager on anything at all.
37. Do not take an oath on either what is true or what is false.
38. When you are about to set up house, first take stock of the expense.
39. Woo the woman who is to be your wife yourself.
40. If you already have property start by buying more irrigated agricultural land, for even if it fails to yield interest, the capital will remain.
41. So far as you possibly can, do not bore your fellow men.
42. Do not seek to be avenged on others, and do not try to cause them loss.
43. Be as generous with your property as you can.
44. Do not deceive anyone, lest you come to grief thereby.
45. Hold your superiors in high esteem, make much of them and listen to what they say.
46. Borrow only from relations and friends.
47. Cherish the woman who is modest and give her in marriage to a clever and knowledgeable man, for such a man is like the good earth which yields good produce when once the seed has been planted in it.
48. Be plain in your speech.
49. Never speak without reflection.
50. Lend money only under agreed conditions.
51. Cherish a wise and modest woman and ask her in marriage.
52. Choose a son in law, who is good natured and honest even though he be poor, for he is sure to come up in life.
53. Do not mock at your elders, for you are subject to them.
54. Do not send a proud and pitiless man to prison but choose prison wardens among big men and set an intelligent man over them.
55. Speak sharply only after much reflection, for there are times when it is better to speakout and times when it is better to hold your peace; on the whole to hold ones peace is better than to speak.
56. Choose a man who tells the truth as your messenger.
57. Do not appoint a bought slave above trustworthy and faithful servants.
58. Spend according to your means.
59. Be courteous in your speech.
60. Do not praise yourself; only so will you perform righteous deeds.
61. Ask the advice of good men of mature age.
62. Accept nothing from a thief, nor give anything to him; drive him away.
63. As you fear Hell, punish others only after due reflection.
64. *Do not put your trust or confidence in anyone or anything at all.*
65. Make good use of authority so that you may obtain a good position there by.
66. *Be without sin so that you may be without fear.*
67. Be grateful so that you may be worthy of good things.
68. Be single minded, so that you may be faithful.
69. *Speak the truth so that you may be trusted.*
70. Be humble so that you may have many friends.

71. Have many friends so that you may enjoy a good repute.
72. *Be of good repute, so that you may live at ease.*
73. Love your religion, so that you be saved.
74. Do not seduce other men's wives, for that is a grievous sin for thy soul.
75. Do not maintain mean and ungrateful men for they will not thank you.
76. Do not destroy your own soul for the sake of anger or vengeance.
77. When you feel an urgent desire to do or say something, ask politely and say a prayer.
78. *Do not address a low born person first.*
79. When you attend a gathering, do not sit next to a wrong-headed man, so that you may not yourself be considered wrong-headed.
80. Whenever you sit in a banquet, do not seat in the highest seat, lest you be moved away there from and made to sit in a lower seat.
81. Do not rely on property and the goods of this world, for they are like a bird that flies from one tree to another, and stays on none.
82. Honour your father and mother, listen to them and obey them, for so long as a man's father and mother live, he is like a lion in the jungle, which has no fear of anyone at all, but he who has neither father nor mother is like a widowed woman, who is despoiled by men and can do nothing about it, and whom all men despise.
83. If you would not be abused by others, do not abuse anyone.
84. Do not be violent or ill-considered in your speech for such a man can be likened to a forest fire which burns up all animals and birds.
85. Do not collaborate with a man who ill treats his father and mother, and with whom they are displeased, lest your justice be turned to injustice and you be deprived of friends and have no pleasant intercourse with any one.
86. Do not out of false modesty or shame, deliver your soul upto hell.
87. Do not say anything that has a double meaning.
88. When you sit in an assembly, do not sit next to a liar, lest you yourself should suffer greatly thereby.
89. Take things easy so that you may be a welcome guest.
90. *Rise before down so that your work may prosper.*
91. *Do not make a new friend out of an old enemy, for an old enemy is like a black snake, which does not forget old injuries, for a hundred years.*
92. Renew your friendship with old friends, for an old friend is like old wine, which becomes better and more fit for the consumption of princes, the older it is.
93. Priase the Gods and be glad of heart, for it is from the Gods, that you will obtain an increase in the good things of this world.
94. I say unto you my son, that in the affairs of men, *the greatest helper and the best is wisdom* for if one's wealth is scattered and lost, or if ones live stock die, wisdom remains.
95. Strive to be firmly anchored in your Religion, for contentment is the highest wisdom and the greatest spiritual hope.
96. Keep your soul ever in mind.

97. *Do not forsake your duty to preserve your good name..*
98. Keep your hands from stealing, your feet from treading the path of undutifulness and your mind from unlawful desires, for who so practices virtue obtains his reward, and who so commits sin receives his punishment.
99. Who so digs a pit for his enemies, will fall into himself.
100. The good man lives at ease, but the bad man suffers distress and grievous woe.
101. Marry a young wife.
102. Drink wine in moderation, for who so drinks wine immoderately falls in to many a sin.
103. Since you know well that a snake has many wiles, do not be over hasty to touch one lest it bite you and you instantly die.
104. Even though you know well a stretch of water much frequented by bathers, do not be overhasty in going in to rough water, lest the water carry you away and you instantly die.
105. Do not on any account be false to a contract, lest you be held accountable.
106. Do not rob others of their property, nor keep what has been robbed, nor add it to your own, for then your own property will be destroyed and vanish away.
107. Do not rejoice for men, for men are like a water skin full of air, when it is deflated nothing remains.
108. Men are like suckling babes, and creatures of habit who cling to their habits.
109. Do not be overjoyed in good times nor overdistressed in bad time, for the good fortune turns to misfortune and misfortune turns to good fortune and there is no 'up' that has not been preceded by a 'down', and no 'down' that is not followed by an 'up'.
110. Do not be gluttonous in eating your food, and do not partake of all foods.
111. Do not be overhasty to attend the feasts and banquets of the great, lest you return from them abashed.
112. *There are four things which are most harmful to the body,* and make them have wrong ideas about their body. They are :
    1. *One is to glory in ones strength*
    2. *Second is the luxury of pride which leads one to pick a quarrel with a well established man*
    3. *Third is the case of the elderly man with a puerile* (immature) *character, who weds an adolescent girl.*
    4. *Fourth is the case of the young man, who weds an old woman.*
113. It should be known that love of one's fellow men proceeds from a balanced mind, and good character from being nicely spoken.
114. *Of all things that give help to man, wisdom is the best.*
115. Strive to hoard up only righteousness, for of all things that one may hoard, only righteousness is good.
116. Do not harbour vengeance in your thoughts lest your enemies catchup with you.
117. Whether you are a defendant or a plaintiff at a court of law, tell the truth so that you

may be more certain of acquittal at the trial.

118. Show moderation in your eating and drinking, so that you may live long, for moderation in eating is good for the body, and moderation in speech is good for the soul.
119. Take a wife from among your kin (ones relatives) so that your lineage may be more protracted.
120. Abstain rigorously from eating the flesh of kine (cow) and all domestic animals.
121. Make the traveller welcome so that you yourself may receive a heartier welcome, in this world and the next.
122. He who gives receives and receives more abundantly.
123. Seat yourself at a banquet where your host bids you be seated, for the best place is where a good man sits.
124. Do not strive for high office, for the man who strives for high office, usually brings disorder on his spirit.
125. 1. Live in harmony with virtue and do not consent to sin
    2. Be thankful for good fortune and be contented in adversity
    3. *Avoid an enemy*
    4. *Do not cause harm in doing good works*
    5. *Do not aid and abet evil.*
126. Even should the most fearful calamity befall you, do not doubt concerning the Gods and the religion.
127. Do not put your trust in life, but put your trust in good works.
128. For the good man, good works are his advocate and for an evil man, his own evil deeds are his accusers.
129. And of thoughts, words and deeds, deeds are the most perfect.
130. Do not plot evil against the evil, for the evil man reaps the fruit of his own evil actions, sooner or later.
    Has there ever been a man, who associated with evil men, who did not regret it in the end?
131. Do good simply because it is good, and even evil men extol goodness.
132. Do not tell your secrets to women lest all your toiling be fruitless.
    Put not your trust in women lest your have cause to be ashamed and to repent.
133. *Do not take orders from the crafty, lest you meet with ruin.*
134. 1. Wisdom combined with courage
    2. Vision combined with knowledge
    3. Wealth combined with generosity
    4. Good deeds combined with good words are most useful to men.
135. *An unbeliever has six signs.* They are :
    1. He has the outward appearance of good character but *his deeds are evil*
    2. He performs the liturgy (public worship in accordance with a prescribed form) correctly, but does evil.
    3. He talks big to others, but is himself stingy though seeming generous

4. *He is a giver of evil gifts*
5. *He is patient of abuse*
6. *His thoughts, words and deeds, do not agree.*

136. All forms of courage need wisdom. Wisdom needs knowledge and knowledge needs experience. *To be respected one should possess a good name.*

137. *All actions depend on the proper time and place.*
Wealth needs to be received and given away.
All enjoyment depends on freedom from fear.

138. Be zealous in the pursuit of culture for culture is an adornment in prosperity, a protection in distress, a ready helper in calamity and becomes a habit in adversity.

139. When you have learnet something, put it in to practice, for the man who knows a lot and believes little is the greater sinner.

140. The wisdom of a learned man if unaccompanied by goodness, turns to injustice and his intelligence turns to unbelief.

141. A man's goodness is revealed in times of anger and his rationality in times of passion which stirs up unrighteousness.
For a man who is assailed by anger and manages to control himself is shown to be good. And a man who is assailed by passion and manages to control himself is shown to be reasonable.

142. *On the drinking of wine :*
Several defects appear in the man who drinks wine immoderately. They are :
1. *His intelligence, wit, blood and seed decrease*
2. *He ruins his liver and stores up sickness for himself*
3. *His colour fades and his strength and endurance fail*
4. *He neglects his prayers and worship of Gods*
5. *His vision, hearing and eloquence of the tongue diminish*
6. *He dishonours his food and drink and gives himself upto sloth*
7. *He leaves undone all he should say and do*
8. *He sleeps with difficulty and rises up listless*
9. *He causes pain to his own body, his wife and children, and friends and relations*
10. *He is uncomfortable, suffers a miserable aftermath, and rejoices his enemies*
11. *The Gods take no pleasure in him; dishonour is the lot of his body, and damnation the portion of his soul.*

Source

A compendium of Zoroastrian Beliefs by R.C. Zaehne.

10

THE TALMUD AND THE VOICE OF WISDOM

The Talmud is a collection of early discussions with the comments of generations of teachers who devoted their lives to the study of scriptures. It is an encyclopaedia of law, civil, and penal, human and divine. *It records the thoughts, rather than the events of a thousand years of the national life of the Jewish people;* all their oral traditions carefully gathered and preserved.

The TALMUD is divided into two parts *MISHNA* and *GEMARAH*. They are the continued works of successive RABBIS. About 311 years were spent in the completion of the entire TALMUD *(3948 – 4253 years)*. The TALMUD is without doubt, the most reliable record of Jewish law and TRADITION.

PROVERBS AND SAYINGS OF THE RABBIS

1. Do not to others what you would not have others do to you.
2. Open not thy mouth to speak evil.
3. To be patient is sometimes better than to have much wealth.
4. The horse fed too liberally with oats becomes unruly.
5. Happy the pupil whose teacher approves his words.
6. When the cucumbers are young we may tell whether they will become good for food.
7. The ass complains of the cold even in JULY (TAMUZ).
8. *First learn and the teach.*
9. *Few are they who see their own faults.*
10. A single light answers as well for a hundred men as for one.
11. Victuals prepared by many cooks will be neither hot nor cold.
12. The world is a wedding.
13. Youth is a wreath of roses.
14. A myrtle (an evergreenshrub of the genus Myrtus with aromatic foilage and white flowers) even in the desert remains a myrtle.
15. *Teach thy tongue to say "I do not know".*
16. *The house which opens not to the poor will open to the physician.*

17. The birds of the air despise a miser.
18. Hospitality is an expression of divine worship.
19. *Thy friend has a friend and thy friend's friend has a friend; therefore be discreet.*
20. Do not place a blemish on thine own flesh.
21. Attend no auctions if thou hast no money.
22. Rather skin a carcass for pay in the public streets than lie idly depend on charity.
23. It is well to add a trade to your studies if you would remain free from sin.
24. The tradesman at his work is the equal of the most learned doctor.
25. He who derives his livelihood from the labour of his hands is as great as he who fears God.
26. *Deal with those who are fortunate.*
27. What is intended for thy neighbour will never be thine.
28. *The weakness of thy walls invites the burglar.*
29. *The place honours not the man, it is the man who gives honour to the place.*
30. The humblest man is ruler in his own house.
31. If the fox is king bow before him.
32. If a word spoken in its time is worth one piece of money, silence in its time is worth two.
33. Drain not the waters of thy well, while other people may desire them.
34. *The doctor who prescribes gratuitously gives a worthless prescription.*
35. The rose grows among thorns.
36. The wine belongs to the master, but the waiter receives the thanks.
37. He who mixes with unclean things becomes unclean himself.
    He whose associations are pure becomes more holy each day.
38. No man is impatient with his creditors.
39. Make but one sale and thou art called a merchant.
40. Mention not a blemish which is thy own, in detraction of thy neighbour.
41. If certain goods sell not in one city, try another place.
42. He who reads the letter should execute the message.
43. A vessel used for holy purposes should not be put to uses less sacred.
44. Ornament thyself first, then magnify others.
45. Two pieces of coin in one bag make more noise than a hundred.
46. Man sees the mote in his neighbour's eye, but knows not of the beam in his own.
47. The rivalry of scholars advances science.
48. If thou tellest thy secret to three persons ten know of it.
49. When love is intense both find room enough upon one board of the bench; afterwards they may find themselves cramped in a space of sixty cubits (*one cubit* = a measure of length approximately equal to the length of a forearm).
50. When wine enters the head, the secret flies out.
51. When a liar speaks the truth, he finds his punishment in the general disbelief.
52. The camel desired horns and ears were taken from him.
53. Sorrow for those who disappear never to be found.

54. The officer of the king is also a recipient of honours.
55. He who studies can not follow a commercial life; neither can the merchant devote his time to study.
56. There is no occasion to light thy lamp at noontide.
57. Let the fruit pray for the welfare of the leaf.
58. Meat without salt is fit only for the dogs.
59. Trust not thyself until the day of thy death.
60. Woe to the army which hath lost its leader; woe to the ship when its captain is no more.
61. He who increaseth his flesh but multiplieth food for the worms.
62. The day is short, the labour great and the workman slothful.
63. Be yielding to thy superior; be affable towards the young; be friendly with all mankind.
64. *Silence is the fence round wisdom.*
65. *Without law civilisation perishes.*
66. Every man will surely have his hour.
67. Rather be the tail among lions than the head among foxes.
68. In to the well which supplies thee with water cast no stones.
69. Many a colt's skin (a young uncastrated male horse usually less than 4 years old) is fashioned to the saddle which its mother bears.
70. Truth is heavy, therefore few care to carry it.
71. *Say little and do much.*
72. He who multiplieth words will likely come to sin.
73. Sacrifice thy will for others, that they may be disposed to sacrifice their wills for thee.
74. Study today delay not.
75. Look not upon thy prayers as on a task; let thy supplications be sincere.
76. *He who is loved by man is loved by God.*
77. Honour the sons of the poor; they give to science its splendour.
78. Do not live near a pious fool.
79. A small coin in a large jar makes a great noise.
80. *Use thy noble vase today; tomorrow it may break.*
81. The cat and the rat make peace over a carcass.
82. *He who walks each day over his estate finds a coin daily.*
83. The dog follows thee for the crumbs in thy pocket.
84. The soldiers fight and the kings are heroes.
85. When the ox is down, many are the butchers.
86. Descend a step in choosing thy wife; ascend a step in choosing thy friend.
87. Beat the Gods and their priests will tremble.
88. The sun will set without thy assistance.
89. Hold no man responsible for his utterances in times of grief.
90. One man eats, another says grace.
91. He who curbs his wrath merits forgiveness for his sins.

92. Commit a sin twice and it will not seem to thee a crime.
93. Study is more meritorious than sacrifice.
94. Jerusalem was destroyed because the instruction of the young was neglected.
95. The world is saved by the education imparted to the children. Even to rebuild the Temple, the schools must not be closed.
96. Blessed is the son who has studied with his father and blessed the father who has instructed his son
97. *Avoid wrath and thou will avoid sin; avoid intemperance and thou will not provoke providence.*
98. *When others gather, do thou disperse; when others disperse gather.*
99. *When thou art the only purchaser, then buy; when other buyers are present, be thou nobody.*
100. The foolish man knows not an insult, neither does a dead man feel the cutting of a knife.
101. The cock and the owl both await daylight 'The light' says the cock "brings me delight; but what in the world are thou waiting for?"
102. The thief who finds no opportunity to steal considers himself an honest man.
103. A Galilean said "when the shepherd is angry with flock, he appoints for its leader a blind *bell wether* (The leading sheep of a flock, with a bell on its neck).
104. Though it is not incumbent upon thee to complete the work, thou must not therefore cease from pursuing it. If the work is great, great will be thy reward, and thy Master is faithful in his payments.
105. There are three crowns: of the Law, the priesthood and the kingship; but the crown of a good name is greater than them all.
106. *Who gains wisdom?*
He who is willing to receive instruction from all sources.
Who is the mighty man?
He who subdueth his temper.
Who is rich?
He who is content with his lot.
Who is deserving of honour?
He who honoureth mankind.
107. Despise no man and deem nothing impossible; everyman hath his hour and everything in its place.
108. Iron breaks stone; fire melts iron, water extinguishes fire; the clouds consume water; the storm dispels clouds man withstands the storm; fear conquers man; wine banishes fear; sleep overcomes wine, and death is the master of the sleep.
But "charity" says SOLOMON "saves even from death".
109. How canst thou escape sin?
Think of three things; whence thou comest, whether thou goest and before whom thou must appear.
The scoffer, the liar, the hypocrite, can have no share in the future world of bliss.

To slander is to commit murder.

110. "Repent the day before thy death "said a Rabbi. His disciples asked him how they could follow his advice as man was unable to tell upon what day his death would occur. Rabbi answered "*Consider every day thy last; be ever ready with penitence and good deeds.*
111. Ten measures of wisdom came in to the world; the Law of Israel received nine measures, and the balance of the world one.
Ten measures of beauty came in to the world;
Jeruslaem received nine measures, and the rest of the world one.
112. Rabbi Simon said "The world stands on three pillars; LAW, WORSHIP and CHRITY.
113. Rabbi ADA said "when he who attends the synagogue regularly is prevented from being present, GOD asks for him.
114. Rabbi Simon, the son of Joshua said "His enemies will humble themselves before the one who builds a place of worship."
115. He who is able to attend synagogue, and neglects to do so is a bad neighbour.
116. Rabbi Jose said "one need not stand upon a high place to pray for it is written "out of the depths have I called unto Thee, oh, Lord".
117. Rabbi Jose prohibits moving about or talking during the progress of prayers.
118. To pray loudly is not a necessity of devotion; when we pray we must direct our heart towards heaven".
119. "I had met with distress and sorrow, I then called on the name of the LORD"–DAVID.
120. "Charity is greater than all".
121. "Who gives charity in secret is greater than MOSES".
122. "A gift given in secret pacifieth anger."
123. "A miser is as wicked as an idolater".
124. "Charity is more than sacrifices."
125. "He who gives charity becomes rich."
126. "A beneficent soul will be abundantly gratified."
127. "If your GOD Loves the poor, why does he not support them?" _ a philosopher inquired of Rabbi Akiba. Rabbi Akiba replied "God allows the poor to be with us ever, so that the opportunities for doing good may never fail."
128. "When one stands at the judgement-seat of GOD" RABBAH said "these questions are asked"
    1. "Hast thou been honest in all thy dealings"?
    2. "Hast thou set aside a portion of thy time for the study of the law"?
    3. "Hast thou observed the first commandment"?
    4. "Hast thou in trouble, sill hoped and believed in GOD"?
    5. "Hast thou spoken wisely"?
129. All the blessings of a household come through the wife, therefore should her husband honour her".
130. Men should be careful lest they cause women to weep, *for God counts their tears.*
131. In cases of charity where both men and women claim relief the latter should be first

assisted. If there should not be enough for both, the men should cheerfully relinquish their claims.

132. A woman's death is felt by nobody as by her husband.
133. Tears are shed on GOD's alter for the one who forsakes his first love.
134. He who loves his wife as himself and honours her more than himself, will train his children properly.
135. Rabbi Jose said: "I never call my wife 'wife' but home for she indeed makes my home".
136. He who possess a knowledge of GOD, and a knowledge of man, will not easily commit sin.
137. The bible was given us to establish peace.
138. He who wrongs his fellow man even in so small a coin as a penny, is as wicked as if he should take life.
139. He who raises his hand against his fellow in passion is a sinner.
140. Be not the friend of one who wears the cloak of a saint to cover the deformities of a fool.
141. One who gives way to passion is as bad as an idolater.
142. Hospitality is as great a virtue as studying the law.
143. "Never put thyself in the way of temptation" advised Rabbi JUDAH; "even DAVID could not resist it".
144. RABBI TYRA, on being asked by his pupils to tell them the secret which had gained him a happy, peaceful old age, replied "I have never cherished anger with my family; I have never envied those greater than myself, and I have never rejoiced in the downfall of anyone.
145. Unhappy is he who mistakes the branch for the tree, the shadow for the substance.
146. Thy yesterday is thy past; thy today thy future; thy tomorrow is a secret.
147. The best preacher is the heart;
The best teacher is time;
The best book is the world;
The best friend is GOD;
148. Life is but a loan to man; DEATH is the creditor who will one day claim it.
149. "Understand a man by his own deeds and words. The impressions of others lead to false judgement.
150. He through whose agency another has been falsely punished stands outside of heavens gates.
151. The sins of the bad tempered are greater than his merits.
152. The man who sins is foolish as well as wicked.
153. The good actions which we perform in this world take form and meet us in the world to come.
154. Better to bear a false accusation in silence, than by speaking, to bring the guilty to public shame.
155. He who can feel ashamed will not readily do wrong.

156. There is a great difference between one who can feel ashamed before his own soul, and one who is only ashamed before his fellow man.
157. GOD'S covenant with us included work; for the command 'Six days shalt thou work, and the seventh shalt thou rest' made the 'rest' conditional upon the 'work'.
158. "Would you have the sun and the moon destroyed because of the foolish ones who worship them? To change the course of nature to punish sinners would bring suffering to the innocent also".
159. "He who refuses to teach a precept to his pupil is guilty of theft, just as one who steals from the inheritance of his father".
160. That house where the LAW is not studied by night should be destroyed.
161. The wealthy man who aids not the scholar desirous of studying GOD'S LAW will not prosper.
162. "He who changes his word, saying one thing and doing another, is even as he who serveth idols".
163. "Thy righteousness will go before thee, the glory of the LORD will gather thee in".
164. "Friends of GOD are those who being offended, yet think not of revenge; who practice good through love for GOD, and are cheerful under suffering and difficulties.
165. *Love thy wife as thyself; honour her more than thy self.*
    He who lives unmarried lives without joy.
    The children of a man who marries for money will prove a curse to him.
    He who sees his wife die, has, as it were been present at the destruction of the sanctuary itself.
166. He who has more learning than good deeds is like a tree with many branches but weak roots; the first great storm will throw it to the ground. He whose good works are greater than his knowledge, is like a tree with fewer branches but with strong and spreading roots, a tree which all the winds of heaven can not uproot.
167. Better is the curse of the righteousman, than the blessing of the wicked.
168. "Wisdom resides with the aged and understanding in length of days.
169. The Angle of Truth approached GOD saying: "cease! oh! GOD, ... with man THOU sendest falsehood to the earth!"
    Divine words came "Thou oh TRUTH, shall go to earth with man, and yet remain a denizen (a foriegner admitted to certain rights in his adopted country) of heaven, 'twixt heaven and earth to float, connecting link between the two!"
170. ON TRADES
    RABBI MEIR said "when a man teaches his son a trade, he should pray to GOD, the Dispenser of wealth and poverty. *For in every trade and pursuit of life both the rich and the poor are to be found.* It is folly for one to say "This is a bad trade, it will not afford me a living because he will find many well to do in the same occupation. Neither should a successful man boast and say "this is a great trade, a glorious art, it has made me wealthy", because many working in the same line as himself have found but poverty, *Let all remember that everything is through the infinite mercy and wisdom of GOD.* "The best doctors are deserving of punishment. In the pursuit

of knowledge, they experiment on their patients and often with fatal result. – RABBI JUDAH

171. ON REPENTANCE

In three ways may we repent.

First, by words of mouth, arising from an honest heart.

Secondly with our feelings, sorrow for sins committed.

Thirdly by good deeds in the future;

GOD is ready at all times to acknowledge true penitence.

SEVEN DEGREES OF REPENTANCE

First, the righteousman, who repents his misconduct as soon as he becomes aware of his (sin). This is the best and most complete.

Secondly of the man, who has for sometime led a life of sin, yet while in the prime of life has abandoned his evil ways.

Thirdly, of the one who was prevented by some cause, from the commission of a contemplated sin, and who truly repents his evil intention.

Fourthly of the one who repents when his sin is pointed out to him, and he is rebuked for the same.

Fifthly, of those who repent when trouble befalls them..

"When thou art in tribulation and all these things have overtaken thee... then wilt thou return unto the LORD, thy GOD".

Sixthly, the repentance of age. Even when man grows old and feeble, if he repents truly, his atonement will be received.

Seventhly is the last degree of penitence of the one who is rebellious against his creator during all the days of his life; turns to GOD only when the hand of death is laid upon him.

Repentance and good deeds from a shield against punishment.

172. ON DEATH

Man is born with his hands clenched; he dies with his hands wide open. Entering life he desires to grasp everything, leaving the world all that he possessed has slipped away. Mourn for those who are left; mourn not for the one taken by GOD from earth. He has entered into the eternal rest, while we are bowed with sorrow.

When the righteous dies it is earth that meets with loss. The jewel will ever be a jewel, but it has passed from the possession of its former owner. Well may the loser weep.

Life is a passing shadow say the scriptures. *The shadow of a tower or a tree; the shadow which prevails for a time? No; even as the shadow of a bird in its flight, it passeth from our sight,* and *neither bird,* nor *shadow remains.*

THE VOICE OF WISDOM

1. *TRUTH is the seal of GOD*—TALMUD.
2. Great is TRUTH and stronger than all things... TRUTH abideth, and is strong for

ever; she liveth and conquereth for evermore... She is the strength, power and the majesty of all ages. Blessed be the GOD OF TRUTH—ESDRAS.

3. ***THE RIGHT LIFE***
   O man! what is good and what doth the LORD require of thee; *only to do justly, to love mercy and to walk humbly with thy GOD—MICAH.*
4. Woe unto them that are wise in their own eyes and prudent in their own sight—ISAIAH
5. The proper study of a wiseman is not how to die but how to live—BENEDICT SPINOZA (1677)
6. ***GOOD and EVIL***
   Many think that the evils are more numerous than the good things. They say that the good is found exceptionally, whilst evils are numerous and lasting. This error is because men judge of the WHOLE UNIVERSE, by examining one single person only. If anything happens to him contrary to his expectation, he concludes forthwith that the whole universe is evil.
   Most of the evils are due to defects existing in themselves, yet they ascribe them to GOD.
   "The foolishness of man perverteth his way and his heart fretteth against the LORD—said SOLOMON—MOSES MAIMONIDES (1190).
7. ***FREEDOM OF THE WILL***
   Free will is granted to everyman. He may follow the path of good or evil. *All the evil deeds one committed have been committed with ones full consent,* it befits us to turn in penitence and to forsake evil deeds; the power of doing so being still in our hands.—MOSES MAIMONIDES (1180)
8. ***WISE COUNCEL***
   The soul when accustomed to superfluous things, acquires a strong habit of desiring others which are necessary neither for the preservation of the individual nor that of the species. This desire is without limit, whilst things which are necessary are few and restricted with in certain bounds.
   Thus you desire to have silver vessels, but golden vessels are still better and vessels studded with sapphires, emeralds and rubies are still better. Those who run after superflous things are constantly in trouble and pain—MOSES MAIMONIDES (1180)
9. Prefer one in hand to two in hope; a little certainty is better than a great perhaps. Sooner a servant among the noble than a leader among the common; for in the first instance, some of the honour of the nobles will sticks to you, white in the latter instance, you have to share the contempt of your contemptible followers. Better enough in freedom than plenty at the table another.
   Love thy children with impartial love; the hope offers that your place on the more promissing, and all your joy, may come from him that you have kept in the background—BENEDICT OF OXFORD (1195)
10. *THE SEVEN MARKS OF A WISEMAN*
    1. The wiseman does not speak before him who is greater than he in wisdom.

2. He is not hasty to answer.
3. He does not break in upon the speech of his fellow.
4. *He questions according to the subject matter and answers to the point.*
5. He speaks upon the first thing first, and upon the last last
6. Regarding that which he has not understood, he says *"I do not understand it"*.
7. *Finally he acknowledges the truth—ETHICS OF THE FATHERS.*

11. ***CLEANLINESS IS NEXT TO GODLINESS***
Carefulness leads to cleanliness;
Cleanliness to purity;
Purity to humility;
Humility to saintliness;
Saintliness to fear of sin
Fear of sin to holiness;
A holiness to immortality—*TALMUD*
12. ***THE CITY OF GOD***
Do not seek for the city of GOD on earth, for it is not built of wood or stones, *but seek it in the soul of man who is at peace with himself and is a lover of true wisdom.* —*PHILO JUDAEUS (1ST CENTURY).*
13. Think not meanly of thyself, and despair not of perfection—MOSES MAIMONIDES (1200).
14. A man should so live that at the close of everyday, he can repeat 'I have not wasted my day—ZOHAR.
15. *Wisdom begetteth humility*—ABRAHAM IBN EZRA (1167).
16. ***HUMILITY***
The man who does good works is more likely to be overtaken by pride in them, and its effect on conduct is injurious in the extreme. Humility is the most necessary of virtues, to banish this pride.
When misfortunes come to the meek, their endurance triumphs over their fear and grief and they willingly submit to the decree of GOD, and own that HIS judgements are righteous.
In matters of justice, the meek will be fearless and punish the wicked without fear or favour. He will help the oppressed, and rescue him from the power of the oppressor—TBACHYA IBN PAKUDAH (1040)
17. The righteous promise little and do much; The wicked promise much and do not perform even a little.
Let your yes be yes and your no be no—TALMID
18. Despise not any man and do not find fault (carp) at anything, for there is not a man that has not his hour, and there is not a thing that has not its place—BEN AZZAI.
19. "If I am not for myself, who will be for me? And being for myself, what am I? and if not now, when?"—HILLEL
20. Separate not thyself from the Community Trust not in thy self until the day of thy death, Judge not thy neighbour until thou art come in to his place—ETHICS OF THE FATHERS

21. *"My Son! thy deeds will bring thee near un to men and your own deeds will drive thee from them."—AKABYA (FIRST CENTURY).*
22. ***WEALTH***
    But if worldly wealth be lent to thee, exalt not thyself above thy brother; for both of you came naked into the world, and both of you will surely have to sleep at last together in the dust —ELEAZAR OR WORMS (1200).
23. Heaven is not to be won by ease, quiet and rest... only those who have suffered and endured greatly have achieved greatly —S. ALFRED ADLER (1906)
24. ***MEETING ADVERSITY***
    "To rail at life, and terrible against adversity is of little avail. *We can not lay down terms to life. Life must be accepted on its own terms. But hard as life's terms are, it never dictates unrighteousness, unholiness, and dishonour —J.H. HERTZ (1900).*
25. *Remember thy last end and cease from enmity* —ECCLESIASTICAS
26. "Reflect upon three things and you will not come within the power of sin; know whence thou comest and whether thou art going, and before whom thou wilt in future have to render account and reckoning. -AKABYA.
27. Whatsoever thy hand findeth to do, do it with all thy might —ECCLESIASTES
28. *Accustom thyself to complete any good work thou hast understaken —DERECH ERETZ ZUTTA (8TH CENTURY)*
29. ***THE THREE FRIENDS***
    Every man has *three friends* when DEATH summons him to appear before his CREATOR.
    His first friend, namely his MONEY, whom he loves most, cannot go with him a single step.
    His second friend, namely his relations and neighbours, can only accompany him up to the grave but cannot defend him before the JUDGE.
    While his third friend - his good works, whom he does not highly esteem - go with him before his CREATOR and obtain his acquittal.
30. ***IMMORTALITY***
    There are those who gain eternity in a lifetime, and others who gain it one brief hour —TALMUD
31. ***TRUE WISDOM***
    But where shall wisdom be found?
    And where is the place of understanding?
    Behold, the fear of the Lord, that is WISDOM;
    And to depart from evil is understanding —JOB.
32. "The day is short and the work is great, but the labourers are idle, though the work is urgent.
    It is not incumbent upon thee to complete the work; but neither art thou free to desist from it...
    But know that the reward unto the righteous is not of this world
    —RABBI TARPHON (2nd CENTURY)

33. ***LESSON OF HISTORY***

One lesson and only one history may be said to repeat with distinctness *that the world is built somehow on moral foundations; that in the long run it is well with the good; in the long run it is ill with the wicked.* It is no more than the old doctrine taught centuries ago by the prophets —J.A. FROUDE (1889).

34. **"*... and the dust returns to the earth as it was, and the spirit returns to GOD, who gave it*" —*ECCLESIASTES.***

Sources

1. The Talmud, translated from the original by H. Polano.
2. A Book of Jewish Thought, J.H. Hertz.

11

WISDOM OF SOLOMON

Introduction

SOLOMON was born in the year 2912 A.M., and reigned over Israel forty years. Solomon wrote three books: PROVERBS, ECCLESIASTES and the SONG OF SOLOMON. When the LORD appeared to Solomon in Gibon and said to him in a dream "what shall I give to thee"? Solomon replied "Give to thy servant an understanding heart".

Then the LORD said "Because thou last asked for wisdom, and requested not wealth or dominion over thy enemies, wisdom and knowledge shall be thine and through them thou shall obtain wealth and power".

If a man possessing brilliant diamonds and precious stones, keeps his jewels concealed, none is aware of their value; but if he allows them to be seen their worth becomes known and the pleasure of ownership is enhanced.

The proverbs of SOLOMON were discovered and copied by the aides of KING HEZEKIAH OF JUDAH.

PROVERBS OF KING SOLOMON

1. How does a man become wise?
   The first step is to trust and reverence the LORD. Listen to your father and mother. What you learn from them will stand you in good stead. Only fools refuse to be taught.
2. "SON! stay away from all who live by violence and murder. Those who live by violence and murder, all will die a violent death.
3. When you are engulfed by anguish and distress, though you search for guidance and wisdom anxiously, you will not be able to find them.
4. If you search for wisdom as you would for lost money or hidden treasure, it will be given to you.
5. Those who do not choose to reverence and trust the LORD, must eat the bitter fruit of having their own way and experience the full terrors of the pathway they have chosen.

6. THE LORD shows you how to distinguish right from wrong, and how to find the right decision everytime. *FOR TRUTH and WISODM will enter the very centre of your being,* filling your life with joy.
7. *In everything you do, put GOD first, and HE will direct you and crown your efforts with success.*
8. The men who enter the houses of prostitutes are doomed. None of these men will ever be same again.
9. Cherish the virtues of loyalty and kindness in your heart.
10. *Good judgement and commonsense are the result of complete trust in the LORD.*
11. Just as a father punishes a son he delights in, to make him better, so the LORD chastens and corrects you, for his punishment is proof of HIS Love.
12. Do not get in to unnecessary fights.
    Do not envy violent men or try to imitate them.
    Do not plot against your neighbour as he trusts you.
    Do not withhold repayment of your debts.
13. GOD gives his friendship to the good only.
14. Avoid the wicked as far as possible. Evil men can not rest unless they cause some one to stumble and fall.
15. *My son! gaurd your affections, for they influence everything esle in your life.*
16. Be faithful and true to your wife.
    Keep away from what is not yours.
17. Son! if you endorse a note for someone you hardly know, guaranteeing his debt you are in serous trouble. Get out of the agreement if you possibly can! Swallow your pride and do not let embarrassment stand in the way. Go and beg to have your name erased. Do not put it off. Do it now, and do not rest until you get out of this trap.
18. *Avoid laziness at any cost.* Take a lesson from the industrious ants.
19. Young man, obey your father and mother, take to heart all of their advice and keep in mind everything they tell you. Their advice will guide you and save you from harm throughout your life.
20. The LORD hates seven things. They are :
    1. Murder 2. Lying 3. Haughtiness 4. Plotting evil 5. Eagerness to do wrong 6. A false witness and 7. Sowing discord among brothers.
21. *The signs of a wicked man are :*
    1. He is a constant liar
    2. He signals his true intentions to his friends with eyes, fingers and feet
    3. He is always thinking up new schemes to swindle people
    4. He stirs up trouble everywhere
    5. *The only solace is that he will be destroyed suddenly.*
22. A man who commits adultery with another's wife shall not go unpunished wounds and constant disgrace are his lot. The woman's husband will have no mercy on you in his days of vengeance.
23. A wise youth makes hay while the sunshines.

A lazy youth sleeps away his hour of opportunity.

24. Bold reproof of sin leads to peace; winking at sin leads to sorrow.
25. The words of a good man are few but worth listening to, the words of a fool are too many and worthless.
26. The good man's goodness delivers him; the evil man's treachery is his undoing.
27. When an evil man dies, all his hopes perish for they are based upon this earthly life.
28. To quarrel with a neighbour is foolish.
29. A gossip goes around spreading rumors while a good man tries to quiet them.
30. Your own soul is nourished when you are kind and it is destroyed when you are cruel.
31. *You can be very sure the evil man will not go unpunished for ever.*
32. By helping others a man helps himself.
33. One who holds on too tightly is likely to lose everything.
34. To learn first you must want to be taught.
35. TRUTH stands the test of time; lies are soon exposed.
36. Self control means controlling the tongue;
    A quick retort can ruin everything.
37. Pride leads to arguments; be humble take advice and become wise.
38. Wealth from hard work grows.
    Wealth from gambling quickly disappears.
39. *It is pleasant to see plans develop. That is why fools refuse to give them up even when they are wrong.*
40. The wise man looks ahead; the fool refuses to face facts and attempts to fool himself.
41. The common bond of the good people is goodwill.
    The common bond of the evil people is their *guilt.*
42. *A wise man is cautious and avoids danger;* a fool plunges ahead with great confidence without a thought for possible consequences and lands amidst danger.
43. *A prudent man understands the need for proof for anything that he is told; only a simpleton believes everything he is told.*
44. The rich have many friends and the poor man is despised even by his own neighbours..
45. A gentle answer turns away wrath but harsh words cause quarrels.
46. *Only the good can give good advice.*
47. Better a little with reverence for GOD than great treasure and trouble with it.
48. *Dishonest money brings grief to all the family.*
49. *If you want your work to succeed, Commit it to the LORD; We can make our plans but the final outcome is in GOD's hands.*
50. When a man is trying to please GOD, the LORD makes even his worst enemies to be at peace with him.
51. A child's glory is his father.
    An old mans grand children are his crowning glory.
52. A bribe works like magic, whoever uses it will prosper.
53. It is useless to pay tuition to educate a rebel who has no heart for truth.

54. It is hard to stop a quarrel once it starts, so don't let it begin.
55. The man of few words and settled mind is wise; even a fool is thought to be wise when he is silent.
56. *Do not decide about anything before you know all the facts.*
57. *Any story sounds true until someone tells the other side and sets the record straight.*
58. *A wise man restrains his anger and overlooks insults.*
59. Discipline your son in his early years while there is hope, if you don't you will ruin his life.
60. *Only fools insist on quarrelling; it is an honour for a man to stay out of a fight.*
61. It is a wonderful heritage to have an honest father.
62. Do not tell your secrets to a gossip, unless you want them broadcast to the world.
63. *An angryman is silenced by giving him a gift.*
64. *The wiseman saves for the future, but the fool spends whatever he gets.*
65. Victory comes from God only
Your own shrewdness and the advice of your counselors are of use only when the LORD assents.
66. Do not move the ancient boundaries. It amounts to stealing.
67. Do not associate with evil men; do not long for their favours and gifts; they want to use you as their pawn and their kindness is only a trick.
68. Be on your guard when you get an invitation to dine from a rich man, for he is trying to bribe you and no good is going to come out of his invitation.
69. Do not weary yourself trying to get rich.
For riches can disappear as though they had the wings of a bird.
70. Avoid all alcoholic drinks.
Blood shot eyes, quarrels, fights, wounds, hallucinations and delirium tremens are the results of excessive indulgence in alcoholic drinks.
71. An enterprise is built by wise planning, becomes strong through commonsense, and profits wonderfully by keeping abreast of the facts.
72. Develop your business first before building your house.
73. O evil man! don't you know that a good man though you trip him up seven times will each time rise again? But one calamity is enough to lay you low.
74. Do not visit your neighbour too often, or you will outwear your welcome.
75. To be happy and cheerful around a person who is sad and suffering, is as bad as rubbing salt in his wounds.
76. It is bad for men to think about all the honours they deserve.
77. Do not priase yourself; let others do it.
78. A man who strays from home is like a bird that wanders from its nest.
79. The man who sets a trap for others will get caught in it himself.
80. A lazy man thinks that he is smarter than seven men.
81. The master may get better work from an untrained apprentice than from a skilled rebel.
82. To interfere in an argument that is not any of your business, is as foolish as to twist (or yank to pull with a jerk) a dog's ears.

83. Fire goes out for lack of fuel, and tensions disappear when gossip stops.
84. Pretty words may hide a wicked heart, just as a pretty glaze covers a common claypot.
85. A man with hate in his heart may sound pleasant enough but do not believe him. Though he pretends to be so kind, his hatred will finally come to light for all to see.
86. Ambition and death are alike in this; neither is ever satisfied.
87. If you shout a pleasant greeting to a friend too early in the morning, he will count it as a curse.
88. The wicked flee when no one is chasing them! But the good are bold as lions.
89. A man who refuses to admit his mistakes can never be successful. But if he confesses and forsakes them, he gets another chance.
90. Sometimes mere words are not enough—discipline and due punishment are necessary-for the words may not be heeded.

Source

The Living Bible, Tyndale House Publishers, 1971.

12

WORDS TO LIVE BY I

1. ***ABILITY***
We judge ourselves by what we feel capable of doing, while others judge us by what we have already done. — H.W. LONGELLOW
2. ***ADVERSITY***
Adversity has the effect of eliciting talents which in prosperous circumstances would have lain dormant.
— HORACE
3. ***ADVICE***
To know one's self is difficult
To advice another is easy.
— THAULES
4. ***AFFECTION***
Those who marry where they do not love are likely to love where they do not marry.
— FULLER
5. ***AMBITION***
Ambition is not a weakness unless it be disproportioned to capacity. One who has more ambition than ability, is likely to be at once weak and unhappy.
— G.S. HILLARD
6. ***APPEARANCES***
Men in general judge more from appearances than from reality. All men have eyes but few have the gift of penetration. — *NICCOLO MACHIAVELLI*
7. ***ATTENTION***
The power of applying attention steady and undissipated to a single object is the sure mark of a superior genius. — CHESTER FIELD
8. ***AVARICE***
Avarice in old age is foolish, for what can be more absurd than to increase ones assets for the road, the nearer one approaches to ones journey's end? — CICERO
9. ***BOLDNESS***
Boldness is everblind, for it sees not inconveniences and dangers; whence *it is bad in council, though good in execution.*
— BACON

10. ***BRIBERY***
GOLD is always better than reason and philosophy. Gold dissipates every doubt and scruple in an instant; accommodates itself to the meanest capacities, silences the loud and clamorous, and makes the most obstinate and inflexible cringe (shrink back in fear). — ADDISON

11. ***CAUTION***
Caution in crediting (enter a sum of money to a person's credit) and reserve in speaking and in revealing one's self to but very few are the best securities for a safe passage in this world and to ones own peace of mind. — THOMAS A KEMPIS

12. It is well to learn caution by the misfortunes of others. — PUBLIUS SYRUS

13. ***COMPANIONSHIP***
Be cautious with whom you associate and never give your company or your confidence to those of whose good principles you are not sure.
— W.H. COLERIDGE

14. ***CONDUCT***
We are never so much disposed to quarrel with others, as when we are dissatisfied with ourselves. — ANON

15. ***COUNSEL***
There is as much difference between the counsel that a friend gives and that a man gives himself as there is between the counsel of a friend and a flatterer.
— BACON

16. ***COVETOUSNESS***
After hypocrites, the greatest dupes of the devil are the covetous. The covetous live miserably and meanly and exhaust themselves in the disappointments and vexations of business. They sacrifice their health, happiness and integrity for the pleasure of dying rich. — COLTON

17. ***CUNNING***
Cunning leads to Knavery (KNAVE = A rouge, a scoundrel) only lying makes the difference; *cunning + LIES = Knavery.* — BRUYERE

18. ***DANGER***
We should avoid unnecessarily exposing ourselves to danger. — CICERO

19. ***DECEIVING***
It is easy to deceive one's self without perceiving it, as it is difficult to deceive others without their finding it out. — ROCHEFOUCAULD

20. ***DEBT***
Run not in the debt. A man who runs in to debt, pays at the latter end a third part more than the principal and is in perpetual servitude to his creditors; lives uncomfortably; is necessitated to increase his debts to stop his creditor's mouth; and many times falls in to desparate courses. — SIR M. HALE

21. ***DECISION***
He that can not say 'NO', when tempted to evil, will be ruined sooner or later. He looses the respect even of those who tempt him to evil. — J. HAWES

When one can say 'NO' not only to sin and evil, but also to things *pleasant* and *profitable* which would *hinder one's primary work, then only one will know how to make the most of life.* — *C.A. STODDARD*

22. ***DISHONESTY***

That which is won by dishonesty will never last. The same corrupt disposition which inclines a man to dishonest gain, will incline him to easy and sinful ways of spending.

— M. HENRY

23. ***DISTANCE***

Distance sometimes endears friendship for separation from those we love shows us by the loss, their real value and dearness to us. — HOWELL

24. ***DISTRUST***

There is no royal road to health but through regular physical exercise so there is no royal road to safety but in constant distrust. — WENDELL PHILLIPS

25. ***DUTY***

I slept and dreamed that life was beauty
I woke up and found that life was duty — ELLEN HOOPER

26. ***QUALITY***

Men are by nature unequal. It is vain therefore to treat them as if they were equal.

— JAMES ANTHONY FROUDE

27. ***ETHICS***

I can not give you a code of conduct, go and watch the best and wisest men you can find and imitate them. — *ARISTOTLE*

28. ***EVIL***

One may cause evil to others not only by his actions, but also by his inactions, and in either case he is justly accountable to them for the injury.

— JOHN STUART MILL

29. ***EVIL***

We sometimes learn more from the sight of evil than from an example of good; it is profitable to learn from the evil which is so common, *while that which is good is so rare.* — *PASCAL*

30. ***EXAMPLE***

Example is the school of mankind; they will learn at no other.

— EDMUNDE BURKE

31. ***EXAGGERATION***

Some persons are exaggerators by temperament – they do not mean untruth, their imaginations vivid and their feelings are strong so that their statements are largely discounted by those of calm judgement and cooler temperament. They do not realize that "*we always weaken what we exaggerate*". — TRYON EDWARDS

32. ***FALSEHOOD***

The telling of a falsehood is like that cut of sabre; for though the wound may heal the scar of it will remain. — SAADI

33. ***FAME***

They who neglect their social duties for their individual life fall into darkness; and those who sacrifice their individuality for social popularity fall in to greater darkness.
— ISHOPANISHAD

34. ***FATHER***

The child is the father of man. — WILLIAM WORS WORTH

35. ***FAULTS***

The fault, dear BRUTUS, is not in our stars,
But in ourselves, that we are underlings — SHAKESPEARE

36. ***FOOL***

A fool may be known by six things. They are :

1. He displays anger without cause
2. *His speech is without profit*
3. He initiates change without progress
4. He inquires without object
5. He puts trust in a stranger
6. He mistakes foes for friends — ARAB PROVERB

37. ***FRAUD***

For the most part, fraud in the end secures for its companions repentance and shame.
— C. SIMMONS

38. ***HASTE***

No two things differ more than hurry and despatch. Hurry is the mark of a weak mind; despatch of a strong one. — COLTON

39. ***HONESTY***

He that loseth his honesty has nothing else to lose. — JOHN LYLY

40. ***IMITATION***

He who imitates evil always goes beyond the example that is set; he who imitates good always falls short. — GUICCIARDINI

41. ***INDEPENDENCE***

It is not the greatness of a man's means that makes him independent, so much as the smallness of his wants. —*COBBET*

42. ***INFLUENCE***

We can not think or act but in the direction pointed out by the soul of someone who has passed before us — The dead never die. — BULWER

Let no man imagine that he has no influence whatever he may be and wherever he may be placed, the man who thinks becomes a source of power and light.
— HENRY GEROGE

43. ***INSULT***

The way to procure insults is to submit to them. A man meets with no more respect than he exacts — HAZLITT

44. ***JUDGE***

The four necessary traits of a judge are :

1. He should listen courteously
2. He should answer wisely
3. He should consider soberly
4. And finally he should decide impartially — SOCRATES

45. *KNOWLEDGE*

The more extensive a man's knowledge of what has been done, the greater will be his power of knowing what to do. — DISRAELI

46. *LIAR*

This is the punishment of a liar; He is not believed even when he speaks the truth.
— BABYLONIAN TALMUD

47. *LIFE*

Life is the art of drawing sufficient conclusions from insufficient premises.
— SAMUEL BUTLER

48. *OBSERVATION*

He alone is an acute observer who can observe minutely without being observed.
— LAVATER

49. *PAST*

Study the past if you would divine the future. — CONFUCIUS

50. *Those who can not remember the past are condemned to repeat it.*
— *GEORGE SANTAYANA*

51. *PRUDENCE*

Prudence implies much gain
Acquired with little pain — PANCHATANTRA

52. *PUNISHMENT*

Penalties may be delayed for the wrongs committed but they are sure to come, sooner or later. — H.W. BEECHER

53. *SELF-DECEPTION*

Nothing is so easy as to deceive one's self, for what we wish we readily believe; but such expectations are often inconsistent with the reality of things.
— DEMOSTHENES

54. *SIMPLICITY*

In character, in manners, in style and in all things, the supreme excellence is simplicity.
— LONGFELLOW

55. *STYLE*

If you wish to model yourself on a great man, you should follow not his style but his training. — V. SAMUEL

56. *SUICIDE*

To commit suicide in order to avoid anything that is unpleasant, disagreeable or an evil, is not the hallmark of a braveman, but that of a coward. — ARISTOTLE

57. *SUSPICION*

Discreet and well found suspicion avoids a multitude of evils, which credulity brings upon itself. C. SIMMONS

58. ***TEMPERANCE***
I have four good reasons for avoiding alcoholic drinks – my health is better, my head is clearer, my heart is lighter and my purse is heavier. — GUTARIE

59. ***TREACHERY***
Fellowship in treason is a shaky ground of confidence. — EDMUND BURKE
TREACHERY though at first very cautious in the end betrays itself. — LIVY

60. ***TRUTH***
Truth is not only violated by falsehood; it may be equally outraged by silence.
— AMIEN

61. ***VIRTUE***
Honour is the reward of virtue. — CICERO

62. ***WISDOM***
Knowledge to become wisdom, needs judgement. — V. SAMUEL

Source

Good Thoughts of Prominent Personalities of the World, Ved Bushan, 1967.

13

JAINISM (MAHAVEERA, 599–527 B.C.)

Life is dear to all creatures, even though it is an admixture of happiness and misery. To explain the cause of misery and to relieve it to the extent possible, and to enhance happiness in ones life is the main function of any religion. The belief in to which we happen to be born is the one which is generally adapted, until through education, travel, criticism and reconstruction it is replaced by the development of a better understanding of ones own religion as well as other religions.

THE JAIN SCRIPTURES are claimed to be the historical records of the lives and teachings of their spiritual leaders, and they are the primary source of *JAIN DOCTRINES. AHIMSA* (NON VIOLENCE) and *DAYA* (Compassion) are the two principles on which JAINISM primarily rests. It affirms that religion is the only thing that can provide true consolation and peace of mind, at the time of affliction and at the hour of death.

THE SPIRITUAL TEACHER

According to Jain scriptures, a spiritual teacher has the following five characteristics; namely :

1. He does not destroy any form of life, animal vegetable or mineral (water for instance) through carelessness of his mind, speech and body.
2. He always speaks truth in a pleasant way and that too only when he thinks that it is beneficial to the person to whom it is spoken.
3. He does not take anything, which is not given to him by its owner, and even when offered he takes only those things which are necessary for the maintenance of his body.
4. H has entirely given up the sex passion.
5. He does not own any property in the sense of ownership, as understood in law.

RULES OF CONDUCT

The purpose of rules of conduct is two fold 1. They help a spiritual aspirant to advance on the path of spiritual realization and 2. They also keep him from sliding down on the path. These relate to ones social life. It is only in society and not in solitude, that a man develops his inter personal relations necessary for progress. The ultimate purpose and outcome of these rules is furthering the welfare of all. These rules are broadly based on AHIMSA, DAYA, love etc.

THIRTY FIVE RULES OF CONDUCT

1. One should follow some kind of business or trade or profession which is not of an ignoble or degrading nature. He should follow it in a just and honest way and in proportion to his capital, or in the case of service under the employment of other people in proportion to his strength, and at anytime not undertaking more than he can perform.
2. The layman should marry; and he should not marry a person from the same ancestors or of the same family; but a person whose character, tastes language and culture etc., are of the same kind; this is to render misunderstandings, discord and inharmony, less likely than otherwise might be the case.
3. He should avoid gambling, drinking, meat eating and lust.
4. He should respect and appreciate the conduct and life of any spiritual teacher. The layman may not be able to act as the teacher, the least he can do is to appreciate and emulate him to the extent possible.
5. He should control the following undesirable traits;
    1. Sexual passion, and the lust full eye towards any girl or woman (not the man's wife).
    2. Anger and its components rashness and injury and the desire to hurt or injure others by ones speech or actions.
    3. Greed
    4. Pride
    5. Boasting about ones family, ancestors and about ones strength, greatness etc.
    6. Gambling, fishing and hunting are to be avoided.
6. He should keep away from a place where famine or plague is; a place of battle; or from a place, where there is much ill feeling towards him by the people around him. If he stays in such places; he will not be able to accomplish, what he wishes to accomplish.
7. He should live in a country where he will have adequate protection of his life and property by the government.
8. He should move in the company of the good and spiritually more advanced people than himself.
9. His house should not be among quarrelsome people or undesirable neighbours. It should not be too concealed and it should not be constructed over a burial ground.
10. He should dress according to his means
    Even when he is rich, his dress should not be showy.
11. His expenses should be in proportion to his income.
12. If there is some particular well established custom in the country where he lives, he

should follow it, if it is not contrary to any of his moral principles.

13. He should avoid meat eating and wine drinking.
14. He should not libel or slander anybody.
15. However exposing fraudulent persons, is not libel or slander.
16. Among equals, he should keep the company of persons of good conduct only.
17. He should always respect his parents.
18. He should avoid ill feeling with others either by his words or actions.
19. He should look after those who are dependent on him. He should assign to them their proper work and make them do it right. He should not ignore wrong doing on their part.
20. One should respect and render service to the 1. GURU (MASTER). 2. GUEST and look after the deserving poor.
21. One should eat and drink at the proper time in conformity with the nature of his constitution. Excessive eating and drinking are to be avoided.
22. When he is physically weak, he should adopt the proper remedy.
23. He should not travel in countries where there are dangers such as 1. Earth quakes 2. Famine 3. Plague 4. Criminals and 5. WILD ANIMALS (such as lions and tigers etc.).
24. He should try to live in peace with people around him. He should avoid unnecessary hostility with others.
25. He must set an example of the good life to those who are in a low state of development, and let them feel the influence of a purer life.
26. He should not be too intimate with anybody.
27. He should respect and render service to those who have taken spiritual vows and those who are known for their knowledge and wisdom.
28. This rule is concerned with aims and goals of life. Broadly speaking, there are four goals in life, namely :
    1. Desires : These are for nice dresses, nice houses name and fame etc.
    2. To acquire wealth.
    3. To do good to society.
    4. To attain spiritual liberation (MOKSHA).

    The ordinary man of the world strives to obtain 1 and 2 objectives only, however a spiritual aspirant should strive to achieve all the above mentioned four goals, but in such a way that a higher one not is sacrificed for the sake of a lower one.
29. In undertaking any task, he should always consider his strength and weaknesses. He should not undertake more than his strength will allow him to carryout.
30. He should always attempt to rise higher and higher on the spiritual path.
31. He should try to perform every work in its proper time and place.
32. One should hear or read holy scriptures every day.
33. He should give up unreasonable obstinacy in all things. He should yield and not be stubborn.
34. He should always strive to acquire virtue.

35. He should use his intelligence and critical faculty to assess and judge beliefs, opinions, philosophies and various religions.

Six Daily Activities:

A spiritual aspirant is expected to perform the following activities :

1. Worship of the master (GURU) or the image of the Master.
2. Rendering homage to ones GURU (Master).
3. Studying holy scriptures every day.
4. Practice of some form of self control every day.
5. Practice of some form of austeriy every day such as control of hunger (UPAVASA) and DHYANA (concentration by assuming a posture etc.).

Twelve Special Rules of Conduct

These rules are meant to bring out the hidden potentialities of the spiritual aspirant. These twelve special rules or vows may be divided in *to three classes,* the first five vows are called the lesser vows as compared with the more strict vows of the monk. The next three vows (GUNA VRATAS) are of a kind, which help and support the first five vows. And the last four vows are disciplinary in nature (SIKSAVRATA); the practice of them forms a sort of preparation for the monk life. The JAIN concept of a vow (or VRATA) differs markedly from the VEDIC concept of a VRATA. In the practice and choice of these vows, there is no oath to a superior or to a Deity. Neither is it a decree or command issued by a Deity to his subjects.

1. FIRST VOW
   STOOTHALA PRANATIPATA VIRAMANA VRATA
   It is a vow to refrain from HIMSA (Killing or destroying life in its various forms). Examples of killing include :
1. Hunting, shooting and fishing for food (fish game, meat etc.) 2. vivi section 3. For dress (skin, feathers etc.) 4. In war 5. For private revenge 6. Animal and fowl sacrifices in the name of religious ceremonies 7. Killing insects and flies which are pests 8. capital punishment 9. In self defence etc.
   One who indulges in HIMSA will have to experience the following sooner or later. They are :
   1. Sorrow 2. Separation from friends and relatives 3. Lameness 4. An incurable disease 5. Decreased longevity and finally 6. in the next birth, he will be born as an animal.
2. SECOND VOW
   STOOLA MRSAVADA VIRAMANA VRATA
   It is a vow to refrain from telling gross falsehoods.
   There are four classes of falsehoods namely :
   1. The denial of a fact
   2. The affirmation of that which does not exist
   3. Designating a thing, something other than what it is

4. Statements that are injurious to others
5. Lies are spoken by reasons of certain states of mind such as 1. deceitfulness 2. greed 3. hatred 4. pride and 5. anger etc.

3. THIRD VOW
STHOOLA ADATTADANA VIRAMANA VRATA
It is a vow to refrain from gross forms of taking what is not given, namely theft.

4. FOURTH VOW
SVADARA SANTOSA- PARADARA VIRAMANA VRATA
It is a vow to moderate sex with ones own wife and to avoid it with other women. Dr NICHOLSON is of the opinion that the act of procreation weakens a person both physically and mentally. According to JAIN SCRIPTURES, CELIBACY facilitates spiritual development, by converting semen in to a higher substance inside the human body. However control of sex passion, gives infact a strong will.
Excessive indulgence in sex has the following deleterious effects
1. One looses sight of his better nature
2. One looses respect and faith in scriptures and ones spiritual teachers and superiors
3. One looses and squanders money
4. one looses interest in good actions and fails to perform them.

The science of breath, according to JAIN SCRIPTURES, explains that in every activity one has to use the force of breath, which in turn is measured by the number of breaths taken for its completion. It is the quantum of psychic and physical energy spent for the execution of a work.

EXAMPLES are :
1. *In DHYANA subtle energy of 4 Breaths*
2. When the mind is filled with good thoughts energy of 6 Breaths
3. While sitting in silence energy of 10 Breaths
4. While speaking energy of 12 Breaths
5. *While sleeping energy of 16 Breaths*
6. While walking energy of 22 Breaths
7. *In sexual intercourse energy of 24 Breaths is consumed.*

For monks complete abstinence from sex and for a layman, moderation in sex are advocated.

5. FIFTH VOW
STHOOLA PARIGRAHA PARIMANA VRATA
It is a vow to reduce ones desire for possessions, and also to limit the extent of ones possessions. It is the uncontrolled desire for possessions, which enslaves a man until his death. By controlling and limiting this raging desire for possessions, in his heart, one acquires contentment and steadiness.
The next three vows are called *GUNAVRATAS* and they complement the first five vows.

6. SIXTH VOW
DIG PARIMANA VRATA
This vow refers to the limitation of the area in which one lives and conducts all his

activities. It is the limitation of the distance and direction beyond which one will not go or send ones men. By undertaking this vow, one proclaims to all living beyond the specified area, that one will not strive with others or hurt them.

7. SEVENTH VOW
   BHOGOPABHOGA PARIMANA VRATA
   It is a vow which imposes limitation of the quantity of things one uses such as foods, drinks, flowers, ornaments, pictures, clothes, furniture and houses etc.
8. EIGHT VOW
   ANARDHANDA VIRAMANA VRATA
   This vow is an undertaking not to incur unnecessary evils. We bring unnecessary evils upon ourselves to no purpose by indulging in thoughts, words, and deeds, which are of no benefit to ourselves, to our friends and to the society.
   The following are some of the examples :
   1. Constantly fearing the loss of the good things we have such as *health, wealth and friends*
   2. Constantly fearing that unwanted things may come upon us such as *pain, disease and poverty*
   3. *Undue anxiety to get rid of pain, disease and poverty*
   4. *Undue anxiety about future*
   5. *Indulging in slander*
   6. *Giving gratuitous advice about matters that are no concern of ours*
   7. *Wishing the death of someone in order to inherit his or her property.*
9. NINTH VOW
   SAMAYIKA
   It is a vow by observing which one acquires equanimity. This is the first of the disciplinary vows, the so called *SIKSHA VRATAS*. By undertaking this vow, *one is supposed to think about his ATMA (the permanent self).* The vow advices the aspirant to sit in a certain place and read or meditate on holy subjects of philosophy and scriptures, and especially to regret misdoings done by self and resolve not to repeat them.
10. TENTH VOW
    DESAVAKASIKA VRATA
    By undertaking this vow, one imposes restriction on ones movements and confines himself to one room, or one house for a day, once a year atleast.
11. ELEVENTH VOW
    PAWSADHOPAVASA VRATA
    This vow is the same as the 9th vow, but continued for 12, or 24 hours, and accompanied by some fasting. It is usual to keep to one place, do no business, and to abstain from food and drink for 12, 24, 48, or 72, consecutive hours once a week, or once a month, or atleast once a year.
12. TWELTH VOW
    ATITHI SAMVIBHAGA VRATA
    This vow is an undertaking to invite some JAIN monk, on the day following the fast

undertaken in the previous vow and to partake of some of the food to be eaten with the guest. This vow if taken, must be practiced at least once a year.

TWELVE REFLECTIONS (ANUPREKSA)

The following twelve reflections help the spiritual aspirant on the path of self realization. The are :

1. *Everything in this world is transient and subject to change (ANITYA).*
2. In this world of pain, misery, disease, old age and death, there is no other protection refuge or help *than our own practice of the truth;* "AS WE SOW, SO WE REAP" *(ASARAVA).*
3. This continual cycle of births and deaths has been going on for countless ages, and one should make efforts to free oneself from this eternal cycle (SAMSARA).
4. *I entered this world by myself alone and I will go out of it myself alone,* I have to do my own work of self moral improvement, and I have to bear my own burden of KARMA alone *(EKATVA).*
5. All the things of the world, including my own body (which is only by MAYA (Delusion) called oneself) are separate from my ATMA (ETERNAL SELF) (ANYATVA).
6. The ATMA (SOUL) is resident in the human body which contains, blood, urine, motion etc. (ASUCHITVA).
7. It is the continual inflow of new thoughts, words and deeds due to delusion and want of self control which is the source of our miseries and pains (ASRAVA).
8. This ASRAVA should be stopped by control of body, mind and senses and by acquiring spiritual knowledge and by practicing DHYANA (concentration) etc. (SAMVARA).
9. By strictly observing the rules of conduct one should eradicate from his mind undesirable qualities such as cruelty, ignorance weakness and misery etc. (NIRJARA).
10. Always reflect on the relation between LOKA (MATTER) and ATMA (SOUL). Know that PANCHABOOTAS (FIVE ELEMENTS namely air, space, water, fire and matter) are permanent and were not created.
11. Know that it is very difficult to acquire right knowledge, right convictions and right conduct (BUDDHI DURLABHATVA).
12. Know that right knowledge, right convictions and right conduct are the source of happiness. (DHARMASVAKHYATANU CHINTANA).

Qualities of an Individual of Higher Religious Life :

According to *JAIN SCRIPTURES,* an individual who aspires to a higher religious life should posses the following qualities.

1. The aspirant should have a sound, strong and a flawless constitution (RUPAVAN).
2. He should have good moral character (LOKAPRIYA).
3. He should not be a cruel person (AKRURA).

4. He should be a cautious man.
5. He should be a honest person (ASATHA).
6. He should be pleasing to others, by nature; and by his very appearance trusted and very easily served by others (PRAKRITISOMA).
7. He must be powerful enough to do good to himself and to others, earnest, a careful observer, and one who puts mature consideration in to actions. *A man of superficial nature is unfit for spiritual life* (AKSUDRA).
8. He should be civil to all. He will try to help others in their meritorious work even at the sacrifice of less important business of his own (SU-DAKSINYA).
9. *He will live up to his principles even to death (LAJJALU).*
10. He is sympathetic and compassionate (DAYALU).
11. He is just and impartial and known for his discrimination. *As he can discriminate correctly between right and wrong, he will not make mistakes of judgement as to conduct.* He will judge all religious beliefs on their individual merits only. (MADHYASTHA SAUMYA DHRUSTIVAN).
12. *He thinks first and talks next* (SATKATHA).
13. He always tries to see the good in others and overlooks their faults, *and if one reiterates the faults and lapses of others, no good comes out of it and hatred is increased* (GUNAGRAHI).
14. He always moves in the company of virtuous, friendly and well behaved persons (SUPASAYULA).
15. *He has foresight. He only takes up work that tells, where the result is great in proportion to the effort and only work that is approved by good men (DEERGHADARSI).*
16. *He discriminates and differentiates minutely right from wrong in all its details and ramifications (VISESHAJNANA).*
17. He tries always to walk in the footsteps of really greatmen (VRUDDHANUGA).
18. He is polite (VINAYI).
19. *He is full of gratitude and always anxious to make use of opportunities to repay kindnesses* (KRUTAJNA).
20. He is always bent upon the good of others without expecting any return, the best good being to bring them to the right path (PARAHITA-NIRATA).
21. He is intelligent and has a quick grasp of matters and is able to learn without much trouble to himself or to his teacher (LABHA–LAKSYA).

CONCLUSION

The universe consists of *JEEVAS* (conscious beings) and *AJEEVAS* (unconscious things). We attract *(ASRAVA)* subtle forms of various matters to ourselves and we assimilate them resulting in a state called *BANDHA*. Because of this phenomenon of BANDHA, the inherent qualities of the ATMA (SOUL) are thus more or less obscured, and as a result of this, various conditions of *PUNYA (WEAL* = welfare, prosperity, good fortune) and *PAPA* (*WOE* = Affliction, bitter grief, calamities) are experienced by the JEEVA.

The unnatural energies generated in the soul may be stopped and destroyed by stopping the influx (SAMVARA) and by ridding the soul of the these extraneous matters (NIRJARA). Rules of conduct mentioned above, self control DHYANA (concentration) etc. help the spiritual aspirant on the path of self realization. He acquires right knowledge, love, strength, wisdom and finally MOKSHA (LIBERATION).

Source

Jainism (Mahaveera, 599 – 527 B.C.) by Herbert Warren, 1912.

14

DHARMAPADAM—GOWTAMA BUDDHA

The Dharmaphadam consists of *423* melodious Pali verses, uttered by the Buddha on about 300 occasions to suit the temperaments of the listeners, in the course of his preaching tours during his ministry of *forty five years.* The gems of truth embodied in these verses aptly illustrate the moral and philosophical teachings of BUDDHA. Three months after the passing away of GOWTAMA BUDDHA, in the year *480 B.C.,* his disciples held a council at Rajagaha, and they arranged and classified his teachings in its present form and named it *"DHARMAPADAM".* In course of time it was translated in to Sanskrit and many other languages. Most of these verses are better understood, when read with context. The greatness of the BUDDHA lies in, in his exposition of profound truths in plain and simple terms.

1. YAMAKA VARGA (CONTRARY WAYS)

1. *Mind is the seat of all KARMAS* (Manaha poorvangamā)
   Mind is the seat of DHARMA (Dharmamanahā)
   Mind is the seat of all evil (manasā chetratpa dustena).
   If one speaks or acts with an evil mind sorrow (DUKHAM) pursues him, even as the wheel follows the chariot (Chakramiva Vahataha padam).
2. Mind is the seat of all karmas
   Mind is the seat of DHARMA
   If one speaks or acts with a pure mind, happiness follows him, even as his own shadow always follows him.
3. "He abused me, he beat me, he defeated me and he robbed me", the hatred of those who harbour such thoughts, is not lessened.
   (Viram nasāmyati)
4. "He abused me, he beat me, he defeated me and he robbed me "the hatred of those who *donot* harbour such thoughts is lessened. (Viram teshu upasyamati)
5. Hatred never ceases by hatred in this world.
   Hatred is conquered by LOVE alone, and *this is an ancient law.*
   (Esha Dharma Sanatanaha)

6. *Fools are not aware that they have to leave this world sooner or later.* The minds of those who understand this Eternal Law, become calm and peaceful.

(Syāmanti medhagāha)

7. A man of unrestraint senses, and one who is lazy and immoderate in his food habits, and who has no ambition, and who is incapable of hardwork, such a one is overthrown by MARA (A devata who is higher than Indra, but lesser than Brahma in Buddhistic lore), just as a weak tree is easily uprooted by wind during a storm.
8. One who is without self control (Dama) and truthfulness (Satyabhýam) even if he wears the yellow robe (Kashayam), he is not worthy of it.
9. One who sees the real as real, the unreal as unreal and who entertains right thoughts achieves the real goal (Samyak sankalpa gocharaha).
10. *Lust (Raga) does not penetrate a well controlled mind, just as rain does not leak through a well Thached house*

(Evam Subhavitam Chittam rāgo nasamati vidhyati)

11. *Evil doer (Pāpakari) grieves and suffers here and hereafter (Ehasōchati, pretasochati) on account of his evil deeds*

(Drustvā karma klista matmanaha)

2. APRAMĀDA VARGA (CAREFUL ATTENTION)

12. Careful attention in doing good deeds is the path to NIRVANA. The life of a man who is devoid of careful attention, is futile indeed.
13. The good fame of one, who is energetic, mindful, pure in deed, considerate, self controlled, and who is known for right and careful living steadily increases.

(yasobhi vardhate)

14. By sustained effort, earnestness, discipline and self control let the intelligent man make for himself an island which no flood of sense pleasures can submerge.

(Dweepam kūryāt medhāveeyam Oghūnābhikirati)

15. Careful (Apramattaha) amongst the careless (pramatteshu), wide awake amongst the slumbering, the intelligent man advances like a swift horse leaving a weak jade (an inferior, worn out horse) behind.
16. *Earnestness is everpraised; carelessness is ever despised.*

(Apramadam prasamsanti, pramādo garhitaha sadā)

3. CHITTA VARGA (THE MIND)

17. The mind is hard to check, the mind is fickle, and the mind is swift. However a well controlled mind is conducive to happiness.

(Sādhu chittam dānta sukhāvaham)

18. *What neither mother, nor father, nor any other relative can do to you, a well directed and controlled mind does to you and facilitates your welfare.*

(Samyak pranihitam chittam sreyāmsum enuntaha kuryāt)

4. PUSPA VARGA (FLOWERS)

19. A wise man investigates and follows the well taught path of virtue (DHARMAPADAM), even as an expert garland maker plucks various beautiful flowers only to make a garland.
(ko dharmapadam sudesitam kusalaha pusphamiva pracheshyati)
20. *Death carries off suddenly the man who is immersed in SAMSARA* (Asakta manasam naram) *just as a sudden flood in the night carries off all the people in a sleeping village.*
21. A sage should move in the village without causing any inconvenience to others, just as a bee gathers honey from flowers without damaging their colour or scent.
22. Do not do any acts enmical to others. Do not waste time in thinking about others lapses and faults. *Always think about your own deeds done and undone.*
(Na pareshām vilomāni na pareshām krutā krutam atmana eva aveksheta krutani Akrutanicha).
23. The words of a man who does not practice what he says are futile just as a colourful flower without any scent is useless.
(Evum subhashita vak aphala bhavati akurvataha)
24. Everyman should perform many good deeds in his life time to make it worthy, just as many beautiful flowers are needed to make a nice garland.
(Evum jatena martyena kartavyam kusalam bahu)
25. The practice of good conduct (Seelam) is better than even the fragrance of sandalwood, agar and jasmine etc.

5. BALA VARGA (FOOLS)

26. Long is the night to the wakeful
(Deergho jagrato rātri hi)
Long is the journey to the weary
(Deergham srāntasya yojanam)
Long is Samsara to the fool who knows not the DHARMA
(deergha balanam samsara saddharmam Avijānatām)
27. If one can not get the friendship of a Sajjana, it is better to be alone. Friendship with a MOORKA should be avoided at any cost.
28. *"I have sons, I have wealth" thinks the fool and worries over them. When his own body is not his (for long), how can the sons and wealth be his?*
(Putrame santi dhanam mesti eti bao vihanyate Atmahe Atmanā nāsti kutaha putraha kuto dhanam)
29. A fool even if he associates with the wise, throughout his lifetime, he will never understand DHARMA, just as a spoon does not know the flavour of a soup even though it is always in it.
(Nasa dharmam vijānati darvee soopa rasam yadhā)
30. An intelligent man understands DHARMA in the duration of a Muhurtam ( ) in the

company of the wise, just as the tongue comprehends the taste of a soup in an instant.
(kshipram dharmam vejānati jehvā sooparasam yadhā)

31. One should not perform deeds which result in difficulties, sorrow and repentance.
(yasya asrumukhū rudan vepākam pratisēvate)
32. One should perform deeds which result in joy pleasure and no repentance.
(yasya prateetaha sumanu vepākam pratisē vate)
33. Even a sinner enjoys the pleasant effects of a deed done by him, until that evil deed ripens, and when it is ripe, he will have to eat its bitter fruit of sorrow and disgrace.
(yadā cha pachyate pāpam adha dukham nigacchati)
34. Just as fresh milk does not curdle at once, an evil deed committed does not immediately bear fruit, but when it has ripened, it consumes the sinner like a hidden fire.
(Nahe pāpam krutam karma sadyaha kseera miva munchati, Dahan bāla manveti bhasmācchanna eva pavakaha)
35. A fool even when he is worldly wise, he is destroyed in the end, because his very worldly wisdom will help to neutralise his better nature (PRAJNA).
(Hanti bālasya suklamsam moordhanamasya vepātayan)

6. PANDITA VARGA (THE WISE)

36. It is better to associate with a Pandita, who points out ones faults and reproves; the welfare of one who associates with the wise is assured.
37. A man who advises, instructs and dissuades one from evil is liked by the good and hated by the bad.
38. Do not associate with evil friends and evil men. Associate with good friends and noble men only.
39. One who is committed to DHARMA abides in happiness and is free from sorrow.
(Arya pravedite dharme sadāramate panditaha)
40. A pandita is undisturbed by praise or blame, just as a mountain is undisturbed by stormy winds.
(Evum nindā prasamsāsu na samuryante panditaha)
41. The Sajjanas never talk about sense pleasures. They show neither elation nor depression when affected by happiness or sorrow.
42. The wise one neither for the sake of oneself, nor for the sake of another, does not desire sons, wealth, and power, or even his own success by unjust means, such a wise one is indeed virtuous and righteous.
(Saseelavān prajnāvān, dhārmikaha syāt)
43. Only very few cross the ocean of SAMSARA, and the rest of mankind, run about on the bank only. (Adhemā etaraha prajāha teeramevānu dhāvati)

7. ARHANTA VARGA (THE WORTHY ONE) (JNANI)

44. Those who are committed to DHARMA are not attached to any abode. They leave their abodes and wander away, just as swans fly away from small pools to wider horizons.

45. Just as trained horses implicitly obey their trainer (Sāradhi), the senses obey the wise man in whom there is no attachment even to his own body. Such a wise one is praised even by DEVATAS.

(Devāpi tasya spruhayanti tādrusaha)

46. In a JNANI who has attained MUKTI, calm is the mind, calm is the speech, and peaceful are his actions.

47. Whether it be a village, or a forest or a vale or a hill, wherever Jeevanmuktas dwell, delightful in deed are those places.

(yatra arhanto vehāranti sa bhoomee ramaneeya)

8. SAHASRA VARGA

48. A single meaningul word which can pacify is better than a thousand meaningless words.

(Ekam artha sadam sreyo yachrutvo upasyamati)

49. One who has conquered his self is better than the one who has vanquished a thousand men in war.

(Ekum cha jayet ātmanam savi sangramajit uttamaha)

50. A single day's life of one who has realised DHARMA is better than hundred years of an AJNANI.

(Ekahum jeevitam sreyaha pasyato dharmam Uttamam)

9. PAPA VARGA (EVIL)

51. Make haste in doing good. Check your mind from evil, for the mind of him who is slow in doing good will eventually become evil.

52. Should a person commit evil, let him not do it again. Painful indeed is the accumulation of evil.

(Sa tasmim chandam kuryāt dukhaha pāpasya ucchayaha)

53. Even an evil doer may find pleasure in evil as long as his evil deed has not given its fruit, and when it bears fruit, he experiences the evil results fully.

(yadā cha pachāyate pāpam adha pāpāni pasyati)

54. Even a good person experiences evil results so long as his good deeds have not given fruit, and when his good deeds ripen and bear fruit, he experiences only the good results.

(yadā pachyate badhrām adha badhrāni pasyati)

55. Despise not evil thinking that "it will not afflict me", just as a water jar is filled by the falling of drops, a man becomes eventually evil by gathring evil little by little.

(Bālaha poorayati pāpam stokum stoka mapāya chinvan)

56. Despise not a good deed thinking "that it is of no importance", just as a water jar is filled by the falling of drops, a man becomes eventually good by gathering good deeds one by one.

(*Dheeraha* poorayati punyam stokumstoka mapyā chinvan)

57. One who wants to live safely, avoids any contact with all poisons.

A merchant carrying great wealth with a small escort, avoids a perilous way, and similarly a man who wants to live happily should avoid all evil.

(Visham jeevitu kama eva pāpāni parivarjayet)

58. Not in the sky, nor in the ocean, nor on entering a mountain cave, can a man escape from the consequences of an evil deed.

(Nā antarikshe, na samudra madhye na parvatanām vivarum pravisya na vidyate nō jagati pradesō yatra sthito muchyeti PAPA KARMANAHA)

10. DANDA VARGA (PUNISHMENT)

59. All creatures tremble at punishment. All fear death considering the welfare of others as ones own welfare one should neither kill nor cause others to kill.

(Sarveshām jeevitam priyam)

60. Speak not harshly to anyone; those thus addressed will retort; painful indeed is vindictive speech and it may result in blows and bruises to self.

61. Neither nakedness, nor matted locks, nor fasting, nor sleeping on the ground, nor covering the body with ashes, can purify a man, who is not free from desires, and doubts with regard to DHARMA.

62. A modest and restrained man does not tolerate any reproach from others, just as a thorough bred horse does not tolerate the lashes of a whip.

11. JARA VARGA (OLD AGE)

63. Even the royal chariots in course of time become dilapidated, and the human body incourse of time is overtaken by old age. But the lustre of DHARMA of the SAJJANAS never decreases.

(Satāmcha dharmō na jarā mupeti santo havi sadbhayaha pravedayanti)

64. Those who have not practiced Brahmacharya, and who have not earned wealth when young and strong, will pine away like old herons in a pond without fish.

12. ATMA VARGA (THE SELF)

65. Let one first establish one's self in the proper principle and practice of DHARMA and then only instruct others. Such a wiseman will not face any difficulties in his ministry.

(Athānya manu sisyāt naklisyet panditaha)

66. It is easy to do things that are evil and not conducive to ones welfare; and very difficult to do things that are good and beneficial to oneself.

(yad vi hetamcha sādhucha tad vi paramadush karam)

67. While trying to do good to others, how so ever great let not one neglect his own duty and his own wlefare. After safeguarding ones welfare only then should one work for the welfare of others.

(Atmanōrtham parardhena bahunāpe sahāpayet Atmanō rtham abhijnāya sadardha prasita ha syat)

13. LOKA VARGA (THE WORLD)

68. In this world, the majority of the people are spiritually blind, and only very few can see and understand TRUTH (SATYA DRUSTI). Just as few birds can escape from a net, few souls only can fly away to heaven.

(Andhabhooto yam lokaha...)

69. One who is not committed to DHARMA, one who is a liar and one who does not believe in a Paraloka, such a one ever ready to do any evil.
(Ekum dharmatee tasya mrushāvādinō janto viteerna paralokasya nāsti pāpamakaryam)

14. BUDDHA VARGA

70. Do not do what is evil. Do what is good. Keep your mind pure. This is the teaching of BUDDHA.
71. Even by a shower of gold coins, contentment éludes a man. All sensual pleasures in the end, end up in sorrow. Knowing thus, the wise one gives up the pleasures of here and hereafter. He strives to root out desire (TRUSHNA) from his heart.
72. Hard to find a superior man; he is not born everywhere and when such a one is born in a caste, that caste thrives.

(yatra sajayate dheeraha tat kulam sukhamedhate)

15. SUKHA VARGA (HAPPINESS)

73. Victory breeds hatred; the defeated live in humiliation and sorrow; Happily, the wise live giving up both victory and defeat.

(Upasāntam sukham sete hetvā jaya parājayāou)

74. There is no fire like lust (Nāsti rāgasamō agnihe)
There is no sin like hate (Nāsti dwesha samaha kavihe)
There is no sorrow like the possession of PANCHAMASKANDAMULU (Roopam + Vedana + Sanjna + Samskaramu + Vijnanamu)
There is no bliss higher than SHANTI (NIRVANA)
75. Heath is the greatest gain (Arogyam paramō hā bhaha)
Contentment is the greatest wealth (Santusti paramam dhanam)
Trust is the best of relations (Viswasaha paramājnati hi)
NIRVANA is the greatest joy (Nirvanam paramam sukham)
76. Good is the sight of sadhus. To live in the company of sadhus leads to happiness. If one seeks to be happy, he should keep away from MOORKHAS (FOOLS).

(Adarsanena balānam nityameva sukheesyāt)

16. PRIYA VARGA (AFFECTIONS)

77. Seeing those that are not liked, and not seeing those that are liked, both lead to sorrow. Hence it is better to discard both likes and dislikes.

(Priyanam adarsanam dukham, apriyānam cha darsanam)

78. From affection spring fear and sorrow. One who is free from affection is free from fear and sorrow.
(Priyato Jayate sokaha priyato jāyate bhayam Priyato viprāmuktasya nāsti sokaha kutō bhayam)
79. The quest of pleasure is the root of fear and sorrow one who is free from the quest of pleasure is free from fear and sorrow.
80. From lust arise fear and sorrow. It one is free from lust, he is free from fear and sorrow. (Kāmato vipra muktasya nāsti sokaha kutōbhayam)
81. From craving arise fear and sorrow. If one is free from craving, he is free from fear and sorrow.
(Trusnaya jayate sokaha, trushnaya jāyate bhayam Trushnāyā vipramuktasya nāsti sokaha kuto bhayam)
82. One who has virtue, DHARMA, Truth and does the work to be done, such a wise man is loved by all.
(Seela darsana sampannam dharmistam, satya vādinam, Atmanaha Karma Kurvānam tumjanaha Kurute priyam).

17. KRODHA VARGA (ANGER)

83. Overcome anger by pacefulness
Overcome evil by good
Overcome the miser by generosity
Overcome a liar by truth
(Akrōdhena jayet krodham asādhum sādhuna jayet, Jayet kadaryam dānena satyenā leeka vādenam)
84. Speak the truth, yield not to anger, give what you can to him who asks; these three steps lead you to the presence of DEVATAS.
85. This is an old saying 'ATULA'.
"They blame the man who is silent,
They blame the man who speaks too much,
They balme the man who speaks too little,
There never was, there never will be, nor does, there now exist a person who is wholly blamed or wholly praised.
(Nacha bhoot na cha bhavishyati nachi tarhi vidyate, Ekantam ninditaha purushaha, ekantam va prasamsitaha)
86. The wise are restrained in their thoughts, words and deeds.

18. MALA VARGA (TAINTS) (A corrupt condition)

87. The evil deeds done by the transgressor lead him to his own destruction, just as the iron is destroyed by the very rust which arises from itself.
88. Life is apparently easy for a man who is shameless, selfish, corrupt and unrestrained, yet in the end, this way of life leads to sorrow.
(Praska nindanā pragalbhena sanklistena jeevitam)

89. Life is apparently hard for a man who is committed to DHARMA, virtue, heedfulness and modesty yet in the end, this way of life leads to happiness.
(Aleenena pragalbhena suddajeevena pasyata)
90. One who is a killer, or a thief, or a Liar, or an adulterer and one who is addicted to intoxicating drinks, such a one destroys his very existence itself.
Thus knowing the ultimate annhilation of the evil doer, the wise root out LOBHA and ADHARMA from their minds.
91. There is no fire like lust (Nāsti rāgasamō agnihe)
There is no devil like hate (Nāsti dwesha samō grahaha)
There is no net like MOHA (Nāsti moha samam Jalam)
There is no river like desire (Nāsti TRUSHNA samā nadee)
92. It is easy to observe the faults of others, but difficult to see one's own faults. One enhances the faults of others, like spreading of chaff during winnowing, but covers up his own faults, like a crafty gambler who conceals his dice.

19. DHARMASTHA VARGA (THE RIGHTEOUS)

93. A wise man calmly considers what is right and what is wrong, and then only proceeds on a task with due care.
One who settles matters without due deliberation and in a violent haste is not a man of DHARMA indeed.
94. One who talks too much can never be a pandita one who works for the welfare of others and who is free from fear and enmity, such a one is termed a PANDITA.
95. In whom are SATYA, DHARMA, AHIMSA, SAMYA MAM (MODERATION) and DAMAM (Self Control), such a one is fit to be called an elder.
(DHEERA - VRUDDAAHA)
96. Not by mere eloquence, nor by beautiful appearance does a man become a SADHU, should he be selfish, jealous and deceitful.
97. Not by a shaven head does an undisciplined man, who utters lies becomes a SANYASI.
One who is not free from desire and greed, can never become a SANYASI.
98. One who kills creatures can never be an ARYA one who is committed to AHIMSA is called an ARYA.
(Ahimsayā sarva praninam Arya eti prochyate)

20. MARGA VARGA (THE WAY)

99. The GREAT of the past only show the way. It is you who must make the effort. Those who think and follow the path become free from bondage.
100. The lazy fellow, though young and strong, strives not when he should strive, and with a mind uncontrolled and aimless, such a one will never acquire PRAJNA (JNANA).
101. Death suddenly snatches away the man immersed in SAMSARA (Sons, cattle etc.), even as a torrent carries away all the people in a sleeping village.
102. Even a father, sons and relatives can not save a man overtaken by death. Realizing

this let the wise one concentrate on the path to NIRVANA.

21. PRAKEERNAKA VARGA (WAKEFULNESS)

103. If by forsaking a small pleasure one finds a greater one, let the wise one give up the lesser in favour of the greater.
(Tyajen matrā sukham dheeraha sampasyan vipulam sukham)

104. He who seeks happiness for himself by making others unhappy, is bound in the chains of enmity and hate forever.

22. NIRAYA VARGA (HELL)

105. Four things happen to the thoughtless man who commits adultery with another's wife
1. He looses Punya (Merit)
2. His sleep is distrubed
3. He is blamed by others
4. He goes to Hell.

If by chance he escapes the above, he will have to experience,
1. Demerit (Absence of PUNYA)
2. Evil destiny (Gatistcha papikā)
3. Brief is the joy of the frightened man and woman involved in adultery.
(Bheetasya Bheetayā ratischa stokika)
4. If detected, the king imposes a heavy punishment on the man.
(Rajācha dandam gurukum pranayati, Tasmāt narō paradārān na seveta)

106. Sanyasa way of life if not followed sincerely will lead to hell, just as KUSA grass if wrongly grasped will cut one's hand.

107. It is better not to do evil dees, as they are sure to result in sorrow and regrets. Do therefore what is right, for good deeds never result in sorrow and regrets.

23. NAGA VARGA (ENDURANCE)

108. *In this world, alas, the majority of people are wicked.* I tolerate the abuse of others, just as an elephant in the battle field withstands the arrows shot from a bow.
(Aham nāga eva sungrāme chāpataha patitam saram, Ativākyam titikshisye *duhseetahi bahu janaha*)

109. It is better to live alone, than to be a companion of a MOORKHA. Let one live alone, doing no evil deeds and wander majestically like a solitary elephant in the forest.

110. Happy is virtue (Seelam) till old age (Jarām).
Happy is steadfast confidence in truth
Happy is to do no evil deeds
Happy is the attainment of wisdom (PRAJNA).

24. TRUSHNA VARGA (CRAVING)

111. Just as a tree sprouts again and again, though cut down if its roots are undamaged,

similarly sorrow overtakes a man again and again, if the roots of craving (TRUSHNA) are not completely destroyed.

(Evamapi trushnā nusaye nihate nirvartate dukha midam punaha punaha)

112. The desire for a wife, sons and for wealth (ornaments, jewels and Dhana) is a much stronger bond (fetter) than any bond made of ropes, wood or iron.

(Saravad rakta manikundaleshu putreshu dāreshu cha yāpeksha)

113. The wise come out of the bonds of desire and move freely untouched by sorrow, where as the rest are entangled in their own desires and immersed in sorrow, just as a silk worm is entombed in the very cocoon it has spun around itself.

114. A man of inordinate cravings, who has a doubting nature and who is interested only in sense objects, in such a man TRUSHNA increases day by day, and the makes the chains of bondage stronger day by day for himself.
(Vitarka pramadhi tasya jantōha Teevra rāgasya subhanu darsinaha, Bhooyaha trushna pravardhate, Esha Khalu drudham Karoti bandhanam)

115. The gift of DHARMA excels all gifts.
The flavour of DHARMA excels all flavours.
The happiness caused by DHARMA excels all other pleasures.
Destruction of craving puts an end to all sorrows.
(Sarvadānam dharma dānam jayāti
Sarva rasam dharma rasō jayāti
Sarvām ratim dharma rati jayāti
Trushnā Kshayaha sarva dukham jayati)

25. BIKSHU VARGA (MONK)

116. There is no DHYANA (Concentration) for one, who lacks PRAJNA (WISDOM), nor is there PRAJNA in whom there is no DHYANA. One who has both DHYANA and PRAJNA, is very close to NIRVANA.
(Nāsti dhyanam Aprajanasya, prajnanastya Adhyataha, yasmin dhayan cha prajna cha savinirvāntike)

26. BRAHMANA VARGA (THE BRAHMANA)

117. One who has his body, speech and mind under control and he who is free from evil, such a one is termed as BRAHMANA.

118. Not by birth, nor by family, nor by having matted hair does a man become a BRAHMANA, but only when he is dedicated to TRUTH and DHARMA.
(Na jatābhirna gotrirna jatyabhavati brahmanaha, yasmin satyam cha dharmascha sasuchihi sa cha Brahmanaha)

119. A man does not become a Brahmana by birth alone. One who has no desire to receive things from others (APARIGRAHA), is termed a BRAHMANA.

120. One who has given up anger, who is dutiful, virtuous self controlled, well versed in all SASTRAS, and who is very close to NIRVANA, such a one is termed a BRAHMANA.

(Akrodhanam, Vratavantam, seelavantam, anusrutam, dāntam, antimasareeram tamaham Braveemi Brahmanam)

121. One who has love and compassion for all living creatures, who neither kills nor causes others to kill, such a one is termed a BRAHMANA.
(Nidaya dandam, bhooteshu tra seshu sthavareshu cha, yona hanti naghātayati tamaham braveemi Brahmanam)

Sources

1. The Dhammapada by Naarada Thera, 1940.
2. Dharmapadam by Bramhachari Ananda Mohan, 1949.
3. Buddha's Teachings, translated from Juan Māscaro, 1979.

15

THE SPIRITUAL QUEST

Every intelligent man is engaged in a perpetual struggle to learn a little more about the universe in which he lives and his relationship to it, and he tries to hand over the torch of his *spiritual quest* to the coming generations. One acquires, chooses, or changes to one particular religious system largely according to ones immediate environment or to ones psychological disposition.

All religions put their emphasis almost exclusively on certain aspects, according to the historical situation at their inception and attending their growth; some for instance on *LOVE* and *CHARITY,* and some on *RENUNCIATION* etc. Some discourse mainly in parables, some use the language of ethical and moral admonition and some stress upon the metaphysical view points.

Modern man with his scientific outlook is wary and tries to distinguish *religious faith from fanaticism and superstition* "you shall know them by their fruits of the Gospel, demarcates them in the two separate entities. Religious faith and vision *transcend* reason, but on the whole they accept reason, whereas famaticism and illusion are *below reason* and they outright reject reason. Beyond the activity of modern man's reasoning mind, there is a vast uncharted ocean of meditation and contemplation. The mind of man can measure the world of matter, but the world of spirit is immeasurable. What he can not know with his reasoning mind, can only be understood by *the spirit within,* and the words of these prophets, philosophers and poets help him to understand his own religious faith better.

I

1. One who studies widely and with set purpose, who questions earnestly, then thinks for himself about what he has heard—such a one will incidentally achieve goodness

   —CONFUCIUS (551 BC – 479 B.C)

2. To learn and never be filled is to acquire wisdom
   To teach and never be weary is to live

   – MENSIUS (372 BC – 289 B.C.)

3. The ultimate end of all is GOD. HE is manifested in the laws of nature. He is the hidden spring. He is in explicable and the unknowable. But by exploring the

unknowns, we understand the known more clearly.

– CHUANG TZU

4. He who knows GOD and man is the one of enlightenment. Knowing God, he knows his own origin, knowing man, he rests in the knowledge of the known, and waits for the knowledge of the unknown.
   Working out ones allotted span and not perishing in midcareer is the sign of wisdom

   – CHUANG TZU (369 BC – 286 B.C)

5. Sincerity is the single virtue that unites man and divinity in to one

   – SHINTOISM

6. "Let there be no evil in your thoughts"

   – CONFUCIUS (551 B.C. – 479 B.C)

7. "Be loyal and true to your every word and be careful in all you do – and you will get on well enough"

   – CONFUCIUS (551 BC – 479 B.C.)

8. The crowd cares for gain
   The honest man for fame
   The good man values success
   The wise man keeps his soul

   – CHUANG TZU (369 BC – 286 B.C.)

9. There are two pathways open for everyone; one is the path of transient pleasures and the other, the path of lasting joy. Pondering on them, the wise one chooses the higher path and the fool takes to the path of transient pleasures

   – KATHOPANISHAD

10. Whenever strife arises amongst men, the sense of possession is the root cause of it. Therefore let a man leave any place where he is tempted to covetousness

    – ANANTAMUKHA (BUDDHISM)

11. One who desires MOKSHA should give up attachment to things living or non living desirable or undesirable, and such an attitude facilitates *non attachment.* And with non attachment, he will be able to sail across the ocean of SAMSARA

    – PANCHASTIKAYA SARA (JAINISM)

12. We see mansions painted in brilliant colours and with ornamented doors
    In course of time, they shall fall to ruin.
    So the human body which is empty within and possesseth no love
    Shall fall and become a heap of dust
    O my brethren, *your bodies and wealth shall not accompany you*
    God's name is the pure wealth; God gives it through the GURU

    – GURU NANAK

13. Fret not over cares of health or mind;
    To loose even life be thou resigned;
    Midst true sincerity find rest,
    In earth and heaven it will make thee blest

    – KUROZUMI MUNETADA (SHINTOISM)

14. A gentleman in his dealings with the world has neither enmities nor affections; but wherever he sees RIGHT, he ranges himself beside it...
    He does not mind failing to get recognition; he is too busy doing the things that entitle him to recognition

    – CONFUCIUS (551 BC – 479 B.C)
15. The superior man clings to virtue and the inferior man clings to material comfort. *The superior man cherishes justice,* the inferior man cherishes the hope of favours to be received —CONFUCIUS
16. To get rich is to be without love;
    To get love is to be without riches – MENCIUS (372 B.C. – 289 B.C)
17. He who has hoarded most will suffer the heaviest loss
    Be content with what you have and are and no one can despoil you
    He who stops in time nothing can harm
    He is safe and secure

    – LAO TSE (571 B.C)
18. All composite things are impermanent
    They are subject to birth and death;
    Put an end to birth and death
    And there is a blissful tranquillity

    – ZEN BUDDHISM.
19. Form no covetous desire, so that the demon of greediness may not deceive thee and the treasures of the nature may not be tasteless to thee, and that of the spirit unperceived

    – ZOROASTER
20. There comes a day or a night, when the master leaves his cattle, or the cattle leave their master, or the SOUL leaves the human body, but his VIRTUE (which he has acquired during his life time) never parts from him

    – ZOROASTER.
21. My friend wisdom lies
    In abandoning heedlessness and
    In turning the heart from the worldly objects
    And in gathering merit for the hereafter
    Before departure from this earth

    – ABDULLAH ANSARI (SUFISM)
22. The essence of the conduct of the sage is that he does not injure any one. One should know only this much, namely that non injury is religion

    – NIR GRANTHA PRAVACHANA (JAINISM)
23. All men are brothers. The suffering of others is my suffering; the good of others is my good

    – KUROZUMI KYO (SHINTOISM)
24. "Loving kindness" is the maxim to guide one throughout his life.
    Do not unto others what you would not they should, do unto you

    – CONFUCIUS (551 B.C TO 479 B.C.)

25. The first principle is to destroy all evils
The second principle is to practice all good deeds
The third principle is to save all living creatures
May we all attain the path of NIRVANA – ZEN BUDDHISM.
26. He who gives succour to the helpless poor, acknowledges the kingdom of GOD.
AHUNAVAR – ZOROASTER
27. Never in sooth does the lover seek without being sought by his beloved.
When the lightning of love has shot in to this heart know that their is love in that heart
When love of GOD waxes in thy heart, beyond any doubt, GOD hath love for thee
No sound of clapping comes from one hand without the other hand
Divine wisdom in destiny and decree made us lovers of one another
– JALALUDDIN RUMI (SUFISM)
28. Let him not desire to die, let him not desire to live, let him wait for his appointed time as a servant waits for the payment of his wages
Let him patiently bear the harsh speech of others, let him not insult anybody and let him not become anybody's enemy for the sake of this perisnable body
Let him forsake anger and spee h devoid of truth
By deep meditation let him recognise the subtle nature of the Supreme Soul, and its presence in all organisms, both the highest and the lowest
– LAWS OF MANU
29. To be long-suffering and meek, to associate with the tranquil, religious talk at due seasons this is a supreme blessing
Self restraint and purity, the knowledge of the Noble Truths, and the realisation of NIRVANA—this is a supreme blessing.
Beneath the stroke of life's changes, the mind that shaketh not, without grief or passion and secure—this is a supreme blessing
– SUTTA NIPATA (BUDDHISM)
30. Conquer your anger by forgivingness
And check vanity by humility
By TRUTH stay all crooked fraud
And vanquish greed by contentment'
– DASA VEYALIYA SUTRA (JAINISM)
31. However numerous one's friends and companions may be in the world
There are no real friends but the GURU and GOD
– GURU NANAK
32. If you desire to obtain help put away pride. Even a tiny bit of pride shuts you off as it were by a great cloud from enlightenment
– Oracle of the Gods Kasuaga (SHINTOISM)
33. Better than outward austerity is the penance of the heart
– KONKO KYO (SHINTOISM)
34. Be reverent, be reverent, heaven is splendid, its charge is not easy; do not say "It is

very high above"; *it ascends and descends in it workings* and daily inspects us who are here ...

– BOOK OF ODES MAO (CONFUCIANISM)

35. Pride bringeth loss; humility increase
This is the way of heaven. He comes to ruin
Who says that others do not equal him

(BOOK OF DOCUMENTS) – CONFUCIUS (551 BC – 479 B.C.)

36. When heaven is going to put a great burden on a man, it first vexes his heart and mind, tires his muscles and bones, and it thwarts and confounds his works. *Thus his heart is stirred his nature is hardened, and his weaknesses are made good.* After this trial, he comes to know there is life in troubles and sorrow, and death in ease and comforts

– MENCIUS (372 BC – 289 B.C.)

37. If thou wouldst become a pilgrim on the path of love,
The first condition is
That thou become as humble as dust and ashes

– ABDULLAH ANSARI (SUFISM)

38. A wise man has four resolves and these are 1. To understand 2. To be truthful 3. To renounce and 4. To win tranquillity

– BUDDHA

39. Subdue your self, for the self is difficult to subdue; if your self is subdued, you will be happy in this world and in the next

–UTTARADHYAYANA SUTRA (JAINISM)

40. *Wealth and rank are* what every man desires; but if they can only be acquired to the detriment of the way he professes he must relinquish them
Poverty and obscurity are what every man detests; but if they can only be avoided to the detriment of the way, he professes, he must accept them
Never for a moment does a gentleman quit the way of goodness

– CONFUCIUS (551 B.C. TO 479 B.C.)

41. A person who is without desires and who is committed to AHIMSA, is free from bondage

– ACARANGA SUTRA (JAINISM)

42. Free yourself from doubt
Open and behold the great broad way of TRUTH
You will find the goodness of GOD all around you

– KONKO KYO (SHINTOISM)

43. If one sincerely believes, one sees more of unseen divine manifestations than the known

–KONKO KYO (SHINTOISM)

44. There is no greater joy than to look in to ones life and find it true;
what do you call true?
What ever we like we call it good; when it is inborn, we call it truth; when it is fully

grown we call it beauty; when it shines brightly, we call it greatness. Greatness that enhances the quality of life, we call it holiness; holiness beyond our understanding, we call it inspiration

– MENCIUS

45. If he shuts his mouth and closes his doors
He can never be exhausted
If he opens his mouth and increases his affairs
He can never be saved
To see the minuteness of things is called clarity of sight
Keep a low profile and it will lead you to a high profile
Use your light, but dim your brightness
Thus you will cause no harm to yourself
This is called following the ETERNAL TAO

– TAO TE CHING (LAO TSE) (571 B.C.)

46. When the sky is clear and when the wind hums in the fir trees, it is the heart of GOD who thus reveals himself

–ORACLE AT A TAIMA SHRINE (SHINTOISM)

47. The characteristic of heaven and earth are to be large; to be substantial; to be high; to be brilliant; to be far reaching; and to be long continuing

– CONFUCIUS

48. When the roses are dead and the garden ravaged, where shall we find the perfume of the roses? In rose water...

(SUFISM)

49. No sounds; the heavens are still,
Where then shall GOD be found?
Search not in distant skies;
In man's own heart GOD lives... – SHAO YUNG (SHINTOISM)

50. Is goodness indeed so far away? If we really wanted goodness, we will find that it is at our very side

– CONFUCIUS (551 B.C. – 479 B.C.)

51. "Can one possess TAO for ones own"?
"Your very body is not your own, and how then can you possess TAO?
If my body is not my own, pray whose is it?
It is a representative image of GOD
Your life is not your own. It is a reflection of GOD, your individuality is not your own. It is the delegated adaptability of GOD.
Your posterity is not your own. ("They are the longings of tomorrow")

(KHALEEL GIBRAN)

You move but know not how. You are at rest, but know not why. You taste but know not the cause
All the above phenomena are the operations of GOD'S laws...

– CHUANG TZU (TAOISM) (369 B.C. – 286 B.C.)

II

1. There are two spirits in the universe: the spirit of Good and the spirit of EVIL. Both work in our thoughts, words and deeds. Between these two, one is free to choose

   – THEZEND AVESTA
2. If by forsaking a small pleasure, one finds a greater joy, the wise one chooses the greater joy

   – BUDDHA (500 B.C.)
3. Why fight with other men? Fight with your own self and attain true joy and glory

   – UTTARADAYANA SUTRA (JAINISM)
4. He who has not peace of mind feels an offence; he who has peace of mind feels it not

   – SAMADHI SATAKA (JAINISM)
5. *What is wisdom?*
   To know what we know, and to know what we do not know
   If a man can not rule himself, how can he rule others
   Nothing done in haste is thorough
   When one works for small gains, big things are left undone

   – CONFUCIUS (550 – 479 B.C.)
6. The first and surest means to enter in to communion with the divine is by sincerity. If you pray with sincerity, you will surely feel the divine presence.

   – YAMAGA - SOKO (SHINTOISM)
7. "O! man, what is good? and what doth the LORD require of thee? but *to do justly* and to *Love mercy* and to *walk humbly with thy GOD*"

   – MICAH (720 B.C.)
8. The heart's vision is what matters and not the tongue's speech. Nothing depends on the creatures everything depends on the CREATOR

   – ABIL - KHAIR (A.D.: 967 – 1049)
9. *Turn, trust GOD and fling away from thee all that is less*

   – GURU NANAK (A.D.: 1469 – 1538)
10. Be able to be alone, loose not the advantage of solitude and the society of thyself in cummunion with the CREATOR. He who is thus prepared, the day is not uneasy, nor the night black unto him. Darkness may bound his eyes, not his imagination. In his bed he may lie and speculate the universe and enjoy the whole world in the hermitage of his own mind

    – SIR THOMAS BROWNE (1605 – 1682)
11. Man goes near to or far away from GOD, but GOD never goes far off from man

    – MEISTER ECKHART (1250 – 1328)
12. If your bonds be not broken while living what hope of deliverance in death? It is but an empty dream that the soul shall have union with GOD, because it has passed from the body. If GOD is found now, HE is found then. If not we do but go to dwell in death

    – KABIR (1440 – 1518)

13. The colour of the water is the colour of the vessel containing it.
A true worshipper would not interfere with the beliefs of others and he would try to perceive GOD in every form and in every belief

– IBNUL - ARABI (1165 – 1240)

14. Whosoever intends to do any good and perfect work, let him depart from himself and his own desires and enter in to resignation, and in to the will of GOD and work with GOD

– BOEHME (1575 – 1624)

15. So whatever the human being can furnish himself by his own efforts, to preserve his existence, may be aptly called the inward aid of GOD, whereas whatever else accrues to man's profit from outward causes may be called the external aid of GOD

– SPINOZA (1632 – 77)

16. To make our soul good and beautiful is to make ourselves like unto GOD, because GOD is the source of the good and the beautiful
Evil and ugliness are contrary to the good and the beautiful

– PLOTINUS (A.D. 205 – 70)

17. And the greatness of spiritual wisdom which is of GOD alone, can not be perceived either by the men of the world or by the men of learning, for *matter* (flesh), *mind* (intellect) and *spirit* (WISDOM), are three orders different in kind...

– BLAISE PASCAL (1623 – 62)

18. A wise man tries to love them that transgress against him; that it is through ignorance and against their wills that they sin; and *that within a few years both you and they shall be no more*. But above all things that they have not done you any hurt; for that by them, your mind and understanding is not made worse or more vile than it was before

– MARCUS AURELIUS (AD 121 – 80)

19. The words of men to you can be of five kinds. They may be
   1. TRUE OR FALSE
   2. At the right time or wrong time
   3. *Gentle or bitter*
   4. *Kindly or resentful*
   5. Profitable or unprofitable

– BUDDHA

20. *We have planted thorns, shall we gather dates?*
our sins are written down, and we have no good works to weigh against our sins ...
Do not think that sins that deserve hell can lead you the Heaven

– SADI (1193 – 1291)

21. A vessel overfull is not easy to carry
A sword oversharpened will soon get blunt
A hall with too much gold and jade is not easy to keep safe
The pride of wealth and honours brings its own destruction
When therefore thy work is done

Withdraw in silence
This is the way of TAO, the way of heaven

– (LAO TSE) (571 B.C.)

22. He who knows others has wisdom
But he who knows himself has inner light
He who conquers others is strong
But he who conquers himself is stronger
He who keeps on his course with energy has will power
But he who knows how to rest where he is endures...

(LAO TSE) (571 B.C.)

23. "Remember therefore that what I have said
I have said, and that what I have not said
I have not said.
And why have I not given an answer to these questions? (such as 1. Is the world eternal or not? 2. whether the body and the life are two things or one thing? 3. whether the one who has reached the goal is beyond death or not? etc.
Because these questions are NOT PROFITABLE and they help not in clearing the way to peace wisdom and NIRVANA

– BUDDHA

24.
1. Many men can utter words of wisdom. Few men can practice what they preach
2. Do today what is good. Do today the work of tomorrow, and do in the morning the work of the evening
3. Even as a jar is filled little by little by drops of water so a man by continual little efforts, acquires, wealth, or learning or virtue
4. Men like the good results of virtue, but they work not to acquire virtue; they like not the evil results of SIN but they work laboriously to accumulate sinful deeds.
5. A man rises or goes down by his own actions, just as a builder of a wall or as a digger of a well

– THE HITOPADESA

25. Deal with events before they come
Put things in order before there is confusion
Even the journey of a thousand miles
Begins with a single foot step
Be careful at the end as at the beginning
And such a careful man will not fail...

(LAO TSE) (571 B.C.)

26. The last words of GOWTAMA BUDDHA
"All composite creatures, disperse in to their components in the course of time ...
"Strive towards perfection"

– (BUDDHA)

27. *Day after day the wind carries away a rose from the garden...*

The LAW OF TIME is the same for all men; murmur not and submit to its justice.
O friend! set not thy heart on this world, for peace undisturbed, is not possible here...
This world is a bridge that leads to ETERNITY
The wise build not their homes on the bridge

–SADI (1193 – 1291)

28. There are four divine seeds in the heart of a man;
    1. A merciful and tender heart is the seed of *Love*
    2. A heart for shame and indignation is the seed *of justice*
    3. A heart to give way and yield is the seed of *courtesy*
    4. A heart for right and wrong is the seed of *wisdom*

– MENCIUS (372 B.C. – 289 B.C.)

29. Blessedness is not the reward of VIRTUE. It is virtue itself. We do not find joy in virtue, because we control our lusts. *But contrariwise, because we find joy in virtue, we are able to control our lusts.*
    Blessedness consists in love towards GOD. In proportion as the mind finds more joy in this divine love, so does it the more understand, and so much more power has it over the emotions which are evil.
    The ignorant man is not only distracted in various ways, by external causes without ever gaining true harmony of his spirit; but he lives as it were, unconscious of himself and of his CREATOR.
    Where as the wise man is scarcely disturbed in spirit, and is conscious of himself and of GOD. The way to GOD seems hard, but it can be discovered. It must be hard, since it is seldom found. If salvation were ready to our hand, and could be found without great labour, how would it be possible, that it should be neglected by almost all men

– SPINOZA (1632 – 77)

30. To endure all things with an equable and peaceful mind, not only brings with it many blessings to the soul; buy it also enables us in the midst of our difficulties to have a clear judgement about them and to apply the appropriate remedy for them

– ST. JOHN OF THE CROSS

31. The pupil who learns not from his teacher goes far astray; and the teacher however learned, who loves not his pupil goes far astray.

– LAO TSE (571 B.C.)

32. And the work of righteousness shall be peace; and the effect of righteousness is quietness and assurance for ever
    In returning and rest shall you be saved
    In quietness and in confidence shall be your strength

– ISAIAH

33. *Reverently care for your body. Carefully preserve your natural purity. Leave EXTERNALS to others. Then you will not be involved* ["Leave externals to others"] means, try to improve yourself, instead of trying to improve others
    Real friendship is unison without the aid of smiles,

Real anger awes without expression,
Real mourning grieves in silence.

– CHUANG TZU (369 – 286 B.C.)

34. By two wings is a man lifted up from earthly things: by *simplicity* and *purity* Simplicity must be in his intention and purity in his affection.
Simplicity aims at GOD; purity apprehends and tastes him. If you intend and seek union with GOD, and the profit of thy neighbour thou shalt enjoy inward liberty. If you are good and pure within, then you would see all things without hinderance, and understand them well. A pure heart pierces into heaven and hell. If there is joy in this world, a pure heart does surely possess it

– THOMAS. A. KEMPIS (1379 – 1471)

35. Next to life, purity is man's greatest good

– VENDIDAD (ZOROASTER)

36. There is nothing more easy to handle than the human soul. It needs but to will, and the thing is done, and the soul is set upon the right path. On the contrary if you do not will it, the thing is not done. *For recovery and ruin are from within.*

– EPICTETUS

37. Whenever a man covets anything inordinately he is presently disquieted in himself. *The proud and covetous are never at rest;* the poor and humble in spirit, dwell in abaundance of peace.
He that is weak in spirit and still in a measure carnal and prone to pleasures of the senses, can hardly withdraw himself altogether from earthly desires. And if he obtains that after which he desires, he is presently stricken with remorse of conscience, for that he has followed his own passion, which helps nothing to the peace that he sought.
In withstanding passions therefore and not in obeying them is found true peace of heart

– THOMAS A KEMPIS (1379 – 1471)

38. If you would foster a calm spirit, first *regulate your breathing;* for when breathing is under control, heart beat will be even. But when the breathing is spasmodic, the heart beat also will be uneven and under strain.
Therefore before attempting any important task, first regulate your breathing and as a result, your temper will be softened, and your spirit calmed
Heaven and Earth do not lose their sublime harmony because of the thunders or stroms, or floods or earthquakes, so likewise a wise man should try to be calm and unruffled, in the midst of a thousand troubles and even when all his dearest hopes and desires are betrayed

– KAI BARA EKKEN (1629 – 1713)

39. In meditation, we consider carefully divine things, so that the heart may feel divine love.
In contemplation, the soul enjoys silence, peace and truth.
Meditation is the means, contemplation is the end. Meditation is the path and

contemplation is the end of the path.
Let a man return in to his own self and there in the centre of his soul, let him wait upon GOD...

– ST. PETER OF ALCANTARA (1499 – 1562)

40. *The first form of prayer is oral,* spoken by word of mouth
The second form of prayer is within the heart
our heart speaks silently with the CREATOR
The third form of prayer is called spiritual
The most pure elements of our soul arise unto
GOD, on the wings of holy longing and love.
The greater is this love, the fewer are its words.
"The true worshipper should worship the Father inspirit, and in truth"

– FRANCISCO DE OSUNA (1540)

VI

41. "Commit no excess; do nothing injurious...
The will should not be gratified to the full;
Pleasures should not be carried to excess"

– CONFUCIOUS

42. *"MEDEN AGEN" (Nothing in excess)* – Motto engraved on the temple of APOLLO at DELPHI
43. *Strive to acquire proper balance* – courage without rashness; caution without timidity; silence without deceit; shrewdness without cunning; patience without carelessness; friendship without favouritism; ambition without selfishness.

– A GREEK PHILOSOPHER

44. To know the eternal is to be close to enlightenment;
Not to know the eternal causes the passions to rise and passions (uncontrolled) will lead one to EVIL...

– LAO TSE

45. Some call it will, and some call it GOD;
Some call it fate, and some call it GOD;
Some call it evolution and some call it GOD;
Some call it chance and some call it GOD;

– A WESTERN POET

46. What the superior man seeks is in himself
What the inferior man seeks is in others

– CONFUCIUS

47. Those who do evil in the open light of day-men will punish them. Those who do evil in secret, GOD will punish them. Who fears GOD and man-he is free and fit to walk alone

– KWANG TZE

48. The five ethical commandments of Confucius are :
    1. Do good to others

2. Truthfullness
3. Propriety, proper conduct, and correct behaviour
4. Trustworthiness
5. Acquire knowledge and wisdom

– CONFUCIUS

49. Filial piety is the basis of virtue and the origin of culture. To do the right thing and walk according to the right morals, thus leaving a good name in posterity, in order to glorify ones ancestors, is the culmination of filial piety

– CONFUCIUS

50. A disciple asked CONFUCIUS "Sir, is there one word, which may serve as a rule of practice for all one's life?
CONFUCIUS answered *"Is "RECIPROCITY" not such a word?"*
Do not to others what you do not want done to yourself
If you act always guided by the principle of RECIPROCITY, your private life and public life will not arouse ill-will"

– CONFUCIUS

51. The main defect of men is this, that they neglect their own fields, and go to weed the field of others and that what they demand from others is great while what they lay upon themselves is light

– MENCIUS

52. He who smites (strike or hit) will be smitten; he who shows rancour (spitefulness) will find rancour; from reviling (criticise abusively) comes reviling, and from him who is angered comes anger

– UDANA VARGA (BUDDHISM)

53. LAO TSE said "Repay EVIL with GOOD" *CONFUCIUS aked* "what then will you return for GOOD? – *Return GOOD for GOOD, and Repay EVIL with JUSTICE".*

– CONFUCIUS

54. "Be straightforward yet mild,
Be gentle yet dignified,
Be mild yet firm,
Be courageous yet just"...

– SHU KING

55. Heaven when about to save one, it will fill his heart with compassion

– TAO TEH KING

56. There are few persons in the world who love yet also know the faults of those they love;
Few also those who hate, yet also know
The virtues of the object of their hate

– TAO TEH KING

57. It is the way of TAO, not to act from any personal motive, and to conduct affairs without worrying about results, to taste without being aware of the flavour, and to account the small as great and great as small, and to recompense injury with kindness

– LAO TSE

58. All those who read ponderous books and do not practice what they read, are only wasting their time in vain pursuit of wisdom, and who acts righteously always is wiser than all those scholars...

—VANA PARVA (MAHABHARATA)

59. Those who aspire to greatness must humble themselves

– TAO TEH KING

60. To share one's wisdom with others is called true wisdom; to share one's wealth with others is reckoned meritorious

– KWANG TZU

61. "In seeking a foothold for self, love finds a foothold for others; seeking light for itself, it enlightens others also"

– CONFUCIUS

Sources

1. An anthology of Religions by Edith B. Schnapper, 1952.
2. Lamps of Fire by Juan Mascaro, 1958.
3. Essential Unity of All Religions by Bhagavan Das, 1932.

16

GURU NANAK AND HIS MESSAGE

Guru Nanak composed about *2949* stanzas, including hymns like JAPJI, ASADIWAR DAKHNI OMKAR, SIDDHA GOSTI AND BARA MAHA TUKHARI.

ADI GRANTH, the BIBLE of the SIKHS was compiled and edited by *GURU ARJAN DEV in 1604 A.D.* It was written in *old PANJABI - HINDI in GURUMUKHI script.*

Guru Nanak observed that humanity was entangled in the meshes of *greed* and *avarice* and the root of the problem was *ego centricity.* The malady and the remedy were suggested in the hymns, which he composed and sang.

GURU NANAK – A BIOGRAPHICAL OUTLINE :

Guru Nank was born in the year *1469 A.D.,* in the village of *TALWANDI,* in the Chief tainship of RAI BULAR, in the reign of BAHLOL LODHI. *This village is now in PAKISTAN.* As a child, he showed no interest in formal education.

As a youth, he worked for some time as a store keeper at SULTANPUR, under DAULAT KHAN, the muslim chief of Sultanpur. It was a sort of a part time job and he had ample time for his spiritual quest.

Nanak was married at the age of 18 to SULAKHANI, daughter of MOOLCHAND of PAKHOKE RANDAWE, in the year *1487 A.D.*. His first son *SRI CHAND* was born in *1494,* and second son *LAHMICHAND* in the year *1479.*

In response to an inner divine call, Guru Nanak, decided to preach his message of the unity of GOD, and universal brotherhood of man, to the people in the year *1500 A.D.*

FIRST TRIP 1500 A.D.–1506 A.D: Guru Nanak's Journeys as a Preacher

After visiting important places in Punjab, Guru Nanak reached *Delhi* in the year *1502,* in the reign of SIKANDER LODHI. From Delhi, he went to Banaras, Patna, Dacca, Manipur, Imphal, Burma, Bengal, Jagannath, Jabalpur and Bhopal. Guru Nanak returned to Punjab is *1506 A.D.*

SECOND TRIP : 1506 – 1510 A.D.

During this journey Guru Nanak visited Southern Punjab, Rajasthan Marwar, *South India* and *Ceylon.* He returned to Punjab via Junagarh and Multan and reached *Talwandi* in *1510.*

KARTARPUR : Guru Nanak stayed at home for about 4 years. During this period, he founded a spiritual centre on the bank of RAVI RIVER, and named it KARTARPUR. He shifted his family to Kartarpur in *1514 A.D.*

THIRD TRIP : 1518 – 1522 A.D.

Guru Nanak spent two years in visiting various pilgrimage centres in Uttar Pradesh and Himalayas.

FOURTH TRIP : 1518 – 1522

For about 3 years, Guru Nanak travelled in countries to the west of India, and visited Mecca, Madina, Bagdad, Tashkand, and Samarkand. He returned to Punjab through Peshawar and Hasan Abdal. He reached Kartarpur towords the end of *1521 A.D.*

LAST YEARS OF GURU NANAK'S LIFE:

He spent the last seventeen years of his life at Kartarpur and died at the age of *70 years,* in *1539 A.D.* While at Kartarpur he visited various religious centres in Punjab, and held discussions and dialogues with the followers of other religious faiths. One such dialogue was recorded in the form of a long hymn entitled *SIDDHA GOSTHI.*

Among the notable disciples of Guru Nanak was *BAHI LEHNA (Guru Angad Dev), who succeeded him as the second Guru of the SIKHS.* Othe notable disciples of Guru Nanak were RAI BULAR, (the Chief of his native village, *MARDANA a muslim minstrel of Nanak's village,* Bebi Nanaki (Guru Nanak's elder sister), DAULAT KHAN (the Nawab of Sultanpur, LALO, the carpenter of Saiyadpur and many others.

THE ESSENCE OF GURU NANAK'S HYMNS AND SONGS

1. ... *Nobody lives for ever,*
   These mortal abodes must be abandoned,
   you will depart as the Master wills ...
2. ...Many lost their lives in the pursuit of riches
   And to many more riches brought only disgrace!
   These riches can be gathered, only through sinful deeds
   These riches will not accompany you in death
   He whom GOD destroys, is first deprived of virtue...
3. ...Says Nanak, the CREATOR ordains justly,
   And everyman gets his lot as ordained.
4. People make serous efforts to acquire wealth

Alas! riches are never faithful to anyone...

5. Greed for wealth is a trap for all...
6. People pray to GOD to acquire wealth
   For the sake of money, they become servants and thieves
   But they get riches, as preordained only...
7. Wealth intoxicated man is deaf and blind
   In the midst of his pursuit of wealth, he does not listen neither to the words of GURU or GOD...
8. All eating, drinking and merry making is futile
   If GOD is not remembered in one's heart...
   A man is as wise as GOD makes him
   God moves him as HE desires...
9. ...wife, sons, wealth and this world are dear to you, and you are entrapped by these baits
   And anxieties about them afflict you
   only when you meditate on GOD, you shall enjoy peace...
10. *Dealth does not wait for opportune time, date or occasion,*
    Countless number of people have gone, others are going, and still others are getting ready to leave
    Says Nanak, that the human body is destined to merge in dust one day or the other...
11. The ignorant man sets his mind on wealth and is worried when it is gone,
    one should offer ones mind and heart to GOD and *have complete reliance on HIM,*
    Then strifes and struggles are no more
    only some rare souls cherish love for TRUTH and GOD...
12. The breaths we take are numbered,
    Limited is the life-span of a man,
    Limited is the number of scenes and sounds of a life,
    Life begins at birth and will end with dealth for all,
    And alas in death, none will accompany you...
    Nanak! I seek not the company of so called the great,
    I am with the lowest among the lowly,
    And with the humblest of the humble
    Because God's grace blesses the humble only
13. With wealth comes evil,
    Joys and sorrows follow it,
    Peace and calm are the fruits which ripen only when you pray to GOD, with a sincere heart
14. The life has been wasted in the pursuit of riches
    once caught in the meshes of greed, one does not know where to stop,
    only the true Guru can protect you by directing you to your CREATOR...
    we see others through our own mind,
    And our own mind is moulded by our desires,

And our deeds mould our passions,
By the grace of the True Guru one enters the abode of peace...

15. The self willed man, trapped by the desire for wealth, engages himself in *evil deeds* and earns *dishonour* through *his own words and deeds.*
One is ruined in the society of the evil minded,
Because evil company leads you away from GOD.
16. A false Sanyasi in a fit of emotional upheaval renounces his home,
And he keeps on wandering and gets tired of reading scriptures,
Alas! he has discarded his own wife, but is enamoured of other's wives,
Outwardly he is composed, but his heart is full of evil
Praise be to that house-holder. Who is devoted to the feet of the LORD.
17. By amassing wealth, one becomes rich
But one suffers many conflicts because of wealth
A sincere devotee gathers only the TRUTH and worships the LORD only...
18. By GOD'S grace one contemplates and acquires wisdom...
As a result of devotion and wisdom, evil and vicious tendencies disappear...
19. *Man's entry in to the world could not be stopped,*
How can his exit be stopped?
Everything happens according to the LORD'S will,
None else can do anything to alter His will,
Just as a pot of a rotating Persian wheel,
One is emptied and the other is filled...
Attachment or detachment of a devotee is judged only by being accepted by one's CREATOR.
20. *Sin is evil, yet the sinner loves it*
Sinner hoard's evil and spreads it all around him
21. *Wife and sons are dear to a man*
And they are the main source of greed for wealth...
22. Yogi! be steady and free yourself,
From the see saw of desires and suffering,...
Are you not ashamed of begging from door to dorr!
23. ...Attachment to wealth is similar to loving a discarded wife, who is notorious and vicious,
Alas! beauty and power last not long!...
24. O! LALO! *falsehood is dominant,*
Modesty and righteousness have disappeared...
25. O! man! you steal what belongs to others,
without knowing that GOD within you sees and hears everything,
when death overtakes you, neither brothers nor sisters accompany you,
you depart singly leaving behind your body, your wealth and your property
26. ...The world is in shackles of greed and too many desires,
Being attached to wives and sons, they forget the LORD'S name...

without a clear vision, one can not achieve one's aim
one who serves the TRUTH is saved...

27. Nanak! what can a man do?
    Everything happens according to HIS will.
28. *Many men claim to be scholars, alas! very few make use of their learning,*
    Many men claim to be wise, alas! very few are virtuous...
29. Brother! Hope and desire both lead to bondage,
    Religious rites and formalities are chains...
    ...And oblivious of the LORD they all perish...
30. NANAK! Be steady, do not run from place to place
    The LORD is in your own heart...
    Discard greed, slander and falsehood
    Then the GURU'S WORD will yield the fruit of TRUTH...
31. You welcome the gains and weep over the losses,
    These profits and losses are all pre ordained by the LORD...
    He who has lost the presence of the LORD, in the lure of wealth
    Has gone astray due to evil counsel...
32. The writ of past deeds is written on the forehead,
    The result of the past deeds can not be erased who knows what will happen?...
    ...you are here for a fewdays,
    Live by the will of GOD,
    By meditating on 'the LORD'S name,
    you will enter the abode of peace...
33. Flowers, youth and wealth do not last long,
    Just as the lotus leaves disappear after the lotus flowers bloom.
34. A man engrossed in wealth, has no time for his creator,
    Attached to wealth and proud of his strength
    He wastes his life in vain pursuits
    And neglects to do any good deeds...
35. *A man may amass crores, but if he does not check his greed,*
    He will go on struggling for more and more wealth, wealth enslaves him in many ways,
    And tosses him hither and thither,
    He *neglects to pray to the LORD, who is the source of all wealth...*
    only a rare one, keeps his greed under control.
36. *Greed, avarice and pride and the desire for a wife, sons, relatives and wealth, lured me to death,*
    Same is true of the whole world!
37. *By forsaking pride, one enters heaven.*
38. *Mad after wealth, man strives for it day and night,*
    He ignores the LORD...
39. *By amassing wealth, you invite curses of the poor*

Those whom you please and yourself will all perish!

40. *None will remain here forever, be he an Emperor or King,*
where are the rich, who had elephants waiting at their doors?
None came with man and nothing will go with him

41. *The poor may try in a thousand ways, but the rich will not adopt him,*
If a poorman goes to the rich,
The rich one turns his back on to him,
And when the rich one calls on the poor,
He is escorted in with respect
Says KABIR, the poor is really he
whose heart is empty of GODS grace.

42. People strive for wealth and property till the end,
Alas! welath and property in the end prove troublesome,
Friends! pray to GOD and He will befriend you in the end.

43. *Overtaken by the greed for money*
one runs in all ten directions...
For the sake of pleasures, he suffers a lot and cringes to one and all,
Like a dog, he waits at the doors,
He wastes his life in vain,
He is not ashamed of peoples jeers,
Says Nanak, why does he not pray to GOD to deliver him from the clutches of greed.

44. The rich man worries over his wealth,
The poor man strives for wealth,
He who is free from craving for (riches and poverty) both is really blessed...

45. ...The coward wanders from birth to birth,
Only the brave knows how to die,
worrying doubts occur while living in the world,
The imperceptible and indescribable is not seen,
He who is guided by the LORD, realises HIM
One renounces wordliness, but it can not be absolutely renounced,
If one is engrossed in worldliness, it leads to fear
Says Nank the LORD is the giver of perfect peace.

46. He, who is proud because of his wealth, should realise that not even a single coin will accompany him in death
He who is proud because of the power he wields, can be reduced to ashes in a moment,
He, who in his arrogance does not acknowledge any body,
Will be humiliated by the yama, (DEATH)
Nanak! he on whom the LORD bestows humility, enjoys peace and freedom here and hereafter.

47. ...As long as a man thinks that he is the doer of some deeds, peace eludes him,

As long as one cherishes friendship with some and enmity with others, his mind cannot remain steady,
So long as he is engrossed in the pursuit of wealth,
he suffers punishment in death.
If a man earns a thousand, he then tries to earn a LAKH,
He is not satisfied and goes on hankering after more money,
He enjoys countless pleasures, yet remains discontented,
and kills himself in these yearnings
Satisfaction comes from contentment only
All our efforts remain directed towards dreamy achievements,
All instructions and understanding come from GOD,
GOD, who is nearest as well as farthest from man,
Does everything according to His own pleasure,
NANAK! always remember GOD,
HE is the cause of all causes...
NANAK! GOD's name is pure and holy
And He is realised only through LOVE in ones own heart.

48. *This world is like a play and none is allowed to continue forever,*
Follow the straight path, otherwise some may trip you up,
Brother! *DEATH will overtake all,* young or old,
rich or poor, ruled or the rulers, none is spared
DEATH is Universal and omnipotent
KABIR! dear soul, listen, you will realise the LORD
By detaching yourself from, wife, sons, wealth and worldliness;

Source

The Malady of Man – Guru Nanak by Sher Sing, 1968.

17

VACHANAS OF BASAVANNA

Basavanna (Basava), the reformer saint of Veerashaiva sect needs no introduction to the Kannada speaking public of our country. *"Vachanas of Basavanna"* are the spiritual out pourings of Basavanna, to the *LORD KUDALA SANGAMA* and are cherished not only by the followers of Veershaiva sect but also by many who belong to other religions.

Biographical Outline of BASAVANNA and His Period:

In the *11th* and *12th centuries Karnataka* was ruled by different dynasties, in different parts the chief among them being the *CHALUKYAS OF KALYAN* and the *HOYASALAS OF DORASAMUDRAM*. Religious tolerance prevailed everywhere. Different communities lived in peace and harmony side by side. However a powerful orthodoxy of those times was opposed to religious tolerance and communal harmony. The society vegetated, and spiritual life was suffocated by numerous meaningless cermonials and fussy rituals.

BASAVANNA was born in a respectable *Brahmin family* of good connections in the year *1125 A.D.*, at *INGALESWARA* – BAGEWADI in the *BIJAPUR DISTRICT OF* erstwhile *MYSORE STATE.* In BAGEWADI, there were five hundred Brahmin families, along with other groups. It was controlled by Brahmins, no doubt, but there were other people belonging to different religious denominations pursuing various occupations. It was a village resounding with VEDIC recitations and devotional songs. Most of the brahmins were *SHAIVITES,* and the centre of activities of the town was perhaps the big SHIVA temple there.

Mandageya Madiraja was the headman of the town and *Madambe* was his wife. They were Shaiva Brahmins of Kamme family, belonging to Sankhyana gotra. The couple had no male issue for a longtime. Basavanna was born to them. The child grew up into a young boy. Basavanna was a very sensitive and intelligent child.

He had some terrible experiences – the pitiable bleatings of a young lamb taken to the sacrificial altar resounded in his dreams. During Nagapanchami people worshipped the stone image of Naga by pouring milk and ghee over it, but when a real snake appeared, they hastened to kill it.

Basavanna himself had assisted his father many times in the worship of fire, but when something caught fire, it was put out by sand and water.

Basavanna saw children, naked and ill-fed and the difference in standards of living between the rich and poor made a deep impression on the tender heart of Basavanna. He was forbidden to mix and play with Children of lower castes.

The dual life of the Brahmins jarred on his sensibilities. They bathed regularly and performed their religious duties; they spoke of GOD, the other world and high ideals. But in their heart of hearts they were selfish and self-centred. *To most of them, the name of GOD was only a tool to achieve their worldly ends.* The innumerable rituals they performed from morning to night throughout the year was the sum total of their religion and alas! Their rituals and ceremonies did not make them better human beings, rather they moved away from the vast suffering humanity. Thus Basavanna grew more thoughtful and introspective. Precocious, sensitive, and devout as Basavanna was, his spirit rebelled against the make believe religious pretensions of his day. Gifted with a precocious mind, *his thinking was much ahead of his period.* He refused to undergo UPANAYANA ceremony in his eighth year. He was convinced that he had already been initiated in to the true faith – VEERASHAIVISM, by the grace of GOD, with out the aid of any ceremony.

Basavanna left his home and settled down at *KUDALA SAGAMA* (*a small village in BIJAPUR DISTRICT* Kudalu and Sangama both mean confluence of rivers. Kudala *Sangama is very beautiful place, where the river MALAPRABHA joins the KRISHNA.* Near the confluence is a temple, and the GOD there is called SANGAMESWARA), along with his elder sister AKKANAGAMMA.

Sangameswara temple was presided over by a STHANIKA (temple official) named ISHANYA GURU. He noticed Basavanna's deep attachment to GOD. He was perhaps the first to recognise the greatness of Basavanna. He permitted Basavanna to stay with him in the temple and assigned to him the duties of bringing fresh water and flowers for worship. Basavanna gladly accepted the temple job. From this juncture, the whereabouts of his elder sister were not known.

Kudala Sangama became the seat of his SADHANA. He worshipped LORD SIVA with his body, mind and soul. In short nothing interested him except GOD. The temple officials and the people appreciated his devotion to LORD SIVA. Basavanna taught them devotional songs. The fame of this God intoxicated man spread all over the region. Basavanna revolutionised old Shaivism and gave it a new form called *VEERA SHAIVISM.*

KING BIJJALA was a feudal lord under CHALUKYAS and his capital was *MANGALIVEDA.* Basavanna had a good knowledge of mathematics and thought that he could become an accountant under King Bijjala. *Siddha dandanatha,* the chief of the treasury of King Bijjala, was instrumental in Basavanna being appointed as a *GANAKA* (Accountant). A Ganaka was an important official in the state adminstration. After some years, the chief treasurer died and King Bijjala made Baravanna, the chief Treasury Officer in his place. Thereafter he was called *Basava Dandanayaka.*

Basavanna had acquired position, power and fame. *Shortly after the death of his benefactor Siddhadandanatha, he married his two daughters Gangadevi* and *Nilalochane* (also called Mayidevi). His married life was happy. Both the sisters cooperated with him in his busy life.

They looked after the innumerable guests and visitors of Basavanna. He threw open the gates of his house and spent his money to the last penny in the cause of his religion.

VEERASHAIVISM

Veerashaivas were expected to develop single minded devotion to one GOD SIVA. To them Siva is supreme. The term LINGAYATA or LINGAVANTA is also used to describe this religion. *Lingayats are those who wear a LINGA on their body.* It is called the *ISHTALINGA,* as opposed to the *"STHAVARA LINGA"* of the temple. Guru is the teacher who initiates a person in to veera shaivism and gives him the Linga.

JANGAMA is the term used to describe a holyperson. He moves from place to place preaching. He is sometimes considered to be greater than GOD himself and hence he should be treated with great respect.

Among BHAKTI, JNANA, and VAIRAGYA, the place of BHAKTI, as a way to realisation of GOD is pre-eminent in veerashaivism.

Brahminism never allowed a low caste man or an outcast to become a Brahmin. Basavanna declared that anybody could become a veerashaiva irrespective of his class, community, creed or occupation. Once he became a veerashaiva, he would be treated as an equal. *However two things were expected of him.* Firstly he should severe connections with his former religion and get initiated in to the new religion and wear *ISHTALINGA* at all times on his body; secondly he should have complete faith in GOD SHIVA. *The religious rites expected of a VEERASHIAVA (are) were :*

1. *He should apply BHASMA* (HOLY ASHES) on the forehead
2. He should give up *meat eating* and *wine drinking* (*He should become a perfect vegetarian*)
3. *He should always speak the TRUTH*
4. *He should avoid stealing, and killing*
5. *He should not be greedy*
6. *He should take up a profession and work hard for* his living (*He should not be lazy*)
7. He should avoid going to a temple, because the body of Siva BHAKTA itself is a temple.

Veerashaivism appealed to the masses, especially to the poor and downtrodden. They felt that a redeemer had a appeared for their upliftment. Thousands of people embraced veerashaivism. Even today lingayats form a bout 20-21% of the total population of Karnataka (Population *27 millions* approximately *(1972).* A large number of lingayats live outside Karnataka in states like Andhra Pradesh, Tamilnadu and MAHARASTRA.

Among these were agriculturists, weavers, shoemakers, fishermen, hunters, basketmakers, barbers, merchants and even Brahmins.

King Bijjala who usurped the Chalukyan throne in 1162 A.D. moved his capital from Mangaliveda to Kalyana. As a result Basavanna also moved in to Kalyana in 1162 A.D. or earlier. The shifting of the capital had a powerful impact on Basavanna and his activities.

Now he had a richer treasury to look after. *Mangaliveda was a small town; Kalyana was a big city teeming with life.* It gave an impetus to the social revolution Basavanna had started in Mangaliveda.

Basavanna at Kalyana

Kalyana was the capital of the Chalukyas in those days. It is now a small town in *Bidar district,* and is named after Basavanna as *BASAVAKALYANA*. At Kalyana there were Shaivites, Vaishnavites, Jains and Buddhists. Trade and commerce flourished in Kalyana. *Basavanna continued to be the treasurer of King Bijjala (1162 A.D.).*

The popularity of veerashaivism posed a great threat to the orthodox, and established religions. Some important officials, a few influential Shaivite and Vaishnavite Brahmins and Jains and others developed enmity towards Basavanna and his veerashaivism. They complained to the king that Basavanna did take out money, jewels and clothes from the King's Treasury and distributed it among the Jangamas. However when King Bijjala checked the accounts of the treasury, they were found to be correct to the last penny. The rift between the king and Basavanna went on widening. The king threatened Basavanna with dismissal and the latter cooly stated that he was not afraid of it.

Last Days of Basavanna

Basavanna's numerous enemies from the orthodox religious groups pleaded before the king that Basavanna and his veerashaivism was promoting VARNA SANKARA (intermingling of various castes) and this was violating *SANATANA DHARMA* and as a king it was his primary duty to uphold *DHARMASASTRAS* and *SANATANA DHARMA*.

Basavanna gave his consent to the marriage of the *son* of one *AILAYYA* (an *untouchable* who became a veerashaivite) and the *daughter* of one *Madhuvayya* (*a Brahmin* who became a veerashaivite). The orthodox conservatives, were totally against the proposed marriage and complained to the king. King Bijjala asked Allayya and Madhuvayya to stop it and they flatly refused to obey the king's order. On *King Bijjala's orders their eyes were plucked out.*

Veerashaiva followers raised a storm of protest against the king's act. In the aftermath of the protest, one *Jagadeva* and *his aides assassinated King Bijjala* and proclaimed that the enemy of veerashaivism was dead (1167 A.D.). Later Jagadeva killed himself and his aides were caught and put to death along with many others.

However *Basavanna* along with his followers left for Kudala Sangama. His mind was perturbed and he wanted peace. He knew that his end was near. *Basavanna died in about* 1167-68 A.D., at the confluence of rivers.

Basavanna (1125 – 1167 A.D.) had left behind him a band of dedicated workers like Channa Basava and Madivala Machayya and they carried on his work. Basavanna brought about a thorough change in the social outlook and had sown seeds of revolution in the minds of the people.

VACHANAS OF BASAVANNA

Basavanna is perhaps the greatest writer of Vachanas in Kannada. Vachana literally means prose. But the Vachanas of Basavanna and others may be termed poetic prose. One advantage about the vachanas was the ease with which they could be composed. The language was simple and there were no rules prescribed in their composition. And therefore scholars as well as ordinary people were able to express themselves effectively.

Though vachana is not a verse it is possible to arrange each vacchana in lines of varying lengths. *A vachana could run from three to thirty or thirty five line. There were no restrictions as regards the number.* Each vachana ends in a *ANKITHA* (An Ankitha is a word or words which the author weaves in to the text of his composition to suggest his authorship). The *Ankitha of Basavanna was 'KUDALA SANGAMA'* his 'ISHTA DAIVAM'.

BASAVANNA composed about *1400 vachanas. They can be classified under the following headings:*

1. *Vachanas which are purely didactic in nature*
2. *Vachanas which are exclusively devoted to social criticism*
3. *Vachanas which contain self criticism and express his inner mental conflict*
4. *Vachanas which narrate the principles of veerashaivism*
5. *Vachanas which describe his mystic experiences*
6. *Vachanas which do not fall into the above 1–5 groups*

Spiritual Evolution According to Veerashaiva Mystics

Spiritual evolution according to veerashaiva mystics takes place in six stages. *The six stages are called SHATSTHALAS* namely 1. *BHAKTA STHALA* 2. *MAHESWARA STHALA* 3. *PRASADI STHALA* 4. *PRANALINGA STHALA* 5. *SHARANA STHALA* and finally 6. *AIKYASTHALA.*

1. *BHAKTA STHALA* : The devotee begins his spiritual apprenticeship
2. *MAHESWARA STHALA* : The devotee does not recognise any other GOD except his own
3. *PRASADI STHALA* : The Divine Gace begins to descend slowly on the aspirant, and a sense of hope fills his mind
4. *PRANA LINGA STHALA* : The devotee feels that GOD resides in his "ISHTA LINGA" and also in his heart
5. *SHARANA STHALA* : The devotee completely surrenders his will to GOD. There is a slow extinction of his separate identity from GOD.
6. *AIKYA STHALA* : The devotee looses his separate identity from GOD and becomes one with HIM.

Some later anthologists of *VACHANAS OF BASAVANNA* and other saints, classified them into the above mentioned six stages, and therefore named them as "*SHATSTHALA VACHANAS*" also.

SELECTED VACHANAS OF BASAVANNA 1. BHAKTA–STHALA

1. O LORD KUDALA SANGAMA
This MAYA has undone my life...

2. This MAYA has enticed me with gold,
with woman and with land
O–LORD, KUDALA SANGAMA!
3. ...where action in accordance with word is found
There truly, LORD KUDALA SANGAMA dwells.
4. ...My courage has been shattered by
the passions of my flesh and mind,
Therefore, O LORD KUDALA SANGAMA!
I surrender to THEE.
5. Greed, lust, sloth, lies,
Infirmity of senses
Roguery and fraud
Anger and meanness heart–Kudala Sangama!
Tear these away from my (tongue!)...
6. ...Let me live as a bee
In the lotus at your feet
Lord Kudala Sangama!

2. GURU KARUNA–STHALA

7. In making a pot,
The clay comes first;
In making an ornament,
The gold comes first...
In the worship of Kudala Sangama,
The fellowship of SARANAS,
Comes first.

3. VIBHUTI–STHALA

8. Bother not how your past sins depart,
will not the bitter bottle gourd,
If filled with sacred ash
within three days loose its bitter taste...
9. Whenever we decide on a good deed
Deem that to be the auspicious time...
And today is better than tomorrow...

4. LINGA DHARANA–STHALA

10. To cancel out all your sins, will not
The name of Siva, uttered once, suffice?
11. A village without BHAKTAS
Is but a ruinous wilderness
O KUDALA SANGAMA!

12. With fraud within and modesty without
Such "HOLY MEN", do not reach at all
The path of righteousness, Kudala Sangama!

5. TAMASA NIRASANA–STHALA

13. A harlot with a child,
Is neither for the lover nor for the child
One moment she will sooth her child
Another, go to bed with the lover
The lust for GOLD persists
O, Lord Kudala Sangama
14. The wife who has no love for her husband,
The bhakta who has no faith in SIVA
They are like a calf that will not suck from the cow
and like a cow that will not yield her milk–
Kudala Sangama!
15. What is the use of a fortune-line
on ones palm, without the life line (longevity)?...
16. A harlot invites one person with her eye
She takes another to her heart
Trust not the wanton who
Beguiles mankind, Kudala Sangama!
17. ... commerce with a lowborn man
No good thing come out of it, Kudala Sangma!

6. BHAKTA JNANI–STHALA

18. Madhavasetti sits in his large shop
Talks about Advaita and Dwita
But he does not lose a single pie
And he will not let go even half a pie
Behold how wise he is, Kudala Sangama!
19. The serverest penances are futile
If ones heart is not pure
Can you kill the snake
If you strike down the ant hill, Kudala Sangama!
20. Make friends with the good
Shun the company of the evil ones
Whatever type the snake may be
Its venom always kills, Kudala Sangama!
21. A trained parrot may utter a few words,
Alas! it cannot warn us, when the cat pounces on it,...
All those who claim to know what others are,

Alas! they are ignorant of themselves—Kudala Sangama!

22. Why should you try to mend,
the failings of others,
First correct yourself by controlling your body and mind...
23. Do you expect perfume in a withered flower?
Where there is no friendship, do you look for goodness?
—Kudala Sangama!
24. Greed begets greed,
One who is born, to beg, will only beg,
And will a harlots child be gentle and nice?
Will the birth-cycle fail to operate? Kudala Sangama!
25. A sheep about to be slaughtered
Nibbles the tender leaves meant for the festoon
Not suspecting its approaching death
Do those who butcher it survive forever?
—Kudala Sangama!
26. A frog caught in a snake's mouth,
Looks hungrily at a nearby fly,
A thief about to be hanged,
How long will he live even when is fed with milk?
Brothers, Do not rely on this perishable flesh...
27. Unless, greed, anger, foul words, fraud and cruelty depart from you
You will not be able to see Kudala Sangama.
28. Avoid the company of those,
Who are half worldly and half pious,
Be the servant of servant of Kudala Sangama.
29. *If an immoral man (Reprobate),*
Tempts you with gold and power,
Do not say 'yes' to him, out of greed,
Better to be the servant of a BHAKTA,
and share his frugal meals
—Kudala Sangama!
30. "A Bhakta's body is my own" said Kudala Sangama
The Bhakta's courtyard is a Varanasi and his body is KAILASA
After the Linga worship
Why ask for a person's caste? Kudala Sangama!
31. One who is a master of words is not wise,
one who recites the GITA is not wise,
He is wise only who has faith in SIVA
—Kudala Sangama
32. This world is but the God's mint;
Those who earn merit here, earn merit in the hereafter also,

And those who earn no merit here, earn neither there
—Kudala Sangama!

33. A rabbit that a huntsman brings,
People buy it eagerly
Alas! none will give even a betel nut
For the dead body of even a king
Dead body of a man is worthless
—Kudala Sangama!

34. The human body is a basket
The mind is the snake
See how they live together
Anytime the snake may bite and kill you
But for the grace of KUDALA SANGAMA!

35. *Do not rely on the perishable body,*
It is like trying to fix an iron frame around a bubble of water,
Live and worship Kudala Sangama!

36. What you call life,
Is a wind blown lamp,
What you call wealth,
Is a crowd in the market place which disperses, and it is like the splendour of the moonlit night which disappears with the dawn
The only thing that does not perish
Is Kudala Sangama's grace

37. When SIVA gives
wealth follows you
It is like the stream
Flooding a tank...

38. ... Before time passes,
Before death carries you away,
worship Kudala Sangama!

39. ... It the body acts against
ones mind and heart
It does not please at all
—Kudala Sangama!

40. ... To do and not to know
The spirit of what you do
Is so much waste of means
If you miss the opportunity when it comes
Kudala Sangama will never wait.

41. They worship a stone image of a snake,
Alas! when they see a real snake,
They hasten to kill it,

When a hungry Jangama comes
They shout "Away", and
They serve their dainties to a LINGA made of stone
That can not eat

—Kudala Sangama!

42. Counterfiet coins are not accepted by any one
Jangama collects the toll
For the wares of piety,

—Kudala Sangama!

43. A devotee who worships SIVA,
with his mind fixed on the safety of his shoes!
Alas! how can his worship be sincere?
Do not save money but to spend it on
The Saranas of Kudala Sangama

44. *You hoard your wealth*
As if you are going to live forever
Or may be you want to leave it to your wife
May be your wife has other plans
The moment life departs from your body
Surely she gives it to another man!
Do not hoard wealth but spend it on
The Saranas of Kudala Sangama!

45. The body, mind and wealth
Are the three swords that hang over you
offer the three to Siva
And become free

46. Shall I say Sastra is great?
It only exalts Karma!
Shall I say Veda is great?
It justifies animal sacrifice!
Shall I say Smriti is great?
It seeks in the future!
One without any blemish is Kudala Sangama alone!

47. Piety of a devotee,
May all perish even with a single sin;
Just as a stack piled up for a long time laboriously,
May be reduced to ashes by a fire;
Even as a son who wastes in vice, in a short time
The wealth his father gathered virtuously over years...

48. Bamboo is pliable and serves,
As a palanquin pole sunshade stick and even as a,
mast of a flag or a tent;

Be humble with all, and as pliable as the bamboo...

49. One who worships ostentatiously,
One who gives alms ostentatiously,
Is only wasting his time and money;
When a harlot's son does obsequies,
His mother's name appears,
And not his father's name

—Kudala Sangama!

50. Do not worship with an ulterior motive,
Nor pray before a crowd;

51. To undertake whatever is come,
That is a vow.
Not to conceal (DISSEMBLE) what one has
That is a vow
Not to betray the word you said
That is a vow
Not to fail in a deed
That is a vow
To look after devotees of Siva
That is a vow

—Kudala Sangama!

52. Thou shall not kill, steal, or lie,
Give up anger, do not scorn another man,
Nor glory in thyself, nor blame others...
This is the way to win the grace of Kudala Sangama!

53. To speak the truth is to enter the world of GODS,
To speak untruth is to be in the mortal world.

54. The worldy man who lies in word,
And fails in deed is far from,
the grace of Kudala Sangama.

55. *You should collect only such goods,*
Which have the touch of truth...

56. ... *Good works is heaven,*
Bad works is hell...

57. Mark you, virtue and sin
Are your own choice
"To say 'SIR' is heaven
To say 'you there' is hell...
Vain is his life who has no courtesy
If you are not insincere
You may even jest at ease even with your own master...

58. What sort of religion can it be

Without compassion?
Compassion towards all living creatures,
Is the root of all religious faith — *Kudala Sangama!*

59. Give up anger,
To show one's anger means,
A loss of dignity, to feel it leads to loss of sense,
The fire in your home, first burns your home,
Then only your neighbour's

– Kudala Sangama!

7. BHAKTA–STHALA

60. When men of every sort,
Are prostate at my feet,
I am puffed with pride and conceit,
Burn away my pride and conceit borax white

– Kudala Sangama!

61. Should any slander you in a strange place
Listen and keep quiet and cool
When resentment leaves your heart
The grace of Kudala Sangama descends on you...

62. Lo! one thing in the heart,
One thing in the mind,
Another still upon the lips,
How can such a hypocrite be the devotee of Kudala Sangama?

63. Even as a washerman fusses over
Clothes which are not his
I foolishly wasted my life in vain thinking such as,
"Mine is the gold, mine is the land, mine is the woman
– Kudala Sangama!

64. It is better to be a servant in a SIVA BHAKTA'S house
Than to be in a King's palace...

65. Can you get milk
Unless you do the meanest tasks?
I do not seek greatness,
Without the lowly state

—Kudala Sangama!

66. when people see mounted guards,
And bearers of royal sun shade,
They prostrate in utter servility;
But when they see a poor Sanyasi
They shout at him to move away

—Kudala Sangama!

8. MAHESA–STHALA

67. No devotee of Siva should beg
 I will not run nor beg, Kudala Sangama!
68. Why should I mind another's business?
 Is not mine own enough for me?
 Whether Kudala Sangama loves me or not
 Is business enough for me...

9. JNANI–STHALA

69. They call him BRAHMA who creates,
 Why then could not Brahma create his own severed head?
 They call him VISHNU, who protects
 Why then could not VISHNU protect his own son?
 The protector of the good and who punishes the wicked,
 is Kudala Sangama only
70. ... Folly to seek fragrance in a flower too long in bloom
 Folly to seek charm in a wizened whore
 Folly to seek depth in a stagnant pool...
71. Because they believed the Brahamnas to be God,
 They had to suffer in various ways;
 1. Gautama the sage did suffer for a cow,
 2. Bali did suffer bondage
 3. Karna did lose his armour
 4. Daksa did earn the head of a lamb
 5. Nagarjuna lost his head
 only devotees who worshipped Kudala Sangama alone
 Now dwell in KAILASA!
72. Cry, cry o goat,
 That you are slain in accordance with VEDAS and SASTRAS
 Lord Kudala Sangama will take a fit toll
 For what you have wept!
73. O Sir, whereever they see water, they dip in it.
 O Sir, whereever they see a tree, they circle it,
 Alas! they rely on water which dries up and a
 tree that withers

—Kudala Sangama!

74. The VEDIC priests who worship fire with Ghee etc.
 When a fire breaks out in their house
 They try to put it out with any dirty water and street dust, and
 Call the whole world to their aid with yells
 Such is the respect they show to their AGNI

—Kudala Sangama!

75. "The outcast is the man who tells a lie"
The whole world knows that the orthodox priests are vile!
You a BRAHMAN? No never
Since it is said "A man is born a SUDRA, and
Becomes a Brahman by his deeds...
76. O look not for caste; in caste
What were you in the past?
Vyasa was a fisherman's son,
Markandeya of an outcaste born,
Mandodari, the daughter of a frog,
Indeed, Agastya was a fowler,
Durvasa, a maker of shoes,
Kasyapa a blacksmith, Kaundanya the sage was a barber,
"What matters one is lowly–born?
Only a SIVABHAKTA is well born!
77. ... *It is the same birth out of the womb for all*
Is there anybody who was delivered through the ear?
"What then is the usefulness of the caste?"
Who sweats in a smithy is a smith,
Who washes clothes is a washerman,
Who weaves is a weaver,
Who reads and teaches is a Brahmin,
What matters one is lowly born?
Only a SIVABHAKTA is well born!
78. ... You claim to be superior by your caste,
Clinging to caste, you seek impurities,
While you cling to light, you live in darkness...
79. A flock of sheep in a sugar cane field,
Are happy to nibble outer leaves, only,
An elephant only sucks up the juice of sugar canes,
Only a BHAKTA can know you KUDALA SANGAMA!
80. ... It is false to say
The Brahman is the Guru of castes
The Guru of castes is Kudala Sangama's Sarana.
81. If Laxmi (TRUTH) and Saraswati (DEVOTION) favour you,
Why worry about caste?
Why should a SIVA BHAKTA depend on any other charm?
82. God is but one, though His names are many,
The faithful wife knows but one lord,
My lord is Kudala Sangama!
83. ... When love is lacking, whatever you do
Is all a waste...

84. Beauty, wealth and the power of kings,
Do not endure O man!...
85. Should I but covet another's wealth or wife
Let me be banished from Thy feet, Kudala Sangama!
86. When you restrain your five senses unnaturally,
The five senses laugh into your face,
Did Bhaktas like SIRIYALA and cangale,
Give up their nights of love as married couple,
Bridling your five senses all you do is starting maladies...
87. ...The association of the vile and noble,
Is not a wholesome thing,
Can a red berry match a ruby
—Kudala Sangama!
88. It is good to practice to follow unfailingly,
Both TRUTH and cleanliness, as well as daily rites:
Fish, frogs and tortoise live in water only and to what purpose?
When the heart is impure, even taking a holy bath
With a hundred pots of water leaves it as impure as a toddy pot...
89. There are men who say that
They will give their wealth, honour and life to Kudala Sangama
But I see no devotee, who has actually given them
DASA gave his cloth but not himself
BALLALA gave his wife but not himself
SIRIYALA gave his son but not himself
It was all an outward thing
SINDHUMARARALA alone did give himself
TO LORD KUDALA SANGAMA!
90. ... You cannot escape
Whatever is written on your brow...
... *Do not do anything*,
Whose consequences and results you cannot enjoy without fear...

10. MAHESVARA – STHALA

91. The undue love of ones relations,
Leads to hell,
Parents, brothers and members of ones clan,
If they are not BHAKTAS, I refuse to own as mine
—Kudala Sangama!
92. What signifies what caste they be?
He who is a SIVABHAKTA, is well born...
Give up your bygone caste
RUDRA is your father, UMA is your mother

ISWARA is your only clan...

11. PRANALINGA – STHALA

93. No living creature will I slay,
Nor eat for pleasure of the tongue,
Nor will I seek adulterous love
Make me steadfast, Kudala Sangama!

94. Does an elephant fear the goad (ANKUSAM)
Save that he thinks it is a lion's claw?...

12. SARANA–STHALA

95. "What is the evidence that GOD exists?" says the atheist
GOD is the one who has created the earth and heaven,
His eyes are everywhere, his arms and feet
Are over all the universe...

96. All wisdom which is ignorant of THEE
Is no wisdom at all – Kudala Sangama!

97. Those who have money, build
Temples to SIVA,
Alas! a poor man like me, what can I
build for you SIVA?
My body is the shrine
Its pillars are my legs
The golden pinnacle, my head
There is destruction for what stands
But not for that which moves! —Kudala Sangama!

98. *If a treasure comes by accident,*
There is none who will refuse,
And Truth is sacrificed, when falsehood saves
Freedom from greed and fear belongs to
None else but to SIVA BHAKTAS —Kudala Sangama!

99. The plate where from we eat,
And the mirror we look in,
Are made of the same metal,
Same size and shape,
You, rub it–lo! a mirror shows,
If one forgets Siva, he becomes an ordinary man
If one worships Siva, he becomes a BHAKTA

– Kudala Sangama!

100. Once butter is melted in to ghee,
It can not be butter again;
A pearl will not become water again,

Once you have become a SIVA BHAKTA
You can not again become or ordinary man!

– Kudala Sangama!

101. *The commerce of the world is at an end*
When the BHAKTA becomes one with SIVA.

– *KUDALA SANGAMA!*

Sources

1. Selected sayings of Basavanna, by C.S. Bagi, 1952.
2. Vachanas of Basavanna – Deveerappa L.M.A. Henezes & S.M. Angadi, 1967.
3. Basavanna, by M.Chidananda Murthy 1972.

18

THIRUKURAL—THIRUVALLUVAR

The Thirukural is one of the oldest of still existing Tamil books. The author of this book *Thiru valluvar lived between 3rd century B.C. and 1st century B.C.* (Dr. M. Rajamanicknar – History of Tamil language and literature—Page 123).

Thirukural is also referred to as 1. MUPP..L (TRIVARGAM) (2) TAMIL MARI (TAMILAVEDAM) (3) DAIVANOOL (DIVYA GRANDHAM), and (4) PODUMARI (SARVA JANEENA VEDAM) etc.

Biographical Outline

Thiruvalluvar lived in *MYLAPORE* (Town of peacocks), which is a part of the present city of *MADRAS (TAMILNADU, INDIA) probably between 3rd century B.C. and 1st century B.C.* There is a temple in MYLAPORE dedicated to the memory of Thiruvalluvar. Thiruvalluvar was a weaver by profession. Thiruvalluvar was married to *VASUKI* daughter of MARGASAHAYAM. They lived a peaceful wedded life for a long time. They brought up their children with love and care. When his wife died, Thiruvalluvar lamented deeply and probably became an Ascetic.

THIRUKURAL

Thirukural of Thiruvalluvar consists of three main divisions, namely :

1. *DHARMA*, 2. *ARTHA* and 3. *KAMA*

I. *DHARMA*: The first book of Kural is perhaps the most widely known and the most appreciated work in Tamil literature. *It consists of 38 chapters and in each chapter are written 10 kurals (a total of 380 kurals). This division deals with the duties of man as a householder* and *as an ascetic.*

II. *ARTHA*: The second book of Kural consists of *70 chapters and in each chapter are written 10 kurals (thus a total of 700 kurals).* This division deals with policy in worldly affairs, including state craft. It contains principles of conduct that should guide all persons engaged in secular affairs.

III. *The third book of Kural consists of 25 chapters and each chapter contains 10 kurals, thus a total of 250 kurals.* This section deals with various aspects of love and marriage. *The three divisions on the whole contain 1330 KURALS.*

THE TIMES OF THIRUVALLUVAR

During the period between 3rd century B.C. and 1st century B.C. TAMILNADU was ruled over by the dynasties of 1. *CHERA* 2. *CHOLA and* 3. *PANDYA KINGS.* It established contacts with countries such as EGYPT, GREECE, ROME, BURMA, MALAYSIA, CHINA HIMALAYAN KINGDOMS, CEYLON etc.

Greeks were employed as palace guards at MADURAI the capital of the PANDYA KINGDOM. Pearls, peacocks and rice and such other indigenous products were in great demand, especially amongst the merchants of the WEST.

It was a period of (Internecine: destructed to one another mutually) internecine wars among CHERAS, CHOLAS and PANDYAS. *Saivism* and *VAISHNAVISM* were the indigenous religions in TAMILNADU of that period. However *JAINISM, BUDDHISM* and *VEDIC BRAHMINISM* also entered in to the picture. Along with their religious tenets, they brought newer linguistic influences in the form of PRAKRIT, PALI and SANSKRIT and they had their impact on TAMIL language.

In that period, TAMILNADU was dotted with PATTIMANRAMS (Debating assemblies), in which various religious and metaphysical issues were debated. Greek Roman and Egyptian Schools of thought, intermingled with those of TAMILS. Different religions vied with one another to obtain political influence and patronage of the TAMIL KINGS.

TAMIL SANGAM

The Tamil Sangam was a literary Academy, which had 49 members, and its centre of activity was *MADURAI,* the capital of PANDY KINGDOM. The Tamil Sangam stood sentinel over the Tamil language and guided its growth and reflected through it literary activities, the best of Tamilian thought of that period. The Tamil Sangam enjoyed such prestige that no new literary work in TAMIL would pass muster, unless it received the approval of the SANGAM (IMPRIMATUR: official approval (LATIN) : Let it be printed). *THIRU VALLUVAR* came to *MADURAI* to get his *THIRUKURAL* approved by the *TAMIL SANGAM.* The orthodox learned members of the Sangam were jealous and would not easily accord recognition to the literary work of THIRUVALLUVAR. According to a legend, they submitted him and his KURAL to the test of the golden bench floating in the tank, inside the MEENAKSHI TEMPLE. THIRUKURAL and THIRUVALLUVAR came out of the test successfully in a grand manner. *THIRUKURAL OF THIRUVALLUVAR was accepted and recognised through out TAMILNADU.* And ever since THIRUVALLUVAR is referred to as one of the divine poets.

Thiruvalluvar was one of those rare and great men, whose catholic spirit rose above all denominations and whose vision was not clouded by dogma or prejudice of any kind. *His teachings elude classification on any denominational basis.* Thiruvalluvar's approach to moral doctrine is marked by a thorough knowledge of human nature and a desire to help people in their struggle against evil.

THIRU KURAL ON DHARMA IN PRAISE OF GOD

1. GOD is the first source of the world. Similarly letter A is the first among all the letters (of all languages)
2. What is the use of one's learning, if one does not worship GOD, who is the source of all learning and wisdom?
3. Those who worship GOD sincerely will lead happy lives.
4. Those who worship GOD, will be rid of all troubles.
5. Those who worship GOD, will be rid of all ignorance.
6. Those who control their five senses and worship GOD, will live long.
7. Those who worship GOD only, can get rid of anxiety of mind, others cannot.
8. Those who worship GOD only can sail safely across the sea of SAMSARA.
9. The (head) *(intelligence)* and the five senses of one, who does not worship GOD are futile.
10. Sincere devotees of GOD only can sail safely across the sea of SAMSARA; others can not.

IN PRAISE OF RAIN

11. Rains are responsible for the continuous existence of this world.
12. Rains produce food and rain by itself serves as a life sustaining water for all (creatures and plants)
13. If there are no rains, famines and hunger will stalk all over the earth.
14. If there are no rains, farmers will cease to plough the land.
15. Rains are responsible for the prosperity or ruin of people.
16. If there is no rainfall, not even a blade of grass sprouts on the earth.
17. Even the unlimited water and wealth of the sea will diminish if the rainfall does not replenish them.
18. If the rains were to fail, there would be no more offerings to Gods, and no more festivals.
19. If the rains were to fail, there would be no DANA (charity) and TAPAS (AUSTERETIES) in this world.
20. This world can not exist without water;
    It the rains were to fail, there can not be any (never ending) perennial source of water in this world.

ON THE GREATNESS OF RENUNCIATION

21. An ascetic who has renounced all desires, is esteemed by all DHARMA SASTRAS.
22. To estimate the number of the dead in this world is impossible, similarly
    To evaluate the greatness of an ascetic who has risen above all likes and dislikes is impossible.
23. An ascetic who has renounced this world and who has realized the nature of birth and liberation is praised by the entire world.
24. An ascetic who has subdued his five senses (comparable to five elephants) with the ANKUSAM of discrimination, is fit to become the seed of (source) HEAVEN (SVARGA).

25. An ascetic who has subdued his five senses is deemed to be an equal to INDRA.
26. Those who can successfully complete difficult tasks, achieve greatness, those who cannot are the inferior sort.
27. One who understands the true nature of taste, sight, touch, sound and smell, understands this world also.
28. The greatness of the saints is borne out by their prophetic utterances.
29. It is difficult to bear the wrath of a saint even for a short time.
30. The saint is the personification of DHARMA (VIRTUE);
    The saint has compassion for all creatures.

ON DHARMA

31. *DHARMA is the source of wealth and liberation also;*
    DHARMA is the greatest source of happiness.
32. *DHARMA is the source of all happiness;*
    To ignore DHARMA is the cause of all evil.
33. *Follow DHARMA in everything to the best of your ability.*
34. *Purity of mind is DHARMA, All else is a vain show.*
35. *Conduct based on DHARMA consists of avoiding*
    1. *offensive speech* 2. *Malice* 3. *Anger* and 4. *Greed.*
36. *Do not postpone the practice of DHARMA;*
    DHARMA will be your only solace and support at the time of death.
37. *There is no need to describe DHARMA in detail*
    Behold the one sitting in the palanquin (PALLAKI) and the palanquin bearers.
38. *The constant practice of DHARMA will itself prevent one's rebirth.*
39. *Happiness springs from DHARMA only; all else is not happiness and merits no praise.*
40. *What one ought to do is DHARMA;*
    What one ought not to do is ADHARMA.

ON FAMILY LIFE

41. A householder *(GRUHASTU)* is the main support of the rest of the three orders of life, namely 1. *BRAHMACHARIS* 2. *VANAPRASTHAS* and 3. *SANYASIS*
42. A householder is the main support of 1. *Ascetics* 2. *destitutes* and (3) *the dead* (The householder helps in the cremation of the dead).
43. A householder should fulfil obligations to Gods, *forefathers, relatives, guests* and *self.*
44. *One should earn wealth by righteous means only.*
    One should share food with others. The progeny of such a virtuous householder will prosper.
45. *Love and virtue (DHARMA) are the main duties of a householder*
    For such a virtuous householder, Love and Dharma are also his rewards.
46. *A householder who follows DHARMA will obtain what all he desires and there is no*

need for him to become an ascetic.

47. *Amongst all those who strive for liberation (MOKSHA), the life of a virtuous householder is the best.*
48. *The householder who does not swerve from DHARMA and who helps the Ascetics is far greater than the latter. (ascetic)*
49. The life of a virtuous householder is an embodiment of DHARMA, if it is free from reproach by others.
50. A virtuous householder is praised as a DEVATA by all the people.

AN IDEAL WIFE

51. *An ideal wife should perform all her domestic duties properly, and especially expend within the means of her husband.*
52. If the wife is devoid of domestic excellence although she may possess other great qualities such a wife is to be regarded as useless.
    (For an ideal wife, the possession of domestic excellence is essential).
53. If a wife is virtuous, her husband has everything,
    If a wife has no virtue, her husband has nothing.
54. To have a virtuous and chaste woman as a wife is the best asset for a man.
55. A wife who worships her husband, as soon as she gets up in the morning, if such an ideal wife says "let it rain", it will rain.
    (A virtuous wife can command even the elements).
56. A wife who protects her virtue (SHEELA) at all times and who also takes care of her husband, is regarded as an ideal wife.
57. *The best protection for a wife is her virtue only.*
58. Even the Gods praise the wife who worships her husband.
59. A husband whose wife is devoid of virtue, will never be able to stand up to those, who revile (criticise abusively) him.
60. The virtue of an ideal wife ensures the welfare of her husband.
    The ornaments of the home of a virtuous wife are her good offspring only.

ON PROGENY

61. *For a householder, the acquisition of intelligent offspring, is one of the greatest advantages.*
62. No evils befall a householder, who is blessed with a good progeny.
63. *A man's riches are his sons; and they are bestowed on him according to his deeds.*
64. The rice in which the little hands of their children have dabbed, tastes far sweeter, to their parents than even nectar (AMRUTHAM).
65. The touch of their little children delights their parents;
    And the words of their little children are a treat to the ears of their parents.
66. The prattle of the little children sounds more melodius, to their parents than even the notes of a VEENA or a flute.

67. The benefit a father can confer on his son is to make him fit to occupy the front rank in the assembly of the learned.
68. There is no greater pleasure in the world for the parents than to have children who are wiser than themselves.
69. A mother feels greater joy when people praise the greatness of her son, than what she felt on the day he was born.
70. The service a son can render to his father is to make the public exclaim "by the result of what great TAPAS (PENANCE) did his father beget such an exemplary son!

THE POSSESSION OF LOVE

71. Is there any fastening that can shut in love?
Tears of the affectionate will surely proclaim the love within.
72. One who has no love in his heart will try to possess everything for himself.
One who has love in his heart is ready to sacrifice everything including his own body for the benefit of others.
73. *The union of love and SUKRUTAM (the result of good deeds done in one's previous birth) causes the entry of life in to a human body in the present birth.*
74. If there is love in ones heart one develops interest in others, and this interest inturn leads to a spirit of friendliness with all.
75. The wise say that a householder who follows the path of DHARMA and LOVE, will be happy here and hereafter.
76. (A) The ignorant say that love leads one to DHARMA only; *but love is a defence against evil too and love helps one to get out of vice also.* (PARIMELAZHAGAR'S interpretation).
(B) "Love inspires the warlike deeds of the brave soldier too" (C. RAJAGOPALACHARI'S interpretation) (Love is the foundation of all virtue)
77. The heat of the sun rays desiccates (dries up) all creatures which have no skeleton, like worms;
Similarly DHARMA destroys one who has no love in his heart.
(Note the comparison between the SUN and DHARMA)
78. The life of a man who has no love in his heart is as futile as the existence and flourishing of a *withered tree in a barren land.*
79. *Mere possession of a human body is futile if there is no love in one's heart.*
80. *The human body which is sustained by love is truly alive, where as*
The human body which is not sustained by love is a mere assembly of bones covered with skin.

ON HOSPITALITY

81. To acquire wealth and to live as a householder is only to exercise the benevolence of hospitality.
82. One should not eat by himself, ignoring the guest waiting at the door.
83. One who looks after his guests, he and his progeny will never suffer from poverty.

84. FORTUNE (LAXMI) smiles on the householder who receives his guests with a cheeful face.
85. The fields of a house holder, who eats only after serving food for his guests, will always yield a rich hearvest.
86. He who cherishes the guests who have come to him and then looks forward to new guests, will be a welcome guest to even GODS.
87. *The advantages of benevolence can not be easily assessed; they are proportionate to the worth of the guests.*
88. *Those who hoard up wealth laboriously and yet do not exercise the benevolence of hospitality, will in the end lament saying "we have laboured and laid up wealth, and are now without human support.*
89. If one does not exercise the benevolence of hospitality although he can afford it, is considered as a stupid one. Such stupidity denotes his mental poverty also.
90. The face of a guest whithers if he is not welcomed just as a ANICHAM flower whithers when smelt.

ON PLEASANT SPEECH

91. Pleasant speech is made up of words that are imbued with love, truth and virtue (DHARMA).
92. To speak pleasantly and with a cheerful countenance is better than to give a gift with a cheerful heart.
93. Words imbued with joy, love, and sincerity, are the contituents of DHARMA (virtue) of pleasant speech.
94. One who speaks pleasantly with others, need never suffer from poverty.
95. Humility and pleasant speech are considered as the true ornaments of a man; all the others are not ornaments at all.
96. If one speaks not only meaningfully but also pleasantly, his virtue (PUNYA) will increase and his vices (PAPAM) will decrease.
97. If one speaks words which are of benefit to others in a pleasant manner, they facilitate ones welfare here and hereafter.
98. Pleasant and in offensive speech is of benefit here and hereafter.
99. Pleasant speech yields joy to all, and observing this, is there any need for unpleasant speech?
100. Avoiding pleasant speech and indulging in unpleasant speech is as senseless as to prefer to eat the unripe to a ripe fruit.

ON GRATITUDE

101. For the help rendered expecting no return, even earth and heaven combined together, will not be able to recompense.
102. The value of a timely help, though small in itself, is considered to be of greater value than this world.
103. The value of a little help rendered expecting no return is considered to be of greater

value than the sea.

104. The help rendered may be as small as a millet seed (NUVVU GINJA) yet the wise consider it to be as large as a palmyra fruit.

105. The benefit conferred in itself is not the measure of the benefit. *The worth of those who have received the benefit is its true measure.*

106. Never forget the benevolence of men of virtue and good conduct; *Forsake not the friendship of those who have stood by you in adversity.*

107. The wise do not forget forever the friendship of those who relieved their afflictions.

108. It is not good to forget the benefit received; but it is good to forget then and there an injury inflicted by another.

109. It is better to pardon even a grievous injury inflicted by another, by recollecting the benefits rendered by him in the past.

110. There is no redemption for the sin of ingratitude though there may be redemption for other sins.

ON IMPARTIALITY (EQUITY)

111. To act impartially with everybody (i.e., relatives friends, strangers and enemies) is a preeminent Virtue (DHARMA).

112. *The wealth of the upright man will not be lost and will pass on to his progeny.*

113. *Give up atonce any ill gotten wealth, though it may seem to be good and make you prosperous.*

114. *The just and unjust among men are known by the existence of worthy or unworthy progeny (The just have worthy offspring* (children)*; the unjust have unworthy offspring.*

115. Loss and gain are inter related with cause and effect (loss and gain are interrelated to one's own KARMA). The wise know this, and maintain an evenness of mind through ups and downs of life.

116. *One who forsakes impartiality, seeks his own ruin.*

117. The wise do not consider an impartial man to be poor even if he is poor. (The virtue of impartiality is an invaluable asset).

118. *To incline to neither side, but to be impartial with all, like a well poised balance, is the characteristic of the wise.*

119. *Freedom from lies in ones speech denotes reverence for truth; Freedom from deceit in the mind indicates absence of bias. (Reverence for TRUTH, and absence of bias in the mind, are both necessary to be impartial).*

120. To guard and to deal with other's goods as ones own, is considered as the mark of proper trade among merchants.

ON SELF CONTROL

121. Possession of self control places one among the Gods. Lack of self control leads one to hell.

122. Let self control be guarded as a precious treasure. Self control ensures ones welfare.
123. Self control leads one to knowledge, and if one conducts himself with that knowledge, it will ensure distinction among the wise.
124. A householder who conducts himself with self control and follows DHARMA (virtue), achieves greatness.
125. Humility is good in all; especially Humility of the rich, is an excellent asset that further enhances the value of their wealth.
126. A tortoise at the sight of its enemy, withdraws all its limbs under it shell and thus remains safe.
   Similarly, If one controls his five senses in one lifetime, he will be ensuring his own happiness even in his future births.
127. *Whatever you may guard or may not guard,*
   guard your speech very carefully.
   Indiscreet speech leads you to repentance and sorrow.
128. If a man's speech results in a single evil to another all the good done by him so far to the latter, will also be turned in to evil.
129. A burn caused by a fire will heal in course of time where as anguish caused by a caustic tongue will never abate.
130. *DHARMA (VIRTUE) follows the man who has controlled his five senses and guards himself against anger.*

ON RIGHT CONDUCT

131. One achieves eminence by means of good conduct.
   Good conduct should therefore be preserved more carefully than ones life.
132. Strive hard to safeguard good conduct inspite of difficulties you may encounter; Good conduct gives surest support to all.
133. Right conduct enhances ones family prestige.
   Improper conduct degrades one family prestige.
134. A BRAHMANA may acquire again, knowledge of VEDAS by further study, but if he looses good character, and distinction of lineage, he will never be able to regain them.
135. One who strays from the right path will never achieve greatness, just as an envious man will never prosper.
136. Any deviation from the right path is fraught with evil consequences. The wise are aware of this, and hence do not stray from the right path.
137. Right conduct leads one to greatness.
   Evil conduct leads one to disgrace.
138. DHARMA (VIRTUE) arises from right conduct.
   Sorrow results from evil conduct.
139. A man of right conduct will not utter evil words even in a forgetful mood.
140. One who can not live in harmony with others, is regarded as an ignorant fool, even if he happens to be very learned in various matters.

ON ADULTERY

141. The sin of adultery is a sign of ignorance.
Those who seek DHARMA (VIRTUE) and ARTHA (WEALTH) will never commit the sin of adultery.
142. There is no greater fool than the man who stands at the door of another man, coveting his wife.
143. One who misbehaves with the wife of a confiding friend is as good as a dead man. (Such a man is unfit to be a human being).
144. One who commits adultery with another's wife forgoes any greatness he may possess.
145. If one enters the house of another man, with the thought of committing adultery with his wife, will obtain eternal disgrace.
146. One who commits adultery with another's wife cannot escape dire consequences of his evil act such as 1. Enmity 2. Sin 3. Fear and 4. Disgrace.
147. A householder who upholds DHARMA (VIRTUE) will never covet another's wife.
148. For the wise. Not to covet another's wife is the essence of good (SEELA). Conduct and Virtue (DHARMA).
149. Prosperity follows the man who does not covet another's wife.
150. To covet another's wife is one of the worst sins.
If one has forsaken DHARMA (Virtue) and has committed evil acts, it is better even for such a one if he avoids the evil of adultery.

ON PATIENCE

151. The earth bears up with those who dig it up. Similarly to bear with those who revile oneself is considered as the best of virtues (DHARMA).
152. To bear with an evil deed committed by another is better; to forget it is the best.
153. Failure in receiving and looking after a guest indicates lack of hospitality.
To bear with the ignorance of a stupid fellow indicates the strength of the mentally strong.
154. *If one wishes to safeguard his greatness, he should be patient under all conditions.*
155. The wise do not esteem the impatient and resentful.
The wise consider the man of patience to be as precious as gold.
156. The pleasure of a reprisal is for a day only;
where as the fame of one who forgives lasts forever.
157. Pity the transgressor since he is adding up to his load of sins;
Never try to repay evil with evil.
158. Let a man overcome those who commit excesses through egotism and pride, with forbearance.
159. Those who bear with the unpleasant speech of the evil ones, are considered to be even greater than the ascetics.
160. Those who give up food and practice austerities are great ascetics indeed;
But those who bear with the unpleasant speech of the evil ones, are considered to be even greater than the ascetics.

ON ENVY

161. Freedom from envy is the essence of one's character.
162. Envy none; there is no other possession greater than ones freedom from envy.
163. DHARMA (VIRTUE) and ARTHA (WEALTH) forsake a man of envious temperament.
164. Those who know that envy causes sorrow, never envy others.
165. Those who envy others, even if they are left unharmed by their enemies, will be ruined by their own envious temperament.
166. Those who envy others and if they cannot tolerate even the DANA (gifts) of others, they and their relatives will perish in destitution. (want of food and clothing)
167. Prosperity (Laxmi) forsakes the envious and poverty (Peddama) (SANIDEVATA) settles down in the house of the envious.
168. The deadly sin of envy not only destroys a man's prosperity but also deprives him of happiness here and hereafter.
169. The cause of poverty of a man of virtue (SAJJANA) and the prosperity of a man of envious temperament are to be pondered over.
170. Freedom from envy leads to greatness;
A man of envious temperament undermines his own position.

ON GREED (Equity: Justice, fairness)

171. If a man departs from equity and covets the wealth of another, not only he will cause the ruin of his family, but also will be entangled in many more evils.
172. Those who stand for equity will not commit evil acts even though they are likely to profit by such deeds.
173. Those who seek sublime happiness, will never commit evil dees, through a love of trifling pleasures; they will never forsake DHARMA (VIRTUE).
174. The wise who have controlled their five senses, and who are free from evil, will never seek anything from others.
175. Of what avail is ones vast learning of SASTRAS, if he acts foolishly through covetousness? (*His keen intelligence and vast learning are of no use, even to himself, because covetousness clouds his judgement*). (COVET: Desire greatly)
176. Even the householder who is interested in virtue (DHARMA) and liberation (MOKSHA), will be destroyed if he does evil acts out of covetousness.
177. Covet not the wealth of another. Even when you enjoy such wealth, many evils will overcome you.
178. Is there any way to safeguard, and acquire wealth? yes, there is one sure way, namely never to covet the wealth of another.
179. One of the best virtues (DHARMA) is not to covet another's wealth. Prosperity (LAXMI = GODDESS OF FORTUNE) seeks such virtuous householders unbidden.
180. Covetousness paves the way for ones own ruin;
Freedom from covetousness ensures ones victory.

ON SLANDER
(A malicious, false and injurious statement spoken about a person)

181. One may be guilty of indifference towards virtue (DHARMA) and may have done many evil deeds, but it is better if such a one avoids atleast the evil of slander.
182. A deceitful smile of a slanderer is a greater evil than even the neglect of virtue (DHARMA), and doing evil deeds.
183. DHARMASASTRAS say that if a deceitful slanderer gives up backbiting, he will acquire merit (PUNYA PHALAM), atleast after his death.
184. If the occasion demands, speak bitter words face to face with another, but never behind his back.
    (Avoid slander at all times).
185. The base slanderer who talks about virtue (DHARMA) to others, reveals his deceitful nature in the very act of backbiting.
186. The faults of others revealed by a deceitful slanderer, will make them reveal the faults of the slander also.
187. As a deceitful slanderer cannot foster friendship between two persons with pleasant speech, he will try his best to ruin a friendship with slander.
188. One who reveals the faults of his own intimate friends, will he be more discreet about others?
189. The earth patiently bears the burden of deceitful slanderers.
190. If one is aware of his own faults as keenly as he observes the faults of others, there will be fewer difficulties in this world.

ON FRIVOLOUS SPEECH

191. He who speaks about frivolous matters, to the disgust of many, will become the laughing stock of others.
192. To talk frivolously in the presence of many is more harmful than committing an evil deed to a friend.
193. Indulgence in frivolous speech atonce betrays ones lack of moral character.
194. Indulgence in frivolous speech not only reveals ones lack of moral character but it deprives him of good qualities also.
195. If a man of virtue and good conduct (SAJJANA) indulges in frivolous speech, his name and fame will be ruined.
196. A man of frivolous speech is regarded as chaff (HUSK) among men.
    The wise never indulge in frivolous speech.
197. If the occasion demands, one may have to utter bitter words. Yet, the wise should avoid frivolous speech at any time.
198. Those who seek after great results from great deeds will never indulge in frivolous speech.
199. Distinguished men of knowledge will never indulge in frivolous speech even in a forgetful mood.

200. Speak useful words only;
Speak not useless words.

ON FEAR OF EVIL DEEDS

201. Men of virtue and good conduct (SAJJANA), do not commit evil deeds, because their conscience forbids them. Whereas the wicked ones, who take pride in their wickedness will commit evil deeds without any scruples.
202. An evil deed produces evil results only; therefore an evil deed is to be more feared than even a fire.
203. Not to return evil to those who do evil unto you is considered as the best of all knowledge.
204. Let none plot to do evil to others even in forgetfulness. If he does so, DHARMA will repay him in kind without fail.
(To plot to do an evil deed to another is to pave the way for ones own ruin).
205. Let none do an evil deed on account of his poverty if he does so, he will become poorer still.
206. If one wants to be free from a afflictions and sorrow let not one do evil unto others. Evil begets evil only.
207. After committing an evil deed, one may escape the vengeance of ones enemies, but the sin of ones evil deeds will pursue and destroy him in the end.
(There is no escape from the sin (consequences) of an evil deed)
208. As your own shadow follows you wherever you go, similarly the sin of an evil deed pursues the evil doer wherever he goes.
209. If a man loves himself dearly, let him not do any harm however little it might be, to others.
210. One who walks always on the right path and avoids all evil deeds, will not be troubled by evil.

ON DECORUM

211. Benevolence seeks not a return.
What does the world give in exchange to the clouds that send down rain.
212. All the wealth one acquires by hard work,
should be spent on benevolence only.
213. Is there anything greater than benevolence either here or hereafter.
214. One who knows what is good and lives by it is truly alive, and the rest are reckoned among the dead.
215. The waters of a full tank are useful to the people in a village, similarly.
The wealth of a man of benevolence is of help to the people of the village.
216. A tree of fruits in the midst of a village is of benefit to all, similarly
The wealth of a man of benevolence is of help to the people of the village.
217. The leaves, roots and the rest of a medicinal herb are of use in the treatment of diseases. Similarly the wealth of a man of benevolence is of help to all.

218. A man of benevolence even when he has become poor will not give up his inherent duty of helping others.
219. The poverty of a man of benevolence is not to be considered as poverty but only as his temporary inability to exercise his inherent duty.
220. A man of benevolence may sustain loss in the exercise of his inherent duty, yet he will do his duty if necessary even by being sold as a slave. (one should not give up his inherent duty of benevolence even when there is a chance of loss or harm to self).

ON LIBERALITY

221. True generosity consists of help given to a destitute.
Everything else is of the nature of barter only.
222. Generosity is good even if it lands you in hell;
Begging is an evil even if it takes you to heaven.
223. A man of noble lineage is ever ready to give to the needy without recourse to lame excuses.
224. It is really painful to watch a beggar beg another until the latter pleasantly relents.
225. To relieve the hunger of others is more meritorious than the endurance of hunger by ascetics.
226. To relieve the hunger of the poor is the duty of the wealthy
(To feed the hungry is the only way to safeguard ones wealth).
227. One who relieves the hunger of others, will never be troubled by hunger himself. Hunger is an unbearable disease. The only remedy for this disease is to relieve the hunger of others and then eat.
228. The callous rich who hoard up money and never give anything in charity, will lose everything in the end.
Alas! what do the callous rich know about the joy in charity?
229. The rich man who eats food without sharing it with others, with the thought of hoarding his money is considered to be worse than a pitiable beggar.
230. Nothing is more unpleasant than death. Yet death is preferable if one can not give in charity to others.

ON FAME

231. Give in charity and live with renown. The purpose of a life is to acquire renown by the exercise of benevolence.
232. A man of benevolence is praised by all.
233. Nothing lasts in this world save ones reputation for benevolence.
234. A man of benevolence is praised not only in this world but also in the heaven.
235. To expend their wealth in charity and to enhance their renown thereby is possible only to men of extra ordinary merit (PUNYA PURUSHAS).
236. The purpose of a life is only to achieve renown. If that is not possible, it is better not to be born at all.

(Renown is essential for a purposeful human life).

237. A man who has not achieved renown, instead of blaming himself blames others for his own lack of distinction.
238. If a man lives without any renown, the world regards his lack of renown as a mark of disgrace only.
239. A man who does not achieve renown is reckoned as a mere burden to the earth.
240. Men who live with renown are said to be really alive whereas the rest are deemed to be dead, though alive.

ON COMPASSION

241. The possession of virtue of compassion is considered to be more valuable than all the wealth in this world, and it is a rare possession, whereas mere wealth can be acquired even by an evil person (DURJANA).
242. Walk on the right path with compassion in your heart whatever might be the different versions of various SASTRAS ON MOKSH, A the path of compassion leads to liberation without fail.
243. Men of compassion need never enter the world of sorrow and darkness. (HELL)
244. The wise say that one who is kind and compassionate towards all creatures, is not troubled by common afflictions.
245. The entire world is a witness to the phenomenon that sorrows keep away from the kind hearted and compassionate.
246. Those who have ignored virtue (Dharma) and forgotten the afflictions they endured in their previous birth, do now live with evil and cruelty in their minds.
247. There is no happiness for the poor in this world. Similarly there is no happiness for those who have no compassion, in the next world.
248. The poor may become rich at some future time; but those who have no compassion here and now will never change.
249. One should be kindhearted if one wants to follow
    (A) the path of virtue (DHARMA)
        one should possess wisdom and knowledge (Jnana) to discover TRUTH (SATYA)
    (B) (A man who has no compassion will never be able to follow the path of virtue, similarly a man devoid of knowledge will never be able to grasp the true message contained in a book).
250. If you remember how you trembled with fear when pitted with an opponent stronger than yourself you will forsake the oppression of the weak.

ON ABSTAINING FROM MEAT

251. How can there be compassion in a man who eats the flesh of other creatures, to increase his own flesh.
252. *One looses his property if he does not take care if it*
    one who eats the flesh of other creatures forsakes compassion.
253. A man with a weapon in his hands is always ready to kill.

one who is fond of meat will never think of compassion.

254. The essence of compassion is to eschew (avoid) killing;
To kill another creature is the height of cruelty;
To kill another creature and eat its flesh is forbidden by DHARMA.

255. Continuance of life is possible only when meat eating is forbidden.
Those who kill and eat the meat of other creatures are sure to rot in the hell forever.

256. If there are none to buy meat, none will sell meat to earn money.

257. The wise consider the meat of any creature to be as repulsive as an ulcer on the body. Therefore meat eating is forbidden.

258. One who is free from delusion (MOHA) will never eat the meat of any slaughtered animal.

259. Not to kill and eat the meat of a creature is more meritorious than performing thousand YAGNAS.

260. The world worships a man who has given up killing and meat eating.

ON PENACE (TAPAS)

261. The essence of penace is to endure self inflicted suffering and not to inflict suffering to others.

262. *To do penace and enjoy its benefits is only possible to those who are truly qualified (i.e., those who have practised austerities in a former birth).*
The penace of the others is useless.

263. To feed the ascetics, perhaps the rest of makind have chosen the state of householder (GRUHASTU).

264. An ascetic, using his spiritual powers, can bring about the ruin of his enemies, or the prosperity of his friends.

265. Penace is done in this world to attain what one wishes to achieve here and hereafter.

266. Only those who do penace, are able to do their duties properly, where as the rest are entangled in their desires (for riches and sensual pleasures) and face dangers and difficulties, because of it.

267. As gold is purified by heating it up in a fire repeatedly an ascetic is purified by the austerities he undergoes.

268. The world worships the ascetic who has controlled his self.
Penace leads to self control.

269. A man of penace can conquer death (YAMA) also.

270. There are a few ascetics and those who are not ascetics are many.
If there are more ascetics, there will be fewer destitutes in this world.

ON IMPROPER CONDUCT

271. The five elements that are in the body of a deceitful man watch his deceitful conduct and hence despise him.

272. Of what avail is a man's external trappings of asceticism when there is evil and guilt in his heart.

273. A cow covered over with the skin of a tiger stealthly tries to feed on grass in a field, hoping that people will mistake it for a tiger.
The external trappings of sainthood of a cheat (who has no control over his senses) are as futile as the camouflage of the above cow.
(There is no spiritual power without control of senses).
274. A cruel hunter hides himself in the bush and traps unwary animals and kills them. Similarly a cheat wearing the external trappings of a saint commits evil deeds.
275. Those who proclaim to the world that they have given up all desires, yet persist in evil conduct, will lament in the end and will be overcome by sorrow.
276. There is none more cruel in the world than a deceitful ascetic.
277. There are many in this world who are fair of face but foul of heart. They can be compared to the bright and attractive seeds of ABRUS PLANT (GURIVENDA GINJA in TELUGU)
(The seeds have a bright red coat and black dot on their bottom).
278. There are many hypocrites with evil in their hearts; in this world, who make a show of sanctity by their dress and going to pilgrimages and bathing in holy waters.
279. An arrow is straight to look at, but it kills a man when released from a bow;
A VEENA (a musical instrument) is curved, but when played, it gives out pleasing musical notes only.
Appearances are deceptive, whereas the conduct of a person reveals his character more accurately.
280. A shaven head or matted locks etc. are not necessary if one abstains from sinful deeds.
(Purity of heart and mind is of more importance than the external indications of sanctity).

ON FRAUD

281. If one does not want to be made fun of or not be despised by others, one should never entertain even the thought of defrauding another of the smallest thing.
282. It is a sin even to entertain the thought of stealing another's money;
Never entertain such evil thoughts in your mind.
283. Ill-gotten wealth while it seems to increase in the beginning will entirely perish in the end.
284. Defrauding of others appears to be profitable in the beginning, but it will lead to sorrow in the end.
285. Those who do not love mercy and have no kindness in their hearts, will be ever ready to defraud the unwary of their money.
(A cheat will never have mercy in his heart towards his victims).
286. Those who have the desire to defraud others in their hearts, will never be able to follow the straight path.
287. Men of rectitude who prefer to walk on the straight path, will never defraud others.

288. Virtue (DHARMA) rules the heart of a man of rectitude. Deceit rules the heart of a man of fraud.
289. A deceitful man will perish the very moment he entertains the thought of a transgression.
290. Even his own body may fail the deceitfulman whereas a man of rectitude is sure to enjoy the bliss even in heaven.

ON TRUTH

291. Truth is defined as to speak words which do not cause even the least harm to others.
292. A falsehood if it confers a benefit without the least blemish of evil, may be considered as TRUTH.
(TRUTH is always beneficial and its benefit is free from the least blemish of evil).
293. Let not a man knowingly tell a lie. His own conscience torments a liar.
294. A truthful man is liked and trusted by all.
295. A truthful man is superior even to a man of penance and generosity.
296. If a man acquires the reputation that he will never speak lies that result in sorrow, that itself will lead him to all virtues (DHARMA).
297. If one speaks TRUTH always, and for such a man of Truth, there is no need for other paths of virtue (DHARMA)
(There is no other virtue more precious than TRUTH).
298. Daily bath ensures cleanliness of the body;
To speak truth always ensures purity of mind.
299. Lamps dispel darkness of a night; but the wise regard the TRUTH as the only lamp that dispels the ignorance of ones mind.
300. Amongst all things we have seen, there is nothing greater than TRUTH.

ON ANGER

301. He who restrains his anger where it can be expressed shows real restraint. What does it matter whether one restrains anger or not, where it can not be expressed.
(To restrain ones anger where it can be expressed with impunity is very difficult).
302. Anger causes evil if expressed where it should not be expressed.
Anger causes greater evil if expressed where it can be expressed with impunity.
303. Do not get angry with anyone, even with those who are weak, helpless and with those who can not defend themselves.
Anger is the main source of many evils.
304. *Anger kills joy and laughter. Avoid anger at all times, as you keep way at all times from an enemy.*
305. If one wants to protect himself, let one avoid anger at all times. If one does not avoid anger it will destroy him.
306. The fire of anger burns up even the pleasant raft of friendship.
307. He who strikes the ground with his palm is sure to be hurt, similarly he who indulges

in anger, thinking that it is beneficial, is sure to be destroyed.

308. It is better if you do not yield to anger even against another, who has inflicted a grievous injury (i.e.) an injury as serious as the one caused by a big fire. To refrain from anger at all times is the best.

309. If ones mind is totally free from anger, one is sure to obtain what all he desires.

310. One who conquers anger becomes a sage,
One who succumbs to anger is no better than a dead man.

DO NOT CAUSE HARM

311. A man of rectitude will never consent to do evil to others even when there is scope of obtaining great wealth. Such is their commitment to virtue.

312. A man of virtue will not repay evil with evil even to those who have cherished enmity and done him evil.

313. If one does evil to an enemy who has not done any harm to him yet, he will have to experience irretrievable sorrow.

314. To repay evil with kindness and shame him is the best way of punishing an enemy.

315. The purpose of knowledge is to make one feel empathetic with the suffering of another and try to alleviate it.
(The knowledge of one who does not relieve the suffering of another is futile).

316. The first thing is to know what deeds cause pain and sorrow to oneself, and the next is not to do them to another at any time.

317. The best of virtues (DHARMA) consists of not doing even the least bit of evil to anyone at any time.

318. Why does a man do acts which by his own experience are sure to cause harm to others?

319. *The pain that a man causes to another in the morning, returns to him that very evening.*
(Evil one does to another is sure to recoil on oneself).

320. Those who inflict suffering on others are sure to suffer themselves. If one wants to be free from pain and sorrow, let him avoid at all cost, acts which are sure to cause pain and sorrow to others.

ON NON-VIOLENCE

321. Non-violence is the greatest of all virtues,
Violence is the root of all evils.

322. The wise say that non-violence and benevolence are the best of virtues.

323. Non-Violence is the best amongst all virtues.
TRUTH is the second best amongst all virtues.

324. The good path is that which leads one to non-violence.

325. A man of non-violence is far greater than an ascetic.

326. The power of non-violence is greater than the power of LORD OF DEATH (YAMA).
(Non-violence is the greatest power in this world).

327. Even when your own life is in peril, do not commit any act of violence against any

living creature.

328. (Although) Animal sacrifices in YAGNAS are said to bestow wealth and prosperity, the wise among the ascetics consider killing (violence) as a sin only.
329. The wise regard those who slaughter living creatures as the basest among human beings.
330. The wise say that those who suffer from poverty, degradation, and incurable diseases at present, are those who slaughtered animals in their previous births.

ON INSTABILITY

331. The wise say that to consider unstable things (such as wealth) as stable and permanent is a sign of disgrace and ignorance.
332. The acquisition of wealth and its expenditure is as fickle and unstable, as an audience that gathers in the night to watch a dance performance and disperses at its close. (*Wealth is a temporary phenomenon*).
333. *Wealth is fickle and unstable; if you acquire wealth spend it on worth while things.*
334. For the ignorant, TIME appears to be dependable and stable, but wise know that TIME can be compared to a saw which relentlessly slices away the life span of all creatures day by day.
    (Time is the eternal saw which slices away relentlessly the life span of all creatures).
335. Let good deeds be done without delay before paralysis of tongue and hiccoughs are evident (i.e.) before DEATH takes you away from this world.
336. Human life is a temporary phenomenon. One who was alive yesterday, is no more today.
337. The ignorant people are tormented by millions of thoughts and desires everyday. Alas! They do not even know for certain that they will be alive on the next day.
338. As the bird flies away leaving its nest, the soul leaves the human body at the time of death.
339. Birth is similar to waking up from sleep, and
    Dealth is similar to going to sleep.
340. The SOUL takes a temporary shelter in a human body and leaves it at the time of death. (Alas! the soul has no permanent abode!)

ON RENUNCIATION

341. As you renounce a thing of this world, you are saved from pain in respect of it.
342. Even after one has renounced desires, many more desires spring up. Let one renounce these desires also;
343. The first step is the control of ones five senses;
    The second step is the total eradication of all desires.
344. An ascetic should be free from all attachments. If he is attached to even one thing, he is likely to fall in to delusion (MAYA) again.
345. For an ascetic striving for liberation (MOKSHA), his own physical body seems to be a hindrance and a burden too what is the need of various things for such a men of

renunciation?

346. One who has conquered attachment to SELF and pride in SELF (MAMAKARA and AHANKARA), will ascend to greater spiritual states than even the DEVATAS (GODS).
347. Desires and sorrows are interrelated. As long as one does not give up desires, sorrows are bound to pursue him.
348. Only those who have renounced everything in this world will attain MOKSHA (LIBERATION). The rest of mankind will remain entangled in the net of cycle of births.
349. As soon as desire is eradicated, one is freed from the eternal cycle of births; if not one is sure to be entangled in the net of eternal cycle of births.
350. Let attachment to GOD be your one attachment;
Attachment GOD will help you to free yourself from all other attachments.

ON TRUE KNOWLEDGE

351. Because of delusion one mistakes the untruth for truth and gets entangled in the cycle of births and experiences untold sorrow.
352. If delusion is destroyed, one will be able to see the goal clearly. For such a one there are no future births and he attains heaven.
353. For one who has realized his true nature and hence he is free from all doubts and for such a one, heaven is much closer than this world.
354. The knowledge which one obtains through his five senses serves no purpose if one fails to realize his true nature.
355. One should not be carried away by the external appearances of a thing, but try to grasp the internal (essential) nature of the thing.
Whatever might be external appearance, to understand the true state (nature) of a thing is said to be true wisdom.
356. Those who have learnt everything that has to be learnt is this world and understood the true nature of things are the liberated souls. They have liberated themselves from the eternal cycle of births.
357. There is no future birth for the one, who after a careful examination, has come to realize his true nature.
358. *Sorrow and ignorance are intermingled in ones birth (life). To eradicate ignorance and to strive for ones liberation (MOKSHA), is said to be essence of understanding the true nature of SELF.*
359. Seek the universal foundation (BRAHMAN) of all things, eradicate all desires, and then live a life untouched by sorrows.
360. Root out the three evils, DESIRE (KAMA), Anger (KRODHA) and Delusion (MOHA), and then only one (you) will be free from sorrows.

RENOUNCING OF DESIRE

361. The wise say that the principal cause of birth of all creatures and resultant sorrow is contained in the seed named DESIRE.
362. If anything is to be desired, liberation from the cycle of births (i.e.) (no more future

births) is to be desired. But this desire can be realized only when one gives up all other desires.

363. Freedom from desires is more valuable than the greatest wealth of this world or even the next.

364. Purity of mind is attained by freedom from desire. And Freedom from desire is attained only when TRUTH is cherished in ones heart.
(Love of TRUTH leads to freedom from desire).

365. Only those who are free from desires are really free and the rest are not free at all.

366. It is the desire that deceives a man. An ascetic must guard himself zealously against desire at all times.

367. For a man who has eradicated desire totally, his life proceeds as anticipated by him on the good path.
(Life proceeds as per the wishes of one who has conquered the desires).

368. Those who are free from desires, are also free from sorrows.
There are many sorrows to be experienced by the one who is not free from desire.

369. Sorrow of the sorrows is the desire. And if this desire is eradicated, one can attain joy and happiness even in this world.

370. Desires can never be satisfied completely as insatiability is its very nature. If desires are destroyed, it confers a state that can never be changed.

ON FATE

371. A prosperous fate bestows perseverance (and success)
An evil fate bestows laziness (and downfall)

372. A prosperous fate faciltates acquisition of knowledge.
An evil fate makes one an ignoramus.

373. One might have studied many books, yet he will be able to understand that portion of knowledge only, which FATE has decreed (alloted) to him.

374. Fate has devided men of this world, according to their temperament in to two groups. One group of men concentrate on the acquisition of wealth and the other group of men concentrate on the acquisition of knowledge.

375. In the acquisition of wealth, because of interference by FATE, favourbale factors become unfavourable and unfavourable factors change to favourable ones.

376. What has not been conferred by FATE, will not remain in your possession, although it be guarded with the utmost care.
What has been decreed by FATE, will not be lost, even if you throw it away.

377. Even those who have hoarded up millions of rupees, will be able to spend only that portion of their wealth as decreed by their FATE.
(They can not spend their wealth as they wish but only as decreed by FATE).

378. Even a poor man will be ready to renounce and become an ascetic if his difficulties and problems are solved, but FATE, and the result of his own past deeds prevent him from doing so.
(It may be easy for the destitute to renounce the world, yet they continue to wallow

in poverty, misery and attachments, because they have not earned by their past deeds a mind inclined to renunciation).

379. When men have good luck, they accept it and enjoy the full benefit of it. But when they get bad luck, they complain and vex themselves. Good, luck and bad luck, pleasure and pain are all ordained by FATE.

380. What is more powerful than FATE? Even if one devises some way of counteracting it, finally it is only the FATE that wins.

THE GREATNESS OF A KING

381. A king to be foremost among other kings should possess the following; 1. Army 2. People 3. Wealth 4. Friends 5. Ministers and a 6. Fortress.

382. A king should possess the following qualities; namely 1. Generosity 2. Courage 3. Perseverance and 4. Wisdom.

383. Vigilance, learning and courage are the essential qualities of a king.

384. A king should never deviate from the path of virtue, avoid evil deeds and conduct himself with self respect at all times.

385. To strive for wealth, to enhance his resources further, to protect the wealth so acquired, and finally to spend it properly, are the duties of a king.

386. A king should be easy of access and avoid harsh speech.

387. A king should cultivate pleasant speech, be generous and protect his subjects at all times.

388. A king who rules his subjects according to virtue (DHARMA) and protects them at all times is worshipped as a GOD by them.

389. A king should listen patiently to (i.e.) even his bitter critics.

390. A king should possess the following qualities namely 1. Compasson 2. Benevolence 3. Rectitude (upright conduct) and 4. Love for his subjects.

ON LEARNING

391. Acquire a thorough knowledge of things that should be learnt, and let your conduct be worthy of your learning.

392. Learning is divided in to two simple divisions mathematics (numbers) and literature (letters). They are like the two eyes to a human being (life). Let every man learn letters and numbers.

393. Only the literate are said to possess the eyes. The unlettered have merely two sores in their face
(To observe and understand the true significance of a thing by ones intelligence is of greater importance than mere seeing).

394. The learned give delight to those whom they meet and on parting they make others, to which for their delightful company in future also.
(The company of the learned is a delight to all).

395. A poor man stands before a wealthy man, eager and trembling seeking help from him. Similarly the seeker of knowledge must stand before the learned, eager and

trembling seeking knowledge from them. He who is proud will remain ignorant and is doomed to inferiority in life.
(Learning has to be acquired in fear and humility)

396. Ones knowledge is in proportion to ones learning just as the depth of water in a well is in proportion to its depth.
397. How is it that many remain ignorant to the end of their lives, even when they notice the value and attention given to the learned even in foreign countries also?
(One should acquired knowledge without wasting any time.)
398. The knowledge that a person acquires in one lifetime yields him prosperity even in his future lives also.
399. The learned man finds delight in his learning whereas others look upon him as a benefactor of mankind. Hence the truly learned are in love with knowledge. (not only because it yields delight to them but also because it is beneficial to the world.)
400. Learning is the only imperishable wealth. All the other assets are next only to learning.

ON IGNORANCE

401. To speak in an assembly of the learned, without sufficient knowledge is as futile as playing at chess on an unmarked board.
402. If an ignorant man tries to speak in an assembly of the learned, he will make himself the butt of ridicule just as the claim of a woman, who has no breasts, to womanhood is ridiculous.
403. It is better for an ignorant man to keep silence when he is in the company of the learned.
404. Even if an illiterate man displays great intelligence the wise do not consider it to be equal to knowledge of the learned.
(It is better for the illiterate one even if he is bestowed with great intelligence, to acquire proper learning.)
405. The self conceit of the illiterate one disappears the moment he speaks in the presence of the learned.
406. An alkaline soil is worthless and yields no produce or any crop.
407. The grand personality of an illiterate man (who is ignorant of great SASTRAS) is as superficial as the beauty of a painted earthen doll.
408. Wealth acquired by the illiterate will cause more sorrow in the end, than the poverty of the learned.
409. A learned man although born in an inferior caste is considered to be superior to an illiterate born in a superior caste.
(A man of learning is always superior to an illiterate)
410. There is a lot of difference between a man and a beast;
Similarly there is a lot of difference between a learned man and an illiterate.

ON KNOWLEDGE THROUGH LISTENING (SRUTAM)

411. Knowledge acquired by listening is considered as an invaluable asset.

412. When a man has not acquired any knowledge by listening, he will be able to get very little food for his stomach also.
413. Those who have acquired a wealth of knowledge by listening, are considered to be equal to even Gods (DEVATAS).
414. Let the illiterate man listen carefully to the words of a learned man, and the knowledge so acquired will sustain him in his days of poverty.
415. A staff supports and prevents a man from a fall on a slippery ground. Similarly the words of a learned and virtuous man, save a man in life.
416. Let a man listen carefully to good instruction however meagre it may be, for out of it great good ensues.
417. Those who have studied widely and diligently listened to instruction, will never speak foolishly even in a forgetful mood, on a matter they have imperfectly understood. (i.e. The wise will never utter meaningless words)
418. The ears which have not listened to any instruction or learning are deemed to be deaf (even when they are physically capable of listening) and useless.
(The ears of the learned only can understand what they hear, and the ears of the illiterate are futile.)
419. Modesty is absent in the ignorant. Only those who have acquired knowledge by listening are modest in their speech.
420. Men who eat are merely alive on a physical plane, where as those who listen carefully and acquire knowledge are considered to be really alive.
(Men of knowledge are really alive, whereas the rest are equal to the dead).

ON WISDOM

421. Wisdom protects one from destruction. Wisdom is an inner fortification that even ones enemies can not destroy.
(Wisdom saves one from destruction and by itself indestructible.)
422. Wisdom does not permit the mind to wander aimlessly, keeps it away from evil, and helps one to keep in the right path.
423. Wisdom helps one to discern the truth in everything by whomsoever spoken.
(To understand the essence and not merely the face of a thing is called wisdom.)
424. To speak lucidly and meaninfully is a sign of wisdom
To discern the subtlest thoughts which may lie hidden in the words of others is a sign of wisdom.
425. True wisdom strives to obtain the friendship of virtuous men (SAJJANAS) and after securing, their friendships, to keep it unchanged through out and not inconstant like the blossoming and fading of a lotus flower.
426. A man of wisdom understands how the world moves and lives accordingly.
427. The wise know before hand what will befall, whereas the ignorant, do not have this capability.
428. Not to fear what ought to be feared is folly.
The wise fear what is truly to be feared and refrain from it.

429. The wise foresee and guard themselves against future evils and hence no terrifying calamity will happen to them.
430. A discriminating mind is the greatest of possessions without it all other possessions are futile.

ON THE CORRECTION OF FAULTS

431. A king who wants to prosper should be free from pride, anger and passion.
432. A king should root out the following faults
1. avarice 2. conceit and 3. avidity for low pleasures
433. Of those who dread dishonour, even a little fault which is as small as a milletseed, looms as large as a palmyra tree.
434. Ones own faults pave the way for ones own downfall; Hence one should guard himself against lapses at all times.
(ones greatest enemies are none but mistakes committed by self only.)
435. The prosperity of one who does not guard himself against lapses, will perish just like straw in a fire
(Errors committed by self are more dangerous than even a fire.)
436. A king should carefully detect his own lapses and correct them and then only he should try to correct others.
437. The hoarded wealth of a miser, who has failed to expend his wealth on benevolence, will totally perish in the end.
438. Avarice (undue attachment to wealth), which prevents one from being benevolent is one of the greatest evils.
439. Avoid self praise at all times;
Avoid the desire even to think about useless and evil deeds at any time.
440. A king should not betray his secrets, and then only will he be safe from the designs of his enemies.

ON FRIENDSHIPS

441. It is better even for a man of virtue to try and secure the friendship of elderly men of virtue and mature knowledge (to advice and guide him).
442. Let one secure the friendship of those who can overcome difficulties when they occur and guard against them before they happen.
443. To cherish the friendship of men of virtue is the rarest of all blessings.
444. The highest power is obtained by one who can secure the help and guidance of men who are wiser than himself.
445. This world is guided by the wise. Hence a king should secure the friendship of the wise for his own guidance.
446. No enemy can destroy a king who relies on capable counsellors for his rule.
447. None can harm the ruler who has brave counsellors that have even the privilege of rebuking him when he goes astray.
448. A king who has no brave counsellors that have even the privilege of rebuking him,

will be destroyed even though he has no enemies.

449. There can be no gain to those, who have no capital. Similarly there can be no permanent status to those who are without the support of like minded people.

450. It is tenfold more harmful to abandon the friendship of virtuous men, than to incur the hatred and enmity of the many.
(The friendship of virtuous men ensures ones welfare and prosperity.)

ON AVOIDING EVIL COMPANY

451. Truly great people are afraid of inferior people and avoid their company, whereas the inferior sort seekout and delight in the company of the base.

452. Water acquires the nature of the soil through which it flows. Similarly the character of a man will resemble that of his associates.

453. The seat of knowledge is in the mind of a man;
But his character is moulded by his associates.

454. The intelligence of a man seems to have origin in his mind only, but in reality it reflects the intelligence of his associates only.

455. Purity of conduct and purity of mind of a person depend on the purity of his associates.

456. A good progeny is a blessing bestowed only to men known for purity of mind and good conduct. All things work for the good of the good.

457. Purity of mind leads the way to wealth.
Pure conduct of ones group yields not only wealth but also fame.

458. One may be known to have good conduct and a pure mind, and even for such a man of virtue, if he moves in the company of virtous men, he will be protecting himself further.

459. A pure mind and good conduct ensures future happiness also. And if such a one moves in good company he acquires great power also.

460. There is no greater source of help than the company of the good.
There is no greater source of sorrow than evil company.

ON ACTING AFTER DUE DELIBERATION

461. In every action there are the three elements of gain, loss and value. Let a man reflect on what will be lost, what will be acquired, and finally what will be the ultimate gain and then only let him act.

462. There is nothing impossible for those who consult trusted and chosen friends, reflect carefully on the task planned and then act.

463. The wise do not launch an undertaking by which for a possible future gain, they will lose what is already acquired.

464. Those who fear reproach will not undertake a task which has not been thoroughly considered and which lacks transparency.

465. To undertake a task without due deliberation will in the end strengthen ones enemies only.
(Such unplanned work is sure to end in failure and disgrace.)

466. One who does not do what is a proper thing will perish.
one who does an improper thing will also perish.
467. Think well before resolving on action. Hesitation after the decision is once taken amounts to folly.
468. A work which is not done properly by suitable methods is bound to fail inspite of the support of many.
469. Even a good work is sure to fail, if it is undertaken without the knowledge of various dispositions of men involved in it.
470. The world will not approve when one does improper things. Therefore let a man reflect carefully and do things which bring no reproach.
(*"The world" means enlightened people in SANSKRIT and TAMIL also*).

ON THE KNOWLEDGE OF POWER

471. Let on estimate his own strength carefully, the strength of his enemy, and the strength of allies of both and then let him act.
472. One who understands thoroughly the task to be done and strives to achieve it, is sure to be successful.
473. One who is not friendly towards alien powers and who does not realize his own limitations and who indulges in self overestimation, will be ruined (dead) soon.
474. One who overestimates his own power and underestimates the power of his enemy will come to grief soon.
475. Although a peacock's feather is very light, yet even an overload of peacocks' feathers will break the axle of the cart carrying their load.
476. A tree climber, having climbed out to the end of a branch of a tall tree, if he ventures to climb further is sure to end up with a fatal fall.
(over vaulting ambition ends in downfall.)
477. *Let one give to others according to his means; and such prudence is essential to safeguard ones wealth.*
478. *Even though ones income be small, he will not be ruined if his outgoings are less than his income.*
479. *One who spends beyond his means is sure to be ruined.*
480. *One who spends money without knowing exactly how much money he has, is sure to loose even that very soon.*

ON JUDGING THE TIME

481. A crow will overcome an owl in daylight. Similarly one should choose a suitable time to overcome ones enemy.
482. To safeguard ones wealth, one should act at a suitable time and thus ensure his own prosperity.
483. One who acts at the right time with the right implements is sure to achieve success.
484. One can conquer even the world, if he acts at the right time, with the right implements and in the right place.

485. One who wants ascendancy in this world, will reflect calmly and carefully about it and bide for the proper time.

486. A fighting ram draws back before it dashes against its opponent. Similarly one should withdraw from an enemy seemingly and then attack at a suitable opportunity.

487. The wise will not hastily and immediately react to the evil committed by their enemies. They restrain their anger within and wait for a suitable opportunity for retaliation.

488. If one meets his enemy, let him show all the respect, and wait for a suitable time (A) to strike him down ruthlessly and (B) to make him bow down his head in subordination).

489. If a rare opportunity comes to you, seize it promptly and accomplish a rare deed without any delay.

490. A crane stands still in a pond and strikes unerringly at the fish; Similarly one should wait patiently and strike at the enemy at an opportune time and place.

ON JUDGING THE PLACE
(To surround with armed forces)

491. Till you find a suitable place for besieging the enemy, it is better to wait patiently. And above all, do not commit the fatal error of underestimating the enemy's strength.

492. The attack and vanquish an enemy from a fortress has many advantages even for a powerful king.

493. Even a relatively weak king is sure to vanquish a more powerful king, if he attacks, after taking due precautions, at the right time and in the right place.

494. If a king is ready to attack at the right time and in the right place, his attacking enemy is sure to withdraw.

495. A crocodile in deepwaters attacks and kills other animals. But alas! a crocodile out of the waters is an easy prey to other animals.

496. Huge chariots with mightly wheels can not move on the seas; and
Ships which sail across the seas can not move on the ground.

497. Firstly one should carefully reflect on the plan of operations, secondly one should select the place for attacking the enemy and thirdly one must proceed with courage to achieve successful outcome.

498. Even a king with a small army entrenched in a right place, will be able to withstand an attack by a larger army.

499. To attack an enemy even if he is a weak one and has no fort to guard him, *on his own native soil is hazardous.*

500. An elephant kills many spear wielding soldiers in war Alas! even such a mighty elephant, if by chance it sinks in to a bog, it becomes an easy prey to a bunch of jackals.

ON CHOOSING THE EXCEUTIVE

501. Let a minister be chosen after he has been tried by means of the following, namely 1. His love of virtue 2. His love for (of) money 3. His love for sexual pleasures and 4. His fear about loosing his own life.

502. The necessary qualifications for being chosen for a high office are 1. Noble lineage 2. He should be free from moral and intellectual defects 3. and a sensitiveness to public censure.
503. Even amongst men of vast learning and who are free from moral and intellectual defects, it is rare to find one who is free from ignorance and incompetence.
504. Test and find out the good and bad points in a candidate for a high office, and see which predominate and then decide.
505. Prosperity or the down fall of a man is determined by the nature of his deeds only.
506. Do not choose men who have no relatives. Such men have no social ties and hence are not sensitive to public censure, and are therefore not to be depended upon.
507. To choose unqualified and unworthy men for high office by affection and partiality will bring every form of disaster.
508. To choose a stranger without a knowledge of his character and conduct will result in sorrow not only to oneself but also to one's successors.
509. Entrust work to men, only after testing them; when once the choice is made, entrust to them appropriate duties unhesitatingly.
510. To select a man without careful consideration and to suspect him later, are sure to cause irremediable sorrow.

ON SELECTION AND EMPLOYMENT

511. One who carefully considers the good and evil aspects of an undertaking and chooses only the good, such a man of discrimination only should be employed.
512. One who can increase the sources of revenue and wealth, and who can anticipate and prevent losses that may occur in future, such a capable man only should be employed.
513. The four essential qualifications for selection of men are :
1. Love 2. Knowledge 3. Clear-headedness and 4. Freedom from covetousness.
514. Even after a careful consideration and selection, many men are found to change and act differently in the performance of alloted duties.
515. Select a man of ability and resourcefulness for the successful completion of a difficult task. If you select one out of mere friendship or admiration, the result is bound to be a failure.
516. One should carefully consider the nature of the work to be done, the proper person for such a task and the suitable time for its execution and then proceed.
517. After a careful selection of a man for an undertaking let him be entrusted with it unhesitatingly.
518. After recognising the aptitude and quality of work of a man, let him be employed in that type of work only.
519. Prosperity leaves the king who suspects the loyalty of a man who is diligent and efficient in his duties.
520. Let a king daily scrutinise the work and welfare of his servants. Any deception or crookedness should not be permitted.

ON LOOKING AFTER ONE'S RELATIVES

521. Even when a man's wealth has all been lost loyal relatives will continue to regard him with their accustomed kindness.
522. Prosperity and wealth arise from the unchanging love and affection of ones relatives.
523. The water in a tank with no bunds all around will not be safe from wastage and pollution. Similarly the life of a man with no relatives around him will not be happy or safe.
524. A man of wealth should look after the welfare of his relatives.
525. An affable and generous man is liked by his relatives.
526. One who is liberal with his money and free from anger is liked and sought after by his relatives.
527. The crows will call out others while they eat and share the pickings with other crows. Similarly a rich man should enjoy his wealth in the company of his relatives.
528. A king should bestow attention and affection on the relatives, according to their special qualities and abilities.
529. Relatives who have forsaken you because of a disagreement will rejoin you, if that disagreement is sorted out.
530. Relatives who have forsaken you, if they return, accept them after careful consideration and look after them.

ON VIGILANCE

531. One is apt to experience great joy after any successful achievement; and this may lead to neglectfulness. This neglectfulness is more harmful than even inordinate anger.
532. Extreme poverty destroys one's intelligence;
Neglectfulness destroys one's name and fame.
533. The wise say that those who are not vigilant will never achieve greatness.
534. One who is negligent will not be able to improve his condition even if he is in an advantageous position at present. There is no safety for king who happens to be a coward, even when he has a fortress, and army etc.
535. One who has no forethought and who does not provide against calamities that may happen in future, will have to repent afterwards for his negligence.
536. There is nothing comparable with vigilance in dealing with everyone and at all times, without any lapse.
537. There is nothing that is impossible if one is vigilant in the performance of an undertaking.
538. One should try always to do deeds, which are praised by the wise; if he neglects to do them, he will have to experience evil and sorrow not only now but also in future births.
539. When you are feeling elated by your prosperity, think of those who in the past were ruined by lapse of vigilance.
540. Every aspiration can be achieved if one never deviates from or forsakes his aim and

works unceasingly for its realization.

ON THE RIGHT GOVERNMENT

541. A just king enquires about all the people involved in a crime, and administers justice impartially.
542.. All the living creatures survive and thrive because of rains;
(All the subjects of a king survive and thrive because of the just rule of a king.
543. The VEDAS, the Brahmans and the DARMA (VIRTUE) are all dependent on the just rule of a king.
544. A king who rules over his subjects with love and DHARMA (VIRTUE), will set an example of others to emulate.
545. Timely rains and plentiful crops are the signs to say that a king rules over his subjects with justice and virtue (DHARMA).
546. Victory is not won by the king with weapons such as spears etc.;
Victory is won by the king with a just rule only.
547. A king defends his entire kingdom; and if he rules over his kingdom with DHARMA (VIRTUE), DHARMA itself will protect him.
548. A king who is not easily accessible, who does not redress the grievances of his subjects and who neglects justice and DHARMA (VIRTUE), will perish in disgrace.
549. A king should protect his subjects, not only against harm from external foes but also from himself or his own officers. To punish the guilty is a primary duty of the king.
550. To protect a crop, weeding is necessary; Similarly to protect innocent subjects in his kingdom, a king should punish criminals and murderers etc. with capital punishment.

ON OPPRESSION AND MISRULE

551. A king whose rule is unjust and who indulges in oppression of his people is considered to be worse than a cruel murderer.
552. A highway robber grabs money and valuables etc. from people with threats and display of sharpweapons;
A king who collects money from people, using his power is no better than the highway robber.
553. A king who does not enquire daily about the welfare of his subjects and administer justice in his kingdom, will be ruined in the course of time.
554. A king who is cruel, and who perverts justice will be ruined.
555. Tears shed by the oppressed subjects of a king will ultimately lead to his ruin.
556. A just rule gives endurance to a king's government. An unjust rule undermine's a king's name and fame.
557. A land becomes arid when there is no rain fall. Similarly The lives of people under the rule of a cruel king are as barren as an arid land.
558. Under the unjust rule of a king to be wealthy is to invite trouble and sorrow for self. (There will be no justice and protection for wealth when the king is unjust)

559. There will be no timely rainfall in a kingdom ruled over by an unjust ruler.
560. When a ruler forsakes DHARMA (VIRTUE) and justice, Brahmans will neglect the study of VEDAS and SASTRAS, in his kingdom and the yield of the cows in the land also will diminish.

ON TYRANNY

561. A king should enquire carefully in to a crime committed and award deterrent punishment to the guilty.
562. The prosperity of a king, who commences his enquiries in to a crime committed with strictness, but tampers his justice with mercy, will endure.
563. A cruel king who terrifies his helpless subjects will be destroyed soon.
564. The life span of a king who is regarded as a cruel rulers by his subjects, will be short and he will be destroyed soon.
565. The wealth and power of a king who is stern and inaccessible to his subjects, is as useless as a treasure guarded by a devil.
(A king should have a pleasant disposition and be easily accessible to all)
566. The wealth of a king who is cruel and whose speech is harsh will perish soon.
567. A piece of iron will be reduced to nothing if it is rubbed constantly with a sharp file. Similarly the power of a king who relies on harsh speech and excessive and cruel punishments also will not last long.
568. A king who does not consult his ministers before undertaking a task, and when failure occurs gives way to anger, will come to ruin soon.
569. In times of war, a king who has no fortress to protect him, will be seized with fear, and destroyed soon.
570. A cruel king who relies on ignorant counsellors will perish soon.
Alas! a cruel king and his ignorant counsellors are to be considered as a great burden to the earth.

ON COMPASSION

571. This world sustained by kings who cherish compassion.
572. Compassion sustains the world; Those who have no compassion, are to be regarded as a mere burden to the earth.
573. What is the purpose of music if it not in harmony with the lyric?
What is the use of eyes, which do not indicate (reflect) compassion?
574. One may have eyes in his face, yet they are futile if they do not indicate (reflect) compassion.
575. The wise regard the eyes that do not reflect compasson as mere sores in the face.
576. Sugarcane stems and bamboo stems have markings suggestive of human eyes;
The eyes of a human being which do not reflect compassion are as useless as the 'eyes' seen on sugarcane and bamboo stems.
577. Men without compassion are to be regarded as blind ones;
Men with compassion only are able to see properly.

578. One who is able to do his duties properly and at the sametime does not forsake compassion, is fit to rule over others.
579. To pardon those who have harmed us indicates the best of all excellent dispositions.
580. One who aspires to enviable reputation of a man of compassion must be ready to swallow even poison if it is given to him (to test his quality).

ON SPIES

581. A spy and a celebrated NEETISASTRA, are to be considered as the two eyes of a king.
582. The duty of a king is to get day to day information about everything that happens to all people through a spy.
583. A king who carefully considers the information given by his spies and profits by it, is sure to be successful.
584. The duty of a spy is to watch 1. All the executive officers of the state 2. Relatives of the king and 3. the enemies of the king.
585. The necessary qualifications of a spy are :
    1. He should be skilled in putting on disguises that raise no suspicion,
    2. He should not be unnerved by the scrutinizing looks of those he observes,
    3. He should be able to guard secrets under all circumstances, and not give himself away.
586. A spy should be able to put on the disguise of an ascetic (SANYASI), to obtain admission in to places usually inaccessible, and should never reveal his purpose even when detected and tortured.
587. A spy should secure information about hidden secrets and reveal them correctly to his master.
588. The information provided by one spy should be accepted only when it is corroborated by another spy.
589. A king while employing spies, should take care that they are not known to one another (i.e.; the engagement of one spy should be kept a secret from another)
    If the information provided by three spies agrees, then only let the king receive it as truth.
590. Let not a king honour a spy publicly; if he does so, he will be divulging not only his own secrets, but also the usefulness of this spy will come to an end.

ON ENTHUSIASM

591. A great and distinct possession of a man is his enthusiasm only; whatever else he may possess, if he has no enthusiasm, are of no use.
592. Ones prosperity resides in the possession of energy of mind
    The possession of all other things, including wealth, is transient and pass away.
593. One who possesses enthusiasm will not grieve over the loss of his wealth.
594. Wealth will find its own way to the man who possesses enthusiasm.
595. *The stems of lotus flowers are proportionate to the depth of water.*

Similarly a man's greatness is proportional to the mental energy he possesses.

596. *In all acts and deeds, let all exertion be towards ones own uplift; even if it is unattainable, one should never give up the effort.*

597. A man with enthusiasm will not give up even when all is lost;
The elephant stands firm, even when wounded in war by a shower of arrows.

598. One who has no enthusiasm will never be able to get recognition for generosity also.

599. Inspite of its huge body and sharp tusks, an elephant is scared when attacked by a ferocious tiger

600. A man's strength rests in his enthusiasm only;
Men who have no enthusiasm are comparable to inert trees.

ON LAZINESS

601. A temple light will go out unless its wick is properly snuffed and looked after. Similarly if laziness is permitted in a family, its prestige and rank will soon be lost.

602. One who aspires to enhance the prestige and rank of ones family, should eradicate laziness totally.

603. The prestige and rank of the family of an ignorant and lazyman will be lost, long before his death.

604. When a man gives way to laziness and gives up totally all energetic effort he will not only ruin his family prestige but also increase his family's defects.

605. Procrastination, forgetfulness, laziness and excessive sleep, are sure to cause the total ruin of anyone.

606. A lazy fellow even when he has access to a king will hardly derive any benefit from it. (one will be benefitted, only when one gives up laziness and works hard for his own uplift, without relying on any external help.)

607. A lazy fellow who has given up every type of dignified exertion, will first meet with censure from friends and finally he will be the butt of ridicule of all.
(laziness deserves to be condemned by one and all)

608. Even a man of noble lineage if he gives way to laziness will ultimately be reduced to an inferior position of a servant under his enemies.

609. If a man overcomes laziness by energetic effort the reproach which has come upon himself and his family will disappear.

610. The king who never gives way to laziness, will be able to conquer the entire world.

ON PERSEVERANCE

611. One should not be discouraged when one is faced with a difficult task. The necessary energy for the completion of the difficult task comes out of the sincere effort itself.

612. Do not give up a task in the middle, and try your best to complete it.
Those who abandon their work in an unfinished state, will be abandoned by the world.

613. The pride of being useful to others can be enjoyed only by those, who are known for persevering effort.

614. A hermaphrodite wielding a sword in a war is only a butt of ridicule;

Similarly a man who is not known for persevering effort; if he attempts to help others, will make himself a butt of ridicule.

615. He who is in love with work and spurns pleasure, will stand as a pillar for the support of his relatives in their troubles and sorrows.
616. Persevering effort leads the way to prosperity and its absence brings in poverty.
617. Prosperity (LAXMI) resides in the house of the industrious;
Poverty (MOODEVI, or PEDDAMMA or SANI DEVATA) dwells in the house of a lazy fellow.
618. Adverse fate is not a disgrace to anyone, but not to know what should be known and to be without persevering effort is disgrace indeed.
619. Though adverse fate, should ordain failure in a task, the effort put in to the task will yield its own reward.
620. Those who work hard, undaunted by obstacles, will even overcome adverse fate.
(Purposeful and unceasing hard work leads the way to success)

ON FORTITUDE

621. Laugh when you meet adversity. There is nothing like the sense of humour to face an adversity and pass on to victory.
622. Misfortunes may come upon one like a flood; but the wise will overcome them by understanding their nature.
623. Do not be perturbed when you meet adversity and this is the only way to overcome adversity.
624. A buffalo draws a cart, undeterred through deep mire
Similarly one should face and overcome adversity undeterred.
625. Do not be scared when adversity meets you;
Overcome the adversity by resolute thought.
626. One who does not give way to undue elation during prosperity, will not give way to undue depression during adversity.
627. Man is born to be the target of adversity. The wise are aware of this and hence do not consider adversity as a misfortune.
628. One who knows that sorrow is natural to human existence will neither seek for pleasure nor experience sorrow when faced with sorrow.
629. If one does not seek for pleasure when enjoying prosperity such a one will not grieve when faced with adversity.
630. If one can regard sorrow as happiness, such a one will be regarded as a great one even by his enemies.
Ref: (*SRI SAMUDRALA. RAGHAVACHARY'S LYRIC "JAGAME MAYA..." for the film "DEVADAS" (1952) SINGER: GHANTASALA ACTOR: A. NAGESWARA RAO*)

THE GOOD MINISTER

631. The good minister is one who selects the time, means and manner of execution of an undertaking and brings it to a successful completion.

632. A good minister should possess the following five qualifications, namely (1) Courage (2) Noble lineage (3) He should be capable of protecting a king's subjects (4) He should possess good learning and (5) He should possess persevering effort.
633. A minister should be skilled in the art of maintaining the good will among friends, restoring to friendship those who have moved away from him, and to bring about discord among his enemies.
634. A minister should be able to comprehend the nature of an undertaking, execute it in the best possible manner, and give his impartial advice, unhesitatingly when needed.
635. A minister should be committed to DHARMA (VIRTUE), possess knowledge, give wise counsel and must be capable of successfully completing any task entrusted to him.
636. A minister should possess a keen intellect, acute observation and wide learning.
637. To successfully complete an undertaking, not only is theoretical knowledge necessary but also an understanding of current ways of the world.
(Theoretical knowledge alone is insufficient for the successful completion of an undertaking and it must be combined with practical ability also)
638. It is the duty of a minister to give sound advice to a king even when he is ignorant and disregards the minister's advice.
639. A treacherous minister by the king's side is more dangerous than seventy crores of enemies.
640. A minister lacking in executive ability, will not be able to successfully complete an undertaking although he has planned it carefully beforehand.

THE ART OF PERSUASION

641. The gift of persuasive speech is a special blessing although one may possess other good qualities.
642. Ones speech is responsible for ones prosperity or downfall. Hence one should be very careful in his speech at all times and on all occasions.
643. The art of persuasive speech consists of talking in a convincing and captivating manner so that even others, who have not heard him so far, are anxious to hear his speech.
644. *Words are the source of power.*
DHARMA (VIRTUE) and ARTHA (WEALTH), come next only to the power of words.
645. Speak after making sure that what you say cannot be refuted by any argument of an opponent.
646. One should not only speak captivatingly with others, but also try to grasp the essence in the speech of others.
647. A convincing style, a good memory and fearlessness are necessary to win a debate.
648. If one can speak on a subject in the proper order and in a pleasing manner, others will readily accept his speech.
649. One who can not convey his message in a few appropriate words, will have to speak too many words.

650. There are flowers that blossom in clusters but bear no fragrance; Similarly there are scholars who have no mastery of expression, to convey their knowledge to others.

PURITY IN ACTION

651. Wealth can be acquired by the support of friends, relatives and those in power, *where as if one has excellence in his work, it will yield to him all that is desired.*
652. Avoid at all times actions which are devoid of DHARMA (virtue) and which do not enhance ones fame (KEERTI).
653. *Avoid at all times actions that are likely to tarnish your name and fame. (Disrepute is a hindrance for ones progress in life).*
654. *The wise will never consent to do disgraceful deeds even in their days of adversity.*
655. *Avoid at all times actions, that you will regret afterwards; if by chance you did such a regrettable deed, atleast do not repeat it.*
656. *The wise will never consent to do disgraceful deeds even to relieve the hunger of one's starving mother.*
657. *The poverty of the wise is to be esteemed than the wealth acquired by doing disgraceful deeds.*
658. *Those who do deeds forbidden by the wise, even if they succeed in doing them, they will have to experience sorrow and suffering from the same deeds.*
659. *Wealth acquired by inflicting suffering on others will inflict suffering to self and disappear in the end. Wealth acquired by fair means, though it might be lost in the beginning, will yield profit in the end.*
660. *Attempts to store water in a vessel of wet clay are futile Similarly attempts to safeguard wealth acquired by fraudulent means are bound to fail, and it is sure to disappear in the end.*

POWER IN ACTION

661. Firmness of mind leads to firmness in action. All the other qualities are of a different kind.
662. The two special features in the performance of a deed by the wise are :
    1. They take necessary precautions to overcome any obstacles that may interfere with their undertaking;
    2. And if they do occur, the wise will not be perturbed and they will face the obstacles boldly.
663. One should reveal an undertaking only after its successful completion to the public; To reveal an undertaking before its successful completion is sure to result in endless suffering.
664. It is easy for anyone to say how an act is to be performed but far difficult to do it in the said manner.
665. The executive ability of a competent minister is appreciated not only by the king but also by the people.
666. One who has determination, if he has firmness in action also, he will be able to successfully complete deeds, which he has planned.

667. Do not despise and underestimate a person by the unimpressiveness of his physical personality, because he may possess great strength of mind and action.
The huge wheels of a mighty chariot are kept in place by a small nail in the axle. (Appearances are deceptive and the true worth of a person is revealed only by the excellence of his work.)
668. Plan a deed after a careful consideration of all factors. Once a decision is made, do it without hesitation and delay.
669. If a deed yields happiness in the end, do it inspite of obstacles that may interfere with its successful completion.
670. One who has no efficiency in action, will never be able to make his mark in the world.

THE METHOD OF ACTING

671. Consider the various aspects of a problem carefully and then take a decision. But once a decision is taken, there should be no delay in its implementation.
672. *There are some undertakings which should be delayed; prolong them accordingly; There are some undertakings which demand promptness; do them promptly.*
673. If all the conditions permit, it is better to complete an undertaking; if conditions do not permit it, *try to achieve the goal by a play (or a ruse) (or a trick).*
674. A fire that is not fully extinguished, will flare up again and consume everything around it. Similarly unresolved hostility, and an unfinished deed and its consequences are bound to escalate and destroy all the concerned.
675. Before launching an operation, the following five factors that are essential for a successful outcome should be carefully considered (i.e.) 1. Money 2. Time 3. Place 4. Means and 5. Execution.
676. Before undertaking a deed, the following factors should be considered carefully. They are :
1. The effort necessary for the task;
2. The obstacles that are likely to be encountered;
3. The ultimate gain that will accrue by successful completion of the task.
677. Before undertaking a deed, one should consult an expert on such matters.
678. A tame elephant is used as a decoy to capture a wild elephant. Similarly the experience gained while doing a task should be used to achieve success in another.
679. It is much more urgent to secure the alliances with your enemy's enemies, than to strengthen existing alliances.
680. A less powerful king should join hands with a more powerful king, at an appropriate time, to avoid defeat and demoralization of his weak army.

ABOUT ENVOYS AND MESSENGERS

681. The qualifications essential for a successful envoy are :
1. An affectionate temperament 2. Noble lineage and 3. Character and conduct admired by royalty.
682. Knowledge of politics, devotion to one's sovereign, discrimination and oratory are

absolutely essential qualifications for an envoy.

683. An envoy to convey effectively the reasons for the victory of his own king to another king, should possess excellent learning.

684. An envoy should possess 1. An attractive personality 2. Knowledge of world affairs and 3. Excellent learning.

685. The speech of a successful envoy is marked by 1. Moderation 2. A pleasing style and 3. Avoidance of harsh words and 4. His speech is always with sole aim of benefiting his own king.

686. The envoy should be learned in political science, persuasive in speech, resourceful, ready witted and he is not cowed down by the angry looks of another king.

687. An envoy should state his case convincingly at the proper time and place.

688. An envoy should possess good conduct, courage and the ability to gain the support of others for his mission.

689. An envoy who bears the message of his king to another should never utter even inadvertently words which may lower the dignity of his king.

690. A true envoy conveys his message loyally, without faltering and even when there is risk of death.

CONDUCT IN THE PRESENCE OF THE KING

691. One who wants to warm himself at a fire will stand neither too close nor too far; similarly a courtier should neither be too close nor be too far from his king (A king's mind is fickle and undependable and as dangerous as a fire, hence a courtier should conduct himself with catuion).

692. If a courtier wants to prosper, let him not covet the things desired by his king.

693. If a courtier wants to be safe, let him avoid errors in his conduct before a king. Once suspicion enters the king's mind, it is hard to dispel it.

694. In the presence of the king, avoid whispering to others or smiling at others.

695. When a king is engaged in secret counsel with others one should neither try to overhear nor pry into it with inquisitive questions, but listen to him if he talks about it himself.

696. Watch the mood of the king and suggest in a pleasing manner, matters that are of interest to him.

697. Speak about matters agreeable to the king, but avoid profitless talk at all times.

698. Do not despise a king on the ground of he being junior in age or because of kinship, but behave at all times as befits his royal status.

699. Simply because one is respected and trusted by the king, taking advantage of the situation, one should never do things that are disagreeable to the king.

700. If one does disagreeable things, taking advantage of his long familiarity with the king, such a one will be ruined.

THE KNOWLEDGE OF INDICATIONS

701. A minister who by looking at the king's face, can understand his mind without being

told of it, is to be considered as an invaluable asset.

702. One who is able to ascertain without a doubt, what is in the mind of another, will be esteemed by all as a God.

703. A king should secure the services of a man, who can ascertain what is within the mind of another, by watching his face and eyes.

704. One who can ascertain what is in the mind of another though physically he is similar to others, but mentally he is of a different kind because of his psychic powers.

705. One should be able to ascertain what is in the mind of another, by carefully observing his face and eyes.

706. As the mirror reflects clearly what is close by, similarly the expressions of the face indicate the emotions of the mind.

707. Love or hatred that are in the mind are reflected in the face. There is no better index than the face to gauge the emotions within.

708. If you come across a man who can read the face of another, it is enough if you watch his face carefully.

709. The eyes of a person reveal clearly love or hatred that is within the mind.

710. *A man's acuteness of observation rests in his eyes only*
(A man's acuteness of observation indicates his level of intelligence also)

THE KNOWLEDGE OF THE ASSEMBLY

711. To address an assembly, one should possess not only a thorough knowledge of the language but also a knowledge of the disposition of the audience.

712. To address an assembly one should possess a knowledge of mental attitude of the audience and also be aware of the suitable time.

713. Those who address an assembly without understanding the mental attitude of the audience, can not be considered as good orators.

714. When you address a discerning audience, let your speech be radiant; and when you address the common people, let your speech be as plain as possible.

715. It is a wise rule to restrain oneself and avoid preceding with ones speech, in an assembly of seniors (in age or accomplishments).
(Modesty of the young and inexperienced in a learned assembly is a praiseworthy quality)

716. One, whose speech is full of blunders in a learned assembly, is considered to have fallen down on the path of virtue (DHARMA).

717. Intelligent criticism in a learned assembly will serve to enhance the knowledge of all in it.

718. To regularly water a growing plant facilitates its growth further. Similarly debating in a learned assembly facilitates the improvement of all in it.

719. *A learned and accomplished orator should not even forgetfully address a mob of illiterates.*

720. To sprinkle honey in a dirty courtyard is futile;
Similarly to address a hostile assembly is futile.

NOT TO BE AFRAID OF AN ASSEMBLY

721. An accomplished orator will not faulter in his speech at any time, while addressing an assembly.
722. Those who can speak about learned matters agreeably before a learned assembly are deemed to be the foremost among the learned.
723. There are many who are ready even to risk their lives in a battlefield, where as there are very few who can speak without any faultering in a learned assembly.
724. Speak about what you have learnt before the learned assembly and at the same time learn from those who are more learned than yourself.
725. One should be well versed in logic and grammar in order to reply fearlessly and effectively in a learned assembly.
726. A sword in the hands of a coward is fultile; Similarly the learning of one who is afraid to face an assembly is futile.
727. A hermaphrodite even with a sword in his hand will never dare to enter a battlefield. Similarly the learning of one who is afraid to face an assembly is useless.
728. The learning of one who can not address effectively a learned assembly, is unprofitable to him.
729. A learned man who is afraid to face a learned assembly will be regarded as an inferior even to the illiterate.
730. Those who can not address an assembly on matters learnt by them already, will be deemed to be dead though alive.

THE LAND

731. People engaged in cultivation, thus ensuring plentiful crops, subjects committed to Virtue (DHARMA) and wealthy merchants, these three constituents are essential to a kingdom.
732. An ideal kingdom should possess 1. Great wealth, coveted even by other kingdoms and 2. Lands which yield plentiful crops and untouched by any pests or rot.
733. An ideal kingdom should be able to look after immigrants from adjoining kingdoms, during emergencies such as war, famines, and epidemics, and its king receives full tribute from his subjects due to him inspite of the additional burden on them.
734. An ideal kingdom should be free from 1. Deaths due to starvation 2. Epidemics and 3. Attacks by neighbouring enemies.
735. An ideal kingdom should be free from 1. Too many groups and divisions (based on castes and religions) with in the kingdom 2. Internal enemies and 3. Hostile chieftains.
736. An ideal kingdom should be free from attacks by enemies and does not experience want during adversity such as a war.
737. An ideal kingdom should possess the following :
   1. Plenty of surface and subsoil water;
   2. Well situated hills and mountain streams and
   3. An indestructible fort.
738. An ideal kingdom is recognised by the following :

1. Its people enjoy good health;
2. They are well to do;
3. The lands yield plentiful crops;
4. The subjects lead a happy life and,
5. There is security for its people.

739. The lands of an ideal kingdom yield good crops, without undue labour, where as lands which yield crops only much toil are not considered as ideal lands.

740. A kingdom may possess all the above mentioned good qualities, yet if it has not right kind of a king, they will all come to nothing.

THE FORTIFICATION

741. A fortress is of great importance not only for a king who is keen about attacking an enemy but also for a timid king, who is satisfied with self defence alone.

742. A fortress should have perennial source of water, open spaces, hills and cool and shady forests around it.

743. The learned say that a good fortress should possess these four qualities namely 1. that its walls should be high, broad and strong and the fortress built so as to be difficult of attack by enemies.

744. An ideal fortress should have small spaces inside it to be guarded, and the rest as an ample open space, and on the whole, a fortress should be inaccessible to enemies.

745. An ideal fortress should have :

1. Plenty of food resources inside it:
2. It should provide security for its inmates;
3. It should afford scope for the garrison to attack the enemy from inside without exposing themselves.

746. An ideal fortress should possess all the qualities mentioned above and most important of all, warriors with courage to defend it.

747. A fort should be built so as to be difficult of being taken by siege, or by assault, or through the betrayal of traitors.

748. An ideal fort should enable its inmates not only in defending themselves but also in driving out the attacking enemy.

749. An ideal fort should enable its inmates to carry out strategems for the rout of the enemy. (defeat of an army)

750. A fortress may possess all the ideal features, yet they will all come to nothing if the commander of the fort is not a man of ability.

WAY OF ACCUMULATING WEALTH

751. There is nothing so effective as wealth, which has the quality of giving worth even to worthless men.

752. *All despise the poor; but all respect the rich.*

753. AKHANDAM (OR NANDĀVILLAKKU) is a light in the SANCTUM SACNTORUM of a temple that sheds light, and dispels darkness around it permanently; Similarly

wealth of a man serves him without a lapse in overcoming difficulties in this world.

754. The wealth acquired by proper means and without fraud will yield virtue (DHARMA) and happiness.

755. Wealth obtained by forsaking compassion (on the part of acquirer) and love (on the part of those who part with money), is not to be sought, as it is sure to cause evil.

756. The following sources of money belong to the royal treasury namely :
1. Money levied as a tax by the king 2. Ownerless property such as
1. ESCHEAT (the reversion of property to the STATE, on the owner's dying without legal heirs 2. TREASURE TROVE (Treasure of unknown ownership found hidden).
3. Transit duties on imports and on internal traffic,
4. Wealth confiscated from a defeated enemy.

757. Love begets mercy and mercy's foster mother is wealth (i.e.)
(one who is wealthy should cherish mercy, in his heart towards the poor)

758. One who watches from a hill top, elephants fighting in the valley down below is secure and safe. Similarly an undertaking of a wealthy man is quite safe from interruptions and obstacles and will be successfully completed. The rich man enjoys all the pleasures of adventure and of triumph without anxiety as to possible reverses.

759. Make wealth and there is no sharper weapon than wealth with which to (cut) (counteract) pride and confidence of the enemy.

760. Make wealth by lawful means. Wealth (ARTHA) is the stepping stone to acquire virtue (DHARMA) and happiness (KAMA) also.

ON THE VALUE OF AN ARMY

761. A king's most important possession is a well manned army in all its component parts (such as 1. Infantry 2. Cavalry 3. GAJA (Elephants) and 4. RADHA (CHARIOTS) and it should be renowed for its indomitable courage.

762. Loyal and experienced soldiers only stand by their king at the time of reduced strength and impending defeat in war, and not the rest.

763. Even a vast army of rats flees at the sight of a hissing cobra.

764. The qualities of an ideal army are :
1. It is victorious 2. It is fearless and 3. It never deserts to the enemy.

765. An army which can stand an attack of an enemy army even when it is led by YAMA himself (king of death) is said to be worthy of its name.

766. The qualities that make a regiment invincible are : 1. Valour 2. Honour 3. Loyalty and 4. Good conduct.

767. The army should know how to receive an attack by the enemy, resist it and then advance on it.

768. An army although may not be bold and not have much strength of resistance, yet it may achieve success by using a clever strategy.

769. An army can achieve success if it is free from 1. Desertions 2. Disaffection (Disloyalty) (hatred for its commander) and 3. Poverty (no dearth of funds for the army).

770. Even when the army has a large number of permanent soldiers, it can not last if it has no able commanders to guide it in a war.

ON VALOUR

771. O, enemies! Do not you dare to challenge my commander! But many did so, and all of them are dead now and statues were installed in their memory.
(Setting up memorials in stone for those killed in battle was prevalent in the times of THIRUVALLUVAR)
772. It is better even to miss the aim while shooting an arrow at an elephant on a battle field than to shoot and kill a rabbit in a forest.
773. Fierceness on the battlefield is a sign of great valour indeed; but when an enemy is in distress, to render him help is considered as the height of valour.
774. A warrior casts (hurls) his spear at an elephant in the battlefield and drives it away and while he is looking for another spear, a spear cast by an enemy pierces his chest. Undaunted, the warrior plucks it out.
775. If the warrior succumbs immediately to a spear cast by the enemy, does it not amount to his defeat?
(i.e., once he is dead, he will never be able to look ferociously on the enemy.)
776. The warrior will reckon among wasted days all those days where in he did not receive grievous wounds in battle.
777. "GANDA PENDARAMU" (THE ANKLET) is a befitting ornament to adorn warriors, who seeking renown fight fearlessly in war even at a risk to their lives.
778. The warriors who fight fearlessly in war even at a risk to their lives, will not let go their zeal (ARDOUR) for war, even when their king restrains them in anger.
779. Who can blame a warrior who sacrifices his life on a battlefield, to fulfil his pledge?
780. Even a king sheds tears for warriors who sacrificed their lives on a battlefield. The death as a martyr on the battlefield is a laudable one. Hence such a glorious death should be sought, even by begging by every warrior.

ON FRIENDSHIP

781. *To acquire the friendship of a SAJJANA (GOOD MAN) is very difficult. Yet such a friendship is the only protection when one is overwhelmed by the strategy of ones enemies.*
782. The friendship with a wise man grows as the days pass just as the young moon waxes as the days pass;
The friendship with an evil person diminishes as the days pass, just as the full moon wanes as the days pass.
783. With deeper study one sees more and more profoundity in a great book. Likewise the friendship with a good man yields more delight, the more it is cultivated.
784. *The purpose of friendship is not mere bonhomie (geniality; good natured friendliness), but to rebuke fearlessly when one's friend swerves from the right path.*
785. *Meeting often and holding frequent dialogue are not essential for a friendship. It is*

the mutual understanding and common ideals which cement the bond of friendship.

786. The face may wear a smile at the sight of one, but he only is a friend whose sight brings delight to ones heart.
(True friendship is an internal phenomenon).

787. *A true friend leads you away from evil and makes you walk on the right path. And he stands by in your misfortune and shares your sorrow.*

788. If your dress slips down in advertently before an assembly one by your side hastens to help you. Similarly a true friend comes swiftly to the rescue in the hour of your trouble.

789. *True friendship consists of support to one at all times and under all circumstances.*

790. *True friendship never publicizes its intimacy with another, and does not differentiate between self and the friend.*

INVESTIGATION IN TO FORMING OF FRIENDSHIPS

791. Indiscriminate choice of friends will cause greatest harm. But once friendship is cultivated after due inquiry it should never be given up.

792. The friendship contracted without repeated inquiry will cause grief to the end of one's life.

793. Let friendship be contracted only after ascertaining a man's good points, his ancestry, his defects and his connections (namely relatives and friends).

794. The friendship of one who is well-born and is sensitive to public opinion about him is worth cultivating even at a cost.

795. The friendship of one who leads you away from evil, who rebukes you fearlessly when you go wrong, and who leads you again in to the good path is to be sought for.

796. Misfortune has its own uses in that it serves as a yardstick for you to assess the reliability of ones friends and relatives.

797. It is indeed a gain if one puts an end to the friendship of fools.

798. Do not think of things that undermine your enthusiasm, and discourage you;
Give up friendship of those who desert you in your days of adversity.

799. The very thought of the friendship of those who have deserted one at the approach of adversity, will rankle in ones heart till his end.

800. Cultivate always friendship with SAJJANAS (the good)
Give up friendship with the evil ones, by giving them even gifts if necessary.

ON FAMILIARITY

801. The sign of intimate friendship is the tolerance of things done by another through the privilege of long-standing intimacy.

802. The wise are pleased by the acts done by friends through the privilege of long-standing intimacy.

803. Of what avail is long-standing friendship if friends do not approve the acts of each other.

804. The wise are pleased and approve the acts of a friend although he (they are) has not

asked him to do them.

805. If a friend acts contrary to one's wishes, it should be attributed to either ignorance or undue intimacy.

806. A true friend will not give up a long-standing friendship even when it was the cause of his ruin.

807. A true friend will not forsake his affection towards his long-standing friend, although he has harmed him.

808. If one does not listen to tales about the faults of his friends, a day will come when he will know for sure the fault committed by his friend.

809. The world applauds long established friendships.

810. Even ones enemies praise the excellent quality of a friendship that has survived for long inspite of lapses on both sides.

ON EVIL FRIENDSHIP

811. An evil person may pretend to be your friend and display a lot of love and affection, yet it is better to allow such an association with an evil person to die out.

812. Of what avail is the friendship of a selfish person, who befriends you when it is profitable and leaves you when it is not?
(A true friend is loyal to you either in prosperity or during adversity).

813. Those who cultivate friendship with the sole purpose of selfish gain, are no better than avaricious thieves and prostitutes.

814. A friend who deserts you in your adversity is no better than a horse which throws down the rider and runs away in a battlefield.
(Solitude is better than such a friendship)

815. It is better to give up the friendship of one, who can not protect his friend even when appointed to do so.

816. The opposition of the wise is ten million times more profitable than the closest friendship of a fool.

817. The hatred of ones enemies is hundred million times more profitable than friendship with those who smile with their faces but have no love or affection for you in their hearts.

818. Allow your friendship to die out with men who fail to help where they could, and obstruct the successful completion of a work.

819. The friendship of one whose words and deeds are at variance will cause distress even in ones dreams.

820. Avoid the friendship of one who is friendly with you in private, but ridicules you in public.

ON UNREAL FRIENDSHIP

821. A grind-stone (Telugu) (PATTEDA OR DIMME in) although very useful to sharpen weapons such as knives and swords in the battlefield,, is discarded at the earliest suitable opportunity and place;

Similarly one should give up the friendship of a deceitful man at the earliest suitable opportunity.

822. The friendship of a deceitful man and the love and affection displayed by a prostitute are totally unreliable.
823. *Although one's enemy is very learned, he will never be able to overcome enmity and hatred, and develop friendship with you.*
(Learning and culture have no effect on hatred and enmity. They do not help to remove enmity).
824. Be on your guard and be not be deceived by those who smile with their lips but plot evil in their hearts.
825. Never rely on the words of a deceitful friend. His words may be pleasant to hear, but there is evil in his heart.
826. A deceitful friend may utter good words to please you, yet you will atonce be able to understand their real purpose.
827. Do not be misled by politeness or courtesy of language on the part of enemies. Just as a bow is bent only as a prelude to shoot an arrow in to the heart of an enemy.
828. Be on your guard and do not be deceived by external signs of friendship. An enemy's hands clasped in salutation may conceal a weapon, and his tears of grief (pretended) are not to be trusted.
829. One should pretend friendship even with an enemy, and allow it to die out.
830. When an enemy smiles and pretends to be your friend, you also smile and pretend to be his friend, and wait for an opportunity to put a stop to this pretension also.

ON STUPIDITY

831. The mark of a stupid man is that he accepts evil things and forsakes the good things.
832. The greatest stupidity is that which causes one to take delight in doing evil things.
833. A stupid man can be recognised by the following traits :
    1. He is shameless;
    2. He is cruel;
    3. He shows indifference to things which must be sought after;
    4. He shows aversion for all good things.
834. There is no bigger fool than the man who has acquired much learning and teaches the same to others, yet who does not walk on the good path.
835. A stupid man undergoes torments of seven future lives in the present life only.
836. A stupid and incopetent man, when he undertakes a work, not only will he fail to complete it properly, but he will land himself in a jail also.
837. If a stupid man happens to get an immense fortune, outsiders are benifited, while his own kith and kin starve.
838. A fool if by chance acquires great wealth, will behave like a lunatic who has drunk an intoxicating liquour like toddy.
839. The friendship of a fool is perhaps the best, for in this case parting brings no grief to both.

840. A filthy fellow with "unwashed feet" if he lies on a clean bed, is sure to make it filthy. Similarly a stupid fellow if he enters in to an assembly of wise men, will ruin the decency and deocrum of the assembly.
("unwashed feet" is an euphemism for one who has neglected necessary ablutions.)

ON IGNORANCE

841. *The world regards lack of wisdom as the greatest deficiency in a man.*
842. If an ignorant man by chance makes a gift with pleasure to another, the cause of it perhaps is the merit acquired by the receipient in the past births.
843. The suffering that fools inflict upon themselves will far exceed the suffering inflicted on them by their enemies.
844. There is no stupidity so great as the stupidity that makes men proud of their own wisdom.
845. If one pretends knowledge of things not learnt, one loses credit for even such knowledge as one really posseses.
846. To forsake ones fault is of greater importance, than even to cover up ones nakedness.
847. A fool of his own accord, invites trouble to self by revealing his innermost secrets to others.
848. A fool neither listens to wise counsel, or does he seek the good path by himself. Such a fool lives as a burden to the earth, to the end of his life.
849. Never try to teach a fool unless you want to become a fool. A fool never gives up his folly and is "wise in his own conceit"
850. He who is out of harmony with the ways of the world will be regarded as a demon on earth.

ON HOSTILITY

851. The wise define hatred as an evil which fosters disunion among men.
852. It is the best not to repay an evil deed with another evil deed.
853. If one intends to acquire name and fame, he should first get rid of hatred, which is the source of sorrow.
854. If one gets rid of hatred, which is the source of sorrow it will yield him greatest happiness.
855. Can anyone cause distress to a man who is free from hatred towards others?
856. One who exults in hatred and revenge is sure to be ruined and fail in life.
857. Those who exult in hatred and revenge will never be able to understand the truth (SATYA) that is the basis of any victory.
858. One who does not indulge in hatred and retaliation is sure to prosper, where as one who exults in them is sure to experience evil.
859. One who is free from hatred is sure to propser;
If one exults in hatred and revenge, it foreshadows decline in his fortune.
860. Hatred is the main cause of all difficulties and misery

Friendship is the main cause (source) of all goodness.

ON THE NATURE OF AN ENEMY

861. Do not offer resistance to the strong and powerful people,
Do not fail to offer resistance to the weak.
862. One who is weak, without any powerful aids and who is cruel, will never be able to overcome his enemies.
863. One who is timid, stupid, unsociable and miserily is an easy prey to his enemies.
864. One who has no control over his mind and who gives way to anger, can be easily defeated by anyone, at anytime and at any place.
865. One who does not walk in the right path, who does evil deeds who is insensitive to reproach and who has no good qualities, such a one is an easy prey to his enemies.
866. One who is full of blind wrath and inordinate desires, such a one is an easy prey to his enemies.
867. It is better to purchase (if necessary) enmity with a man who engages himself in deeds that are bound to fail.
868. One who has no good qualities and whose faults are many will be forsaken by all, and such a one is an easy prey to his enemies.
869. If one is ignorant and timid, such a one will yield delight to his enemies.
870. It is easy to overcome an illiterate antagonist. If one fails even in such an easy task, such a one is unworthy of any name or fame.

ON ENEMIES

871. Even in jest do not entertain the wish to make an enemy of anyone.
872. You may incur the hatred of archers (Warriors), but never incur the hatred of men whose weapon is their word (such as plotters, politicians and writers).
(A Pen is more powerful than a weapon such as a bow and arrows) (ARCHER)
873. One who has no allies, if he incurs the hatred of many such a one is considered to be worse than a mad fool.
874. The greatness of a man who has converted an enemy in to a friend by his behaviour is praised by the world.
875. If you have no allies and when you are faced with two enemies, you must befriend one of them.
876. When you are down in luck, make neither friends nor enemies; be neutral even as regards those whom you have found reason to trust or to distrust.
877. Do not reveal your problems even to friends who are not aware of them already,
Do not reveal your weaknesses to an enemy.
878. If one acquires allies and improves his strength for the proper completion of a deed, the pride of his enemies will be destroyed.
879. A thorny shrub should be destroyed when it is yet young and easy to pull it out. But when it is fully grown it is difficult to destroy it and it will hurt your hands.
(Procrastination is dangerous in certain tasks).

880. Those who can not destroy their enemies by timely action will in the end pay with their own lives.
(i.e.) (They will be killed by their enemies).

ENMITY WITHIN

881. Shade of trees and water of a village, wholesome as they are, if they do not suit your constitution, it is better to keep away from them;
If the qualities of your own relatives are not agreeable it is better to avoid them.
882. Fear not open enemies who move about with drawn swords;
But guard yourself from relatives, who outwardly are cordial but internally bear enmity towards you.
883. A potter's knife can slice through a mudpot in the making, in an instant. Similarly internal enmity of your relatives and associates will destroy you, unless you are on guard.
884. The internal enmity of a person will cause many evils and disaffection among his relatives.
885. If there is internal enmity in a family, not only will it cause many evils, but also will not end until there is a death.
886. A man's ruin is certain if his own relatives harbour enmity towards him.
887. A casket with its lid in place seemingly looks like a single piece, but can be separated into two pieces;
Similarly a family with internal dissension (want of harmony), seemingly may present a picture of harmony to an outsider, but alas! there is no true harmony among its members.
888. A piece of iron if it is rubbed constantly with a file will disappear in the course of time, to become a small heap of iron filings; Similarly a family which harbours internal dissension, will in the course of time become powerless and ultimately ruined.
889. Although internal dissesion in a family be as minute as a crack in a gingili seed (Indian Sesame or NUVVULU) it is sure to cause evil to the family.
890. If one lives in a hut in which a cobra also dwells one is sure to die of the cobra bite sooner or later;
Similarly to live in the company of people who harbour internal enmity towards you, is dangerous.

NOT OFFENDING THE GREAT

891. The best way of protecting oneself from the wrath of the powerful and accomplished ones is not to disregard or offend them in any manner.
892. If one disregards and offends the powerful and accomplished ones, such a one is sure to experience endless trouble and sorrow.
893. If one wants his own ruin and destruction, let him disregard, offend and commit crimes against the powerful and accomplished ones.

894. One who is weak and less accomplished if he disregards and offends the powerful and accomplished ones, such a one will be courting his own death.
895. Those who have incurred the wrath of a king will not be safe wherever they may hide.
896. One may perhaps survive, though he was caught in a forest fire and sustained burns on his body;
But one will not survive if he has committed crimes against the powerful and mighty.
897. If a powerful and wealthy king incurs the wrath of a saint, such a one is sure to be destroyed inspite of his power and wealth.
898. A king who incurs the wrath of saints, will be totally destroyed, although he was secure and well settled at that time.
899. Even INDRA (The King of Devatas) will lose his power and celestial throne, if he incurs the wrath of saints.
900. Even a king with many allies, is sure to perish if he incurs the wrath of saints.

ON DOMINATION BY ONE'S WIFE

901. In-ordinate attachment to one's wife is not only an impediment to the attainment of virtue but also to achieve excellence in ones work.
902. One who neglects his duty because of his inordinate attachment to his wife, such a ones conduct will be regarded as shameful and disgraceful by others.
903. The cowardice of one who always obeys his wife, will make him feel ashamed, when he is in the company of distinguished people.
904. The undertakings of one who fears his wife will never be applauded by others.
905. He that fears his wife, will be afraid even to do good things to virtuous people (SAJJANAS).
906. A man's life style may be grander than even that of a DEVATA, yet if he fears his wife, he will never be esteemed by others.
907. Natural modesty of a woman is more admirable than the shameful conduct of a husband who always obeys his wife out of cowardice.
908. One who is led by his wife will neither be able to help his friends nor perform good deeds.
909. Deeds of Virtue (DHARMA), Wealth (ARTHA) and others (KAMA or pleasure) are not to be expected from one who is led by his wife.
910. Those who have intelligence and discrimination and who plan great undertakings, will never succumb to the weakness of being led by women.
(Domination by one's wife leads to narrowness of outlook and initiative. No man or woman can serve two masters satisfactorily. One who holds a public responsibility can not permit himself or herself to be guided by another, who has not been entrusted with the responsibility. The danger of a clouded judgement is all the greater, when it is a case of *uxoriousness* (undue attachment to one's wife).

ON PUBLIC WOMEN

911. The sweet words of a public woman who approaches a man not out of affection but

out of desire to get some money from him, are sure to cause sorrow in the end.

912. One should keep away from a woman who approaches him, after ascertaining his wealth and with a profit motive only.

913. To seek pleasure in the embrace of a public woman is as futile as to seek it in the embrace of an unknown corpse in a dark room.
(For a public woman, money and not love or affection is always the motive in her contacts with men)

914. The wise who seek the grace of ALMIGHTY, will never seek the favours of public women, who live only to make money.

915. The wise and intelligent people will never seek the favours of public women who sell their favours to all.

916. The wise who value good character will never seek the favours of public women, who are proud of their beauty and accomplishments and sell their favours to all.

917. Men who lack discrimination and a steadfast mind only seek the company of public women who always think of money only.

918. One who lacks discrimination and a steadfast mind when he seeks the company of a deceitful and greedy public woman, he is said to be possessed by a devil called "MOHINE PISACHE".

919. The delicate and beautiful shoulders of a public woman sought by an inferior fellow who has no desire for his own uplift, will ultimately lead to his ruin.

920. Liquor, gambling and deceitful public women are the associates of a wretch forsaken by FORTUNE.

ON AVOIDING LIQUOR

921. Those who are addicted to liquor will not only loose their name and fame but also will not be able to inspire fear in the hearts of their enemies.

922. Keep away from liquor; for a drunkard will never be able to get any respect or regard from the wise.

923. The conduct of a drunkard causes distress and sorrow even to his own mother, not to speak of the elite of the world.
(An indulgent mother may put up with the obnoxious conduct of a drunkard, but the wise will not).

924. Modesty forsakes a man addicted to liquor.

925. Only an ignorant fool spends his money on liquor and purchases the state of intoxication and finally unconsciousness also.

926. They that sleep resemble the dead;
Those who drink liquor and become unconscious also resemble the dead.
(Addiction to liquor is as lethal as taking a poison to kill oneself.)

927. Those who drink liquor in secret soon become the laughing stock of the village for the effects of the indulgence, can not for long remain unknown.

928. Let not a drunkard boast that he has not tasted wine so far; for the moment he drinks, he will betray to others, what he has tried to conceal.

929. To reason with a drunkard is as stupid as to get into water with a torch to search for a man who is drowned in deep waters. Both are futile.
(The light of reason can not pierce through the darkness that pervades an alcoholic mind.)

930. If an alcoholic in his sober moments observes the disgusting conduct of another alcoholic, will he not realize that his own conduct will be equally disgusting?

ON GAMBLING

931. Gambling, even if you win occasionally is a thing to be avoided;
The bait on a fish hook tempts the fish to swallow it and ultimately kills it. Similarly that occasional win in gambling will tempt and ultimately ruin the gambler.

932. A gambler may win once but he is sure to loose a hundred times. (His winning chances are about one in a hundred.)
That is why gamblers will never prosper.

933. If one is a gambler and addicted to rolling of dice not only will he loose his wealth but it will also fall into other's (enemies) hands.

934. Gambling causes misery, destroys ones reputation and brings in disgraceful poverty.

935. Those who do not give up gambling, are sure to end up as paupers in the end.

936. One who is addicted to gambling is said to be a victim of MOODEVI (OR SANI DEVATA OR PEDDAMMA); such a one will always go hungry and suffer and will have to experience many difficulties on account of gambling.

937. A gambler who spends all of his time in gambling is sure to loose not only his ancestral wealth, but also his reputation.

938. Addiction to gambling destroys wealth, teaches deceit and dishonesty, results in many difficulties and puts an end to all benevolent acts.

939. A gambler forgoes the following on account of his addiction to gambling namely 1. Timely meals and clean clothes 2. Reputation 3. Learning and finally 4. Money.

940. A sick man inspite of excruciating physical suffering, holds on to life and tries to avoid death. Similarly a gambler hods on to the vice of gambling the more he looses by it.

ON THE ART OF HEALING

941. Those learned in the medical sciences have postulated that there are three humours in a human body (Vata, Pitta and Smlesha) and health is a state when there is harmony and balance amongst the three humours. If this harmony and balance amongst the three humours is upset either by an excess or deficiency of one of the components, this imbalance results in disease.

942. If one eats only after making sure that what has already eaten been digested, such a one will not need medication to maintain good health
(MORAL: Eat only when you are hungry and that too with moderation.)

943. Even after assuring oneself what has been eaten has already been digested, let one eat with moderation. To eat moderately is the only way to ensure a long life.

944. Eat only when you are hungry, that too with moderation and only the food that agrees with your constitution and health.
945. One who eats moderately and only the food that agrees with his constitution and health, will be safe from life threatening diseases.
946. One who eats with moderation is sure to enjoy health and happiness;
One who is a glutton is sure to develop many diseases.
947. One who eats voraciously irrespective of hunger is sure to be afflicted with many diseases.
948. Let the physician first make a diagnosis of the disease, then let him carefully consider the cause of the disease and then only let him commence the treatment that is best suited to the constitution of the patient.
949. Let the physician ascertain carefully the age of the patient, duration of illness, and the season of the year, and then commence the treatment.
950. There are four elements that go to make effective treatment of a disease of a patient namely 1. The patient 2. The physician 3. The medicine (treatment) and 4. The attendant.

ON NOBILITY

951. Consistency in thought, word and deed and a quick reaction against anything mean or improper are natural to persons of noble lineage (high or well born).
(To be born in a noble family is an asset)
952. Truthfulness, good conduct and modesty are the three traits that distinguish persons of noble lineage.
953. A cheerful countenance, pleasant speech, generosity and an unreviling disposition (avoiding of fault finding) are the traits that distinguish persons of noble lineage.
954. Men of noble birth will never stoop to do anything mean or improper, though they may there by gain many millions of rupees. (Men of noble birth will never consent to do anything unbecoming that might tarnish the name, fame and prestige of their family).
955. Ancient families though poor now and unable to be munificent, will not forsake generosity and right conduct.
956. Those who seek to preserve the irreproachable honour of their families, will never consent to do fraudulent undertakings.
957. Any faults of persons of noble lineage however small are observed by the world, and they stand out in contrast like the dark spots on a full moon.
958. If there is want of affection in a man, although he may possess all other good qualities, the world even suspects his claim of noble lineage.
959. The sprouts and plants indicate the nature of the soil. So does softness of speech indicate a good family.
960. If one desires a good name, one should be modest
If one wants to ensure the prosperity and prestige of ones family, one should cultivate the spirit of true humility towards all. (towards not only those placed above, but equals and those below.)

ON HONOUR

961. One who wants to safeguard the name and prestige of his family should never consent to do deeds, (although they are important and the best) if they are likely to tarnish the name and fame of one's family.
962. One who wants to safeguard the name and prestige of his family, even with a desire to enhance them further will not consent to do deeds that are likely to tarnish the name and fame of one's family.
963. When you have wealth cultivate humility;
When you are poor, do not let go dignity, and self respect.
964. The hair on the head is a thing of beauty and when it is removed from the head, it becomes filth. Similarly men who forsake their honourbale conduct and demean themselves are sure to loose their original status.
965. Even those who are now in an exalted position, if they consent to do a trivial or mean deed which is as little as an ABRUS SEED (TELUGU: GURUVINDA GINJA), they are sure to loose their original status.
966. Do not approach those who revile you. Your will not only loose your self respect but also your name and fame, and there are no other gains from them.
967. Dath by starvation is preferable to survival and servitude under those who scorn you.
968. A man of honour is prepared even to sacrifice his life when overtaken by dishonour.
969. According to a legend, the YAK (a long-haired humped Tibetan ox) kills itself at the loss of even one of its hairs; Similarly a man of honour sacrifices his life when overtaken by dishonour.
(For a man of honour, to safeguard his honour is of more importance than his very existence).
970. The world admires and worships the glory of men who sacrifice their lives when overtaken by dishonour.

ON GREATNESS

971. To achieve name and fame through ones own effort imparts glory to a man's life;
To think of a mere survival without achieving name and fame in one's life is a disgraceful thing indeed
(*Lack of earnest endeavour (STRIVING) is the root cause of a man's failure in life.*)
972. All human beings are equal in birth; but depending on the quality of deeds performed by them, a few achieve greatness, and the rest, rest in mediocrity.
973. Though raised above the superior ones by chance, the inferior ones cannot equal the former;
Though brought low by chance, the superior ones will never lose their greatness.
974. Chastity adorns a lady who safeguards her virtue;
Similarly greatness belongs to one, who safeguards his virtuous conduct. (Note that chastity of a lady and greatness of a man are compared here).

975. Only the great can accomplish in the proper way deeds difficult for others to do.
976. The inferior sort have no respect or regard for the superior ones, and refuse to learn from them.
977. There is no limit to the pride of an inferior person if by chance, he achieves greatness.
978. A greatman cultivates humility;
An inferior fellow is always arrogant.
979. Greatness is never tinged with conceit;
Inferiority and conceit, always go together.
980. The great do not reveal the faults of others;
The inferior fellow is ever ready to reveal to faults of others.

ON GOOD CONDUCT

981. One who is conscious of his responsibilities and duties (DHARMA) and fulfils them properly, such a one, will regard as natural all that is good and proper. (Good conduct is natural for a man of virtue).
982. Good conduct is the only asset of the great; all the other assets are next only to good conduct.
983. Affection, modesty, mercy, avoiding of slander, and truthfulness are the five constituents of good conduct.
984. Non violence (AHIMSA) is the best of all penaces (TAPAS)
Avoiding slander (the evil of finding faults in others) is the basis of good conduct.
985. The power of the great rests in their humility;
It is by cultivating humility, one can convert even an enemy in to a friend.
986. The touchstone of greatness is the ability to recognise and accept the greatness of another who is not socially equal to him.
987. Of what avail is ones nobility, if evil is repaid with evil, but not with good?
(The noble sort repay even evil with good only)
988. Poverty is no disgrace to one who abounds in good qualities
(A poor man is one who has no good qualities.)
989. A man of nobility will remain steadfast in his conduct, though the times may change.
990. If there is a lack of virtue in the men of virtue of this world, even the earth which bears the burden of all, will disintegrate.

ON COURTESY

991. The wise say that if one is easy of access to all, and is affectionate towards all, for such a one, good conduct and a good life are natural and easy.
992. Birth in a good family and an affectionate temperament are the two qualities that ensure good conduct of a person.
993. Similarity of physical features will not lead to affinity among men;
Similarity of behaviour only will lead to affinity among men.
994. The world applauds the character of those committed to equity, virtue and benevolence.

995. Do not mock at others even in a sportive mood, as it is sure to cause unpleasantness and suffering to them. To be courteous even to an enemy is the mark of a gentleman.

996. The earth exists because there are good men;
If there are no good men in the world, the earth would have disintegrated long ago.

997. If a man has no good qualities although he may be as sharp as a file (in intelligence), such a one's life is as devoid of wisdom as that of a tree.

998. To be courteous even towards those who are not one's friends and who do only evil deeds, is a sign of wisdom.
(The wise are courteous even towards the evil ones)

999. For those who can not rejoice and live happily with others, there is only gloom and darkness even in broad daylight.

1000. Pure milk stored in a dirty vessel gets spoilt soon. Similarly the wealth of one, who has no good qualities will perish soon.

WEALTH WITHOUT BENEFACTION

1001. If a man amasses immense wealth and dies without enjoying it, such a man's immense wealth has not served him at all.

1002. The wise say that a miser who hoards up wealth with the thought it will yield everything in this world will be born as a PISACHE (DEMON) in his next birth.

1003. Men who live only to a mass wealth and not to acquire a good name, are regarded as a burden to the earth. (Wealth should used to do good deeds and thereby acquire a good name.)

1004. One who does not help others when alive, will never be able to acquire name and fame after his dealth.

1005. Those who neither help others with their wealth, nor enjoy it by themselves, are considered as the poorest among the poor, thought they may possess millions of rupees. (The immense wealth of such a miser serves neither the society nor him).

1006. One who neither helps a deserving person with his wealth, nor enjoys it by himself, is considered as a rot on his wealth (as a disease to society).

1007. The beauty of a woman who grows old without a marriage (and a husband) is futile; Similarly the wealth of a man, that is not spent on the deserving poor is futile.

1008. The fruits of a poison-tree, which is in the centre of a village are not only lethal but also not eaten by the villagers; Similarly the wealth of a miser is not only disliked by all but is futile.

1009. Strangers will inherit the riches that have been acquired without regard for DHARMA (VIRTUE) felicity of others, and basic bodily needs of self such as (happiness) food and water.

1010. Clouds loose their moisture after raining, but they regain their moisture in a short while and again rains follow; Similarly the generosity of the noble rich, makes them poor temporarily, but their wealth gets replenished.

ON MODESTY

1011. To be ashamed of oneself, when one does a wrong or an improper deed is the essence of modesty. The natural modesty of a woman differs from the above mentioned modesty of men of virtue.

1012. The need for food and clothing etc. are common to all. But spontaneous repugnance to evil is a distinct quality found in men of virtue and modesty only.

1013. Body is the abode of the spirit. Similarly
Modesty is the basis of all other good qualities of a man

1014. Modesty is a quality that adorns the noble.
The haughtiness of the noble would be unbearable if not for their modesty.

1015. One who is sensitive to public censure not only on himself, but also on others, is regarded as the abode of modesty in this world.

1016. Men of virtue regard the quality of modesty as essential for an honourable existence.

1017. The modest would rather sacrifice their life for the sake of modesty, than loose modesty to save their lives.

1018. DHARMA (Virtue) will leave a man, who shamelessly does what others are ashamed of.

1019. If you break the rules of a caste or (a group), you are lost to your caste (group);
But if you act against the dictates of honour, you are lost to virtue itself.

1020. A puppet is made to move by pulling on strings attached to it by the puppeteer; Similarly the actions of a man who has not a sensitive conscience, are governed by external forces, and resemble the mechanical movements of a puppet (i.e., there is no inner urge for his actions. (Marionette : a puppet worked by strings)

ON THE UPLIFT OF A COMMUNITY
(KUDI - A Social unit or Community)

1021. Nothing is more exalted than one's dignified efforts directed towards the uplift of a community.

1022. Industriousness coupled with knowledge and insight ensure the prosperity of a community.

1023. Even GODS help a man who sincerely resolves to work for the uplift of a community.

1024. Success comes unbidden to those who work sincerely for the uplift of a community.

1025. People will eagerly seek the friendship of one who has sincerely worked for the uplift of a community.

1026. True valour consists in taking up the responsibilities of the community in which one is born.

1027. Only a few soldiers gain recognition for bravery in a battlefield during a war; Similarly the burden of the family (or a community) is borne by those, who are the most efficient in a family (or a community).

1028. He who is bent on service to the community, should not wait for the proper time or waste energy in thinking over points of dignity;
Laziness and false dignity on his part are sure to cause the ruin of a community.

1029. One who resolves on the uplift of his community must be preapared for great suffering.
He must look upon his body as a receptacle to hold griefs and sufferings for the

benefit of others.

1030. That community will fall uprooted by misfortune which has no men of virtue (SAJJANAS) to support it by public spirited sacrifice.

ON AGRICULTURE

1031. Agriculture, though laborious, is the most excellent form of labour; Many other professions may be taken up by the people, but ultimately they all depend on the farmer for their needs of food.

1032. An axle pin keeps the wheel in place of a cart. Similarly the farmers sustain all others who do not till the soil.

1033. They only live by right that till the soil and produce food materials for all; all the others are dependent on them.

1034. Farmers who produce plentiful crops are not only the source of wealth and power of their king, but also help to bring other states, under the control of their king.

1035. Farmers who till the land and live by agriculture will never beg for their needs, but are everready to give to those who beg for their needs.

1036. The ascetics though they say that they have given up everything in this world, alas! they can not give up eating as long as they are alive. Hence if farmers do not till the land and produce food materials, even the ascetics will cease to exist!

1037. If the ploughed soil is left to dry to a fourth of its bulk, it will yield a plenteous crop, without even a handful of manure being put in.

1038. Manuring a field is more important than ploughing;
After weeding a field guarding of the crop is more important than even watering it.

1039. It there is any lapse of attention or affection on the part of a husband, the wife turns away from him in anger. Similarly if a farmer does not personally attend to his cultivation, the yield from the land will cease.

1040. The earth scorns the sight of those men who plead poverty and lead an idle life.

ON POVERTY

1041. Poverty causes sorrow.

1042. Poverty robs one of happiness here and in the future also.

1043. Poverty destroys not only the name and fame of a person's family but also robs him the dignity of speech.

1044. Poverty will reduce the status of even a man of noble lineage and make him convese in a base manner.

1045. The misery of poverty brings in its wake many more miseries.

1046. The advice of a man may be based on vast experience, sound in thought and clear in expression, yet it is ignored by all if the happens to be poor.
(The wise counsel of a poorman is ignored by all.)

1047. Poverty forces a man to forsake DHARMA (VIRTUE). Even a mother will treat her own son as a stranger, if he is reduced to a state of absolute poverty.
(Poverty affects even a mother's love for her son.)

1048. "Is the poverty that almost killed me yesterday, to meet me even today too", laments a poor man every day.

1049. One may sleep and survive in the midst of a fire. But none can endure and survive the afflictions of poverty.

1050. Those who are absolutely poor can easily renounce the world and become ascetics; yet they do not renounce the world and become ascetis as they hanker after their daily need of salt and gruel.

ON BEGGING

1051. If you meet people who are generous and ready to give alms, you may beg of them; If they refuse to give alms, the blame will be their's and not yours.

1052. Even begging may be pleasant, if what is begged for is obtained without grief to him that begs.

1053. There is a sort of beauty in begging of one who is noble and generous.

1054. There are a few who never think of with holding their charity even in their dreams; To beg of such persons is infact the same as giving charity to oneself.

1055. As there are many who do not withhold their charity under any condition, there are many who prefer to beg of such generous people.

1056. All the indignities of begging vanish in the presence of generous people who never withhold their charity.

1057. A beggar rejoices when he sees those who give alms with kindness and courtesy.

1058. The world will resemble a mere puppet show, if there are no beggars, to give us an opportunity to be charitable.

1059. If there were no beggars in this world, what praise would there be to (givers of alms) men of charity.

1060. A beggar should not be angry at a refusal and to suffer resultant misery, since it is his own poverty that is mainly responsible for his condition.

ON FEAR OF BEGGING

1061. It is a million times better not to be a even from persons who cheerfully give for charity.

1062. If God has decreed begging as a means of livelihood for some may HE too go a begging and perish.

1063. There is no greater folly than the thought that begging will eradicate ones poverty. (To give up hard work to improve ones lot and to beg is one of the greatest evils).

1064. Not to beg even when one is in the midst of utter destitution is a mark of extra ordinary dignity.

1065. Nothing is sweeter than thin gruel earned by one's hard work.

1066. Begging for water to quench the thirst of even a cow is a disgraceful thing.

1067. I, Implore beggars not to beg of people who hide their money and refuse to give anything in charity.

1068. The unsafe raft of begging will split when it strikes on the rock of refusal.

1069. To think of misery in begging is enough to melt one's heart; but to think of refusal is enough to break it.

1070. A refusal depresses a beggar to the utmost; But where can the conscience of one who refuses to give charity hide?

ON MEANNESS

1071. The unscrupulous men resemble others in physical appearance completely; (It is only in character and conduct, the men of virtue differ from the unscrupulous men).

1072. Blessed indeed are the unscrupulous, for they do not suffer from anxieties and troubles of those who have a sensitive conscience.

1073. Gods, according to legends, do what they please and are bound by no restraints of conduct unlike human beings. Similarly the unscrupulous men do as they please and are bound by no restraint of conscience or conduct.

1074. An unscrupulous man fells proud of himself when he sees another who is more unscrupulous than himself.

1075. Unscrupulous men are motivated only by fear of punishment. They observe restraints only under the threat of punishment. Sometimes, they are motivated by operating on their greed.
(Fear of punishment and greed are the Two principal motives to move unscrupulous men).

1076. Drum beating precedes any announcement in a village. Similarly a base fellow is ever ready to reveal to others all the secrets he has heard.

1077. The inferior man will not part with anything except to those who would hit him on his cheek.

1078. A sugar cane yields juice only when it is crushed; Similarly an inferior man gives alms reluctantly and that too when there is no other alternative; where as a man of Virtue gives alms as soon as a request is made for them.

1079. An inferior man will try to find faults with others out of envy, as soon as he sees them enjoying better clothing and food than himself.

1080. An inferior man hastens to sell himself as soon as a calamity overtakes him. For what else is he fitted?

Sources

1. Thirukkuaral by Rev. Drew, 1840
2. Tirukural by V.R. Ramachandra Dikshitar (1949)
3. Kural by C. Raja Gopalachari, 1947
4. Tiruvalluvar by S. Maharajann, (1979)
5. Tirukural by Challa Radha Krishana Sarma, M.A., M.Lit., Ph.D (1989)
6. Sreevani by G. Gali. Gunasekhar, M.A., M.Phil., Ph.D., (1993).

19

SRI SANKARACHARYA AND HIS MESSAGE

Sri Sankaracharya, one of the greatest of Indian philosophers and religious reformers was born in *788 A.D.* (1210 years ago) on the banks of the *PURNA river* in *Kerala* in the small village of *KALADI,* about six miles from ALWAYE.

SHIVAGURU and *ARYAMBA* were his parents. *They were Namboodri Brahmins.* Shivaguru was a great devotee of LORD SIVA, as was Aryamba. Sankara was a precocious child. He was remarkably intelligent and had an excellent memory that surprised even elders. By the time he was *eight,* he had become conversant with the SASTRAS, and completed his formal education.

About this time Shivaguru, his *father died.* The responsibility of bringing up the boy was now solely on the mother Aryamba. She brought him up with great care an affection. Sankara also loved his mother deeply.

One morning when Sankara was bathing in the Purna river, a *crocodile* caught hold of one of his legs. Sankara shouted for help, but to no avail. Sankara cried out to his mother "Mother! the crocodile may release me from its hold, if I renounce the world and become a *SANYASI* (ASCETIC)". Aryamba was put in to a dilemma. She wanted to see her son alive at any cost, so she reluctantly gave her permission to Sankara's request. Sankara chanted the mantra of Renunciation, and before he had uttered the mantra thrice, the crocodile released its deadly hold, and disappeared in to the river. Sankara came out of the river safely.

Young *Sankara* barely *eight years in age,* renounced the world and took leave of his mother after promising to his mother, that he would hasten to her side in her last moments wherever he was, and perform her funeral rites.

Sankara proceeded north, ward in search of a *GURU.* He reached the banks of *NARMADA RIVER* where lived a philosopher-saint named GOVINDAPADA. *GOVINDAPADA* accepted Sankara as his disciple and initiated him into Sanyasa. *For eight years* Govindapada taught Sankara, the DARSHANAS, and the VEDANTA, and the mystic processes of SADHANA and DHYANA etc.

One day the river NARMADA was in spate. The flood threatened the villages on its banks, including the ASHRAMAM of Govindapada with inundation. *According to the legend,* Sankara stopped the fury of the flood, using his "YOGIC POWERS". The flood receded and all were saved. Gonvindapada needed no further proof of the greatness of his extraordinary disciple. *Govindapada* commanded Sankara to go to *KASHI (Present day VARANASI)*, and write a commentary on the *BRAHMA SUTRAS*". *Sankara* set out for *KASHI.*

SANKARACHARYA AT KASHI

In those times, Kashi was a great centre of learning and spirituality. In those days, no teacher ever became great, till his learning was accepted by the PANDITS in KASHI. *Sri Sankaracharya* wrote his commentaries on the *GEETHA, UPANISHADS,* and the *BRAHMASUTRAS OF VYASA, at Kashi.* Pupils gathered around him, to hear his exposition of the VEDANTA. Many came to see him, and became his ardent followers.

From Kashi, Sri Sankaracharya went to *PRAYAG,* where lived *KUMARILA BHATTA.* Kumarila Bhatta was a great authority on *PURVA MIMAMSA.* This school of thought considered ritualism (Karmakanda) as the only way to liberation (MOKSHA). Sankaracharya wanted to have a debate with him. Kumarila Bhatta was about to end his life by *self immolation* in a fire, to atone for the sin of trying to learn Buddhist doctrine from Buddhist teachers, and he directed Sankaracharya, to his disciple, *Mandana Misra,* and to have his dialectical contest with him.

Sankaracharya travelled from Prayaga to *Mahismati* on the banks of *Narmada River* to meet *Mandana Misra. Mandana Misra* and his equally learned wife, *Ubhaya Bharati,* were held in the highest esteem by the scholars of the time. Sankaracharya challenged Mandana Misra for a debate to which the latter agreed. Ubhaya Bharati was appointed the judge. It was agreed that Sankaracharya, if defeated in the debate, would give up Sanyasa and marry. If Mandana Misra was defeated, he would renounce the world and become a Sanyasi.

The debate began in right earnest and continued for many days without any break. The debate lasted for *seventeen days.* At last, Ubhaya Barati declared, that Sankarcharya had defeated her husband. However as she was Mandana Misra's ARTHANGINI (wife), her contention was that Sankaracharyas's victory was therefore not complete, until she was also defeated in the debate. Sankaracharya took up her challenge. Ubhaya Bharati questioned him in detail about Kamasastra, and various aspects of the art of making love. Sankaracharya was now puzzled, and was not able to answer her. He requested her to give him *a month's time,* and promised to return and resume the debate.

According to the legend, at that time *KING AMARUKA,* (the king of Bengal) had just died. Shankaracharya left his own body in charge of his disciples, and by means of yogic powers entered the dead body of King AMARUKA. The king came back to life. Sankaracharya lived in the king's physical body and soon learnt all about the Kamasastra and the art of making love. Sankaracharya left the king's body and re-entered his own physical body left in charge of his disciples by means of a *"yogic vidya"* called *"PARAKAYA PRAVESAM"*. Sankaracharya resumed the incomplete debate with *UBHAYABHARATI* and answered all her questions, and finally defeated her in the debate. *Mandana Misra and ubhayabharati* accepted *Sankaracharya* as their GURU, and joined his ascetic order.

Sankaracharya now toured all over *India,* and met the leaders of different schools of thought.

He convinced them, with arguments and established the supremacy and truth of *ADVAITA,* which he expounded in his commentaries. Sankaracharya was honoured by the royal courts, and the people of India, as the preeminent leader among the scholars and ascetics of his day.

Sankaracharya's tour took him to the *SOUTH INDIA.* When he reached *SHRINGERI,* he knew by intuition, that his mother's end was near. He remembered the promise he had given her. Leaving his disciples, Sankaracharya rushed to his mother's side. On seeing her son, Aryamba shed tears of joy. She had also heard of her son's great spiritual victories. It was the supreme moment of her life. Sankaracharya composed the *"VISHNU BHUJANGA STOTRA",* and enabled his mother to have the vision of *MAHAVISHNU (NARAYANA).* With the divine name of MAHAVISHNU on her lips, and her son by her side *ARYAMBA* passed away.

Sankaracharya requested, his relatives the Namboodri Brahmins of his village, to help him carry his mother's body to the cremation ground. But they refused to cooperate on the ground, that a Sanyasi should not perform funeral rites, according to scriptures. Sankaracharya was unable to remove the dead body of his mother, out of his house. He made a pyre of plantain stems, in the backyard of his house. He then cut the dead body in to pieces, carried the pieces one by one, and laid them on the pyre and completed the funeral rites. The dead body was soon consumed by the flames.

Sankaracharya now set on another journey from *Rameswaram* to the *HIMALAYAS.* He composed hundreds of devotional poems. Wherever he went, he sanctified all the places, by his holy presence – *temples, mathas* and *rivers.* When he was at *KEDARNATH,* he realized that his earthly life had come to an end. *He was only thirty two years old.* One morning he entered a cave in the *HIMALAYAS,* and never again was he seen in the world of mortals. On that eve, a comet moved slowly across the sky, reached *MOUNT KAILAS,* and disappeared behind it.

Sankaracharya established *MATHAS* in *SHRINGERI, BADRINATH, DWARAKA* and *PURI.* They stand to this day, a lasting homage to his revered memory. He reorganised the ancient order of SANYASIS, and prescribed the vows and rules for its ten sub orders. He also reorganised the *KUMB MELA* at *PRAYAG,* where for centuries people have been going *every twelve years,* to bathe at the *TRIVENI SANGAM.* Sri Sankarcharya was one of the greatest religious leaders, and spiritual thinkers of all time. He was an *ascetic,* a *saint,* a *philosopher* and a *religious reformer.* As a philosopher- saint of INDIA, Sri Sankaracharya will be remembered for all times to come.

VIGNANA RATNAMALIKA – SRI SANKARACHARYA

1. KO ANDHO? YO KAARYA RATAHA
   Who is a blind man?
   One who performs deeds not prescribed by DHARMA.
2. *KO BADHIRO? YO HETAANI NASRUNOTI*
   Who is a deaf man?
   One who refuses to listen the voice of wisdom.
3. *KO MOOKO? YAHA KAALE PRIYANIVAKTUM NA JAANATI*
   Who is a dumb man?
   One who does not discuss about spiritual matters with those who know more than himself.

4. *KIM DAANAM? ANAA KAANKSHUM*
   What is meant by a DAANA?
   Daana is a gift given to another, even without a request from the other for such a gift.
5. *KIM MITRAM? YO NIVARAYATI PAAPAAT*
   Who is a friend?
   One who keeps you away from EVIL.
6. *KO ALANKAARAHA? SEELAM.*
   What is an adornment?
   A man's good character and conduct are his adornments.
7. *KIM VAACHYAM MANDANAM? SATYAM.*
   What imparts credibility to one's speech?
   Truth imparts credibility to one's speech.
8. *KIM SOCHYAM? KAARPANYAM*
   What is the root of sorrow?
   GREED and AVARICE are the source of sorrow.
9. *SATI VIBHAVE KIM PRASASTAM? OUDAARYAM.*
   What is the most excellent of all qualities? GENEROSITY
10. *KIM POOJYO VIDVADBHIHE? SWABHAAVATAHA SARVADA VINEETOYAHA*
    Who is esteemed by the PANDITAS? A man of humility.
11. *KIM AHARNISAM ANU CHINTAM? BHAGAVACCHARANAM NA SAMSARAHA*
    On what should a man reflect through the day and night?
    One should reflect on and worship the creator of the universe and not waste time thinking about this world.
12. *CHAKSHUSMANTO PYAANDHAHA KOSYUHU? YE NAASTIKA MANUJAHA*
    Who is a blind man, inspite of possessing eyes?
    One who is not aware of the creater of universe, is deemed to be blind, inspite of possessing eyes.
13. *KAM PANGUM EHA PRADHITO? VRAJATI CHA YO VAARDHAKE TEERDHAM*
    Who is a lame fellow?
    One who sets out on a spiritual pilgrimage in his old age.
14. *KIM TEERDHAM APICHA MUKHYAM? CHITTA MALAM YAN NIVARTAYATI*
    Which is the best place for a pilgrimage?
    Any place, where one can get rid of all impurities of ones mind.
15. *KIM SMARTAVYAM PURUSHIHI? HARINAMA SADAA NA YAVANEE BHASHA*
    On what subject should a man constantly think about?

One should never waste his time in frivolous speech.

16. ***KOHINA VAACHYAHA SUDHIYAA? PARADOSHA CHAANRUTAM TADVAT***
What should a wise man avoid at all times?
A wise man should avoid SLANDER and LIES in his speech at all times.
17. ***KIM SAMPAADYAHA MANUJIHA? VIDYA, VITTAM, BALAM, YASAHA, PUNYAM***
For what things should a man strive for in his life?
1. WISDOM 2. WEALTH 3. POWER 4. NAME AND FAME and 5. PUNYAM (MERIT).
18. ***KAHA SARVAGUNA VINAASEE? LOBHAHA***
What is the evil quality that destroys all other good qualities of a man?
AVARICE is the evil quality, that destroys all other good qualities of a man.
19. ***SATRUSCHA KAHA? KAMAHA***
What quality can be considered as an ENEMY of a man?
"UNCONTROLLED DESIRES" (Kama), are to be considered as enemies of a man.
20. ***KAA KALPALATAA LOKE? SACCHISHYARPITA VIDYAA***
What is the most fruitful thing in this world?
The most fruitful thing in this world, is the knowledge imparted to a deserving disciple.
21. ***KO KSHAYA VATAVRUKSHAHA SYATT? VIDHIVATSA PAATRA DATTA DAANAM YAT***
What is the best amongst the gifts?
A gift that is given to a deserving person is to be considered as the best of gifts.
22. ***KIM SASTRAM SARVESHAAM? YUKTIHE***
What should a man possess, to guide him in his life?
KNOWLEDGE AND DISCRMININATION. (where power alone is futile, success can be achieved by using knowledge combined with discrimination).
23. ***MAATAA HAKA? DHENUHU***
What should be revered as a mother?
A cow which saves an infant, with its milk, should be revered as a mother.
24. ***KIM NU BALAM? YADDHIRYAM.***
What is the source of a man's power?
The source of a man's power is his courage only.
25. ***KO MRUTYUHU? YAD AVADHAANA RAHITATVAM***
What is DEATH?
"CARELESSNESS" leads to DEATH.
26. ***KUTRA VISHAM? DUSTAJANE***
Where do you find EVIL?
Evil is found in the hearts of the DECEITFUL men.
27. ***KIM EHA ASOWCHAM? RUNAM NRUNAM.***
What is an undesirable evil?
Indebtedness is an undesirable evil.
28. ***KIM ABHAYA MIHA? VIRAGYAM***

What is the source of fearlessness?
"DETACHMENT" is the source of fearlessness.

29. *BHAYAMAPE KIM? VITTAMEVA SARVESHAAM*
What is the source of fear?
WEALTH is the source of fear.
(To protect and safeguard the wealth one has acquired is the main source of fear)

30. *KADURLABHAA NARAANAAM? HARI BHAKTEHE*
What is the quality, that is most difficult to cultivate?
Reverence to the creator of the universe is the quality that is the most difficult to cultivate.

31. *PAATAKIM CHA KIM? HIMSAA*
What is the greatest evil?
VIOLENCE (CRUELTY) is the greatest evil.

32. *KOHI BHAGAVAT PRIYA HA SYAAT? YO ANYAM NO DVIJAYE ANUDYIGNAHA*
Who deserves the love of GOD?
One who is not unsettled by ups and downs of life and who imparts his mental poise, to those around him, deserves the love of GOD ("STHITAPRAJNA)".

33. *SARVA SUKHAANAAM BEEJAM KIM? PUNYAM*
What is the source of all happiness?
MERIT (PUNYAM) is the source of all happiness.

34. *DUKHAMAPI KUTAHA? PAAPAAT.*
What is the source of all sorrows?
EVIL (DEEDS) are the source of sorrow.

35. KASTIY ISVARYAM? YAHA KILA SANKARA ARAADHAYED BHAKTYA
Who is a rich man?
One who worships SIVA is to be regarded as a rich man.

36. *SAADHU BALAM KIM? DIVAM.*
Who is the source of strength of DEVOTEES?
GOD is the source of strength of DEVOTEES.

37. *DIYAM KIM? YAT SUKRUTAM.*
What is meant by divinity?
Divinity is the sum total of all good deeds done by SELF only.

38. *KAHA SUKRUTEE? SLAAGAYATE YAHA SADBHIHE*
Who is a man of virtue?
One who is esteemed by good men is to be considered as a man of virtue.

39. *KO DHANYA HA? SANYAASEE*
Who is a liberated soul?
One who has renounced the world is a liberated soul.

40. *KO MAANYAHA? PANDTAHA SAADHHU*
Who deserves the respect of all?
A learned ascetic deserves the respect of all.

41. *KAHA SEVYO? YO DAATAA*
Who deserves the services of all?
A man of generosity deserves the services of all.
42. *KO DAATAA? YORDHI TRUPTI MAA TANUTE*
Who is to be considered as a DONOR?
one who gives a gift to a deserving needy person is to be regarded as a donor.
43. *KAHA SOORO? YO BHEETA TRAATA.*
Who is a man of valour?
One who comes to the rescue of terror-striken, is called a man of valour.
44. *TRAATAA CHA KAHA? SAHA GURUHU*
Who is a saviour?
One who shows you the path of liberation is called a saviour
45. *KOHE JAGADGURU RUKTAHA? SAMBHUHU*
Who is the master of the universe?
SAMBHU (SIVA) is the master of the universe.
46. *JNANAM KUTAHA? SIVADEVA*
Who is the source of all knowledge?
"PARAMASIVA" is the source of all knowledge.
47. *MUKTIM LABHATE KASMAAT? MUKUNDA BHAKTEHA.*
What is the way to MOKSHA?
The way to MOKSHA, is through devotion and worship of MUKUNDA.
48. *MUKUNDAHA KAHA? YASTAARAYED AVIDYAM.*
Who is MUKUNDA?
One who shows you the path of liberation is called MUKUNDA.
49. *KAA CHAA VIDYAA? YADAATMANO SPOORTHIHE*
What is meant by ignorance?
Ignorance is a state where one is not aware of his SOUL.
50. *KASYA NA SOKO? YAHA SYADKRODHAHA*
Who is free from sorrow?
One who has conquered 'ANGER', is said to be free from sorrows.
51. *KIM SUKHAM? TUSTHI*
What is happiness?
Contentment leads to happiness.
52. *KO RAAJAA? RANJANAKRUT*
Who is a king?
One who has conquered his five senses, and realized his true nature is a king indeed.
53. *KASCHASVAA? NEECHASEVAKOYAHA SYAAT*
Who is said to be worse than a dog?
One who serves an inferior person is said to be worse than a dog.
54. *PAATRAM KIM ANNADANE? KSHUDITAM*
Who deserves a gift of food?
One who is hungry deserves a gift of food.

55. ***KO ARCHOHE? BHAGAVAD AVATARAHA***
Who deserves worship by all?
Any AVATARA of GOD, deserves devotion and worship by all.
56. ***KASCHA BHAGAVAAN?***
Who is a GOD?
MAHESA, SANKARA, NARAYANA etc. are all the various names of GOD.
57. ***PHALAMAPI BHAGAVAD BHAKTE HE KIM? TALLOKA SVAROOPA SAAK SHATVAM***
What is the result of devotion towards the CREATOR OF UNIVERSE?
Self-realization is the end result of devotion to and worship of the creator of universe.
58. ***MOKSHACHA KO? HYAA AVIDYAASTAMAYAHA***
What is meant by MOKSHA?
When IGNORANCE about SELF is rooted out,
MOKSHA is experienced.
59. ***KAHA SARVAVEDA BHOOHA? ADHACHOM***
What is the origin and end of VEDAS?
"OM" is the origin and end of VEDAS.
60. ***KIM UPAADEYAM? GURU VACHANAM.***
What should be implicitly obeyed?
The instructions of a GURU should be implicitly obeyed at all times.
61. ***HEYAMAPTI CHA KIM? AKAARYAM***
What should be avoided?
EVIL DEEDS should be avoided at all times.
62. ***KO GURUHU? ADHIGATA TATVAHA SISHYA HITAA YODYATAHA-SATATAM***
Who should be regarded as a GURU?
One who earnestly works for the welfere and uplift of his disciples should be regarded as a GURU.
63. ***TVARITAM KIM KARTAVYAM VIDOOSHAAM? SAMSARA SANTATI CHEDAHA***
What should be the immediate concern of a PANDITA (learned man)?
To be liberated from the eternal cycle of births and deaths, should be the immediate concern of a PANDITA.
64. ***KIM MOKSHA TARORBEEJAM? SAMYAGNANAM KRIYAASIDDHAM***
What is the way to MOKSHA?
1. To realize the true nature of existence.
2. Not to be swayed by likes and dislikes.
3. And to be steadfast, under all conditions, these three steps, lead the way to MOKSHA.
65. ***KIM SAMSAARO SAARAM? BAHU SOPI VICHINTANAMAANA MIDAMEVA***
What is the purpose of existence in the world?
To reflect about the temporary nature of human existence and suffer sorrow.

66. ***KIM MANUJESHVISTA TA MAM? SVA PARAHITAA YODYATAM JANMA***
What should a man aspire for?
To strive not only for his welfare, but also for the welfare of those associated with him, should be the aim of a man.
67. ***MADIREVA YEHA JANAKAHA? SNEHA HA***
What is that clouds the mind like an intoxicating drink?
Indiscriminate indulgence in sense pleasures (the activities of the five sense organs), clouds the mind like an intoxicating drink.
68. ***KECHA DASYAVO? VISHAYAHA***
What ruins a life?
Indiscriminate indulgence in sense pleasures ruins a life.
69. ***KA BHAVA VALLE? TRUSHNAA***
What are the roots of a creeper called 'SAMSARA'?
'Inordinate Desires' are the roots of a creeper called 'SAMSARA'
70. ***KO VIREE? YASTVANUDYOGA***
Who is the enemy of a man?
INODOLENCE (LAZINESS) is the enemy of a man.
71. ***KIM JEEVITAM? ANAVADYAM***
What is the purpose of a human life?
To lead an examplary life is the purpose of existence here (in this world)
72. ***KIM JAADYAM? PATHATOPYA ANABHYASA***
What is meant by a mental disease?
One who does not practice, what he has thoroughly studied, is said to be a victim of a mental disease.
73. ***KO JAAGARTE? VIVEKEE***
Who is a man of DILIGENCE?
One who possesses discriminating intelligence, is said to be a man of diligence.
74. ***KAA NIDRAA? MOODHATO JANTO***
What is meant by sleep?
One who is not aware of the purpose of his existence, is said to be asleep, even though he is physically awake.
75. ***NALINEE DALAGATA JALA MATTARALAM KIM?***
YOUVANNAH, DHANAH CHA AYUHU
What are as transient as water drops on a LOTUS/LEAF?
Youth, wealth and human life are as
Transient as water drops on a lotus leaf.
76. ***KADHAYA PUNAHA KE SASINAHA KIRANA SAMAAHA? SAJJANAAEVA***
Whose company is more pleasant than even the moonlight?
The company of men of virtue is more pleasant than even the moonlight.
77. ***KO NARAKAHA? PARAVASATAA***
What is meant by hell?
One who is a slave to another, is said to be worse than one who lives in a hell.

78. *KIM SOUKYAM? SARVASANGA VIRATIRYAA*
What is happiness?
Happiness consists in renouncing the world to become an ASCETIC
79. *KIM SATYAM? BHOOTAHITAM*
What is the nature of TRUTH?
One who works for the welfare of all, realises the nature of TRUTH.
80. *PRIYOCHA KIM PRAANINAMM? ASAVAHA*
What is the most precious thing for any living creature?
The most precious thing for any living creature is its own existence (or life).
81. *KO ANARDHA PHALO? MAANAM*
What is the evil quality that is sure to ruin a man?
Egoism is the evil quality, that is sure to ruin a man.
82. *KAA SUKHAD? SAADHUJANA MITREE*
What is the source of happiness?
Association with men of virtue, is always a source of happiness.
83. *SARVA VYASANA VINAASE KODAKSHA? SAVADHAA TYAAGEE*
Who can extricate a man from the clutches of all vices?
A SAINT who has renonced the world, can extricate a man from the clutches of all vices.
84. *KIM MARANAM? MOORKHATVAM*
What is equal to DEATH?
IGNORANCE is equal to DEATH.
85. *KIM CHAA ANARDHAM? YADAVASARE DATTAM*
What should be considered as an invaluable help?
Any timely help rendered by another should be considered as an invaluable help.
86. *AMARANAANTIKAM SALYAM? PRACHANNAM YATKRUTAM PAPAM*
What torments a man until his death?
An evil deed done by him in secrecy, torments a man until his death.
87. *KA AHARNESA MANU CHINTYA? SAMSAARAA SAARATAA NATU PRAMAADAA*
On what aspect of the world, should one think about, throughout the day and night?
One should think about MAYA of this SAMSARA throughout the day and night.
88. *KAA PREYASEE VIDHEYAA? KARUNAA DEENESHU SAJJANE MITREE*
What qualities deserve our love and worship?
Compassion for all destitutes deserves our love at all times.
Association with men of virtue should be sought after at all times.
89. *PAATUM KARNAAM JALIBHIHE KEM AMRUTAM EHA UJYATE? SADUPADESAHA*
What should be considered as the best advice?
Advice given by a man of virtue should be regarded as the best advice.

BHAJA GOVINDAM (FROM MOHA MUDGARAHA)

(MOHA = DELUSION, MUDGARAHA = Heavy Hammer MOHA
MUDGARAHA = A Heavy Hammer which destroys Maya or DELUSION)

– SRI. SANKARAACHARYA

1. BHAJA! GOVINDAM BHAJA! GOVINDAM
GOVINDAM BHAJA MOODHAMATE
SAMPRAPTE SANNIHETA KAALE
NAHE NAHE RAKSHATI "DUKRUN KARANE"!!

Worship Govinda, whorship GOVINDA,
Worship Govinda, oh, foolish mind,
When you are at death's door,
The rules of grammer, which you are trying to master will be of no avail.
"DUKRING" is an aphorism in the famous grammer of 'Paanini'.

2. MOODHA! JAHEEHE! DHANAAGAMA TRUSHNAAM
KURU SADBUDDHIM MANASI VITRUSHNAAM
YALLABHASE NIJAKARMO PAATTAM
VITTA TENA VINODAYA! CHITTAM!!

Fool! give up this insatiable desire for wealth,
Be wise and cherish contentment,
Be happy, and content with the fruits of your own labour.

3. NAAREE STANABHARA NAABHEEDESAM
DRUSTVAA MAAGAA MOHAAVESAM
ETAN MAAMSAVASAADI VIKAARAM
MANASI VICHINTAYA! VAARAM VAARAM

Enticed by woman's beauty, her breasts and the region of her navel,
Do not allow yourself to be lost,
They are only forms of mere flesh,
Think of them as such, every time you look at them.

Sankaracharya says "Do not get overpowered by lust (Maayaa Mohaavesam). You must pause and think on this beauty of a woman, which captivates the mind to such an extent. Is it not mere flesh and skin? and it is wise not to be taken in by external appearances". Control of senses leads to a sense of freedom in the mind, and tranquillity is the end result. Craving and lust are apparent pleasures, which conceal inevitable pain and sorrow.

4. NALINEEDALAGATA JALA MATITARALAM
TADVAT JEEVITA MATISAYA CHAPALAM
VIDDHI VYADHYABHIMAANA GRASTAM
LOKAM SOKAHATAM CHA SAMASTAM!!

"Water drops on a lotus leaf move hither and thither and disappear,
So too is human life, precarious and unstable,
Anxiety, sorrow and diseases are its constituents"
Seek refuge in GOD to face the afflictions of existence.

5. YAAVAD VITTOPAARJANA SAKTA
STAVA DRAKTO NIJAPARIVĀRAHA
PASCHAA JEEVATI JARJARA DEHE
VAARTAAM KOPI NA PRUCHATI GEHE!!

"As long as you are able to earn, so long will your relatives be attached to you.
After that, when your body has become weak and old and disease ridden,
None will speak to you, even in your own home."

The love that your relatives show to you, and their interest in your welfare, depend on the benefit they can derive or hope to derive from you. Do not be deceived seeing relatives and others gather round you now. When you have become weak, old and disease-ridden and no longer able to earn money, all of them are sure to abandon you to your fate.

6 YAAVAT PAVANO NIVASATI DEHE
YAAVAT PRUCCHATI KUSALAM GEHE
GATAVATI VAYOU DEHAA PAAYE
BHAARYA BIBHYATI TASMIN KAAYE!!

"People at home enquire about your welfare, so long as you are alive,
when life-breath takes leave of your body, even your wife is afraid of your lifeless body"

Sankaracharya warns against undue attachment to any person including the wife. Go about your life fully aware of the TRUTH about things. Think about the following deeply a Who is a wife? Who is a son? What is the nature of bondage between your life and theirs? *These bonds subsist only so long as life lasts. It is wise to know the limitations of every relationship.* It is futile to mistake the fleeting for the permanent.

7. BAALA STAAVAT KREEDASKTA
TARUNA STAAVA TARUNEESAKTAHA
VRUDDHA STAAVA CHINTAA SAKTAHA
PARE BRAHMANI KOPI NA SAKTAHA!!

"Childhood passes away in play,
youth passes away in pursuit of love and women,
old age passes away in endless worries,
Alas! at no stage does a man worship GOD".

8. KAATE KAANTAA? KASTE PUTRAHA?
SAMSAAROYA MATEEVA VICHITRAHA?

KASYA TVAM? KAHA KUTA AAYAATA
STATVAM CHINTAYA! YADEDAM BHRAATAHA!!

"Who is your wife? Who is your son?
These relationships are inscrutable indeed.
Who are you? To whom do you belong?
From where did you come
Brother! think deeply on these bonds".

Sankaracharya asks you to think deeply on the following: "From where did you come? Where were you prior to this existence? Who is your wife? What is the permanent relation between the wife and yourself? Who is your son? What is the permanent relation between the son and yourself? Why all this anxiety and attachment? *Do not confuse the perishing body with the imperishable soul;* Human existence is a wonderful, enigma. Reflect on all this for a while and your delusions will slowly loose their grip on you. *Finally remember that the relation between this world and yourself is temporary.*

9. SAT SANGATVE NISSANGATVAM
NISSANGATVE NIRMOHATVAM
NIRMOHATVE NISCHALATATVAM
NISCHALATATVE JEEVANMUKTIHE!!

"The company of men of virtue destroys all undue attachments;
when attachments are gone, there is no delusion;
when there is no delusion, the mind is steady;
when the mind is steady, liberation is close by."

As attachments loose their grip, infatuation is reduced. When infatuation is reduced, one attains equanimity and peace. These changes evolve one from the other, like the leaf, flower and fruit of a tree.

10. VAYASIGATE KAHA KĀMA VIKAARAHA?
SUSKHE NEERE KAHA KAASAARAHA?
KSHEENE VITTEKAHA PARIVAARO?
JNATE TATVE KA SAMSAARAHA!!

"When youth is gone, where is the scope for sexual relations;
There is no lake, when its water has dried up;
When wealth is gone, there are none with you;
When the SELF is realized, there is no SAMSAARA"

As old age creeps, sexual relations vanish of their own accord; As water dries up, the lake becomes a mere parched ground; *when your money is gone all your relatives and associates disappear;* when the ATMAAN (SELF) is realized, the existence in this world comes to an end.

11. MAA KURU DHANA JANA YOUVANA GARVAM
HAARATI NEMESHAT KAALA SARVAM
MAAYAAMAYA MIDAM AKHILAM HETVAA
BRAHMAPADAM TYAM PRAVESA VEDETVAA!!

"Do not be proud of your wealth, youth and kinsmen
Death may snatch you away in a minute from all;
Realise that youth, wealth and kinsmen are all a part of Maaya (DELUSION);
Renounce MAAYA and enter the path of liberation (BRAHMA PADAM)

12. DINAYAA MINYOW SAAYAM PRAATAHA
SISIRA VASANTOW PUNA RAAYATAHA
KALAHA KREEDATI GACCHAT AAYU
STADAPI NA MUCCHAT ATYAASAAYAYUHU!!

Day and night, morning and evening,
Winter and spring come and go in a cycle,
Thus while TIME moves on inexorably, the life span of all living creatures is relentlessly cut down;
yet, a man is not able to overcome "DESIRE".

13. KAA TE KAANTAA DHANAGATA CHINTAA?
VAATULA KIM TAVA NAASTI NIYANTAA?
TRIJAGATI SAJJANA SANGATI REKAA
BHAVATI BHAVAARNAVA TARANE NOWKAA!!

"O! you! fickle minded fool! why do you worry about your wife and wealth? know you not, that in all the three worlds, the association with men of virtue, is the only means to sail across the sea of SAMSARAA".

One should think on the attachments that bind us to the world, and examine them carefully. Take the case of the wife. What is the connection between her soul and mine. Why should one depend on the other? What is the relationship between her and myself in the present, past and future lives of both of us? Do souls have kinship? Once you are dead, what is the relationship between your wife and yourself? *Why this undue worry about a relationship of a single life in the eternal cycle of births and deaths?*

When this is the case with the wife, what needs be said about wealth? *It is something inanimate.* What is the relationship of wealth to you, once you are dead? Why do you worry about it?

14. JATELO MUNDEE LUNCHITA KESAHA
KAASHAAYAAMBARA BAHUKRUTA VESHAHA
PASYANNAPI CHA NA PASYATI MOODHO
UDARANIMITTAM BAHUKRUTA VESHAHA!!

"The sanyasis with the matted locks, shaven heads and kasshaya robes, all these are mere disguises to cheat the people and to fill their bellies. These 'Sanaysis' have eyes but fail to see the SELF"
Renouncing is not a matter of external show. It is a victory that has to be won by rooting out desires from ones mind. The show of renunciation of most of the sanyasis is quite often a means to fill the belly. *Sankaracharya urges* such people to give up their vain pretensions.

15. ANGAM GALITAM PALITAM MUNDAM
DASANA VEHEENAM JAATAM TUNDAM
VRUDDHO YATTI GRUHEETVAA DANDAM
TADAPE NA MUNCHAT ATYAASAA PINDAM!!

"Old age has overtaken the body; the hairs on the head have all turned grey; all the teeth have dropped off;
The old man moves about leaning on a stick;
yet this decrepit old fellow, is not able to come out of the clutches of "DESIRES".

16. AGRE VAHANEHE PRUSTE BHANOO
RAATROU CHUBUKA SAMARPITA JAANUHU
KARATALA BHIKSHA TARUTALA VAASA
STADAPE NA MUNCHAT ATYAASAA PAASAHA!!

"Sitting before the fire or with the sun at the back sleeping at night with the knees tucked under the chin, begging for alms, living homeless under the trees, and *even in this state of utter destitution, he is not able to come out the clutches of DESIRE".*

17. KURUTE GANGAA SAAGARAGAMANAM
VRATA PARIPAALANA MADHAVAA DAANAM
JNAANA VEHEENA SARVA MATENA
MUKTIM NA BHAJATE JANMASATENA!!

"one may bathe in the Ganga or the sea
one may observe every austerity and VRATAS; one may make gifts lavishly;
yet none of these will bestow on him MOKSHA even in a hundred lives, if he does not acquire true knowledge".
The state of mind free from desires is what is known as "JNANA". If desires are vanquished and eliminated "JNANA" will arise of itself.

18. SURAMANDIRA TARUMOOLA NIVASSAHA
SAYYAA BHOOTALA MAJENAM VAASAHA
SARVA PAREGRAHA BHOGATYAAGAHA
KASYA SUKHAM NA MAROTI VERAAGAHA!!

"If one can sleep happily in temples, or under the trees, or on the bare ground;
If one can be happy, to move around wrapped in skins;

If one has renounced all attachments, possessions and pleasures, who can rob such a man his happiness that arises from "RENUNCIATION".

19. YOGARATO VAA BHOGARATO VAA
SANGARATO VAA SANGAVEHEENA HA
YASYA BRAHMANI RAMATE CHITTAM
NANDATE NANDATE NANDATYEVA!!

"One who has merged his soul in PARABRAHMAM, will always be happy, whether he is practising YOGA, or enjoying some pleasures, or whether in company or in solitude; such a one is indeed truly happy.

Pleasure is a state of mind. Pleasure obtained through the sense organs is of one kind. But the bliss that results from the union of SOUL with GOD is a joy that knows no limitations of time, place and duration.

20. BHAGAVAGEETAA KINCHI DADHEETAA
GANGA JALA LAVA KANEKAA PEETA
SAKRUDAPI YENA MURAARI SAMARCHAA
KRIYATE TASYA YAMOPI NA CHARCHAAM.

"A little study of BHAGAVADC EETA, drinking a drop of GANGA WATER, and worship of MURARI – these will save you even from death".
KINCHIT ADHEETAA = (read at least a little bit – of Bhaghavad GEETA)

21. PUNARAPE JANANAM PUNARAPI MARANAM
PUNARAPE JANANEE JHATHARE SAYANAM
EHA SAMSAARE BAHU DUSTAARE
KRUPAYAA PAARE PAAHE MURAARE!!

"Birth and then death,
And getting in to a mother's womb, over and over again Oh! MURAARI! please save me from this eternal cycle of births and deaths".

22. RADHYAA KARPATA VERACHITAKANDHAHA
PUNYA PUNYA VESARJITA PANDHAAHA
YOGEE YOGANIYOJITA CHITTO
RAMATE BALO UNMATTAVA DEVA!!

"A yogi renounces both the good and evil, and moves around clad in rags, lost in meditation. His SELF is merged in PARABRAHMAM. Such a yogi plays around sometimes like a child, and sometimes behaves like an insane fellow".

23. KASTVAM KOHAM KUTA AAYAATAHA
KA ME JANANEE KO ME TATAHA
ETI PARIBHAVITA NIJA SAMSAARAHA
SARVAM TYAKTVAA SVAPNA VICHAARAHA!!

"Who are you? Who am I? Who is my mother? and who is my father? Reflect on this, The world and its cares are but the cares and anxieties of a dream. If you realize the dream like nature of this world, then you will be able to free yourself from the grip of that dream"

Sankaracharya says "Think about the following deeply; who were you in your previous birth? Prior to this birth in how many wombs had you been confined? Who were you parents in your previous birth? Do you see all those fathers and mothers now? Even if you saw them would you recognise them? or would you feel love and affection for them? *All these illusory forms that you see in this world, arise from one SUBSTACE. Wake up from this dream and try to see the ONE REALITY behind them all. The mirage projected by your KARMA will disappear before BHAKTI. Devotion to, and worship of GOVINDA is the key to open the lock of MAYA of this existence.*

24. TVAYA MAYE SARVATRIKO VISHNU
RVYARDHAM KUPYASI MAYYA SAHESHNUHU
BHAVA SAMACHITTTAM SARVATRA TVAM
VAANCHA SYACHIRAADYADI VISHNUTVAM!!

"There is but one "VISHNU" in all,
Unable to bear with me, you get angry with me in vain,
Try to see your own self in all creatures,
Give up this false sense of difference from others".

25. SATROU MITRE PUTRE BANDOU
MAA KURU YATNAM VIGRAHA SANDHOV
BHAVA SAMACHITTAM SARVATRATVAM
VAANCHA SYACHIRAADYADE VISHNUTVAM!!

"Do not think in terms of friend or enemy, son or relative;
Do not waste your energy in friendship or enmity;
If you wish "MOKSHA", be of equal mind with all".
Attachments are the root cause of all sorrows and MAYA. Friendship or enmity with any one will only add a further load to the already existing attachments. The only way to liberation is by gradually reducing and getting rid of all attachments *one must cultivate a sense of impartiality in dealing with others, at all times.* This attitude of impartiality paves the way to equanimity and helps us to see the essential oneness in everyone and everywhere. *Sankaracharya describes this attitude as "VISHNUTVA".*

26. KAMAM KRODHAM LOBHAM MOHAM,
TYAKTVAA ATMAANAM PASYATE SOHAM,
ATMA JNANA VEHEENAA MOODHA,
STE PACHAYANTE NARAKA NEGOODHAHA!!

"Root out lust, anger, greed and attachments from your mind,
Meditate on who you are; Ask of yourself "who am I",

The fools who fail to realize their "SELF", end up in hell.

A desire takes hold of a man's heart. He thinks that he can be happy if that desire is satisfied. He exerts himself to the utmost for that purpose. But there is no end to the steps on the ladder of desire. This is the inscrutable MAYA of the DESIRE and *once it gets a firm hold on the mind of a man, it leads him on and on and to his end.*

Desires are of various kinds. We would feel ashamed openly to express some of them. We proclaim some of our other desires with pride. Both types of desires grow by what they feed on. Feed the desire; it becomes more hungry. *The hunger of desires is insatiable.*

The moment an evil desire springs in the mind at once it must be eschewed. By merely ordering it to go it will not go. The mind must be diverted to something else. *An evil thought should be replaced by a good thought. This is the secret of the working of a human mind. At any given moment, there is no room in a human mind for two divergent thoughts.* Profiting by this secret of the nature of the mind, one should try to get rid of evil thoughts and desires, by substituting good thoughts and righteous deeds in their place. If one yields to a desire even in the slightest measure, one is lost. If one thinks "My desire lies concealed in my heart; no one need know about it", and thus if one fails to realise the danger, one is sure to be ruined. Once a thought is entertained in ones mind, it easily takes the shape of action very soon. Even if an evil thought remains dormant, it is sure to have its latent effect on the mind.

Kama is a state of mental agitation which desires sexual indulgence.

LOBHA is a state of the mind, which hankers after wealth.

MOHA signifies the futile pursuit of things unaware of their real nature and lack of value. It is the wrong value that we give to things, not knowing what is good and what is evil. *EXAMPLE*: Most of us hanker for the praises of our fellow-men. We know that these are empty words; yet we believe that there is something of value in them, and strive hard to obtain them. However, these time serving praises and cheap flatteries lack any permanent value, and should be eschewed at any cost. Because one finds that he can not get rid of all vices, one should not get discouraged and give up his attempts to eradicate them. Even if one occasionally fails in overcoming evil thoughts and deeds, the very attempt to overcome them will do good on the whole. *The effort one puts in to overcome an evil thought or a deed will rescue him from many more evil the thoughts or deeds.*

If KAMA, LOBHA, and MOHA and KRODHA (Anger) are given a free hand over ones mind, life itself will become unbearable; grief and sorrow will increase. Hence discrimination is indispensable for those who have renounced the world; it is essential for the GRUHASTU, in fact, he needs it a little more, to reduce grief and sorrow in his life.

27. GEYAM GEETAA NAAMA SAHASRAM
DHYEYAM SREEPATI ROOPAM AJASRAM
NEYAM SAJJANA SANGE CHITTAM
DEYAM DEENAJANAAYA CHA VITTAM!!
"Read Bhagavadgeeta and recite the thousand names of "VISHNU,"
Meditate and worship "SREEPATI" in your heart,
Associate always with men of virtue,
Give away your wealth to the destitutes".

28. SUKHATAHA KRIYATE RAMABHOGAHA,
PASCHATD ANTA SAREERE ROGAHA,
YADYAPI LOKE MARANAM SARANAM,
TADAPE NA MUNCHAATI PAPAACHARANAM!!

"Man easily takes to sexual enjoyment,
then alas! many diseases overtake the human body and death ends the show,
yet men do not give up sinful ways".

29. ARTHAM ANARDHAM BHAAVAYA NITYAM
NASTITATA SUKHALESA SATYAM
PUTRAADAPE DHANA BHAAJAAM BHEETEHE
SARVATRISHAA VEHITAA REETEHE!!

"Weath is sure to ruin you in the end,
There is no happiness in the pursuit of wealth,
A wealthy man comes to fear even his own sons,
This is the end result of wealth every where".

One cane work hard and earn to make a living. But *"AVARICE"* comes under a different category. *Avarice is the insatiable hunger to make more and more money irrespective of ones requirements.* The end result of avarice is only grief and sorrow. To acquire wealth and the efforts, to safeguard the wealth acquired go together. One has to safeguard his wealth not only from thiefs, cheats etc. but also from his sons and other heirs to his wealth and property. Natural love and affection are sullied, scheming and calculated manouvres take their place and the end result is the poisoning of all human relationships.

Money is not an end in itself, it is only a means to and end. Money is not a source of happiness by itself. There is a limit to the sum of money, that each man needs. If that limit is exceeded, the end result will be oppressive weight of the excessive money and anxiety on that score. *What every one seeks is happiness.* Forgetting this fundamental principle, we sincerely believe and act in the way, *that money itself is happiness, and become its bond slaves until our end.* What exactly is the reason why you hoard money? You may think "My son is a simpletion, or my daughter is poor and helpless (if she happens to be a widow etc.) and the money I leave to them after may demise will support them". This line of thinking shows that you are not fully aware of the ways of the world. If you observe and enquire carefully, you will learn *that cunning and deceitful relatives* and people gather round the rich but hapless men and women, who have come by money, *defraud them of* what they have, and totally ruin them in the process. It is foolish and naive to think that everything will be all right, if you leave behind (bequeath) a lot of money to your heirs. *Experience belies this hope.*

Do not delude yourself in to the thinking that you can secure everything in this world with money. Do not ruin your life in the endless quest for wealth. Perform your duties without undue attachments. Do not become a miser. IF you can afford, give your money to the deserving poor and needy, and experience the joy in giving to others.

30. PRAANAA YAAMAM PRATYAHAARAM
NITYA NITYA VIVEKA VIHARAM
JAPYA SAMETA SAMADHI VIDHAANAM
KURVA AVADHANAM MAHADAVADHANAM!!

"Pranayamam (Breath Control), control of senses (Pratyahara), discrimination, JAPA, and meditation and finally to enter the state of SAMADHI – attend to these steps on the path of liberation *with care, with great care*"

Sankaracharya says "you are not the body. You are ATMA. The body in which ATMA resides is certainly careworthy; but it is the mind that must be primarily attended to. *The mind is the seat of all our thoughts and activities.* The mind must be guarded very carefully with the help of intelligence and discrimination and control of senses". – "Attend to these things with care, with great care" says Sankaracharya, repeating himself in order to emphasize the importance of the above mentioned steps.

31 GURU CHARANAAMBUJA NIRBHARA BHAKTAHA
SAMSAARAA DACHIRAADBHAVA MUKTAHA
SENDRIYA MAANASA NIYAMAA DEVAM
DRAKSYASI NIJA HRUDAYASTHAM DEVAM!!

"Trust yourself whole heartedly to your GURU,
Freed from the shackles of existence,
with the control of senses and mind,
you will realise the GOD, residing in your heart'

Sankaracharya says "Put your faith in the GURU; your whole faith; you will be freed from the eternal cycle of births and deaths."

At present, it is not possible for everybody to receive instruction from a GURU in person. The practice of being directly instructed by a GURU has almost ceased. A book may serve as a Guru; the sight of a temple tower, an idol of GANESHA,

VENKATESWARA, or ANJANEYA or any of the many forms of VISHNU or SIVA, may help to bring about spiritual awareness and enlightenment.

Human society is based on the principle of *DHARMA* (cooperation). If GREED, AVARICE and EVIL are allowed to replace DHARMA, human society cannot progress for long. Men will not have faith in one another. Every one will have to be suspicious about others, and live in dread of others, and be afflicted by anxiety and hatred. Co-operative life will come to a halt. To stop this disastrous trend of the present day, DHARMA and BHAKTI (DEVOTION to, and worship of GOD) should be ushered in to dethrone EVIL and AVARICE from our hearts.

Sources

1. Bhajagovindam by C. Rajagopalachari and P. Sankaranarayanan, 1965.
2. Sages and Saints of India by B. Manu, 1982.
3. Vignana Ratanmalika by Swami Sundara Chaitanyananda Swamy, 1985.
4. Moha Mudgaraha by B. Rama Mohama Rao, 1989.

20

YAKSHA PRASNA

Mahabharata is one of the greatest epics, that India has produced. *VYASA,* the great sage is the author of the Mahabharata. The Socratic method of question and answer is an ancient method for imparting knowledge, and it has been in vogue in India also for thousands of years.

The Yaksha Prasna episode is described in the *Aranya Parva,* which in turn is a subdivision of the *Vana Parva. Dharamaputra* and *his brothers* were residing in the *DWAITA VANA,* at the time related to this episode. A deer in the forest picked up with its horns, the sticks called ARANI used for making fire and also the churning staff called 'MANTHA', belonging to a Brahmana. (The sticks and staff are used to make a fire, in which Angnihotra oblations are offered, during a yagna). The deer taking these sticks with its antlers, ran away and disappeared in to the forest.

The Brahmana approached Dharmaputra and his brothers and requested their help in tracing the elusive deer and his articles needed for the yagna. As it was the duty of Kshatriya to help a Brahmana in distress, Dharmaputra and his brothers went in pursuit of the deer. They were wearied by the chase and thirsty. Nakula was sent out by Dharmaputra, to look out for a source of water. Nakula found a pond close by. He went to the pond and began to drink, when he heard a *voice saying "The pond is mine. First answer my questions and them drink."* But Nakula disregarded the voice, drank the water in the pond and dropped down *dead.*

Sahadeva, Bhimasena, and *Arjuna* who followed Nakula, drank the water in the pond and died in the same manner. Finally Dharmaputra went to the pond and to his utter dismay found his dead brothers. *YAKSHA* appeared before Dharmaputra and spoke to him "your brothers did not heed my warning, drank the water in the pond and died. *If you wish to live, first answer my questions, and then drink as you please*".

Dharmaputra agreed and then follows YAKSHA PRASNA, consisting of questions of Yaksha and Dharmaputra's answers to them. The questions are sometimes in the nature of puzzles and riddles and can be answered only by a Pandita well versed in the subject. The answers are often as brief and cryptic as the questions and convey a wealth of meaning for the layman as well as for a spiritual aspirant.

YAKASHA PRASNA

1. *What is it that makes the Sun rise up?*
Brahma (vedam) makes the SUN rise up.
BRAHMA ADITYAM UNNAYATI (Uunnayati = To rise up)
2. *Who are his attendants?*
The DEVAS are his attendants
DEVA TASYA ABHITAHA CHARA (Abhitaha = on all sides, Chara-move)
3. *Who makes the sun set?*
Dharma makes the Sun set.
DHARMAHA ASTAM NAYATE
4. *In which is the Sun firmly placed?*
Sun is firmly established in TRUTH
SATYE CHA PRATETISHATATE
5. *By what does a person become a SROTRIYA (or a vedic scholar)?*
By the study of Vedas only a person becomes SROTRIYA
SRUTENA SROTRIYO BHAVATI
6. *By what does a person achieve greatness?*
By Austereties (TAPAS) only a person can achieve greatness
TAPSA VINDATE MAHAAT (Vinaate = Attains, Mahaat = Greatness (or BRAHMAM)
7. *By what does a person acquire a dependable friend?*
By cultivating STEADFASTNESS (DHRUTI), a person acquires a dependable friend
DRHRUTYA DVETEEYAVAN BHAVATI
8. *How does a man become wise?*
A person acquires wisdom by serving the elders
BUDDHIMAN VRUDDHA SEVAYAA
9. *How does a Brahmana acquire excellence?*
A Brahmana acquires excellence by the study of VEDAS
SVAADHYAYA ESHAAM DEVATVAM
10. *What is the good tradition of a Brahmana?*
Performing austerities (TAPAS) is the good tradition of a Brahamana
TAPAHA ESHAAM SATAAMEVA
11. *What is the ordinary human trait of a Brahmana?*
Death is the ordinary human trait of a Brahmana
MARANAM MANUSHO BHAAVAHA
(If one loves his body and sense organs and fails to realise the true nature of his soul, such a man is deemed to be dead, though he is physically alive)
12. *What are the evil qualities found in a Brahmana?*
The two evil qualities found in a Brahmana are :
1. To find faults in Divam and Brahmajnanis, and
2. To disregard tradition
PARIVAADO SATAMEVA
(Every Brahmana should avoid the above two evil qualities)

13. *What imparts excellence to a Kshatirya?*
Military prowess (skill in archery and in the use of other weapons) imparts excellence to a Kshatiriya
ESHVASTRA ESHAM DEVATVAM
14. *What is the good qualtiy of a Kshatriya?*
To perform yagnas for the welfare of all is the good quality of a Kshatriya
YAGNA ESHAM SATAMEVA
15. *What is the ordinary human trait of a Kshatirya?*
The fear of their rival kings is the ordinary human trait of a Kshatriya
BHAYAM YI MAANUSHO BHAAVAHA
16. *What is the evil quality of a Kshatriya?*
Abandoning the afflicted is the evil quality found in a Kshatriya
PARITYAAGO SATAA MEVA
17. *What is the 'SOMA', which is beneficial for the yagna?*
'PRANA' is the soma which is beneficial for the yagna
PRANAHA YI YAGNIYAM SAAMA.
18. *What is the YAJUS which is beneficial for the yagna?*
'MANAS' (or the mind) is the YAJUS which is beneficial for the yagna
MANO YI YAGNIYAM YAJU HU
19. *Which among them is chosen for the yagna itself?*
It is the RUKKU, which chooses for the yagna itself
(RUKKU = VAAKKU = RUGVEDA MANTRAS)
RUGEKA VRUNUTE YAGNAM
20. *What is that which the yagna can not be without?*
It is the "RUKKU" alone which yagna cannot do without
TAAM YAGNO NA ATIVARTATE
(control of Prana (or Breath) and the manas (or the mind is the first step, worship of DEVATAS (Such as INDRA, VARUNA, AGNI etc. by "RUKKU" (RUGVEDA MANTRAS) is the next step, and realising the true nature of Self (or ATMA) with the help of UPANISHAD MANTRAS is the final step)
TAM TVOW UPANISHADAM PURUSHA
21. *What is that which pleases the DEVATAS?*
Rain is that which pleases the Devatas
VARSHAM AAVAPATAAM SRESTHAM (Aaavapataam = which satisfies completely)
22. *What is the best in the "PITRU TARPANA* (NIVA PATAAM)
Seeds are the best offerings in the 'PITRU TARPANA' ceremony.
BEEJAM NIVAPATAAM VARAM
23. *What is the best for one who seeks prestige?*
Protecting the cows is the best for one who seeks prestige
GAAVAHA PRATISATA MAANAANAM
24. *What is the best for one who seeks progeny?*
Begetting a son is the best for one who seeks progeny

PUTRAHA PRASAVATAAM VARAM

25. *Who is the man, though alive, endowed with intelligence and respected by all and loved by all is deemed to be dead?*
    One who does not propitiate by offerings 1. Devatas 2. guests 3. dependants 4. PITRUDEVATAS and one's ownself, is deemed to be dead, though physically alive
    DEVATA ATETHE BRUTYAANAAM ATMANA CHAYAHA
    NA NIRVAPATI PANCHAANAM UCHVASAN NA SA JEEVATE
    (Everyone is expected to do (perform) the following yagnas (*PANCHA YAGNAS*) everyday namely :
    1. BRAHMA YAGNA
    2. PITRU YAGNA
    3. DEVA YAGNA
    4. BHOOTA YAGNA
    5. MANUSHYA YAGNA
26. *Who deserves reverence and worship more than the earth?*
    A mother deserves reverence and worship more than the earth
    MAATA GURUTARAA BHOOMEHA
27. *Who deserves reverence and worship more than the sky?*
    A father deserves reverence and worship more than the sky
    Khaat Pitaa Uttchatara Tadha (khaat = sky)
28. *What is swifter than the wind?*
    The mind is swifter than the wind (hence try to control the mind)
    MANAHA SEEGRATARAM VAATAT (vattaat = wind)
29. (YOGAHA CHITTA VRUTTI NIRODHAHA)
    What are more numerous than the blades of grass?
    Cares and worries of an ordinary man ar more numerous than all the blades of grass
    CHINTAA BHUTAREE TRUNAAT (CHINTA = SORROW)
30. *What is the creature which does not close its eyes while asleep?*
    A fish does not close its eyes while asleep
    MATSYAHA SUPTA NA NIMISHATI
31. *What is that which does not move after birth?*
    An egg does not move after birth
    ANDAM JAATAM NA CHOPATI
32. *What is that which is without a heart?*
    A stone is without a heart
    ASMANO HRUDAYAM NAASTI
    SMA = Sareera (human body) which eventually disintegrates
    ASMA = which does not disintegrate namely ATMA or soul.
    A yogi is untouched by DWANDAS (such as joy or sorrow, heat or cold etc.) and his heart is impervious to all emotions and afflictions, *just as though his heart is made up of stone.*
    ASAREERAM VAD VASANTAM NAHA PRIYAPRIYE SPRUSATAHA (For a yogi who is not conscious of his own sareera, even if it is existing, is said to be without a body)

33. *What is that which swells by its own force?*
A river swells by the force of its own current.
NADEE VEGENA VARDHATE
34. *Who is the friend of one who goes on a jorney?*
A group of travellers (CARAVAN) is the friend of a person going on a journey
SAARDHAHA PRAVASATO MITRAM
35. *Who is the friend of one, who remains at home?*
The wife is the friend of one who remains at home
BHARYAA MITRAM GRUHE SATAHA
36. *Who is the friend of a sick man?*
The physician is the friend of a sick man
AATURASYA BISHAK MITRAM
37. *Who is the friend of one, who is about to die?*
DANAM made by self is the friend of one who is about to die
DAANAM MITRAM MARISHYATAHA (Marishyataha = one who is about to die)
38. *Who is the guest of all creatures?* (SARA BHOOTAS)
AGNI, which consists of 1. AAHAVANEEYAM 2. DAKSHINA MU and GARHA PATYAMU, is the guest of all creatures.
ATIDHIHE SARVABHUTAANAA AGNIHE.
39. *What is the eternal Dharma?*
SOMA YAGA is the eternal dharma
SOMO GAVAA AMRUTHAM
40. *What is AMRITAM?*
Sanaatana Dharma is Amrutam
(SANAATANO AMRUTO DHARMO)
41. *What is this entire universe?*
The entire universe consists of VAAYU
VAAYUHU SARVA MIDAM JAGAT.
42. *What is that which journeys alone?*
The sun journeys alone
SOORYA EKO VICHARATE
43. *What is that which is born again?*
The moon is reborn
CHANDRAMAA JAAYATE PUNAHA
44. *What is the remedy against snow or fog?*
The fire is the remedy for snow or fog
AGNIHE HIMASYA BISHAJYAM (Bhishajyam = Remedy)
45. *What is the great receptacle?*
Earth is the great receptacle (to sow the seeds)
BHOOMI AAAVAPANAM MAHAT (Aaavapanam = to recieve the seeds) (Mahat = great)
46. *What is the main source of DHARMA?*
Integrity combined with ability is the main source of Dharma (*DAAKSYAM = Integrity*

+ Ability)
DAAKSHYAM EKA PADAM DHARMYAM
(Daakshyam = capacity to accomplish quickly
Virtuous deeds always demand quick desision and action. The man who hesitates, doubts and delays cannot accomplish righteous acts.

47. *What is the main source of fame?*
Dana is the main source of fame
DAANAM EKA PADAM YASAHA.
(It is well-known that one's name is perpetuated by charity alone, while everything else about him may be forgotten)
48. *What is the important source of heaven?*
TRUTH is the only important source of heaven
SATYAM EKAPADAM SVARGAM
49. *What is the important source of SUKHAM (HAPPINESS)*
Virtuous character is the important source of happiness
SEELAM EKAPADAM SUKHAM.
50. *Who is the soul of a man?*
The soul of a man is his own son
PUTRA AATMAA MANUSHYASYA
51. *Who is the friend bestowed by GOD (DIVA KRUTAHA)*
The wife is the friend bestowed by GOD
BHARYAA DIVAKRUTAHA SAKHAA
52. *On what does the existence of man depend upon?*
The existence of man depends upon RAIN
UPAJEEVANAM CHA PARJANYO (Parjanyaha = God of Rain)
53. *What is the most important duty of a man?*
DANA is the most important duty of a man
DANAM ASYA PARAAYANAM(Paraayanam: Primary Duty)
54. *What is the outstanding quality that is present in men of distinction?*
Integrity combined with ability, is the outstanding quality, that is present in men of distinction.
DHANYAANAM UTTAMAM DAAKSHYAM (DAAKSHYAM = Integrity combined with skill and ability in the performance of one's duty)
55. *What is the best among all assets?*
Learning is the best asset
DHANAANAAM UTTAMAM SRUTAM (DHANAANAAM: RICHES)
56. *What is the best of all gains?*
Health is the best of all gains
LAABHANAAM SREYAHA AAROGYAM (SREYAHA = THE BEST)
57. *What is the best among all things that cause happiness?*
Contentment is the best among all things that cause happiness
SUKHAANAAM TUSTE UTTAMA (TUSTE = CONTENTMENT)

(Integrity + Skill + Ability + Learning + Health + Contentment, are needed to acquire JNANA (OR WISDOM)

58. *What is the highest Dharma in the world?*
The highest dharma is kindness to all creatures
ANRUSAMSYAM PARO DHARMA (Anrusamsyam = Kindness to all creatures; Paraha : The best)

59. *What is that DHARMA, which always yields great results?*
The DHARMA ordained by the three VEDAS, always yields great resutls.
DHARMA TRIYEE DHARMAHA SADAA PHALAHA
(TRIYEE = OMKARAMU; Moksha mantram Triyee (VEDAMANTRA))

60. *What is that by controlling which one never grieves?*
One who controls his mind, avoids grief and sorrow
MONO YAMYA NA SOCHANTI (Mano = mind; Yamya = controlling which; na sochanti = avoids grief)

61. *With whom does an association never break?*
Association with the good never breaks SANDHIHI SADBHI NA JEERYATE (Sadbhihi : men of virtue; na jeeryate = never breaks; Sandhihi = Association or friendship. (control of mind is the result of association with men of virtue)

62. *By forsaking which quality does one become lovable?*
By giving up pride, one becomes lovable
MAANAM HITVAA PRIYO BHAVATI (Maanam = Pride; Hitvaa = forsaking)

63. *By forsaking which quality does one never suffer grief?*
By forsaking anger, one never suffers grief
KRODHAM HITVAA NA SOCHATI

64. *By renouncing which quality does one become rich?*
By renouncing DESIRE (KAAMA), one becomes rich
KAAMAN HITVAA ARDHAVAAN BHAVATI (Ardhavaan = Rich)

65. *By forsaking which quality, does one become happy?*
By forsaking AVARICE, one becomes happy
LOBHAM HITVAA SUKHEE BHAVET (LOBHAM = GREED AND AVARICE)

66. *Why shoulld one make gifts to a Brahamana?*
It is to acquire DHARMA, one makes gifts to a Brahmana
DHARMARDHAM BRAHMANA DAANAM

67. *Why should one make gifts to actors and dancers?*
It is to acquire fame, one gives to actors and dancers
Yasus Artham nata nartake

68. *What for does one give presents to servants?*
It is for their sustenance that one gives presents to servants.
BHRUTYESHU BHARANAARDHAM

69. *What for does one make gifts to a King?*
It is on account of fear (of punsihment) that one makes gifts to a King
BHAYARDHAM CHIVA RAJASU

70. *By what is the world enveloped?*
The world is enveloped by AGNANA
AGNAANENA AVRUTAHA LOKAHA
71. *What is the quality that interferes with its lustre?*
It is on account of TAMAS, that things do not shine. TAAMASAA NA PRAKAASATE
AGNANA has two componetns namely 1. *AVARANA SAKTI* This prevents one from seeing things that actually exist 2. *VIKSHEPA SAKTI* : This aspect of AGNANA, projects the false as TRUTH
72. *For what reason does one give up friends?*
It is due to AVARICE, that friends are abandoned
LOBHAAT TYAJATI MITRANNE
73. *What is it that prevents one from entering heaven?*
MAMAKAARA (Attachment to one's wife and children etc.) prevents one from entering heaven
SANGAAT SVARGAM NA GATTCHATI (Sangaat = Attachments)
74. *Who should be considered as dead, although he is yet alive?*
A man who does not perform DANA DHARMAS (who does not make gifts to the poor and deserving needy) is to be considered as dead, although he is yet alive
MRUTO DARIDRAHA PURUSHO (Daridraha = a miser)
75. *When will a kingdom be considered as dead?*
A kingdom without a king to rule over it, is to be considered as dead
MRUTAM RAASTRAM ARRAJAKAM
76. *When will a SRADDHA CEREMONY be considered as dead?*
A Sraddha ceremony performed without SROTRIYAS
(Brahmanas learned in VEDAS = VEDAVETTAS)
MRUTAM ASROTRIYAM SRAADHAM
77. *When will a yagna be considered as dead?*
A yagna performed without giving any DAKSHINA
(or renumeration) to the RITVIKS may be considered as futile
MRUTAHA YAGNAHA ADAKSHINAHA
(Dakshate eti Dakshinaa). Here the verb Daksha means Vruddhi (or increase of efficacy)
(TE DAKSHNATA DAKSHINAAM PRATI GRUHYATA)
("Receiving the Dakshina, they increase in efficacy" –VED MANTRA
78. *Who is the proper Aacharya (GURU) to guide and show the way (to self-realisation)?*
One who is well-versed in VEDAS (SANTAHA), is the the proper person to guide and show the way to self-realisation.
(SANTAHA DIK) Santaha : Men of Virtue
(those who are well-versed in VEDAS, and live according to its standards) DIK–The way
79. *What has been spoken of as water?*
AKAASA (or space) is spoken of as water (Jalam Akaasam)
(PANCHAMYA MAAHUTAA VAAPAHA PURUSHA VACHASO BHAVANTI – CHANDOGYO-PANISHAD)

(Veerya when it gains entry in to the womb, becomes the starting point of a human life)

80. *What is meant by ANNAMU (or food)?*
The cow is mentioned as Annamu (or food)
Gowha (Cow) (Annamu) = "Gowrannam"
(In this context Govu means = sense organs which experience Sabda, Sparsa, Roopa, Rasa and Gandha sensations and not a cow. As Annamu or food when eaten becomes One with the body, sense objects should be absorbed and made to merge in the sense organs. Finally even the sense organs and their perceptions also should be merged in the self (or ATMA)
"ATRA HYETE SARVA MEKAM BHAVANTI" – SRUTI

81. *What should be eschewed as if it is a poison?*
Desire should be eschewed as if it is a poison
PRAARDHANA VISHAM (Praardhana = Desire)

82. *What is the proper time for SRADDHA?*
Arrival of a SROTRIYA (a brahmana well-versed in vedas) is the proper time for SRADDHA.
SRADDHASYA BRAHMANAHA KALAHA

83. *What is meant by TAPAS?*
The proper performance of ones own duty is said to be TAPAS
TAPAHA SWADHARMA VARTITVAM

84. *What is meant by DAMAM?*
The control of mind is DAMAM
MANASO DAMANAM DAMAHA (Damanam : Control)

85. *What is said to be the excellence in patience (KSHAMA)*
One who puts up with opposites like joy or sorrow, and heat and cold, and praise or criticism etc. with equanimity is said to possess excellence in patience
KSHAMAA DVANDA SAHESHNUTVAM (DVANDA = Pairs of opposits : SAHESHNUTVAM: TOLERANCE)

86. *What is meant by shame?*
Shame is the quality which restrains one from evil conduct
HREE AKAARYA NIVARTANAM (HREE = SHAME
(AKAARYA = EVIL DEEDS)

87. *What is said to be knowledge (OR JNANA)?*
Jnana is the perception of the nature of one's own soul
JNANAM TATVAARDHA SAMBODHAHA

88. *What is meant by SAMAM (or TRANQUILITY)*
Samam is defined as peace of mind (or Tranquillity)
SAMA CHITTA PRASAANTATAA

89. *What is the highest compassion?*
One who seeks the welfare of all creatures is said to possess the highest compassion
DAYAA SARVA SUKHISHITVA

90. *What is meant by ARJAVAM (Straight forwardness)*

Arjavam is defined as equitable conduct
ARJAVAM SAMA CHITTATAA.

91. *Who is the enemy unconquerable to man?*
Anger is the most invincible enemy to man
KRODHAHA SUDURJAYAHA (Durjayaha = unconquerable) (Krodhaha = Anger)

92. *What is the disease that has no end?*
Covetousness is the disease that has no end
LOBHO VYAADHI ANANTAKAHA
LOBHO = Avarice (Anantakaha = That has no end)

93. *Who is said to be a good man (SAADHU)?*
SAADHU (or a good man) is one who seeks the welfare of all creatures
SARVA BHOOTA HITAHA SAADHU

94. *Who is said to be a cruel man (ASAADHU)?*
One who has no compassion in his heart is said to be a cruel man
ASASDHU NIRDAYAHA SMRUTAHA
(Asaadhu = cruel) (smrutaha = should be considered as)

95. *What is meant by MOHA (or delusion)?*
Ignorance about DHARMA is said to be MOHA
MOHO HE DHARMA MOODHATVAM

96. *What is meant by MAANAM (or PRIDE or conceit)*
(EGOISM : AHANKARA : Egotism : Self-praise)
Maanam is defined as Ahankara or Egoism
MAANAS AATMABHI MAANITAA

97. *What should be considered as laziness?*
Neglect of ones own DHARMA, should be considered as laziness
DHARMA NISHKRIYATA AALASYAM
(NISHKRIYATA = Neglect of) (Aalaysyam = Laziness)

98. *What is meant by SOKA (or grief)?*
SOKA (or grief) is caused by AGNANA
SOKAM AGNAANAM UCHYATE

99. *What is the steadfastness (STHIRYAM) spoken of by the RISHIS (RUSHIBEH HE PROKTUM)?*
Not swerving from one's own duties is the STHIRYAM
(Steadfastness), spoken of by the RISHIS
SVADHARME STHIRATAA STHIRYAM

100. *What is meant by courage (or Dhiryam)?*
Courage is defined as the control of the senses
DHIRYAM INDRIYA NIGRAHA HA.

101. *What should be considred as the best in clealiness?*
Cleansing the mind of all impure thoughts, should be considered as the best in cleanliness
SNANAM MANO MALO TYAAGO

102. *What is meant by DANA (or charity)?*

Dana is defined as the protection of all living creatures
DAANAM YI BHOOTA RAKSHANAM
(In this context Daanam = Serving or seeking the welfare of)

103. *Which man should be regarded a learned man (or a PANDITA)*
One who knows thoroughly about all aspects of Dharma should be regarded as a PANDITA (or a learned man)
DHARMAGNA PANDITO JNEYAHA (Jneyaha = who knows all about)

104. *Who is said to be a NASTIKA (or ATHEIST)?*
There is no greater MOORKHA (STUPID FELLOW) than a Nastika.
(One who believes in a world above (PARALOKA) is called an AASTIKA, and one Who believes that this material world alone exists and there is no PARALOKA, is called a NASTIKA)
NAASTIKO MOORKHA UCHYATE

105. *Who is said to be a MOORKHA (STUPID FELLOW)*
A Naastika should be considred as MOORKHA.

106. *What is meant by Kaama (or desire)?*
Kaama (or Desire) is the origin of eternal cycle of births and death
KAMAHA SAMSAARA HETUSCHA (Hetuhu = origin of)

107. *What is meant by MATSARA (OR ENVY)?*
One who is afflicted with jealousy by seeing the wealth, power etc. of others, is said to be a victim of envy
HRUTTAPO MATSARAHA SMRUTAHA
(The remedy for Matasara is to cultivate *joy, friendship* and *compassion,* depending On the situation. *NARADA in SRIMAD BHAGAVAT* in his Upadesa (or advice) to *UDDHAVA* says as follows :
"GUNAADHIKAAN MUDAM (JOY) LIPSET, ANUKROSAM GUNAADHAMAAT, MITRIM SAMAANA DANVICCHETH NATAA BY RABHI BHOOYATE"
Seeing a person of nobler qualities, one must try to experience joy. Seeing another of inferior quality, one must show compassion, and towards person of the same quality, one must cultivate friendship. In this way one will never be affected by TAAPA (or Affliction).

108. *What is AHANKARA (EGOISM)?*
Boundless Ignorance (AGNANA) leads the way to Ahankara
MAHA AGNANA AHAJKARAHA (Ahajkaraha = Ahankara or Egoism)

109. *Define DHAMBHAHA (or CONCEIT)?*
One who advertises about his performance of DHARMA, just as flying aloft of the flag of Dharma, is said to be a victim of DHAMBHAHA (or conciet). (DHAMBHO DHARMO DHVAJA UCCHARYAHA. (Uccharayaha: Flying Aloft of a flag)

110. *What is meant by Parama Daivam (Supreme divine nature)?*
Parama Daivam is nothing but the result of DANA (or charity) performed by self
DAIVAM DAANAPHALAM PROKTUM
(DANA DHARMAS done by self only, eventually pave the way for ones welfare)

111. *What is meant by PYSUNYAM (or slandering)?*
Talking evil of others is called PYSUNYAM (or slandering)
PYSUNYAM PARADHOOSHANAM
"AAHO KHALA BHUJANGASYA VICHITRO YAM VADHA KRAMAHA
ANYASAY DASATI SROTRAM ANYAHA PRAANIRVI MUCHYATE"
– BHARTRUHARI
"A slander bites the ear of another and a third person is deprived of his life. Like the snake which bites his victim in the dark, the slanderer carries tales and indirectly causes injury to another, without himself being known as the cause of it."

112. *Dharma, Artha and Kama are opposed to one another and how do these three constituents coexist in one situation?*
When one's practice of DANA and DHARMA are not interfered with and when there is wholehearted cooperation by the wife for such activities, Dharma, Artha and Kama can coexist.
YADDA DHARMASCHA BHAARYA CHA PARASPARA VASANUGAON TADAA
DHARMARDHA KAMAANAM TRANAM API SANGAMAHA
(Trianam Api = These three constituents
Sangamaha = Union is possible)
"DHARMARTHA KAMAHA ELA TATA LOKE SAMEEKSHITAA DHARMA PHALODAYESHU
YE TATRA SARVESYURA SAMSAYAM, ME BHARYEVA VASYABHIMETAA SUPUTRAA" –*VAALMIKE*
"A ttainment of fruits of Dharma, Artha and Kama are possible only when the wife is cooperative, obedient and endowed with a good son"–VAALMIKE

113. *Who deserves to be put in to everlasting hell?*
A. One who voluntarily invites a poor Brahmana and then refuses to make any DAANA to him, deserves to be put in the everlasting hell
B. one who does not believe in and who ascribes falsehood to 1. VEDAS 2. DHARMA SASTRAS 3. DVIJAATESHU (BRAHMANAS), 4. DEVESHU (DEVATAS) and 5. PITRU DHARMESHU (ceremonial rites done to Ancestors) deserves to be put in to everlasting hell.
C. He who is rich, yet is devoid of DAANA or enjoyment, owing to avarice, deserves to be put into everlasting hell.
"VIDYA MAANE DHANE LOBHAA DAANA BHOGA VIVERJITAHA
PASCHAAT NA ASTI ETI YOU BROOYAAT SO KSHAYAM NARAKAM VRAJET
(LOBHAAT = Due to avarice; Dhane Vidya Manu = inspite of possessing wealth)

114. *How does one become a BRAHMANA? Is it by (i) KULA (or ANCESTRY), (2) VRATA (or CONDUCT) (3) SWADHYAYA (Reciting the VEDAS) and (4) SRUTENA* (Thorough study and understanding of the VEDAS)?
A. It is not by kula, (or Ancestry), or by reciting the Vedas (Swadhyaya), or by the study of Vedas (SRUTENA), one becomes a BRAHMANA. Without doubt, *it is by exemplary (outstandingly good) conduct only, one can be regarded as a BRAHMAN*

"SRUNU YAKSHA KULAM TAATA NA SVAADHYAYO NACHA SRUTAM
KARNAM HE DVIJATVE CHA VRUTTAM EVA NA SAMSAYAHA
(DVIJATVE = To become a Brahmana
VRUTTAM = CONDUCT ONLY is the criterion)

B. Ones conduct should always be safeguarded, especially by a Brahmana. One who safeguards his conduct, can never be ruined. One, who has sullied (tarnished) his conduct, is deemed to be already dead).
"VRUTTAM, YATNENA SAMRAKSHYAM BRAHAMENENA VISESHATAHA
ADKSHEENA VRUTT NA KSHEENAHA, VRUTTATASTU HATO HATAHA"
(Hataha = Deemed to be already dead)

C. The teachers and pupils and others, who, read, study and discuss the VEDAS and SASTRAS are only to be regarded as misguided fools. But he alone who practices what he has read and studied in VEDAS and SASTRAS, is to be regarded as a really learned PANDITA
"PATHAKAHA PATHAKAASCHIVA EVA ANYE SASTRA CHINTAKAAHE
SARVE VYASANINO MOORKHA YAHA KRIYAAVAAN SA PANDITAHA"
Pathakaha = Those who study Vedas : Pathakaa cha Eva = Those who make others (their students) to read Vedas : Saastra chintakaaha: Those who reflect on the contents of Sastras: Kriyavaan : whose conduct is according to the traditions of Vedas and Sastras)

D. A BRAHMANA even if he has studied the four vedas if his conduct is tarnished (sullied) , such a one is to be regarded as inferior even to a SOODRA. One who performs Agnihotra with all SRADDHA (Sincerity) and who has his mind and senses, under control such a one only should be considered as a true BRAHMANA.
CHATURVEDO API DURVRUTTAHA SA SOODRAA ATIRICHYATE
YAHA AGNIHOTRA PARAHA DAANTAHA SAHA BRAHMANA ETI SMRUTAHA
Durvruttaha: Evil conduct; Atirichyate = worse than; Daantaha: one who has control over his mind and senses; Agnihotra paraha=one who performs Agnihotra with SRADDHA.

115. *What does one gain who speaks pleasant words?*
He who uses pleasant words is liked by all
PRIYAVACHANVAADEE PRIYO BHAVATI

116. *What does he gain that acts after due deliberation?*
He who acts with due deliberation, succeeds to a great extent
Vimrusita Kaaryokarodhikam jayati
Vimrusita Kaarya Karaha = one who undertakes a task only after due deliberation

117. *What does he get that makes many friends?*
He who has many friends lives happily. BAHUMITRA KARAHA SUKHAM VASATE

118. *What does he gain who loves or devoted to DHARMA?*
He who is devoted to Dharma, attains hapiness here and in the hereafter.
YASCHA DHARMARATAHA SUGATIM LABHATE

yaha: who is; Dharmarataha : Devoted to Dharama

119. *Who is the man that lives happily?*
One who is free from debts, who has no need to leave his house for his sustenance, and who cooks and eats Vegetables every fifth or sixth day in his own house, such a One is truly happy.
PANCHAME HANI SHASTE VAA SAAKAM PACHATI SVE GRUHA ANRUNEE CHA PRAVAASEE CHA SA VAARICHERA MODATE Panchame: Fifth; Ahani : Day; Shaste vaa : Sixth day; Sve : One's own; Gruhe : house; Saakam : Vegetables; Pachati : Cooks; Anrunee : one who s free from debts; Pravaasee : who has no need to depend on others for his living and who has no need to go to foreign places for his sustenance.
(one who is content, lives happily)

120. *What is the most surprising thing in this world?*
Day after day, creatures (men women and children and other creatures) die to enter the abode of YAMA (King of DEATH), yet those that are alive, believe that they will live forever. This is the most surprising thing in this world.
"AHANYAHAANI BHOOTANI GATCHANTEEHA YAMALAYAM
SESHAHA STHAAVARAM ECCHANTI KIM ASCHARYAM ATAHA PARAM
Ahani Ahani = Every Day; Bhootaani = creatures; Gatchanti = Depart; Seshaaha = Those who remain; Sthavaram = wish; to to live forever = Ecchanti; Desire to Ataha Param Ascharyam. No greater wonder than this.
(Ones own body and life are bound to end in death sooner or later. Realising this eternal truth, one should give up luxuries, and strive to attain MOKSHA (Or liberation).

121. *What is the best way?*
TARKA SASTRA (or LOGIC) is uncertain,
SRUTAYAHA (or VEDAS) are contradictory,
There is not one RUSHE, whose opiniion is authoritative,
The true nature of DHARMA is inscrutable (or hidden)
That alone is the path, which great men tread
TARKAHA APRATISHTAHA SRUTAY. VIBHINNA NIKO RUSHI RYASYA MATAM PRAMANAM
DHARMASYA TATVAM NIHITAM GUHAAYAAM
MAHAAJANO YENA GATAHA SA PANDHAHA
(As even the vedas are contradictory, opinions of Rushis vary, and as the true nature of Dharma is inscrutable, *the only way for anyone is to follow in the footsteps of great men (of the past and present times)*

122. *What is the news?*
This world is similar to a huge vessel filled with MOHA (illusion). TIME (or KALA) Cooks in this vessel of MOHA all the creatures in the fire of the SUN, with fuel of days and nights, and with the ladle constituted by months and seasons. This is news.
ASMIN MAHAA MOHAMAYE KATAAHE SOORYAGNINAA RAATRI DIVAA ENDHANENA

MAASA RUTU DARVEE PARIGHATTANENA BHOOTAANI KALAHA PACHATI ETI VAARTAA

Mahaa Mohamaye = This world filled with Illusion

Kataahe = huge vessle; Raatri Divaa; Night and day; Endhanena = as fuel; Sooryagninaa = By the heat of the sun; Maasa rutu = months and seasons; Darvee = with the ladle of; Parighattanena = stirring up; Bhootaani = All the creatures; Pachati = cooks; ETI Vaartaa = This is news

(one should not be carried away by the pleasures of this world such as wealth, women, power etc. and realise that all of them are transient and mere play things in the hands of TIME, and renounce all of them to attain PEACE)

123. *Who is a PURUSHAA? (or who is the man that is really alive?)*

Puram = Human body; PURUSHAA = JEEVA (SOUL) who resides in the human body

Who should be regarded as still alive, although his Jeeva has departed from the Puram (humanbody)?

As long as one's KEERTI (or FAME) (resulting from good deeds done by him) touches heaven and earth, one will be called a PURUSHAA.

DIVAM SPRUSATI BHOOMIN CHA SABDHAHA PUNYENA KARMANAA
YAAVAT SA SABDHO BHAVATI TAAVAT PURUSHA UCHYATE

124. *Who is a SARVADHANEE? (or who is the richest among all?)*

He to whom the things likable and not likable, or sorrow and happiness, or the past and the future are the same, such a one should be regarded as a SARVADHANEE

TULYE PRIYA APRIYE YASYA SUKHA DUKHE TADHIVA CHA
ATEETA ANAAGAE CHA UBHE SA VI SARVADHANEE NARAHA

yasya = For whom; Atteta Anaagate = Paste and future; ubhe = Both; Tulye = are equal; Sahavi = such a one; Sarvadhanee = Richest among all; Naraha = man.

(one who realises the true nature of the SOUL, also attains SARVALOKAS (or all the worlds) and obtains all that he desires (SARVA KAMAS), hence a SARVADHANEE in this context, is none but a BRAHMAVETTA.

"YASTA MAATMAANA MANUVIDYA VIJAANAATI
SARVAAMCHA LOKAANAA PNOTE SARVAAMCHA KAAMAAN" – VEDA MANTRA

A person who is devoid of attachments and desires, attains poise, tranquillity of mind and contentment. Such a one is neither afflicted by sorrow, nor elated by joy. He never shrinks from any thing disagreeable to him, nor does he run after things which he likes. He is never worried about the past, nor does he pine for what he may not get.

Such a one indeed is a SARVA DHANEE.

Sources

1. Yaksha Prasna by K.B. Iyer, 1963
2. Yaksha Prasnalu by J.R. Sarma, 1997
3. Yaksha Prasnalu by D.S. Rao.

21

SARVAJNA AND HIS MESSAGE

There are many stories in circulation about the early years of Sarvajna. A brief account of his early years presented here is most probably very close to the few facts known about him.

Sarvajna was born in the year A.D. *1570* in a village called *AMBALOORU,* in *HIRIA KARUR* Taluk of *DHARWADA DISTICT* of the present day *KARNATAKA*. The village is close by the RIVER KUMUDVATI (Ref. Dr. B. Ramakrishna Rao's introduction to SARVAJNA VACHANAMULU BY SRI KALAGODU ASWATHA RAO *(1966)*.

Sarvajna's father was a AARAADHYA BRAHMANA named *BASAVARASU* (or MALLARASU and his mother was *MAALE,* and she belonged to the *potter's* (KUMMARI) community. The boy was given the name *"GUNDAPPA"* by his parents when the boy was only a child of two years, his mother MAALI died. After a few years, his father BASAVARASU, also died, leaving the boy as an orphan.

The boy wandered from village to village in that part of KARNATAKA. He came to know about people, their habits, and their traditions and their religious practices. Thus the world was his school experience his teacher and life itself, his book. In his wandering, he met his GURU, who initiated him into the *VEERASAIVA RELIGION*. Eventually he became a great saint moralist and a poet in *KARNATAKA* of the *16th CENTURY,* and became renowned as *"SARVAJNA"*.

1. *REV. FATHER WIRTH* (A German Missionary) in *1868,* collected some 300 poems of SARVAJNA and published them in a book form

2. *REV. UTTANGI CHENNAPPA* in *1924*, collected the poems of SARVAJNA and published them in a book form. This edition contained 1928 TRIPLETS (OR TRIPAADIS), which grew in number to *2,100* in the revised second edition (Not available now). The people of Karnataka and the rest of INDIA, are indebted to *Rev. U.CHENNAPPA* for bringing to light, the complete collection of *"VACHANAS OF SARVAJNA"* which were scattered out in crumbling palm leaf manuscripts lying in some dark and dusty store rooms and attics. Rev. U. Chennappa compiled and edited these sayings of SARVAJNA and wrote a long and inspiring preface to it. This book revived the public interest in SARVAJNA.

"SARVAJNA": All the poems of SARVAJNA end with the "ANKITANAAMA" of SARVAJNA. Most probably Sarvajna was influenced by the tradition *of VEERA SAIVA*

VACHANAKARTAS, who ended each of their Vachanas with the name of ESWARA OR SIVA.

Examples are

1. *KOODALA SANGAMA DEVA! – BASAVANNA 12TH CENTURY*
2. *Chenna Mallikarjuna!*
3. *Someswara!*
4. *SARVAJNA!* The word literally means "one who knows everything" – namely PARAMASIVA
5. All the poems of YOGI VEMANA. END WITH *"VISWADAABHIRAMA VINURA VEMA."* (*17th century* TELUGU Poet–Reformer–YOGI) Literally means VISWADUDU = creator of the world; ABHIRAMA = one who is dear to all; VEMA = Name of the poet; VINURA : Listern to this)

SARVAJNA VACHANAS

1. All human beings have similar organs,
   How can you separate them into
   Chandalaas, Soodraas and others?

   – SARVAJNA

2. All of us live on the same earth,
   Drink the same water, and in the end are consumed by the same fire
   Then what is the basis for KULA and GOTRA?

   – SARVAJNA

3. A donkey even if it rolls on and smears itself with ashes,
   Does it become a saint?
   One who is not aware of his SELF, even if has smeared himself with ashes, is no better than a donkey.

   – SARVAJNA

4. Hypocrites may wear many RUDRAKSHA MALAAS,
   Just as "ATTI" "tree's branches may be loaded with ATTI fruits,
   One who is not aware of his SELF is futile.

   – SARVAJNA

5. Do not be misguided by the shaven heads of false ascetics,
   Follow and be guided by the true GURU,
   who has realised his SELF.

   – SARVAJNA

6. There is no need of matted hair, or POOJAS OR NOMUS
   For one who has realised his SELF,
   If he is committed to TRUTH (SATYA), that is enough.

   – SARVAJNA

7. Fools worship idols, unaware of
   SIVA, who is in their own hearts
   All of you, reflect on this.

   – SARVAJNA

8. Stone upon a stone, a temple is built
And a stone idol is installed and worshipped
one who worships a stone idol is no better than a stone.

– SARVAJNA

9. Sivalinga is decorated with flowers,
And when a fool knocks his head on it during a Pooja
The only result of his pooja is a bump on his forehead.

– SARVAJNA

10. A fool who smears his forehead with SREEGANDHAM
Does he attain MOKSHA?
If so, the stone on which Sreegandham is prepared everyday, should also attain MOKSHA.

– SARVAJNA

11. One who comes uninvited, one who reads and reads but never writes,
One who walks barefooted, such fools are difficult to change,
The only way to teach them, is to beat them with a shoe.

– SARVAJNA

12. One who is rich shines like the sun,
One who is poor is regarded as worse than a dog,
Earn, become rich and be respected by all.

– SARVAJNA

13. Is there any difference between a DAATA (DONOR) and a GOD?
Does a GOD come down from heaven and make a gift for you?
One who makes a gift for you is none else but a GOD on earth.

– SARVAJNA

14. One who makes a gift to the deserving and needy
Attains the everlasting abode of SIVA (KAILASA).

– SARVAJNA

15. One who gives "DAANA" (gifts) without discriminating people in to good and bad ones,
And at all times, deserves to be called a DHARMADAATA.

– SARVAJNA

16. There is no GOD greater than ANNAM (FOOD),
None can survive without ANNAM,
Give ANNADAANA and save the lives of hungry.

– SARVAJNA

17. One who gives ANNAM (FOOD) to the hungry,
One who is committed to SATYA (TRUTH),
One who treats his sworn enemy as a friend attains KAILASA.

– SARVAJNA

18. A miser who never gives a gift,

A cow which yields no milk, and one who walks barefooted – all these three are useless.

– SARVAJNA

19. Some eat the animals, some eat the plants,
None can survive without eating either of them
The doctrine of AHIMSA is difficult to sustain.

– SARVAJNA

20. Creatures survive by eating other creatures,
All survive by eating things endowed with life;
The doctrine of AHIMSA is difficult to sustain.

– SARVAJNA

21. Who has painted the beautiful colours of a peacock?
Who has painted the beautiful colours of a rainbow on the sky?
Who has painted the beautiful colours on flowers and who has given them such sweet scent?

– SARVAJNA

22. Who has given a special scent to ASOFOETIDA?
How does water enter a green coconut?
Who has endowed such enchanting musical notes to the nightingale?

– SARVAJNA

23. One who is to be found even in the finest particles of sand and stones,
One who is worshipped in all paintings,
Is he not to be found in you and me?

– SARVAJNA

24. Do not be taken in by numbers,
A thousand meaningless words remain after all a thousand meaningless words,
Vigorous braying of a donkey is after all the Vigorous braying of a donkey.

– SARVAJNA

25. A comfortable house, money enough for your needs
And a cooperative and obedient wife, if you have them, there is no need for any other heaven.

– SARVAJNA

26. A pair of oxen, a milch cow, five sons,
Industrious daughter-in-laws and an old grandmother,
If you have them, there is no need for another heaven.

– SARVAJNA

27. One who knows and shows you the path,
One who knows and walks on the path,
One who knows and anticipates the events will be esteemed by all.

– SARVAJNA

28. One who works hard acquires wealth,

Wealth seeks the hard working man,
Wealth leaves the lazy man.

– SARVAJNA

29. Love and marry the woman of your love,
Love in such a happy married life is as
Delicious as tasting the cream of AMRUTAM. (Divine Nectar)

– SARVAJNA

30. Never touch a woman, who is not yours
To touch another's woman is a great sin.

– SARVAJNA

31. SADAACHARA (GOOD TRADITIONS), SATKARMAS
(GOOD DEEDS) and VAIRAGYA (RENUNCIATION).
Lead one to MOKSHA (LIBERATION).

– SARVAJNA

32. One with a shaven head, clad in a thick blanket
One who is free from pride, and who moves around solitarily, like an elephant which has left its herd, look out for such a JNANI. (Liberated Soul)

– SARVAJNA

33. A wick called "DHYANA" put in clear ghee called "SILENCE",
And when lit with a taper called "EXPERIENCE"
Dispells the darkness called "AJNANA".

– SARVAJNA

34. In the 'anthill' called the human body
There is a 'snake' called the tongue, with a 'poison' called ANGER
And the only remedy *(GARUDAMANTRA)* for this poison is *PATIENCE (KSHAMA).*

– SARVAJNA

35. A street dog is more useful than a shoe that bites
A raging fire is preferable to a vilemouthed wife.

– SARVAJNA

36. Even a big lump of Camphor when burnt
Leaves no residue, similarly by the grace of one's GURU, all the attachments and sins are destroyed without leaving a trace.

– SARVAJNA

37. The speech of an orator will be
As spontaneous and smooth, as the flow of water from a full ARAGHATTA (in SANSKRIT) or ETAMU (in TELUGU), and the speech of one who is not an orator is as futile as an empty ARAGHATTA (or ETAMMU).

– SARVAJNA

38. The lamp lit in the house of a low caste man
Does it give less light than the one in the house of a high caste man?
One who is dear to GOD is the one who is a high born.

– SARVAJNA

39. One who hides his own lapses,
yet always on the look out for others lapses, should be regarded as inferior even to a dog.
– SARVAJNA

40. To live under a tree is safer, than to live under a leaky roof,
To die of a disease is better than to live with a SHREW (A woman of violent temper).
– SARVAJNA

41. "ETTIYA" fruit has an attractive red outer coat,
ALAS! its inside stuff is very poisonous, just as an evil man may have an attractive personality Beware! his heart is full of evil thoughts.
– SARVAJNA

42. One may mend a piece of iron in a forge
But one will never be able to repair the harm done by cruel words.
– SARVAJNA

43. Anger is a SIN, Anger ruins a man,
A bucket of water is lost while drawing it form a well, if its rope gives way, just like that, a man is lost and lands in hell, if he gives way to ANGER.
– SARVAJNA

44. The world hates the man who tells the TRUTH,
ALAS! It is almost impossible to find one who is committed to TRUTH in this world.
– SARVAJNA

45. Is there anyone in this world not tempted
At the sight of a beautiful woman, gold and delicious fruits.
– SARVAJNA

46. One who worships stone idols of SIVA and KALI,
and fails to realise SIVA, who is in his own heart is no better than a fool.
– SARVAJNA

47. There is no greater DANA than ANNADANA,
There is nothing greater than ANNAM
ANNAM is what sustain all.
– SARVAJNA

48. Yogis perform ASANAS and strain their muslces to the utmost,
Tet they fail to get rid of their evil thoughts,
Can you kill the snake by beating on the ant hill?
– SARVAJNA

49. Salt and camphor look alike,
But they differ in taste,
Good and Evil men look alike, but they differ in conduct.
– SARVAJNA

50. Is there any need to secure a SIVALINGA
with so many threads and hang it around ones neck,
First restrain your eyes and then control your mind
– SARVAJNA

51. A miser hoards money and never spends it on himself, or to make DANADHARMAS, just as a honey bee hoards all the honey it gathers for the benefit of a passer by.
– SARVAJNA

52. An ox goes round and round grinding oil seeds in an oil mill throughout the day. Its labour is as futile as that of one who goes on pilgrimages, without ever realising Siva, who resides in his own heart.
– SARVAJNA

53. How did SARVAJNA become a great JNANI?
It is by giving up pride and by learning from all.
– SARVAJNA

54. Do not waste your time to extol the greatness of VEDAS
There is no greater VEDA, than ones own experience
(EXTOL = Praise, glorify).
– SARVAJNA

55. All the discussions about VEDAS are futile,
If they are not tempered with discrimination,
All the VEDAVETTAS are as futile as the VIBHOOTI
(on their bodies), if they are ignorant of essence of VEDAS.
– SARVAJNA

56. JNANA bestows everything here and hereafter
If one has no JNANA, he is in danger, though he may possess everything else.
– SARVAJNA

57. If a fool makes fun of a JNANI,
It is no loss to the JNANI,
A dog barks at an elephant passing by.
– SARVAJNA

58. Difference of opinion with a JNANI
Is as pleasant and as sweet as tasting Jaggery,
The same with a fool, is as dangerous as hurling stones at each other.
– SARVAJNA

59. One who realises his SELF
will be free from all fears and Evil.
– SARVAJNA

60. *Do not beg for anything from GOD,*
GOD is none but yourself if
you root out GUNAS and DESIRES from your heart
– SARVAJNA

61. There are five enemies in everyone, namely
ROOPA, RASA, GANDHA, SPARSA and SABHDA,
(Vision, Taste, Smell, Touch and Sound)
If they are conquered, one becomes a GOD himself. – SARVAJNA

62. Does one attain MOKSHA after one's DEATH?
One can attain MOKSHA even before one's DEATH if one pursues JNANA.
– SARVAJNA

63. One who is content to eat what is given to him, and wear clothes given to him, and
One who lives and sleeps, wherever he wants,
Is he not as happy as a KING.
– SARVAJNA

64. Do not presume that your own mind, eyes and tongue are harmless
And that others only can harm and destroy you
If unchecked, your own mind, eyes and tongue can destroy you.
– SARVAJNA

65. Wherever you go, your mind accompanies you with all its qualities, and
None can overcome you if you possess JNANA.
– SARVAJNA

66. One who avoids gluttony, lives long, and
A glutton is very close to Disease and DEATH.
– SARVAJNA

67. Control over ones tongue,
And good conduct enhance one's prestige.
– SARVAJNA

68. A lamp when lit dispels darkness
TRUTH and GOOD CONDUCT, if cherished dispel darkness called AJNANA.
– SARVAJNA

69. Those who weep excessively for the departed dead Alas! they foget that they also will have to join the departed dead, may be TEN or TWENTY years later.
– SARVAJNA

70. If one has renounced all attachments,
where is the need for gold and power
And if one has not renounced the woman
where is the need for another fetter.
– SARVAJNA

71. A river with fish and frogs, how does it become a THEERTHA?
Where you find SAJJANAS is a THEERTHA
Their presence is as desirable as nicely cooked RICE (when you are hungry).
– SARVAJNA

72. Truth spoken by those committed to TRUTH,
GOOD conduct of those committed to GOOD CONDUCT,
and the presence of SAJJANAS, all these should be there, to call a place a THEERTHA,
without them a river simply does not become a THEERTHA.
– SARVAJNA

73. Dirt on the body can be cleaned away by water
But SINS committed by SELF, can not be removed so easily.

– SARVAJNA

74. If a BRAHMANA can go to heaven
by simply bathing in a holy river
why can not a frog that lives in the same holy river go to heaven?

– SARVAJNA

75. If one can attain heaven by smearing holy VIBHOOTI
on his face and body, why can not a donkey
that rolls on ashes go to heaven?

– SARVAJNA

76. Devotees bring PRASADAMS and offer them to idols and beseech them to eat them, and they do not give any thing to eat, to hungry JANGAMAS, ALAS! the fools do not comprehend that idols can never eat.

– SARVAJNA

77. One who is born in a high caste is not the only one who deserves distinction,
One who treats all alike is the one who deserves distinction.

– SARVAJNA

78. A skeleton covered over with muslces and skin
Inside full of waste, worms and urine
Such is the nature of the human body and
where is the place of caste in it?

– SARVAJNA

79. Abandon the friendship of one, who refuses to eat with others, because of pride in his own caste.

– SARVAJNA

80. If a man shows you the right way to a village
Does it matter to which caste he belongs?
If a GURU shows you the right way to MOKSHA
Does it matter what his origin is?

– SARVAJNA

81. Relatives come to visit you, eat with you and then leave,
They can not help you to come out of the bondage of SAMSARA,
Only a GURU can help you to come out of the bondage of SAMSARA

– SARVAJNA

82. By churning CURDS, one obtains BUTTER
Just like that, GURU'S UPADESA, makes the way to MOKSHA to become clearer.

– SARVAJNA

83. Some GURUS repeat their advice again and again,
Some speak in riddles and puzzles,
Some want you to listen to the same advice again and again,

Out of listening, some attain peace and happiness.
– SARVAJNA

84. If one waters orange trees now,
others will eat and enjoy their fruits in future,
Just as we eat and enjoy the fruits of trees watered by others in the past.
– SARVAJNA

85. A father who fails to educate his son,
A GURU who fails to teach his student,
A mother who fails to nurse her sick son,
are to be considered as worse than an enemy. – SARVAJNA

86. When one is hungry, his speech falters, sleep eludes him, until a meal is eaten.
– SARVAJNA

87. A face that looks liked a lustre less moon,
Sunken eyes, down cast face and discomfort are the signs of a famished fellow.
– SARVAJNA

88. There is a fire which is ever alight;
This fire emits no smoke or heat,
yet it is a fire which always burns ones inside.
And it is the fire of hunger. – SARVAJNA

89. Even the foolish words of a rich man
are listened to with attention by all
where as even the wise advice of a poor man is discarded, just as one spits out a pebble that was in his morsel.
– SARVAJNA

90. One who eats only after feeding the hungry
is the one, who is a high born;
one who eates by himself, without feeding the hungry
is the one who is a low born. – SARVAJNA

91. A dana should be given with devotion and Egoism should be avoided
And when Egoism disappears, teachings of one's GURU (GURU BHODHA) becomes fruitful.
– SARVAJNA

92. The demarcation between a generous and a poorman, JNANI and an AJNANI, and an Egoist (AHANKARI) and one with no Egoism (NIRAHANKARI) is as wide as that between a lion and a street dog.
– SARVAJNA

93. A miser hoards wealth
He neither enjoys his wealth nor gives it to others
Alas! when a miser dies, all the gold which he has hoarded, will not be buried along with him.
– SARVAJNA

94. What you give as a DANA to others is yours
What you hoard will go to others after your death
Do not regret after you give a gift,
It will return to you later multiplied manifold.

– SARVAJNA

95. A superior man gives a DANA without any talk about it
An ordinary person gives when he has promised it
An inferior person talks and talks about it but never gives anything.

– SARVAJNA

96. One who gives promptly, and without making the poor fellow go round him again and again, the gift of such a good man is more precious than gold and he is sure to attain SVARGA (or Heaven).

– SARVAJNA

97. Among all gifts, "ANNADANAM" is the best
Nothing is more precious than "ANNAM"
Is it not "ANNAM" that sustains the lives of all?

– SARVAJNA

98. GOLD is used to make "KANKANAMS" (a wrist ornaments)
Gold is used to make many other ornaments
If one fails to see the source of all these
such a one should be regarded as worse than a dog.

– SARVAJNA

99. A crow when it sees some food stuff, it crows
gathers other crows and shares it with them
crows, and fowl, have a better social etiquette than a man.

– SARVAJNA

100. Family attachments and wealth, are all trasient,
As all the villagers disperse from a Fair by nightfall
Family attachments and wealth also vanish in the end. – SARVAJNA

101. If one works hard and saves, wealth accumulates with him
IF one is lazy, WEALTH takes leave of him. – SARVAJNA

102. A full tank or a well, will become dried up in the course of time
Do not trust and rely on the wealth, which will disappear sooner or later.

– SARVAJNA

103. Ones own speech causes, smiles, enmities and even murders
Ones own speech brings in wealth
Ones own speech rewards one with prestige and distinction. – SARVAJNA

104. For one who is a master of words
words are more precious to him than diamonds
For one who is not such a master of words
His very life is a chequered (with varied fortune) one – SARVAJNA

105. Even if one is a master of words,
It is wiser to avoid arguments, for the end result of all arguments is ill will and ill, luck only.

– SARVAJNA

106. An appropriate word at the right time and place is appreciated by all; they joy felt is akin to what one feels when a dead man comes to life again, where as a wrong word at the wrong time and place is a loss as great as a pearl slipping away from ones hand.

– SARVAJNA

107. Appropriate words are liked by all
Just as everyone prefers to eat a sweet ripe fruit
Inappropriate words are sure to cause harm and headache to all.

– SARVAJNA

108. Sandalwood sticks give out fine fragrance while they are burnt to ashes,
A man of virtue (SAJJANA) bears his misfortunes with fortitude and at any time he never gives up his good conduct.

– SARVAJNA

109. Precious articles like pearls, LAC (a dark red gum)
Asofaetida (a medicinal gum resine (Enguva in Telugu)
Honey and Musk (KASTOORI obtained from Musk deer) are difficult to procure, yet they are sought after by all.

– SARVAJNA

110. One who treats all other women
with respect and regard that he shows towards his own mother has no cause to be afriad of, from anyone and prosperity seeks such a one.

– SARVAJNA

111. A woman who treats all other men
with respect and regard that she shows towards her own father, is sure to attain SVARGA (HEAVEN).

– SARVAJNA

112. A son who loves his parents and treats them with affection, respect and regard, such a one is free from all dangers and is sure to attain happiness here and in the hereafter.

– SARVAJNA

113. Born warriors are never afraid to lay down their lives, in the cause of their belief, for they are aware of the eternal law that all creatures born are sure to die sooner or later and then where is the cause of fear in such valiant people?

– SARVAJNA

114. The world persecutes the man who is committed to TRUTH, and
the world loves the man who flatters and praises.

– SARVAJNA

115. A fool boasts about what little he knows
A wise man keeps quite about what he knows and is safe.

– SARVAJNA

116. A proud man comes to ruin sooner than an ordinary man,
when a storm rages, tall and big trees are uprooted first, where as the smaller trees and shrubs remain safe.

– SARVAJNA

117. One who knows how to serve well is fit to rule over others,
One who knows not how to serve well will be destroyed soon.

– SARVAJNA

118. One who spends his borrowed money, feels like
One who eats a meal of milk and rice with relish,
But when the lender (CREDITOR) demands the return of his money, he will feel the ignominy and agony of it (Shame or discredit)
more painful than when his ribs are smashed in.

– SARVAJNA

119. Keep away from contagious diseases and gambling,
Diseases undermine ones well being, whereas gambling makes one a pauper.

– SARVAJNA

120. KAMA (DESIRE) and KRODHA (ANGER) not only afflict the body but also the mind
If one eradicates Kama and Krodha, peace and happiness are his. – SARVAJNA

121. One who walks a hundred feet
in a cool breeze after his meal and
one who sleeps on his left side will never need a physician.

– SARVAJNA

122. One who reads and reads without any reflection, is as futile as a squeezed out sugar-cane; one who reads and reflects on what he has read is like the man who sips sugarcane juice at leisure.

– SARVAJNA

123. Do not commit A sin which you committed in the past out of ignorance
one who commits an evil deed again and again
even out of forgetfulness, destroys himself soon.

– SARVAJNA

124. Keep away from a man who not only fails to correct his faults but also indulges in slander, to safeguard your own welfare.

– SARVAJNA

125. One who fails to correct his own hundred faults
yet is so keen to detect even a single fault in an another
Such a one growls like a tiger, when in fact he is worse than a dog.

– SARVAJNA

126. Evil men who are worse than vultures and pigs deride (laugh at) men of virtue, yet the latter are unaffected by their revilings.

– SARVAJNA

127. Do not make fun of an ascetic
Do not revile (abuse) a generous man
Remember DAKSHA lost his head by reviling SIVA.

– SARVAJNA

128. Dogs bark when an elephant passes by
And if the elephant reacts to their barking
it is sure to loose its dignity.

– SARVAJNA

129. A beggar commands no respect or regard,
The mind (of a yogi) is untouched by all impurities,
There is no fear for one who has renounced the world
There is no AJNANA in a YOGI.

– SARVAJNA

130. Try to associate with men of virtue
If you associate with evil men
you are sure to reap unlimited grief and sorrow.

– SARVAJNA

131. Devotion and detachment facilitate salvation
If there is no devotion or detachment, there is no salvation.

– SARVAJNA

132. Alphabet is for writing, logic for disputation
All other studies enable one to make a living
To attain salvation two letters are enough namely SIVA.

– SARVAJNA

133. A rascal who associates with men of virtue, he himself changes into a man of virtue
But a good man who associates with rascals turns in to a real knave (rogue).

– SARVAJNA

134. Pride in ones family, quarrels and fights are indulged in only as long as there is strength in the body
when a man becomes sick and weak, the very
ground rises as if to hit him.

– SARVAJNA

135. If a braggart (vain boaster) says that a rabbit can outrun a chasing dog, it is wiser to agree
Let there be no quarrel with a fool and a braggart.

– SARVAJNA

136. The wise value quality,
conversation with a saint is inspiring,
For a virtuous woman, her husband is important,
And the man who endures to the last is the best.

– SARVAJNA

137. As long as you are healthy and wealthy
your wife and children love to be with you
when wealth is gone and when life departs from
your body, they take leave of you, the very next day.

– SARVAJNA

138. Even those who are pure, brave and saintly
can they remain unmoved at the sight of a
beautiful woman, a sharp weapon or gold.
(Unmoved = not affected by emotion).

– SARVAJNA

139. GOLD perverts even the mind of an ascetic,
endangers the Chastity of a wife,
and confounds even men of substance.
(confounds = puzzles).

– SARVAJNA

140. *For the sake of gold, strangers are glorified*
one's own relatives are forgotten and even murders are committed.

– SARVAJNA

141. Knowledge is vast, wisdom is priceless,
who causes disunion among men is far from salvation
Alas! there is no remedy on earth for DEATH.

– SARVAJNA

142. One who conducts himself always in keeping with his words
commands the world from where he sits.

– SARVAJNA

143. *Knowledge and wisdom are more precious than ones own parent sand brother,*
one who comes to your help in distress is to be regarded as more precious than an affectionate relative,
where one lives happily is his own native place.

– SARVAJNA

144. Borrow if you have to, in towns distant
creditor comes once or twice in three or six years
demands his money and interest, and goes back by the same way.

– SARVAJNA

145. A husband who is afraid of his wife is similar to a fox which pounces on a flock of fowls but runs away when it sees a dog.

– SARVAJNA

146. One who kills animals (and fish) and eats them will know the agony of the creature being killed when his only son dies.

– SARVAJNA

147. Greed warps the mind
A man of avarice ruins his own welfare

CARNAL (SENSUAL) pleasures ruin the wife and children.

– SARVAJNA

148. A diversity of pleasures keep the wife and children in mirth,
Alas! when you die, they consign your dead body to the burning pyre, and go home.

– SARVAJNA

149. TRUTH has no equal to it and UNTRUTH has no basis,
None is more beneficent than one's own mother,
and there is none immortal among men.

– SARVAJNA

150. A horse, a bullock, and a wife living away from her husband, are sure to be used by others.

– SARVAJNA

151. One who leaves his wife, Jewels, mango fruits and sugar cane, for safe keeping in another's hands is a stupid fool.

– SARVAJNA

152. Do not run after another's woman,
Do not waste time in futile gossip,
Do not you ever quarrel with your neighbours
and do not submit to the whims of others.

– SARVAJNA

153. Do not wade in to unknown waters, and thus avoid a watery grave,
Learn to grasp the essentials in a problem,
realise the truth, and aim to be an outstanding personality among all.

– SARVAJNA

154. To deliver one's arms to strangers, is to invite an attack from behind.

– SARVAJNA

155. From woman comes the new life on earth and woman is the source of all prosperity here and hereafter.

– SARVAJNA

156. Scholars, monks and ascetics, all of them
Pray from whom did they come in to this world, if not form a woman?

– SARVAJNA

157. Love of a woman, honour and dishonour and knowledge of truth, one comes by, should not be revealed to another.

– SARVAJNA

158. Worship without a symbol, a garden without a source of water, and the household affairs of one without a woman, all these are doomed to fail.

– SARVAJNA

159. Eyes fail to see, ears can not hear
your own legs can not carry you, if for one day your meal is missed.

– SARVAJNA

160. Sleep keeps away, mind wanders
Loving words cease to appeal if for one day your meal is missed.

– SARVAJNA

161. Eat not when you have no appetite, when hungry fail not to eat,
Do not eat cold dishes mixed with hot dishes
one who eats once a day is a saint, twice a day
a healthy man, and a glutton is sure to fall ill.

– SARVAJNA

162. One's tongue remains safe though it is always surrounded by teeth,
Just like the tongue, be vigilant and live safely amidst the wicked in the world.

– SARVAJNA

163. Better to survive with a little gruel and be free
Instead of eating plenty of food in humiliation
To be free is the best.

– SARVAJNA

164. Seeming to trust, be on guard,
Be alert, after ascertaining the basis of trust,
Trust no public woman. (STREE)

– SARVAJNA

165. Greed makes one to tell lies, perverts justice
Makes one to forego food and sleep,
Such is the retinue of GREED (Body of Attendants). – SARVAJNA

166. How can a hungry man who eats a carcass be called an out caste?
one who exploits others everyday for his own selfish gain is the unrivalled out caste.

– SARVAJNA

167. My father is not a BRAHMANA,
My mother in not MAALI
I am the son born of CHANDRASEKHARA'S grace. – SARVAJNA

168. Truth leads one to glory now and forever
In this world, TRUTH and falsehood are found counfusedly mixed
yet it is TRUTH alone that triumphs here and hereafter.

– SARVAJNA

169. *TRUTH is PUNYAM (MERIT), Falsehood is PAPAM (SIN)*
Never take to the crooked and deceitful course
Hold fast to the TRUTH,
RELY NOT ON THIS PERISHABLE HUMAN BODY.

– SARVAJNA

Sources

1. Anthology of Sarvajna's Sayings by D. Seshagiri Rao, 1978.
2. Vemanna–Sarvajnulu by Gandham Appa Rao, 1979.
3. Sarvajna by K.B. Prabhu Prasad, 1984.
4. Sarvajna Sukti by Nalluri Basavalingam, 1998.

22

AMARAVĀNI

Here is a collection of 140 POEMS and 100 Sanskrit Slokas) (139 SANSKRIT and 1 TELUGU POEM translated in to simple modern ENGLISH), and they give us a glimpse in to the wisdom of these great poets of the past.

1. **WELFARE**

   SULABHAHA PURUSHĀ RĀJAN! SATATAM PRIYA VĀDINAHA
   APRIYASYA TU PATHYASYA VAKTĀ SROTĀ CHA DURLABHAHA

   —VALMEEKI

   Oh! King! It is quite easy to find those who speak pleasantly with you on all occasions, whereas to find one who will tell you what will facilitate your welfare, although it is unpleasant and not welcomed by you is almost impossible. Even if you find such a one, where will you find one who is ready to listen to his wise counsel?

2. **THE WAY**

   TARKO APRATISHTAHA SRUTAYO VIBHINNAHA
   NIKO RUSHIRYASYA MATAM PRAMANAM
   DHARMASYA TATVAM NIHITAM GUHAYAM
   MAHAJANO YENA GATASSA PANDHAHA

   —MAHABHARATA

   Logic is uncertain, and VEDAS give different interpretations on DHARMA. There is not a single RUSHI (SAINT), whose words are authoritative on DHARMA. The essential nature of DHARMA is inscrutable. The only way for the mankind is to follow in the footsteps of the great ones of the past.
   (Refer : YAKSHA PRASNA No. : 121 - Page No. : 536)

3. **A PANDITA**

   ASOCHYAN ANVASOCHAHA TVAM
   PRAJNAVĀDĀMSCHA BHASHASE
   GATASOONA GATĀ SOOSCHA
   NANU SOCHANTI PANDITAHA

   —SRIMAD BHAGAVADGITA

Arjuna! you are lamenting for those, one should not lament for, and also you are talking in a clever manner. A PANDITA never grieves for the departed dead, or for those who are still alive.

(PANDITA in the context means, one who is unaffected by the DVANDAS (or opposites, such as joy or sorrow, heat or cold etc.) and not the usual meaning of a learned man)

Asochyan = lamenting for those one should not lament for; Anvasochaha = lamented Gata + Asoon; Departed dead = Agatasoon = Those who are still alive; Na anusochanti = will not grieve.

4. **JOY AND SORROW**

SUKHAM HE DUKHANI ANUBHOOYA SOBHATE
GHANANDHAKARA DIVA DEEPADARSANAM
SUKHATTU YO YATI DASAM DARIDRATAM STHITAHA SAREERENA MRUTAHA SA TEEVATI

—BHASA (FROM CHARU DATTA)

When one experiences joy after grief, it is similar to stepping in to bright light from utter darkness. When one becomes poor, after enjoying wealth in the past, such a one will be considered as a dead one although he is still alive.

Anubhuya = after experiencing; Daridratam Dasare = when one becomes poverty stricken; Mrutaha = Dead; Jeevati = even though still alive.

5. **EXEMPLARY QUALITIES**

JNANE MOUNAM KSHAMĀ SAKTOU TYAGE SLAGAVIPARYA YAHA
GUNAHA GUNĀNUBHADITVAT TASYA SA PRASAVAHA EVA

—MAHAKAVI KALIDAS (FROM RAGHUVAMSAM)

Exemplary qualities like restraint in exhibiting his knowledge, prowess, and self praise are present in KING DILEEPA.

slaga viparya yaha = Free from self praise

Guna + Anubandhi tvat = in the company of qualities such as MOUNA, KSHAMA etc.

Saktou = Prowess : Sa presavaha eva = are found in harmony just like the harmony found in the members of a family

6. LOUKIKANAM HE SADHUNAM ARTHAM VAGĀNUVARTATE
RUSHI RĀM PUNARADYA NAM VACHAM ARTHAHA ARTHAHA ANUDHAVATI

—BHAVA BHOOTI (FROM UTTARA RAMA CHARITAM)

The words of an ordinary sage convey the ordinary meaning of those words, whereas the words uttered by a great saint are extra ordinarily powerful and their meaning will be fulfilled.

Anuvartate = conveys; Loukikanam = ordinary

Adyanam = great : - affairs of the word

Rushinam = saints; Anudhavati = follows.

7. **MEN OF ACHIEVEMENT**

PRARABHYATE NA KHALU VIGHNA BHAYENA NEECHIHA
PRARABHYA VIGHNANI HATA VIRAMANTI MADHYAHA
VIGHNIHA MUHURMUHURAPI PRATIHANYA MANAHA
PRARABDHHA UTTAMAJANAHA NA PARITYAJANTI

—BHARTRU HARI

An inferior man never takes up any task, as he is scared of the obstacles that might interfere in its successful completion

An ordinary man takes up a task, but gives it up in the middle, as soon as he encounters obstacles in its completion.

A superior man once he takes up any task, he will successfully complete it, inspite of obstacles.

Vignabhayena = scared of obstacles; viramanti = gives up

Muhuhu + Muhuhu = inspite of repeated upsets

Pratihanyamanaha = by the interference of

Prarabdham = The task they have taken; Parityajanti = never leave it without a successful completion.

8. **CONCENTRATION**

UPAYAM ASTHITASYA API NASYANTI ARDHAHA PRAMADYATAHA
HANTI NO UPASAYASTHAHA API SAYALUHU MRUGAYUHA MRUGAN

—MAGHA (FROM SISUPALA VADHA)

Even for a skilled and experienced man, success in a task eludes, if he is not vigilant (ALERT) and if he lacks concentration. Just as a hunter will never be able to trap an animal, if he is sleepy and lacks concentration, whatever might be his skill and experience

Upayam = Skill; Asthitasya + Api = inspite of possessing; Pramadyataha = one who is careless

Nasyanti = become useless (or fails); Mrugayuha = Hunter; upasayasthaha + Api = inspite of hiding patiently in a hideout to hunt animals

Na hanti = will not be able to kill them.

9. **THE ESSENCE OF KNOWLEDGE**

ANANTA SASTRAM BAHU VEDITAVYAM
ALPASCHA KALO BA HU VASCHA VIGNAHA
YAT SARABHUTAM TADU PASI TAVYAM
HAMSO YADHA KSHEERAM AMBU MISRAM

—VISHNUSARMA (FROM PANCHATANTRA)

SASTRAS are many and vast, and the time to read and master them is limited, and there are many obstacles on the way to acquisition of knowledge.

Hence a wise man concentrates on acquiring the essence of knowledge, just as a swan drinks milk only and discards water, when it is given diluted milk to drink.

Veditavyam = To study and learn; sarabhutam = Essence of; Vighnaha = obstacles;

Upas Tavyam = To acquire; Ambu misram = diluted with water Ksheeram = milk.

10. **ON FRIENDSHIP**

ARAMBHA GURVEE KSHAYINEE KRAMENA
LAGHVEE PURA VRUDDHI MUPITI PASCHAT
DINASYA POORVARDHA PARADHA BHINNA
CHAYEVA MITRU KHALA SAJJA NANAM

—BHARTRUHARI

The friendship of an evil person to begin with is impressive and it is similar to the big shadow cast by the morning sun, but as the day progresses the shadow size dwindles and by noon, it altogether disappears.

Whereas the friendship with a man of virtue, to begin with is unimpressive, like the small shadow cast by the after noon sun, and as the day comes to a close the size of the shadow goes on increasing, and similarly the friendship with a man of virtue progresses gradually and becomes more dependable and reliable, as time passes.

Khala = An evil person; Sajjananam = Man of virtue

Dinasya = Morning; POORVA + ARTHA = First half of the day (i.e. up to noon); PARA + ARTHA = Second half of the day (i.e. from noon to evening); Chaya + eva = like the shadow of; Arumbha gurvee = To begin with impressive; Lagvee = Decreases in size; Paschat = Later; Vruddhim = increases; Upite = in size.

11. **ON PATIENCE**

DURJANA VADANA VINIRGATA VACHANA BHUJANGENA SAJJANO DASTAHA
OUSHADA SATIHA ASADHYAHA CHIKITSA TYE KSHĀNTI MANTRENA

—SUNDARA PANDYA (6TH CENTURY POET)
FROM (NEETI DVISHASTIKA)

There is no remedy for the cruel words uttered by an evil person. His words are more poisonous than even the venom of a snake. The only remedy for such a provocation is to be patient. A man of virtue saves himself from the poisonous words of an evil person by the 'MANTRA' called 'PATIENCE'

Bhujangena = Snake; Dastaha; Bitten by; oushada satiha = Even by using hundreds of medicines; Asadhyaha = impossible; KSHANTI MANTRENA = A mantra called Patience; Chikitsa tye = will be cured by.

12. **ON CONTENTMENT**

MODHA! JAHEEHE DHANA AGAMATRUSHNAM
KURU TANU BUDDE MANASI VITRUSHNAM
YALLABHASE NIJA KARMOPATTAM
VITTAM TENA VINODAYA CHITTAM

—SRI SANKARACHARYA
(FROM "BHAJAGOVINDAM SLOKAS)
(REFER PAGE NO : 489 SLOKA NO : 2)

Give up the desire to a mass more and more of wealth

Be contented with what you obtain by your own efforts, and enjoy peace of mind.

Dhana + Agamatrushnam = Avarice; Tanubudde = Do not be stupid; Jaheehe = give up = Nijakarma + Upattam = obtained by ones own effort.

13. **DISCRIMINATION**

SAHASĀ VIDADHEETA NA KRIYAM
AVIVEKAHA PARAMĀPADĀM PADAM
VRUNATE HE VIMRU SYAKARI NAM
GUNA LUBDHAHA SVA YAMEVA SAMPADAHA

—BHARAVI (FROM : KIRATARJUNEEYAM)

One should not undertake a task impulsively and without carefully assessing the advantages and disadvantages of it. One who works without discrimination and foresight is sure to land himself in many predicaments.

Wealth and prosperity seek the man of discrimination and foresight by themselves.

Sahasa = on impulse; Kriyam = A TASK; Na Vidadheeta = should not be undertaken; VIMRUSYAKARI = A man of discrimination and foresight; SVAYAM EVA = By themselves; Vrunate = Seek him.

14. **TRUTH AND FALSEHOOD**

PRANAHĀNI VACCHU PATTUNA SARVADHA
NĀPAHĀRA VELA YANDU NADAPU
ASATYAM ANRUTA MANDRA SATYAM BU SOONRUTA
MANI PARIGRAHINTURU ARYAJANULU

—TIKKANA (TELUGU) (FROM ANDHRA MAHABHAARATAM)

When one's life is in danger, or when all of one's wealth is likely to be robbed, one may tell lies to safeguard ones life and wealth.

The lies uttered under such dire (EXTREME) conditions should be taken as TRUTH only. If even one tells TRUTH under such dire conditions, because of misguided zeal for TRUTH, it should be taken as falsehood only.

15. **SEA SHELLS AND DIAMONDS**

NA ARGANTI RATNANI SAMUDRA JANI
PAREEKSHA KAHA YATRA NA SANTI DESE
ABHEERA PALYANCHITA PADMARAGAM
TRIBHI HE VARATIHA PANAYANTI GOPYAHA

—PANDITARAYALU - JAGNNA DHUDU
(FROM BHAMINEE VILASAMU)

Even diamonds obtained from the depths of the sea, remain unnoticed if there are no Diamond assessors (in that sea shore) near by.

PADMARAGAM (A precious stone) commonly available in villages of shepherds, is exchanged for three sea shells by the women, as they are not aware of the real value of PADMARGAM.

yatra dese = in which country; Pareekshakaha = assessors of diamonds; Na santi = are not available; Na Arghanti = not valued; Samudrajani = obtained from the ocean; Ratnani = Diamonds; Gopyaha = Shepherd women; Abheerapalli = Villages of shepherds; Padma Ragam = A precious stone; Tri bhihe varatiha = for 3 sea shells; Panayanti = are able to buy.

16. **ON MARRIED LIFE**

ADVITAM SUKHA DUKHAYOHO ANUGATAM
SARVASU AVASTHASU YAT
VISRAMO HRUDAYASYA YATRA JARASA
YASMIN HARYO RASAHA
KALENA AVARANA ATYAT PARINATE
YAT SNEHASĀRE STIHTHAM
BHADRAM TASYA SUMĀNUSHASYA KATHA
MAPYEKAM HE TAT PRĀPYATE

—BHAVA BHOOTI (FROM UTTARA RAMACHARITAM)

The happiness that one obtains in the married state has no equal to it. It is unaffected by the ups and downs of life. It consoles a man in the vicissitudes of life.

This happiness in the married state is unaffected even by the approach of old age and even by inevitable separations, which occur in the course of time However, such unsullied happiness for the wife in the married state is rare indeed.

Advaitam = without separation; Sarvasu Avasthasu = on all occasions; Anugatam = follows; Jarasa = onset of old age; Avarana + Atyat = shame, inhibitions and separation etc.; Sumanushasya = for a Virtuous wife; Bhadram = Happiness; Hrudayasya = for the mind; Visramaha = rest; kadham + Api = rarely; prapyate = is attained = Rasaha; LOVE: Na HARYAHA = will not diminish in intensity

17. **ON GREED**

ASHĀ BALAVATEE BHEEMA! KĀCHIDĀSCHARYA SRUNKHALA YAYĀ
BADDHĀHA PRADHAVANTI MUKTAHA TISHTANTI PUNGUVAT

—(FROM JAIMINI BHARATAM)
(ASVAMEDHA PARVAM : 6th chapter 55th SLOKA)

Bheemasena! GREED is a very powerful instinct. It is a strange and strong fetter self imposed on a man. One who is in those fetters keeps on running till the end of his life, whereas one who has freed himself from those fetters, limps on as a cripple.

18. **OLD AGE - DISEASE - DEATH**

JARA SAMĀ NASTI AMRUJĀ PRAJĀNAM
VYADHEHA SAMO NASTI JAGATI ANARDHAHA
MRUTYOHA SAMAM NASTI BHAYAM PRUDHIVYAM
ATAT TRIAM KHALVA VASENA SEVYAM

—ASVA GHOSHUDU
(FROM SOUNDARANANDANAM)

1. To maintain the cleanliness of the body in old age is rather difficult;
2. Disease of the human body is one of the greatest threats to its survival.
3. Fear of DEATH is the greatest fear, one experiences on the earth.

A VIVASA (one who has no control over his body, mind and soul) is subject to the above mentioned afflictions.

Amruja = Dirt; Avasena = one who has no control over himself; Prudhivyam = on the earth.

19. **GOOD CONDUCT**

GUNESHU AVA ADARMA KURYĀT
NA JATOU JATU TATVAVIT
DROUNIHE DVIJOBHAVAT SOODRAHA
SOODRASCHA VIDURAHA KSHAMEE

—KSHEMENDRA's CHARU CHARYA

One who knows the true nature of things (TATVA) gives importance to a man's conduct, rather than to his ancestry

ASWADTHAMA, son of ACHARYA DRONA lost his preeminent position and prestige as a BHAHMANA and became a SOODRA because of his evil conduct and cruel deeds. Where as VIDURA, though born as a SOODRA, became renowned for his PATIENCE and exemplary moral conduct.

Jatu = never consider; Jatou = Ancestry;
Geneshu Ava Adaram = Give importance only to good qualities and good conduct; DVIJAHA = Being a Brahamana; Drounihi = son of DRONA (ASVADTHAMA); Soodraha = Became a SOODRA; Viduraha = VIDURA; KSHAMEE = A man of patience.

20. **COLLECTION OF TAXES**

MADHUDOHAM DUHET RASTRAM
BRAMARAHA EVA PĀDAPAM
VATSĀPEKOSHI DUHECCHIVA
STANASCHA NA VIKUTTAYET
JALOU KAVAT PIBET RASTRUM
MRUDUNIVA NARĀDHIPAHA
VYAGHREEVA CHA HARET PUTRAN
SANDASENNA CHA PEEDAYET

—MAHABHARATAM
(FROM SANTI PARVAMU - 8th chapter)

A King should collect taxes from his subjects without causing any undue inconvenience or hardships to them. The proper way of collection of the taxes can be learnt from the examples given below.

1. A butterfly gently extracts honey from the flowers without causing the least damage to them
2. One milks a cow gently and always leaving enough milk for the sustenance of its calf
3. A tigress carries her cubs by their scruff (Loose skin at the back of neck) from place to place, without causing the least injury to them
4. A leech extracts blood from its victim, silently and in a pain free manner.

Padapam = Tree; Bramaraha Eva = Like the butterfly; Duhet = extract; Vatsa + Apekshee = one who wants to ensure the welfare of the calf;
Stanaat = Udder of the cow; Na Vikuttayet = should not pull on it unduly; Naradhipaha = A king; Jalou Kāvat = Like a leech; Mruduna + Ava = gently; Vyaghree + Eva = A tigress; Haret = carries; Na sandaset = should not bite them

21. **ANCIENT AND MODERN POETRY**
PURĀNAMITYEVA NA SADHU SARVAM
NA CHAPI KAVYAM NAVAMITYAVADYAM
SANTAHA PAREEKSHĀ ANYATARAT BHAJANTE
MOODAHA PARAPRATYA YA NEYA BUDDHIHI

—MAHAKAVI KALIDAS
(FROM MALAVIKAGNIMITRAM)

Ancient poetry should not be applauded simply because it is ancient. Modern poetry should not be underestimated simply because it is modern. A man of discernment (good insight), critically evaluates both of them, and approves only the best among the two, where as a fool approves them only on the recommendation of others.

Puranam + Eti = Simply because it is ancient; Na SADHU = not all of it is the best; Navam + Eti = modern; Na Avadyam = underestimate; SANTAHA = Men of virtue; Pareekshya = critically evaluate; Anyatarat = choose one among them; Para pratyaya neya buddhihe = relies on the judgement of others.

22. **TEACHER AND THE STUDENT**
PATRAVISHESHE NYASTUM GUNANTARAM VRAJATI SILPĀMA DHATU HU
JALAMIVA SAMUDRA SUKTOU MUKTĀPHALATĀM PYODASYA

—MAHAKAVI KALIDAS.

Knowledge imparted to an outstanding student in the course of time, attains greater brilliance, because of the inherent genius of the student.

Just as a rain drop if it by chance falls in to an oyster shell in the sea, it eventually turns in to a pearl, where as the rest of the rain drops merge in the sea.

Patravisheshe = An outstanding student; Nyastum = imparted to; Adhatuhu = Teacher's; silpam = knowledge; Samudra suktou = oyster shell in the sea; Muktaphalatam Vrajati Eva = turns in to a pearl

23. **MAN OF VIRTURE**
BHAVANTI NAMRĀ TARAVAHA PHALODGAMIHA
NAVA AMBUBHIHI DOORA VILAMBINO GHANĀHA
ANUDDHATAHA SATPURUSHAHA SAMRUDDHI BHIHI
SVABHAVA AVISHA PAROPA KARINĀM.

The branches of trees laden with fruits, (under their weight), bend down and become more accessible.

Clouds laden with rain spread far and wide in the sky, similarly

Men of virtue never forgo their inherent noble qualities such as generosity, humility etc., even when they have become prosperous and wealthy

Taravaha = Trees; Phala + Udgamiha = Laden with fruits; Namraha = Bend down; Ghanāha = clouds; Nava + Ambubhihe = Laden with new water (Rain); Dooravilambinaha = Spread far and wide in the sky; Samruddhibhihe = prosperity; Anuddhataha = do not become short tempered or loose their humility

24. **SOIL AND THE SEEDS**
CHEEYATE BALISASYA API

SAT KSHETRA PATITĀ KRUSHIHI
NA SĀLEHA STAMBAKARITĀ
VAPTUHU GUNAMAPEKSHATE

—VISAKHADATTUDU (AD 6TH CENTURY)
(FROM MUDRĀRĀKSHASAM)

Seeds sown in a fertile soil yield a rich crop. The yield of the crop does not depend upon the intelligence of the sower, but on the feritility of the soil.
Balisasya api = one who is ignorant;
Krushihe = Cultivation; Satkshetra patita = Fertile field; Chuyate = yield a rich crop; Saleha = Paddy Crop; Stamba Karita = paddy stems become stout and robust; Vaptuhu = A sower; Gunam = Skill; Na apekshate = does not depend upon.

25. **GENEROSITY**
GUNĀNĀM VĀ VISĀLANĀM
SATKĀRĀNĀM CHA NITYASAHA
KARTĀRAHA SULABHĀHĀ LOKE
VIGNATĀ RASTU DURLABHA HA

—BHASA (FROM SVAPNA VASAVADATTAM)

There are many endowed with good qualities such as generosity and those who felicitate others, but there are very few, who gracefully acknowledge and give credit to the good qualities of others.
Gunānām = qualities; Nityasaha = Always; Kartārahā = Those who posses; Vignatrastu = Those who acknowledge and give credit; Durlabhaha = are rare indeed.

26. **NATURE AND DEATH**
KAHA KUM SAKTO RAKSHITUM MRUTYUKĀLE
RAJJU CHEDDHE KE GHATAM DHARAYANTI
AVUM LOKAHA TULYADHARMO VANĀ NĀM
KALE KALE CHIDYATE RUHYATE CHA

—BHASA.

O! King! none is capable of saving another from DEATH, just as none is capable of retrieving a pot of water, which drops in to a well suddenly, when the rope of the pot gives way unexpectedly.
Trees in a forest are cut down and in the course of time, new sprigs and shoots spring up from the remaining stumps.
Man that is born is sure to die sooner or later
This is an ETERNAL LAW
Kaha = who; Kum = whom; Mrutyukale = at the time of death; Saktaha = capable of; Rajjuche dhe = when the rope gives way; Ghatam = pot; Dharyanti = can retrieve it; Chidyate = cut down; Ruhyate = again put forth new sprigs and shoots

27. **FATE AND DESTINY**
DVEEPAT API ANYASMĀT
MADHYĀ DAPI JALANIDHEHA DISAHA ANTĀTAPI
ANEEYA JHUTATI GHATAYATI

VIDHIRABHIMATAM ABHIMUKHEE BHOOTAHA

—HARSHAVARDHANA (A.D. : 606 - 646)
(FROM "RATNAVALEE")

The object which one desires to possess, if FATE decrees, will reach self, even if it is in a far off island, or in the middle of the ocean or in a remote corner of the world. Abhimukhee bhootaha = Favourable; Vidhi = FATE Anyasmat = From another; Dveepat api = island; Jalanidheha = ocean; madhyatapi = from the middle of; Antat api = even from a far off corner; Abhimatam = what one desires; Jhutiti = immediately; Aneeya = so arranges; Ghatayati = that is reaches you.

28. **DANAM**

TYAGE SATVANIDHIHE KURYĀT
NA PRATYUPAKRUTI SPRUHAM
KARNAHA KUNDALA DĀNEBHOOT
KALUSHAHA SAKTI YĀCHAYĀ

—KSHEMENDRA (A.D. 1029 -1064)
(FROM 'CHARUCHARYA')

A man of virtue, if he makes a gift to another is not supposed to expect a return for the gift he has given to another.

KARNA made a gift of his KUNDALAMS (ornaments of the ear) to INDRA, and he wanted A 'SAKTI' (A special power which can be used against an enemy in a war) in return for his KUNDALAMS.

And because of this request for a 'SAKTI', KARNA's 'DANA' of Kundalams, lost its pristine glory.

Satvanidhihe = A man of virtue; Tyage = while making a gift; Prati + Upakruti + Spruham = should not expect a return; Sakti yāchaya = By requesting for a 'SAKTI'; Kalushaha = Karna's fame was sullied.

29. **ENCOURAGEMENT**

GUNASTAVENA KURVEETA
MAHATAM MANAVARDHANAM
HANUMANA BHAVATI STUTYU
RAMAKARYABHARA KSHAMAHA

However great and powerful person one might be, even such a powerful and great one hesitate to undertake a stupendous task, unless there are others who have faithin his capability and greatness and who give him support and encouragement at the right time.

30. **CONDUCT - SPEECH - APPEARANCE**

ACHARAHA KULAMĀ KHYĀTI
DESAMĀ KHYĀTI BHĀSHANAM
SAMBRAMAHA SNEHAMA KHYATI
VAPURĀ KHYATI BHOJANAM

A man's conduct reveals his ancestry
A man's speech reveals the place where he was brought up

A man's affection and regard for others, reveals his friendliness
A man's physique (bodily structure and strength) reveals his food habits
Acharaha = conduct; Kulam = Ancestry; Akhyati = Reveals; Bhashanam = Speech; Sambramaha = regard; Sneham = friendship Vapuhu; PHYSIQUE (Bodily structure and strength)

31. **BODY AND SOUL**
PUSPHE GANDHAHĀ TILE TILAM
KASTE VAHNIHE PYOGHRUTAM
EKSHA GUDAM TĀDHA DEHE
PASYA ATMĀNUM VIVEKATAHA
As there is scent in a flower,
as there is oil in gingili seeds (Indian sesame OR NUVVULU),
as there is fire in a nascent form in firewood,
as there is ghee in milk,
as there is jaggery in the juice of sugarcane,
one who is wise, comes to realize that SOUL (OR GOD) is imminent (close at hand) in his own body.
Vahnihe = Fire; Dehe = in ones own body; Atmānum = Realise the soul; Vivekataha = with intelligence; Pasya = See.

32. **DHARMA AND DANA.**
JALABINDU NIPĀTENA
KRAMASAHA POORYATE GHATAHA
SA HETUHU SARVAVIDYANAM
DHARMASYA CHẠ DHANASYACHA
A pot gets filled up eventually if water is allowed to drop in to it, drop by drop. In the same manner, even if one acquires VIDYA, DHARMA and DHANA, little by little, and gradually, in the end such a one will be renowned for his Vidya, Dharma and Dhana.
Ghataha = pot; Jalabindu = water drops; Nipātena = By the drops of; Kramasaha = gradually; Pooryate = gets filled up; Saha = in the same manner.

33. **MĀNAM (SELF RESPECT) AND DHANAM (WEALTH)**
ADHAMAHA DHANAMICCHANTI
DHAĀNAM MĀNAM CHA MADHYAMĀHA
UTTAMAHA MĀNAM ECCHANTI
MANO HE MAHATĀM DHANAM
An inferior man lives to earn money
An ordinary man lives to earn money and at the same time wants to retain his self respect
A superior man tries to safeguard his self respect at all cost, for such an exemplary man, to safeguard his self respect is of greater importance than to earn money.
Adhamaha = An inferior person; Mahatam = for the great one; Mānam = Self respect

34. **THE THREE DIAMONDS**
PRUDHIVYAM TREENI RATNĀNI
JALAM ANNAM SUBHASHITAM
MOODHIHA PĀSHĀNA KHANDESHU
RATNA SANKHYA ABHIDHEEYATE
In this world there are three priceless diamonds.
They are : 1. Water (JALAM) 2. ANNAM (FOOD) and MORALS (SUBHASHITAMS), where as stupid fools regard pieces of stone as diamonds.
Prudhivyam = on the earth; Treeni = Three
Pāshāna Khandeshu = pieces of stone
Ratna sankhya = as diamonds; Abhidheeyate = consider them as

38. **A LEARNED MAN AS A FRIEND**
SUHRUTTCHA VIDVĀNAPI DURLABHA STADHA
YADOUSHADAM SVĀDU HITAMCHA DURLABHAM
It is almost impossible to acquire the friendship of a learned man (PANDITA), as he is endowed with intelligence, discrimination and foresight, where as to cultivate the friendship of an ordinary person is relatively easy, as he lacks the above qualities of a PANDITA.
Most of Aurvedic Medicines are bitter to the taste, but they help in restoring health. Similarly, though to cultivate the friendship with a PANDITA is not easy, but once cultivated, it proves to be more fruitful for all.

39. **RENUNCIATION**
BHOGE ROGA BHAYAM, KULE CHYUTI BHAYAM VITTE NRUPALAD BHAYAM
MĀNE DINYA BHAYAM, BALE RIPU BHAYAM, ROOPE JARAYA BHAYAM
SASTRĀ VĀDI BHAYAM, GUNE KHALABHAYAM, KAYE KRUTĀNTĀT BHAYAM
SARVAM VASTU BHAYANVITAM, BHUVI NRUNĀM VIRAGYAMEVA ABHAYAM

—BHARTRUHARI

One who leads a life of ease, comfort and luxury is scared of their effect on his health and longevity.
One who is proud of his ancestry, is scared of loosing his social status.
One who is wealthy is afraid of the taxes that will be levied on him by the King.
One who is proud of his status is afraid of loosing it.
One who is proud of his physical strength is afraid of loosing it in the hands of his enemies (when they attack him).
One who is proud of his handsome personality is afraid of loosing it with the onset of old age.
One who is proud of his learning is afraid of other learned men, as they may defeat him in a debate in a learned assembly.
A man of virtue is afraid of dangers from evil persons.

one who is alive, is afraid of DEATH, which may strike at any time and place.
The only one who is free from all the above fears is the one, who has renourced the world.

40. **DHARMA**

DHANANI BHOOMOU PASAVASCHA GOSTE
BHARYA GRUHADVĀRI JANAHA SMASĀNE
DEHASCHITAYAM PAROLOKE MARGE
DHARMĀNUGO GATCCHATI JEEVA EKAHA

When a man dies, he leaves behind all of his wealth, cattle etc.
Alas! his wife takes leave of the dead body at the front door only.
Relatives and friends accompany the funeral journey up to the burial ground, and consign the dead body to the flames of a burning pyre and depart.
Ones own lifeless body, (which was the sole basis of existence on earth during your life time) is reduced to ashes.
In the final and solitary journey, the SOUL is accompanied only by DHARMA.

41. **PARAMATMA**

MRUTPINDAM EKO BAHU BHANDAROOPAM
SUVARNAM EKUM BAHU BHOOSHANI
GOKSHEERAM EKUM BAHU DHENU JATAM
EKAHA PARAMATMA BAHU DEHAVARTEE

Pots vary in size and shape, but they are all made up of mud,
Ornaments are of many types, but they are all made up of GOLD,
Cows vary in colour but the milk they all yield is white in colour
Living creatures are many, but only one PARAMATMA pervades in all of them.

42. **ARTHA, KAMA, VIDYA AND KSHUDA**

ARTHĀTURĀNĀM NA GURU NA BANDHUHU
KĀMĀTURĀNĀM NA BHAYAM NA LAJJĀ
VIDYATURĀNAM NA SUKHAM NA NIDRĀ
KSHUDHATURANAM NA RUCHI NA PAKVAM

One whose sole aim in life is to earn money, will not hesitate to get money out of any one, including his own GURU, or relative or friend
One who is overtaken by sexual passion, will not be restrained either by fear or by public ridicule
One who wants to acquire VIDYA, will have to forego ease, comfort and sleep in its pursuit
One who is hungry will eat up anything and will not bother about its taste or whether it is cooked properly or not.

43. **DHARMA AND ADHARMA**

AKI VA GOW TRIA SIMHAHA
PANCHA VYAGRA PRASOOTIBHIHE
ADHARMO NASTA SANTANAHA
DHARMA SANTANA VARDHANAHA.

A cow gives birth to a calf at a time, a lioness gives birth to three cubs, and a tigress gives birth to five cubs, yet as years pass by, the number of cows is increasing, and the number of lions and tigers is decreasing day by day.
Tigers and lions survive by killing and eating other defenceless creatures, whereas a cow is a harmless and useful creature that survives on grass.
Those who walk on the path of ADHARMA are sure to be ruined in the end, whereas those who walk on the path of DHARMA, are sure to prosper in the end.

44. **A DURJANA**
SAKATAM PANCHA HASTESHU
DASA HASTESHU VĀJINAM
GAJAM HASTA SAHASRESHU
DURJANAM DOORATAHA TYAJET
   1. For your own safety, keep a distance of about 5 five feet between yourself and a moving CART
   2. For your own safety, keep a distance of about 10 feet between yourself and a horse
   3. For your own safety, keep a distance of about 1000 feet between yourself and an elephant
   4. And when you see an evil person, keep away from him at any cost.

45. **VIDYA AND DHANAM**
PUSTAKESHU CHA YĀ VIDYA
PARAHASTE CHA YAT DHANAM
SAMAYETU PARIPRĀPTE
NASĀ VIDYĀ NA TADDHANAM
Knowledge contained in a book, and money kept in the custody of others, are of no use for immediate purposes. The only remedy is to learn the subject contained in the book, thoroughly and memorise it, and to keep ready cash in ones hand for emergency needs.

46. **A DURJANA**
VRUSCHI KASCHA VISHAM PUCCHAM
MAKSHI KASYA VISHAM SIRAHA
TAKSHA KASYA VISHAM DAMSTRA
SARVANGAM DURJANE VISHAM
A scorpion has a venomous sting in its tail
A fly has venom in its head
A cobra has venom in its fangs in the head
A Durjana (or an EVIL PERSON) has venom in his entire body.

47. **THE BEST THINGS IN THE WORLD**
STREE YO RATNĀ ANYADHO VIDYĀ
DHARMA SOUCHAM SUBHĀSHITAM
VIVIDHĀNI CHA SILPANI
SAMĀDEYANI SARVATAHA

Vidya, Dharma, Morals, good conduct, attractive sculptures and beautiful women, whereever and with whomsoever they might be, are worth possessing.

48. **VEDAM - MATRU**

NASTI VEDĀT PARAM SASTRAM
NASTI MATRU SAMO GURUHU
NASTI MATRU SAMAHA POOJYO
NASTI MATRU SAMAHA SAKHA

VEDAM is the greatest among all SASTRAS
MOTHER is the greatest among all GURUS
There is none more worthy of reverence than a mother
There is no friend more sincere than ones mother.

49. **SATYAM**

SATYAM BROOYĀT PRIYAM BROOYA
NNA BROOYAT SATYAM APRIYAM
PRIYANCHA ANRUTAM BROOYA
AVAVA DHARMA SANĀTANAHA

Always speak the TRUTH. Speak truth in a pleasant manner. But do not reveal unpleasant truths.
Do not tell lies to please anyone. This is the eternal law about TRUTH.

50. **DHARMA - ARTHA - KAMA**

PARITYAJET ARTHA KAMOU
YOU SYĀTĀM DHARMA VARJITOU
DHARMAM CHAVYA SUBHOD KARAM
LOKA NIKRUSTA MEVACHA

Do not try to earn money by unscrupulous means.
Do not try to possess anything forbidden by DHARMA though it may make you happy in the beginning, it is sure to ruin your reputation and cause sorrow in the end.

51. **MARGAM**

YENĀSYA PITARA YĀTĀ
YENA YĀTAHA PITĀMAHĀHA
TENA YĀ YĀ SATAM MARGAM
TENA GACCHANNARISHYATI

Follow the path trodden by your parents, grand parents and ancestors. By following in their foot steps, you will not only gain in mental satisfaction but also will not loose anything.

52. **SHĀRADDHA AND BHAKTI**

NĀ VRUSTĀHA KASYA CHIDROODBHOOYA
NNĀ CHĀNYO ANA PRUCCHATAHA
JANANNAPIHEE MEDHĀVI
JADAVALLOKA ACHARET.

Do not volunteer (reveal) any information to another, unless it is asked for. Even when asked for, do not reveal any information if that person lacks SHĀRADDHA

(INTEREST) and BHAKTI (REVERENCE). A wise man although he knows what is going on around him, moves on as if he is a dumb and ignorant man.

53. **DHARMA AND ADHARMA**

NA SEENNAPICHA DHARMESHU
MANODHARMĀ NIVESAYET
ADHĀ KARMINĀM PAPĀNĀ
CHOOSU PASYAN VIPARYAYAM

One who follows DHARMA, has to suffer from poverty and many afflictions, where as if one follows ADHARMA, such a one will experience success and prosperity in the begining, yet this success and prosperity will come to an end, and he will have to pay for all his evil deeds.

Aware of this truth, one should never deviate from DHARMA.

54. **PĀPAM AND PUNYAM**

NĀ DHARMAS CHARITE LOKE
SADYAHA PHALATI GOURIVA
SANI RĀ VARTA MĀNASTU
KARTUR MOOLANI KRUNTAYĀ

A cow eats grass and yields milk only after a certain time. Similarly good and evil deeds committed by self, yield their results after a certain time

None can escape the result of an evil deed and the ruin that follows.

55. **PAPAM AND PUNYAM**

YADE NĀTMANI PUTRESHU
NACHETPUTRESHU NAPTASHU
NITYEVATU KRUTO DHARMAHA
KARTURBHAVATI NISHPHALAHA

One who follows ADHARMA may be successful and prosper in the begining, but the results of his evil deeds, are sure to afflict his children, grand children, great grand children and descendants.

None can escape from the consequences of his own evil deeds. This is an eternal law.

56. **PAPAM AND PUNAYAM**

ADHARME NI TATETĀVA
TTATO BHADRĀNI PASYATI
ATATSA PATVĀN JAYATI
SAMOOLASTU VINASYATI.

One who follows ADHARMA will become wealthy, prosperous and conquer (overcome) his enemies in the begining. But in the course of time when his evil deeds bear fruit, he is sure to lose everything.

57. **NASTIKA**

NASTIKYAM VEDA NINDĀCHA
DEVATĀNAM CHA KUTSANAM
DVESHAM DAMBHANCHA, MANANCHA
KRODHAM TI KSHVANCHA VARJAYET.

To argue about and refute the existence of GOD and to criticize VEDAS and DEVATAS is forbidden.

One should eschew (AVOID) evil qualities such as Anger, hatred and Egoism (AHANKARAM)

58. **SATYAM - DHARMAM - SOUCHAM**

SATYAM DHARMA ARYA VRUTTESHU
SOUCHE BIVĀRA MET SADĀ
SISHYAN CHA SISHYĀ DHARMANE
VĀGBAHODARA SAMYUTAHA

One should be always careful in the practice of SATYAM, DHARMAM, SOUCHAM (cleanliness) and about ones food.

If one's wife, or children, or servants or disciples fluot (mock) discipline, they should be corrected with moderation, avoiding harsh treatment.

One should be contented with his status and never commit evil deeds for one's needs.

59. **ABHIVADANA**

SAYYASANEDHYĀ CHARITE
SREYASĀ NA SAMĀVASET
SAYYASANASTHA SCHI VINAM
PRATYUTHĀ ABHIVADAYET

When a person who is older and wiser than you approaches you and if you are seated on a chair or a bed, it is proper and polite to get up, greet him with a namaskaram and invite him in.

60. **ABHIVADANA**

ABHIVĀDANA SEELASYA
NITYAM VRUDDHOPA SAVINAHA
CHATVARI TASMĀ VARNANTA
AURVIDYĀ YASO BALAM.

One who respectfully greets the elders, is sure to have not only a long life but his Vidya, Yasassu (FAME) and Balam (POWER) are likely to be increased.

61. **AKSHEPANA**

HEENĀNGĀ ATIRIKTĀNGĀN
VIDYĀHEENĀN VAYODHI KAN
ROOPA DRAVYA VIHEENĀMSCHA
JĀTI HEENAMSCHA NĀKSHEEPET

When one comes across men who are cripples or who have too many fingers or toes, or who are illiterate, or who are too old and decrepit or who are destitutes, and who are born as "out castes" one should not make fun or mock at them.

62. **AGNI**

PITĀ YI ĠARHAPATYAGNI
MĀTĀ AGNI DAKSHINĀS TADHA
GURU AVAHANEEYASTU
SAAGNI TRETĀ GAREEYASE.

There are three types of AGNI namely : 1. Garhapa tyagni 2. Dakshina Agni and 3. Avahaneeya Agni and they represent 1. FATHER 2. MOTHER and 3. GURU respectively, hence they should all be worshipped with reverence.

63. **DHARMA AND KARMA**

EKAHA PRAJAYATE JANTU
EKA AVA PRALEEYATE
AKON BHUJYE SUKRUTAM
AKA AVACHA DUSHKRUTAM.

Every creature enters this world singly and departs singly. During its lifetime it has to experience the results of its good and evil deeds. Neither mother, father, relatives nor friends, can alter this inexorable law of KARMA, except DHARMA.

64. **DHARMA AND PARALOKA**

NA MUTRAHE SAHAYARDHAM
PITĀ MATĀCHA TISTATAHA
NA PUTRA DARĀ NA JNATI
DHARMA TISTATI KEVALAHA

When the JEEVA departs from this world to PARALOKA neither the mother, father, wife, sons or relatives accompany and help it except DHARMA.

DHARMA alone accompanies a JEEVA in its solitary journey to PARALOKA.

65. **LAXMI**

BHEETĀ LAXMIHE KURAMGEEVA DOORAM DOORAM
PALĀYATE GUNINAM JANA MĀLOKYA
NIJA BANDHANA SANKAYĀ

Laxmi keeps away from men of virtue. Like a deer afraid of being caught, Laxmi runs away from men of virtue.

66. **LAXMI AND SARASWATI**

SVALPA SATVAM UNNATI KAROTI SARASWATEE PARI
GRUHEETA ERSHYA YEVA NĀLINGATEE JANAM

Laxmi is very fickle minded. It elevates an inferior man in to a superior status and degrades a superior man in to an inferior status.

Laxmi is very jealous of SARASWATI, and never consents to reside along with her.

67. **DURJANA**

KANTAKĀNĀM KHALĀNĀNCHA
DVIVIDHIVA PRATIKRIYĀ
UPĀNAN MUKHABHANGOVĀ
DOORATOVĀ VISARJANAM.

There are only two ways of dealing with (1) evil persons and (2) thorns. The first method is to punish them severely, and to crush them out with a shoe, respectively. If this method is not suitable for the occasion, the second and simpler method is to keep away from EVIL PERSONS and THORNS.

68. **AHANKARAM**

JARĀ ROOPAM HARATI DHIRYAM ASHĀ

MRUTYUHU PRĀNAN DHARMĀCHARYĀ ASOOYA
KRODHAHA SRIYAM SEELAM ANARYA SEVA
HRIYAM KAMAHA SARVAMEVĀ ABHIMANAHA
Old age destroys ones handsome features
Greed undermines ones courage
Death puts an end to one's life
Jealousy prevents one from pursuing DHARMA
Anger destroys the accumulation of riches, one looses ones conduct, by serving inferior people
Uncontrolled sexual passion robs one off his modesty and manners
AHANKARAM (EGOISM) destroys all the virtues of a man.

69. **UTTAMA**

KURVĀNAHA KRUTI AMITĀ MITAM SAYĀNAHA
BHUNJANO MITA AMITAM PARAM DĀNAHA
JĀNANO BAHU VISHAYAN MITAM BRUVĀNAHA
UTKARSHAM BHUVI LABHATE SA VARDHAMĀNAHA

One who follows the precepts given below is sure to prosper and succeed in life; 1. He should work hard 2. He should exercise moderation in food and sleep 3. He should be guarded in his speech 4. He should cultivate hospitality and 5. He should not reveal matters which he has come to know, indiscriminately to others.

70. **GURU AND SISHYA**

DHARMA ARTHOU YATA NASYĀTĀM
SUSROOSHĀ VAPI TATDVIDHĀ
TATRA VIDYA NA VAPTAVYA
SUBHAM BEEJAMI VOSHARE.

A Guru should not impart Vidya to a SISHYA who is not committed to DHARMA, who has no ARTHA and who does not perform SUSROOSHA (service to his GURU) Imparting Vidya to a Sishya who is devoid of DHARMA, ARTHA and SUSROOSHA, is as futile as sowing seeds in a barren and brackish soil.

71. **GURU AND SISHYA**

VIDYA YIVA NAMUM KĀMUM
MARTAVYAM BRAHMA VĀDINĀ
APADYA PIHE GHORAYAM
NATVENA MIRINE VAPET

A GURU, even under a great threat or danger to his life, should not impart his VIDYA to an undeserving disciple. If a GURU has not come across a deserving disciple, it is better even if he dies without imparting his knowledge to another.

72. **BALAKA VACHANAM**

YUKTI YUKTAM UPĀDEYAM
VACHANAM BALAKĀ DAPI
VIDOOSHATU SADĀ GRAHYAM
VRUDDHA DAPI NA DURVACHAHA

A wise counsel from even a young person should be preferred to an evil counsel from an older person.

73. **DHARMA - RAVI - CHANDRA**
SARVAREE DEEPAKA CHANDRAHA
PROBHATO UDDEEPAKO RAVIHE
TRILOKYĀ DEEPAKO DHARMAHA
SUPUTRAHA KULA DEEPAKAHA
Sun illuminates the world in the day time
Moon sheds moonlight over the earth in the night time
A wise son enhances the prestige of his parents and ancestors
DHARMA sustains the entire universe

74. **TASMAT BHĀVOHE KARANAM**
NA KAASTE VIDYATE DEVO
NA PASHANE NA MRUNMAYE
BHAVE HE VIDYATE DEVA
TASMAT BHAVO HE KARANAM
GOD is not to be found in idols made up of mud, wood, stone (or other various metals such as gold, silver etc.)
The existence of GOD is a concept, that one should discover in ones own heart.

75. **NA PHALO HOTE KASCHANA**
YADHAPI RUCHIRAM PUSHPAM
NANNAVANTAM AGANDHAKAM
AVUM SUBHASHITĀ VĀCHĀ
NA PHALOHOTE KASCHANA
A flower devoid of perfume is futile; words unsubstantiated by deeds are futile.

76. **TATTABRUNKA PHALAM BAHAM**
YADHAPI PUSPHA RĀSINĀ
MUDĀMALĀ GUNE BAHOO
APUM JATENA MACCHENA
TATTABRUNKA PHALAM BAHAM
One selects the best among the flowers to make a nice garland. Similarly one should select the best among SADGUNAS (good qualities), and cultivate them for his own uplift.

77. **INHERITED QUALITIES**
DATRUTVAM PRIYA VAKTRU TVAM
DHEERATVAM UCHITAGNATĀ
ABHYASENA NA LABHAYANTE
CHATVARA SAHAJA GUNAA
Certain traits such as : 1 Generosity 2. Pleasant speech 3. Courage and 4. Discretion (SOUND JUDGEMENT) are inherited qualities and cannot be cultivated so easily by others.

78. **INHERITED QUALITIES**
VIDYASCHAT SROU SADHĀSU
RĀJAMANĀ SAHA SAMBHAVĀHA
GĀNDHARVAM CHA KAVITVAM CHA
SOORATĀ DĀNASEELATĀ
Certain traits such as 1. Talent for singing 2. Poetry 3. Courage and 4. Generosity are inherited, and can not be cultivated so easily by others.

79. **BĀLĀNĀM RODANAM BALAM**
PAKSHINAM BALAM AKASAM
MATSYANAM UDAKAM BALAM
DURBALASYA BALAM RAJA
BĀLĀNĀM RODANAM BALAM.
The strength of a bird lies in its ability to fly
The strength of a fish lies in its ability to swim
The strength of a weak fellow rest in the support
of more powerful people for him;
The strength of a baby lies in its vigorous cry to draw attention to itself.

80. **VIDVADJANA PARISRAMAM**
VIDYANEVA VIJANĀTI
VIDVADJANA PARISRAMAM
NAHE VANDHYĀ VIJĀNATI
DURNEEM PRASAVAVEDANAM
An illiterate fellow is not aware of the years of study and hard work, that go in to the make up of a learned man (A PANDITA). Similarly a barren woman is not aware of the travails of child birth.

81. **VIDVĀN SARVATRAPOOJYATE**
SVAGRUHE POOJYATE MOORKHAHA
SVAGRĀME POOJYATE PRAHUHU
SVADESE POOJYATE RAJA
VIDVAN SARVATRA POOJYATE
Even a stupid fellow is respected in his house
A ruler is respected in his small territory such as a village
A king is respected in his kingdom only where as a PANDITA is respected by all, in all places and in all countries.

82. **SEELA VRUTTI PHALAM SRUTAM**
SEELA VRUTTI PHALAM SRUTAM
The purpose of education is to inculcate good character and conduct.

83. **KRUSHITO NĀSTI DURBHIKSAM**
KRUSHITO NĀSTI DURBHIKSAM
JAPATO NĀSTI PATAKAM
MOUNENA KALAHAM NĀSTI
NĀSTI JAGARATO BHAYAM.

One who works hard to make a living, will never suffer from poverty
One who repents and prays for redemption will get rid of his sins
One who is careful, cautious in his speech and silent for most of the time, will be free from all quarrels
and one who is careful about all matters has no cause to be afraid of

84. **MARDAYE GUNA VRUDDHAYE**
DURJANAM, KĀNCHANAM BHEREE (DUNDUBHI)
DUSTA STREE DUSTA VĀHANAM
EKSHU KHANDĀN TILOSHADHĀN
MARDAYE GUNA VRUDDHAYE
Evil men, evil women and wild horses can be controlled only by stringent punishment. The quality of (1) GOLD (2) Bheree (A percussion musical devise) (3) Sugarcane juice (4) Oil obtained from seeds of Indian sesame (gingeli or NUVVULU (TELUGU) (5) Medicines obtained from medicinal herbs, improves the more one grinds and crushes them.

85. **PUSTAKAM VANITĀ VITTAM**
PUSTAKAM VANITĀ VITTAM
PARAHASTAM GATAM GATAHA
ADHAVĀ PUNARĀ YATAM
JEERNAM BRASTACHA KHANDASAHA
When a book, money or a woman, if they are given to others, they will never come back to the owner in the same condition.
A book is likely to be returned in a dilapidated ana torn condition
Money loaned to others, is likely to be repaid if at all in very small instalments
A woman who was in the custody of others, is likely to loose her chastity and character.

86. **DHARMAPATNI**
KARYESHU DĀSEE KARANESHU MANTREE
ROOPECHA LAKSHMI KSHAMAYĀ DHARITREE
BHOJYESHU MĀTĀ SAYANETU (VESYA) RAMBHA
SHATKARMA YUKTĀ KULA DHARMAPATNEE
An ideal wife should possess the following :
1. Beauty 2. Intelligence 3. Patience 4. Hard work and 5. she should look after the needs of her husband such as food, rest and relaxation.

87. **VIDYA HEEÑO NA SHOBANTE**
ROOPA YOUVANA SAMPANNĀ
VISUDDHA KULA SAMBHAVĀ HA
VIDYA HEENO NA SHOBANTE
NIRGANDHĀ EVAHA KIMSUKĀ
Kimsuka (MODUGA FLOWERS) flower are rather large and red in colour, and are attractive to look at but they lack scent, and hence they are not sought after.
Similarly, a man even if he is well born, young, handsome and rich, if he has no education, such a one will not be respected in the society.

88. **BUDDHI HE KARMANUSARINI**
ABHYANUSREE VIDYA
BUDDHI HE KARMANUSARINI
UDYOGĀNU SAREE LAKSHMI
PHALAM BHAGYĀNUSARINI
Repeated study and efforts put in to acquisition of knowledge are bound to be fruitful.
The direction of ones efforts follows one's inherited tendencies,
The money one earns, depends on ones profession
However, the final result of any human endeavour is decreed by FATE only.

89. **MAN'S FINAL JOURNEY**
ARTHĀ GRUHE NIVARTANTE
SMASĀNE MITRA BHANDHAVAHA
SUKRUTAM DUSHSKRUTAM CHIVA
GACCHANTA MANUGACCHATI
When a man dies, he has to leave his money, gold and his house also. Relatives and friends accompany his dead body, to the burial ground. The dead body is reduced to ashes in the burning pyre. Finally what does remain of the man?
In its final and solitary journey, the SOUL is accompanied by the results of its own good and bad deeds.

90. **RUNĀNUBANDHA ROOPENA**
RUNĀNUBANDHA ROOPENA
PASUPATNEE SUTĀLAYA
RUNAKSHYE KSHAYAM YĀTI
KĀTATRA PARIVEDANĀ
Every type of relationship that involve a man such as one between himself and an animal, or between himself and a woman or a son, are all predestined and on account of debts incurred in an earlier birth and once the debt is cleared, the relationship comes to an end, and to grieve over such inevitable, and predestined separations is futile.

91. **ATI VINAYAM DHOORTA LAKSHANAM**
MUKHAM PADMA DALA KARAM
VACHAS CHANDANA SEETALAM
HRUT KARTAREE SAMANCHA
ATI VINAYAM DHOORTA LAKSHANAM.
A deceitful man may have a pleasant personality, and talk in a gentle and persuasive manner, but his heart is full of deceit and cunning, and his mind is as sharp and dangerous as a scissors.
Do not be taken in by mere externals, and watch a man's deeds, which reveal his true character, to a greater extent.

92. **UTSAHAM - SAHASAM - DHIRYAM**
UTSAHAM - SAHASAM - DHIRYAM
BUDDI SAKTI, PARAKRAMAHA

SHADITE YATRA TISHTANTI
TATRA DEVOPI TISHTATI

In whomsoever one notices the following exemplary qualities such as : 1. Enthusiasm 2. Daring 3. Courage 4. Intelligence 5. Power and 6. Invincibility, such a one is sure to have divine support and guidance.

93. **SISHYA PAPAM GURURVAJET**
RAJA RASTRAKRUTAM PAPAM
RAJA PAPAM PUROHITAHA
BHARTACHA STREE KRUTAM PAPAM
SISHYA PAPAM GURUR VAJET.

A king is responsible for any sins committed by his subjects
A purohita is responsible for any sins commited by the King
The hunband is responsible for any sins commited by the wife.
The teacher is responsible for any sins commited by the student.

94. **DHANA MOOLAM EDAM JAGAT**
DHANA MOOLAM EDAM JAGAT

Money is the ultimate basis for all activities in this world.

95. **KALOU YUGE SHADGUNAM ASRAYANTI**
DANĀ DARIDRAHA KRUPANO DHANADYAHA
PAPI CHÉRĀYU SUKRUTEE GATĀYUHU
RAJA KULEENA SUKULEENA BRUTYAHA
KALOU YUGE SHADGUNAM ASRAYANTI

KALI YUGA is recognised by the following six characterestics. They are :

1. A generous man will be poor,
2. A miser will be rich,
3. A SAJJANA will not have a long life,
4. A man of SIN will have a long life,
5. A low born man will occupy a high position,
6. A high born man will occupy a low position.

96. **NA STREE SVĀTANTRYAM ARHATI**
PITA RAKSHATE KOUMARE
BHARTĀ RAKSHATE YOUVANE
RAKSHANTI VĀRDHAKE PUTRĀ
NA STREE SVATANTRYAM ARHATI

A girl is protected by her father in her childhood days. After her marriage, she comes under the protection of her husband. In her old age, she comes under the protection of her sons. At all stages of her life, a woman needs protection for her own welfare.

97. **PITĀ - MATĀ - PUTRA**
PITĀCHA RUNAVĀN SATRU
MATĀCHA VYABHICHARINI
BHARYĀ ROOPAVATI SATRUHU
PUTRA SATRU APANDITAHA

A father who leaves behind him after his death debts to be cleared by his sons, is to be regarded as an enemy only

A mother who indulges in adultery, is to be regarded an enemy only

A wife who is extraordinarily beautiful, is likely to cause jealousy, suspicion and enmity in her husband

A son who is an illeterate will be the cause of shame and disgrace to his father.

98. **ASVA MEDHA SAMAM VIDUHU**

DARIDRĀYA KRUTAM DĀNAM
SOONYA LINGASYA POOJANAM
ANĀDHA PRETA SAMSKARĀM
ASVA MEDHA SAMAM VIDUHU

One who gives a gift to a destitute;

One who worships an uncared for SIVALINGAM and one who performs the last rites to an unknown dead body, acquires the merit equal to that of performing a ASVAMEDHA YAGAM.

99. **JIHVAGRE VARTATE LAXMI**

JIHVAGRE VARTATE LAXMI
JIHVAGRE MITRA BANDHAVAHA
JIHVAGRE BANDHA SAMPRAPTIHE
JIHVAGRE MARANAM DHRUVAM

By means of gentle and pleasant speech, one acquires wealth, friends and relatives. If one's speech is harsh and cruel, one may be imprisoned, or even put to death.

100. **VIDYA**

VITTAM BANDHU VAYAHA KARMA
VIDYĀ BHAVATI PANCHAMEE
A TĀNI MĀNYA STHĀNANE
GAREEYO YAD UTTARAM

Wealth, relationship, seniority, excellence in one's profession and education, are assets which command respect and regard from all. However the value of each quality increases over its predecessor from left to right (i.e.)

1. Relationship has more value than wealth
2. Seniority has more value than relationship
3. Excellence in one's work has more value than seniority
4. VIDYA has more value than excellence in one's work VIDYA is held in the highest esteem by all.

101. **LAXMI**

AJAGĀMA YADĀLAKSHMI
NARI KELA PHALAMBUVAT
NIRJAGĀMA YADĀLAXMI
GAJA BHUKTA KAPITHAVAT

Laxmi has a very strange and fickle nature. None can predict accurately about when wealth comes in to ones hands or when it disappears. When it enters, it enters

unnoticed, like water that enters in to a green coconut.
It disappears without any notice, like the pulp of a VELAGA FRUIT, which was swallowed by an elephant (The shell of a Velaga fruit remains intact inside the gastrointestinal tract of an elephant, but the pulp is digested away by the gastric juices of the elephant.)

102. **MRUTYO SARVATRA TULYATAHA**
PANDITE CHIVA MOORKHECHA
BALAVATYAPI DURBALE
DHANIKO DARIDRE CHIVA
MRUTYO SARVATRA TULYATAHA
Death is an impartial and universal phenomenon
Death does not discriminate between, a learned man or an illiterate, a robust man or a weakling, a rich man or a poor man.
Death is impartial towards all creatures.

103. **LOBHA**
MĀTARAṂM, PITĀRAM, PUTRAM
BHRĀTARAM VĀ SUHRUTTAMAM
LOBHONISTO NAROHANTEE
SVĀMINAM VA SHAODARAM
There is no greater evil than AVARICE (Inordinate desire for wealth). An avaricious man will not hesitate even to murder his own mother, father, son, brother, friend and his own master, if he stands to gain.

104. **DHANAM**
DANAM BHOGO NĀSTHISRO
GTAYO BHAVANTI VITTASYA
YONA DADATI NA BHUNKTE
TASYA TRUTEEYĀ GATIRBHAVATI.
There are three ways of spending money
The first one is to spend one's money on and for self
The second one is to donate it to a deserving person or a cause.
If one does not use his wealth in the above mentioned ways, it is bound to be stolen by thieves.

105. **SARVO GUNAHA KANCHANAM ASRAYANTI**
YASYASTHI VITTAM SAVARAHA KUVANA
SAPANDITAHA SA SRUTA VAGNI DHIGNAHA
SA AVA VAKTA SACHA DARSANEEYAHA
SARVO GUNAHA KANCHANAM ASRAYANTI
A man who is wealthy is considered to be
1. Well born 2. Handsome 3. a Pandita 4. well-versed in all SASTRAS 5. an orator 6. and a man of ability and discrimination.
All the exemplary qualities are attributed to a man of wealth, whether he possesses them or not. Such is the power of wealth.

106. **YAT AYAVYADHIKOVYAYA**
EDE MAY HE PANDITYAM
EYA MEVA VIDAGTHATA
AYAMEVA PARODHARMAHA
YAT AYA VYADHIKO VYAYA
One's expenditure should never exceed one's in come. One who scrupulously follows this rule in his expenditure, can be regarded as a man of prudence, thrift and as a PANDITA.

107. **SEELAM SARVATRA VI DHANAM**
VIDE SESHU DHANAM VIDYA
VYASANESHU DHANAM MATIHE
PARALOKE DHANAM DHARMAHA
SEELAM SARVATRA VI DHANAM
Vidya (EDUCATION) helps one to survive even in a foreign country,
When one is overwhelmed by afflictions, one's own intelligence will help in overcoming them, when one leaves this world, DHARMA accompanies and supports,
Whereas one's own good conduct sustains him in this world and PARALOKA also.

108. **YAT SVALPAMAPI TAT BAHU**
AKRUTVĀ PARA SANTAPAM
AGATVĀ KHALA MANDIRAM
ANỤLLANGYA SATĀM MARGAM
YAT SVALPAMAPI TAT BAHU
The best and proper way of earning money is one which inflicts no suffering on others, which does not necessitate any sort of association with evil persons and which is obtained by following the path of DHARMA.
Money earned by following the path of DHARMA, even if it is little, should be considered as great.

109. **SATYAM MĀTĀ PITĀ JNANAM**
SATYAM MĀTĀ PITĀ JNANAM
DHARMO BHRATĀ DAYĀ SAKHĀ
SANTIHE PATNEE KSHAMĀ PUTRAHA
SHADITE MAMA BANDHAVĀ
Satyam (TRUTH) and JNANAM (KNOWLEDGE) are to be revered as one's own parents;
Dharma should be revered as ones own brother; DAYA (Compassion) should be regarded as one's own friend; SANTI (PEACE) should be regarded as important as one's wife;
KSHAMA should be regarded as important as one's on own son.
"SATYAM, Jnanam, Dharmam, Daya, Santi and Kshama are as important to me as my dearest relatives" --- said DHARMARAJA.

110. **ATMAVAT SARVA BHOOTANI**
MATRUVAT PARA DARAMSCHA

PARADRAYANI LOSTAVAT
ATMAVAT SARVA BHOOTANI
YAHA PASYATI SA PASYATI
One who reveres all the women as he reveres his own mother,
One who treats the money that belongs to others as worthless as mud (i.e. who will not touch others money at any cost), and who regards all the creatures, as important as himself, is fit to be called a "BRAHMAJNANI"

111. **KARTA DHARMA SANGRAHA HA**
ANITYĀNI SAREERANI
VIBHAVO NIVA SASVATAHA
NITYAM SANNIHITO MRUTYUHU
KARTA DHARMA SANGRAHAHA
All creatures are bound to disintegrate and die sooner or later,
Wealth and prosperity do not last long,
Death approaches every creature relentlessly day by day
Aware of the above eternal truths, one should strive to acquire DHARMA, before death overtakes him.

112. **BAHUGNO JAYATE NARAHA**
ADEEYANO BAHOON GRANDHĀN
SEVAMANŌ BAHOON GUROON
LOKAMANO BAHOON DESAAN
BAHUGNO JAYATE NARAHA
One who has studied many SASTRAS, who has pursued his studies under many GURUS, and who has travelled widely in many countries, will be wise.

113. **VIDYA - VUPASSU - VASTRAM - VAKKU - VIBHAVAM**
VIDYAYĀ VAVUSHĀ VĀCHĀ
VASTRENA VIBHAVENACHA
VAKARIHA PANCHABHI HE YUKTAHA
NARO BHAVATI POOJITAHA.
A man who is handsome, well dressed, well educated, who is wealthy and whose speech is polite and pleasant, is respected by one and all.

114. **CHALĀ LAKSHMI - CHALĀHA PRANA**
CHALA LAXMI - CHALAHA PRĀNĀ
CHALAM JEEVITA YOUVANNAM
CHALA CHALECHA SAMSĀRE
DHARMA AKOPE NISCHALAHA
Wealth has no permanency,
Life has no permanency
Youth lasts but for a few years
Family relations have no permanency
Only DHARMA stands and lasts forever.

115. **MAYACHARO MAYAYA VĀRANEEYAHA**
YASMIN YADHĀ VARTATE YO MANUSHYAHA
TASMIN TADHĀ VARTITVYAM SADHARMAHA
MAYACHARO MAYAYA VARANEEYAHA
SVĀDĀCHARAHA SADHUNĀ PRATYU PEYAHA
In day to day affairs, one should be guided by the character and conduct of the person, one has·to deal with. If the other person relies on cunning and deceit, such a one should be tackled with cunning and deceit only. If the other person is straight forward in his dealings, such a one should be dealt within a straight forward manner only.

116. **VIDYA - DHANAM - MITRAM - SUKHAM**
ALASASYA KUTO VIDYA
AVIDYASYA KUTO DHANAM
ADHANASYA KUTO MITRAM
AMITRASYA KUTAHA SUKHAM
One who is lazy will never acquire VIDYA (EDUCATION)
One who is uneducated will never acquire wealth
One who has no wealth, has no friends
One who has no friends will never be happy.

117. **ECCHATI SATEE SAHASRAM**
ECCHATI SATEE SAHASRAM
SAHASREE LAKSHA MIHATEHA
LAKSHADHIPA STADHĀ RAJYAM
RAJYASTHA HA SVARGA MIHATE
The desire for the acquisition of wealth is insatiable,
One who has a hundred rupees, wants to earn a thousand rupees,
One who has a thousand rupees wants to earn a Lakh rupees,
One who has a Lakh rupees wants to earn a crore of rupees, or he wants to be a King,
One who is a King, wants to rule over HEAVEN (INDRALOKA) also.

118. **NA SUVARNE DHANISTĀ**
NA SUVARNE DHANISTĀ
DRUGYĀ DRUKKA KAMSYA PRAJĀYATE
GOLD is a precious metal and it does not produce any sound when struck,
Bronze is a cheap alloy of Copper and Tin and gives out a loud note, when struck with a hammer.
(NOTE : 1. BRASS : An alloy of Copper and Zinc
2. BRONZE : An alloy of Copper and Tin)

119. **YADARDHA VĀDEE LOKA VIRODHEE**
YADARDHA VĀDEE LOKA VIRODHEE
One who reveals the TRUTH about any matter, will be considered as an enemy by all.

120. **AJNATA KULA SEELASYA**
AJNATA KULA SEELASYA
VASO DEYO NA KASYACHIT
It is not safe to permit a man to reside in ones own house, whose name, caste, character, conduct and native place are not known.

121. **VIDYĀ VIVĀDAYA, DHANAM MADĀYA**
VIDYĀ VIVĀDAYA DHANAM MADĀYA
SAKTIHE SARESHAM PARAPEEDANĀYA
KHALASYA SADHOHA VIPAREETA METAT
JNANAYA, DĀNĀYACHA, RAKSHNĀYA.
If an evil man aquires Vidya, he will use his Vidya in futile arguments;
If an evil man aquires DHANAM, he will act in an Egoistic manner;
If an evil man aquires SAKTI (POWER), he will use it to torment others;
On the other hand
If a SAJJANA acquires VIDYA, he will use it to acquire more knowledge
If a SAJJANA acquires DHANAM, he will use it to make gifts to the deserving and needy;
If a SAJJANA acquires SAKTI (POWER), he will use it to protect those who are weak and helpless.

122. **ATI PARICHAYĀT AVAGNĀ**
ATI PARICHAYĀT AVAGNA
SANTATAAGAMANA ANADARO BHAVATI
MALAYE BHILLA PURANDHREE
CHANDANA TARUKASTAM ENDHANAM KURUTE
Any undue intimacy with another person is likely to result in indifference, and one's qualities and services are likely to be taken for granted and even underestimated;
There are plenty of SANDALWOOD TREES on the MALAYA MOUNTAINS. Tribal women who live in those mountains, use these sandalwood trees as firewood
Alas! they are not aware that sandalwood is a precious commodity.
Avoid undue intimacy with any one

123. **NEECHO VADATI NA KURUTE**
GARJATI SARA DINA VARSHATI
VARSATI VARSASU NISSVANO MEGHAHA
NEECHO VADATI NA KURUTE
NA VADATI SUJANAHA KAROTYEVA
In the autumn season, clouds and thunder do not necessarily indicate rain, whereas in the rainy season it will rain suddenly even when there are no clouds or thunders.
An inferior person talks and promises to do a work, but he will never do it promptly and completely.
A superior person will not talk unnecessarily about a work, but he will keep up his word, and will complete the work silently and efficiently.

124. **ASAYA DASĀ YE DASASTE SARVALOKASYA**
ASĀYA DASĀ YE DĀSASTE SARVALOKASYA
ASA DASEE YESHAM DASĀYATE LOKAHA
If a man is possessed by greed, in the course of time he will be enslaved by one and all. One should check this impulse of greed from the start. He should be the master and the impulse of greed should always obey the master. Then he will be able to face the world as a master.

125. **VYAVAHARENA MITRANI JAYANTE RIPAVASTADHĀ**
NA KASCHIT KASYA CHIN MITRAM NA KASCHIT KASYA CHIDREPUHU,
VYAVAHĀRENA MITRĀNI JĀYANTE RIPAVASTĀDHĀ
None comes in to this world, as a specific friend or an enemy to another man. It is by the nature of his conduct and dealings with others, that a man may be regarded as a friend or an enemy.

126. **KSHANA TYAGE KUTO VIDYA**
KSHANA TYAGE KUTO DHANAM
KSHANASHAHA KANASCHIVA VIDYĀ ARTHANCHA SADHAYET
KSHANA TYĀGE KUTO VIDYA
KSHANA TYĀGE KUTO DHANAM
One should acquire VIDYA and DHANAM without wasting even a single moment. If one is slack even for a single moment in such acquisition, he is sure to fail.

127. **GĀTRANI SIDHILAYANTE TRUSHNIKA TARUNAYATE**
VALIBHIRMUKHA AKRĀNANTAM PALITE NANKITAM SIRAHA
GATRANI SIDHILAYANTE TRUSHNIKA TARUNAYATE
As a man grows old, his hair turns to white in colour, wrinkles develop on his face, and his limbs loose their strength and coordination.
Inspite of all these changes in his body, the impulse of GREED, in his heart, goes on increasing its hold on him until his death.

128. **A PANDITA**
YASTU PARYATATE DESAN : YASTU SEVETA PANDITĀN
TASYA VISTĀRITA BUDHI HE : TILA BINDU RIVAMBHĀSI
To become a PANDITA one should study many KAVYAS and SASTRAS for many years. He should travel widely, look out for other PANDITAS, and please them, by his services (SUSHROOSA) and then partake of their knowledge. Only by such a laborious, and painstaking method, one becomes a PANDITA
For such a PANDITA to unravel a problem becomes simpler and his understanding is quick and far reaching, like the spread of an oil drop on water.
An ingnoramus who is an illiterate, and who never travels to other places, and who lives like a frog in a well, will never become a PANDITA.

129. **HITAM BHUMJYA MITAM BHUMJYĀT**
HITAM BHUMJYA MITAM BHUMJYĀT
NA BHUMJYA AMITAM HITAM
HITAM ESTANCHA BHUNJEEYĀT

ASHA DHARMA SANĀTANAHA
One should eat food which suits him, that too in moderate quantity. Simply because one likes a particular food stuff, one should not consume it in excess. To eat the food of his choice, that too in moderate quantity is the secret of enjoying good health and longevity.

130. **DOORASTOPI SAMEEPASTO**
DOORASTOPI SAMEEPASTO
YOYASYA HRUDI VARTATE
YOYASYA HRUDAYE NASTI, SAMEEPASTHOPI DOORAGAHA.
One who is constantly in your thoughts, although he is physically far off, should be considered to be very close to you.
One who is not constantly in your thoughts, although he is physically very near to you should be considered to be far off.
Love and friendship with another do not depend on physical proximity but on spiritual affinity.

131. **NASYATYA NĀYAKAM KĀRYAM**
NASYATYA NĀYAKAM KARYAM
TADHIVA SISU NĀYAKAM
STREE NĀYAKAM TADHONMATTA
NĀYAKAM BAHUNĀYAKAM
An able leader is essential for the success of any undertaking. Any task whose control and supervision and execution, if it is entrusted to a child, or a women or a lunatic, is sure to fail.

132. **SĀNTI ECCHANTI SĀDHAVAHA**
MAKSHIKĀ VRANAM ECCHANTI
DHANAM ECCHANTI PARDHIVĀHA
NEECHAHA KALAHAM ECCHANTI
SANTI ECCHANTI SĀDHAVAHA
A fly seeks out an open sore to feast on it
A wealthy man strives to acquire more and more wealth
An inferior person always prefers to quarrel with others on some pretext or the other.
A superior person always prefers peace and quiet and tries to avoid quarrels at all times.

133. **YĀNTI NYĀYA PRAVRUTTASYA**
YANTI NYĀYA PRAVRUTTASYA
TIRYAM CHOPI SAHAYĀTAM
APANDHANANTU GACCHAMTUM
SODAROPI VIMUNCHATI —MURARI
Those who walk on the path of DHARMA, are trusted and helped not only by men but also by birds, beasts and monkeys etc. whereas those who walk on the path of ADHARMA, are not trusted not only by men but (and) even their own brothers will desert them in a crisis.

SREERAMA was helped in the search for missing SITA by (1) JATAYUVU (BIRD) (2) HANUMAN and others (Monkey warriors)

RAVANA who abducted SITA, was deserted by his own brother VIBHEESHANA.

134. **LAKSHMI HE SVAYAM YĀTI NIVĀSA HETO**

UTSAHA SAMPANNA ADEERGHA SOOTRAM
KRIYĀ VIDHIJNAM VYASANESHVAKTAM
SOORAM KRUTAGNAM DHRUDHA SOUHRUDANCHA
LAXMI HE SVAYAM YĀTI NIVASA HETO

Laxmi (or wealth) likes to be with and will not leave a man, who has the following virtues :

1. He is full of enthusiasm and is prompt and competent in his work;
2. He is free from all vices;
3. He has courage;
4. He is loyal and steadfast in his friendships.

135. **DĀTA LAGHURAPI SEVYO BHAVATI**

DĀTĀ LAGHURAPI SEVYO BHAVATI
NA KRUPANO MAHĀNAPI SAMRUDDHYA
KOOPONTAHA SVĀDUJALA HA
PREETYE LOKASYA NA SAMUDRAHA

It is better to seek help from a generous man, though he may not be wealthy, he is sure to help.

It is futile to seek help from a miser, though he may be wealthy, he will not part with anything

One seeks out a well, however small it might he to slake (quench) ones thirst, and none approach the sea, though it may be vast in size and close by.

136. **ASAHAYAHA SAMARDHOPI TEJASVI KIM KARISHYATI**

ASAHAYAHA SAMARDHOPI TEJASVI KIM KARISHYATI
NIRVATE JVALITO VAHNIHE SVAYAMEVA VINASYATI

One may possess extra ordinary abilities, yet to succeed in life, one needs the cooperation and help from others.

Just as a fire needs air currents to keep it burning, even the man with extra ordinary abilities needs the cooperation and help from others, to succeed in life.

137. **ALASYAM HE MANUSHYĀNĀM**

ALASYAM HE MANUSHYĀNĀM
SAREERASTHO MAHAN RIPUHU
NAASTU UDYAMA SAMO BANDHUHU
KURVANO NAVASEEDATI.

Laziness is one of the most powerful internal enemy of a man. A lazy fellow never dares to commence any task and even if he commences, he fails to complete it and there by he is ruined.

A man of industry is sure to succeed in life.

138. **NA JATU KAMAHA KĀMĀNĀM**

NA JATU KAMAHA KĀMĀNĀM

UPA BHOGENA SYAMATI
HAVISHA KRISHNA VARTMEVA
BHOOYA AVAABHI VARDHATE

The more one satisfies his desires, they become more numerous, pernicious and insatiable. There is no end to the desires that arise in a man's mind. Hence a wise man seeks peace of mind by limiting and controlling the desires.

Just as when ghee is poured in to a fire, it escalates it further, and the only way to contain the fire is to stop pouring ghee in to the fire.

(Pernicious = Destructive or ruinous)

139. **SUKHĀRTHEE TYAJATE VIDYĀM**

SUKHARTHEE TYAJATE VIDYAM
VIDYARTHEE TYAJATE SUKHAM
SUKHARTHENAHA KUTO VIDYĀ
KUTO VIDYARDHINAHA SUKHAM

One who is fond of ease, comfort and luxuries will never be able to acquire Vidya. One who wants to acquire VIDYA should forego ease, comfort and luxuries.

140. **ANĀYĀSENA MARANAM**

ANĀYĀSENA MARANAM
VINA DINYENA JEEVANAM
DEHEE MAY KRUPAYĀ DEVA
TVAYE BHAKTIR ACHANCHALĀ
SARVESWARA!

1. Please grant me steadfast devotion towards you
2. Please grant me my daily needs of food and clothing
3. Please grant me an easy death when it is due

In this simple prayer, one finds devotion, reverence and moderation.

Sources

1. *Manimala* by D. N. Deekshit, 1990
2. *Amrutavani* by K. Chandra Sekhara Sarma,1991.
3. *Subhashita Ratnavali* by R. Gopala Krishna, 1980.
4. *Neeti Padyalu* by S. Narasimha Swamy.

23

KABIR AND HIS MESSAGE

Kabir, who lived in the *fifteenth century*, was one of the greatest saints, mystics and poets of that era. Kabir brought Hinduism and Islam nearer by condemning the meaningless rituals and ceremonies in both, and by preaching that the ultimate goal of both the religions is one and the same.

BIOGRAPHICAL OUTLINE

NIRU, a weaver of KASHI and *NIMA*, his wife, came upon a foundling (a deserted child, whose parents are not known), at a place called *LAHARTARA*, *in the year 1456.* The boy was named *KABIR*. Kabir called himself a *JOLAHA* and a *KORI.* During the MUSLIM RULE, many castes such as *NATH PANTHIS* (wandering mendicants and their followers such as JUGI, or JOGI or GOSAI) were converted to ISLAM, but their earlier habits and ways of worship continued.

JOLAHA means a weaver and most of the weavers in VARANASI are MUSLIMS. KORI is a kind of weaver and in UTTAR PRADESH, they are considered a lower caste. Kabir refers to his father as GOSAI, who were weavers converted to ISLAM (*Refer 'KABIR' - DR. HAZARI PRASAD DWIVEDI (1960).*

Even as a child KABIR displayed signs of extra ordinary spirituality, and devotion to and worship of RAMANAMA. In his pursuit of spirituality, Kabir often neglected his vocation, which was weaving. Muslims of KASHI found Kabirs' ways perplexing and annoying. *Many commented that Kabir was an infidel* (*Unbeliver of any religion*). Kabir replied to them that an infidel was one who was a hypocrite, who appropriated (STOLE) other's property and one who killed innocent and harmless animals such as cows and goats etc. and not one who was devoted to and worshipped 'RAMANAMA'.

KABIR was very severe in his criticism of VEDAS, PURANAS, IDOL WORSHIP and other obsolete HINDU rituals and ceremonies. Muslims were displeased with Kabir because of his devotion to and worship of RAMANAMA.

SWAMI RAMANAND and Kabir's Initiation

Kabir, outwardly lived as a Hindu Vaishnava devotee. Brahmins of KASHI, were annoyed at Kabir's ways, and they thought as he belonged to a MUSLIM family it was presumptuous on his part to imitate the manners of VAISHNAVAS. *They questioned Kabir about his GURU.* Kabir felt harassed.

Swami Ramanand, one of the greatest VAISHNAVA saints was then living in KASHI. It occurred to KABIR to seek initiation in to the Vaishnava sect through Swami Ramanand. But would he consent to initiate a weaver doubted KABIR. Kabir found a way out of the problem Swami Ramanand used to bathe in the GANGA every day in the early hours of dawn. Kabir went and planted himself in the path of SWAMIJI. Swami Ramanand came down the path in due course, repeating 'RAMA' - 'RAMA' and passed KABIR. 'RAMANAMA' was more than enough for Kabir's initiation. Kabir came home and let it be known that Swami Ramanand had accepted him as his disciple. The Hindus were displeased that Swami Ramanand consented to initiate a Muslim in to the Vaishnava sect. The controversy reached the ears of the saint. He was surprised, for he knew that he had done nothing of the sort. Swami Ramanand bade kabir appear before him. When Kabir went to meet him, Swami was engaged in a Puja inside a curtained enclosure and he was waiting for holy basil leaves (BASIL = TULASI), to perform worship of RAMA. Kabir shouted from outside the enclosure 'O Saint! you have not yet offered holy basil leaves to RAMA'. Swami Ramanand was amazed at the yogic powers of KABIR. However *Swami Ramanand asked Kabir :* "when did I ever initiate you as my disciple"?

Kabir gave his account of initiation in to RAMA NAMA, in the early hours of dawn on the bank of Ganges. The saint was not satisfied.

Swami Ramanand : "This is not the traditional way of initiation between a master and a disciple"

Kabir : "Is there anything more precious than RAMANAMA in all the Puranas and Sastras"?

Swami Ramanand agreed "that there is nothing greater than the name of GOD"

KABIR : "Then what other mystery do you reveal to those you initiate as disciples?"

Swami Ramanand was pleased with the replies of KABIR, and accepted him as a disciple.

SIKANDER SHAH OF DELHI AND THE ORDEALS OF KABIR

SIKANDER SHAH of Delhi a *King of LODI DYNASTY*, paid a visit to *Kashi. Kazis, Mullas, Brahmins and Banias of Kashi* gathered together and complained to the King about KABIR. They complained that Kabir had given up his own religion, namely ISLAM, and he criticized the rituals and ceremonies of Hindus and Muslims also. Kabir condemned Vedas, Puranas, fasting on EKADASHI DAYS and pilgrimages. Kabir considered himself neither as a HINDU or as a MUSLIM, and started his own RELIGION. So long as KABIR remained at large, none in KASHI would care either for a Brahmin priest or a Muslim KAZI. They beseeched the King to have KABIR exiled from Kashi.

Kabir was summoned to the presence of the King. *The Kazi ordered Kabir to prostrate himself before the King. Kabir refused.* The King was furious. *King* thundered "O! you wretched weaver, why have you given up ISLAM, and taken the road to perdition?" (Perdition = Ruin)

Kabir calmly replied "I care nothing for criticism either of Hindus or Muslims. By the grace of my GURU I live in devotion to Rama and sing praises of Rama watched over by Rama I fear neither King nor anyone". The King was beside himself with rage and *ordered Kabir to be tied up and thrown in to the Ganga.* The order was executed. But KABIR survived this test by the grace of RAMA. King and the people were amazed at Kabir's survival. *In the second attempt* Kabir was tied up and thrown in to a house, which was then set on fire. Kabir survived this trial also. *In the third attempt* on Kabir's life, Kabir was tied up and thrown before a mad elephant, to be trampled to death. Kabir came through this trial also unscathed.

KABIR was further tested by the King no less than fifty two times and KABIR survived all the trials and ordeals. The king realized at last that KABIR was no ordinary weaver but a great SAINT. He fell at the feet of KABIR and asked him to forgive his misdeeds. After the successful out come of these ordeals, KABIR's fame as a saint spread far and wide.

LAST DAYS OF KABIR

In his last days KABIR left Kashi for MAGHAR (which is now in BASTI DISTRICT) KABIR delivered his last discourse to the assembled throng, and retired to his hut, and shut himself in. *KABIR's earthly sojourn was over in the year 1575.* Then followed an unruly squabble amongst his followers. *RAJA VIRSINGH DEV of KASHI* and HINDUS, asserted that KABIR was their GURU and that his mortal remains should be cremated according to HINDU RITES. Where as *NABOB BIJILIKHAN* and the MUSLIMS, insisted that KABIR was their PIR and that his body should be buried according to ISLAMIC RITES. The tension and tempers mounted in both the groups and they were about to clash with arms. *Then a voice was heard from the sky "Oh!* My *disciples*! Do not *kill each other for my mortal remains*! *Please look inside the hut first*". The throng looked inside the hut. But there was no sign of KABIR's BODY. There were instead a few flowers and a sheet of white cloth. The Hindus and Muslims devided the flowers and the white cloth amongst themselves and HINDUS cremated their portion according to HINDU RITES and the MUSLIMS buried their portion according to ISLAMIC RITES.

What is important in the brief outline of SAINT KABIR's life, is not the mere factual account of his life, (i.e.) where he lived, in which year, how he lived and how he died etc. but *his religious, philosophical and poetical contributions to mankind and his spiritual influence on millions even today*, and the same can be said about other great saints and poets of India ancient or medieval, such as TIRUVALLUVAR, KALIDAS, JNANESWAR, NAMDEV, CHAITANYA, YOGI VEMANA, SARVAJNA and other.

KABIR GRANDHAVALI : "KABIR GRANDHAVALI"—published by THE ALLAHABAD UNIVERSITY - TIWARI PARASNATH (1961) is *one of the most authentic collection of KABIR's,* PADAS (200), RAMAINIS (20) and SAKHIS (750).

SELECTIONS FROM KABIR

1. Streams that merge in to the GANGA, become Ganga, *Do not worry about the caste or clan of a SAINT,*

   —Says KABIR

2. One who is free from lust, anger, greed and attachments

One who cares not for praise or blame, honour or dishonour
One who treats gold and iron alike
Such a one only sees RAMA

—Says KABIR.

3. SANAKA, SANANDANA, JAIDEV and NAMADEV were great BHAKTAS,
But, they knew not the ATMAN,
where does ATMAN go, when your mortal body has perished?
Always seek the ATMAN

—Says KABIR

4. As all ornaments of gold, dissolve in to one molten metal,
When we leave this world, we will all mingle in the void
In the end SWAN will meet the SWAN

—Says KABIR

5. Many parts I have played in my life and I am tired
I can not act any more,
Friends, companions and all the others have forsaken me
GOD's NAME is the only jewel, I possess now

—Says KABIR

6. Do not rely on traditions, rituals, family's name and prestige,
They are in the end similar to a noose around your neck,
Climb on and on, even if you fall.

—Says KABIR

7. When you are in the company of GOOD, listen
When you are in the company of EVIL ONES, speak not,
Discourse with the good and the learned brings prosperity
Speech with the ignorant is futile
A half filled jar makes a lot of noise,
A full jar makes no noise

—Says KABIR

8. The human body perishes sooner or later, be not proud of it,
It will start disintegrating the moment life departs from it,
The body which you have pampered when alive with milk, butter and sweets
When life departs from it, is taken out and burnt to ashes,
The head which you adorned with a turban, will be pecked at by vultures
The bones burn as faggots, and the hair burns just like dry grass
But none wakes up, before the club of DEATH
Comes down on his head

—Says KABIR

9. Do not fret merely to make a living
You take by the measure, the fruits of your own good work
To some HE gives pearls, to some rags
A miser hoards much wealth and proudly says "It is all mine"

The club of DEATH descends on his head and the matter is set right

—Says KABIR

10. When you are dead, nothing accompanies you
The SHROUD, and even your under clothing are snatched away
And your own dead body is burnt to ashes

—Says KABIR

11. To reflect any image, a mirror's surface should be clean
If the mirror's surface is dirty, its reflections also will be dirty

—Says KABIR

12. *Who can be saved without relying on RAMANAMA?*
Without RAMANAMA, all is vain

—Says KABIR

13. Merit and Sin are constant companions throughout one's life,
Rare are men who can comprehend GOD's ways

—Says KABIR

14. O! Crazy fool! pray to RAMA,
Your own physical body will not endure forever *whose is the wealth? with whom it will go? Like a village fair, prosperity is there for some time* and *then disappears*
Mighty RAVANA of LANKA and his city of gold, DURYODHANA and his empire and countless others. *Vanished in to ETERNITY*
Short is human life and will come to an end just as abruptly as a dream
KABIR cries from the housetops that none is immortal in this world.

15. Man enters this world, beats his drum for a few years and then he is no more
His dead body is carried away on an upturned string bed
The wife wails (loud weeping) but *stops at the door*
The mother wails and *goes up to the outer gate*
Kinsmen accompany the dead body *up to the cremation ground*
Beyond that the SWAN goes alone
He sees not again his mother, wife, sons and his money and the rest
O! man! life is futile without devotion to Rama

—Says KABIR

16. *Who is not born, nor dies, who is formless,* and *who has neither father nor mother, such a one is KABIR's GOD*

17. The human body is in GOD and GOD is in the human body
GOD is in everything and everywhere

—Says KABIR

18. One who keeps his conduct pure,
One who has knowledge of BRAHMA is a BRAHMIN,
One who is a true HINDU is also a true MUSALMAN

—Says KABIR

19. Smearing holy ashes on ones body, matted locks, or dwelling in forests or caves are all futile

If one's mind is conquered, the world is conquered

—Says KABIR

20. What is the use of oblations (*NIVEDYAM*) (anything offered in worship)?
What is the good in kneeling in a mosque?
The Brahmin fasts on EKADASHI and the KAZI during RAMZAN,
Why is it that only one month in a year is singled out for good works? Why not the whole year be marked out for good works?
And if ALLAH dwells in the mosque alone, what about he rest of the world?
HINDUS says that GOD is in idols, temples and piligrimage centres, and *none has seen HIM in them*
They say that HINDU'S GOD is in the EAST and the MUSALMAN's GOD is in the WEST
Seek HIM in your own heart and nowhere else; RAM and RAHIM are both there.

—Says KABIR

21. In a previous (preceding) birth, I too was a BRAHMANA, but alas! my deeds were unworthy
I turned away from RAMA's FEET and HE let me be born as a weaver in this birth

—Says KABIR

22. Mere recitation of VEDAS and PURANAS is as *futile* as the *labour of a laden Donkey,*
How can you obtain MOKSHA, if you do not Cherish RAMA in your heart?

—Says KABIR

23. *O! BRAHMIN! tell me which place is clean for me to sit for a meal!*
Floor smeared with cow dung is unclean
Unclean is the mother, unclean is the father, the children too are unclean,
Unclean are those that come and go,
Unclean too are those that die,
Clean are only those that Cherish RAMA in *their hearts*

—Says KABIR

24. *One turns a MALA, and the other turns a TASBIH*
Both of them are mere professionals
one goes to KASHI and the other goes to MECCA
Alas! both have nooses only round their necks

—Says KABIR

25. Brahmana says that he is high born, but eats with the low,
On the days of eclipse and on AMAVASYA days, *he begs as much as he can*
You are a Brahmana and I am a weaver of KASHI
Though you relied on VEDAS, you were not saved
I relied on "RAMA" and 'RAMA' saved me

—Says KABIR

26. KABIR says O! People! listen to me and do not fall in to error,
To depart from this world, KASHI or MAGHAR, are the same if there is 'RAMA' in

one's heart

—Says KABIR

27. By HIS grace alone things happen; VEDA and KORAN, both are futile,
False is that which is born of the womb; false too that which bears a name
False are the yagnopaveetha (Sacred thread) and also the SUNNAT
Neither the HINDUS nor the MUSLIMS know HIS secret
Both have fallen in to error and mistake it for true religion
Pray to 'RAMA' constantly and be free of joy and sorrow

—Says KABIR

28. Relying on the VEDAS, the BRAHMIN has gone astray
SANDHYA, TARPANA, and the six rituals are performed in his house without fail and the GAYATRI MANTRA's recitation has been going on since ages,
Alas! none of them helped any one to attain MOKSHA,
When others touch him, he bathes; ask him who is lower than himself?
Of his own birth and virtues, he is supremely proud
Oh! BRAHMIN! Give up this conceit and inordinate pride in your birth and caste and Cherish 'RAMANAMA' in your heart

—Says KABIR

29. The heart that knows not the pain of parting is similar to a house of the dead

—Says KABIR

30. A saint is like a white cloth, which can not stand soiling
A wicked man is like a black blanket, which can stand soiling easily

—Says KABIR

31. I have found none with whom to establish a bond
All seem to be burning, each in his own fire

—Says KABIR

32. Nothing is mine; every thing belongs to RAMA

—Says KABIR

33. "LOVE" does not grow in a field, nor can it be purchased in a BAZAR
He who wants 'LOVE', may offer his heart and have it

—Says KABIR

34. The ripe fruit fallen from the tree will grow no more

—Says KABIR

35. *Today, tomorrow or a few years later, you will quietly lie in your grave,* and *on the ground above your mortal remains, animals* (cattle) *will roam about and graze quietly*

—Says KABIR

36. As a weaver, weaving a garment comes at last to its end
So does 'DEATH' overtake you in the end, flee from it if you can

—Says KABIR

37. Man's existence is as evanescent (quickly fading) as a bubble on the surface of a water pond,

One moment he was there, and in the next moment he has vanished, like a star in the morning sky

—Says KABIR

38. The mourners are dead; those who cremated the body are dead,
Those that wailed around the dead body are dead *who will show me the path?*

—Says KABIR

39. A king who ruled in a palace yesterday is today a dead body in the cremation ground

—Says KABIR

40. Do not display a diamond in a village bazar,
Keep it safely and proceed on your way

—Says KABIR

41. Death is better than life if one knows how to die
He who dies before death conquers age and *death*

—Says KABIR

42. What harm is caused by the hair on your head that you shave it off so often,
Why not get rid off passions that arise in your mind continuously

—Says KABIR

43. Do not waste your time in mere book reading of the fifty two letters in the language
two letters, RA MA are enough to lead you to MOKSHA

—Says KABIR

44. Alas! people worship idols of STONE;
Why do not they worship the GRINDSTONE which
grinds and gives them the flour to eat

—Says KABIR

45. Beyond VEDAS, Beyond KORAN,
Beyond virtue or sin,
Beyond knowledge, beyond meditation,
Beyond dress, beyond alms,
Beyond all snobbery and ceremonies,
Is the ETERNAL ESSENCE.

—Says KABIR

46. If a BRAHMANA can become a DVIJA by wearing a yagnopavitha (a holy thread)
Why not call the iron pulley of a well, which always has a rope around it a BRAHMANA?

—Says KABIR

47. *The old parents, while alive are neglected, abused and cursed*
When they are dead, 'SHARADDA' ceremony is performed to show off honour and respect due to them,
Dainties fed to the crows, how do they reach your dead parents?

—Says KABIR

(*Similar question was posed by YOGI-VEMANA* (17 CENTURY SAINT & POET REFORMER)

48. The beads of a Japamala are of wood, the Gods you worship are made up of stone,
The holy GANGES and the JAMUNA are water only
Rama and KRISHNA are dead since ages,
The four VEDAS are full of fictitious stories.

—Says KABIR

49. If thou art a BRAHMANA, born to a Brahmin woman
Why have you not come by another way (Ref : No. 52 also)

—Says KABIR

50. If bathing in water can liberate you
Why do not the frogs attain 'MUKTI', as they bathe continuously

—Says KABIR

51. For all the creatures, when they are in the womb, there is no caste or clan
From the SEED OF BRAHMA, the whole creation springs up

—Says KABIR

52. Brahmanas are born in the same way as others are born
And where is his distinction?
Brahmana pours ghee in to the sacrificial fire while performing a yagna
It may or may not bestow MUKTI to him, but the smoke it produces is sure to blind his eyes

—*Extract from SAHAJAYANI SIDDHA*(*FROM SARAHAPAD* - 8TH CENTURY)

(NOTE : Such straight forward and forthright criticism of orthodoxy and rituals by the above mentioned SIDDHAS OF 8TH CENTURY, could have inspired KABIR and others)

53. Finish tomorrow's work today
Today's work - do it now
If DEATH overtakes you suddenly
How will you finish your work?

—Says KABIR

54. First tend your field
And then help in tending your brother's field
First practice what yours preach
And then teach others

—Says KABIR

55. As you plant, so shall you reap
Be careful about what you sow now
A thorn tree can not and will not yield managoes in future
Regret for the past wont help, whatever might be your excuses
So be careful, and plant well today for tomorrow

—Says KABIR

56. When there is no love for GOD in the heart
One lives and dies, unwept, unknown and unsung

—Says KABIR

57. Why are you so enamoured of your body,
It is sure to perish in the course of time
One touch, an illness or a stroke
Your earthly sojourn is over

—Says KABIR

58. Where there is pride, there is no love
Where there is LOVE, there is no pride
Two swords can not stay in a SCABBARD (sheath)

—Says KABIR

59. Do not take pride in your strength or intelligence
or money you are paid for your services
The date tree may be laden with fruits
Yet it is too high to reach, and gives no shade

—Says KABIR

60. Be kind to all while you may
You are here today
But tomorrow you may not be there

—Says KABIR

61. The dog just eats a morsel and runs away in a hurry
The majestic elephant waits patiently and eats his fill
It is the patient man who gets the prize

—Says KABIR

62. Only an ant can find sugar in the sand
and not an elephant
If you are really humble, GOD takes you by the hand and guides you on

—Says KABIR

63. He who serves for gain
Does not really serve
Only selfless service
Does deserve merit

—Says KABIR

64. Love is not grown in the fields
Nor sold in the market by measure
If you give yourself wholeheartedly to LOVE
Then only you will find this priceless treasure
(Refer Page No. : 652, No. : 33)

—Says KABIR

65. A house without a light is dark indeed
A SOUL without a GOD is dark indeed

—Says KABIR

66. Every one prays when he is afflicted with sorrow and adversity
But one who prays when he is happy and prosperous is the best

—Says KABIR

67. A crane even when it is in MANA SASAROVER LAKE looks for and eats fish only
Whereas a SWAN looks for and eats pearls only
—Says KABIR

68. Sandalwood trees are very rarely found in forests,
Real saints are very rarely seen in this world
—Says KABIR

69. Why do you shave off the hair on your head
A sheep is shorn off its wool every summer and yet it never attains MOKSHA
It is better to get rid off desires and attachments, that arise in your mind
—Says KABIR

70. Selfishness rules the world,
None will accompany you when you depart from this world
—Says KABIR

71. The human body is similar to a cage with ten outlets
The SOUL in the cage is the SWAN
It is a wonder that the SWAN concedes to reside in the cage
It is no wonder, when the SWAN flies away from its cage
—Says KABIR

72. Do not deceive others, even when they deceive you
Sorrow and affliction follow in the footsteps of deception
—Says KABIR

73. Avarice and greed are insatiable
They torment their victim to the end
—Says KABIR

74. Where there is KAMA (DESIRE) there is no RAMA
Where there is RAMA, there is no KAMA
—Says KABIR

75. Food and water you consume everyday, influence your mind and its way of functioning
So be careful about your food and water everyday
—Says KABIR

76. Do not beg for any thing
Begging is worse than dying
—Says KABIR

77. Where there is mercy, there is DHARMA,
Where there is patience, there is GOD
Where there is greed, there is SIN
Where there is anger, there is DEATH
—Says KABIR

78. There is no virtue greater than TRUTH
There is no sin greater than UNTRUTH
—Says KABIR

79. If "TRUTH" is enshrined in one's heart
GOD also is enshrined in him

—Says KABIR

80. Milk is sold from door to door, where as Toddy (Liquor) is sold from a shop only,
Alas! the world believes more easily in FALSEHOOD than the TRUTH

—Says KABIR

81. If you are proud of your birth as a BRAHMANA
Why were you born in the same way as others?
(Ref : 49, and 52 also)

—Says KABIR

82. If you are a MUSLIM by birth, why were you born
Without any CIRCUMCISION (SUNTI), in the same way as others

—Says KABIR

83. Mullah! why do you pray so loudly? Is your ALLAH deaf?
No! 'HE' can hear even the rustle (make a soft sound) of a tiny ant

—Says KABIR

84. 'DIGAMBARAS' go about naked to seek MOKSHA
If so, the wild animals such as deers, foxes and others which are always naked, do they attain MOKSHA?

—Says KABIR

(Digambaras : A sect of spiritual aspirants who go about naked (such as in JAIN RELIGION)

85. One wears JAPAMALAS, one reads holy books
One lives in KASHI, one drinks GANGAJAL
One marks his forehead with TILAK, one performs VRATAS
All the rituals and ceremonies are futile
If there is no 'RAMA' in your heart

—Says KABIR

86. When you leave this world, your parents, wife, children, brothers, sisters, relatives and others
None will accompany you in your final journey
They are all with you and around you to further their own welfare
Rely only on 'RAMA' -Says KABIR

87. Cows vary in colour but the milk they yield is white in colour
Ornaments are many, but they are all made of gold
RAHIM and RAM are only names
One is called a MUSLIM, and the other is called a HINDU
One reads the KORAN, the other reads the GITA,
One does NAMAZ and the other does POOJA
One kills cows and the other kills goats
Their skin is alike, bones are alike, muscles are alike, their excretions are alike, and their birth and death are the same

One buries the dead and the other burns them
There are no MUSLIMS and there are no HINDUS
There is only one HUMANITY

—Says KABIR

88. When a man is about to die, he gasps for his breath,
The sight and gasps of the dying man are terrifying to all around him
When the SOUL (SWAN) leaves the body,
The mother wails "Oh! my son"; The wife wails "Oh! my hushand"!, the sister wails "Oh! my brother"!
The mother laments for her departed son *all the rest of her life*,
The sister lament for her departed brother for *ten months*,
The wife laments for her departed husband *for thirteen days*,
The dead body is wrapped in four yards of thick cloth, and consigned to the burning pyre
The bones burn like dry faggots and the hair burns
Like dry grass, and in a short while, all that remains is a heap of ashes

—Says KABIR

89. I do not pray for my *BHUKTI* (daily needs of food)
I do not pray for *MUKTI* (DELIVERANCE)
I pray to RAMA to fill my heart with *BHAKTI* (DEVOTION) *PRAYS KABIR*

THE TEACHING OF KABIR

REV. G. H. WESTCOTT, M. A. (1907) in his book *"KABIR AND THE KABIR PANTH"*, is of the opinion, that the teaching of KABIR was delivered orally and not reduced to writing till a later age. The earliest writings in which KABIR's teaching is recorded are the "*BIJAK*", and the "*ADIGRANDH*", probably *50 years after KABIR's death*, and they can hardly be regarded as retaining in all passages, the actual words of KABIR much less such words without additions.

About *2,500 SAKHIS are* attributed to *KABIR. SAKHI means a rhyming couplet and it is derived from the SANSKRIT word "SAAKSHI" which means "evidence"* literally.

90. I neither touched ink nor paper, nor did I take a pen in to my hand;
to the sages of all four ages, KABIR declared his word by mouth

91. The Guru is the *potter* and the disciple *the* pot
The Guru places '*SAHARA*' within before he fashions the vessel in to shape

—SAYS KABIR

('*Sahara*' is an instrument of wood or stone which with one hand the potter holds within the pot while with the other he strikes)

92. A man steals an *anvil*, and offers a *needle* as alms
and he thinks, that GOD will be so pleased with his generosity that HE will at once send a chariot to fetch him to heaven

—SAYS KABIR

93. A vulture soars high up in the sky, but it always looks down, to locate corpses down below
A man may preach excellently, but he is futile if he does not practice what he teaches
—SAYS KABIR

94. Strain your water before you drink it
Test your GURU, before you commit yourself to him
—SAYS KABIR

95. The door of *BHAKTI* is smaller than a *mustard* seed
A proud man whose heart has swollen to the size of an elephant, how can he pass within
—SAYS KABIR

96. The worship of a devotee in prosperity, and a rushing stream in the rainy season are impressive
But a devotee who worships GOD even in adversity and a stream that continues to flow even in summer are the best
—SAYS KABIR

97. By the puffs of the bellows of a black smith, even iron is consumed,
The sighs of the oppressed poor will destroy even the mighty ruler
—SAYS KABIR

98. The GHĀT (HEART) in which love dwells not, know that
GHĀT (HEART) to be worse than a burning GHĀT (CEMETERY) (SMASAN)
One who has no love in his heart, is worse than a blacksmith's bellows which puffs, but has no life
—SAYS KABIR

99. Covetousness destroys sound judgement,
Pride destroys devotion to GOD,
A GURU destroys ones ignorance,
when the SUN rises, night ends.
—SAYS KABIR

100. Live on friendly terms with all; be ready to speak with all
Be ready to agree with all, but live in your own way
—SAYS KABIR
(Be tolerant of religious beliefs of others but do not surrender your own religious belief)

101. All men speak of the mill, but fail to notice the pin in the centre,
The grain that remains close to the pin remains safe
—SAYS KABIR
(The two stones of the mill represent HEAVEN and EARTH, and nearly all the people who live on earth are tainted with evil to some extent or the other, and only those who sincerely worship GOD are fit to attain MOKSHA.)

102. The disciple should be willing to give everything to his GURU
And the Guru should refuse to take anything from the disciple
—SAYS KABIR

103. One who kills another man, will himself be killed one day or the other
In GOD's Durbar, every account will be settled —SAYS KABIR

104. The earth said to the potter "why do you trample on me? the day will come, when I shall cover your mortal remains"

—SAYS KABIR

105. All help the strong; none helps the weak
A breeze gives fresh life to a fire but it extinguishes a candle

—SAYS KABIR

106. A sieve allows the flour (SAR) to pass but it retains the husk (ASAR)
Sugarcane juice flows out of the press but the waste is retained
Men remember futile worldly matters and ignore spiritual wisdom

—SAYS KABIR

107. In a poppy field, there are *many* white poppy heads and *a few red flowers,*
There are many SADHUS and they all look alike but among them "TRUE SADHUS" are very few (*POPPY* = *Papaver Somniferum* or opium plant)

—SAYS KABIR

108. If you sit close to a perfume seller, even if he does not sell anything to you, yet you enjoy the scent of his perfumes,
If you associate with a SADHU, even when he does not teach you anything, yet you become a better man

—SAYS KABIR

109. To an ant when it comes across a grain of DHAL (RED GRAM) while it is already carrying a grain of rice
Oh! Ant! as you can not carry both, take the one and leave the other

—SAYS KABIR

110. A fool beats on the hole of a snake in an ant hill whereas the snake is safe deep inside its hole
To root out evil from ones mind is more difficult than to practice external austereties and rutuals

—SAYS KABIR

(NOTE : Similar ideas were expressed by
1. YOGI VEMANA (17TH CENTURY) - Ref. Page No. :
2. SARVAJNA (16TH CENTURY) - Ref. Page No : 549)

111. Everything is from GOD; and nothing from man
He can change a mustard seed in to a mountain and a mountain in to a mustard seed

—SAYS KABIR

112. You came in to this world with a purpose
Do not while away your time; this hour will not return again,
The green grass of today is the dried fuel of tomorrow
Worship 'RAMA' and attain MOKSHA —SAYS KABIR

113. Should all the earth be turned in to paper and all the trees in to pens; should the seven seas be turned in to ink, it is impossible to write down all the attributes of the CREATOR OF THE UNIVERSE

—SAYS KABIR

114. The pride of intellect makes one a swindler, a thief, a liar and even a murderer
Men, sages and even Gods have run after it in vain;
Its mansion has a hundred gates
Root out the pride of intellect

—SAYS KABIR

115. It by wearing a sacred thread (YAGNOPAVEETHA) a man becomes a BRAHMANA, then
What do your women wear?
If they are SOODRAS by birth, how can you being a Brahmana, eat the meal cooked and served by them;
If a man becomes a MUSLIM if he is circumcised, why not your ALLAH send you in to this world already circumcised?
Your women are not circumcised, and how can we regard them as MUSLIMS;
Whence have the HINDUS and MUSLIMS come?
Who has started this division of mankind according to religious systems?
There are no HINDUS and there are no MUSLIMS,
There is only one HUMANITY

—SAYS KABIR

116. People practice rituals and ceremonies, so long as perfect knowledge of GOD is not obtained;
The STARS sparkle in the sky, as long as the SUN does not rise —SAYS KABIR

Sources

1. Kabir by Parasnath Tiwari, 1969.
2. Kabir Vachanavali by Puttaparti Narayana Charyulu, 1967
3. Kabir - Prabhakar, Machwe, 1968
4. Kabir - Simply Wonderful by R. H. Lesser, 1985
5. Kabir and The Kabir Panth by G. H. Westcott, 1901.

24

SELECTED PROVERBS FROM NINE RELIGIONS

Proverbs from nine religions were selected and rewritten and arranged chronologically for the convenience of the reader.

1. HEBREW PROVERBS
(*DATE OF ORIGIN : 13TH CENTURY B.C.*)

1. He who performs a single good deed gains for himself an advocate;
   He who commits a single sin procures for himself an accuser
2. If you faint in the day of adversity, your strength is small
3. It is not good that man should be alone
4. We generally reproach others with blemishes similar to our own
5. *The borrower is servant to the lender*
6. Except the LORD build the house, they labour in vain that build it
7. *The weakness of your walls invites the burglar*
8. There are many old camels that are laden with the hides of young camels
9. In three things a man's character is recognized; in the vine cup, in his purse and in his anger
10. Charity given in health is gold; in sickness silver; after death lead
11. *A man shall be known in his children*
12. Two pieces of coin in one bag make more noise than a hundred
13. *Cleanliness is next to godliness*
14. In the city I am known by my name, out of the city by my dress.
15. The chastisements of GOD, are afflictions of love
16. *Spend more on your clothes than on your food*
17. Gold and silver make the foot stand sure; but counsel (advice) is esteemed above them both.
18. *In multitude of counsellors, there is safety*
19. That which is crooked can not be made straight
20. The days of our years are three score and ten (1 score = 20 years : (i.e. 70 years), or

even by reason of strength, four score years (i.e.: 80 years), yet is their pride but labour and sorrow

21. As thy days, so shall thy strength be
22. The father shall not die for the children; neither shall the children die for the father, but every man shall die for his own sin
23. No man dies and has the half of his wishes realized
24. A man only dies to his wife, and a woman to her husband
25. What ever you have to your discredit, be the first to tell it
26. Seest thou a man diligent (hard working) in his business? He shall stand before Kings; he shall not stand before mean men
27. What so ever thou takest in hand, *remember the end* and thcu shall never do amiss (wrong)
28. *The end does not justify the means*
29. Remember thy end and let enmity cease
30. Men reap the evil that they plough and the trouble that they sow
31. Fret not thyself because of evil doers; neither be thou envious against the workers of iniquity (injustice), for they shall soon be cut down like the grass, and wither as the green herb
32. Be strong as a leopard, brave as a lion, swift as an eagle and fleet as a gazelle, to do the will of thy LORD
    (Gazelle = A small graceful antelope)
33. One father willingly maintains ten sons, but ten sons are not willing to support one father
34. For fear is nothing else but a betraying of the succours (succor = Aid, relief) which reason offereth.
35. Ponder the path of thy feet, and let all thy ways be established
36. Where no wood is there, there the fire goeth out; so where there is no tale bearer, the strife ceaseth
37. A reproof enters more in to a wise man, than a hundred stripes in to a fool.
38. A whip for the horse, a bridle for the ass, and a rod for the fool's back
39. The most beautiful of all things, man can do is to forgive wrong — (ROKEACH)
40. *Deal with those who are fortunate*
41. *A friendship that can grow old should never die*
42. He gives little who gives much with a frown; he gives much who gives a little with a smile.
43. At the first glass—a lamb, at the second glass a lion and at the third glass—a swine
44. *He who is loved by man, is loved by GOD*
45. *Be first in greeting every man*
46. *He who denies his guilt, doubles his guilt.*
47. *What so ever thy hand findeth to do it, do it with all thy might.*
48. *He that gives should never remember;*
    He that receives should never forget.
49. The happiness of the impious and the unhappiness of the righteous are

incomprehensible things. (not capable of being understood)
50. Conquer thy hearts desire before it conquers thee and breaks thee
51. Even when the gates of heaven are shut to prayer, they are open to those of tears
52. My son! gather instruction from thy youth up; so shall thou find wisdom till thine old age.
53. *Happy is he who hears an insult and, ignores it, a hundred evils pass by him*
54. For the ear of jealousy heareth all things; and the noise of murmuring is not hid
55. *Burden not thyself above thy power while thou livest*; and have no fellowship with one that is mightier and richer than thyself; for how agree the Kettle and earthen pot together
56. *Great is labour for it honours the labourer*
57. *According to the labour is the reward*
58. Be not ashamed to learn and seek knowledge follow the wise, so that you may become wise
59. *He who adds not to his learning, diminishes it*
60. Say not when I am at leisure I will study perchance thou will have no leisure
61. *Everyone who does too much detracts from the whole*
62. The penalty of the liar is that he is not believed even when he speaks the truth
63. *Life is but a loan to a man; DEATH is the creditor who will one day claim it*
64. *And what doth the LORD require of thee, but to do justly and to love mercy, and to walk humbly with thy GOD-MICAH*
65. Trust in the LORD with all thine heart and lean not unto thine own understanding; in all thy ways acknowledge HIM, and *HE shall direct thy paths*
66. *LOVE without rebuke (check, reprove) is no love*
67. The life of a man is similar to a flower in a field; as the wind passes over it and it is gone; and the place there off shall know it no more.
68. *In a place where there is no man, strive to be a man*
69. A merry heart doeth good like a medicine; but a broken spirit drieth the bones
70. Attend no auctions if thou hast no money
71. Thou shall not follow a multitude to do evil
72. For better is a neighbour that is near, than a brother far off
73. Observe the opportunity
74. The house that does not open to the poor, shall open to the physician
75. A physician whose services are obtained gratis (for nothing, free), is worth nothing
76. The place honours not the man, it is the man who gives honour to the place
77. The (A) poorman is hated even by his neighbour, but the rich have many friends
78. Prayer is worship in the heart
79. Better is a little prayer with devotion, than much without it
80. Let the property and honour of another be as dear to you, as your own
81. *Questioning is half way to wisdom*
82. Without religion, there can be no true morality, without morality there can be no true religion
83. Who is rich? He who rejoiceth in his portion

84. Be not righteous over much; neither make thyself overwise
85. A little with righteousness is better than much with unrighteousness
86. The righteousness of the righteous man will not save him on the day when he transgresses
87. All the rivers run into the sea, yet the sea is not full; unto the place from whence the rivers come thither they return again
88. *In returning and rest shall ye be saved;*
    In quietness and in confidence shall be your strength
89. Thy secret is thy slave; if thou let it loose, you become its slave
90. If thy secret oppresses thine own heart, how can you expect the heart of another to endure it
91. *Silence is a fence round wisdom*
92. *Silence is good for the wise; how much more so for the foolish*
93. Eye and heart are the brokers of SIN
94. So long as a man does not sin he is feared; as soon as he sins, he himself is in fear
95. Words may occasion regret, but silence will avoid it.
96. It is better to have ten inches to stand upon than a hundred yards to fall,
97. *Thrift is half way to wealth*
98. *TRUTH is heavy, therefore few care to carry it*
99. *TRUTH is the seal of GOD*
100. Two are better than one; because they have a good reward for their labour, for if they fall, the one will lift up his fellow; But woe to him, that is alone when he falleth, for he hath not another to help him up ...
     And if one prevail against him, two shall withstand him; and *a three-fold cord is not quickly broken*
101. *Use the best VASE today, for tomorrow it may perchance be broken*
102. *In the way in which a man wishes to walk, he is guided.*
103. He who walks over his estate daily, finds a coin daily.
104. In to a well out of which one has drunk, one should not cast a stone.
105. *He who has no wife lives without happiness, without religion, and without blessing*
106. If the wife sins, the husband is not innocent
107. *The greatest wisdom is to know thyself*
108. *He is not called wise who knows good and evil, but he who can recognize of two evils, the lesser*
109. Men should be careful lest they cause women to weep, for GOD counts their tears
110. He who can not hear one word will hear many
111. Ten measures of speech descended to the world; women took nine and men one
112. God did not make woman from man's head, that she should rule over him; nor from his feet, that she should be his slave; but from his side that she should be near his heart
113. Stumble not at the beauty of a woman, and desire her not for pleasure
114. GOD endowed woman with more intelligence than man.

115. Commit thy works unto the LORD, and thy thoughts shall be established
116. Let your 'YES' be 'YES', and your 'NO' be 'NO', lest you fall into condemnation.
117. If you have gathered nothing in your youth, how can you find anything in your age?
118. Your yesterday is your past; your today is your future; but your tomorrow is a secret.

2. CONFUCIANISM
(*DATE OF ORIGIN: 6TH CENTURY B.C.*)

1. The bird chooses the tree; the tree does not choose the bird
2. A crooked man can never make others straight
3. If the upper beam leans to one side, the lower ones also will give way
4. *Without tasting the bitterest, we never reach* the *highest*
5. A bow never unbent is useless
6. *The cautious seldom err*
7. To see what is right and not to do it is want of courage.
8. Men neglect their own fields and go to weed the fields of others; what they demand from others is great, while what they lay upon themselves is light
9. *The path of duty is close at hand, but men seek for it in what is difficult and remote*
10. *The end must be attended to, even as the begining*
11. If a man is telling the truth, the pupils of his eyes are bright, otherwise they will be dull. While listening to a man's word, look at his eyes. How can a man conceal his deceit?
12. *Pardon inadvertent (carelessness) faults however great and punish preplanned crimes however small*
13. If the flower is good, the fruit will be good
14. Friendship with a man is friendship with his virtue and does not admit of assumptions of superiority
15. *A gem is not polished without rubbing, nor a man perfected without trials* (Inscription in the temple of everlasting harmony)
16. The superior man is friendly but not familiar
    The inferior man is familiary but not friendly
17. To do one good act is better than building a nine storey pagoda.
18. The great man is he who does not loose his child's heart
19. To be happy see no evil, hear no evil and do no evil
20. That which is done without a man's involvement is from HEAVEN
21. He who likes to put questions, becomes wiser;
    He who uses only his own views, becomes smaller
22. Roman (or Recompense) Evil with justice and Repay Kindness with Kindness.
23. Better do a good deed near home than walk a thousand miles to burn incense in a temple
24. When you know, to know that you know, and when you do not know; to know that you do not know is the essence of wisdom.

25. (A) Those who labour with their minds govern others
(B) Those who labour with their muscles are governed by others
Those who govern (A) others are supported by the latter (B)
And the latter (B) are supported by the former (A)
26. While you do not fully understand life, how can you understand DEATH?
27. If you love men and they are unfriendly, look into your love
If you are courteous to them, and they do not respond look into your respect
If what you do is vain (fruitless), always seek within.
28. *He who requires much from himself and little from others, will be secure from hatred*
29. Human nature is common to all, but those who follow noble qualities become great and those who follow inferior qualities become inferior.
30. If a man himself does not walk in the right path even his own wife and children will not walk on the right path
31. *He who attains to sincerity is he who chooses what is good, and firmly holds it fast*
32. *Small men never think they are small;*
Great men never know they are great.
33. By promoting the straight, and degrading the crooked, you can make even the crooked straight
34. *A man can do things, properly only when he knows what things he should not do*
35. *Only from a good tree, comes a good fruit*
36. Fix the mind on TRUTH; cling to virtue; give play to loving kindness; recreate yourself with arts.
37. Firmness and resolution, simplicity and slowness of speech, are qualities that make for perfect virtue
38. Virtue practiced to be seen is not real virtue vice which fears to be seen is real vice
39. When a man does not trangress the boundary line in the great virtues, he may take some liberty in the smaller virtues
40. The wise man will be slow to speak, but quick to act
41. It is only the truly virtuous man, who can love or hate others
42. *The wise through not thinking become foolish and the foolish by thinking become wise*

3. TAOISM
(DATE OF ORIGIN: 6TH CENTURY B.C.)

1. If you would take, you must first give and this is called the law of life
2. A small bag can not be made to contain what is big
A short rope can not be made to draw water from a deep well.
3. He who grudges expense pays dearest in the end.
4. Do not precede others, follow them
5. The superior man abides by what is solid, and eschews (avoids) what is flimsy;
He concentrates on the fruit and not on the flower.
6. *He who thinks tasks are easy to perform is sure to find them difficult*

7. *He who is conscious of being strong, is content to be weak*
8. *The three important precepts (instructions) are :*
   1. *Be gentle* and you can afford to be bold,
   2. *Be frugal* and you can afford to be generous,
   3. *Be humble* and avoid putting, yourself before others, and you can become a leader among men
9. Good words shall gain you honour in the market place
   Good deeds shall gain you friends among wise men
10. The way of TAO is easy and straight, but the people love to loose themselves in the bypaths.

4. SHINTO
(DATE OF ORIGIN: PRE HISTORIC)

1. *The path of DUTY is near at hand, but men seek it in what is remote and difficult*
2. *Set up a fence between even intimate friends*
3. If the heart is upright such a ones deeds also will be upright
4. One good deed is better than three days of fasting at a shrine
5. Although HEAVEN says no word, it points the way
6. *Esteem loyalty and uprightness, higher than life*
7. *DO NOT FORGET THE LIMITATIONS OF YOUR OWN PERSON*

SHINTO PRECEPT

8. To admit a fault is the begining of righteousness
9. *Although the sage may hate the fault, he will not hate the man.*
10. Sympathy is from above; respect is from below
11. Sincerity is the single virtue that binds DIVINITY and MAN in ONE
12. *VIRTUE goes hand in hand with happiness*
13. *So long as a man cherishes (keep in the mind, take care of , protect) TRUTH in his mind, HEAVEN will guard him, though he may not pray.*

5. JAINISM
(DATE OF ORIGIN: 6TH CENTURY B.C.)

1. By ones own actions, one becomes a BRAHMANA, or a KSHATRIYA, or a Vysya or a SOODRA.
2. *Difficult to conquer is ones own self, but when SELF is conquered, everything else is conquered*
3. One who has identified himself with his physical body, is extremely afraid of DEATH, seeing there in his own destruction, and separation from relatives and friends.

6. ZOROASTRIANISM
(DATE OF ORIGIN : 6TH CENTURY B.C.)

1. A man with no off spring is deemed to be one with a *severed bridge*, that is, the way

for him to that other world is severed

2. *Root out (ERADICATE) greediness from your heart, otherwise it will render the wonders of the world tasteless to thee, and that of the spirit unperceived*
3. *By eating every creature lives, by not eating it dies away*
4. One should not be a partner with a greedy man
   One should not walk on the road, with a drunken man
   One should never take a loan from an ill-natured man
5. To live in fear and falsehood, is worse than DEATH.
6. *Men of good deeds are known in their children*
7. One may heal with 1. Holiness 2. THE LAW 3. THE KNIEF 4. THE HERBS and 5. THE HOLYWORD... *The best healing of all remedies is by THE HOLY WORD*
8. Even the swiftest horse requires the whip; the sharpest steel knief requires the whet stone
   And the wisest man requires counsel
9. *What you are able to do today, do not postpone for tomorrow, for you do not know, when DEATH will snatch you away.*
10. *One truthful man is better than a multitude speaking falsehood.*

7. CHRISTIANITY
(DATE OF ORIGIN: A.D. 30)

1. A wise man gains his wisdom from the experience of others
2. Wisdom enables one to know what is true, and to detect (or discern) what is false
3. A child may not inherit his parents' genius or talents but he is sure to absorb their values on life and men
4. For every man shall bear his own burden
5. In necessary things unity, in doubtful things liberty, but in everything charity
6. Charity is a stately plant, its very rare flower is gratitude
7. Charity begins at home, but should not end there
8. *One does EVIL enough, when one does nothing GOOD*
9. The nearer the church, the farther from GOD
10. Pray to GOD, but continue to row to the shore
11. God delays but does not forget
12. God does not give to all alike; to one he gives the goose, and to another the egg
13. God does not love a man , who never suffered
14. In a little house GOD has a corner, but in a big house, HE has to stand in the hall.
15. *God helps the poor, but the rich help themselves*
16. Next to GOD, it is better to rely on oneself
17. Whom GOD means to punish, HE first deprives a man of his reason
18. To GOD one limps, to the devil one jumps
19. GOD promises a safe landing, but not a calm passage
20. *GOD rules (reigns) in heaven, and money on Earth*
21. When one can do no more, GOD sends DEATH

22. *If you fear GOD, you will not fear man*
23. Good is recognized, when it is lost (goes), and Evil, when it comes
24. The good that is done today, constitutes the happiness of tomorrow
25. *He who is not good to himself, how can he be good to others*
26. They will be hushed by a good deed, who laugh at a wise speech
27. If you would live long, open your heart.
28. *What does not come from the heart, does not reach the heart*
29. *Where a man's heart is, there is his GOD.*
30. *Behold! the kingdom of GOD is within you*
31. Thou shall not muzzle the mouth of the OX, that treads out the corn
32. *He preaches well, that lives well.*
33. A prophet is not acceptable in his own country; nor doth a physician do cures upon them, that know him — A.N.T. OXYRHYNCHUS PAPYRUS
34. The measure of our sacrifice is the measure of our love
35. Behold! I send you forth as sheep in the midst of wolves; Be ye therefore wise as serpents, and harmless as doves.
36. A sin even if committed by many, remains a sin
37. If any would not work, neither should he eat
38. Work as if thou art to live a hundred years and pray to GOD, as if thou art to die tomorrow.

8. ISLAM
(DATE OF ORIGIN: A.D. 622)

1. The value of an act, is according to its intention
2. A man is safe when alone, and safety is a sufficient advantage
3. Help thou thy brother's boat across and lo! thine own has touched the shore
4. A branch tells of what stock it comes
5. When GOD wishes a man well, he gives him insight into his faults
6. To choose good is to avoid evil
7. Hospitality is for three days
8. *GIVE THE LABOURER HIS WAGE, BEFORE HIS PERSPIRATION BE DRY.*
9. The law of life requires, sincerity to GOD, severity to self, justice to all people, service to elders, Kindness to the young, generosity to the poor, good counsel to friends, forbearance with enemies, indifference to fools and respect to the learned
10. *Men grow eager for that, which is with held*
11. Paradise is under the shadow of swords — MUSLIM BATTLE CRY
12. He is no perfect man, who has not fallen into trouble; *for there is no skilful physician but experience*
13. *Sleep is the brother of DEATH*
14. You think you are but a small thing, where as in you is involved the whole universe
15. Visit seldom and you will get more love
16. A man is free, when he gives up this world, even before he has left it

17. This world is a BRIDGE; pass over it, and build no house there ...
(carving by AKBAR over the gate of a mosque at FATHEPUR SIKRI)

B. PERSIAN PROVERBS

1. The arrow that has left the bow never returns (Words once spoken can not be recalled),
2. Death is a camel that kneels once at every man's tent
3. *Patience is bitter, but its fruit is sweet*
4. Woman is a torment, but O! GOD! let no home be without a torment.
5. He most values safety, who experiences danger
6. Escape may lie between this pillar and that
7. If you talk by night lower your voice;
If your talk by day keep your eyes open
8. Hearing is never as good as seeing
9. Use your enemy's hand to catch a snake.
10. It takes a needle to remove a thorn from one's foot
11. Trust in GOD, but tie your camel
12. Necessity turns even a lion into a fox
(Necessity turns even the noblest man into a deceiver)
13. A fruit that hangs out of the garden, will be stoned by every passer by
14. Look after your money and do not make your neighbour a thief
15. Live together like brothers, but do business like strangers.
(Personal relations should not be allowed to interfere in business transactions)
16. A sponsor will be caught by the purse or caught by the collar (It is not worthwhile to give surety for anyone)
17. Do not judge a pepper corn by its small size, crack it and taste it and you will know its sharp taste (An insignificant looking man may have sharp wits)
18. War at the begining is better than peace at the end (An ounce of prevention is worth a pound of cure)
19. *What is cheaply obtained is despised*
20. He who wants a rose must respect the thorn
21. You must start by night, arrive by day
22. *To walk and sit is better than to run and burst.*
23. *You must climb a ladder step by step.*
24. *A hasty man does his work twice over.*
25. GOD is the PROVIDER for all, but HE needs a nudge (a push gently with the elbow)
26. The master's eye has its own effect.
27. To die with honour is better than to live in disgrace
28. *No one sees his own faults*
29. *EVERY ONE THINKS OF HIMSELF*
30. The donkey works and the horse eats
31. *The oppressor's wrongs fall on his childrens heads*
32. The neighbour's morsel has goose fat on it (other people's possessions always seem better than one's own)

33. Even the QAZI will drink free wine (Most men will sacrifice principle for GREED)
34. A stone is as good as gold for hiding (A miser's son says to his father "Gold is for spending and for mere hiding a stone is just as good)
35. When the snake is old, even a frog will tease him (when a powerful man falls, no one has respect for him anymore)
36. Kindness to evil men is as bad as injury to a good man (Harshness in return for harshness is an act of justice. — *SADI (1184-1291)*
"To spare the ravening leopard is an act of injustice to the sheep"
37. Above every hand, there are other hands (*Every oppressor will himself be oppressed*)
38. A hollow drum makes a great noise
39. *You may sow thorns, but you wont reap Jasmine*
40. *For what you have done yourself there is no remedy*
41. *GOD seizes late, but seizes harshly*
42. A house with two mistresses, will be deep in dust
43. Every spring has an autumn, and *every road an end*
44. Drunkenness brings out the truth (A man who is off his guard gives himself away)
45. *Reticence is a sign of wisdom.*
46. *Do not answer until you are questioned.*
47. He who talks of others with you, will talk about you, with others (*Beware of gossip-mongers*)
48. You can shut the city gate, but you can not shut the mouth of men.
49. It is easier to make a promise, than to fulfil it
50. The quick witted die young (A warning to someone, who tries to be too clever)
51. *Heart finds a way to heart* (LOVE and friendship are always mutual)
52. Who is lost from sight, is lost from the heart
53. *DISTANCE PRESERVES FRIENDSHIP*
54. A wise enemy is better than a foolish friend
55. The liar is forgetful
56. Nature not spite gives the scorpion its sting (A scorpion stings whether it be the back of a friend, or the breast of an enemy)
57. *Ripeness is in wisdom, and not in years*
58. Youth is too wild to worship GOD, and age too weak
59. *To a wise man, a nod is enough*
60. One stroke is enough for a noble horse
61. *KNOWLEDGE IS POWER*

9. SIKHISM
(DATE OF ORIGIN: 15TH CENTURY)

1. The woe (grief, misery) and weal are according to thine acts.
2. There is no devotion without virtue.
3. God will not ask man of what race, community or caste he is, but he will ask what he has done.

4. "Turn my feet in a direction in which GOD is not" — NANAK
5. Revile (abuse with words) not dust, when we are alive it is beneath our feet, but when we are dead, it is above us. — FARID
6. "None can erase what is written on the forehead" — NANAK
7. *He who forgetteth GOD, is already dead*
8. "They who worship the GOD in their hearts possess wisdom, honour and wealth" — NANAK
9. Naked man cometh, naked he departeth—such is the will of GOD —AMAR DAS
10. "The fruit of SIN is sweet, but only for four days; it then grows bitter" — NANAK
11. All the creatures are made out of one material, but the CREATOR has fashioned it into myraid varieties. — AMAR DAS (Myraid : an immense number)

Sources

1. The Eleven Religions and their Proverbial Lore by Selwyn Gurney Champion, 1944.
2. Sutton's Persian Proverbs by L. P. Elwell, 1954.

25

MORALS FROM MAHABHARATA

Mahabharata, also known as '*JAYA*' was originally written by *VEDAVYASA* in *SANSKRIT* and it contained about *8,800 SLOKAS.*

Mahabharata dealt not only with the historical events of its period, but also various aspects of 1. *DHARMA SASTRAS* 2. *PURĀNĀS* 3. *AGAMAS* and 4. *KNOWLEDGE* AND *WISDOM* OF ITS PERIOD. *MAHABHARATA* is also renowned as *'PANCHAMA VEDAM'*.

1. *PERINDEVANAAR*, in *8th century A.D.*, wrote the *TAMIL VERSION* of Mahabharata
2. *ADIKAVI PAMPA* in *10th century A.D.*, wrote the *Kannada version* of Mahabharata, and named it '*VIKRAMARJUNA VIJAYAM*'
3. *NANNAYABHATTU, TIKKANA SOMAYAJI* and *YERRAPRAGADA*, in *11-14th century* wrote the *TELUGU VERSION* of Mahabharata

   Here is a collection of 148 TELUGU POEMS from ANDHRA MAHABHARATAM, each elucidating a moral principle.

A. POEMS WRITTEN BY NANNAYA BHATTARAKUDU

1. Tagunidi Taganidi yedalo
   Vagavaka Sadhulaku bedavārala keggul
   mogi jeyu durveneetula
   Kagu Animittā gatam bulayena Bhayambul.

   Vagavaka = without any discrimination; Mogin = intentionally; Eggulu cheyu = who do evil deeds; Durveneetulaku = Evil persons; Animittā gatambulayena = Unexpected; Bhayambulu = Dangers and afflictions; Agun = happen

   Men who do evil deeds intentionally and cause suffering to men of virtue and to the poor, are sure to face unexpected afflictions and dangers.

2. Tana yerigina yardhamboru
   danagha edi yetlu sepumani yadiginaje
   ppani vādunu Satyamu se
   ppani vādunu ghora naraka pankamuna padun

Anagha! = one who is free from all moral defects

One who does not speak the truth, and who does not explain a matter with which he is fully conversant with, to another, even when the latter prayerfully requests him to explain, is sure to land in the hell.

3. Yenta Sāntulayyu nenta jitendriya
Layyu gadu vivaktamayena chota
Satula gosti jitta chalanamondudu rendu
Gāṃu sakti norva galare janulu

Gadu vivak tanayena chota = in an isolated private place; satula gostin = when a man meets a woman; Endu = at any time; Chitta chalanamondudu = are likely to loose self control; orva galare = will be over come by passion

Even a man renowned for his forbearance and control of senses, will be overcome by passion, if he happens to meet a woman, in an isolated private place.

4. Aligina nalugaka yeggulu
Valikina mari vinaniyatlu prativachanam bul
Valukaka bannamu vadiyeda
Dalapaka yunnatada choove Dharmagnu delan

Bannamuvadi = Although one has been insulted; yedan dalapaka = who does not harbour any resentment in his heart

One who does not loose his temper even under provocation, and who does not harbour any resentment in his heart, towards another though the latter has insulted him, is fit to be called a man of DHARMA.

5. Kadu nanuraktiyu nerpunu
Gada Kayu galavāri nuraka Kadavaga neggul
Nodivedu viveka soonyula
Kadanundedu nanta kante gastamu galade
Kadu Anuraktiyu = with a lot of enthusiasm

Nerpunu = Skill; Kadakayu = Effort; Kadav; Vagan = just to while away time; yeggulu no divedu = who finds faults in the work of

It is very difficult to serve a stupid master who finds faults in the work of a servant even when the latter does his work with all the enthusiasm, effort and skill.

6. Tanayundu talli dandrulu

Panichina pani seya deni Balukedalu je

Konadeni Vādu tanayun

danabadune Pitru dhanamuna karhunda gune

Panichina pani = a work entrusted to him by his parents; Che konadeni = who does not listen to the advice given by his parents

A son who does not perform the work entrusted to him by his parents and who rejects the advice given to him by them, is unfit not only to be called a son, but also to inherit their wealth.

7. Eruka gala vāri charitalu
Garachuchu sajjanula gosti gadalaka Dharmam
Beruguchu nerigina dānini

Maruvaka nushti nchunadi samanjasa buddhin

Eruka galavari charitalu = Life histories of wise men; Karachuchu = getting acquainted with; Kadalaka = without leaving the company of sajjanas, while they are discussing

Anustinchunadi = Practising the wisdom learnt from sajjanas

One should get acquainted with life histories of greatmen, and also listen carefully to their discussions on DHARMA; After understanding Dharma, one should practice it without fail.

8. Manamunaku briyambunu hita
munu badhyamu dadhyamunu namoghamu madhuram
bunu barimitamunu nagu palu
Konaraga balu kunadi dharma yutamuga Sabhalan

Pathyamunu = Acceptable; Tadhyamu = Truth; Amoghamu = which is not futile

Parimitamunu = Concise

One who addresses an audience, should take care to see that it (his speech) is 1. Based on DHARMA 2. Pleasant to hear 3. Truthful 4. Useful 5. Concise and 6. Acceptable to all.

9. Madamu gāmambu grodhambu matsarambu
Lobhamunu mohamunu nanu loni sahaja
Viri vargambu nodichinavāda yeduchu
Nasramambuna velupali yahi tatula

Bada china vada = who has destroyed; Asramambuna = easily; oduçhu = will be able to defeat.

One who has conquered his internal evil qualities (or enemies) such as 1. PRIDE 2. DESIRE 3. ANGER 4. JEALOUSY 5. GREED and 6. PASSION will also be able to conquer his external enemies easily.

10. Etti Sadhvukulanu buttina indlanu
Bedda Kalamuniki tadda tagadu
Patula Kadana uniki satulaku dharmuvu
Satula Kedugadayu batula choove

Pedda kalamunini = To live for a long time; Tadda tagadu = it is forbidden; Edugadayu = Protection; Patula choove = Husband is the sole protector for a chaste wife

An ideal wife should not live for a longtime in her parents' house, away from her husband. At all times, the husband is the sole protector for a wife. According to DHARMA, a wife should live with her husband only.

11. Marachina dalapimpaga nagu
Nerugani nadella patla nerigimpadagun
Mari yerigi yeruga nollani

karatim delupanga gamalagarbhuni vasame

Marachina = one who has forgotten; Ellapātlan = By all means; Karatim = A stupid fellow
It is easy to teach one who is ignorant;
It is easy to remind one who has forgotten, what he has learnt already
But even BRAHMA, will not be able to teach a stupid fellow, who refuses to learn.

12. Satiyunu gunavatiyu brajā
Vatiyā nanuvratayunina vanita navagnā
Nvita drusti joochu notidu
rmati kihamun baramu galade mati bari kimpan

Prajā vatiyu = who has borne children; Anuvratayu = who is cooperative; Avagnanvita drustin = to look down with contempt

An evil man who ill treats his wife who is chaste, cooperative and who has borne children with him, is sure to forego happiness here and in hereafter.

13. Velayanga nasvamedham
Bulu veyunu nokka satyamununiru gadalan; dula nide toopaga satyamu
Valanana mulu soopu gouravambuna permin

Erugadalan = when weighed in a balance; Toopagan = when weighed;

The greatness of TRUTH, surpassess even the merit acquired by performing a thousand "ASVAMEDHA YAGAS"
TRUTH is an incomparable quality

14. Etti Visista Kulambuna
Buttiyu sada sadvivekamulu galgiyu mun
gattina karmaphalambulu
Nettana bhogimpa kunda nerture manujul

Mangattina = the fruits of ones past karma; Nettana = without fail

One has to experience the results of his past KARMA, irrespective of his noble ancestry, intelligence and discriminatory powers.
The law of KARMA is inexorable (unyielding) for all.

15. Mati dalapaga samsarum
Bati chanchala mendāmavulattula sampa
tpratatu lati Kshanikambulu
gatakālamu melu vacchu Kalam Kanten

Sampat pratatulu = Wealth and prosperity

The pleasures of this world are all temporary. All the wealth one acquires here, is as evanescent (quickly fading), as a mirage in the desert. The past life of any one will be better than his future, by any measure.

16. Palumaru Sapathambulu nan
jaleyunu nabhi vadamunu sama priyabha
shalu midhya vinayambulu
gala yavi dusta savabhāva kapuru shulakun.

Anjaliyun = Repeatedly bringing the hands together in an attitude of supplication; Samapriya bhashalu = Pleasant speech; Midhya vinayambulu = Deceitful humility

An evil fellow can be recognised by the following traits; 1. Frequent oath taking; 2. Repeatedly bringing the hands together in an attitude of supplication 3. Pleasant speech and 4. deceitful humility

17. Tana kimmagunantaku du
rja nudistuda pole nundi sarpamu polen
dana kimma gudunu garechunu
ghana daruna karma garala ghāṇa dāmstralachen

Tana kimmagunantaku = Until his work is done; Estuda pole nundi = he will pretend to be a friend; sarpamu polen = like a venomous snake; Ghenadaruma Karma = By cruel deeds; garala ghana damstralachen = He will bite with his poisonous fangs

An evil fellow will pretend to be a friend until his work is completed; once his work is over, he will repay with only evil deeds, which are much more dangerous than the bite of a venomous snake.

18. Kadunalukayu goormiyu ne
rpada nериginchunadi vāri phalakalamu penpidugunu gādpunu janulaku
badatayu veechu tayu neruka padiyedu bhangin

Penpidugunu gādpunu = Thunders and stormy winds; Kadu nalu kayu = Excessive anger; Koormiyu = affection

Clouds, and rain, precede thunders and storms; similarly, the display of excessive anger or affection precede the unfolding of one's Karma.

19. Tana kapakāramu madije
sina janudalpudani nammi chekoni yundan; janadoka enchuka mullaye
nanu bāda talamuna nunna nadavaga nagune

Chekoni yundajanadu = one should not be indifferent; Pāda talamuna = in the sole of the foot

One should not underestimate and ignore an enemy simply because he is an insignificant fellow. A thorn may be little in size, but when it is stuck in the sole of a foot, one will not be able to walk until it is removed completely.

20. Monasi yapakāri gadanidi
Koni yundedu Kumati deergha kuja sākhāgrambe
buna nundi nidravoyedu
Manujunaku samānudagu bramattatvamunam

Monisi = Inspite of; Kadanidukoni = having an enemy close by; Kumati = stupid fellow; Pramattatvamunan = indifferent or negligent

One who is proud and indifferent to an enemy who is close by, can be compared to a stupid fellow, who carelessly goes to sleep on the top most branch of a very tall tree (i.e. he is sure to fall down sooner or later and die.)

21. Kulapamsanulaye yahitam
bulu seyuchunundu chuttamula bondaka ye
mmulanundu vādu punyudu
Velayaga gra masti thika Vrukshama polen

Kulapamsanulay = Those who have brought an evil reputation to their community; Ahitamulu = Evil deeds; Pondaka = without joining them; Emmulanundu vadu = who keeps away from them; gramastitha = in the centre of the village; Eka vrukshama polen = like a solitary tree

One who keeps away from evil minded kinsfolk (relatives) can be compared to a solitary tree in the centre of a village (i.e. it is the only source of shade for all the villagers).

22. Parahita balavantulu su
sthira moolānvitula pāpadheeratu lu para
spara samsrayamuna jeevin
turu manujulu vanamuloni drumamula polen

Parahita balavantulu = Those powerful people, who wish the welfare of others; Apāpadheera tulu = Those who eschew (avoid) evil at all times; Susthira moolanvitulu = Those who have huge and solid trunks; Drumamula polen = like the trees in a forest; Paraspara samsrayamuna = wishing the welfare of each other

Men of virtue and power always wish the welfare of others, and try to live in cooperation with people. They can be compared to tall trees with huge trunks, which flourish in forests.

23. Apadayenanu Dharmuva
Prapuga rakshim pavalayu baramardhamu Dha
Rmāpayama dharmikulaku
Nāpada janmantaramuna nanu gata magutan

Dharmuva prapuga = protect and favour Dharma only; Dharma payamu = when Dharma is in danger; Janmāntaramuna = in the next life also; Anugatu magutan = follows

One should try to favour and protect DHARMA at all times, inspite of difficulties and obstacles one may encounter on this path, as any violation of Dharma, is bound to have an adverse effect on one's next life also.

24. Kruta meruguta punyamusa
nmati dāniki samamuseta madhyamu mari ta
tkru tamuna kaggalamuga sa
tkrūti seyuta yuttamambu kruta buddhula kun

Kruta buddhu lakun = For men of virtue; Kruta meruguta = to remember a good deed done to him with gratitude; sanmatin = with good intentions; Samamuseta = To reciprocate with another good deed; Tat Krutamunakun = For a benefit received; Aggalamuga = greater

One who remembers with gratitude a benefit conferred on him acquires merit (PUNYAM); one who reciprocates with an equivalent good deed is an ordinary person (MADHYAMA) one who reciprocates with a greater benefit is indeed a superior person. (UTTAMA)

25. Adini samyoga viyo
Gādi dvandamulu dehi yagu vānikisam
pādillaka takkavu poo
rvodaya karmamuna netti yogi kinayenan

Adini = Even from the begining; Dehi yaguvāniki = for any human being; Sampādillaka takkavu = They are bound to affect him; Samyogadi viyogadi = Union and separation; Poorvodayakarmamunan = As a result of ones past Karma

Even a YOGI, as long as he is (EXISTS) in a human body, has to experience the effects of unions and separations, which are caused by his own past KARMA (Law of Karma is inexorable (unyielding) for all)

26. Dhrutisedi Vededu Vānini
natidhini nabhyagatuni bhayasthuni saranā
gatu jam paga nodabadu du
rmati kiha mum baramu galade madi parikimpan

Dhrutisedi = who has lost his courage; Vededu = who prayer fully requests; Champanga noda badu = who tries to kill

An evil doer who tries to kill (1) a man who seeks refuge under him, after he has lost his courage (2) a man who requests for food and shelter (3) a man who is terror stricken and (4) a refugee, is sure to loose every thing here and in the hereafter.

27. Erukagaladeni marisaktudeni yanyu
lanyulaku himsagavin chunapuda dāni
booni vārimbakunna nappurushudegu
himsa chesina vārala yegu gatiki.

Erukagaledeni = if he is a wise man; Saktūdeni = if he is a powerful man; Pooni

Vārimpakunna = if he does not oppose such oppression.

One who is wise and powerful, if fails to oppose and prevent others from tormenting helpless creatures, is sure to reap to same consequences, that are in store for the oppressors themselves, in the course of time

28. Arambharahitu bondune
yāraya sampadalu hee nu dayyunu pureshun
dārambha seeludaye yakru
tārambhula norchu nenta yadhikula nayenan

Arayan = if one observes carefully; Aramba rahitun; One who lacks enthusiāsm and effort; Aramba seeludaye = if he possesses the necessary effort and enterprise; A Krutrambhulan = those who lack enthusiasm and effort; orchun = he will surpass them

Wealth and prosperity always seeks out a man of effort and enterprise; Even an inferior man is sure to surpass those who are now in an exalted position, if he displays more enthusiasm and enterprise than the latter.

29. Kadunadhiku toda dodarina
Bodichina nodichinanu buru shu purusha gunambe
rpadu gāka heenu noduchuta
Kadidiye pourushamu dāna kalugune chepuma

Kadunadhiku toda = one who is more powerful than self; Todarinan = if one fights; Podichinan = if one kills; odichinan = if one defeats; Purushu = such a man's; Purushagunam berpadugaka = then only his valour is recognized; Heenu nodachuta = To defeat an inferior and weaker man; Kadidiye = Is it a mark of valour? No!

If one fights, defeats and kills an opponent who is more powerful than self, is sure to gain recognition for his valour. To defeat an inferior and weaker enemy is not considered as a mark of valour.

30. Kularoopa guna dravyam
bulu vikrama vantunandu Bhoo viditamuli
niluchu navikramunaku navi
galigiyu leni kriya naprakasambulagun

Kula, roopa, guna, dravyambulu = Ancestry, personality, character and wealth; Vikrama vantunandu = in a man of valour; Bhooviditamuli niluchu = add renown to his name; Navikramunaku = to a coward; A prakasambulagun = will not impart renown to his name

To a man of courage, qualities and assets such as 1. noble ancestry 2. an attractive personality 3. a good character and 4. wealth enhance his name and fame; whereas the same qualities and assets are futile in a coward.

31. Kāranambu leka dārunambagu sadhu
himsaseyu kujanu dellavaru
Kapriyundu Kaka yapriya lakshanam
Bondugalade talapa nuttamulaku

An evil fellow who torments men of virtue without any reason, will be hated by all. Men of virtue regard the tormenting of SAJJANAS, as one of the most heinous (very wicked) crimes.

32. Sakala bhoota sanghambu parjanyu bakshi
samiti bahuphala vrukshambu namaru lindru
nanisamunu nupa jeevinchunaatlu bandhu
janulu ninnupa jeevimpa manumu permi

Sakala bhoota sanghambu = All the living creatures

Parjanyu = clouds and rain; Amarulu = Devatas; Indru = Indra (God and ruler of Devatas); Anisamunun = at all times; upajeevinchu natula = survive with the support of

All the living creatures survive because of rains; All the birds survive because of fruit laden trees; All the DEVATAS survive because of the rule by INDRA; One should live and support ones kith and kin; And thereby acquire renown. (Kith = friends; kin = relatives)

33. Kutila mārgu layena kutsita Kitavula
toda gadagi jooda māda janadu
dana jesi yardha dharma vivarjitu
lagudu rettivāru jaga mulona

Kutila margu layena = Deceitful men; kutsita kita vula toda = Evil minded gamblers; Kadagi = particularly with

One should never gamble with deceitful and evil minded rascals; one who gambles with such men, is sure to loose not only his wealth but also his virtue (DHARMA).

34. Priyamu palikedu vārina peddamettu
ra priyamubunu bathyambunina paluku
Vinaga nollaru gāvuna vedka dāni
baluka revvaru nuttama prati bhulayyu

Peddametture = are praised greatly; Pathyambunina = appropriate and conducive; (Conduce = contribute) to ones welfare; Apriyambunu = unpleasant; Vedkan = with pleasure.

People prefer to listen to those who talk about pleasant matters, and not to those who talk about unpleasant truths. Hence even distinguished men avoid talking about unpleasant truths.

35. Madamalina manasku darun
tududu nrusamsudanabaragu durjanunaku sampada peddayayyu nātani
modaliti sanchayamuto samoolambu chedun

Madamalina manskudu = An arrogant fellow; Aruntududu = a merciless fellow; Nrusamsudu = a cruel fellow modaliti; sanchayamutodan = all the wealth he has accumulated so far; samoolambu chedun = will lose it totally.

One who is arrrogant, merciless and cruel, although he possesses great wealth, is sure to loose in the end all the wealth he has accumulated so far.

36. Manamuna veramidalapami
yunu sakshamachittu dagutayunu gunamulu ki
Koni doshambulu viduchuta
Yunu nuttamudayena purushu nuttamagunamul

Manamuna = even in his thinking; Vera midalapami yunu = who does not differentiate between self and others; Sakshama Chittudagutayunu = who is known for his forbearance

(1) Non discrimination between self and others (2) forbearance and (3) giving credit for good qualities found in others and overlooking their lapses, are the characteristics of a man of virtue (superior man)

37. Sokabhayastanambu la
nekambulu Kaliginanu Viheena Vivekun
dākulata bondunatlu Vi
Vekamugala vādu buddhi vigatundagune

Sokabhayastanambulu = Events which cause grief and terror; Heena Vivekundu = A stupid fellow; Akulata = loosing ones equanimity; Buddhivigatundagune = will not forego his intelligence and equanimity

A stupid fellow looses his equanimity (calmness of mind) as soon as he encounters events which cause grief and terror; where as an intelligent man will not forego his composure and will face such events with courage.

38. Saareera manasa mahā
dāruna dukha mulajesi tarigi Sareerul
Krooratara badha bondudu
rārentini jeru tu raryulamalina buddhin

Sareera manasa maha daruna dukhamulajesi = Physical and mental afflictions, Sareerul = ordinary people; Tarigi = become enfeebled; Amalina buddhin = with composure; Jeruturu = they overcome.

Ordinary men are overwhelmed by physical and mental afflictions, whereas superior men do not loose their composure and try to over come such afflictions.

39. Snehārnava magnundaye
Dehi mahā dukhamula nadhruti bondunu du
Kha hatudu soka tapa vi
mohi yagun sneha moolamulu rāgādul

Snehernava magnundeye = one who is steeped in (immersed in) attachments; dehi = a human being; Adhrutin = looses his courage; Dukha hatude = one who is overcome by grief; Vimohiyagun = looses his intelligence; Ragāadulu = affections etc.

A man who is overwhelmed by undue attachments with people around him, is sure to be overtaken by grief and as a consequence of this grief, he looses his discrimination also.

Undue attachments are the source of human bondage

40. Adi sarvadosha mula kā
spadamadi durita kriyanubandhambulakun
modalu nirantara dukha
pradamani madi nerigi trushnaba turu sumatul

Adi = greed (or desire); Sarvadoshamulaku = for all sins: Aspadamu = basis; Duritakriyānu bandhambu lakun = it is the main motive for all evil deeds; Nirantara dukhaprādamu = its end result is always grief; Trushna = greed (or desire); pāture = give up sumatul = men of virtue

Greed (or desire) is the root cause of all sins, and all evil deeds and its end result is always sorrow. Aware of its consequences, wise men avoid it by all means.

41. Jalamulandu matsyambulu jadala bakshu
ta misham bethlu bhakshinchunatlu diviri
yella vārumu jeri yaneka vidhula
na nudinambum bhakshintu rardhavantu

Chadalan = in the sky; Amishambun = food; Tiviri = try by all means; Arthavantun = a wealthy man; Bakshinturu = try to grasp his wealth

Fish search for their food in water;

Birds search for their food in sky.

Similary all the people seek out a wealthy man, and try their level best of grasp his money.

42. Arthama yanardha moolam
Barthamā māyā vimoha nā vahamu narun
dartharjana dukhamunana
parthee kruta janmudaguta paramartha milan

Arthamu = Wealth (money); Anardhamoolambu = Root cause of all evil; Maya

Vimohana vahamu = its end result is Maya (Delusion); Artharjana dukhamunana = Acquisition of wealth results in sorrow; A partha Krutajan mudaguta = he will be misunderstood and will be considered as an evil person by others; Paramardhamu = it is certain.

Wealth is the root cause of all evil, delusion (MAYA) and attachment (MOHA) One who is regarded as a good one, as soon as he becomes rich, is sure to loose his erstwhile good name also.

43. Hari Vishayābhilāshamu
Karanamuga nenta yerukagalāvārunu du
rvāra vikarmu bondedu
Varu nijendriyamula viya vasyamu laguten

Nijendriyamulu = Ones own sense organs; Avasya mulagutan = are impossible to check and control; Hari = which destroys everything; Vishayabhi lashamu = desire for pleasure to be enjoyed through sense organs; Enta eru kagalavarunu = even for wise men; Durvara = uncontrollable; Vikaramunu = experience MOHA (DELUSION)

To check and control one's sense organs is almost impossible. The craving for pleasures to be enjoyed through the sense organs, persists and as a consequence of this hankering for pleasures, even wise men become victims of MOHA (Attachment).

44. Kāryagatula teragu kala roopu seppina
nadhinamatulu dani nādarintu
ralpa karya buddhulagu vāralaku nadi
Virasa karanambu vishama pole

Karyagatula teragu = The consequences of a particular line of action; Kala roopu = described as it is : Adhikamatulu = intelligent people; Alpa Karyabuddhu lagu varalaku = for evil minded people; Vishama pole = as undesirable as a poison; Virasa karanambu = It causes enmity

When one explains the consequences of a particular line of action, intelligent people accept it; whereas the evil minded people reject it, thinking that it is as undesirable as a poison, and also they develop enmity towards the person who gives sound advice.

45. Ella neyyamulaku dalli dandru layandu
sutulavalani neyya matisayambu
dhanamu lenta galigina nu sutarahitula
Kemmeyini manaha priyammu ledu

Ella neyyamulakun = Among all types of friendships; Neyyamu = affection; Atisayambu = it is unsurpassed; Sutarahitulakun = Those who have no progeny (or descendants); Emmeyin = By any means; Manaha priyambu = have no happiness

The affection of parents towards their sons is preeminent (unsurpassed) among all types of affections or friendships. Those parents who have no sons, do not have peace and happiness in their minds, although they may possess great wealth.

46. Kshamagalavāniki brudhvee
samunaku nityambu vijaya samsiddhiyagun
Kshamiyina vāni bhuja ve
Kramamugadun velayu sarva karya kshamami

Prudhvee samunaku = one who has forbearance equal to that of the BHOODEVI (EARTH); Kshamagalavanikin = to a man of patience; Bhuja Vikramamu = Valour

Sarva karya kshamami = it will enable him to successfully complete all his tasks; Kadun = greately; velayun = shines brilliantly.

A man of forbearance is sure to succeed in all his tasks. Forbearance adds lustre to his valour.

47. Dheera mati yukti jesi vi
Charimpaga nikkuvambu sarvajana sva
rgārohana sopānam
baraga dharmamba choove yati ramyambi

Dheeramati yukti jesi = The way followed by wise men; Svargārohana sopanambu = The way to heaven; Aragan = if you carefully study it; Nikkuvambu = certainly.

The path of DHARMA is the only excellent way to reach the heaven, if one is willing to follow in the footsteps of wise men.

48. Tagili nityambu nekānta dharmaniratu
daguta yuktame purushuna katti vāni
velaya dharmakā mambulu viduchu brāna
Vigatu sukha dukhamulu rendu viduchu natlu

Tagili = Concentrating all his efforts on it; Ekanta dharma niratudaguta = To be interested in DHARMA; Pranavigatu = a dead man; Yuktame = a proper thing

A man who concentrates all his energy and efforts to realize DHARMA, will not be affected even by DHARMA and KAMA (DESIRE) just as a dead man is no longer affected by any joy or sorrow.

49. Balamugalavāni baluvuru balaviheenu
lokkti koodi nirjintu rutsahinchi
madhuvugona nutsahinchina manujubatti
Kutti nirjinchu madhu kara kulamu natlu

Madhuvugonan = to collect honey; utsahinchina = when enthusiastic attempts are made to; Nirjinchu = Kill; Madhukara Kulamunatlu = swarm (a collection of insects) of Bees

Many weakings if they conspire and join in a group, they will be able to kill even a stronger man, just as a swarm of bees kill a man who tries to collect honey from a honey comb.

50. Antakundu janula kāsannudi yunda
nimisha mātra meni nischayinpa
dagani jeevambu dadda susthiramuga
jesi karya medaya jeya dagune

Antakundu = YAMA; Edayajeyadagune = one should not delay; susthiramuga jesi = thinking that one is going to live forever; Tadda = greatly

Death (YAMA) approaches all living creatures relentlessly minute by minute. Aware of this eternal truth one should never delay or postpone any task he ought to do.

51. Adhika dukharogartuna koushadhambu
suruchirambuga bharyaya choove yendu
nonara bharyā sametudi yunna vāni
Kenta layyunu nāpada lerukapadavu

Dukharogār tunaku = one who is grief stricken; Suru chirambuga = appropriate; ou shadhambu = medicine (or remedy); enta layyunu = any afflictions; Eruka padavu = will not affect him

The company of one's wife is the best remedy for one who is grief stricken and overtaken by afflictions.

52. Alacinaneda dassineda nā
Kali trushnayunina yedala gadukoni dharanee
tala nādha purūshunaku ni
mmula bharya ya pāchu jichittamunā Dukhambul

Alasinaneda = when tired; Dassina eda = when thirsty; Immula = with pleasure; Akali = when hungry; Trushnayu nina yedala = when passion strirs up inside him; Pachun = wife is the solace of her husband; Dhaneetalanadha = oh! King

Oh! King! One's own wife is the only solace for a man who is tired thirsty, hungry and or in need of sexual satisfaction.

53. Tilago suvarna danām
bulu nupavāsamulu deer thamula sevayu ni
mmula jeyani vāru dari
drulu niratemu nagudu rātmadoshamu permin

Tila = gingili (Indian sesame or NUVVULU)(TELUGU); GO = COW; Suvarna = gold; upavasamulu = fasting; Teerthaseva = pilgrimages; Immulan = with pleasure;

Duratma doshamu permin = Because of evil pervading in their minds.

Those who do not make gifts of 1. gingili 2. cows and 3. gold to the deserving and needy, and who do not willingly fast on auspicious days, and who do not undertake pilgrimages willingly, are sure to be cursed with poverty for ever, because of the evil in their minds.

54. Anavadya teerthasevana
munu gapila svarna dānamulu nugratapam
bunu jeyani variki bo
lune padayaga bermi nubhayaloka sukhambul

Anavadya = renowned; Teerdhasevanamu = pilgrimages; Kapila svarna dānamulu = making gifts of KAPILA Cow, and gold etc.; Ugra tapambu = austerities; Polune = is it possible; permin = greatness; ubhayaloka sukhambul = happiness here and in the hereafter

One who does not make gifts of KAPILA cows and gold to the deserving and needy, who does not undertake pilgrimages, and who does not undergo severe austereties, is sure to forego happiness here and in the hereafter.

55. Dharmagnulina purushulu
Dharmuvunaku bādhaseyu dharmuvuninan
Dharmamugā madi dalaparu
Dharmuvu sarvambunaku hitambuga valayun

Dharmagnulina purushulu = Those who are well-versed in DHARMA SASTRAS; Badhaseyu = when it undermines; Sarvambu naku = for all; Hita mbuga valayun = should ensure the welfare of all

Those who are well-versed in DHARMA, will discard even a dharma if it undermines DHARMA itself.

A DHARMA should contribute to the welfare of all

56. Alayaka yendlu gadun be
kkulu jeevinchuta naragalugutayun daguvru
ddhula lakghaname jnānamu
gala denin bāludayene gadu vruddhu mahin

Alayaka = without getting tired; Naragalu guta yun = with hair on the head which has turned white

Living to very old age, and having white hair on the head, are not the only signs of wisdom. Even a boy if he happens to be intelligent and wise, should be considered as a wise man.

57. Guru susroosha yonarchuchu
Barama klesamuna jesi padasina vidyal
Spuriyinchugāka guru mukha

Virahitamuga badasinavi velayune yendun

Guru susroosha yonarchuchu = Reverently serving one's Guru; Paramaklesamuna = undergoing many difficulties; spurinchugaka = can be recollected; Guru mukha virahitamuga = skills obtained without the guidance of a Guru; Velayune yendun = will not be recognized by others;

Reverently serving one's Guru and undergoing many difficulties in the acquisition of knowledge is the only way to acquire VIDYA, and only this VIDYA (VIDYA = Education and Knowledge) will come to ones rescue when the need arises.

All the various types of vidya acquired without the guidance of a GURU (GURU = Teacher or Preceptor), will not be appreciated or recognized by others.

58. Karyasiddhi bonda kālambu desambu
nerigi buddhi mantulella proddu
sahasambu vidichi sāmādupāya pra
yukti cheyuduru yadho chita muga

Karyasiddhi bonda = To successfully complete a task; Ella proddu = at all times; Sahasambu vidichi = Avoiding recklessness; Samadupaya prayakti = Employing (1) SAMA (conciliatory or peace making) (2) DANA (making gifts) (3) BHEDA = pitting one antagonist against another and (4) DANDA = Threat of punishment or punishment.

A wise man very carefully assesses the proper time and place for any task he undertakes. He avoids recklessness in the completion of his tasks at all times. He uses SAMA, DANA, BHEDA and DANDA manoeuvres, as and when indicated for the successful completion of a task.

B. POEMS WRITTEN BY ERRA PREGGADA

59. Vinu manujuna Kevvidhamuna
dana chesina sukruta dush krutambulunerayan,
dana kanubhavimpa bālivi
tanuvu sedungāni karmatali seda danagha

Anagha! = one who is free from all faults; Nerayan = Completely; Sukruta dush Krutambulu = good and evil deeds done by self; Pālivi = has to experience without fail; Tanuvu = human body; sedungani = disintegrates; Karmatali = sum total of his own KARMA

One has to experience fully the results of good and evil deeds done by self; ones own human body disintegrates in the course of time but the sum total of his KARMA is indestructible.

60. Ee lokamayagu gondara
Kā lokama kondaraku nihambunu paramun

Melagu gondara kadhipa!
yelokamu ledu vinave ela gondarakun

Eelokama yagun = some experience happiness here; Aalokama = in the next world; Ehambun = in this world; Paramun = in the next world

Some experience happiness in this world only, whereas some attain it in the next world only; whereas some attain happiness here and in the hereafter also; whereas for some there is no happiness here and in the hereafter also.

61. Satyamunu Samambu Souchambu leka nā
stikyamunu nishiddhaesvanambu
galigi tirugu dushtakasta janasreni
poliyu nubhayaloka mulaku gāka.

Satyamunu = TRUTH; Samambu = forbearance; Souchambu = cleanliness; Nastikyamunu = Refuting the existence of GOD (ATHEISM); Nishiddha sevanambu = displaying keen interest in forbidden things; Dushta kasta janasreni = Evil men; Poliyu = will be totally destroyed.

Evil men who have forsaken (given up) 1. TRUTH 2. FORBEARANCE 3. CLEANLINESS 4. Belief in the existence of GOD, and who display keen interest in forbidden things, are sure to experience destruction not only in this world but also in the next world.

62. Tana keerti yenta kālamu
Vinabadu nijjagamunandu velayaga nandā
kanu bunya loka soukhyam
bunu nentayu nullasillu burushun dana gha!

Ejjagamunandu = in this world; Ullasillunu = he will experience fully the heavenly pleasures.

As long as a man's name and fame are remembered in this world, such a one is sure to enjoy heavenly bliss for an equivalent period in the next world also.

63. Tanayugani talli dandrulu damaku natadu
Bhaktudagutaku dharmarthasa ktudaguta
Kasa paduduru vinumatti yāsa siddhi
Bondajeyu natada chuvve nandanundu

Bhaktudagutaku = to have respect and reverence for elders; Dharmarthasuktu dagutaku = to be interested in DHARMA and ARTHA; Siddhi bondajeyu natade = one who fulfils the expectations of his parents

Parents bring up a son with the fond hope that he will display reverence and respect for elders and that he will show keen interest on (in) DHARMA (DUTY) and ARTHA (WEALTH). An ideal son should strive his level best to fulfil the expectations of his parents.

64. Jananiyu janakudu nevvani
Yanuvartanamuna briyambu nandudu redada
TTanayudu dharmamu geertiyu
Nanoonamuga bondu badayu nakshaya gatulan

Anuvartanamuna = whose character and conduct is approved by his parents; Anoonamuga = to a great extent; Akshayagatulan = the best of the next world also.

A son whose character and conduct are approved by his parents, is sure to attain DHARMA (MERIT) name, and fame not only in this world, but also the best of the next world.

65. Tana Kuladharmamu viduvaka
Manuta paramadharmandru mānyulu chittam
buna grupagaluguta mukhyapu
bani siranavalayu nakhila bhavamulandun

Mukhyapubani = is an essential trait; Krupagaluguta = to possess a merciful heart; Akhila bhavamulandu = in all matters; Siranavalayu = Forbearance is an ideal quality

(A) one should fellow the DHARMA as shown by one's ancestors

(B) one should cultivate mercy at all times in one's heart

(C) In all matters one should display forbearance

66. Vidupu valayu sakala Vishayavānchala yandu
Vidupubolu gunamu vedaki yendu
gānarire budhulu galade parityāga
seelunaku nasādhya siddhi yendu

Sakala vishaya vānchala yandu = in all pleasures experienced through the sense organs; Vidupu = renunciation; Parityagaseeluna kun = one who can renounce all desires at any time

"Renunciation" is one of the best qualities. All should strive to achieve the excellent quality of renunciation.

Nothing is impossible for a man of renunciation.

67. Eggusesina vāriki hitamu seta
yāryajanamulu geertintu ranya dosha
Kāri danapapa mana dāna kalipovu
Vera vāniki keedu gavimpanelā

Aryajanulu = men of virtue; Eggusesinavariki = those who have harmed others; Hitamuseta = to recompense evil with good; anyadosha kari = one who has done evil to others;

Superior men appreciate if a man repays evil with good. There is no special need to punish an evil doer as his own evil tendency will destroy him eventually.

68. Dharmi kulu salupu nuttama
Karmamu jedanādu nāsti kajanamu vinumā
durmatula teragu gani koni
dharmamuneda breeti vadala dagadu budhunākun

Dharmikulu = those who are committed to DHARMA; Uttamakarmamu = deeds of merit; Nastikajanamu = Those who do not believe in the existence of a God; Durmatula = evil minded fellows; Teragu = method

NASTICAS (ATHEISTS) always try their level best to foil (obstruct or undermine) the good deeds undertaken by men of DHARMA. Aware of this inherent tendency of evil minded fellows, good men should never give up their committment to DHARMA.

69. Madimarapuna bāpamu danu
Kodavutayunu bidapa vagachi yoka sagamun
nidi seyaninka nani yedu
madi berasagamunu narundu malugu naghabun

Madimarapuna = done in a forgetful mood; tana kodavutayunu = sin that accrues (happens) to self; Perasagamunu = the other half of Aghambun = the sin; Malugun = will get rid of it

By repentance, one will be able to get rid off half of the results of a sin, and the rest of it by resolving not to commit the sin again.

70. Papa mula Kella nekkudu pātakamulu
Suvve krodha lobhambulu suvratātma
vāni renti jayinchina vādugāni
Yendu barama dhārmikudani yennabadadu

Suvratatma! = oh! man worthy of worship by all; Krodha lobhambu = Anger and greed; Patakamulu Suvve = abominable (Hateful) sins; Paramadharmi kudani = to be considered as a man of DHARMA.

Among all the evil qualities, anger and greed are the worst of the lot. Unless one is able to conquer these two evil qualities one will never be fit, to be considered as a man of DHARMA.

71. Vinu sista cherita gikoni
yanapāyata nadava nadava natah karnam
buna bodalu natti sammada
managha! durlabhamu soove yanya padhamulan

Anagha! = one who is free from all faults; sistacharitan = those who walk in the foot steps of SAJJANS; Anāpayatan = without experiencing any dangers; Nada nadavan = as one walks along such a path; Podalunatti = one experiences; Sammadamu =

happiness or joy; Anyapathamulan = By following various other ways; Durlabhamu soove = impossible to attain.

If one adopts and follows the path chosen by men of virtue, one is sure to achieve happiness eventually. And such happiness can not be achieved by any other means.

72. Vinu mahimsa dharmavitati kellanu meti
yadiyu satya yuktamina velayu
nanagha sistacharita landu satyama kadu
nadhikamaniri srutula narasi budhulu

Anagha! = one who is free from all defects; Dharma vitalikellanu = The best among all DHARMAS; Ahimsa = Non violence; Strutula narasi = Those who have studied vedas thoroughly; Budhulu = wise men Non violence is the greatest among all DHARMAS

Non violence if it is practised with TRUTH (SATYA) leads to the pinnacle (or zenith) of DHARMA.

Those who are well-versed in VEDAS, are of the opinion, that TRUTH (SATYA) is the basis for excellent conduct among all distinguished men.

73. Vedavihitambulunu sastravihitamulunu
sista charitambulunu nana jeppa noppi
dharmamulu moodu vidhamula danaru chundu
gadagi enniyu sadgati karanamulu

DHARMAS are broadly classified in to three groups. They are :

(A) DHARMA as explained (or expounded) in the VEDAS

(B) DHARMA as expounded in the SASTRAS

(C) DHARMA as followed by SAJJANAS

All the above mentioned ways to DHARMA lead one to the best in the world.

74. Munu tanu chesina karmam
buna joove nasinchu bhootamulu sampedu vā
du nimitta matramintaye
yani cheppaga viname yanchitācharulachen

Nimittamatram = one is only an agent in the deal; Anchitācharulachen = Wise men

All the creatures are destroyed eventually by their own inexorable (unyielding) KARMA. One who kills another man is only an agent of the KARMA of the latter, according to wise men.

75. Panivadi yahimsa vrata muga
goni vanamuna nunna munulako dodarade him

sanamu taru moola phala sa
Ka nipeedana madiyu himsa gadoko talapan

Panivadi = especially; Todarade = does it not affect; Himsanamu = is it not committing violence on; Taru moolaphala sāka = roots, fruits and leaves of trees; Nipeedanamu = consuming the above

Ascetics (or hermits), who are especially committed to AHIMSA (NON-VIOLENCE) to realize this (vow of non-violence), they choose to live in forests; and even they survive there, by eating the roots, fruits and leaves of the trees.

Do they not indulge in a type of HIMSA (VIOLENCE) towards the trees?

76. Himsa seyanivādu ledijjagamuna
nokkadinanu tamatama yopinatlu
himsateruvuna kedagalgi yegavalayu
nadiyachoove yahimsana natisayillu

Tama tama yopinatlu = as far as possible; Edagalgi = avoiding; yegavalayu = should proceed; Adiye choove = it is this only; Ahimsann = it is termed AHIMSA; Atisayillu = becomes renowned;

There is none in this world who does not indulge in HIMSA (violence), to some extent or the other wittingly or unwittingly. To avoid HIMSA (or violence) as far as possible is termed AHIMSA (Non-violence).

Ahimsa (Non-violence) imparts renown to all who practice it.

77. Oppedu nadiyinanu gadu
noppani yadi yina nija kulochita padhamun
dappa dagadandru dhārmiku
lappani nija bhagya vihitamani yundadagun

Dharmikulu = Those who are committed to DHARMA; oppedu nadiyinanu = a profession to ones liking; oppenidiyinanu = a profession not liked by self; Nija = his own; Kulochita padha muna = the way followed by ones own ancestors; Tappadagadandru = one should not give up; Nija bhagya vihitamani = one should think that it has come to him as ordained.

Whether the profession of his own ancestors is to his liking or not, one should not forsake it, and one should accept it, thinking that it has been ordained by his own luck (or KARMA).

78. Vinu poorva karmaphalamulu
danaku vasamugāka pondu darito vānin
gani kona neraka moodhudu
dana kāpadayina chota divamu doorun

Tanaku Vasamugaka = when he is not able to overcome the results of his own KARMA; Kanikona neraka = not understanding and not accepting; Doorun = he reviles (or abuses)

The law of KARMA is inexorable and is universal in its operation. A stupid fellow fails to understand and accept it and reviles GOD for the afflictions he undergoes now.

79. Kāryaphalamula yeda dāna kartananuta
Kadu nerungami juvve tā gartayeni
dagili ta nadina kārya jatambu nella
jedaka phaliyinchu natluga jeyarade

Kāryaphalamula yedā = To perform a task and to be the sole cause of its completion; Kadun = bound less or height of; Erungamijuvve = ignorance; Karyajata mbulanella = all his works.

To perform a task and to bring it to a successful completion are two separate aspects of the problem. To assume that the doer is responsible for both these aspects is the height of ignorance.

If the doer is responsible for both these aspects in a task undertaken, why can not he ensure success in all his works? He succeeds in some and fails in some, and this clearly shows that many other factors are also involved.

80. Purushudu Karmādheenata
narugaka tana vasama yanina nāpadalu rujal
maranambunu nivi yemiyu
Borayaka yundanga bradu kabolade chepuma

Karmādheenata = A man is subject to KARMA at all times; Tanavasama yanina = if one thinks that he is in full control of his own karma; Apadalu = Afflictions; Rujal = Diseases; Maranambunu = DEATH; Porayaka yundanga = without being affected by the above

If anyone thinks that it is not KARMA, but he himself is responsible for all events in his life then why he is not able to get rid off afflictions, diseases and death, which undermine his happiness, and welfare and put an end to his existence on earth?

None is exempt from the laws of KARMA.

81. Karmavasata joove kalugu dehamu deha
vartanambu karmavasata buttu
Deha pātamina dehastu dagu jeevu
darugu garmavihitamina yedaku

Dehamu = Human body; Karmavasatan = one acquires as a result of KARMA; Deha vartanambu = A man's conduct; Dehapatamine = when the human body disintegrates; Dehastu daga jeevudu = JEEVA OR PRANA which was in the human body; Karma vihitamina yedaku = HIs prana proceeds to a destination chosen by his own KARMA.

One is born as a human being because of is KARMA. His conduct also is as dictated by his Karma. His death occurs as ordained by KARMA. His PRAANA (OR JEEVA) leaves the body after his death and proceeds to a destination as chosen by KARMA

82. Vinu jeevundu sanatanu
danaghudu nijakarmavasata nadhruva deham
bunu bondu dehapātam
buna neppudu jedadandu vinte kumārā

Jeevundu = A jeeva or a prani or a soul; Sanātanudu = Ancient; Anaghudu = The soul is free from all defects; Nijakarmavasatun = as ordained by his own KARMA;

Adruva dehambunu bondun = Human body is a temporary abode for the SOUL; Dehapatambunan = when the human body disintegrates; Chadadu = The soul is not affected.

Jeeva or Prana (or SOUL) is quite ancient and is free from all defects. As a result of its own Karma, it enters and lives in a human body, which is only a temporary abode for it. At the time of DEATH, human body disintegrates, but the SOUL is not affected.

83. Ee yodalu vidichi veroka
Kāyamu gikoni sareeri garmavasagatim
Boyi sukhadukhamulu ganu
Bāyaka vendiyunu dehabandhamu bondun

Sareeri = JEEVA or PRANA or SOUL; Ee yodaluvidichi = giving up this human body; Karmavasagatin boyi = as ordained by his own KARMA; Pāyaka = without fail; Vendiyun = Again

A soul (JEEVA) leaves the human body at the time of death, and it enters and experiences weal (welfare) and woe (grief) again and again in another body.

This cycle of birth and death revolves on and on until the souls KARMA is completely worked out.

84. Anagha sabedādi vishayamulandu dagili
Eccha jariyinchu neppudu nindriyamulu
budhudu tatsvabhavamu dana buddhi nerigi
yemaraka vānidaga gudiyinpavalayu

Anagha! = oh! man of merit (Punyātma);Tagili = interested; Ecchan = without any control; Kudiyinpavalayu = should be kept under check

Human sense organs have an inherent tendency towards uncontrolled wandering. A wise man is aware of this trait, and he tries his level best to keep the sense organs under check.

85. Svarga narakambu lindriya
varga samācharanamuna vacchunu vinave
Svarga magu dannivārana
durgatiyagu dannirodha durbalata meyin

Indriya varga samācharanamuna = Depending on the conduct of ones five sense organs; Tannivaranan = control of; Tannirodha durbalata meyin = because of failure in the control of sense organs; Durgati yagu = one is ruined and ultimately lands in the hell

One enters the heaven or hell, as a result of control of the sense organs, or failure in their control respectively.

One who succeeds in the control of sense organs enters the heaven.

One who fails in the control of sense organs goes to hell.

86. Indriyambulu divichina yedaka paru
chundu manasepdu dadvegamudu pakunna
nedali chedipovu buddhi yudurnapavana
hati payonidhilo galā maviyunatlu

Indriyambulu = sense organs; Tivichina yedaka = wander about; Paruchundunu = run after; Tadvegamudupakunna = if the uncontrolled wanderings of sense organs are not checked; Buddhiyun = intelligence and discrimination; Udeerna pavanahatin = when struck by stormy winds and gales; Payonidhilon = in the sea; Kalamu = a ship; Aviyunatlu = sinks Edali = disintegrates : Chedi povunu = destroyed

Human sense organs have an inherent tendency to wander about in an uncontrolled manner and one should always keep them under control otherwise, one is sure to loose his intelligence and discrimination (or BUDDHI), just as a ship is destroyed and sunk, when it is struck by stormy winds in the midst of the sea.

87. Anindriyamulu manasunu
booni tana vasambina burushundu sadā
dhayana samādhi samagrudu
vanin geertintu ramara varulun munulun

Enu = five; Indriyamulu = sense organs; Pooni = using all his powers; Dhyana sumādhi samagrudu = one who has realized his self through DHYANA and SAMADHI states of YOGA; Amaravarulu = celestial beings (DEVATAS); MUNULU = SAGES

One who has achieved the complete control of his five sense organs, and who has realized his self through 'DHYANA' and 'SAMADHI' states of YOGA is praised (extolled) by even by DEVATAS and sages.

88. Chetana rahita kshetramu
jetanamun borayajeyu jeevātma daso
petudu paramātmudu vi
khyātudu trilokya samprakalpanu danagha

Anagha! = one who is free from all defects; chetana rahita Kshetramu = this lifeless human body; chetanamunu = is activated with life; Porayajeyu = imparts; Jeevatma dasopetudu = Paramatma takes on the existence of a Jeevatma; Paramatma = CREATOR; Vikhyatudu = renowned; Trilokya samprakalpanudu = He is the creator of the three worlds.

PARAMATMA (creator of the Universe) imparts life to a lifeless human body, and takes on the existence of a JEEVATMA (INDIVIDUAL SOUL)

A JEEVATMA is one of the many manifestations of PARAMATMA.

PARAMATMA is the CREATOR of all the three worlds.

89. Bhootamula yandu veligedu
Bhotatmuni neru guduru prabuddhulu nitya
jyotirmayu navyayu na
Advitambagu buddhi sookshma dharmamu valanan

Prabhddhulu = men with intelligence; Nityajjyotirmayun = one who shines with everlasting brilliance; Avyayun = one who is indestructible; Bhootamula yandu veligedu = one who exists as the life force in all creatures; Advitambagu buddhin = A mind (or a way of thinking) which does not differentiate an individual SOUL (JEEVATMA) from the UNIVERSAL SOUL (PARAMATMA); Sookshma dharmamu valanan = By their thorough understanding of ADVAITA and DHARMA.

PARAMATHMA (UNIVERSAL SOUL) is indestructible, ever present (everlasting) and shines with everlasting brilliance in all living creatures.

Intelligent men who are well-versed in ADVAITA and DHARMA, are able to see the manifestations of PARAMATMA in all JEEVATMAS

90. Kāmambunu Krodhambunu
nemaraka jayimpavalayu nellavidhamulan
Dheemahita ediya satata
kshemam karamina pathamu krutabuddhulakun

Dheemahita! = one who is renowned for his intelligence; Kamambunu = DESIRES; KRODHAMBUNU = Anger; Kruta buddhulakun = for intelligent men; Patham = way; Kshemam karamina = ensures the welfare of

One should root out DESIRES (KAMA) and ANGER (KRODHA), from one's mind, using all methods possible. This is the only way to ensure one's welfare, at all times.

91. Janani janakudu sadguru danalu dātmu
danaga niyye vurunu ne gruhasthu cheta
sugati vāncha brasadu laguduratti
Vādachoove dharmātmundu vasudha meeda

Analudu (Agni or GOD OF FIRE); Atmudu = Atma (or SOUL); Eyyevurun = These five; Sadgativān; chan = with the desire of attaining uttama lokas (Higher worlds); Prasāditulaguduru = satisfied

A house holder who satisfies the following five namely 1. Mother 2. Father 3. GURU 4. AGNI and ATMA (or SELF) is not only fit to be called a DHARMATMA (a man committed to Dharma), but also fit to enter the higher worlds (UTTAMA LOKAS).

92. Priyamuli vāyutayunu na
priyamulu vesa bondutayunu belluga nagu da
t Kriyalandu moodhamatiki hru
dayatāpamu vāyadepudu dari konuchundun

Priyamulu = Pleasant events; Pāyutayunu = loosing them; Apriyamulu = unpleasant events; Vesan = follow each other; Pellugan agu = happen very frequently; Tatkriyalandu = when unpleasant events happen after pleasant events; Payadu = will not leave him; Darikonuchundun = mental distress will enhance

In the course of a lifetime, losses, afflictions happen quite frequently to all. But a stupid fool reacts unduly to such events and suffers from great mental distress.

93. Vagatumanna nevvariki vagavajanadu
Chittamuna nemitiki santasimparādu
Kāna gata munandunu nanāgatamunandu
Vagava rāryulu santoshavantu laguchu

Evvari kin = for all; Vagatumannan = to grieve; Vagavajanadu = to grieve is forbidden; Chitta munan = for any event; Gatamu = past; Anāgatamu = future; Vagavaru = do not grieve; Aryulu = Superior people

Weal (Joys) and woe (Sorrows) are natural events for all. One should avoid elation when experiencing joys and depression when faced with afflictions.

Superior people never loose their equanimity thinking about the past or the future, and they always try to be cheerful under all conditions.

94. Vagapuna tejoheenun
dagu nātmahita kriyalaku nakshamudaguna
vvagapu doragi yudyogamu
daga jeyaga galugu nanchitamulagu subhamul

Vagapunan = because of grief; Tejoheenundagun = becomes weak; Atmahita kriyalakun = even to do tasks beneficial to self; Akshamudagun = becomes in capable of; Avvagapun = because of grief; Toragi = avoiding; udyogamu = Effort; Anchitamulagu = plenty; subhamulu = good things (or prosperity)

Grief robs a man of his energy, and he becomes incapable of doing tasks even beneficial to himself.

One who overcomes grief and relies on his own effort is sure to prosper.

95. Aadidevudagu mahādevu meeda ne
vvāni manasu bhakti vibhavamuna
nullasillu natani nella karyamula da
ggaravu soove grahā vikara krutulu

Adidevudagu = one who is first among DEVATAS; Mahadeva = LORD SIVA; Ullasillun = Shines; Graha vikara krutulu = Pervert effects caused by evil planets (GRAHAS); Daggaravu soove = will not approach him.

A sincere devotee who worships 'LORD SHIVA' (ADIDEVA) with the utmost reverence is sure to succeed in all his undertakings. Pervert effects of evil planets will not affect him at all.

96. Saranambani vacchina bhee
Kara satruvunina breeti gāvagavalayun
garunā parula terangidi
eravuga sarigāvu deenike dharmambul

Saranambani = if any one seeks refuge under you; Bheekara satruvunina = even when a deadly enemy; Eruvugan = definitely

One with a merciful heart will protect even a deadly enemy if the latter seeks refuge under him.

There is no DHARMA greater than protecting even a deadly enemy if he seeks refuge.

97. Vinu durvinayātmakudagu
janu dujjvalamina siriyu sadvidyayuga
lgina nandu melaga neraka
chenati terangunaku jochi chedipovududin

Durvinayetmakudagu janudu = An evil minded fellow; Ujjvalamina siriyun = great wealth; Sadvidyayun = excellent education; Andu melaganeraka = he fails to make the best use of his great wealth and excellent education; Chenati terangunaku = he pursues the evil path; Chedipovu tudin = he will be ruined in the end

An evil minded fellow even if by chance acquires great wealth and good education, not only will fail to make the best use of them, but he also will pursue an evil path, and will be ruined in the end.

98. Kshamayu nahimsayu satyamu
samatayu nindriya jayambu samamu barityā
gamunu dapolakshanamulu
gramamuna ninniyunu noordhvagati kāranamul.

Kshamamu = Patience (Forbearance); Ahimsayu = non-violence; Satyamu = TRUTH; Samatayu = Equality; Indriya jayambu = control of senses; Parityagamu = renunciation; SAMAMU = SHANTI (or peace); Tapo lakshanamulu = qualities of a saint (or an ascetic); oordhvagati kāranamul = All the above mentioned qualities eventually pave the way for liberation (or MOKSHA)

Qualities such as 1. Patience 2. Non-violence 3. Truth 4. Equality 5. Control of senses 6. Peace and 7 Renunciation are found in a man of TAPAS (Austerity). All the above mentioned qualities eventually pave the way for liberation (or MOKSHA).

C. POEMS WRITTEN BY TIKKANA SOMAYAJE

99. Erigedu vāriki ninanu
garapaka takka ruchita prakāramu subhamun
goralu hitulatlaguta nan
darakunu jeppangavalayu dagiyedu buddhul

Karapaka = to teach; Takaru = will not stop; Tagiyedu buddhul = proper conduct.

Those who wish your welfare will not stop giving you sound advice (counsel), although you are already aware of the proper course of action.

Those who are well-versed in DHARMA should deem it their duty to counsel others who are in need of advice and guidance.

100. Vunnaroopa paluku nannaru lekkada
galaru tochinatlu paluku valuka
nina chandamayye nantiyaka kanta
patti choodagalare yettivāru

Vunnaroopa = Those who can judge correctly; Paluku = explain; Annarulu = such men; Ekkadagalaru = where can you find them; Ayena chandamayye = things happen as they are bound to happen; Anta patti choodagalare = they will not be able to explain events accurately.

There are very few persons who can judge events accurately. The vast majority of people placidly accept events in a matter of fact attitude only. Those who give sound advice and guidance are very rare indeed.

101. Nānāvidha bhoota mayamu

Menati chanchalamu manamu meyikoni nikkam
be narunaku jellimpa
gānagu satyambu nadapu krama matlunden

Menu = Human body; Nanavidha bhoota mayamu = is made up of five elements namely AIR, WATER, EARTH, FIRE and SPACE; Manamu = mind; Ati chanchalamu = very fickle; A narunaku = to any man; Chellimpaganagu = impossible to explain; Satyambu nadapu kramamu = the path of TRUTH is so difficult to explain and to follow

Human body is made up of different elements;

Human mind is a very fickle one;

It is almost impossible to explain the TRUTH about any matter to any one;

The path of TRUTH is so difficult to explain and to follow.

102. Saranu socchina rakshimpajāli yundi
Kadapi pucchina noordhvalokamulu dappu
bunya karmambula phalata bondu nanade
Kamala garbhundu tolli jagaddhitamuga

Saranu socchina = when somebody prays for protection; Kadapi pucchina = fails to protect; Tolli = in the past; Oordhvalokamulu = Higher worlds; Punya karmambulu = meritorious works; Aphalata pondun = will not bear fruit; Jagaddhitamuga = wishing the welfare of the world

BRAHMA once said "that if one fails to protect those who seek refuge under him although he is capable of protecting them, he not only is sure to forego the results of any meritorious works, he has already done, but also he will be denied entry into higher worlds".

103. Madi sukhamu gori dukham
bodavam gala kārya mulaku nutsahamuse
yudu roppani trushnanbadi
chadu remiyuleni yatti janu lāturuli

Chaduru = skill; Aturuli = anxiously; Oppani trushnan badi = overcome by greed; utsahamu seyuduru = They try their level best to get involved in; Dukham bodavamgala; karyamulaku = Tasks which are sure to cause sorrow and grief

Men lacking the necessary skills, overcome by greed, try their level best to do tasks, which are sure to cause sorrow and ruin.

104. Edirin damayattula ka
madidalachina bosagugāka makun gudumin
dide meeru vrakka gonudani
Chaduradichina manasu pondu chakkambadune

Edirin = while dealing with others; Tamayattulakan = dealing with others as one would like to be dealt with; Manasu pondu = intimate friendship; Posagun = is possible; Kudumu indu = taking a major slice or portion of a thing; vrakka gonudu = leaving a small portion of a thing; Chaduradichina = when equity (Justice, Fairness) is overlooked

If one grabs the major portion of anything (example : such as a sweet meat like a KUDUMU), and leaves only a minor portion for the other, in such an unfair relationship, friendship will not flourish.

There can be no intimate friendship between two persons without fair dealing.

105. Balavantudu pinettina
balaheenudu dhanam golu padina yatadu mru
cchila vechuvādu gāmā
kula chittudu nidra leka kundudu radhipa

Balavantudu pinettina = when a powerful enemy attacks a weak opponent; Dhanamu golupadina yatadu = one who has lost his wealth; Mrucchilan Vechuvadu = one who is waiting to commit a theft; Kāmākulachittudu = one who is overwhelmed by passion; Nidraleka kunduduru = will not be able to sleep and suffer thereby; ADHIPA! = O! King

The following kinds of people will not be able to sleep soundly and suffer thereby

1. A weak opponent when attacked by a more powerful enemy;
2. One who has lost his wealth;
3. One who is waiting to commit a theft; and
4. One who is overwhelmed by passion

106. Janulaku nodabātagu vidha
muna nadachuchu lokanindyamula nuduguchumā
dani yokani kalimi kulukaka
manujulato bondi posagi manutoppu nrupa

Nrupa! = O! King; Janulakun = the people; Odabātagu vidhamunan = conduct approved by the people; Loka nindyamulan = giving up all evil activities; Okani kaliminan = other's wealth; Kulukaka = without spending the wealth of others; Pondi posagi = to live in cooperation and friendship.

1. One's conduct should be agreeable to all,
2. One should give up all evil activities,
3. One should not spend the wealth of others, and
4. One should try to live in a spirit of friendship and cooperation with the people.

107. Kopamu nubbunu garvamu
napōvaka yunikiyunu durabhimanamu ni

rvyapratvamu nanunavi
kapurusha gunambulandru kourava nadha!

Kouravanadha! O! King DRUTARASTRA; Kopamu = Anger; Ubbunu = Susceptibility to flattery; Garvamu = pride; Apovaka yunikiyunu = dissatisfaction (DISCONTENT) Durabhimanamu = Undue Egoism; Nirvyaparatvamu = Laziness (INDOLENCE); Kapurushagunambulandru = Qualities found in evil men

The qualities that are characterestic of an evil man are : 1. Anger 2. Susceptibility to flattery 3. Pride 4. Dissatisfaction 5. Egoism and 6. Indolence.

108. Alinavanini divamu
nalini bandhulanu samuchitaārādhana sem
seelata breetulajeyani
pālasu dāphalamu lāsapadu manujendra

Manujendra! = Oh! King; Alinavanini = one's own king; Divamun = one's own GOD; Alini = one's own wife; Bandhulanu = ones relatives; Samuchita aradha na samseelatan = to satisfy them in a suitable manner; preetulan cheyani = who fails to satisfy them; Palasudu = Evil fellow; Aphalamulasapadu = he will be interested in evil qualities.

One who fails to give satisfaction in a suitable manner to his own 1. King 2. GOD 3. Wife and 4. Relatives, will be drawn to evil qualities such as anger, pride, egoism etc.

109. Nemmigalavāri nollaru
tammollani vari venuka daguludu radhika
tvammerigi yerigi todarudu
rimmerugani yattivara libhapuranadha

Ebhapuranadha! = Oh! King DRUTARASTRA!; Emmerugani yatti vāru = those who lack discrimination; Nemmigalavārin = Those who love them sincerely; Ollaru = reject them; Tammollani vari venuka daguluduru = they run after those, who treat (regard) them with all the contempt; Adhikatvamu = knowing fully which is the best; yerigi yerigi = thoughtfully aware of; Todaruduru = try to follow them

Men who lack discrimination reject the friendship of those people who love them sincerely. On the other hand they run after and seek the friendship of those people who treat them with all the contempt.

Knowing well that they are inferior (unsuited) to claim the friendship of the great ones, they do not give up their efforts.

110. Dhanamunu vidyayu vamsam
bunu durmatulaku madambu bonarinchunu sa
jjanulinavāri kadakuva

yunu vinayamu niviya tecchu nurveenadha

Urveenadha! = Oh! King; Dhanamuna = Wealth; Vidyayu = learning; Vamsambunu = noble lineage; Durmatulaku = for evil men; Madambu bonarinchunu = enhance his pride; Ada kuvayunu = Humility; Vinayamu = modesty

Wealth, learning and noble lineage, will enhance pride and egoism in an evil fellow, whereas the same qualities will enhance humility and modesty in a man of virtue (SAJJANA).

111. Aridi Vilukāni yujjvala
sara mokkani nonchu dappi chaninanjanu ne
rpariyina vāni neeti
spuranamu pagarāju natani bhoomin jerachun

Aridi = skilled; Vilukani = Archer; YUJJVALA SARAMU = Powerful (or great) arrow; On chun = kills; Tappichaninanjanun = or even it may miss the target; Nerpariyinavani = An expert; Neetispuranamu = STRATEGY (the art of war); Pagarajun = an enemy King; Atani bhoomin = and his kingdom also; Cherachun = will destroy.

An arrow released by a skilled archer may strike and kill an enemy or it may even miss the target; whereas the strategy of an expert in the art of war, will not only destroy an opponent but also even his kingdom.

112. Okatigoni renti nischalayukti jerchi
mooti nalginta gadu vasyamuluga jesi
yenitini gelchi yarinti nerigi yedu
vidichi vartinchuvadu vivekadhanudu.

Okatigoni = taking the soul (or ATMA) as the basis; Nischalayuktin = with a clear mind; Rentini = Love (Raga) and hatred (Dvesha); Mootin = The three qualities namely SATVA, RAJAS and TAMO gunas; Nalgintan = By using SAMA, DANA, BHEDA and DANDA strategies; (kadun vasyamuluga chesi = control of); Anitini = Five sense organs (1. Eye, 2. Nose, 3. Ear, 4. Taste and 5. Touch); Gelchi = conquering; Arintin = six evil qualities; namely 1. Kama (Desire), 2. Krodha (Anger), 3. Lobha (Avarice), 4. Moha (Passion), 5. Mada (Egoism) and 6. Matsarya (JEALOUSY) Erigi; fully aware of

Aduvidichi = by giving up seven evil habits (SAPTA VYASANAMULU) namely 1. VELADI (Debauchery) 2. JOODAMU (Gambling) 3. PANAMU (Addiction to alcoholic drinks) 4. VETA (Hunting) 5. PALUKU PRALLADANAMU (Harsh speech) 6. Dandambu parushadanamu (Excessive punishment) 7. Sommu Nishprayoja-namuga vammuseta (spending money recklessly on useless things) (*Refer Poem No. : 119*)

Vartinchuvcdu = whose conduct is based on the above mentioned principles; Viveka dhanudu = A wise man.

1. A wise man considers the SOUL (ATMA) as the basis for all existense.
2. He gives up opposite emotions like Raga (LOVE) and DVESHA (HATRED).
3. He gains the full control of three GUNAS ((1) SATVA; (2) RAJAS, and (3) TAMAS) with the help of (1) SAMA, (2) DANA, (3) BHEDA, and (4) DANDA, strategies
4. He gains the full control of the five sense organs.
5. He is fully aware of the consequences of six evil qualities (ARISAD VARGAS) (1. Kama, 2. Krodha, 3. Lobha, 4. Moha, 5. Mada and 6. Matsarya)
6. He keeps away from the seven evil habits (SAPTAVYASANAMULU) (Refer Poem No. : 119)

113. Vinu madhurā harambulu
gonutayu bekkandru nidra goorina yeda me
lkani yunikiyu garyālo
chanamu deruvu nadachutayunu janadokkani kin

Vinu = please listen to me; Madhurāharambulu gonutayu = Eating sweet meats (CONFECTION); Pekkandru nidragoorina yeda = when most of the people are asleep; Melkani yunikiyu = To be awake; Karyalochanamu = To think and plan about important matters; Teravu nada chutayunu = To walk singly on a road; Chanadu = it is forbidden

The following ways of conduct are forbidden by the wise :

1. One should not eat sweet meats (CONFECTION) singly (it is better to share and eat it with others)
2. One should not be awake when most of the people around are asleep
3. One should not think and plan about important matters singly
4. One should not walk singly on a road (for his own safety)

114. Nadavadiyanu munneetin
gadavam bettanga noda karani dagi tā
nodagoodu nanina satyamu
gadachina gunaminka nondugalade yarayan

Nadavadiyanu = conduct; Munnutin = sea; Kadavam bettaga = To sail across; oda Karanindagi = like a ship; odagoodunanina = helps one; Arayan = if one sees carefully; Nondu gunamu = There is no other quality

To sail across a sea safely, a ship is essential, similarly in the proper conduct of a human life, TRUTH is essential. There is no greater quality than TRUTH to help and guide all.

115. Kshamiyinchu varigani cha
lami vettudu rinanu dalampa nanoona
kshamaya kadu merayu todavu
ttama roopamu goruvāru dālturu dānin

Kshamiyinchu varigani = Those who are not vindictive and full of forbearance; Chalami vettuduru = people regard them as weak and powerless; Anoona kshamaya = a high degree of forbearance (EXEMPLARY); Todavu = ornament; uttama roopu goruvaru = those who aim at an excellent personality

Those who are not vindictive and are full of forbearance, are considered by others to be weak and powerless. Yet forbearance is an excellent quality and those who aim at embellishment (Decoration) of their personality, cultivate it.

116. Purushundu rendu deragula
dhara nutta mudanaga baragu dāneyyadalam
bārusamulu valukakunikin
duritambulu vorayu panulu doraguta katanan

Purushundu = a man; Rendu terangulan = By adopting the two ways; Dharan = on the earth; Uttamudana baragu = he is called a superior person; Ayyedalan = at anytime; Parushamulu = Abusive language; Palukakunikin = not uttering; Duritambulu = sanful deeds; Porayu = which result in; toraguta katanan = by giving up.

One is considered as a superior person if

1. he never utters abusive words and if

2. he never indulges in sinful deeds.

117. Chelliyundiyu sirana seyu natadu
beda vadiyunu nardhiki briyamutoda
danakugala bhangi nicchunatandu bunya
purushulani cheppirāryulu kuruvarenya

Kuruvarenya! = Oh! King Drutarastra! Chelliyundiyu = Inspite of having the capacity to retaliate; Sirana seyu natadu = one who bears the provocation with forbearance; Peda vadiyunu = although he is now poor; Arthiki = one who begs for assistance; Priyamu toda = with affection; Tanaku galabhangin = to the extent he can afford; purushulani = man of merit

A man of merit will not retaliate when provoked, although he has the necessary strength and power; and although he is now poor, he will try to help another to the extent possible, when the latter begs him for assistance.

118. Pādi dappa kunda badayu sommulaku na
patramulaku neegi patramulaku
betta kuniki yanaga nettana rendu vi

dhamula geedu dodāru dharani nādha

Dharani radha! = oh! King; Padidappakunda = without violating any DHARMA; sommulakun = for the wealth acquired; Apatramulakun = undeserving; Eegi = by giving; Patramulakun = deserving; Petta Kuniki = By not giving; Nettanan = total; Keedu = destruction; Todaru = is sure to occur.

The wealth although acquired by not violating any DHARMA will be totally destroyed if

(1) it is spent on the undeserving, and if
(2) It is not spent on the deserving subjects.

119. Veladi joodambu pānambu veta paluku
pralladambunu dandambu barusadanamu
sommu nish prayojanamuga vammuseta
Yanedu sapta vyasanamula janadu tagula

Veladi = Debauchery; Joodambu = gambling; Panambu = addiction to alcoholic drinks; Veta = practice of hunting; Paluku pāralladambunu = foul speech (or abusive speech); Dandambu parusadanamu = Undue punishment (or punishment meted out of proportion to the offence committed); Sommu nishprayōjanamuga; Vammuseta = Spending money recklessly on useless things; Saptavyasanamulu = seven vices; Tagula = to get into the habit of; Chanadu = is forbidden

The seven evil habits (SAPTAVYASANAS) are forbidden for all. They are (1) Debauchery (2) Gambling (3) Addiction to alcoholic drinks (4) Foul speech (5) Undue punishment (6) Practice of hunting and (7) spending money recklessly on useless things.

(Ref Poem No. : 112)

120. Tagina veshambu danudana pogadu konami
Nocchiyunu geedu valukami ecchi vagava
Kuniki danakenta nadavakayunna badhamu
dappa kunduta nadavadi koppuseyu

Tagina Veshambu = Decent and suitable dress; Tanu tana pogadu konami = Avoiding self praise; Nocchiyunu = Inspite of being offended; Keedupalukami = not abusing others; ecchi = after giving a gift (or making gift); Vagava kuniki = not regretting; Tanaku enta nadavaka yunnanu = even when he is poverty stricken (or even when he is in straitened circumstances); Pathamu tappa kunduta = not forsaking the path of DHARMA; Nadavadiki = to his conduct; oppuseyun = enhance his name and fame.

The name and fame of a man are enhanced by the following:

1. Decent and suitable dress 2. Avoiding self-praise 3. Not abusing others although

he has been offended by them 4. Not regretting after making a gift and 5. Not forsaking the path of DHARMA, even when he is in straitened circumstances.

121. Chelimiyu sambhashanamunu
balimi vivādambu dropu bādiyu damayan
tala varitona tagu nadhi
kula heenula todanina goragā dadhipa!

Adhipa! = Oh! King; chelimiyu = friendship; Sam bhasha namu = Conversation; Balimi Vivadamu = physical confrontation; Tropu = Insult (an affront); Pādiyu = Transaction; Koragadu = is futile (bound to fail)

(1) Friendship, (2) Conversation, (3) Physical confrontation (4) An affront and (5) Transactions, are bound to be fruitful, if they are conducted with those who are on the same social level; whereas if they are conducted with those who are in a higher or lower social level, such social intercourse or transactions are bound to fail.

122. Konchminanu dagabanchi kudupumelu
Panulayeda dukha morchi yalpambu sukhemu
nanubhavinchuta hitamu satru nakunina
nicchutaya lessa yadigina yeda nrupala

Nrupala! = Oh! King; Kudupumelu = to share and eat; Ecchutayu lessa = to give is the best

1. It is better to share the food although it is little in quantity and eat it, with others
2. While working hard at a task, it is better to put up with many inconveniences, and attain (experience) even a little joy in the end
3. It is better to give something even to an enemy if the latter begs of you.

123. Tanu lokamu goniyādaga
Vini yubbadu sajjanundu vendiyu gadu ne
lo narinchu geedo hinchuka
yunu dana desa dopaneeka yudupuchu vacchun

Sajjanundu = a man of virtue; Vubbadu = will not be carried away by praises; Vendiyu = after wards; Kadun = great; Keedu = harm; Okinchukayunu = even a little bit of; Tanadesan = on his part; Topaneeyaka = to happen; Vudupuchuvacchu = takes care to prevent any harm

A man of virtue will not be carried away by the praises of people. He always strives for the welfare of all. He takes great care to see that no harm is caused by him to others.

124. Mālakari pusphamulu goyu madki deti
puvvudeniya goni yedu polki neduru

ganda kundaga gonunadi kārya phalamu
boggulakupole modalanta boduva janadu

Mālakari = A garland maker; Koyu madki = the way he plucks the flowers; Teti = A bee; Pavvu deniyan = Honey in the flowers; Koniyedu polkin = the way the bees extract honey; Eduru kanda kundaga = without causing any resentment to others; Konunadi = one should achieve his purpose; Boggulaku pole = just as one pokes at coals; Modalanta poduva janadu = poking crudely is to be avoided.

A garland maker very gently plucks the flowers he needs to make a garland; and a bee very gently sucks the honey from various flowers, without causing the least damage to them. Similarly one should deal with others, with tact and should not give any scope for resentment. Crude tactics (STRATEGY) which are similar to "poking of coals" are bound to be futile.

125. Parula dhanamunaku vidyā
parinatikim dejamunaku balamunaku manam
beriyaga nasa hyapadu na
nnarudu devulu leni vedanambadu nadhipa

Adhipa! = Oh! King; Vidyaparinatikia = learning; Tejamu = Valour; Balamu = Prowess (courage); Asahyapadu = Jealous (Envious); Eriyagan = Intolerant; Annarudu = such a man : Tevulu; Leni Vedanan = will suffer from untold misery although he has no disease

One who is jealous of another's wealth, learning valour and prowess will suffer from untold misery and grief, although he has no disease.

126. Adiriki hitamunu briyamunu
madi kimpunugaga baluku mātalu pekki
yodavinanu lessa yatu gā
Kidi yadiyana koora kanuki yentayu noppun.

Hintamu = welfare; Priyamu = pleasant; Impunugaga = words which are pleasant to hear; Pekki yoda Vinanu = although such words are many; Lessa = it is fine; Atugāka = if one can not speak in the manner described above; Edi yadi yanaka = to be non committal; Oorakuniki = to be silent; Entayu noppun = it is the best policy.

One speech should always be pleasant and contribute to the welfare of the other person. If one is unable to talk in such a proper manner, it is better to be non committal and to be silent.

127. Chelimiyu bagayunu deliviyu
galakayu dharmambu bāpagatiyunu bempun
duluvatanambunu vacchunu
baluka badina kāna posaga balukaga valayun

Chelimiyun = friendship; Pagayunu = Enmity; Teliviyunu = Knowledge; Kalakayunu = difficulties; Dharmambu = Dharma; Papagatiyu = SIN; Pempun = greatness; Tuluva tonambunu = Evil; Palukubadina = The way or manner of talking; Posagen- proper manner

One should cultivate the proper manner of speech, as the manner of ones own speech is the main cause of the following; 1. Friendship 2. Enmity 3. Knowledge 4. Difficulties (or afflictions) 5. Merit 6. SIN 7. EVIL and 8 Greatness.

128. Bedidamuga kaati goddata
Boduvadegina mrana jiguru vodamu balukulam
jeda dunisina karyambu ne
guda neradu pidapa nettu guru vamsanedhee

Kuru vamsanedhee = Oh! King Drutarastra! Kattin = By a sword; Goddatan = By an axe; Bedidamuga = cruelly; Poduvan = when cut; Mranan = a tree; Chiguru vodamun = will sprout; again; Palukulan = By words; Chedadunisina = A task which has failed; Ettun = by any means; Nigudaneradu = will never be set right.

A tree which was ruthlessly cut down by a sword or an axe, will sprout again in the course of time;

However a task ruined by inappropriate words, can never be set right.

129. Tanuvuna virigina yalugula
nanuvuna bucchanga vacchu nati nishturatan
manamuna nātina mātalu
Vinu menni yupayamulanu vedalune yadhipa

Adhipa! = Oh! King; Tanuvunan = in the human body; Virigina = embedded; Alugulan = arrows; Anuvunan = skillfully; Pucchanga vacchun = can be extracted; Atinishturatan = Very cruel; Vedalune = will not be forgotten

Arrows embedded in the human body can be extracted by a skilled man, where as cruel words which have hurt another's mind are never forgotten or forgiven.

130. Chetukalamina jetta mātalu neri
gāni teravuvattu karjamulunu
dagavulatla tochu degiyedunavi yavi
neetulani manambu nischayinchu

Chetukalaminan = when man is living in an evil period; Chettamātalu = futile words; Nerigāni = lead to unsuitable; Teravuvattu = ways; Karjamulunu = suitable tasks; Tagavulatla tochu = Appear to be leading to quarrels and confrontations; Tagiyedunavi = even proper deeds; avineetulani manambu nichayinchu = His mind will decided (or mistake) even proper deeds to be corrupt.

When a man is over taken by an evil destiny, he

1. Utters futile words,

2. Prefers to proceed along improper ways,
3. Mistakes even proper deeds for futile deeds, which are sure to land him in quarrels and confrontations,
4. and he mistakes even proper deeds for corrupt deeds.

131. Sakala punya karmachayamunu noka desa
Vinumu pādidappa kuniki yokka
dikku deeni srutulu telipedu neda badi
Kalimi yendu beddagā nutinche

Vinumu = Please listen; Samasta punya karma Chayamunu = sum total of all meritorious deeds; Okadesan = on one side; Pādidappakuniki = not forsaking DHARMA; SRUTULU = VEDAS; Pādi kalimini = greatness of DHARMA; Endun = in every context; nutinche = Extolled (or praised)

While comparing the relative merits of (A) all meritorious deeds and (B) not forsaking DHARMA, VEDAS have proclaimed and praised in every context the greatness of DHARMA.

132. Pādigaligina nihaluka phalamulella
Jerutoya kādu keertiyu chendu purushu
dharani bogadita yendāka baragunanta
Kālamunu bunya lokambu galgu nandru

Pādikaliginan = if a man pursues DHARMA; Pogadita = he will be praised; Endāka baragunanta = as long as; Antakalamunu = up to that period; Punyalokambulu = he will stay in higher worlds

If a man pursues DHARMA, he is sure to attain name, fame and happiness in this world. As long as his name and fame are remembered on the earth, such a one is sure to stay in the higher worlds also for an equivalent period.

133. Papambulu karjamulani
yepuna jeyanga naviyu nimpagu dharma
vyaparambu lakaryamu
li parinati bondeneni yattula chellun

Papambulu = Evil deeds; Karjamulani = thinking that they are proper deeds; Apunan = with all the enthusiasm; Dharmavyaparambulu = Deeds of merit; Akaryamuli = they appear to be improper deeds; Parinati bondeneni = if one decides in his mind; Attulan = in that manner; chellun = appear to him

If a man prefers to do evil deeds with enthusiasm, in the course of time, he will prefer to do only evil deeds at all times;

And if a man decides not to do deeds of merit, in the course of time, he will prefer not to do them at all.

134. Karanamu lekayunu nupa
Kāra paratvamuna norula karyambulakun
Vārani yalajadi badi yedu
Vārala choo yedu gadayu vāri ki nadhipa

Adhipa! = Oh! King; Vupakara paratvamunanu = with the sole aim of helping others only; Vorula Karyam bulakun = to help others; Varani = unlimited; Alajadi = Anxiety; Edugadayu = Such a one's life; Varala choo = is Exemplary (= worthy to be followed)

There are some rare men, who always try to help others in their afflictions, and suffer great anxiety to further the welfare of them;

The lives of such rare men are exemplary indeed.

135. Braduku chetu pogadu vaduta dooronduta
eegi vedukonuta etlu mariyu
galugu soukhya dukhamulu vacchu nedapadi
Vānikinta yela vagava nadhipa

Adhipa = Oh! King; Bradukuchetu = danger to one's life; Pogadu vaduta = being praised; Dooronduta = being criticised; Eegivedu konuta = to beseech (ask earnestly) for a gift: Edapadii = one after; another, Vagavan = grieve.

During the course of a human life, events and experiences such as

1. Joys and sorrows 2. Dangers to life 3. Praises 4. Criticisms and 5. Requests for gifts, follow one another, and to grieve unduly over them is futile.

136. Vaga balamu darugu rooparu
vagachina matidappu devulu vacchun dooran
vagachi nalangina briyamagu
bagaturakunu vagachutudugu pārdhivamukhya

Pardhiva mukhya = Oh! King; Vagan = because of grief; Balamu tarugun = one's energy is depleted; Roopu = Personality; Arun = is affected; Mati dappun = stability of mind is lost; tevulu vacchun = one will be prone to diseases; Dooran = when scandalized (when discredited); Nalangina = when one is emaciated; Pagaturakun = to one's enemies priyamagu = will be pleased; Vudugu = give up.

One should not give way to grief as it is the cause of many untoward (unfortunate) changes in ones constitution such as:

1. Depletion of energy 2. Affected personality 3. Loss of mental stability 4. Pronness to diseases and finally 5. One who is sick and emaciated because of grief, will be the object to rejoice and ridicule, to his enemies.

137. Niyata tapamunu nindriya nigrahambu
Bhoori vidyayu santiki garanamulu

Vāni yannitikante melina sānti
Karanamu lobhamuduguta, kouravendra

Kouravendra = Oh! King Drutarastra; Niyata tapamunu = Penance; Bhoorividyayu = Vast learning; Sāntiki = to lead a happy and peaceful life; Lobhamuduguta = By giving up greed

(1) Penance (TAPAS), (2) Control of senses and (3) Vast learning contribute to a happy and peaceful life. Above all to root out greed from ones heart, is the best way to achieve a happy and peaceful life.

138. Divamba nerchu gākitu
Vovaga ne nertu nera bommani paluken
gā vasame naruna kekkudu
Divamu pourushamu kante dharaneenadha

Dharaneenadha! = Oh! King; Etu vovagan = to behave in this manner; Divamba = for GOD only; Nerchugaka = such a thing is possible; Ne nertu = I can do this; Ne neran = I can not do this; Pommani palukanga = to talk as one pleases; Narunaku = for an ordinary man; Vasame = is it possible; Pourushamu kante = human effort; Diva mu = GOD's WILL; Ekkudu = is more powerful.

An ordinary man will never be able to say "I can do this", or "I can not do this". Only a GOD can proclaim in such an emphatic manner. GOD's will over rules all human endeavour.

139. Ekkada nadachunu satyam
bekkada dharmambu varagu nekkada galugum
jakkati niluchun grushnun
dakkada natadunna kadana yagu jaya madhipa

Adhipa! = Oh! King; Paragun = is well established; Chakkati = Justice; Jayamu = Victory

Whereever one finds TRUTH (SATYA), DUTY (DHARMA) and JUSTICE, well established, there one finds SRI KRISHNA.

Victory always chooses the side supported by SRIKRISHNA.

140. yellayandunu dāvasi yinchu tella
yadiyu danayandu vasiyinchutandru Vāsi
danu peri kardhambu dellaminta
yerugu janulandu daga vasiyinchu subhamu

Ellayandu = in all things; Vasudevudanu perikin = The meaning of the word Vasudeva; Ellayadiyu = all things; Tellamu = it is very clear; yinta yerugu janulandu = Those who understand the meaning of the word "Vasudeva"; Subhamu = prosperity

The meaning of the word "VASUDEVA" is that VASUDEVA is imminent (close at hand) in all, and all are imminent in VASUDEVA.

Those who understand the subtle (fine) meaning of the word "VASUDEVA", are bound to prosper.

141. Kalahamaguta lakshmi garinchu branahā
niyunu jeyu ninta nikkuvambu
paluvu rokani kodiparuta ballidu
lanada cheta jedutayunu ghatinchu

Kalahamaguta = In the event of a war; Laxmi garnchun = Wealth is lost; Pranahaniyunu cheyu = many loose their lives; Balidulu = powerful men; Anadachetan = in the hands of a weaker opponent; Chedutayu = will be defeated and destroyed; Ghatinchu = is sure to happen

War is the main cause of manifold (several) havoc (or destruction). It results in 1. Loss of wealth 2. Loss of many lives 3. Many will face defeat in the hands of one man and 4. even powerful men will be destroyed by a weaker opponent.

142. Pagaya kaligeneni pamunna yintilo
nunnayatlakaka yoorudilli
yundunetlu chitta moka mātu gāvuna
Valava dadhika deergha vira vrutti

Pagaya = Enmity; valavadu = forbidden; Deerghavira Vrutti = Long standing enmity; Chittamu = mind; Yooradilli = how can it be at rest or peace;

One will never be able to live peacefully in a house infested by a snake;

Similarly one will never be able to live with peace of mind, if he harbours enmity in his heart towards someone. Hence it is forbidden to harbour, especially long standing enmity towards anyone.

143. Pagavāri yinta gudichina
nagu dama kanumāna mamrutaminaṇu dārun
bagaturaku guduva bettaga
daga dodalula kippu devvidham vatilunā

Pagavari yintan = In the house of an enemy; Kudichinan = if one eats; Odalulaku = To the human body; Kuduve bettagan = To feed an enemy; Tagadu = is forbidden (not permitted)

If one eats a meal which excels (surpasses) even AMRUTAM (NECTAR OF DEVATAS) in taste, yet the fear that it may contain a poison, lurks (lie concealed) in one's mind;

Not only this, the general condition of any body at any time is unpredictable and one may be overtaken by an unexpected illness.

Hence it is forbidden to feed an enemy in one's own house, to avoid unnecessary suspicions and risks.

144. Dorakoni punyamu bapamu
narudardhin jeyu chunda naduma nokata na
vvera vedali tāp pinanu da
tparinati phala mondu nandru dharma vidhignul

Dorakoni = with all the earnestness; Punyamun = deeds of merit; Papamun = sinful deeds; Arthin = with a desire; naduman = in the middle of; Okatan = at one place; Avveravu = in that method; Dharma vidhignul = Those who are well versed in DHARMA; Tat periniti phalamondu nandru = They are sure to reap the consequences of their deeds.

Those who are well versed in DHARMA are of the opinion, that those who do deeds of merit or sin, are sure to reap the consequences of their deeds, although they may not be able to complete their deeds, due to some reason or the other.

145. Chuttamulalona noppami puttinappu
dāddapadi vāritoda gotladiyina
dāni yudupanga jora kunnavani groora
Karmudam cheppuduru karma Kandavidulu

Chuttamulalonam = Among kinsfolk (Relations); Oppami = misunderstanding; Udupangan = to resolve it; Chora kunnan = who fails to take any initiative; Kroora Karmudu = a cruel fellow; Karmakandavidulu = Those who are well-versed in KARMA KANDA (RITES OF KARMA)

Those who are well-versed in KARMAKANDA are of the opinion that one who fails to take the initiative to resolve any misunderstanding that arises among kinsfolk is sure to be branded as a cruel man

146. Balavantula balamulu na
ggalamagu bala medura galugagā geedpadu ne
Koladula vāriki garvamu
niluchune nayamarga vrutti nilichina bhangin

Aggalamagu = limitless (or more powerful); Keedpadunu = will be defeated; Akoladulavari kin = even for men of extra ordinary abilities; Naya margavrutti = conduct as dictated by morality and justice; Garvamu niluchune = can egoism stand up to.

A powerful man is sure to be defeated, when he confronts a more powerful enemy;

Even those who are full of egoism (AHANKARA) and bestowed with extraordinary abilities, are sure to be subdued in the long run, by men committed to morality and justice.

147. Garviyi karyamitti dakaryamitti
dani yerungaka lokambu chanupadhamuna
diruga kunmadavrutti vartinchunatti
vāni gurunina dandimpavalayu nandru

Garviyi = one who is full of pride; Vunmada vruttin = with boundless egoism

One who has lost his discriminatory powers and who has forsaken the proper ways of the people, because of boundless egoism, deserves to be punished, even if he happens to be a GURU.

148. Karuninpumu samstrita bhaya
harana dhureena sahimpu magnanbun
Saranambu vededa bhava
ccharanambulu ganugono brasādim pagade

Samsrita = refugee; Bhayaharana = one who allays fears and anxieties; Dhureena = one who is capable of; Saranambu vededa = I seek refuge under you; Bhavacchara nambulu = your holy feet; Kanugonan prasādim pagade = to see and worship your holy feet.

LORD! You are renowned to allay the fears and anxieties of all, who seek refuge in you. Please bear with my ignorance and have mercy on me.

Please grant me the privilege of worshipping your holy feet.

Source

1. Bharata Sooktulu from Kavitria Bharatamu by Bulusu Venkata Satyanarayana Murthy, 1983.

26

YOGI VEMANA AND HIS MESSAGE

Yogi Vemana was a mystic, poet and saint of the 17th century. Yogi Vemana lived in the neighbourhood of Gandikota, Cuddapah District of the present day Andhra Pradesh, India.

Government of India issued a commemorative postal stamp, in the year 1972, to mark the tricentinary celebrations of yogi Vemana.

Charles Philip Brown : C.P. Brown (1824) while he has working as a sub-judge at cuddapah in the year *1824*, was the *first* to discover the poems of yogi Vemana and bring them to light. The present day readers especially Telugu speaking people of India are all indebted to C.P. Brown, a literary savant and a pioneer.

C.P. Brown collected about *2,100 verses* of yogi Vemana, from different parts of the present day Andhra Pradesh such as Bellary, Cuddapah, Madras, Visakhapatnam etc. In the year 1829, C.P. Brown selected and published some *693 poems* of yogi Vemana.

C.P. Brown was born at Calcutta in the year *1798. David Brown* (A missionary) and *Kale* were his parents. David Brown died when C.P. Brown, was only a boy of 14 years. He left for England, along with his mother and brothers. C.P. Brown was already acquainted with Hebrew, Arabic, and Hindustani. C.P. Brown continued his studies at Hailbury College, London, and he was awarded a Gold Medal for his proficiency in *Sanskrit.*

C.P. Brown was recruited in the year 1871, by East India Company. He reported for work at Saint-George Fort Madras, India. As per the regulations of The East India Company, in those days, every recruit was expected to learn two Indian languages. C.P. Brown chose to learn *Telugu* and *Marathi* languages. *Sri Velagapoodi Kodanda Ramapandita was C.P. Brown's first teacher in Telugu Language.*

Sir Thomas Munroe (1817) was the Governor of Madras, in those days. His knowledge of Indian languages and his spirit of enquiry and his quest for good will with Indians, inspired C.P. Brown throughout his career.

C.P. Brown worked as the Court Register, at Cuddapah from the year 1826--1829. His monthly salary was Rupees 500 per month. He spent his own hard earned money in the collection of various Sanskrit and Telugu manuscripts, rewriting them and bringing them to light. He appointed and paid from his own pocket. Writers and Panditas, to do the above mentioned literary work. The writers were paid at the rate of (1) one rupee for writing down 200 poems (or 800 lines) (2) Rupees 5/- for writing down 1000 poems and (3) Rs 6/- for writing down 1000 Sanskrit Slokas.

C.P. Brown collected about 36 *Puranas and Itihasas* such as 1. Manu Charitra 2. Vasu Charitra 3. Padma Puranam 4. Bharatam 5. Bhagavatam and 6. 84 Satakas. He spent Rs 2714/- of his own money and got a good copy of ANDHRA MAHABHARATAM prepared. C.P. Brown also translated SUMATI SATAKAMU into English.

In the year 1825, the glory of Telugu literature was at its lowest ebb and was very close to oblivion. Thanks to this British literary savant's untiring efforts spread over a period of 30 years starting from 1825 Telugu Literature, was able to regain its erstwhile pristine glory. Above all, Telugu speaking people of Andhra Pradesh, in India and others, are able to read today the "POEMS OF YOGI VEMANA", because of the selfless, pioneering work done by one of the outstanding British officers of East India Company, namely *C.P. Brown.*

LITERARY WORKS OF C.P. BROWN available to the modern reader are :

1. VERSES OF VEMANA (296 pages) (1829) Rs. 80.00
2. TELUGU ENGLISH DICTIONARY (1424 pages) Rs. 150.00
3. ENGLISH TELUGU DICTIONARY (1416 pages) Rs. 150.00
4. A GRAMMAR OF THE TELUGU LANGUAGE (392 pages) Rs. 95.00

(Available at "ASIAN EDUCATIONAL SERVICES" C-2/15, SAFDARJUNG DEVELOPMENT AREA, NEW DELHI 110016)

YOGI VEMANA (A.D. 1672)—A BIOGRAPHICAL SKETCH

No authentic records of the life of Yogi Vemana are available. Even among scholars and critics, there is controversy about the year of birth of yogi Vemana.

However C.P. Brown surmised that yogi Vemana was born in the year A.D. *1672* in the neighbourhood of Gandikota, Cuddapah district, of the present day Andhra Pradesh, India. Yogi Vemana was born in a powerful family of Reddy community.

EARLY LIFE OF VEMANA

According to a widely believed popular legend, Vemana was brought up in an atmosphere of luxury and comfort. He fell into bad company and took to wine and women. He fell a victim to the charms of a courtesan (a dancing girl). He spent most of his time in the house of the dancing girl. His mother, and sister-in-law were worried about his wayward behaviour, tried to get him married, but their persuasions had no effect on Vemana.

One day the dancing girl demanded a diamond nose ring called '*MUKKARA*' in Telugu. Vemana approached his sister-in-law for help in getting this diamond nose ring. She consented to give her own 'MUKKARA' to Vemana, provided the courtesan presented herself naked in the day light to receive the nose ring from Vemana. Vemana hurried with the 'MUKKARA', to the house of the courtesan, and told her about the precondition laid by his sister-in-law for the costly gift. The dancing girl readily agreed to the precondition, as there was only greed in her heart and the rest of finer sentiments such as decency, decorum had long ago taken leave from her wanton dissipated life. She appeared before him completely naked in the broad daylight and grabbed the 'MUKKARA' from the hands of Vemana.

When Vemana saw her thus with flesh corrupted by a life of dissipation the veil of infatuation dropped from his mind. In the transformation of the sinner to sainthood, this was the first step.

At this juncture Vemana was entrusted with the supervision of the making of jewellery for the royal household. Abhiramaiah and Laxmanna, two expert goldsmiths worked in this jewellery. Vemana noticed that Abhiramaiah every day came late for work. Inspite of repeated warnings, Abhiramaiah continued to come late for work. Vemana became curious to know the reason behind Abhiramaiah's late coming. One morning Vemana reached Abhiramaiah's place before day break and closely watched his movements. Abhiramaiah woke up early that day, bathed in a nearby lake, collected various flowers and fruits. Abhiramaiah then proceeded to a mountain cave not far away. In that cave a saint called *LAMBIKA SIVA YOGI*, had been living and doing TAPAS (spiritual austeretics) since many years. Abhiramaiah prostrated before the saint and offered him the flowers and fruits, which he had brought along with him.

The saint came out of the SAMADHI (Meditation) and saw Abhiramaiah and said "I am satisfied with your devotion and service to me of several years. Tomorrow is the last day for my earthly existense. Come early and receive the 'UPADESHA' (Initiation into the spiritual life). Abhiramaiah took leave of the saint and hurried back to his house and then to the jewellery workshop and set about his work for the day.

Vemana who had secretly followed Abhiramaiah to the cave, overheard their conversation with great interest and hastened home. Vemana thought very deeply about the saint and whole episode involving Abhiramaiah, and decided to receive the 'UPADESHA' himself, instead of Abhiramaiah. Vemana decided to detain Abhiramaiah on some pretext or the other. Vemana ordered Abhiramaiah to come to the jewellery workshop at day break next day and start working on some gold ornaments, that the queen urgently wanted. Abhiramaiah was thoroughly depressed by this order of Vemana, yet he dared not to disobey it.

Vemana woke up at day break and meticulously followed the daily routine of Abhiramiah, went to the cave of the saint and offered the various flowers and fruits to the saint, who was in the state of 'SAMADHI', and prostrated himself before the saint, when the saint awoke from the 'SAMADHI', he was surprised to see a stranger instead of Abhiramaiah.

Vemana explained "O! Venerable saint! Abhiramaiah had been detained in the fort, on some urgent work, and he bade me to go to your cave and serve you with all the reverence and devotion". The saint waited for sometime and asked Vemana to see if Abhiramaiah was coming. Vemana looked out and replied in the negative. The saint repeated the above query thrice and he received the same answer thrice from Vemana.

At last Lambika Siva yogi said "As I am to leave this human body today I wanted to give 'UPADESHA', to Abhiramaiah, who had served me with all the devotion all these years.

Instead of him, you have come. The ways of Almighty are inscrutable". So saying, the saint drew Vemana close to him, and whispered the HOLY MANTRA (UPADESHA) into his ear and disappeared into the cave and was never seen again.

Vemana returned to the fort and called Abhiramaiah and told him everything that happened in the cave, and requested Abhiramaiah to pardon him, as he had deprived him of the Upadesha of the Saint. Vemana said "Abhiramaiah it is by your grace, that I was able to receive the Upadesha from Lambika Siva yogi and now I am a JEEVAN MUKTA (A liberated Soul)". Noble Abhiramaiah forgave Vemana and blessed him.

Vemana now lived like a VAIRAGI (an ascetic or a Sanyasi or a Yogi). Yogi Vemana began to give utterance to his ideas in extempore verses. Most of the verses of yogi Vemana were composed in 'ATAVELADI' metre (Chandassu), which consists of four lines, out of which the last and fourth line is a mere refrain "VISVADABHIRAMA VINURAVEMA" Most of the "SATAKA poets" in the past also followed the tradition of a refrain in their poems. The word 'VEMA' is in the form of an address to his own 'SELF', and the word 'ABHIRAMA' probably suggests his eternal gratitude, he felt for the man, who was instrumental in he becoming a "JEEVAN MUKTA".

There is no authentic account of the several stages of Vemana's spiritual growth however it is evident from his poems that he was familiar with ALCHEMY, RAJAYOGA and HATAYOGA etc. Yogi Vemana became a wandering mendicant, roaming from place to place preaching his gospel in verse, composed in simple, easy to recite, read and write ATAVELADI POEMS. Yogi Vemana toured the entire Southern India, and scattered his priceless poems, whereever he went. People began to call him a 'YOGI', who possessed miraculous psychic powers and a 'BHAKTA' (A devotee of SIVA) of a high order.

Finally yogi Vemana settled in the neighbourhood of 'PAMOORU' *Mountains* in cuddapah district of the present day Andhra Pradesh, India. In the last phase of his saintly career, probably yogi Vemana discarded all his clothes. This was symbolic of his attaining the highest peak of renunciation, for he had now discarded all that of this earth. Most of the portraits of yogi Vemana available to us depict him as a 'DIGAMBARA'.

One day when he was aged 68 years, yogi Vemana took leave of his disciples and entered into one of the caves of Pamooru Mountains, and he was never seen again. Every year on the Sree Ramanavami Day, yogi Vemana's Anniversary is celebrated with great devotion, and thousands of devotees from the nearby villages attend this annual festival and pay homage to yogi Vemana.

POEMS OF YOGI VEMANA

Till today about *2,500* poems attributed to yogi Vemana, are available to the modern reader in different editions. "Verses of Vemana" published by C.P. Brown in the year 1829 contained 1215 poems. A majority of scholar and critics are of the opinion that poems written in 'ATAVELADI' Metre were composed by yogi Vemana and the rest of the poems were later additions.

Yogi Vemana popularised ADVAITIC school of Vedanta, through brevity of expression and a graceful style. Yogi Vemana was a critic of the corroding caste system, blind beliefs, idol worship, meaningless religious rites, pilgrimages and cruelty towards dumb creatures. He advocated AHIMSA (Non violence) and laid great stress on the purification of the mind than on formal Idol worship. Spiritual life according to yogi Vemana should culminate in the realization of ESWARA (SIVA) within ones own self.

Yogi Vemana as a mystic, yogi, and as a people's poet stands like a colossus through the centuries and he has few parallels in greatness, except perhaps *Tiruvalluvar*, the Tamil poet, saint, (*3rd century B.C.*) *BASAVESWARA*, KANNADA Poet, saint (*12th centruy*) and *SARVAJNA*, Kannada poet saint (*16th century)* Yogi Vemana's fame as a peoples poet will last as long as 'TELUGU' is spoken and written in India and elsewhere.

POEMS OF YOGI VEMANA

Poems of Yogi Vemana were traditionally classified into *16* Sections. Here also, the same order was followed. In each section, poems which impressed me most either because of their poetical brilliance or philosophical content or both, were selected and written down in Roman Script and their English translation given below each poem. Out of 2495 poems of yogi Vemana available to the modern reader, 316 poems were selected and their English translation is given below.

1. THE WAY OF THE MOORKHA *(THE WAY OF THE FOOL)*

1. Adavi yadavi tirigi yasanu vidaleka
Gasi padedu vādu ghanudu kādu
Rosi rosi madini roodhiga nilpina
Vade para muganna Vādu vema
(Gāsi = Exhaustion)
One who roams about forest and gets exhausted, without first destroying all the desires from his mind, will never be able to realize his SELF.
2. Alimatalu vini yannadammula rosi
Veru paduchunundu verrijanudu
Kukkatoka batti godavariedunu
Visvadabhirama vinura vema
A man, who by listening to his wife's advice and stops all his association with his own brothers is sure to suffer grief in the end; just as a man who tries to swim across the Godavari River, by catching hold of the tail of a dog, is sure to be drowned.
3. Enti yali vidichi ela jāra kāntala
Venta dirugu vādu verrivādu
Pantachenu vidichi parigayeri nayatlu
Visvadabhirama vinura vema
(Pariga = Gleanings of corn)
One who gathers a few gleanings of corn scattered around a cornfield, leaving alone

all the grain in the cornfield is a fool; similarly a man who runs after an adulteress, leaving alone his wife is a greater fool.

4. Ennija tulandu nejati mukhyaman
Eruka galguvare hetcchuvaru
Eruka lenivara lejatinunnanu
Heena jatiyanchu nerugu vema

(ERUKA = Knowledge)

Those who possess knowledge, though not well born, should be respected, than the well born if the latter do not possess knowledge.

5. Vuttatitti deeni yupayogamulu levu
Titti koraku chedunu devuladi
Kattimeedisāmu kadaterabodaya
Visvadabhirama vinura vema

(Sahu = Gymnastics; TITTI = bellows; DEVULADU = To be in search of)

Human body is similar to a pair of bellows, and once life departs from it has no more value or use for any one.

A man who pursues an evil path for his living is sure to perish sooner or later, just as one who tries to per form gymnastics on the edge of a sword is sure to get killed sooner or later.

6. Rushu lerunga natti vishayambu bhuviledu
Varu cheppinanta varusa nagunu
Teliya kanedu vāru debelu vinumaya
Visvadabhirama vinura vema

(DEBELU = A poor wretch)

Saints know about everything that is in this world. Every event happens as they predict; poor wretches, who deride the saints are to be pitied.

7. Edde delpa vacchu nedādikinanu
Mouni delpavacchu masamunane
Moppe delparādu muppadendlakunina
Visvadabhirama vinura vema

(EDDE = an ignorant man; MOPPE = An obstinate man; MOUNI = Ascetic)

An ignorant fool can be taught and trained in one year
An ascetic can be taught in one month;
But it is impossible to teach an obstinate fool even in thirty years.

8. Entachaduvu chadivi yenniti vinnanu
Heenu davagunambu mānaledu
Boggu palagaduga bovunā nilyambu
Visvadabhirama vinura vema

(AVAGUNAMU = An evil disposition; NILYAMU = darkness of colour)

An inferior fellow will not be able to overcome his evil tendencies, inspite of having the advantages of a good upbringing and good education, just as a lump of charcoal does not loose its black colour even when it is rinsed in milk.

9. Okani jeruchu manchu nulla mandenturu
Tamaku galugu chetu tā merugaka
Tammu jeruchuvādu divambu kadoko
Visvadabhirama vinura vema

A man plans in his mind to do some evil deed to another and as soon as he plans to harm another, alas! he is not aware that a greater harm (or evil) is already in store for him, which the Creator has ordained for the evil doer.

10. Ogu nogu metcchu nonaranga nagnani
Bhava micchi metcchu barama lubdhu
Bandi burada metcchu banneru metcchunā
Visvadabhirama vinura vema

OGU = A wicked man; Agnani = An ignorant person; Lubdhudu = A greedy and avaricious man; PANNEERU = Rose water, perfumed water)

A wicked man prefers to be an associate of another wicked man only,

An ignorant person prefers to be an associate of a greedy and avaricious man only; just as a pig relishes to wallow (role about in mud, sand and water) in mire (thick mud), but not in perfumed water.

11. Kandakavaramuna gānadu maranambu
Madamu cheta datva mahima ganadu
Bhogakanksha cheta buraharu ganadu
Visvadabhirama vinura vema

A stupid person is not aware of the fact that he had to face death sooner or later, because of his pride in his muscular strength. Because of arrogance, he does not appreciate the greatness in the study of the human soul and its relation to its creator.

Because of his carving for sensual pleasures, he fails to realize the creator of the world (SIVA).

12. Kannulandu madamu kappi kānarugani
Nirudu mundatedu ninna monna
Daghdulinavaru tomakante takkuva?
Visvadabhirama vinura vema.

Because of boundless egoism, men are not aware that death is a universal phenomenon. They fail to recognize that many greater men than themselves left this world for ever, yesterday, the day before yesterday, last year and the year before that.

13. Kasavunu dinuvādu ghana phalam bula ruchi
Ganaledu gade vaniyatlu

Chinna Chaduvulakunu minna gnanamuradu
Visvadabhirama vinura vema

(KASAVU) = Grass

One who is accustomed to eat grass, will not be able to relish delicious fruits; similarly one who has acquired a little learning, is not likely to possess profound knowledge and wisdom.

14. Kunda chillipadina gudda dopagavacchu
Paniki veelupadunu bāgugānu
Koolabadina narudu kuduruta yarudayā
Visvadabhirama vinura vema

A leaky earthen pot can be reused after sealing the leak with a piece of cloth, however a man who has given up all effort to improve his lot in life, either due to laziness or despondency, is not likely to stand up again and face the struggle of life with courage and enterprise.

15. Grāsa mintaleka kadugashta paduchunna
Vidya yela niluchu? vedalugāka
Pacchi kunda neellu pattina niluchunā?
Visvadabhirama vinura vema

A man who has to struggle hard throughout the day for his daily food, will never be able to acquire any learning; just as a freshly made earthen pot will not hold any water poured into it.

16. Gooba gruhamujera gunisi pādugabetti
Velli podurenta verrivare?
Gooba gruhamulemi koorchurā karmambu
Visvadabhirama vinura vema

(GOOBA : Owl; GUNISI = To grumble)

Fools desert a house if by chance an owl roosts in it, thinking that the presence of the owl heralds ill luck to the family;

Alas! they are not aware of the fact, that every thing they experience in their lives is on account of their own KARMA, and not because of an owl.

17. Janana maranamulaku sarisvatantrudu kadu
Modata gartakādu tudanukādu
Naduma gartananuta nagubātu kadoko
Visvadabhirama vinura vema

A man is not free to decide about his birth (time, place and parents) or about his death (time, place and mode of death); Is it not ridiculous to assume that he is responsible for all events that happen in the interval between birth and death?

18. Talli yunna yapude tanadu gārābamu
Lame pova dannu naraya revaru

Manchi kala mapude maryada narjimpu
Visvadabhirama vinura vema

A man's welfare will be looked after by his mother as long as she is alive, and when she is no more, there is none left to look after his welfare, with such unselfish love; one should strive to acquire respect and honour in the society, when the time and circumstances are favourable; when the proper time and circumstances have been ignored, wasted or abused, all the efforts at a later and an unfavourable time are bound to be futile.

19. Tumma chettu mundlu todaneputtunu
Vittulonanundi vedalu natlu
Moorkhunakunu buddhi mundugā buttunu
Visvadabhirama vinura vema

(TUMMACHETTU = (BOT) ACACIA ȦRABICA (Babool tree)

Evil tendencies in a wicked man are quite evident even from his early days, just as the thorns are present on a Babool Tree even from its seedling stage.

20. Dānamarasi cheyu dāta daggarajeri
Vakrabhashanamulu paluku moraku
Chandana tarunandu sarpamunnatlayā
Visvadabhirama vinura vema

(MORAKU = An obstinate and foolish man; VAKRAMU = Perverse, wicked, cruel)

An obstinate and foolish man, if he is the companion of a generous man, he is sure to prevent the latter from making gifts, by his perverse suggestions; just as a cobra by coiling around a sandal wood tree, scares away any one who wants to approach the sandal wood tree.

21. Neellu posi kadigi nityamu shodhinchi
Koodu petti meeda gokakatti
yenni patlo paduduree dehamuna kaye
Visvadabhirama vinura vema

A man washes his body with water, inspects it carefully, covers it up with clothes and feeds it every day. He undergoes any number of hardships in its care forgetting the eternal truth, that every human being is ultimately destined for disintegration and death.

22. Paraga dānosagadu parulu cheppinina
Niyya jalaka vidhi nesagu vadu
Pottu tinedi landi buvvanu pettunā
Visvadabhirama vinura vema

(POTTU = The husk of grain; LANDI = A mean fellow)

A wicked person never gives any gifts to the deserving and needy either by himself or even when others suggest it; just as miser who eats bran (husk) daily, will never feed the hungry with boiled rice.

23. Potlakaya raye poduga drātānugatta
Laela toda vanka leka perugu
Kukkatoka gatta gudurunā chakkagā
Visvadabhirama vinura vema

To prevent the curling up of the end of a snake gourd, farmers tie up a small stone to its end; similarly one may tie up the curved tail of a dog with thin wodden splints, to straighten it, yet alas! as soon as the splints are removed, the tail of a dog, assumes its original curved shape. Similarly a stupid fellow will never become wise, inspite of excellent education.

24. Manchivaru leru mahimeeda vedakina
Kashtu lendarina galaru bhuvini
Pasidi ledugani padadenta ledayā
Visvadabhira Vinura Vema

(Kashtulu = Wicked men; PADADU = Ashes or Rubbish)
SAJJANAS are very few in number, whereas DURJANAS are many.
There is plenty of rubbish on the earth, but very little precious gold.

25. Lekkaleni yasa leelami yundagā
Tikka yetti narudu tirugugaka
Kukka vanti manasu koorchunda nicchunā
Visvadabhirama vinura vema

When numerous desires overwhelm the mind of a man, he roams about from place to place in search of their fulfilment, just as a dog roams from place to place in search of food.

26. Vishnu bhaktulella veliboodi palire
Vadamela? matavibhedamela?
Teliya lingadharulu tirumanipalire
Visvadabhirama vinura vema

(TIRUMANI = A kind of white clay used by Vaishnavas in making the mark on the forehead; LINGADHARI = one who follows the SAIVA religion and wears a Sivalingam, suspended by a cord round the neck)

All men are born in the same way. As they grow up, some become devotees of Vishnu and some become devotees of Siva. Alas! they quarrel and fight with each other about their religious faith. At times some of them even change in to opposing sects.

27. Sravanaputa mulunna sārdhakyamemirā
Vinaga valayu bedda lanedivanni

Vinaga vinaga neeke visadamulou summu
Visvadabhirama vinura vema

One should carefully listen to the discourses of wise men, then only one will be able to understand the meaning and importance of their teachings.

2. THE WAY OF THE DHAMBICA THE WAY OF THE HYPOCRITE

1. Alla Bodi talalu tellani gongallu
odala booti poosi yundu repudu
Etti veshamul lila botta kootike sumee
Visvadabhirama vinura vema

(POTTAKOODU = Food given instead of wages or pay)

Hypocrites roam about with clean shaven heads, smear their bodies with ash and wrap themselves in white blankets. All these guises are meant to hoodwink the credulous public and to fill their bellies.

2. Akatiki dolangu nāchara vidhulella
Jeekatiki dolangu chittasuddhi
Vekatiki dolangu venukati bigiyella
Visvada bhirama vinura vema

A hungry man while eating will not pay any attention to traditional rules and regulations about food (ACHARA).

A man as the night approaches, will ignore all moral restraints and seeks the company of a woman.

A pregnant woman looses the attraction of her once youthful figure.

3. Aadudanijooda nordhambu joodaga
Bammakina buttu dimma tegulu
Brahmayali tradu bandi revuna drempa
Visvadabhirama vinure vema

(TRADUTENCHU = To become a widow (since the marriage cord is then snapped)

A beautiful woman and gold are sure to tempt even a god like BRAHMA. Alas! BRAHMA was infatuated with SARASWATHI (who was a daughter to Brahma by relationship).

Let the Mangalasootram of the wife of Brahma be snapped at BANDLAREVU (This is a curse commonly used by villagers in Rayalaseema in Andhra Pradesh, India).

4. Aaru matamulandu nadhi kamina matambu
Linga matamukanna ledu bhuvini
Lingadhar lakanna dongalu lerayā
Visvadabhirama vinura vema

(Aaru matamulu = 1. SAIVA 2. VAISHNAVA 3. SAKTEYA 4. KAPALIKA 5. JAINA and 6. CHARVAKA—these six religious sects were popular in the days of yogi Vemana (17th century)

Among the above mentioned religious sects, SAIVA sect is the greatest; Alas! yet there are no greater rogues than its followers (LINGA DHARIS)

5. Oddu podugu galgi gaddam podavina
Dāna gunamu leka dātā yagune
Enumu goppadina nenugu bolunā
Visvadabhirama vinura vema

(ENUMU = A she buffalo; DATA = Donor)

A man becomes renowned as a DATA (A charitable man) only when he makes gifts to the deserving and needy, not simply because he is tall in stature and sports an impressive beard; just as a she buffalo, though big in size, can never be compared to an elephant.

6. Chakkani satiyina sarasuralinanu
Menorulaku gāna neeyakunna
Sandegrunki nanta sayyata ladadā
Visvadabhirama vinura vema.

(Sarasata = good manners; SAYYATA = Play or Dalliance)

A beautiful woman will display good manners and may pretend to be home bound during day time, yet as the night approaches, she will be eagerly on the look out for dalliance with a man.

7. Chaduvu chaduvanela? sanyasi kanela?
Shanmata mula jikki chavanela?
Atanu bhajana chesi yatmalo deliyudee
Visvadabhirama vinura vema.

(ATANUDU = The bodiless, Cupid; SHANMATAMULU = Six Religious Sects

The study of vedas, renouncing the world to become an ascetic, and to follow one of the six religious sects (SAIVA, Vaishnava, Sakteya, Kapalika, Jaina and Charvaka), are all second only to worshipping the creator and realize him in one's own soul.

8. Tanuvu lasthiramani dhanamu lasthiramani
Telupagaladu tānu teliyaledu
Cheppavacchu banulu cheyuta kastamou
Visvadabhirama vinura vema

A hypocrite glibly tells others that wealth and life are all mere temporary phenomena, yet he himself is not aware of it;

It is easy to talk about a precept, but difficult to understand and practice it.

9. Tolu kadupulona dodda vādundaga
Rāti gulla nela rasidoya
Rayi devudina rasulu mringada?
Visvadabhirama vinura vema
(DODDA = Great; RASI = A heap stack, pile)

A soul is imminent in every human being, Alas! yet men labour under the delusion that God is imminent in stone idols;

If a stone idol is really a God, will it not eat all the offerings, kept before it.

10. Desa desa mulanu tiruganga tiruganga
Atmayandu dhyana mantu konune?
Kaasulakunu diruga galgunā mokshambu
Visvadabhirama vinura vema

Hypocrites go round different places and collect money in the name of God, from devotees;

Their minds are always engaged in money making, and DHYANA (meditation) and MOKSHA elude them.

11. Neebla munuganela? nidhula bettaganela?
Monasi velpulakunu mrokka nela?
Kapata kalmashamulu kadupulonundaga
Visvadabhirama vinura vema
(Monakoni = to begin with; NIDHI = A treasure)

Bathing in holy rivers, offering hoarded money to Gods, and worshipping various Gods, are all futile, if one does not rid his mind of all deceit and evil thoughts.

12. Paraga pratimalakunu prana pratistalo?
Prana mosaga bratima paluka valada
Modativani srusti moorti mantambina
Visvadabhirama vinura vema
(PRATIMA = Idol; MOORTIMANTAMU = having a bodily form)

Idols are installed in temples, and priests perform a ritual called "PRANAPRATISTA" in which invoking life and consecrating it are done.

Alas! if the idols so installed, have life in them, will they not talk? (Hypocrites have no answer for this question for Yogi Vemana)

13. Parula mosapucchi paradhana mārjinchi
Kadupu nimpukānuta kani paddu
Runamu cheyu manujudekkuva kekkunā?
Visvadabhirama vinura vema

One who earns money by deceiving others is sure to loose his honour sooner or later; one who incurs debts, is sure to loose his honour if he does not repay the debts.

14. Matapu veshadharlu mahe meeda padivelu
Moodhajanula galapa moogu chundru
Kongalu gumikoodi korakava bodelu
Visvadabhirama vinura vema

(BODELU = Stems of Corn)

Thousands of hypocrites wearing the garb of religious preachers, deceive credulous people; just as flocks of cranes descend on fields laden with ripe corn and eat to their fill.

15. Mosamunanu danadu modati mukhyata haani
Mosamunanu danadu muruvu tappu
Mosamunanu danadu mokshamu tappurā
Visvadabhirama vinura vema

(MURUVU = Liking)

One who relies on deception is sure to endanger himself in the first place.

One who relies on deception is sure to lose his respectability in the second place

And finally MOKSHA eludes a deceiver.

16. Raati bommakela rangina valuvalu?
Gullu gopuramulunu kumbhamulunu
Koodu gudda tanu gorunā devundu
Visvadabhirama vinura vema

Devotees construct temples and towers for Gods;

They decorate the idols with colourful silk brocades and offer various NIVEDYAMS.

Does a God really want these?

17. Verribattu vani vinayamu ladhikamul
Cheddamunda musugu chelagu chundu
Chedipe koduku migula jeyu nacharambu
Visvadabhirama vinura vema

(Chedipa = an unchaste woman; unctuous = unpleasantly flattering)

A mad fellow displays excessive (unctuous) humility

An unchaste woman displays excessive modesty, by covering her face with a veil, when others watch her; a son born to an unchaste woman displays an excessive interest in rituals and ceremonies.

18. Sakala teerdhamulanu sakala yagnambula
Talalu gorugukunna phalamu kalade
Mantrajalam kante mangali jala mecchu
Visvadabhirama Vinura Vema

(YAGNA = An act of worship)

Devotees get their heads shaved, while performing YAGNAS, and at various places of pilgrimage; perhaps, they assume the water that is sprinkled on their heads by the barber prior to shaving is more holy than "MANTRA JALAM" (water consecrated by magical incantations).

19. Sandhya varvanemi? japamu cheyaganemi?
Veda sastramulanu velayanemi?
Paramu ganani vadu bapadu kādurā
Visvadabhirama vinura vema

(SANDHYA = Morning or evening twilight; VARCHU (Achamanamu) = Sipping water, before religious ceremonies, from the palm of the hand repeating at the same time 15-24 principal names of VISHNU; JAPAMU = Repeating prayers in an undertone; PARAMU = The supreme spirit

A BRAHMANA may perform religious ceremonies and rituals such SANDHYA VARPU, and JAPAMU, and may achieve renown by the study of VEDAS, yet all these are of no avail if he does not realize the supreme spirit (OR PARAMU)

20. Mrucchu gudiki poye mudivippune kani
Posaga swami jooda bodandu
Kukka ellu socchi kundalu vetukada?
Visvadabhirama vinura vema

(Mrucchu = A thief; Mudi = A bundle)

A thief enters a temple not to worship but to steal any thing, he can lay his hands upon; a street dog as soon as it enters a house, it starts to search various pots in the kitchen for eatables.

3. THE WAY OF VIDYA THE WAY OF KNOWLEDGE

1. Atmaloni sommu nanjanamuna joochi
yanti tirugunatti yatadu yogi
Punju goota nundi prodderingeye kooyu
Visvadabhirama vinura vema

(Anjanamu = A magic ointment for the eyes by which the operator is enabled to find hidden things, or which gives him the power of creating illusions; Punju = A COCK; ROOST = Pole where birds rest at night (Hen house)

A yogi realizes the supreme spirit in his own Soul, with the help of knowledge, which helps him just as an "Anjanamu" helps a Tantrik to find hidden things;

A cock crows at the crack of dawn, from its roost unerringly, inspite of the utter darkness of the night all around it.

2. Vuddharimpa galgu nuttamundu kulambu
Madhya mundu dāni māta ganadu
Adhamudina vadadanginchu nokkata
Vishvadabhirama vinura vema

A superior man tries to improve the caste in which he is born;
An ordinary man ignores it and is indifferent to the caste in which he is born;
An inferior man tries to ruin and bring disrepute to the caste in which he is born.

3. Vuppu kappurambu nokka polikanundu
Jooda jooda ruchula jada veru
Purushu landu bunya purushulu veraya
Visvadabhirama vinural vema

Common salt and camphor are alike in appearance but their taste differ;

Similarly men of virtue and ordinary men are alike in appearance, but they differ in character and conduct.

4. Kanaga sommulenno kanakamba dokkati
Pasula vanne lenno palokatiye
Puspha jatulenno pooja yokkate sumee
Visvadabhirama vinura vema

Ornaments are of various designs, but they are all made up of gold;

Cows are of various colours, but the milk they yield is always white in colour;

Flowers are of various colours and shapes, but their purpose is only to be offered in the worship of the creator.

5. Kasturi natu chooda ganti nallaga nundu
Parimalinchu dani parimalamlu
Guruvulina vari gunamuleelagurā
Visvadabhirama vinura vema

(Kasturi = MUSK —A strong smelling reddish-brown substance produced by a gland, in the male musk deer and it is used as an ingredient in perfumes and Aurvedic medicines)

Kasturi is almost black in colour, but it exudes a fine fragrance;

A GURU may not be impressive to look at, but the knowledge he possesses, makes him great.

6. Kunda kumbhamanna konda parvata manna
Nuppu lavanamanna nokati kāde
Bhasha litlu veru; para tatva mokkate
Visva dabhirama vinura vema

(Kunda = POT; KONDA = Mountain; Vuppu = Common salt)

Kunda or Khumbhamu,

Konda or parvatamu, and

Vuppu or Lavanamu are synonyms; similarly there are many languages in the world yet there is only one supreme spirit for all mankind.

7. Chitta suddhi Kaligi chesina punyambu
Konchemina nadiyu goduva kadu
Vittanambu marri vrukshambunaku nenta?
Visvadabhirama vinara vema

(MARRI = Banyan Tree or Indian fig tree (FICUS INDICA)

The seed of a Banyan tree is very tinv in size, but it grows over the years into a mighty banyan tree, similarly a little deed of virtue done with a pure mind is to be regarded as a great one.

8. Jati neeti veru janmam badokkati
Araya dindlu vere younu gāka
Darsanamulu veru divamou nokkati
Visvadabhirama vinura vema

(Jāti = Race; NEETI = Morals; DARSANAMULU = Systems of philosophy)

There are many human races and many moral codes, yet all human beings are born in the same way; There are many food habits in the world, but there is only one mankind;

There are many religions and systems of philosophy, but there is only one CREATOR.

9. Jeeva bheda merigi chediponi varalu
Brahma bhavamondi paragu chundru
Neeru mutyamina neerugā marunā?
Visvadabhirama vinura vema

(Mutyamu = Pearl; oyster = various marine; Bivalve molluses of the genus PINCTADA, bearing pearls)

A water drop when it fall into an open pearl oyster, it turns in to pearl in the course of time; once it changes in to a pearl, the pearl so formed will never change again into a water drop.

Similarly one who has realized the supreme spirit in his own soul, will never again fall into the delusion he (JEEVATMA) is separate from the supreme spirit (PARAMATMA).

10. Taruva daruva buttu daruvunan danalambu
Taruva daruva buttu dadhini venna
Talapa dalpa buttu danuvuna datvambu
Visvadabhirama vinura vema

(ANALAMU = Fire; TARUVU = Tree (a piece of dry fire wood)

By constant friction between two pieces of dry fire wood, sparks of fire are produced; By repeated churning of curds, butter is produced, similarly by repeated meditation, one comes to realize the essential nature of the human soul in its relation with the supreme spirit.

11. Pālalona bulusu leelagā galisina
Virigi tunakalagunu virivegānu
Telivi nella nasa kalaginchi cherachura
Visvadabhirama vinura vema

(From LOKAKAVI VEMANA YOGI - Page No : 26, Poem No: 146 - Kalaprapoorna Marupooru-Kodandarama Reddy 1983)

When a drop of TAMARIND JUICE is added to milk, it cause the whole lot of milk to congeal; similarly when a man's mind is overcome by DESIRE, it (desire) neutralizes all his intelligence thus he becomes an easy prey for deceivers.

12. Bahula Kavyamulanu barikimpagā vacchu
Bahula Sabdhachayamu baluka vacchu
Sahanamokka tabba jala kastamburā
Visvadabhirama vinura vema

(Kāvyamulu = Poetical compositions; SABDHA CHAYAMU = collection of words (GRAMMAR); SAHANAMU = Patience or forbearance)

One may have studied many poetical compositions one may have participated in many discourses dealing with words and grammar, yet to be patient under all conditions is very difficult.

13. Brahmanunaku sakala bhagyambu leevacchu
Goura vimpa vacchu, galiya vacchu
Gnana mosagi janula gada terchinatlina
Visvadabhirama vinura vema

If a BRAHMANA imparts spiritual knowledge to people and shows them the path of liberation (MOKSHA), such a BRAHMANA deserves all the respect and regard from the people.

14. Manasu gupta parachi manyudou vibudhudu
Tarachu paluka Kunta dharma mandru
Tarachu mata cheta datvambu chedipovu
Visvadabhirama vinura vema

(VIBUDHUDU = A wise man OR A JNANI)

A wise man always prefers to be sparing in his speech;
Moderation is speech is a mark of virtue;
A chatter box undermines his own value.

15. Mātatāda vacchu manasu delpagaledu
Telupavacchu dannu teliyaledu
Suriya batta vacchu soorudu kaledu
Visvadabhirama vinura vema
(SURIYA = A Knief) (BRANDISH = Wave with a flourish)
It is easy to converse with another, but difficult to fathom his thoughts;
It is easy to teach another, but difficult to do a task by oneself
It is easy to brandish a sword, but difficult to become a renowned soldier.

16. Modatanu matamun vadalaka
Tuda nevvari matamunina dooshimpaka ta
Padiludayi korke goraka
Mudamuna jari yinchu budhude mukhyudu vema

A wise man never gives up his own religion and he never derides (scorns or langhs at) other religions; He gets rid of all desires from his heart, and is always serene and happy under all conditions.

17. Vadamadadepudu varusa nevvaritoda
Jerarādu tanu chetudedu
Jnani yaguchu budhudu ghaneta bondegajoochu
Visvadabhirama vinura vema

A wise man never wastes his time in futile arguments will others;

He never approaches others to while away time;

He never causes any harm to others;

He tries to get the respect and regard from others, by his own exmplary character and conduct.

18. Vidyalenivadu vidvamsu cheruva
Nundagane panditudā Kādu
Kalani hamsala kada gokkeralunnatlu
Visvadabhirama vinura vema

(KOKKERA = CRANE)

An illiterate fellow, even if he associates with eminent scholars, will never become a renowned scholar;

One sees many cranes and a few swans on the surface of a lake, though the cranes mingle freely with swans, yet a crane is a crane only and a swan is a swan only.

19. Vidyalekayunna vittamu lekunna
Moodhudina dudaku moogayina
Esta bandhuvina gastame kalugunu
Visvadabhirama vinura vema

Ones own close relation (Kinsman) if he happens to be 1. An illiterate or 2. Poor or

3. Stupid or 4. and a dumb fellow is sure to cause troubles and difficulties.

20. Veerudina rāvu vibudhula gunamulu
Chaduvulandu rāvu jatala rāvu
Janma pakamunane saphalamou narunaku
Visvadabhirama vinura vema.

(KARMA PHALAMU = The fruit of good and evil actions performed in former lives)

A man's renown as a soldier, his learning or he having long plaits of hair on his head, are all of no avail, if he has no 'KARMA PHALA', to his credit;

A man becomes a 'JNANI' as a consequence of his 'KARMAPHALA' only.

4. THE WAY OF ARTHA (THE WAY OF WEALTH)

1. Adhamudina manuju dardhavantudina
Atani mata nadachu navanilona
Gaja patinta nunna gavvalu chellavā
Visvadabhirama vinura vema

(GAVVALU = Cowries = Any gastropod mollsc of the family CYPRAEIDAE, having a smooth, glossy and usually bright coloured shell; They are used as money in parts of Africa and South Asia) (Gajapati Kings : In the 15TH century during the reign of Gajapati Kings, COWRIES were used as money)

The words of even a base fellow (mean or inferior), carry weight, if he happens to be rich;

Even a COWRY (SEA SHELL) from the house of Gajapati Kings, commands a certain value of exchange.

2. Kāni vāni cheta kasu veesamulicchi
Venta dirugu tella verritanamu
Pilli batta kodi pilichina palukunā
Visvadabhirama vinura vema

To pester (to persistently request) an Evil fellow asking him to repay money, after lending him money is as futile as any attempt to save a fowl caught by a cat.

3. Appulenivade yadhika sampannudu
Tappulenivāru dharani leru
Goppaleni buddhi konchemi povurā
Visvadabhirama vinura vema

(TAPPU = Fault; GOPPALENI BUDDHI = one who has no forgiving disposition; Konchemipovu = mean or petty)

A man who has no debts, is to be considered as a very rich man;

Every one on this earth has some fault or the other; A man who has no forgiving disposition is to be regarded as a mean one.

4. Araya darachu kallaladedi varinta
Vedala kela lakshmi visraminchu?
Neeramotakunda niluvani chandāna
Visvadabhirama vinura vema.

Wealth disappears from the house of a habitual liar sooner or later; just as water leaks out, when poured into a leaky pot.

5. Arthavantu sommu nasinturardhuli
Arthikeeya sommu vyardhamagunu
Vyardhamina sommu vyardhula jerurā
Visvadabhirama vinura vema.

(VYARDHAMU = Useless; VYARDHULU = useless men)

People beg money from a man of wealth; but money so acquired, is sure to be wasted; superfluous money is sure to fall in the hands of useless men and misspent.

6. Aaduvāriganna nardhambu bodaganna
Sāramina ruchula chavulaganna
Ayyavarikina nasalu galugurā
Visvadabhirama vinura vema

(AYYAVARU = A Brahmana)

Even a learned man (Brahmana) is attracted and tempted at the sight of a beautiful woman, money and delicious food.

7. Apadandu joodu māraya bandhula
Bhayamu vela joodu bantu tanamu
Pedapadda venuka bendlamu matijoodu
Visvadabhirama vinura vema

A true relation (Kinsman) comes forward to help, when one is beset with afflictions;

A loyal soldier stands by his master, when the latter's life is in danger;

A good wife respects her husband, even in his days of poverty.

8. Entiloni dhanamu nidi nādi yanuchunu
Mantilona dachu manku jeevi
Konchu bodu venta gulla kāsunu rādu
Visvadadhirama vinura vema.

(MANKU JEEVI = A stupid fellow)

A man quarrels with his own brothers for his share of property and money and he buries his share of money very carefully in a secret hole in the grounds of his home; Alas! the stupid fellow when he dies will not be able to take even a single coin along with him.

9. Ehamuna sukhiyimpa hemataraka vidya
   Paramuna sukhiyimpa brahma vidya
   Kadama vidya lella kalla moodhulakurā
   Visvadabhirama vinura vema.

   To lead to comfortable life in this world, one should earn money;

   To lead a happy existence in the next world, one should learn BRAHMAVIDYA (about the relationship between the Soul and the Supreme Spirit)

   All the rest of the branches of knowledge are for all the rest of the stupid fellows.

10. EEtakanna lotu nenchanga baniledu
    Chavukanna keedu jagati ledu
    Gochipatakanna konchem bikanu ledu
    Visvadabhirama vinura vema

    For an expert swimmer, the depth of water (in a well, river or sea) is not a matter of concern;

    For an impoverished man, his tatters are the sign of his destitution;

    For any man, his own death is the greatest calamity he has to face on the earth.

11. Runamosangunāta dinudagu doludolta
    Nadiyu marala naduga yamuduga nagu
    Appu chesi teerpa narayani variki
    Visvadabhi rama vinura vema

    A borrower flatters a lender to get a loan from him; And when the latter insists on recovery of the loan, the borrower avoids him as if he is the very personification of YAMA (King of Death)

12. Enta bhoomi tirigi yepatu paduchunna
    Antaneeka prapti venta derugu
    Bhoomi krottadina bhoktalu krottalā
    Visvadabhirama vinura vema

    (PRAPTI = Fortune (Lot, Luck); BHOKTA = An eater, an enjoyer)

    A man moves from country to country and tries his level best to get rid of his poverty; Alas! poverty never leaves him; whereever he goes his own ill-luck pursues him;

    The country may be a new one but the man is the same old one, with the same old ill-luck.

13. Ojamalu maguva oli madala chetu
    Patuleni magadu kooti chetu
    Paniki mālu dasi battembu cheturā
    Visvadabhirama vinura vena

    (OLI = Dowry; OJAMALU = Unruly, Disorderly)

An unruly wife is not worth the dowry given to her at the time of marriage;
A worthless and unemployed husband is not worth the food he eats everyday;

A servant maid who shirks her work is not worth the wages given to her.

14. Kadupuninda davudu gampalo bettina
Channu batta neeka tannu gede
Varakanta lettu valatura yooraka
Visvadalhirama vinura vema

(TAVUDU = Bran; Varakanta = a prostitute)

A she buffaloe never yields any milk, unless it is given plenty of feed such as Bran;
Similarly a public woman never loves anyone unless there is money for her in it.

15. Vunna ghanata batti manninture kani
Pinna peddatanamu lennaboru
Vasudevu vidichi vasudevu nentura
Visvadabhirama vinura vema.

Mere seniority does not bestow eminence (distinction) to any one;

SRIKRISHNA's father VASUDEVA is a non entity, where as SRIKRISHNA is worshipped by all.

16. Kaligina manujudu kāmudi somudi
Migula tejamuna merayu chundu
Vittaheenudina nutta sanyasirā
Visvadabhirama vinura vema

A rich man glitters with the brilliance of God of Love and the moon;

A poor man is despised by all and is regarded as a mere penniless mendicant (SANYASI)

17. Kalimi Kaligi yundi kathina bhavamu chendi
Teliyaleru prajalu telivileka
Kalimi vennelagati ganangaleraya
Visvadabhirama vinura vema

There are some who become arrogant and merciless, when they acquire wealth;

Alas! these stupid fellows are not aware that the acquisition of wealth is as unreliable and as fickle as moonlight (Moonlight appears from nowhere and disappears as fast)

18. Kalimi galuga sakala kulamula kekkuva
Kalimi bhoga bhagyamulaku nelavu
Kalimi lenivāni kulamemi kulamaya
Visvadabhirama vinura vema

A rich man although he is low born is respected by all;
Wealth is the source of all comforts and luxury

A poor man, although he is high born is despised by all.

19. Kalimi joochi eeya gaya micchinayatlu
Samuna keeya nadiyu sarasatanamu
Pedakicchu manuvu penavesinatlundu
Visvadabhirama vinura vema

To give ones daughter in marriage to a rich man is certain to cause many difficulties, because of disparity in social status;

To give her in marriage to a man of equal social status is better, yet

To give her in marriage to a poor man is the best, as the poor man is bound to be more devoted and affectionate towards her.

20. Kāvavalayu dhanamu ganta nellappudu
Kavalenivadu chava valayu
Kapulenidani kapura madugan̄ā?
Visvadabhirama vinura vema

A man should strive (endeavour earnestly) to safeguard his wealth and his wife at all times, and who fails to do so is unfit to live as a man;

A woman who is not protected and guarded by her husband is sure to be ruined.

21. Kulamu kaluguvāru gotrambu kalavaru
Vidya cheta virra veeguvaru
Pasidi kalguvani banisa kodukulu
Visvaabhirama vinura vema

Those who are high born, those who are proud of their noble ancestry and those who are proud of their vast learning, all have to obey the commands of a wealthy man, just as promptly as the son of a slave obeys the commands of his master.

22. Kooli nāli chesi gullamu panichesi
Tecchipetta jalu mecchu chundu
Lemi jikku vibhuni vemāru tittunu
Visvadabhirama vinura vema

As long as a man works hard at some job or the other, and brings home some money, his wife praises and respects him;

Once he becomes poor, his wife begins to scold him and to ignore him.

23. Komati madigoru kshamame yellada
Vidyu dorulakepudu vyadhigoru
Voorivadu dhanikuni jeragā gorunu
Visvadabhirama vinura vema

A merchant (or a Vaisya) always wishes and hopes a famine to overtake the land (So that he can make more profits by selling scarcity items at higher prices);

A physician always wishes and hopes the rise in the incidence of disease, (so that he may get more number of patients to treat and thus make more money)

An ordinary villager always tries to be in the good books of the rich man, to improve his social status.

24. Chaduvulandu badi soukhyamulandunu
Pedavulandu rajya padavu landu
Ashaludiginatti yayyalu Kalaroko
Visvadabhirama vinura vema
(MODAVU = A Milk Cow)

Men who are not interested in (1) Learning (2) Wealth (obtained through cattle and cultivation) (3) Beautiful young women (4) and Power (obtained through the patronage of a King), are very rare indeed.

25. Chamuru galgu divve santoshamuga velgu
Dhanamu galgu vani talapu jelagu
Dhanamu leni vani talapulu teerunā?
Visvadabhirama vinura vema.

A lamp with plenty of oil in it, shed bright light all around it;

The plans of a rich man are readily carried out, whereas the plans of a poor man remain unfulfilled.

26. Tankamaduka Kunna bon kambugārādu
Svarna bhooshanambu; jaga merungu
Bhatudu ventaleka prabhudu sobhinchunā?
Visvadabhirama vinura vema.

(TANKAMU = Soldering) (SOLDER = A fusible alloy used to join less fusible metals or wires)

To makes and finish a gold ornament, soldering (with an alloy of baser metals such as Copper or Borax) is necessary; Even a man of certain importance and social status, is respected by others only when he is accompanied by a servant.

27. Taruni satulu dhanamu dhanyamul sampada
Lenta chuttu konina nanta chetu
Pasirikaya purugu paddati kanaro
Visvadabhirama vinurav vema

(Cocoon = A silky case spun by many insect larvae for protection as pupae; Pasari kaya purugu = A green cater pillar)

More a man is engrossed in earning (making) money, more deeply he is attached to his wife and sons, the more difficult it will be for him, to free himself from these bonds of attachment; just as a green caterpillar weaves a cocoon around itself for its own protection and finally it entombs itself.

28. Tāmu tirugu bhoomi kshamapeeditamina
Porugu desamunaku jaruga valayu
Kolanatendi pova gokkera lundunā
Visvadabhirama vinura vema

(KOKKERA = A Crane)

It is wiser to leave a famine stricken land and move on to a nearby country;

Just as cranes fly way to a distant lake leaving behind a dried up lake.

29. Teepikella deepi teliyanga branambu
Prānavitatikanna basidi teepi
Pasidikanta migula badati matalu teepi
Visvadabhirma vinura vema.

Every man regards his own life to be the most precious thing in this world;

Yet he is swayed by the delusion, that to amass wealth is of more importance than his very existence;

Finally he is swayed by another delusion, that the company of a beautiful young woman is better than mere amassing of wealth.

30. Dasayananga mendu dhanamundute yandru
Koodu nidra leka kundu tayekada
Rāgamundabova bagugā nedpinchu
Visvadabhirama vinura vema.

(DASA = Good Fortune; KUNDU = To grieve, sorrow, to sink under affliction)

The world regards wealth as a mark of good fortune and special status; Alas! to a mass, wealth men forego even their food and sleep and toil day and night;

Undue attachment to the amassing of wealth, punishes a man very severely till his end.

31. Dhanamu lekayunna dhiryambu chikkadu
Dhirya modavadeni dhana modavadu
Dhanamu dhirya marayadagu bhoomi narulaku
Visvadabhirama vinura vema.

A poor man usually will be lacking in courage;
Yet if a man has no courage, he will never acquire wealth;
Hence to succeed in life, both wealth and courage are necessary.

32. Hariyananga vacchu harayananga vacchu
Meluvani joochi mecchavacchu
Kongu kasu vidichi gobbuna neerādu

Visvadabhirama vinura vema

(GOBBUNA = at once, instantly, quickly, swiftly)
One may recite the names of Gods such as HARI or HARA;
One may appreciate the virtues of a SAJJANA
yet, if it is a matter of parting with one's money one should not part with it at once, without judging the pros and cons involved in it.

33. Paragalemicheta bandhuvul pagavaru
Paraga lemicheta paramu tappu
Paraga lemicheta parapatiyunu dappu
Visvadabhirama vinura vema

For a poor man, his own relations (Kinsmen) will change and become his enemies;
A poor man also looses his chance of entering the higher worlds of the hereafter;
None will trust and give credit to a poor man.

34. Dhanamulemi sutulu, tappulu niduduru
Dhanamu lemi patni tākaradu
Dhanamu lemevaniki tālika neeyadu
Visvadabhirama vinura vema

(TĀLIKA = Patience, endurance)
Even his own sons find fault with a poor man;
Even his own wife prefers not to be close to a poor man;
His own poverty robs him off any patience which he may posses.

35. Puttadigalavāni pundu badhayu gooda
Vasudhalona jala varta kekku

Pedavani enta bendlina nerugaru
Visvadabhirama vinura vema

Even a marriage celebrated in the house of a poor man goes unnoticed, where as the news of a boil on the back of a rich man (CARBUNCLE = A severe abscess in the skin) gets wide publicity.

36. Poorvajanma mandu punyambu cheyani
Pāpi ta dhanambu badayaledu
Vitta marachi koya vedakina chandambu
Visvadabhirama vinura vema.

A man acquires wealth only as a result of good deeds performed in a previous birth;
An evil fellow who wants to possess wealth now, is similar to a man who wants to reap a crop without even sowing the seeds.

37. Prapti galguchota phalamicchu divambu
Prapti leni chota phalamu ledu
Prapti leka pasidi paramatmudicchunā?

Visvadabhirama vinura vema.

(PRAPTI = Luck, fortune, destiny)

One acquires wealth here only as a result of ones SUKRUTAM (good deeds performed in previous births) if one has no SUKRUTAM to his credit, there is no wealth now for him. Wealth eludes a man even if Almighty (Paramatma) is ready to bestow it to him, if he has no SUKRUTAM, to his credit.

38. Magani kalimi balimi maguvakunu balambu
Kalimi leni magadu kasukadu
Pani kirāni magani patinchi choodadu
Visvadabhirama vinura vema

(KASU = A pie, money in general)

A rich and powerful husband is the main source of strength to his wife;

A poor man is ignored not only by his wife but also by the world.

5. THE WAY OF A DURJANA THE WAY OF AN EVIL MAN

1. Antarangamandu naparadhamulu chesi
Manchivanivalene manujudundu
Etaru lerugakunna neesvaruderugadā
Visvadabhirama vinura vema

An evil fellow commits many evil deeds in secrecy and he thinks that he has hood = winked all the people around him;

He might have fooled others, but how can he hoodwink the Almighty, who knows all his transgressions.

2. Alpabuddhivāni kadhikaramicchina
Doddavarinella tolagagottu
Chepputinedi kukka cheraku teperugunā?
Visvadabhirama vinura vema

An evil fellow if by chance comes into power, is sure to dismiss all the men of virtue around him;

Alas! a dog always prefers to nibble an old leather shoe than a juicy sugar cane.

3. Alpu depudu balku nādambaramuganu
Sajjanundu palku jallagānu
Kanchu mrogu natlu kanakambu mrogunā?
Visvadabhirama vinura vema

(*KANCHU* = Bronze = *An alloy of copper and Tin;* ETTADI = Brass = An alloy of Copper and Zinc)

An evil fellow always talks in a loud and boisterous manner;

A SAJJANA's (talk) speech is always gentle and pleasant;

A Bronze vessel, when struck gives out a louder note than a golden vessel.

4. Adi karanamula nalpudettu lerungu?
Cheppaledugāni tappu battu
Troya nerchu kukka dontulu pettunā?
Visvadabhirama vinura vema

(DONTI = Column; ADI = Primacy, chief-principal)

An evil fellow is ever ready to find fault with all the deeds of a SAJJANA although he is not aware of the primary motive of the latter;

A dog enters a house, searches the pots and pans for any eatables and breaks them up, but it can never restore them to their prior shape and order.

5. Enumu virigeneni enumaru mummaru
Kachi yatuka nerchu gammareedu
Manasuvi regeneni mariyanta nerchuna?
Visvadabhirama Vinura Vema

(KAMMARA = Blacksmith)

A vessel or an implement made up of iron when broken, can be repaired twice or thrice, in a forge by a smith;

One affection, sympathy and trust are gone from one's heart towards another, these sentiments can never be restored.

6. Entaseva chesi yepatu padinanu
Racha mooka nammarāduranna
Pāmutodi pondu padivelakinanu
Visvadabhirama vinura vema

A king will be kind and considerate towards a servant as long as the latter serves him sincerely and as long as it suits him,

Taking a ruler (King) for granted is akin to assuming that any type of association with a snake is free from all danger.

7. Eddukanna dunna yelāgu takkuva?
Vivaramerigi choodu vrutti yandu
Nerpulenivani nerayodhudandurā?
Visvadabhirama vinura vema

(EDDU = OX; DUNNA = male buffalo)

Farmers commonly use oxen or buffaloes to plough the land; yet they prefer an ox to a buffalo as the former is more adept (skilled) than the latter similarly one who has no skill in the art of war will never acquire the reputation of a renowned soldier.

8. Erukamaluvadi kemevi chadivina
Chadivinantasepe sadguniyagu
Kadisi tamarandu kappa koorchunnatlu
Visvadabhirama vinura vema

(ERUKA = KNOWLEDGE)

Even a stupid fellow displays good conduct as long as he is under the influence of strict instruction, and once it is over, he reverts to his original stupid ways;

Just as a frog sits still on a lotus leaf in a pond for a moment, only to jump into the pond the next moment.

9. Kanda chakkerayunu galiya balposina
Tarimi pāmu tannu dāku gāde?
Kapala munna vāni ganpettavale sumee
Visvadabhirama vinura vema

(KANDA CHAKKERA = Sugar Candy)

A snake bites even the man who feeds it with a mixture of sugar candy and milk; similarly a deceiver will not hesitate to harm even a benefactor.

10. Kaliyugambunandu ghanataku nichyamu
Ghanata nichyamunaku galugu chundu
Shraddha bhaktuludigi janu lundre kavuna
Visvadabhirama vinura vema

(KALIYUGA = KALI AGE)

In Kaliyuga, a superior, quality is regarded as an inferior quality and vice versa, as the people in this era have little or no faith (SHRADDHA) and devotion (BHAKTI)

11. Kallu kunda kenni ghanabhooshanamulidda
Aunduloni kampu chindulidade?
Tulava padavigonna doli guna memagu
Visvadabhirama vinura vema

(KALLU = fermented juice of various palms : TULUVA = a low, wicked and impudent person)

The obnoxious smell that emanates from a pot of TODDY (KALLU), cannot be covered up by decorating the pot with ornaments and garlands;
similarly an evil fellow even if by chance occupies a high post at present, he will not be able to overcome his inherent evil qualities.

12. Kāni vāni toda galasi melangina
Hāni vacchu nenta vānikina
Kaki goodi hamsa kastambu pondadā?

Visvadabhirama vinura vema

Even a man of virtue is sure to be wounded or even killed if he moves in the company of evil men; Just as a swan is sure to be wounded or even killed if it is found in a flock of Crows.

13. Kullu botu nodda goodi mātādina
Goppa marmamulanu chepparādu
Peru teerudelpa noorella muttinchu
Visvadabhirama vinura vema

(KULLU BOTU = a man of envious temperament)

One should not reveal important secrets to a man of envious temperament; if revealed, he is sure to give them wide publicity, out of spite.

14. Kipu meeru vela gadaku jera garādu
Anuvudappi māta ladaradu
Samaya merugana tadā sarasundu kadayā
Visvadabhirama vinura vema

One should keep away from an intoxicated man for ones own safety;

One should be discreet in ones speech at all times;

One should always adopt his conduct to suit the time and place

15. Koti batti tecchi krotta putta mugatti
Konda mrucchulella golichinatlu
Neeti heenunodda nirbhagyulunduru
Visvadabhirama vinura vema

(KONDA MRUCCHU = A large black faced monkey (Baboon); PUTTAMU = Vesture (Ceremonial Robe)

Destitutes gather around a man without any morals or scruples; just as

Baboons in the forest gather around a monkey and serve it.

16. Kondegadu Chava gompa vakitikini
Vacchi podurinte vagapu ledu
Dooda vagachune bhuvi dodelu chacchina
Visvadabhirama vinura vema

(KONDEGADU = A slanderer or a backbiter)

When a wicked slanderer dies, neighbours just peep in and go away; None really grieve when a wicked man dies; just as:

A calf does not grieve, when a wolf dies.

17. Ganga pāruchunda gadalani gatitoda
Murikivagu paru mrota toda

Adhikudorchunattu ladhamudorvagaledu
Visvadabhirama vinura vema

River Ganga flows on with grandeur and silently where as a gutter full of dirty water flows on noisily;

A superior man has forbearance, where as an inferior man is always impatient.

18. Champadalachu raju chana vagga lambicchu
Cherupanunna pagara chelimi cheyu
Garavanunna pamu nerigachukoniyundu
Visvadabhirama vinura vema

(AGGALAMU = Excessive; CHANAVU = Intimacy, familiarity, freedom)

A king who plans to kill an enemy, first feigns (pretends) friendship with him and gives him a lot of leniency as well;
An enemy who wants to harm another, first feigns (pretends) friendship with him; Just as

A snake hides itself in a crevice, before it strikes down its victim.

19. Takkarulanu goodi yekka sakkemulāda
Nikkamina ghanuni neetichedunu
Vullithota berugu malle mokka karani
Visvadabhirama vinura vema

(TAKKARI = A cheat; YEKKA SAKEMU = A joke; joking, mockery)

A man of virtue, if he moves in the company of cheats and makes fun of others, is sure to loose his respectability; Just as

A Jasmine creeper if it grows in a field of onions is sure to be pulled out as a weed.

20. Tanara nrupatitoda daga durjanunitoda
Agnitoda baruni yali toda
Haasya mādutella nagunu prānaantumu
Visvadabhirama vinura vema

It is not safe or wise to jest or play with a king, or an evil fellow, or a fire or with the wife of another man as they are inherently dangerous, and one may even loose ones own life.

21. Tanayu dodave nanuchu dā bongu chundunu
Vādu dusthudina gōdu goorchu
Tuluva vandra goōdi melaga neeyaga rādu
Visvadabhirama vinura vema

(PONGU = Elation, pride; GODU = grief, affliction)

A man is elated, when a son is born to him, if the son takes up to evil ways, as he grows up, such an evil son will cause grief to his father;

A father should take care to see that his son does not fall in to evil company at any time.

22. Dooradrusti ganaru toogina danukanu
Bāru patteru garu padinadanuka
Dandasaadhyu laraya dharmasaadhyu lukāru
Visvadabhirama vinura vema

(TOOGU = To swing, to rock, to reel; PATTU = Hold, grip)

An evil fellow never thinks about the consequences of any action but only when he reels under the impact of those consequences; Evil men alas! have no foresight;

An evil fellow if he stumbles while running, looks for the cause of it, only after he has stumbled and not before it;

Evil men can only be controlled by punishment and not by an appeal to their sense of reason or virtue or honour.

23. Pala needIginta groluchundina
Manjulella choochi madyamandru
Niluvadagani chota neluva nindalu puttu
Visvadabhirama vinura vema

(EEDIGA = A man of the toddy drawer caste; NINDA = Blame, censure, reproach)

Even if a man drinks milk only in a toddy drawer's hut, people assume that he has drunk toddy only;

If a man is seen in a forbidden place, he is sure to face calumny (a false charge)

24. Matalādu tokati manasulo nokkati
Odaliguna madokati nadata yokati
Etlu kalugu mukti ettlulunda tānu
Visvadabhirama vinura vema

An evil fellow talks about some thing, but he takes care to conceal his real thoughts;
His nature is one thing and his conduct is another thing;
Such a man's words, thoughts, nature and conduct are always at variance and can not be relied upon;
Such an evil fellow will never attain MOKSHA.

25. Ramanama pathanache mahevalmeeki
Pāpi boyadayyu bapadayye
Kulem ghanamu kādu guname pradhānamu
Visvadabhirama vinura vema

(BOYA = A huntsman, a savage, barbarian; BAPADU = A Brahmana)

Vālmeeki was a savage and a huntsman in his younger years; But he gave up his evil ways, and changed into one of the greatest devotees of SRI RAMA, and wrote the epic RAMAYANA (which is read with great devotion by millions even today)

A man's character and conduct are of more importance than his caste (Lineage)

26. Enta chaduvu chadivi yenni nerchinagāni
Heenudavagunambu mānaledu
Boggu palagaduga bovunā malinambu
Visvadabhirama vinura vema

(AVAGUNAMU = A bad quality, an evil disposition; HEENUDU = A low, base, mean or vile person)

A vile person even if he has had the advantage of excellent learning, will not be able to overcome his inherent evil tendencies; just as

A piece of charcoal even if it is rinsed repeatedly in milk will not loose its black colour.

27. Satpurushula mitri jālimpagārādu
Prakruti neruga kunna bhakti ledu
Paluva letti reeti bhakti nilpuduraya
Visvadabhirama vinura vema

(PALUVA = A wicked man; PRAKRUTI = Cause, origin, source of the creation)

One should not give up the friendship of a SAJJANA. Unless one realizes the cause, origin and source of the CREATION, devotion, and reverence towards the CREATOR, will not dawn in ones heart;

An evil fellow will never be able to develop steadfast devotion.

28. Heena narulatoda nintulatodanu
Paduchu Vandra toda brabhuvutoda
Brāgnajanula toda balukangarādāya
Visvadabhirama vinura vema

It is safer and wiser not to take the initiative and talk with (1) A vile person, (2) Women (3) Young men (4) A King and (5) Learned men.

6. THE WAY OF A SAJJANA (THE WAY OF A MAN OF VIRTUE)

1. Anuvugānichota nadhikula manarādu
Konche mundutella goduva kadu
Konda yadda mandu gonchemi yundadā
Visvadabhirama vinura vema

A Sajjana assumes a low profile, when the time and place are not suitable, yet his own worth is not affected by such a strategy;

Just as a big mountain is seen as a little one in a mirror.

2. Asuvinasamina nānanda sukhākeli
Satyanista paruni santarinchu
Satyanista chooda sajjana bhavambu
Visvadabhirama vinura vema

A Sajjana will not forego his committment to TRUTH even when his very existence is at stake; Such total committment to TRUTH is the very characterestic of a man of virtue.

3. Aaryu lina vāralanu bhava roodhini
Deliya jeppu chundru tetapadaga
Guru tugananivādu guriyoppa jeppunā
Visvadabhirama vinura vema

Only a Sajjana is capable of understanding and explaining clearly to others, the various experiences of his own life;

One who has merely blundered through the various experiences of his own life, will not be able to explain them to others or guide them.

4. Kadupu chicchu cheta gāmanalamu cheta
Krodhavahini cheta gutilapadaka
yuktamanasu toda nundunu sujanudu
Visvadabhirama vinura vema

(KADUPU CHICCHU = Hunger; KAMANALAMU = Lust; KRODHAVAHNI = Anger; KUTILAPADAKA = Not to suffer from, not overcome by)

A Sajjana always tries to keep (1) Hunger (2) Lust and (3) Anger under check; And he keeps his mind always in a proper and reasonable state.

5. Kadupukela meeru kalavalapadedaru?
Kadupu challabadaga kaladu bhukti
Kadaku ratiloni kappaku ledoka?
Visvadabhirama vinura vema

(KALAVALAMU = Anxiety, distress)

Do not be distressed or over anxious about your sustenance (maintenance); There is sustenance even for a frog encased in a rock.

6. Kanulu povuvadu kallu poyina vādu
Vabhayu laraya goodi yundu natlu
Peda peda goodi penagoni yundunu
Visvadabhirama vinura vema

(PENAGONI = To join, unite)

A blind man and a lame man (Cripple) live together, and help each other;
A poor man lives near another poor man to seek help and cooperation.

7. Kama mohamulanu galigiyundu narundu
Esta deva gurula nerugaledu

Estu neriginataade ela sajjanundu
Visvadabhirama vinura vema

(ESTUDU = A friend)

A man who is a slave to his sexual desires and engrossed in worldly attachments, will not heed and revere his own well wishers, GURU and or even GOD; whereas a sajjana only heeds and reveres them.

8. Koora yuduku venuka koodunā kasavera?
Yeruka galgi munupe yeravalayu
Sthalamu tappu venuka dharmambu puttunā?
Visvadabhirama vinura vema

(ERUKA = Knowledge; KASAVU = grass)

It is easy to pick out and discard unwanted grass shoots and leaves etc. from any leafy vegetable before cooking it, whereas the same can not be done after the cooking is over;

One should never miss any opportunity to do a good deed as it is impossible to do it, once the opportunity is lost.

9. Kopamunanu ghanata konchemi povunu
Kopamunanu gunamu koratapadunu
Kopamunanu bratuku konchemi povunu
Visvadabhirama vinura vema

(GHANATA = Dignity, respectability; GUNAMU = character, virtue; BRATUKU = Livelihood; KONCHEMU = Deficiency)

A man who is overcome by uncontrolled anger foregoes his dignity and virtue; Anger endangers even a man's very livelihood.

10. Khalulu tittiranchu galavara padanela?
Varititla nemi vasi chedunu?
Sajjanundu titta sāpambadounaya
Visvadabhirama vinura vema

(KHALUDU = An evil doer, a wicked man; SĀPAMU = A curse; TITTU = Abuse, revile, rail at)

One need not be unduly distressed, when a wicked man reviles you, but one should take care not to kindle the wrath of a SAJJANA as the curse of a SAJJANA is sure to cause formidable consequences.

11. Gangigovu palu gantedinanu chalu
Kadavedina nemi kharamu palu?
Bhakti galgu koodu pattedinanu chalu
Visvadabhirama vinura vema

(GANGA GOVU = A cow of superior sanctity; KHARAMU = An Ass; BHAKTI = Devotion, love, affection; MORSEL = A mouthful, a small bit)

A spoonful of a cow's milk is to be preferred to a large pot of donkey's milk; Just as even a morsel of food given with love and affection is cherished.

12. Gunayutunaku melu goranta chesina
Kondayagunu vani gunamu cheta
Kondayanta melu guna heenu derugunā?
Visvadabhirama vinura vema

A little benefit conferred on a Sajjana, will be considered by him as a great benefit and he cherishes gratitude whereas a Durgana regards even a great benefit conferred on him as a little one and rank ingratitude is his very characterestic.

13. Gunamu teeruleka kulamella jedipoye
Streela nadata valana siggu poye
Chaviti nela valana jalamella chedi poye
Visvadabhirama vinura vema

(Chaviti nela = Brackish soil)

The reputation of a caste is ruined by the disgraceful conduct of its members;
By the evil conduct of women, one is burdened with shame;
By seeping through a brackish soil, entire water becomes unfit for drinking purpose.

14 . Chittasuddhi yokati srestalanchanamagu
Nikhila punya karya nirvahanamu
Naddileka Cheya nanuvugā deriki?
Visvadabhirama vinura vema

For the successful completion of any deed of merit one should concentrate and focus all his physical and mental powers, or else failure is a certainty

15. Chadivinayya Kanna Chakaliye melu
Gruhamu velpukanna gede melu
Bapana yya kanna bineedu melaya
Visvadabhirama vinura vema

(BINEEDU = One who beats drums or special occasions such as marriages, festivals etc.)

A DHOBI should be preferred to a learned man devoid of common sense;

A she buffalo which gives milk should be preferred to a GOD, who does not respond to prayers;

A "BINEEDU" should be preferred to a wicked BRAHMANA.

16. Chadu vulanni chadivi chala vivekiyou
Kapati kennadina galade mukti?
Nirmalatmunake nischalampu samādhi
Visvadabhirama Vinura Vema

A cheat (DECEIVER) will will never attain 'MOKSHA' inspite of his keen intelligence and vast learning;

Only a man with a pure soul will be able to attain 'MOKSHA'.

17. Champadagina yatti satruvu tanacheta
Jikkeneni keedu cheyarādu
Posaga meluchesi pommanute chalu
Visvadabhirama vinura vema

Even when a mortal enemy is delivered to a Sajjana he will not only free him unharmed, but also confer a benefit on him.

18. Chooragonumu doraku sugnana mellanu
Paaraveyu mella papagunamu
Daariteliya budhula daapuna melagumu
Visvadabhirama vinura vema

Try to acquire knowledge and wisdom from every possible source;

Discard all evil qualities;

To know the path, follow in the footsteps JNANIS (WISE MEN).

19. Janudu telivinonda sanchalimpadu madi
Dayayu neeti galuga dagulu buddhi
Tivuru Bhaanujoochi timirambu nilchunā?
Visvadabhirama vinura vema

When a man acquires wisdom, fickleness of mind disappears;

Mercy and morality overtake his mind; just as the rising sun dispels darkness.

20. Daagu padina venuka daaga nasakyamu
Arasi Cheyumayya yanni panulu
Teliyakunna nadugu telisinavārini
Visvadabhirama vinura vema

(DAAGU = A stain, spot, Blot, mark)
One is sure to be disgraced if there is a failure in the performance of a task, inspite of secrecy maintained, as all will come to know about it sooner or later;
Hence it is wiser to undertake a task only after a thorough deliberation (careful consideration);
If the course of action is not clear, it is wiser to seek the help and guidance of more experienced people.

21. Tanaku bole naviyu dhara buttinavi kavo
Paraga dannu boli bratuku gade
Jnani prani jampa garana memayā?
Visvadabhirama vinura vema

All the creatures on the earth, are born and exist, just as you do;

Is there any reason to kill ancther creature?

22. Tappu lennu varu tandopatandamu
Lurvi janula kella nundu dappu

Tappuennuvaru tama tappu lerugaru
Visvadabhirama vinura vema

(TAPPU = and error (short-coming), mistake, a fault); Tandopatandamulu = great numbers)

Those who criticise and find fault with others are in great numbers;
All the people on the earth have some short-coming or the other;
Alas! the zealous (ardent or enthusiastic) fault finders are not aware of their own short-comings.

23. Talli neduruko nuta tandri neduru konuta
Anna nedurukonuta yanedi moodu
Patakamula nerigi vartimpagavale
Visvadabhirama vinura vema

(EDURUKONU = To oppose, act against; PATAKAMU = Sin)

To oppose and act against the advice of one's father, mother and brother is a sin;
A Sajjana takes care to avoid it at all times.

24. Doolamula natekki dommari gada nekka
Jaaludu nanadepdu sajjanundu
Veelu manu panulu verriyi cheyunā?
Visvadabhirama vinura vema

(ATUKA = A loft under the roof of a house; DOMMARI = A rope dancer, an acrobat; DOOLAMU = Beam)

An agile man may climb up the beam of a loft under the roof of his house;
yet even such an agile man will not dare to do the feats done by a street acrobat such as climbing up a vertical beam, wire walking etc. There are specific limitations to every man's abilities and skills;
A wise man is fully aware of his own limitations of ability and skill, and will never attempt the impossible, and what is beyond his ability and skill.

25. Nera nannavādu nerajana mahelona
Nertu nanavadu vārta kadu
Voorakunnavade Yuttamottamudaya
Visvadabhirama vinura vema

(NERAMI = Ignorance; NERAJANA = clever person; VAARTA-KADU = A Chatter-box)

A man who is aware of his ignorance and admits that he is ignorant is not an ignorant fellow;
A man who says that he knows every thing is only a chatter box;
A man who knows everything and who is silent is the best of the lot.

26. Phakki telisi paluka nokka vakyamechalu
Pekku lela vatti prelpulela?
Dikku kaligi mrokka nokkati chaladā

Visvadabhirama vinura vema

(PHAKKI = manner, mode, method, way, style, fashion; DIKKU = Direction, refuge, protection)
Few meaningful words are better than many meaningless words;
To pray once with all the devotion, is better than to pray many times without any devotion.

27. Maratunemo yanuchu madi sujanundepdu
Nevaro narchu meladentayina
Marumelujechi maryada ganchunu
Visvadabhirama vinura vema

A Sajjana whenever he receives a benefit from another reciprocates with another benefit, without fail and thus safeguards his own good reputation.

7. THE WAY OF DAIVA (THE WAY OF DESTINY)

1. Alpudinanemi? Adhikudinanemi?
Cheppa valayu reeti Cheppināda
Haruni yerukaleka yakullādunā?
Visvadabhirama vinura vema

Everyone on this earth whether great or little, is sustained only by the grace of God; Indeed even a leaf does not move without the knowledge of God.

2. Aakumeedi vrāta yandari kideliyu
Chetiloni vrata jeppa vacchu
Tolu krindi vrata doddavāderugunā
Visvadabhirama vinura vema

(AAKU = A palmyra leaf; TALAPATRAS = Inscriptions on palmyra leaves; DODDAVADU = the great one (BRAHMA)
Many can read TALAPATRAS;
Some can read the lines on a palm and foretell the fortune of a man;
But who can foretell what BHRAHMA has ordained for a man.

3. Eeyanatani cheta nippinchu dana prapti
Ecchu vanicheta neeyaneedu
Eyya gikonanga neesvarude karta
Visvadabhirama vinura vema

(PRAPTI = Luck, fortune, lot, destined, or preordained)

What is preordained for you, that you are bound to receive inspite of any reluctance and resistance from a donor; what is not preordained for you, that you will never receive, inspite of all the willing cooperation from a donor;

It is ESVARA only that gives or takes from any one.

4. Enni bhoomulu gani yepaatu padinanu
   Antaneeka saniyu venta dirugu
   Bhoomi krottayina bhoktalu krottalā?
   Visvadabhirama vinura vema

   (SANI = The planet SATURN or its regent (governor), a deity causing ill-luck; BHOKTA = An Enjoyer.)

   A man moves from place to place in search of better luck and prospects; Alas! whereever he may go, and whatever means of livelihood he takes up, his misfortune (SANI) follows him;

   The place chosen by the man may be a new one, but the man is the same old one with the same old misfortune (SANI) following him.

5. Evvarerugakunda neppudu povuno
   Povu jeevamakata! bondi vidichi
   Antamatra munake yapakeerti ganaleka
   Virugabadunu narudu verri vema

   (VIRUGABADU = To be proud or haughty; APAKEERTI = Infamy, disgrace; BONDI = The body)

   Life departs from a human body at any time and without giving any prior notice;

   Not aware of the transitory nature of life, a man struts, (walk about with pride and vanity) about, ignoring all infamy.

6. Edi kulamu neeku? Edi matamburā?
   Padukonumu madini pakvamerigi
   Yadarinchu; dāni yantamu teliyumu

   (KULAMU = caste, race, tribe, class; MATAMU = Religion, faith, creed; PADUKONU = to become firm or fixed, to be established to take root, to stand; PAKVAMU = Ripe, mature)

   What does the word 'CASTE' mean to you?

   What does the word 'RELIGION' mean to you?

   Ponder deeply on these two problems and try to get at the root of them and then only take a firm stand.

7. Okari keedu verikokkari keeyadu
   Okari melu vera yokani keedu
   Keedu melu Vāru podimi deliyaru
   Visvadabhirama vinura vema

   (PODEME = Manner, mode)

   The creator does not inflict afflictions on one, which are preordained for another;

   He does not award prosperity meant for one to another;

   Every one experiences WEAL (WELFARE) or WOE (GRIEF), as ordained by his

"KARMA" only.

8. Katteyandu nippuganani Chanda mee
Tanuvunandu nātma dagiliyundu
Marugu telisi pidapa mar konavalenayā
Visvadabhirama vinura vema

(MARUGU = Hidden, concealed, scret; MARKONU = To attack, to face or front, to oppose.)

As there is fire in an invisible form in a piece of firewood, SOUL (ATMA) is imminent in a human body

Aware of this concealment (close at hand), one should try to realize it.

9. Kadagi patti yasa kadatera neeyadu
Edumalandu betti eedchugani
Pudami janula bhakti podamanga neeyadu
Visvadabhirama vinura vema

(KADAGU = to endeavor, strive, attempt; KADATERU = To be saved; AASHA = Desire, attachment, avarice, ambition; EDUMA = Trouble, hardship, misfortune)

Desire is an evil quality.

Desire leads on a man into more and more of troubles, and to grief;

Desire is the main obstacle that prevents the dawn of devotion in a man's heart.

10. Kanaka mrugamu bhuvini Kalugunan cherugadā
Ramu deruka kalgu rajukādo?
Chetu kalamunaku chedu buddhi puttedu
Visvadabhirama vinura vema

(CHETUKALAMU = The time at which the doom of a person is ordained to overtake him; CHEDU = to be ruined or destroyed)

SREE RAMA went in pursuit of a "GOLDEN DEER", was he not intelligent enough to know that a "golden deer" does not exist on the earth;

when the time is ripe for a man's down fall, even his own intelligence lets him down.

11. Kanaledu nuduru karnamul veepunu
Nerulu kānaledu netti meeda
Tanne kanaledu divamu nerugunā?
Visvadabhirama vinura vema

(NERULU = Hairs)

A man can not see his own brow, ears, back and the hairs on his head;

One who can not see himself, how can such a one come to know God

12. Kalachakra meruga galeka yeppudu
Sandhya japamu cheyu janalara
Sandhya japamuloni jada letlundunu?
Visvadabhirama vinura vema

(SANDHYA = morning or evening twilight; JAPAMU = Repeating prayers in an undertone)

Time is the most precious possession of a man; yet not aware of this fact many spend a lot of time every day performing rituals such as SANDHYA and JAPAMU.

13. Kori drupadu patti koppu patteedchina
Simhabaluni chavu jeppa darame
Mugiyu kalamunaku monagādu neelgadā
Visvadabhirama vinura vema

DRUPADUPATTI = Daughter of King Drupada namely Droupadi; SIMHABALUDU = Brother in law of King Virata, known for his valour and prowess) (namely KEECHAKA); (BHEEMASENA = one of the five Pandava Brothers)

Keechaka once dragged Droupadi by the hair of her head in the court of King VIRATA; (MAHABHARATA)

Even a mighty man like Keechaka, had to die when his time was up, in the hands of BHEEMASENA.

14. Gatamu chesinatti karmabandha mulella
Barisi povu satyaguruni Valana
Kummari kokayedu gudiyaku nokanādu
Visvadabhirama vinura vema

(KARMABANDHAMU = The bond of action that ties a human soul down to the cycle of births and deaths; GUDIYA = a club; SATYAGURU = A true preceptor)

By the grace of a SATYAGURU, all the accumulated results of a man's past actions are destroyed; Just as all the pots made by a potter in a year can be smashed down in a day with a club.

15. Chakra dharuni vedi jaladhi dataga vacchu
Vikrutamina buddhi vetala bettu
Nakramenna gajamu nayamara bhakshinchu
Visvadabhirama vinura vema

(CHAKRADHARI = Vishnu; NAKRAMU = A Crocodile; VIKRUTAMU = Corrupted, changed, altered, affected by strong passion or emotion)

Prayers addressed to VISHNU, will enable one to cross the ocean of "SAMSARA" safely; A corrupted mind affected by a strong passion or emotion leads a man into difficulties and dangers; Just as even a huge elephant, if it is inattentive, will be dragged down to a watery grave by a crocodile.

16. Chippaalona badda chinuku mutyambayye
Neetabadda chinuku neella galase
Praptamu gala chota phalamela tappurā
Visvadabhirama vinura vema

(CHIPPA = Pearl oyster (Mother of pearl); PRAPTAMU = Luck, fortune, destiny)

A water drop which falls in to a pearl oyster will become a pearl in the course of time, where as the rest of the water drops mingle and merge in the sea;

A man is sure to receive the fruit (fortune) that has been ordained for him.

17. Neellaloni mosali nigidi yenugu battu
Bayata kukka cheta bhanga padunu
Sthanabalmi kani tana balmi kadayā
Visvadabhirama vinura vema

A crocodile as long as it is in a river or a stream, can easily drag down even an elephant, whereas on the land it can not even protect itself from the attacks of a dog; similarly a man is invincible (unconquerable) when he is in his own place, and when he moves out of his place, alas! he becomes vulnerable. (Capable of being wounded)

18. Maranamanna verichi madi kalangaga nela?
Nirudu, mundatedu ninna monna
Tanuvu vidichi natadu tanakanna takkuvā?
Visvadabhirama vinura vema

(NIRUDU = last year)

Do not be scared of 'DEATH', as it is universal;

Those who died yesterday, the day before yesterday, the last year and the year before the last year, are they in any way inferior to you.

19. Mariyu dadhini ghrutamu mraku landanalamu
Soumya sumamulandu sourabhambu
Tilala tilamatlu tejarillu chidātma
Visvadabhirama vinura vema

(NASCENT = In the act of being born; just begining to be; not yet mature)

Curd contains ghee in a nascent form;

Firewood contains fire in a nascent form;

Gingelli seeds contain oil in a nascent form;

Fragrance is imminent (close at hand) in flowers;

Manifestations of the 'CREATOR' are evident in magnificent (resplendent) brilliance in the universe.

20. Lankapovunādu lankādhipati rajya
manta keesasena lakra minche
Chetukalamina jerupa nalpude chalu

Visvadabhirama vinura vema

(KEESAMU = A monkey; ALPUDU = A mean or low person; CHETU KALAMU = The time at which the doom of a person is ordained to overtake him)

Lanka, the capital of 'RAVANA' was destroyed by a horde of monkeys;
When the time is ripe for (his) (a man's) down fall, even
a mean fellow will be able to overcome him.

21. Vellivacchuvadu vellipoyeduvādu
Tenuledu Konchu bonuledu
Tanadedapono dhanameda povuno
Visvadabhirama vinura vema

No man brings any wealth along with him at the time of his birth;
No man takes any wealth along with him at the time of his death;
Where does he go after his death?
What happens to the wealth after his death?

22. Velakoladi bhuvini veshamul dalturu
Pralumali buvva phalamu koraku
Melukādu; madini minnandi yundumu
Visvadabhirama vinura vema

(PRALU MALIKA = Laziness, indolence; MINNAKA = Silently, quietly, coolly)

Thousands of lazy fellows, put on various guises to hoodwink others and to fill their bellies;
But their's is not a good path;
It is better to be contented and to be at peace with oneself.

23. Vyādhi peeditambu vyasana santāpambu
Dukha sambhavamuna dodaru bhayamu
Lenivaralunda lenatikinanu
Visvadabhirama vinura vema

(TODARU = To follow, accompany)

There are none in this world who are not subject to the following, to some extent or the other, namely 1. Disease 2. Vice 3. Grief and 4. Fear which results as a consequence of 1, or 2, or 3 or all.

24. Saativaru ninnu saadhimpaga leru
Divamepudu neeku dappakunna
Bharātambuloni paramardha midekāda
Visvadabhirama vinura vema

(SAADHINCHU = to conquer, overcome, subdue, to master; SAATIVĀDU = An equal, a rival)

Rivals will never be able to overcome you, if God's mercy protects you, in your trials and tribulations;

In MAHABHARATA, 'KOURAVAS' (hundred) failed to conquer 'PANDAVS', (five) as the latter had the guidance and protection of 'SRI KRISHNA'.

8. THE WAY OF KARMA (THE WAY OF KARMA OR DUTY)

1. Rutuvu nanusarinchi stithi kalamuna noppu
Gatini batti manuju matiyu noppu
Svecchа batti yuvida cherlatamunu noppu
Visvadabhirama vinura vema

(GATI = Fate, lot, destiny; VUVIDA = a woman; CHĀRALĀDU = To sport, play, rove about for pleasure, to jaunt)

Climate changes with the change of seasons;

A man's mind works as preordained by his destiny;

A woman's dalliance (a leisurely or frivolous passing of time) depends on the freedom given to her.

2. Chāki koka lutiki cheekaku padajesi
Mila teesi lessa madichinatlu
Buddhi cheppuvadu gruddina melaya
Visvadabhirama vinura vema

A washerman thrashes a dirty cloth repeatedly on a stone to drive out the dirt, rinses it in water, dries it up in the sunlight and finally he folds it in to a proper shape and thus makes it ready for use;

A man who has a mind to help and improve you, has a right to correct and even punish you if necessary.

3. Tanadu bhratalella danambu cheyanga
Danaku phalamatanchu minukarādu
Tanaku Kalugoya tana tammuded chunā?
Visvadabhirama vinura vema

(BHRATA = A Brother; MINAKARINCHU = To be in a fix or dilemma, to be non-plussed)

The merit that accrues (arise, grow naturally) because of gifts made by your brothers will be credited to them only and not to you;

Just as when your leg is cut off, you alone feel the pain of it, and not your brothers.

4. Ningi negayuvādu neri lokamuna ledu
Bangi dragu vādu baliyabodu
Konga yogamulanu gorku ladangunā?

Visvadabhirama vinura vema

(BANGI = GANJAYE = Dried leaves of Indian hemp plant (CANNABIS SATIVA) used in smoking along with opium, or in making an intoxicating drink)

No man can fly or stay aloft in the air like a bird; yet imposters make such tall claims to deceive credulous devotees;

Addicts who drink 'BANGI' will never put on fat;

These imposters and addicts are a prey to their own unchecked desires and halluccinations.

5. Puttu mugdha tirigi poyeducha mugdha
Tera mugdha tannu teliyaledu
Vunna natikinanu nupakari kaledu
Visvadabhirama vinura vema

(MUGDHATA = Ignorance, stupidity; TERA = unconnectedness or unconcerned)

When a man is born, he is ignorant about the world;

When a man leaves this world also, he is ignorant about his whereabouts

Even during his life time, he does not strive to acquire 'SELF KNOWLEDGE'

Even during his life time, he fails to be helpful to others.

6. Matamu lenniyina satamulu kavavi
Satamu karmamagunu Jagatiyandu
Anni matamulandu naraya nokkati ledu
Visvadabhirama vinura vema

(MATAMU = Faiths, creed, religious sects; SATAMU = Permanent, lasting, eternal)

All the religions are mere interpretations about the CREATOR and CREATION; They are all subject to change where as the 'KARMA' is the only unchanging inexorable (unyielding) law;

None of the religions have the final answer.

7. Manasuloni mukti mari yokka chotanu
Veduka bovuvādu verrivādu
Gorre jankabetti golla Vedaku reeti
Visvadabhirama vinura vema

The way to 'MOKSHA' is in your mind only;

Yet a man searches for it elsewhere than in his mind

Just as a shepherd searching for a lamb everywhere when it is cradled in his own arms.

8. Marma merugaleka matamulu kalpinchi
Yurvi janulu dukha mondu chundru
Gaju tinti kukka kalvala padu reeti
Visvadabhirama vinura vema

(KALAVALA PADU = to be perplexed, or confused, or to be anxious; MARMANU

= A Secret or mystery)

As men (they) have failed to unravel the mystery of a soul, they have propounded (propose, put forward) Various religions, and as a result of these various interpretations they are steeped in confusion and sorrow;

Just as a dog gets confused, when it sees its own reflections in a house of mirrors.

9. Mooti neeshanamula modalanta jerupaka
Chitta mela niluchu sthiramugānu
Chitta shuddhi leka sivudu kaanpinchunā
Visvadabhirama vinura vema

There are three main obstacles on the path of MOKSHA; They are (1) DAARESHANA (Attachment to ones wife), (2) PUTRESHANA (Attachment to one's son) and (3) DHANESHANA (Attachment to wealth)

Unless these bonds are totally destroyed, one will not be able to see 'SIVA'

10. Moodha bhakticheta mukkanti boojimpa
munnu boyavarudu muktudaye
Pooja kemi? tanadu buddhi pradhanamu
Visvadabhirama vinura vema

(MUKKANTI = Siva) (BOYA = A huntsman; MOODHABHAKTI = Blind faith)

BOYA TINNADU, a hunts man, worshipped SIVA with unmatched sincerity and devotion and attained MOKSHA, although he was unaware of any rituals or ceremonies;

Sincere devotion to SIVA is of more importance than rituals and ceremonies.

11. Raayiyi yahalya raamu pādamu soki
Aadudayye nandu ravani janulu
Cheyu sukrutamulitlu silalina dappavu
Visvadabhirama vinura vema

(SUKRUTAMULU = Spiritual merit)

(acquired due to his or her virtue and piety in previous lives)

"Ahalya", the wife of Sage Goutama, who was in the form of a rock, regained her human form when SRI RAMA's feet touched that rock; (From the epic (RAMAYANA)

If one has spiritual merit (SUKRUTAM), one is sure to reap its fruit, even if one is in the form of a rock.

12. Vākku cheta dappu vavulu varusalu
Vākku cheta dappu vanita gunamu
Vākku cheta galgu varakarmamulu Bhuvi
Visvadabhirama vinura vema

(VAKKU = speech; VAVI = Relationship; VARUSA = Same; VARA KARMAMULU = best or excellent deeds)

By one's own improper speech, one spoils the relations among kith (friends) and kin

(relations)

By her own improper speech, a woman acquires a bad reputation;

Even to perform excellent deeds of merit, one should first cultivate a proper manner of speech.

13. Vāna rakada mari pranambu pokada
Kāna badadu kala karma vasata
Ganabadinameeda kali etlu nadachunā?
Visvadabhirama vinura vema

None can predict exactly the time of a rain or the time of death of a person; Both are dictated by (under the control of) TIME and FATE;

If one can predict exactly their occurrence the state and course of 'KALI YUGA' would have been quite different.

14. Vraata ventagani varameedu divambu
Cheta koladigani vrata raadu
Vraata kajudu karta cheta ku daa gartā
Visvadabhirama vinura vema

(AJUDU = Brahma; VRAATA = writing; VARAMU = a boon, blessing, divine gift; reward)

A man's destiny is decreed by what BRAHMA has written on his forehead;

Yet a man's good deeds can influence his own destiny;

Destiny of a man is in the hands of BRAHMA whereas good deeds are to be performed by ones own hands.

15. Satini choochi choochi soukhyambu dāgoru
Gatini kānaledu karmajeevi
Gatulu satulavalana gananga lerugā
Visvadabhirama vinura vema

A man hopes to attain all the happiness in this life through the companionship of one's wife;

Alas! such a man is not aware of his own fate;

One will never be able to realize his own fate with the help of the companionship of a wife.

16. Sutulacheta bunya sukhamu nondudunani
Manujudundu garma matamu dagili
Enugu padiyunna nettunā masakambu?
Visvadabhirama vinura vema

(MASAKAMU = A mosquito, a gnat, any fly that bites or stings)

Men believe that they will attain higher worlds (PUNYAGATIS), in the hereafter, as they have begotten sons here;

Alas! how mistaken they are in their hopes;
Can a mosquito lift up a prostrate (lying flat on the ground) elephant.

9. THE WAY OF DHIRYA (THE WAY OF COURAGE OR FORTITUDE)

1. Aadi nevaru puttirani teliyangora
Sodiyagunu pidapa sukhamu ledu
Aaadi sakti yanna nadi bayalani nammu
Visvadabhirama vinura vema

(SODI = fortune telling)

All discussions about the origin of creation are as futile as 'SODI' (fortune telling);
Believe that there is only one cosmic energy, from the begining of creation.

2. Eduti tama balambu lenchu koneraka
Deekoni chalamunane deercheneni
Elugu divite seva kerpadu chandamu
Visvadabhirama vinura vema

(DEEKONU = To oppose; CHALAMU = unfixed, unsteady, fickle, inconstant; TEERCHU = To settle, decide, a dispute etc.; ELUGU = A bear)

One should carefully assess the strength and weaknesses of an opponent and self and then only proceed on a course of action;

A bear even if it is allotted the duty of a torch bearer, it will never do it and it is sure to run away.

3. Taamu velayu noora kshamambu vātilla
Natti yooru vidichi yavala bore?
Kolaku lendinanta gokkera lundunā?
Visvadabhirama vinura vema

(KOKKERA = Crane)

People leave famine stricken villages and move on to better places;
Just as cranes fly away from dried up lakes and seek lakes with plenty of water

4. Ramudokadu putti ravi kulam beederche
Gurupatiyunu putti kulamu jeriche
Ela nadharma dharmamula reeti ettula
Visvadabhirama vinura vema

SRIRAMA pursued DHARMA and enhanced the name and fame of his ancestors (RAGHUVAMSA); whereas DURYODHANA pursued ADHARMA (The evil path) and destroyed not only the name and fame of his ancestors, but also his Kith and Kin, and in the end himself also (in KURUKSHETRA WAR);

One who pursues DHARMA is sure to prosper;

One who pursues ADHARMA is sure to be destroyed.

5. Raayi raayi goorchi raayaga raayaga
Nunna nina yattu lanni panulu
Paatu chesinanta paripāti yagunayā
Visvadabhirama vinura vema

(PARIPATI = Method, practice, habit)

By repeatedly rubbing and polishing a stone on another stone, it acquires a smooth polished surface;

By repeated sincere efforts to accomplish a task, one acquires superb skill in performing it.

6. Vedu chunna yatte vishayambu joopuchu
Gota dimpu summu kondegadu
Chercharadu vāni jerachunu tudi netlo
Visvadabhirama vinura vema

(KONDEGADU = A Tale bearer; VISHAYAMU = An object of sense, any thing perceptible by the senses, the object of concern)
A tale bearer approaches you as a humble petitioner (SUPPLICANT) and should never be trusted; if trusted he is sure to ruin you by some means or the other.

7. Sakala vidyalandu sampannuli yunna
Natti vāru parichayamuna jouka
Perati chettu mandu parikimpa meccharu
Visvadabhirama vinura vema

(PARICHAYAMU = Acquaintance, friendship, Knowledge; CHOWKA = (a) Cheap)

Acquaintance lessens the respectability of even a great scholar;

A rare medicinal herb, if it is found in one's own backyard, is not valued at all.

10. THE WAY OF MOHA (THE WAY OF DELUSION)

1. Aalu biddalanuchu nati mohamuna nunna
Dhanamu meeda vāncha tagili yunna
Natti narula keila navani muktiyeledu
Visvadabhirama vinura vema

(Vancha = wish, desire, longing, craving)

One who is unduly attached to his wife and children and of avaricious temperament will never be able to achieve 'MOKSHA'.

2. Aalu sutulu maya annadammulu maya
Talidandri maya taanu maya
Teliyaneedu maya deenillu padāye

Visvadabhirama vinura vema

(MAYA = Illusion (the indescribable power of the infinite)

Maya is an all pervading cosmic phenomenon; wife, sons, brothers, mother and father and even one's own SELF, are all a part of it.

It is impossible to come out of the spell of Maya, let Maya be damned.

3. Aashalanedi tralla namara goyaga jesi
Pāravivagani paramu ledu
Kokku tindi yasa jikki chacchinayatlu
Visvadabhirama vinura vema

(KOKKU = Pandikokku = A species of very large rat (Bandicoot)

Unless one destroys totally all the desires in ones mind, one will never by able to achieve 'MOKSHA';

Alas! a bandicoot is lured into a trap by a morsel of food and gets killed.

4. Vooru kondaveedu; vuniki paschima veedhi
Moogachinta palle modati ellu
Edde reddikula mademani cheppudu
Visvadabhirama vinura vema

YOGI VEMANA writes about himself "I hail from a REDDY family in "KONDAVEEDU", and my first residence was in the western street of a village called, 'MOOGA CHINTAPALLI'.

5. Ruta manruta merunga nevvari taramagu
Sthitiyu gatiyu deliya detapadunu
vinna matravunane vivarimpagā rādu
Visvadabhirama vinura vema

RUTAMU = Truth; ANRUTAMU = Falsehood.

To differentiate truth and falsehood of any matter is not an easy task for any one; one should carefully enquire in to all the details (such as the time, place etc.), before coming to a conclusion one should never decide on any matter, as soon as one comes to know to it.

6. Kaayamunna epude kamadulanu gosi
Jnanamargamunaku gadagavalayu
Jaagu cheya gaaya megina nemagu?
Visvadabhirama vinura vema

One should strive to eradicate KAMA (Desires) and MOHA (Attachments) etc. from one's heart and pursue the path of JNANA (Wisdom), before death overtakes the human body;

There is nothing one can do after the dissolution of the human body.

7. Chamuru rāchi konna jarmambu merugekku
Saamu cheya mena sattu vekku
Jnanamarga meruga gadateru janmambu
Visvadabhirama vinura vema

When oil is massaged on the skin, it acquires a shiny look;
Physical exercise improves ones physical fitness;
when one pursues the path of JNANA, one achieves MOKSHA.

8. Jeevi jeevi jampa sivuni champute yagu
Jeevudarasi teliya sivudu kaade?
Bhaavamandu deeni barikinchi choodumu
Visvadabhirama vinura vema

Every creature is a manifestation of the CREATOR;
To kill a creature is to destroy a manifestation of the CREATOR;
One should ponder on this aspect and come to a conclusion.

9. Talli dandru levaro tanaku janmamu lenno
Tiruga neruga natti dikkulenno
Sthiramu nasthi ramunu teliyaledagnāni
Visvadabhirama vinura vema

A man who is devoid of 'JNANA', is not aware of his own innumerable previous births, his parents in those births and innumerable number of places in which he lived in those lives;

Alas! he is not aware of what is of permanent value and what is of temporary value.

10. Teliya tanadu bharya tega bāru sankela
Chinna sisuvulella cheela laraya
Arasi chooda danuve ela cherasā lara
Visvadabhirama vinura vema

(SANKELA = A Chain, a fetter)
The 'SOUL' is a prisoner in a human body;
The 'wife' is a 'big iron chain' that immobilizes a man;
The 'little children' are the 'screws' on those shackles.

11. Tolughatamulona dolagaka yunnappu
dālumagalu preeti nalaru chundru
Jeevi ghatemu viduva jikkoodi povurā
Visvadabhirama vinura vema

As long as a husband and wife are alive, they life together happily;
when one of them dies, their union comes to an end.

12. Dasami ekadassiyani vratamulu pooni

Meduku tinakunna durgu namadi yadagune
Puttapi gotta nuragambu getta bodu
Teerungani moudhya mee teragu vema

Many devotees fast on 'DASAMI', 'EKADASI' (Auspicious days) days to acquire merit;

Alas! these hypocrites are not aware that to eradicate all the evil qualities is of more importance, than fasting on certain days;

It is similar to beating with a stick on an ant hill, to kill a snake, hiding safely deep down in one of the many underground recesses.

13. Neela munugu vadu nirmalatmudu Kadu
Poornamina mukti bondaledu
Neerukodi yepudu neella mungadā
Visvadabhirama vinura vema

(NEERUKODI = A water fowl)

Many devotees take pride in bathing in holy ri 'ers and hope to acquire spiritual merit;

Alas! these hypocrites are not aware, that these rituals are all futile unless they first purify their minds;

A water fowl repeatedly dives into water and a devotee who repeatedly bathes in a holy river without first purifying his mind, is no better than the water fowl.

11. THE WAY OF THE YOGI (THE WAY OF AN ASCETIC)

1. Aaru gurunijera natyanta dukhambu
Edugurini gooda nedu payye
Vadiga veeri pondu viduchutā yogambu
Visvadabhirama vinura vema

(AARUGURU = Arishad vargas, namely 1. KAMA (Desire) 2. KRODHA (Anger) 3. LOBHA (Avarice or greed) 4. MOHA (Delusion or attachment) 5. MADA (Egoism) and 6. MATSARYA (Jealousy)
2. EDUGURU = SAPTAVYASANAS (seven vices) namely 1. Womanize 2. Gambling 3. Addittion to intoxicating drinks, such as alcohol 4. Hunting 5. Harsh speech 6. Punishment meted out of proportion to the offence committed 7. Spending money on useless things.)

One who aspires to become a yogi, should first conquer 'ARISHADVARGAS', and eschew (AVOID) 'SAPTAVYASANAS' also.

2. Enta bhagyamunna nanta kastapu jinta
Chinta cheta manasu chivuku manunu
Chinta leka yunta chediponi sampada
Visvadabhirama vinura vema

Wealth is the main source of all worries and troubles; (i.e.) in safeguarding it)

Sorrow and grief are the end results of wealth.
A man who is free from sorrow and grief is said to enjoy incorruptible wealth.

3. Gattu ralla decchi kallu chetulu trokki
Kachi yulula cheta gasi jesi
moraku ralla keragu moppela nemandu?
Visvadabhirama vinura vema

GATTU RALLU = Huge boulders from the shores of a river, or from a range of hills; GASI = Toil or labour, fatigue, exhaustion; VULI = a chisel; MORAKU (OR MOPPE) = An obstinate and foolish man; ERAGU = To salute or to prostate one's self

Men chisel and toil over huge boulders and sculpture them into the idols of various Gods;

And fools worship these stone idols; can there be greater stupidity than theirs?

4. Galigali galase gaganambu gaganambu
Mannu mannu galase manta manta
Neeru neetagalase nirmalambiyunde
Visvadabhirama vinura vema

There are five primary elements (PANCHA BHOOTAS) in a human body, namely 1. VAYU (Air) 2. AKASAMU or GAGANAMU (Space) 3. PHRUDHVI (Mannu = Earth) 4. AGNI (Warmth or Fire) and 5. JALAMU (Water);

When life departs from a human body, the above mentioned five elements disperse, and the JEEVA (Soul) attains its pristine (original) pure state.

5. Chadivi chadivi chadivi chavanga netiki?
Chavuleni chaduvu chaduvavalayu
Chaduvuleka koti janulu chacchiri kadā
Visvadabhirama vinura vema

Millions of people died in the past, and none of them had any inkling (sign) of any learning; Many scholars spend many years on studies;
The study on the nature of one's Soul is the only one that liberates (him) a man.

6. Narudeyina leka narayanundina
Tatvabaddhudina dharani naraya
Maranamunna danuchu madini nammagavale
Visvadabhirama vinura vema

Every human being, whether he is an ordinary person or a philosopher, or even when he thinks that he is a God, should always bear in mind, that death is the final destination for all.

7. Badugu nerugaleni prabhavam badiyela?
Yoga merugaleni yogi yela?
Vyadhi nerugaleni vidyudu nelayā?
Visvadabhirama vinura vema

BADUGU = Helpless or devoid of protection; PRABHAVAMU = Rule, government, power, authority;

A ruler who does not use his power (or authority) to protect his helpless subjects is futile; An ascetic who is ignorant of yoga is futile; A physician who can not diagnose a disease is futile.

8. Bondi yevari sommu poshimpa balumāru
Prana mevari sommu bhakti seya
Dhana madevari sommu dharmame tana sommu
Visvadabhirama vinura vema

Every human being (body) is destined for eventual disintegration and death irrespective of the care and attention bestowed on it; life (or PRANA) is sure to depart from every human being, irrespective of devotion shown towards it; wealth does not accompany a man after his death 'DHARMA' alone accompanies a man after his death.

9. Bratuku nityama nuchu vadaruchu Vagameera
Viriveeguvādu Verrivādu
Pranulella yamuni bariki gorrelu
Visvadabhirama vinura vema

(VADARUCHU = to chatter, to prattle; VAGA = Pretence, manner, mode, way; VIRRA VEEGU = to be proud, haughty or conceited)

Because of pride and ignorance, a fool thinks that he is going to live for ever;

Alas! he is not aware that all the living creatures are destined to die sooner or later, just as all the sheep are destined for slaughter sooner or later.

12. THE WAY OF BRAHMA SVAROOPA (BRAHMA = The creator of the world) (SVAROOPA = The real form)

1. Kopamunanu naraka koopamu jindunu
Kopamunanu gunamu korata vadunu
Kopamunanu bratuku konchemi povunu
Visvadabhirama Vinura Vema

Anger paves the way to hell;
Anger depletes the good qualities;
Anger reduces the life span also.

2. Pinna vandra svecch a mannana jerachunu
Aadu vandra sveccha godonarchu
Purushavaruni sveccha bhootini goorchura
Visvadabhirama vinura vema

PINNA = young; BHOOTI = Prosperity, power, grandeur; GODU = grief, affliction, distress; VARUDU = one who is best

Undue freedom given to youngsters is sure to pave the way for indiscipline and lessen the respectability of their parents;

Undue freedom given to woman is sure to cause grief for all the concerned;
Freedom given to a man of excellence promotes prosperity.

3. Puttinadiyu modalu purushuderpadu daka
Mantrasani goodu maragi yanta
Poyerāve yanuchu butturu selavicchi
Visvadabhirama vinura vema

MANTRASANI = a mid wife; GOODU = A nest, a cage; MARAGU = to become familiar with, to take to; PUCCHU KONU = To take, receive; SELAVICCHU = give leave or permission

A mid wife attending on a woman in labour, is given all the attention and respect by the relations; Once the baby is delivered, the relations stop giving any attention and respect to the midwife and ask her to leave the house.

4. Perata jettu petti parikimpakundina
Velugu dāti teega vedala baru
Aadudāni gunamu natuvale nundurā
Visvadabhirama vinura vema

PARIKINCHU = To examine, To investigate; VEDALU = Come out, issue forth; TEEGA = Creeper or vine; TEEGALU VARU = To spread, extend in different directions

A creeper in ones own backyard, will grow out of its confines and spread out into open spaces, if it is not pruned regularly, similarly a woman who is not kept under check is sure to be ruined if she is exposed to evil influences of the outside world.

5. Phalaka medanu cheta batti Khadgamboona
Bantu tanamu rādu prati bhalemi?
Veedhilona diruga veladi purushudoune
Visvadabhirama vinura vema

(PHALAKAMU = A shield, a disc, or round piece of metal; PRATIBHA = genius)

A man who is devoid of valour and skill in warfare even if he sports (or carries) a sword and shield will never be considered as a soldier;

Just as a woman will never be considered as a man although she may move around boldly in a street.

6. Janana maraaana vela svatantryamā ledu
Tenu ledu munnu ponuledu
Naduma gartananuta nagu batu kadate
Visvadabhirama vinura vema

NAGUBATU = ridicule, mockery, derision

Man is not free to choose the time of his birth and death;

Man does not bring any wealth along with him at the time of his birth, nor can be take any wealth with him after his death;

Is it not ridiculous to assume that he is the master of the interval.

13. THE WAY OF GURU BHAKTI (REVERENCE TO GURU)

1. Annidānamulanu nannadāname goppa
Kanna vāri kante ghanulu leru
Enna guruni kanna nekkuva lerayā
Visvadabhirama vinura vema

Among all the gifts, the gift of ANNAMU (Boiled rice or any food) is the greatest; Among all the people, ones own parents are the greatest; among all the great one's, there is none greater than the GURU.

2. Guruni siksha leka gurutetlu kalguno
Ajunakina vāni yabbakina
Talapujevi leka talupettu looduno
Visvadabhirama vinura vema

(GURUTU = a mark, sign, token, a limit; AJUDU = BRAHMA)

A student may be as intelligent as BRAHMA or even more intelligent than BRAHMA'S father, yet even such a one needs the guidance of a Guru if he wants to acquire knowledge; can a lock be opened without its key?

3. Talli tandri meeda daya leni putrundu
Puttanemi? vadu gittanemi?
Puttalona jedalu puttadā? gittadā?
Visvadabhirama vinura vema

(CHEDALU = Termites (Small antlike insects of the order ISOPTERA; DAYA = Kindness, compassion, sympathy, love)

A son who is devoid of love and kindness for his mother and father is futile;

The existence of such a son is as futile as the existence or non existence of thousands of termites in an anthill.

4. Darsanambu nandu dhara shanmatamulandu
Varnamasramamunu vadala kepudu
Tirugu chunna vādu dharalona nagnani
Visvadabhirama vinura vema

DARSANAMU = A system of philosophy (SASTRAMU); SHANMATAMU = Six system of Religion, namely

1. Vishnavamu 2. Saivamu 3. Bouddham 4. Jainamu 5. Chārvākamu 6.Kapalikamu)

(Varnamu = Caste, class, tribe, race, species)

(ASHRAMAMU = Period of life in a religious point of view. Life being divided in to four such periods viz.

1. Brahamacharyamu 2. Garhasthyamu 3. Vānaprasthamu 4. Sanyasamu)

One who is devoid of JNANA (Wisdom) will never be able to overcome the limitations of 1. DARSANAS 2. SHANMATAS and 3. VARNASRAMAS;

Only a JNANI will be able to overcome their limitations.

5. Noru palukavacchu nudi vrayagāradu
Vratakanna sākshi valavadanna
Paraga leni vrata bhangapātundecchu
Visvadabhirama vinura vema

NUDI = A word or expression, a promise; SAKSHI = A witness; VALAVADU = Vaddu = need not; do not, is not required or needed)

(PARAGU = to be, exist, remain, to fare, to shine, to be agreeable); (PALUKU = to speak, to utter, pronounce)

One may converse on any matter in an informal manner; but while writing down any matter, one should be very careful; any falsification while writing down is bound to have serious consequences and one is sure to be burdened with regret.

6. Bhakti yunnachota baramesvarun dundu
Bhakti leni chota papamundu
Bhakti kaluguvadu paramatmudagunaya
Visvadabhirama vinura vema

Where there is devotion and reverence to God, there is Paramesvara;

where there is no devotion and reverence to God, there is bound to be sin;

one who has devotion and reverence to God will eventually realize God in himself.

7. Ledu ledaninanu ledu lene ledu
Kadu kadatanna gane kadu
Todu todannanu todane todagu
Visvadabhirama vinura vema

God does not exist for a man, who refutes the existence of God; but for a devotee who sincerely believes in the existence of God, and prays to him for help and guidance, God, exists, helps and guides him.

8. Vaakku valana galugu paramagu mokshambu
Vaakku valana galugu Varalu ghanata
Vaakku valana galugu nekku disvaryambu
Visvadabhirama vinura vema

GHANATA = greatness, nobility, respectability; VARALU = To shine, to behave, to spread)

One who has mastered the art of conversation acquires respectability, wealth and MOKSHA.

14. THE WAY OF PRAPANCHA SVABHAVA (THE WAY OF THE WORLD)

1. Aalivanka vaara laatmabandhuvulire
Talli vanka vaaru taginapaati

Tandri vanka vaaru dayaaduliraya
Visvadabhirama vinura vema

(DAYAADUDU = An agnatic cousin who has a claim for a share in the property (an enemy; a foe; TAGINA = PROPER, BECOMING, FIT, SUITABLE, APPROPRIATE; BANDHUVU = a relation, relative, kinsman)
Relations of one's wife are valued as very close relations;
Relations of one's mother are treated as ordinary relations;
Relations of one's father are considered as potential enemies.

2. Aalinonchaleka yadhamata nonduchu
Venukanunti nanuta verritanumu
Chettu mudurunāni chidimina bovanā?
Visvadabhirama vinura vema

If a man fails to keep his wife under check, from the begining, such a one is sure to be disgraced in society by her rudeness and mannerless behaviour;
It is easy to bend a young plant in the direction of one's choice and the same is impossible, when it has grown in to a big tree.

3. Vutta mottamudagu nurvi tatvagnudu
Mahima joopuvadu madhyamundu
Veshadhāri yudara poshakudadha mundu
Visvadabhirama vinura vema

(TATVAGNUDU = one who knows the real nature of the human soul in its relation with the supreme spirit pervading the universe)
One who has realized the nature of the Soul is the best;
One who displays certain spiritual powers (such as producing flowers, ash, etc. out of air), belongs to the second category;
One who dons (puts on) the garb (dress) of an ascetic to fill his belly is the worst of the lot.

4. Ekkudina yaasa enumadiyi yunda
Dikkupatti narudu tiruguchundu
Kukkavanti yaasa koorchunda neeyadu
Visvadabhirama vinura vema

When a man's mind is obsessed with innumerable (countless) desires, he becomes restless and roams about from place to place, in search of fulfilment of those innumerable desires, just as a dog roams about from house to house in search of food.

5. Kaavavalayu magadu kānta nellappudu
Kaavaleni vādu chaavavalayu
Kaapulenidani kaapurambadugana
Visvadabhirama vinura vema

(KAAVALI = guard, protect, watch, custody)
A husband should protect and safeguard his wife at all times;
A husband who fails to protect and safeguard his wife at all times is deemed to be dead, although he is alive;
A wife without the protection of a husband is sure to be ruined.

6. Chaduvulandu rāja padavulandunu pādi
modavulam streela pedavulandu
Naasalu diginatti yayyalu muktulu
Visvadabhirama vinura vema

CHADUVU = reading, learning, education; PADAVI = high position, station or rank; MODAVU = a milch cow

Those who have given up the craving (hankering) for the delight that accrues from (1) Learning (2) Wealth (that results from the possession of milch cows) (3) holding (Power) high positions in a Kingdom (4) the company of beautiful women, are the really liberated ones.

7. Chanuvarellanu janulan
Janipoyina vāri punya satkadhalellan
Vinavale, ganavale manavale
Nanimishulaku delupagooda dantyamu vema

(ANIMISHULU = one who does not wink; a deity, a God; ANTYAMU = last, final, ultimate, concluding)

One should carefully listen to the life stories of the great men of the past and try of follow in their footsteps;

But one should not reveal even to Gods, one's own final conclusions.

8. Jihvalampatambu jeevanambiyundu
Jihva lampatambe jeeva posha
Jihva cheta narulu cheekaku vadiraya
Visvadabhirama vinura vema

(LAMPATAMU = trouble, bother, object of attachment or fondness; CHEEKAKU = Vexation, disgust, annoyance disturbance; JEEVANAMU = life, living)
As long as a man is alive, he has to satisfy the vagaries (whims) of his palate;
To satisfy the vagaries of the palate, he undergoes many vexations, until his end.

9. Ekkadi sutu lekkadi satu
Lekkadi bandhulu sakhulu nekkadi bhrutyul
Dokku padipovu velala
Jakkatihini nevaru raru sahajamu vema

(DOKKU = to perish, die; OKATIGA = together, in one, unitedly, conjointly)

When the appointed time of death approaches a man, none of the people around him such as 1. Sons 2. Wife, 3. Relations 4. Friends and 5. Servants, will be able to provide any succour (aid or relief) to him.

Every man has to face his death all by himself.

10. Kipu vastuvulanu kankshinchi sevimpa
Kani panu lonarchu menerugaka
Atlu poonu vāri nadhamula tanduru
Visvadabhirama vinura vema

(KIPU VASTUVULANU = Intoxicating drugs and drinks; ADHAMUDU = A despicable fellow (a mean fellow, fit to be treated with scorn)

A man who consumes intoxicating drinks or drugs, foregoes his discrimination, and is likely to commit evil deeds; The world regards such a man as a despicable fellow.

11. Dhanamecchina madamecchunu
Madamecchina durgunambu mānaka hecchun
Dhanamudigina madamudugunu
Madamudigina durgunambu mānunu vema

When a man acquires wealth, evil qualities such as 1. Egoism 2. Pride 3. and Conceit overtake his mind; when a man looses his wealth, the evil qualities also abate (lessen).

12. Bhuktini mikkili vishayā
Sktata da diruguchundu satramulandun
Bhuktini mukti labhimpadu
Bhaktini jeevunaku mukti bhadramu vema

(BHUKTI = food; BHAKTI = Devotion and reverence to God; VISHAYASAKTI = Sensuality, addiction to sensual pleasures; SATRAMU = A choultry, a lodge, a hotel)

People go to various choultries in search of free food and sensual pleasures;

Alas! These hypocrites are not aware that 'MUKTI' (Liberation) is only for those devotees who cherish reverence to God, in their hearts and not for the hypocrites who go round in search of food etc.

13. Kalimi galganemi karuna lekundina
Kalimi tagune dusta karmu lakunu
Tene goorpa neega teruvuna bovada
Visvadabhirama vinura vema

A man who has no kindness in his heart, even if he possesses great wealth, will not be able to retain it for long;

A honey bee gathers and stores a lot of honey in the beehive and while it is away gathering more honey, the honey in the beehive is sure to be stolen by a passerby.

14. Theevi ledatanchu dendambulo nenchi
Jnani yerugaleni manavundu

Dhambi kunaku longi dayyunu gadapata
Visvadabhirama vinura vema

(DHAMBICUDU = A cheat or a hypocrite or a charlatan; DAYYU = To be tired, or fatigued)

A stupid fellow will not recognise and respect a JNAANI (a wise man), if he is not showy and pompous;

A stupid fellow willingly serves a showy and pompous charlatan, and is sure to be deceived in the end by him.

15. Tana kulagotramu lakruti
Tana sampada Kalimi balimi tanakelanaya
Tana venta ravu nijamidi
Taṇa satyame todavacchu dana to vema.

KULAMU = family, class, caste; GOTRAMU = lineage)

A man's caste (family), lineage, personality wealth and power he (wielded) commanded none of these assets, are of any solace to him at the time of his dealth;

His own committment to TRUTH is the only one quality that is of any solace to him, at the time of his dealth

16. Tanadu bhratru varulu dhara neluchundagā
Tanaku nundu nandru venukāvaru
Tanadu kalugoya dammudu nedchunā?
Visvadabhirama vinura vema

(BHRATA = a brother)

One who assumes that he is powerful in a country because his own brothers are the rulers of the country is really mistaken;

When a man's leg is being amputated, does his brother weep because of pain? No.

17. Tanu valachina dā valachunu
Tanu valavaka yunna nevadu ta valavadilan
Tanadu patā topambulu
Tana mayalu panikirāvu dharalo vema

(VALACHU = love, to wish, desire; PATĀTOPAMU = pomp, show, grandeur; MAYA = deception, fraud, trick, illusion)

If one loves another sincerely, the other person also will reciprocate sincerely; the other person also will not reciprocate sincerely; if one does not love another sincerely;

One's show, pomp, cunning and deception are all futile in loving and being loved.

18. Talli dandri chāva tanayundu ta nedchu
Magadu chāva nālu vagachuchundu
Karya vasame kani kalugunā mohamu
Visvadabhirama vinura vema

(KARYAMU = work, act, duty, which ought to be done or performed; VASAMU =

subject to, influenced by; MOHAMU = love, passion, state of being enamoured)

A son grieves when his parents die;

A wife grieves when her husband dies;

Each grieves for his or her loss only and none really grieve for the departed dead.

19. Tirigi vacchuvela marali poyedi vela
Venta deru dhanamu nantaboru
Tenetaku januno dhanamendu bovuno?
Visvadabhirama vinura vema

No man brings wealth along with him, at the time of his birth;

No man takes wealth along with him, at the time of his death;

Where does he go after his death?

What happens to his wealth after his death?

20. Dehamanedi enti dina dinambunu noodchi
Aliki, pooni, metti yanuvu parachi
Kāpu vidichi povu gadapata nee jeevi
Visvadabhirama vinura vema

(PRANAMU = life, vitality; JEEVUDU = the soul, a living being)

A soul resides in a 'house' called a human body;

It keeps the 'house' clean, tidy and looks after its maintenance in every possible manner;

At last, when the appointed time approaches, the soul takes leave off the 'residence', and the residence crumbles in to dust.

21. Parama bhagavatulu prajalu santoshinchu
Nāta pāta nerchi neetuganu
Kotla koladi tecchi kootiki lekundru
Visvadabhirama vinura vema

(BHAGAVATUDU = An actor, a player, the chief actor in a Harikatha performance; KOTI = a crore, ten millions)

Entertainers (Actors, players, singers etc.) earn crores of rupees, by means of their much sought after talents;

Alas! yet most of them die in utter poverty.

22. Paapa jaati narudu parasati goruta
Chepa jihva ruchiki jikku natlu
Teepunanti eega teguvato neelgadā
Visvadabhirama vinura vema

(EEGA = a fly; TEGUVA = Daring, boldness, Venturesomeness)

An evil minded, lustful fellow, who seeks the intimacy and pleasure with the wife of another man is certain to face many dangers and may even loose his life as well; Just as

1. a fish lured by the bait on the fishing hook swallows it and looses its life; and
2. A fly lured by the sweet taste of honey, lands on honey and looses its life.

23. Mukhamu joochinanta mohambu ghanamounu
Disa molanu gananga deeru naddi
Koodina valapella kustarimpagarāde
Visvadabhirama vinura vema

(DISAMOLA = nakedness, nudity; KUSTARINCHU = to pacify, to adjust)

The beautiful face of a woman attracts a man
But when he sees her naked, attraction gives way to repulsion.

24. Raati basavani gani rangugā mrokkuchu
Roodhi basava gaala ruddu chundru
Basava bhaktulella paapulu tala poya
Visvadabhirama vinura vema

(BASAVANA = the bull on which Siva rides; RANGUGA = finely, nicely, beautifully, elegantly gallantly; ROODHI = True, sure, certain)

People worship Basavanna's sculptured out of stone;
Alas! these hypocrites treat 'live' Basavannas very cruelly;
These 'Basava' worshippers are the worst sinners.

25. Lavanamenta? daani laabhambu gananenta?
Koddi danuchu nenna goodunayya?
Bhogametiki? nupabhogambe lekkagu
Visvadabhirama vinura vema

(BHOGAMU = Enjoyment, pleasure, wealth; UPABHOGAMU = use; LAVANAMU = common salt)

Common salt is a very useful and essential item in cooking, although its cost is little;
Common salt's utility (usefulness) outweighs its cost.

26. Lobha mohamulanu prabhava mulu tappu
Talachina panulella tappi Chanunu
Tanokati dalachina divamondagu chundu
Visvadabhirama vinura vema

(PRABHAVAMU = power, authority, supremacy; LOBHAMU = Avarice, greed; MOHAMU = Delusion, infatuation)

Supremacy eludes a man whose mind is overwhelmed by greed and undue attachment to sensual pleasures;

Whatever work such a man plans to carry out is sure to fail;

What such a man proposes, God disposes.

27. Viduvavaluyu nooru visrānti gakunna
Viduvavalayu naali vidham chedina

Viduvavalayu raaju vitarani gaakunna
Visvadabhirama vinura vema

(VISRĀNTI = rest, repose; VIDHAMU = manner, way, mode; VITARANI = Charitable, liberal, or bountiful person)

One should leave a village if it is not possible to lead a peaceful life in it;
One should leave a wife if her conduct is evil;
One should leave the service of a King if he is not generous.

28. Vitta heenamina velalandunu talli
Tanayu lalu suhrudu lanedi vāra
lella satrulagudu rendina nijamidi
Visvadabhirama vinura vema

(SUHRUDUDU = a friend or a well wisher)

When a man is poverty-stricken, his own mother, sons, wife and friends, change in their attitude towards him, and alas! they become hostile.

29. Venna chetabatti vivarambu teliyaka
Ghrutamu korunatti yatani bhangi
Tānu divamayyu divambu dalachunu
Visvadabhirama vinura vema

(GHRUTAMU = ghee)

Man searches for God everywhere except in his own self; Just as a man who searches for butter everywhere, (not aware) although he has it in his own hands.

30. Verrivānikina veshadharikinina
Rogikina parama yogikina
Streela joochi napudu chittamu ranjillu
Visvadabhirama vinura vema

A beautiful woman attracts and fascinates all types of men including 1. Lunatics 2. Actors and players 3. Sick fellows and 4. even great ascetics.

31. Veshadhāri nepudu visvasimpagarādu
Vesha doshamu loka vidhame yagunu
Rattu kade munupu ravanu veshambu
Visvadabhirama vinura vema

(VESHADHARI = an actor, a man in disguise, an imposter, a pretender; RATTU = Divulging a secret, exposure, scandal)

A man who puts on different guises to hoodwink the public should never be trusted; as guise and deceit go together;

In the epic Ramayana, Ravana kidnapped Sita, approaching her in the guise of an ascetic.

32. Vyadhi nerugaleni vidya madelarā?
Kodava teliyaleni korkulela?

Manasu teliya leni marmagnu letiki?
Visvadabhirama vinura vema

(MARMAGNUDU = one who knows a secret or secrets one who has a deep insight in to any thing or any subject)

A physician who cannot diagnose a disease,

A man who can not restrain and moderate his desires and needs, and a 'MARMAGNA', who can not divine (foretell) what is in the mind of another, are all futile.

33. Vratamu lenniyina vatti chikkulekani
Atma chikku gava nalivikadu
Atma chiku bapunatade po ghana yogi
Visvadabhirama vinura vema

(VRATAMU = a religious vow, religious observance; CHIKKU = entangled, intricate, complicate; CHIKKU DEEYU = to disentangle, unravel)

Devotees perform 'VRATAS' to acquire spiritual merit and enlightenment, yet they do not succeed, because to realize the nature of one's Soul is not an easy task;

Only a great yogi is capable of realizing the nature of ones Soul.

34. Santāme janulanu jayamu nondinchunu
Sāntamunane gurini jāda teliyu
Sānta bhāva mahima jarchimpalemaya
Visvadabhirama vinura vema

(SANTAMU = calmness, tranquillity, patience, endurance; JADA = A sign, trace, track, hint, intimation)

Tranquillity and endurance are necessary for the successful completion of any task;

Tranquillity and endurance are essential to obtain spiritual enlightenment from a Guru

To extol (praise) the efficacy of tranquillity and endurance is almost impossible.

35. Silanu pratima jesi cheekatilo betti
Mrokka valavadikanu moodhulara
Vullamandu brahma munduta deliyudee
Visvadabhirama vinura vema

(VULLAMU = the heart, mind; PRATIMA = an image, a figure, idol) Men install idols of Gods sculptured in stone in a dark room of a temple (i.e. = SANCTUM SANCTORUM), and worship them;

Alas! these fools are not aware that stone idols are only stone idols and they should strive to realize 'BRAHMA' who is ever present in their own hearts.

36. Silala joochi narulu sivudani bhavintru
Silalu silale kani sivudu kādu

Tanaduloni sivuni danela teliyado
Visvadabhirama vinura vema
Men mistake stone idols for 'Siva';

A stone idol is only a stone idol and there is no "SIVA" in any of them; why can not they realize the 'SIVA' is ever present in their hearts only.

37. Sakala sastramulanu jadiviyu vrasiyu
Teliya galaru chāvu teliyaleru
Chavu deliyaleni chaduvula velarā?
Visvadabhirama vinura vema

Men study and master various branches of knowledge (religion, science, law etc.), by means of reading and writing;

Yet none of them known anything about death;

All their studies are futile, as none of them throw any light on Death.

38. Satyavantula yeda sarasamadagarādu
Peda varitoda benagarādu
Kalimi kalugu vari galiyane radayā
Visvadabhirama vinura vema

(SARASAMU = joking, jesting, fun; PENAGU = fight, to wrangle, dispute; KALIYU = to meet, unite with, join)

Never make fun of a man committed to truth;

Do not quarrel or fight with a poor man;

Never seek the friendship of a man of wealth.

39. Sandramunaku jooda sari yediyunu ledu
Atti jaladhi neera manuvugādu
Anuvugāni neere yadi yemicheyunu?
Visvadabhirama vinura vema

A sea contains limitless quantity of water, which is brackish (Salty) and unsuitable for drinking purposes;

Alas! such limitless quantity of sea water is futile to slake (satisfy, quench) the thirst of even a single man

(Just like the brackish water of a sea, the wealth of a miser is of no use to others)

40. Satini joochi choochi soukhyambu gorunu
Gatini kānaledu karma jeevi
Gatulu satulavalana ganangalerayā
Visvadabhirama vinura vema

(GATI = Fate, lot, destiny; KARMA BANDHAMU = The bond of action that ties a human soul down to the cycle of births and deaths; JEEVI = a living being)

A man assumes that he will be able to attain (obtain) all the happiness through the association with a woman;

Alas! he is not aware, that he will never be able to realize his final destiny, through the association with a woman.

41. Sādhujanula chelimi chalimpagā rādu
Prakruti vidakayunna baramu ledu
Pindegosi chooda beejambu kalugunā?
Visvadabhirama vinura vema

(PRAKRUTI = Nature, character, constitution; PARAMU = Succeeding, following, future, highest, greatest, best, supreme, pre-eminent)

One should never give up the friendship of a SAJJANA;

Unless one renounces the nature, one will never be able to attain the highest goal;

To cut open an unripe fruit (the fruit just formed after the flower (PINDE) and to look for ripe seeds is futile, (as ripe seeds are to be found in a ripe fruit only)

42. Alpudina vani kadhika bhagyamu kalga
Dodda vāri ditti tolaga drolu
Alpa jati vara ladhikula neru gunā?
Visvadabhirama vinura vema

(DODDA = great, fine, excellent)

If an inferior man acquires great wealth and power, such a one is sure to revile and dismiss all the superior men around him;

How can an inferior man recognise the excellence of a superior man?

15. THE WAY OF SVABHAVA (THE WAY OF HUMAN NATURE)

1. Aadu dāni bonku goda pettina yatlu
Purusha varuni bonku poori tadaka
Streela nerpu magala jeekāku parachurā
Visvadabhirama vinura vema

(BONKU = A lie, falsehood; Poori = Straw, thatch; TADAKA = A screen made of bamboos)

When a woman tells a lie, it is very difficult to see through it; A woman's lie can be compared to a wall (i.e.) it is strong, solid and secure where as the falsehood of a man is easy to see through; it can be compared to a screen made of bamboos (i.e.) it is weak, thin and full of gaps;

The skill of a woman in telling lies, lands a man in many difficulties.

2. Aali doli venta nadhamudi tā venta
nela povutella neddetanamu
Chetu muduranicchi chidimina bovunā?
Visvadabhirama vinura vema

(TOLINCHU = to cause to be driven, to cause to be sent; NELAKONU = to become firm, to stay, to be, stand; EDDETANAMU = stupidity)

If a man given undue freedom to his wife out of stupidity, she is sure not only to be ruined but also to ruin him in the end;

A tender plant can be easily plucked out, where as it is impossible to pull out a big tree.

3. Kika putti cherichegā rāmu pattambu
Seeta putti lanka cherichagade
Kouravulanu jeriche gada droupadiyu gooda
Visvadabhirama vinura vema

Kikeyi prevailed upon King Dasaradha to cancel the coronation ceremony of Sri Rama; Sita was the main cause that led to the destruction of Lanka; (In the epic Ramayana)

Droupadi was the main cause that led to the death of Kouravas (In the epic Mahabharata)

4. Jagadamunaku bodu jarini yeppudu
Maya jesi purushu mamata bettu
Kāni mātaladu gayyali satatamu
Visvadabhirama vinura vema

(JARINI = an adulteress; GAYALI = a shrew, termagant a woman of violent temper)

An immoral woman, always avoids quarrels with a man. She feigns (pretends) affection for him and makes use of duplicity (cheating), to manipulate him; whereas a shrew (termagant) always nags and quarrels with her husband.

5. Naatipine prema nanatikini rota
Jyoti pine prema choodaganu
Matru prema yokate maryada dalchunu
Visvadabhirama Vinura Vema

(JYOTI = light, lustre, brightness, luminary (an object that sheds natural light); MARYADA = the bounds of morality or propriety, respect, honour)

The love for a woman decreases day by day and ends in repulsion;

The affection shown towards a mother acquires respect and honour day by day;

The ardent desire to realize the light in ones own soul (ATMAJYOTI) is the best.

6. Siggu gala datandru srusti lopalivaru
Verri vemana gani veragupadiri
Tanaku galugu siggu diva merungadā?
Visvadabhirama vinura vema

(VERAGUPADU = fear, terror, surprise; VERRI = mad, insane, crazy; SRUSTI = Creation, the world, the universe, nature)

People think that they are full of modesty as they cover their nakedness with clothes;

They are surprised to see VEMANA, who wears no clothes (DIGAMBARA) and call him as (VERRI VEMANA)

Does not the 'CREATOR' know what they have underneath their clothes?

(NOTE : Most of the portaits of YOGI-VEMANA available today depict him as a "DIGAMBARA";

Most probably YOGI VEMANA discarded all his clothes, when he attained the zenith of SELF REALIZATION and in the last days of his earthly sojourn)

7. Svā nubhooti leka sastra vasanalache
Samsayambuvidadu sādhakunaku
Chitradeepamunanu cheekati ponatlu
Visvadabhirama vinura vema

(SVĀNUBHOOTI = direct or personal experience; SASTRAMU = science, law, a sacred precept, any sacred book; VASANA = association, recollection, knowledge derived from memory; SAMSAYAMU = Doubt, uncertainty, irresolution, hesitation, scruple, misgiving, suspicion)

Study of sastras, to yield the best possible results should be combined with direct or personal experience otherwise a student will never be able to overcome hesitation and doubts; (in making use of knowledge he has acquired)

Just as the picture of lamp in a painting is futile in dispelling darkness around it.

8. Alluni kagu mrutiki nātma chintinchunu
Tanayu mrutiki tānu talladillu
Punya purushu mrutiyu bhoomiki mrutiyagu
Visvadabhirama vinura vema

One suffers grief at the death of one's Son-in-law;
One grieves bitterly at the death of one's son;
The death of a saint is mourned by all.

9. Ikamatya mokkatāvasyakam bepdu
Dāni balimi nentayina goodu
Gaddi venta betti kattarā yenungu
Visvadabhirama vinura vema

(IKAMATYAMU = unanimity, agreement, harmony; VENTI = a twist, or rope of straw)

Unity is necessary for the successful completion of any task;
Unity and invincibility go together;
A rope made up of dried grass blades, by twisting them, is used to tie up even a huge elephant.

10. Iduvrella balimi hastambu panicheyu
Nandokatiyu veeda bondika chedu
Sveeyu dokadu vidina jedu gadā panibalmi
Visvadabhirama vinura vema

A hand with five fingers can do its tasks very well yet, the loss of even one finger tells upon the efficiency of the hand;

Similarly even if one trusted member of a team, leaves it, the efficiency of the team is bound to suffer.

11. Inavāralanchu naptu latanchunu
Bandugulanu namma pādi gadu
Tanaku ninavādu tānokade yagu
Visvadabhirama Vinura Vema

(Inavaru = relations and friends; Padi = Justice, equity, propriety)

One should not repose trust blindly in one's relations, friends and associates;

One should repose trust on one's own self only.

12. Kalla nijamu rendu Karakantu derugunu
Neeru palla merugu nijamugānu
Tanayani janmambu talli tanerugunu
Visvadabhirama vinura vema

(KARAKANTUDU = Siva)

(an EPITHET of Siva)

Siva (GOD) only knows the truth and falsehood;

water always seeks the lowest level;

A mother only knows the real father of her son

13. Chikkiyanna vela simhambuninanu
Bakka kukkayina badha seyu
Balimi leni vela pantamul chellavu
Visvadabhirama vinura vema

(BAKKAR = lean or thin; BADHA PETTU = annoy, vex, trouble, torment; PANTAMU = obstinancy, stubborness, rivalry)

A lion which has grown old and weak, is teased and tormented even by a lean dog;

When one's strength is on the wane (Decline, decrease) one has to lie low, and give up obstinancy (unreasonable firmness).

14. Jhushamu neeru vādala jacchute siddhamu
Neeta nunde neni nikki padunu
Anda tolagu nedala nandarapani yatle
Visvadabhirama vinura vema

(JHUSHAMU = FISH; ANDA = Support, assistance, protection, patronage)

A fish in the water swims freely and at times even leaps up for short distances in water; yet when it is taken out of water, alas! the fish is sure to die;

Similarly a man struts about if he has patronage and protection, and when these are withdrawn he becomes a non entity (a person of little importance)

15. Deekonanga dagadu denda merungaka
Yaduga vacchi konta yanina vaani
Cheppunanta viniyu meppugā baluku
Visvadabhirama vinura vema

(DEEKONU = oppose attack; DENDAMU = the heart, the mind, wish, intention; MEPPINCHU = to conciliate, to please, to satisfy obtain or gain the approval, approbation, or admiration of)

If any one approaches you to talk about any matter, it is better to listen to the end, and then give a reply in a gentle and conciliatory manner;

To oppose and quarrel with any one is not a wise move.

16. Tappu paluku paliki tātota chesina
Koodiyunna lakshmi krungipovu
Noti kunda neellu nonaragā niluchunā?
Visvadabhirama vinura vema

(TAPPU = an error, mistake, incorrect, faulty, false, wrong; TATOTU = Deceit, knavery, deceitful, knavish)

The wealth of a man who tells lies and deceives others, is sure to be lost sooner or later;

Just as water leaks away from a leaky pot sooner or later.

17. Taruni punyavatiga varuni battiyi yagu
Papini yagu magani prapu valana
Bharta vartanambe padatula yandundu
Visvadabhirama vinura vema

(TARUNI = A young woman; VARUDU = A husband; PAPI = a sinner)

Husband's good and bad traits are to be found in the wife also because of example and association;

If the husband is a good one, wife also will be a good one;

If the husband is a sinner, wife also will be a sinner.

18. Nikkamina manchi neela mokkati chalu
Taluku beluku ralu lattedela
Chaduva padya maraya jalada yokkati
Visvadabhirama Vinura Vema

(NEELAMU = A dark blue semi precious stone; a sapphire; NIKKAMU = True, real, certain; TALUKU = glitter; BELAKU = to shine, gleam, glitter)

to possess one valuable and genuine sapphire is better than to possess many, glittering and worthless pebbles;

To read one worthy poem is better than to read many worthless poems.

19. Nijamu lādu vani nindinchu jagamella
Nijamu balkarādu neechula kada
Nija mahatmu gooda nijamāda valayurā
Visvadabhirama vinura vema

(NIJAMU = Truth, reality, fact; NINDINCHU = to blame, censure, reproach, to accuse; JAGAMU = people, mankind, the world; NEECHUDU = a low, base, mean or vile person; MAHATMUDU = a great man, a man worthy of honour or reverence)

People blame a man who reveals the TRUTH about any matter;

One should not reveal the truth about any matter to a Vile (or mean) person;

However, one should utter TRUTH only with a MAHATMA. (a great man)

20. Pandi pilla leenu padunidu nokatini
Kunjaramba deenu godama nokati
Vuttama purushudatu lokkadu chaladā?
Visvadabhirama vinura vema

(KUNJARAMU = An elephant; PANDI = a pig or a hog; EENU = bring forth, bear, to produce)

A pig gives birth to 15 or 16 piglets, whereas an elephant gives birth to one baby elephant only;

A (single) great man is to be preferred to many worthless fellows.

21. Pālapakshi sakuna phalamicchu nanduru
Palapakshi kemi phalamu teliyu?
Tanadu melu keellu tanatoda nundagā
Visvadabhirama vinura vema

(PALE PITTA = A species of Jay (Bird) a blue and green feathered bird; SAKUNAMU = an omen determined by the flight or cry of a bird, any omen, augury, prognostic)

People consider it a good omen if by chance they see a Palapitta (A blue and green feathered bird);

Alas! a bird is a bird only and what does it know about the good or bad luck of a man?

The cause of a man's good or bad luck is in him only.

22. Anna madhikamina naraya mrutyuvu nijam
banna mantakunna nātma nocchu
Champa bempa buvva chālada veyela?
Visvadabhirama vinura vema

(Buvva = food, rice; NOCCHU = to ache, pain, smart)

Gluttony (excessive liking for food) will surely kill a man sooner or later; Similarly
Fasting (abstain from taking food) will surely kill a man sooner or later;
To sustain the life or to put an end to it depend upon the intake of food or abstaining from it respectively.

23. Bhoomi peru Valla punya teerdhamu laye
Velaya ralla valla velpulaye
Neella peru Valla nikhila teerdhamulaye
Visvadabhirama Vinura Vema

(PUNYATEERDHAMU = Holy water of a river, tank or lake; NIKHILAMU = all, entire, whole, complete; VELUPU = a Good or Goddess; VELAYU = to be renowned, to be known.)

Various pilgrimage centres are renowned because of the locations and the names of the places;
Various idols of Gods and Goddesses sculptured out of rocks are worshipped in those centres;
Various rivers are renowned as holy waters and named after the rivers.

24. Medipandu chooda melimi yundunu
Potta vicchi chooda burugu lundu
Piriki vani madini binka meelagurā
Visvadabhirama vinura vema

(MEDIPANDU = Fig fruit - pulpy fruit of a fig tree
(FICUS CARICA) a soft pear shaped fruit with many seeds, eaten fresh or dried)
BINKAMU = pride, arrogance, haughtiness)

A ripe fruit of a fig tree is very attractive to look at and when it is crushed open, the inside of the fruit is found to be full of wriggling worms;
A coward may pretend to be bold, but in a crisis his cowardice comes out to the fore (front)

25. Rajjulada rādu rana bhoomi lopala
Bujjagimparādu bonku vani
Nojja toda vadu lonaranga manarā
Visvadabhirama vinura vema

(RAJJU = useless talk; BUJJAGINCHU = to coax, flatter lull, soothe; OJJA = a teacher, tutor, master, instructor, a priest)

One should not indulge in frivolous talk in a war field;
One should not oblige a liar;
One should never argue with ones GURU.

26. Laxmi yelinatti lankādhipati puri
Pilla koti fouju kolla bette
Kalisi vacchu vela ghanuloudu ralpulu
Visvadabhirama vinura vema

(FOUJU = an army, force, troops; KOLLA KOTTU = to plunder pillage; VELA = time, day)

Lanka, fabulously rich capital of Ravana was plundered by a horde of monkeys (From the Epic Ramayana) when the time is ripe, even a vile fellow will assume a superior (greater) position, and will be able to torment even a more powerful man than himself.

27. Vavi vartanalunu varusalu maryāda
Tappi nadache neni tagulu keedu
Vadala dapudu taku vandura dappadu
Visvadabhirama vinura vema

(VAVI = relation, relationship; VARTANA = conduct, behaviour; VARUSA = relation, relationship; MARYADA = limits or the bounds of propriety or morality; VANDU, VANDURU = to grieve, to sorrow, to be afflicted)

Those who disobey social regulations and the bounds of propriety and morality, are certain to face consequences of such evil conduct, and will experience grief sooner or later.

28. Chatramunna dakina chaya yerpadi yundu
Sastra meruga dagina jnana modavu
Abbayunna vani kanda yunnattule
Visvadabhirama vinura vema

(CHATRAMU = An umbrella, as an ensign of royalty; TAGINA = proper, suitable, becoming, fit, appropriate)

One who has an umbrella is sure of a shade from the sun;

One who has studied 'SASTRAS', acquires knowledge

As long as one's father is alive, a son is sure of support from his father.

29. Parula mosapucchi dhara dhana marjinchi
Kadupu nimpukonuta kanipaddu
Runamu cheyu manujudekkuva kekkunā?
Visvadabhirama vinura vema

(MOSA PUCCHU = to deceive, cheat; KANI = Bad, impure, vile improper, wrong, objectionable, wicked; PADDU = an item, an entry in an account, a vow, or promise; EKKUVA = Superiority, greatness, eminence; Runamu = debt, obligation; RUNAGRASTUDU = one who is indebted, or involved in debt)

To earn money by cheating and deception is an evil,
to incur debts is another evil.

30. Nerpu galugu vadu neratanamu galādu
Vidyacheta virra veeguvadu
Pasidi galugu vaari bānisa kodukulu
Visvadabhirama vinura vema

(NERPU = skill, dexterity; NERATANAMU = Respectability)

One who is renowned for his skill in a job and one who is renowned for his

respectability in society and one who is renowned for his extra ordinary learning all have to bow down to a man of wealth.
Alas! all the above, are far more servile to a man of wealth than even the son of a slave.

31. Mataladagalugu marmamu lerigina
Pinna peddatanamu lennavaladu
Pinna cheti divve peddagā velugadā?
Visvadabhirama vinura vema

(MATALADU = to speak, to converse, discourse, confer; MARMAMU = a secret, a clue, anything hidden a weak or vulnerable part; PINNA = young, small, little; PEDDA = older, elder, senior; DIVVE = a light, a lamp)
The suggestion of a young man, if he is wise and well-versed in the art of conversation should be heeded;
His suggestion should not be brushed aside on the grounds of his youth and inexperience.
Does not a lamp in the hands of an young man shine with great brightness?

32. Malakanniyalanu manchiroopambunna
Muttene trisanku pattinadu
Kanipanulu cheya ghanulasa padudurā?
Visvadabhirama vinura vema

(ROOPAMU = Beauty; KANNIYA = Virgin, maiden; TRISANKU PATTI = Harischandra; MALA = out caste; GHANUDU = A great man, an important personage, a man of rank or high station)
Sage Visvamitra compelled King Harischandra to marry two beautiful MATANGA KANYAS (beautiful maidens belonging to an out caste group);
King Harischandra, refused to marry them, inspite of coercion from sage Visvamitra;
Great men always decline to do forbidden things (deeds)

33. Vitudu dāgu chesi vidichipettina yadi
Peda penimitigani priyamucheyu
Kuppaloni cheppu gukka tinnatlayā
Visvadabhirama vinura vema

(VITUDU = a lover, paramour; DAGU = a stain, spot, blot, mark; PENIMITI = husband; KUPPA = rubbish heap; CHEPPU = a shoe, slipper)
A woman used (seduced) and rejected by her lover, seeks her 'poor' husband and feigns (pretends) a lot of affection for him;
Her behaviour is just like that of a dog which picks up an old leather shoe from a rubbish heap and nibbles it.

34. Vesha bhasa linka gashaya vastramul
Bodi nettu loppa borayu chundru
Talalu bodulina dalapulu bodula?
Visvadabhirama vinura vema

(VESHAMU = dress, attire, costume, habit, garb; BHASA = a language, a dialect; KASHAYAMU = A reddish cloth, an ascetic's dress; BODI = bold, wholly shaven; OCHRE COLOUR = A pale brownish yellow colour)

Many hypocrites wear the ochre coloured dress of an ascetic and they move about with clean shaven heads; Their speech, dress and clean shaven heads are only a guise to hoodwink others;
Their heads may be clean shaven, alas! their minds are not as clean as their clean shaven heads.

35. Satula gavayutayunu sutula badasedamani
Vetala boduta yento verritanamu
Nelanunna rayi nettikettina yatlu
Visvadabhirama vinura vema

(SATI = a wife; SUTUDU = a son; KAVIYU = to approach; BANDA = a rock, a slab of stone; VETA = pain, distress, affliction; VERRI = madness insanity, lunacy)
A man marries a woman, begets sons by her and undergoes any number of afflictions to ensure their welfare;
Alas! he is like a mad man who lifts up a rock on to his head, and hopes to be happy.

16. PHALA SRUTI

(PHALAMU = Result, fruit, profit, benefit
SRUTI = Hearing, intelligence, revelation)
Eha parambulakunu nidi sadhanambani
Vrasi chadivi vinna vVarikella
Mangalambu lonaru mahilona nijamidi
Visvadabhirama vinura vema.
(EHAMU = the present world, this life
PARAMU = subsequent, succeeding, following, future
MANAGALAMU = prosperity, welfare, felicity, success)
Those who write, read and listen to the poems of Yogi Vemana will attain peace and prosperity here and in the hereafter also.

Sources

1. Verses of Vemana by C.P. Brown, 1829.
2. Sages and Saints of India by Manu Bhagat, 1982.
3. Vemana Padya Ratnakaramu by B. Venkata Ramanaiah, 1976.
4. Loka Kavi Vemana Yogi by Kalaprapoorna M. Kodanda Rami Reddy, 1983.
5. Vemana Bhavana by S. Gangappa, 1986.

27

CHĀRU CHARYA (EXEMPLARY CONDUCT)

Poet Kshemendra hailed from *KASHMIR*, and probably lived in *the second half of 11th century*, during the *reign of KING ANANTADEVA of KASHMIR (A.D. 1028-1063)* Historians are of the opinion, that Poet Kshemendra wrote his works *in SANSKRIT*, probably between *A.D. 1025-1066.*
Nanniah Bhattu, *King Bhoja*, and *Mammatacharya* (the well known Rhetorician) were some of the contemporaries of *Poet Kshemendra.*

CHĀRU CHARYA

Chāru Charya is a collection of *100 SANSKRIT SLOKAS* composed by *Poet Kshemendra.* The first half of each SLOKA enunciates a moral principle or a DHARMA, and the second half of each sloka gives an example or an episode to illustrate the moral principle of Dhrama stated in the first half of each sloka.
Poet Kshemendra drew his examples for his slokas mostly from 1. *MAHABHARATA* 2. *RAMAYANA,* 3. *BHRUHADKADHA MANJARI* and 4. *BODHISATVA-VADANA KALPALATA.*
KSHEMENDRA perhaps inspired latter day poets to write 'SATAKAS' in this fashion, examples are :
1. *Bhaskara Satakamu* (in Telugu)
2. *Jagannayaka Satakamu etc.*
Kshemendras '*CHĀRU CHARYA*' and its SLOKAS are renowned for their *brevity elegance* and *apt illustrations from the various epics.*

1. *Greatness of SADĀCHARA* (Fair and just conduct)

   "SREE LĀBHA SULABHAHA SATYASAKTAHA SVARGĀ PAVARGADAHA JAYATĀT TRIJAGAT POOJYAHA SADACHARA EVĀCHU TAHA"

   Sadachara leads the way to prosperity;

   Sadachara is based on commitment to TRUTH; Sadachara leads the way not only to heaven but also to liberation (MOKSHA)

Sadachara is equal to ACHUTA (OR VISHNU) in glory and greatness.

2. ***One should get up from sleep before the rising of the Sun (i.e.) at BRAHMA MUHOORTAM***

"BRAHME MUHOORTE PURUSHASTYA JENNIDRAMA TANDRITAHA PRATAHA PRABUDDAM KAMALAH SRAYE SREERGUNASRAYA"

(Muhoortam: 48 minutes; 30 Muhoortams = 24 Hours (1 Day)
(Brahmamuhoortam = 96 minutes prior to sun rise (i.e.) 4:30 A.M.)
Every day one should get up from sleep before the rising of the sun (at Brahmamuhoortam = 4:30) A lotus which blossoms early in the dawn is renowned for its beauty;
LAXMI (wealth and prosperity) seeks out a man who gets up before the rising of Sun.

3. ***One should bathe every day to keep the body free from impurities***

"PUNYA POOTA SAREERAHA SYAT SATATAM SNANA NIRMALAHA TATYAJA VRUTAHA SNANAT PAPAM VRUTẠ VADHARJITAM

One should bathe everyday to keep the body free from impurities
One should perform PUNYAKARYAS (Deeds of merit) everyday;
One upon a time *INDRA* killed a *RAKSHASA* name '*VRUTA*'. INDRA was able to get rid of the sin that accrued to him because of killing the rakshasa 'VRUTA', by bathing in various holy rivers.

4. ***One should commence a task only after worshipping 'MAHESVARA'***

"NA KURVEETA KRIYAM KANCHIDANA BHYARCHYA MAHESVARAM EESARCHANARATAM SVETAM NABHOONNETUM YAMAHA KSHAMAHA"
One should commence a task only after worshipping 'MAHESVARA'.
Even '*YAMA*', King of Death, was not able to snatch away the life of *SVETAMUNI*, as the latter was worshipping 'MAHESVARA', at that time.

5. ***"SHRADDHA" ceremony should be performed as dictated by 'SASTRAS' only.***

(SHRADDHA CEREMONY = A funeral rite or ceremony performed at various fixed period in honour of departed spirits or ancestors)

"SRADDHAM SRADDHANVITAM KURYA SASTROKTENIVA VARTMANA

BHUVI PINDAM DADOU VIDVAN BHEESHAMAHA PANOU NA SANTANOHA"

Bheesma, while he was performing the 'SHRADDHA' ceremony in the honour of his departed father "*King Santana*", on the banks of River Ganga, as he was about to drop the PINDAS (PINDAMU: Ball of meal, or rice mixed up with milk, curds etc., dropped on to the ground, while reciting the names of the departed dead), BHEESMA saw the "hand" of late King *Santana*. *Bheesma* was in a dilemma either to drop the

'PINDAS' on to the ground, as dictated by the Sastras, or to drop them into the hand of late king *Santana*, which did materialize in a magical manner. Finally and wisely *Bheesma* decided to follow the dictates of the Sastras only and dropped the 'PINDAS' on to the ground only.

(*A SASTRA* = The main constituents of any SASTRA are (1) *JNANA* (Knowledge) and (2) *VIVEKA* (Discrimination) whenever there is a diiemma as to one's course of action, one should follow the SASTRAS only, as they are untainted by *MOHA* (Delusion) and *EERSHYA* (Jealousy). As *MOHA* and *EERSHYA* might in fluence the interpretation of a SASTRA even by (1) *A GURU* (2) *one's own parents* (3) *or even by one's own SELF*)

6. ***One should not sleep with ones head pointing towards the NORTHERN or the WESTERN directions***

"NOTTARASYAM PRATEECHYAM VĀ KURVEETA SAYANE SIRAHA
SAYYA VIP ARYAYAD GARBHO DITEHA SA KRENA PATITAHA"

One should not sleep with one's head pointing towards the Northern or the Western directions;

Once upon a time *DITI*, the wife of *KASYAPA*, and the mother of *RAKSHASAS*, obtained a boon from her husband *KASYAPA*, to bear a child by him, who when he grew up, would be capable of destroying *INDRA*.

One day when *DITI* was found inadvertently sleeping with her head pointing towards a forbidden direction, *INDRA* destroyed her foetus named '*DITYA*', with his *VAJRAYUDHAMU*.

7. ***One should eat only after feeding the hungry and needy.***

"ARTHI BHUKTAVASISTAM YAT TADASNEE YANMAHASAYAHA
SVETORTHI RAHITAM BHUKTVA NIJA MAMSASANO BHAVAT"

One should eat only after feeding the hungry and needy;

Once upon a time *King SVETA* performed TAPAS for *three thousand years*, and during the period of his TAPAS, *King Sveta never cared to feed others except himself.* By the spiritual merit so acquired, *King Sveta* gained entry into *BRAHMALOKA*. However, even in *BRAHMALOKA*, *King Sveta* had to suffer from pangs of hunger, for the lapse he committed during his TAPAS (i.e.) not feeding the hungry and needy. *King Sveta was forced to eat his own flesh to appease the pangs of hunger.*

8. ***One should perform JAPA, HOMA and DEVATARCHANA, only after cleaning and thoroughly washing one's feet***

"JAPA HOMARCHANAM KURYAT SUDHOUTA CHARANAHA SUCHIHE
PADA SOUCHA VIHEENAM HE PRAVIVESA NALAM KALIHE"

(1) *Japa* = Repeating prayers in an undertone

(2) *Homa* = An oblation to the Gods consisting in the casting of clarified butter etc.,

accompanied with prayers and invocations

(3) Devatarchana = Ceremonial worship of DEVATAS (or Gods)

(4) *Sandhya Varchu* = To sip water as a religious rite at *morning or evening twilight.* One should perform JAPA, HOMA and DEVATARCHANA only after cleaning and thoroughly washing one's feet; once upon a time *King Nala* performed "SANDHYA VARCHU" ceremony, inadvertently without cleaning and washing thoroughly his feet.

'*KALI*' (the tutelary genius of the *KALI AGE*, being all evil personified), who was waiting for such an opportunity, entered the body of King Nala and from that moment, *King Nala's downfall began.*

9. ***One should not roam about carelessly in the dark of a night as it might endanger one's life***;

"NA SANCHARANA SEELAHA SYANNISI NISSANKA MANASAAHA
MANDAVYAHA SOOLALEENO BHOODA CHOURAS CHOURASANKAYA"

One should not roam about carelessly in the dark of a night as it might endanger one's life;

Once upon a time *MAHARSHI MANDAVYA*, was roaming around in the dark of a night, near the outskirts of a city in a state of spiritual estacy. Soldiers on the night watch of the city mistook him for a robber and they took him in to custody. On the orders of an officer of guards MAHARSHI MANDAVYA was impaled on a sharp spike (This mode of punishment was also termed KORATA). *Later the soldiers came to know that their prisoner was a MAHARSHI MANDAVYA and not a robber.*

10. 1. ***One should not covet (desire) another's wife***;
 2. ***One should not blindly trust even one's wife***

"NA KURYAT PARADARECCHAM VISVASAM STREESHU VARJAYET
HATO DASASYAHA SETARDHE HATAHA PATNYA VIDOORADHAHA"

1. *Ravana* coveted and kidnapped *Sita*, the wife of *Sree Rama*, and this event eventually led to a war between *Sree Rama* and *Ravana* and finally Ravana was killed by *Sree Rama*.
2. *Vidooradha* was deeply in love with his wife and trusted her implicitly; Alas! Vidooradha was killed by his wife only, with a knief which she had hidden in her Chignon (Hair on the head tied into a tuft and worn on the back of head)

(*SOURCE: VATSAYANA's KAMASUTRAS*)

11. 1. ***To drink intoxicating liquors is forbidden***;
 2. ***Intoxication leads to quarrels, fights and even to death.***

"NA MADYAVYASANEE KSHEEBAHA KURYAD VETALA CHESTITAM
VRUSHNAYO HE YAYUHU KSHEEBAS TRUNA PRAHARANAHA KSHAYAM"

1. To drink intoxicating liquors is forbidden;
2. Intoxication leads to quarrels, fights and even to death.

Once upon a time, there was a tribe among *YADAVAS* (*Relations of SRI KRISHNA*) named "*VRUSTI GANAMU*" Under the influence of intoxicating liquors, *Vrusti Ganamu*, quarrelled among themselves, fought with each other using "*TUNGA* grass blades" as weapons (Botanical name this grass is *CYPERUS ROTUNDUS*) and all were destroyed in the end.

12. 1. ***Jealousy leads to quarrels;***
    2. ***Forbearance leads to prosperity.***

"EERSHYA KALAHAMOOLAM SYAAT KSHAMA MOOLAMHE SAMPADAM
EERSHYA DOSHAD VIPRASAPAMA VAPA JANAMEJAYA HA"

1. Jealousy leads to quarrels;
2. Forbearance leads to prosperity.

Emperor Janamejaya (a descendant of Pandavas) was cursed by a BRAHMANA, because of his inordinate jealousy;
Emperor Janamejaya and *his capital Hastinapuri* were destroyed by hordes of locusts and *inundated* with floods of *River Ganga*.

13. ***One should endeavour to protect DHARMA even under adverse conditions***

"SA TYAJED DHARMA MARYADA MAPI KLESADASAM SRITAHA
HARISCHANDRO HE DHARMARDHEE SEHE CHANDALA DASATAM"

One should endeavour to protect DHARMA even under adverse conditions;
Harischandra, because of his commitment to Truth agreed to be the servant of an *outcaste* (*CHANDALA*)
Thus *Harischandra* acquired eternal renown as "*SATYAHARISCHANDRA*"

14. ***One should never forsake TRUTH even to achieve success in a task.***

"NA SATYAVRATA BHANGENA KARYAM DHEEMAN PRASADAYET/DA
DARSA NARAKAKLESAM SATYANASAD YUDHISTRIRAHA"

One should never forsake Truth even to achieve success in a task;
Yudhistira, though he was committed to Truth, throughout his life, yet he conceded to a lie concocted by *Sri Krishna* during *Kurukshetra War*, namely "*ASHWATHAMA MRUTAHA... NAROVA KUNJARAHA*".
Dronacharya was able to hear clearly the first half of the statement of Yudhistira (namely "*ASHWATHAMA MRUTAHA*") but he was unable to hear the second half namely "*NAROVA KUNJARAHA*" because, at this critical juncture, *Sri Krishna*" and *the rest of the Pandawas blew their CONCHES* (SANKHAMULU), to drown and mask the voice of Yudhistira, while he was uttering "*NAROVA KUNJARAHA*".
Dronacharya had implicit faith in the committment of Yudhistira to Truth and believing *really that his son Ashwathama was killed*, he was grief-stricken and threw away all his *bows*, *arrows* and *weapons*. *Drustadumna* then killed *Dronacharya*.
Yudhistira had to enter the hell first, and experience the punishment for the sin that

accrued to him in the killing of *Dronacharya.*

15. ***One should cultivate the friendship of SAJJANAS (Men of Virture); and one should give up any association with DHRJANAS (Evil Men)***

"KURVEETA SANGATAM SADBHIRNA SADBHIR, GUNA VARJITIHA PRAPA RAGHAVASANGATYA PRAJYAM RAJYAM VIBHEESAANAHA"

One should cultivate the friendship of SAJJANAS, and one should give up any association with DURJANAS;
Vibheeshana, brother of *Ravana*, left the court of *evil Ravana*, sought the protection and friendship of *Sree Rama*. Ravana was killed by Sri Rama, in the *RAMA-RAVANA SANGRAMA*, that followed. *Vibheeshana* was crowned as the king of *Sri Lanka* by Sree Rama

16. ***Serve your parents with all the reverence and affection and give no occasion for them to be angry with you.***

"MATARAM PITARAM BHAKTYA TOSHAYENNA PRAKOPAYET MATRUSAPENA NAGANAM SARPASATRE BHAVAT KSHAYAHA"

Serve your parents with all the reverence and affection, and give no occasion for them to be angry with you;
Once upon a time *NAGAS*' (Semi divine beings of HINDU MYTHOLOGY living in PATALA, half man and half serpent) mother *KADRUVA*, was displeased with her offspring as they disobeyed her on one occasion. *KANDRUVA* cursed all of them to perish in the "*SARPAYAGA*" to be performed by "*Janamejaya*"

17. ***The reward and benefit of a sacrifice is extraordinary and unexpected,***

"JARAGRAHANA TUSTENA NIJA YOUVANADAHA SUTAHA/KRUTAHA KANEEYAN PRANATAHA CHAKRAVARTEE YAYATINA"

The reward and benefit of a sacrifice is extraordinary and unexpected;
King Yayati became prematurely old (SENILE) on account of a curse given to him by *Sukracharya Yayati* requested all *his five sons* to exchange his senility with their youth and thus give him a chance to be young again; All his sons, except the youngest named '*PURU*' refused this extraordinary request of *king Yayati*. King Yayati was extremely pleased with the extraordinary sacrifice made by his youngest son *Puru*, and crowned him as an Emperor, in preference to his four *older brothers.*

18. 1. ***Give a DANA (Gift) with a virtuous disposition*; (SATVICA BHAVANA)**
 2. ***Have no regrets, after giving a DANA*;**
 3. ***However a DANA should never jeopardize (or endanger) ones very existence.***

"DANAM SATVAMITAM DADYANNA PASCHHATTAPA DOOSHITAM BALINATMARPITO BANDHE DANASESHASYA SUDDHAYE"

1. Give a Dana with a virtuous disposition (SATVICA BHAVANA);
2. Have no regrets after giving a DANA;

3. However, a DANA should never jeopardize (endanger) once very existence;

Once upon a time "*VISHNU*" disguised as a "*VAMANA*" (A Brahmachari and a Dwarf) approached *Emperor Bali* and begged him for a gift. *Emperor Bali* bestowed as a gift (1) The world (BHOOLOKA) (2) The sky and (3) finally even himself *to VAMANA* Thus Emperor *Bali* endangered his very existence by conceding to the request of *MAHAVISHNU* disguised as "*VAMANA*"

19. 1. ***Bestow a gift (DANA) with a virtuous disposition (SATVICA BHAVANA);***
2. ***One should not expect a return for the gift one has bestowed;***

"TYAGE SATVANIDHINE KURYANNA PRATUPAKRUTI SPRUHAM
KARNAH KUNDALADANE BHOOT KALUSHAHA SAKTI YACHĀYA"

1. Bestow a gift (DANA) with a virtuous disposition (SATVICA BHAVANA)
2. One should not expect a return for the gift (DANA) one has bestowed.

During the *Kurukshetra War, Indra* approached *Karna,* in *the guise of a Brahmana* and begged him to give away his "SAHAJA KAVACHA KUNDALAMULU" (Magical ear rings with which Karna was born and which made him invincible in war)

Karna gave Indra his 'Ear Rings' but requested a '*SAKTI'* (a magical ASTRA (weapon) capable of destroying any one in a war), in return for his '*Ear Rings*'. *And because of this counter request, Karna's gift of "Ear Rings" to Indra lost its pristine glory and assumed the mundane (worldly) nature of a barter.*

20. 1. ***Do not insult a BRAHMANA (one who possess Brahmajnana);***
2. ***The curse (SAPAMU) of a BRAHMANA is irrevocable***

BRAHMANNAVA MANYETA BRAHMA SOPO HE DUHSAHA
TAKSHĀGNOU BRAHMA SAPAT PAREEKSHI DAGAMAT KSHAYAM

Once upon a time, *King Pareekshit, son of Abhimanyu,* while hunting in a forest, became very thirsty. He saw a *MUNI,* doing *Tapas* in the shade of a tree in the forest. The King asked the *MUNI* to guide him to a source of water. The *MUNI engrossed in Tapas, did not answer* the King. The King was very angry at the silence of the MUNI. The King picked up a dead snake lying nearby, dropped it around the neck of the MUNI, and left;

After a while, the son of the MUNI come to attend on him. He was enraged to see a dead snake around the neck of his father, and he cursed the man who was responsible for such an insolent deed *to die of a snake bite within seven days. King Pareekshit* died of a snake bite (*bitten by a snake called TAKSHAKA*) *inspite of all his precautions, on the seventh day.*

21. ***Any knowledge of an "ASTRA" (Magical weapon) acquired in an attitude of arrogance, and through deception, will be ineffective when needed***

"DAMBHARAM BHODDHATAM DHARMAM NANCHAREDANTA NISHPHALAM
BRAHMANYA DAMBHA LABDHASTRA VIDYA KARNASYA NISHPHALA"

(*Dambhamu* = Deceit, fraud, cheating, *feigning*)
(*Ouddhatyamu* = *Arrogance, insolence*)
Any knowledge of an 'ASTRA' (Magical weapon) acquired in an attitude of arrogance, and through deception, will be ineffective when needed
Parasurama, the son of Jamadagni, was a renowned teacher of *BRAHMASTRA* and *other ASTRAS*, but he was also an *implacable* (*unforgiving*) *enemy of all KSHATRIYA Kings.*
Karna, who was a Kshatriya by birth, was eager to acquire the knowledge about the *BRAHMASTRA* from *Parasurama. Karna* became a disciple of *Parasurama in the guise of a Brahmana Student*, and learnt *every aspect of BRAHMASTRA from Parasurama.*
One day *Parasurama* dozed off to sleep, resting his head on the thigh of *Karna.* Strangely at this juncture, an insect started to bore a hole into the thigh of Karna and caused excruciating pain to Karna and blood began to drip out of the hole bored by the insect. *Karna though tortured by the strange insect, did not stir so as not to disturb the sleep of his Guru Parasurama.*
However *Parasurama* woke up and saw instantly the entire scene (i.e.) the insect, blood dripping out through a hole in the thigh of Karna and *realized that Karna was not an ordinary Brahmana student* (*no brahmana student would have tolerated such a torture silently*) and cursed him, for the deception played on him.
And because of this curse of Parasurama, Karna was not able to recollect from memory BRAHMASTRA and use it during Kurukshetra War and finally perished.

22. 1. ***Do not serve an unworthy master to earn money.***
    2. ***One acquires wealth only to that extent as ordained by the God.***

"NA SEVYA SEVAYA DADHYAD DIVADHEENE DHANE DHIYAM
BHEESMA DRONADOYO YATA: HA KSHAYAM DURYODHANASRAYAT

1. Do not serve an unworthy master to earn money.
2. One acquires wealth only to that extent as ordained by the God.

Even renowned warriors like *Bheesma* and *Drona*, as they served *an evil minded Duryodhana*, had to undergo many tribulations, and finally perished in the Kurukshetra War.

23. 1. ***Cherish the quality of mercy in hour heart;***
    2. ***Try to protect and save the lives of others;***

"PARA PRANA PARITRANA PARAHA KARUNYAVAN BHAVET
MAMSAM KAPOTA RAKSHAYI SVAM SYENAYA DADOU SIBEHE"

1. Cherish the quality of mercy in hour heart;
2. Try to protect and save the lives of others;

Once upon a time *Emperor Sibi*, to save the *life of a dove* which sought refuge under him, cut up his own thigh, and gave the flesh to the *eagle* which was in pursuit of the dove. *Emperor Sibi thus acquired eternal renown as a man of mercy.*

24. 1. ***Forsake evil qualities like jealousy and hatred;***
    2. ***Let your mind become as soft and tender as that of a flower;***

"ADVESHA PESALAM KURYANMANAHA KUSUMA KOMALAM BABHOOVA DVESHA DOSHENA DEVA DANAVA SAMKSHA YAHA"

1. Forsake evil qualities like jealousy and hatred;
2. Let your mind become as soft and tender as that of a flower;

The father of *DEVAS* (celestial beings) and *DANAVAS* (DEMONS) was *Kasyapa* and *their mothers* were *the daughters of Daksha.* Even this close bond of relationship was of no avail in preventing the *internecine* (*destructive to one another mutually*) wars among themselves. *Devas* and *Danavas* were overcome by mutual hatred and jealousy fought with each other and finally both perished.

25. 1. ***Do not forget any favour or benefit conferred on you***
    2. ***Forsake an evil quality like ingratitude.***

"AVISMRUTOPAKARAHA SYĀNNA KURVEETA KRUTA GHNATAM HATVOPAKARINAM VIPRO NADEE JANGHAMADHAS CHUTAHA"

1. Do not forget any favour or benefit conferred on you
2. Forsake an evil quality like ingratitude;

A *renegade* (a deserter, an apostate = one who has given up his religious faith) *BRAHMANA killed and ate up NAADIJANGHA*, a *crane renowned for DHARMA* who gave food and shelter to this renegade Brahmana.
This renegade Brahmana, thus acquired everlasting infamy for his rank ingratitude.

26. 1. ***Do not be a victim of inordinate (excessive) love and attachment towards a woman;***
    2. ***Do not forego discrimination and freedom of action on account of such inordinate (excessive) love and attachment towards a woman.***

"STREEJITO NA BHAVED DHEEMAN GADHA RAGA VASEE KRUTAHA PUTRA SOKAD DASARADHO JEEVAM JAYAJITO TYAJAT"

1. Do not be a victim of inordinate (excessive) love and attachment towards a woman;
2. Do not forego discrimination and freedom of action on account of such inordinate (excessive) love and attachment towards a woman;

King Dasaradha loved and was deeply attached to *Kikeya*, who was one of his wives. Once upon a time *King Dasaradha* fought a war with a great and powerful *RAKSHASA* named "*TIMIDWAJUNDU*" OR " *SAMBARUDU*". During the war, *Kikeyi* rescued *King DASARADHA from the Rakshasas.* King Dasaradha was pleased with the timely help and bravery shown by Kikeyi and granted her two boons. Later, *King Dasaradha was* forced to banish *Sri Rama* to forests at the behest of *Kikeyi.* King *Dasaradha* died of grief, caused by the separation of his beloved son *Sri Rama.*

27. ***Self-praise is an evil quality and it should be eschewed (avoided).***

"NA SVAYAM SAMSTUTI PADIRGLANIM GUNAGANAM NAYET
SVAGUNASTUTI VADENA YAYTIRAPATAD DIVAHA"

Self-praise is an evil quality and it should be eschewed;
King Yayati, who was in the *DEVALOKA* at that time on account of the spiritual merit acquired through "Tapas", *indulged in self-praise in the presence of Indra. Indra was enraged with the impudence (immodesty) of King Yayati and banished from DEVALOKA. King Yayati had to descend to BHOOLOKA.*

28. ***Avoid harshness and severity in words or deeds.***

"KSHIPED VAKYASARAM STEEKSHANNA PARUSHYA VUPAPLUTAN
VAKPARUSHYA RUSHA CHAKRE BHEEMAHA KURU KULA KSHAYAM"

Avoid harshness and severity in words or deeds;
Enraged by the harsh and insulting words of *Duryodhana, Dussasena* and *Karna, Bheemasena,* made a vow to kill all *the Kouravas,* in the ensuring war.

29. ***Calumny and to slander others is an evil quality and it should be avoided.***

"PARESHEM KLESADAM KURYANNA PISUNYAM PRAABHOHA PRIYAM
PISUNYENA GATOU RAHOSCCHANDRARKOU BHAKSHANEEYATAM"

Calumny and to slander others is an evil quality and it should be avoided;
Once upon a time, when *DEVA DANAVAS* were churning the *ocean (PALAKADALI), AMRUTAM* was obtained and it was being distributed by *Vishnu* (in *the guise of Mohini*) to all *Devatas.*
RAHUVU (*A RAKSHASA*) partook of AMRUTAM in the guise of a *DEVATA. SOORYA* (Sun) and *Chandra (Moon)* informed *Vishnu* about the deception of RAHUVU. Vishnu was enraged at *Rahuvu's deception* and severed the latter's head with his *CHAKRA. The severed head of RAHUVU and his body* (*KETUVU*), *from that time onwards become two GRAHAS* (*or Planets*). *During every eclipse, RAHUVU and KETUVU try to swallow up SOORYA* (*Sun*) *and CHANDRA* (*Moon*) *in vengeance.*

30. ***Begging is a despicable (mean or fit to be treated with scorn) trait, and it undermines one's respectability;***

"KURYANNECHA JANABHYASTAM NA YACHAM MANA HARINEEM
BALIYACHA PARAHA PRAPA LAGHAVAM PURUSHOTTAMAHA"

Begging is a despicable (mean or fit to be treated with scorn) trait, and it undermines one's respectability;

Mahavishnu assumed the guise of *Vamana* (A brahmachari and a dwarf) and begged an extraordinary gift from *Emperor Bali.*
Mahavishnu, the supreme being, had to assume not only *the guise of Vamana* (a brahmachari and a dwarf) while begging from *Emperor Bali, but also acquired the disrepute of a cheat and a deceiver.*

31. ***Do not insult or forsake relations;***

"NA BANDHU SAMBANDHI JANAM DOOSHAYENNAPE VARJAYET
DAKSHA YAGNA KSHAYA YABHOOT TRINETRASYA VIMANANA"

Do not insult of forsake relations;
Once upon a time, *Daksha Prajapati,* father of *Satidevi* and *father in law of Siva,* was conducting a "*YAGNA*" but he ignored and insulted *Siva* and *Satidevi,* by not inviting them to the "*YAGNA*".
Satidevi attended the YAGNA, though she was not invited to the YAGNA. *Daksha Prajapati* insulted and ignored her. *Satidevi died by self immolation in that YAGNA. Siva* was enraged at *Daksha Prajapati* and to destroy him, *Siva* created one "*Veerbadhara*". *Veerbadhara destroyed Daksha Prajapati and his YAGNA.*

32. 1. ***Quarrelsomeness (contentiousness) is an evil quality;***
    2. ***To give way to jealousy and envy at the respect and regard shown to a great man will eventually lead to once own ruin;***

"NA VIVADA MADANDHAHA SYANNA PARESHA MAMARSHNAHA
VAKPARUSHYACCHIRA CHINNAM SISUPALASYA SOURINA"

1. Quarrelsomeness (contentiousness) is an evil quality;
2. To give way to jealousy and envy at the respect and regard shown to a great man will eventually lead to one's own ruin;

Dharmaraja while conducting an *YAGNA* called "*RAJASOOYAMU*" offered *the prestigious seat* (*AGRASANAMU*) to *Sri Krishna* and worshipped him with all the reverence.
Sisupala, King of Chedidesa, and an arch enemy of *Sri Krishna,* was jealous and envious about the preferential treatment shown to *Sri Krishna. Sisupala carried on a tirade (strain of censure or reproof) against Sri Krishna.*
At last *Sri Krishna* used his weapon called "*CHAKRAMU*", and *severed the head of Sisupala, and thus saved the "RAJASOOYAM" from disruption and chaos.*

33. ***Extol (praise) and glorify the exemplary (worthy of a high degree) qualities of greatmen and thus encourage them to perform even greater deeds.***

"GUNASTAVENA KURVEETA MAHATAM MANAVARDHANAM
HANUMANA BHAVAT STUTYA RAMA KARYA BHARA KSHAMAHA"
Extol (*praise*) and glorify the exemplary (worthy of a high degree) qualities of greatmen and thus encourage them to perform even greater deeds;

Hanuman, the monkey warrior, was renowned for his valour, intelligence and wisdom, *yet Hanuman was strangely unaware of his prowess and distinction*;

JAMBAVANTA and other monkey warriors recognised the greatness and inherent potential of *Hanuman*, extolled and glorified the exemplary qualities of him, *and thus encouraged him to leap across the ocean and commence the rescue of Sita from Ravana.*

Hanuman thus commenced "RAMAKARYA".

34. 1. ***Repeated and persistent begging is a disgusting and despicable (fit to be treated with scorn) trait;***
    2. ***It will eventually cause not only emotions like anger and disgust in the donor, but also will end in one's own ruin;***

"NATYARTHA MARTHARTHA NAYA DHEEMANU DVEJAYEJJANAM
ABDHIRDATTA SVA RATNA SREER MADHYA MANO SRUJAD VISHAM"

1. Repeated and persistent begging is a disgusting and despicable (fit to be treated with scorn) trait;
2. It will eventually cause not only emotions like anger and disgust in the donor, but also will end in one's own ruin;

Once upon a time, *DEVA DANAVAS* (Celestial beings and demons) churned the *ocean* (*PALAKADALI*). PALAKADALI was pleased with them and gave them precious possessions such as 1. *VUCCHISRAVAMU* (A horse) 2. *KOUSTUBHAMU* 3. *CHINTAMANI* 4. *KALPAVRUKSHAMU* 6. *KAMADHENUVU* 7. *LAXMIDEVI* 8. *CHANDRUDU* (MOON) and many other precious items.

Yet *Devadanavas* went on churning PALAKADALI. Palakadali was enraged at Devadanavas and yielded "*HALAHALAM*", a terribly destructive poison which was capable of destroying the entire world, *Siva* swallowed "*HALAHALAM*" and thus saved the world from destruction. Siva from then onwards acquired the title "*SREE KHANTA*".

35. ***Do not seek the friendship of a crooked, cruel and greedy man***

"VAKRIHE KROORATA RIRLUBHDIRNA KURYAT PREETI SANGATIM
VASISTA SYAHARAD DHENUM VISVAMITRO NIMANTRITAHA"

Once upon a time *Visvamitra* was the guest of *Brahmarshi Vasista.* VASISTA gave a grand feast to Vishvamitra and his soldiers, with the help of "*KAMADHENU*". (A celestial cow)

Visvamitra wanted the "KAMADHENU" for his own use and tried to take it by force. But Brahmarshi Vasista saved the Kamadhenu from the evil design of Visamitra, by the use of "*TAPAS SAKTI*" (spiritual powers).

36. 1.***Never should one take (his) ones own sense organs for granted;***
2.***It is almost impossible to have total control over (one's own) sense organs.***

"TEEVRE TAPASI LEENANAMINDRIYANAM NA VISVASET
VISVAMITROPI SOTKANTHAHA KANTHE JAGRAHA MENAKAM"

1.Never should one take (his ones own) sense organs for granted;
2.It is almost impossible to have total control over (ones own) sense organs.
Once upon a time *Visvamitra* was doing intense *TAPAS* in order to acquire the title of *BRAHMARSHI* and become equally renowned LIKE *Brahmarshi Vasista*; *Indra* deputed an *Apserasa* named "*Menaka*" to entice (*allure, tempt*) Visvamitra and detract him from the *Tapas*. *Visvamitra* was captivated by the charm and beauty of *Meneka*, gave up his Tapas and began to live with her. "*Sakuntala*" was born out of their union.

37. ***Do not forego your courage and become a victim of dejection, when you are grief stricken because of the loss of a dear and near one.***

"KURYADVIYOGA DUKHESHU DHIRYAMUTSRUJYA DEENATAM
ASVATHAMA VADHAM SRUTVA DRONO GATA DHRUTIRARHTA HA"

Do not forego your courage and become a victim of dejection, when you are grief stricken because of the loss of a dear and near one;
During *Kurukshetra war*, *Dronacharya* when he heard the concocted news of his son's (*Aswathama's*) death from *Yudhistrira*, was grief-stricken, and totally dejected. Dronacharya, was overwhelmed by grief and dejection, and he discarded all his bows, arrows and other weapons. *Pandavas* anticipated such a reaction from Dronacharya and made the best use of it. *Drustadumina, son of Drupada*, instantly killed *Dronacharya*.

38. ***A wise man should never allow himself to be overpowered and overwhelmed by uncontrolled wrath;***

"NA KRODHA YATU DHANASYA DHEEMAN GACCHEDA DHEENATAM
PAPOU RAKSHSAVAD BHEEMAHA KSHATAJAM RIPU VAKSHASAHA"

A wise man should never allow himself to be overpowered and overwhelmed by uncontrolled wrath;
During *Kurukshetra War*, *Bheemasena* killed *Dusyasena*. At this juncture, Bheemasena was overpowered and overwhelmed by uncontrolled wrath. He ripped open the chest of his victim and *drank his blood like a RAKSHASA* (*Demon*).

39. ***Forsake hunting; hunting is an evil habit; By its very nature, it involves cruelty to and killing of living creatures.***

"TYAJED MRUGA VYASANAM HIMSAYATE MALEEMASAM
MRUGAYA RASIKAHA PANDUHU SAPENA TANU MA TYAJAT"

Forsake hunting; hunting is an evil habit; By its very nature, it involves cruelty to and killing of living creatures;
Once upon a time *King Pandu*, while hunting in a forest, killed an antelope (male)

which was making love with another antelope;
The antelopes were in fact a *Rishi Couple* in disguise, namely *Rishi Kindamudu and his wife.* Rishi Kindamudu, before dying cursed King Pandu to die in a similar manner like himself (i.e.) when he was making love to his woman.
The death of King Pandu occured later as ordained by Rishi Kindamudu

40. ***One should never endanger one's own safety and existence, what ever might be the cause of one's elation and satisfaction.***

"SIVENEVA NA TUSHTENA BUDDHIRDEYA VINASINEE
BHASMASURAYA VARADAHA SA HE TENA VIDAMBITAHA"

One should never endanger one's own safety and existence, whatever might be the cause of one's elation and satisfaction.
Once upon a time *Siva* was extremely pleased with the *Tapas*, of a *Rakshasa*, and wanted to reward him with a boon. The Rakshasa wanted a boon by which he could change and reduce any one in to a heap of powder (*BHASMA*), as soon as he laid his hands on the head of the selected victim.
Siva granted the *Rakshasa* such a *lethal boon even without a second thought.* From then onwards the Rakshasa acquired the title "*BHASMASURA*".
Bhasmasura wanted to test the efficacy of the boon granted by '*Siva*', on *Siva*himself. *Siva* was finally rescued by *Vishnu* from the clutches (strong hold) of *Bhasmasura.*

41. ***One should not cause annoyance and grief to SAJJANAS (Men of Virtue) by Vehemently contradicting their opinions and thus pave the way for one's own ruin***

"NA JATOOLLANGHANAM KURYAT SATAM MARMA VIDARANAM
CCCHEDA VADANAM SAMBHUR BRAHMANO VEDAVADINAHA"

Do not cause annoyance and grief to SAJJANAS (Men of Virtue) by Vehemently contradicting their opinions and thus pave the way for one's own ruin.
Once upon a time, *Brahma*, who was an authority on "VEDAS", argued vehemently with Siva and caused him annoyance and grief. Thereby *Siva was enraged with Brahma and severed the four heads of Brahma.*

42. ***Give credit to a man's virtue and his exemplary character, rather than to his lineage or high birth.***

"GUNESHVA VADARAM KURYANNA JATOU JATU TATVAVIT
DROUNIRDVIJO BHAVACCHOODRAHA SOODRASCHA VIDURAHA KSHAMEE"

Give credit to a man's virtue and his exemplary character, rather than to his lineage or high birth;
Asvathama, son of *Dronacharya*, was by birth a *Brahmana*, yet by, his cruel and infamous deeds such as the *Killing of "UPAPANDAVAS"* who were asleep at that time, and others, *Asvathama lost the dignity and status of a Brahmana.*

Vidura was born as a "*SOODRA*". *VIDURA's mother was the servant maid of Vichitraveerya*. Though *Vidura* was born as a "*SOODRA*", he excelled even many wise brahmanas in learning, wisdom and forbearance.
Even today "VIDURA NEETI (Wisdom of Vidura) is read by all seekers of WISDOM.

43. ***One who desires to acquire learning and knowledge from a GURU (Teacher), should be willing to hear, obey and serve the GURU, without any anxiety, agitation or fear.***

"VIDYODYOGEE GATODVEGAHA SEVAYA TOSHAYED GURUM
GURUSEVA PARAHA SEHE KAYAKLESADASAM KACHAHA"

One who desires to acquire learning and knowledge from a GURU (Teacher), should be willing to hear, obey and serve the GURU, without any anxiety, agitation or fear;
Once upon a time *Kacha*, *son of Brihaspati*, became a disciple of *Sukracharya*, who was renowned teacher for all *Rakshasas*. Sukracharya was the only one who was well versed in "*MRUTA SANJEEVINI VIDYA*" (*The art and science of resurrecting the Dead*). *Devatas* deputed *Kacha*, to undergo training under *Sukracharya* and learn every thing about Mrutasanjeevini Vidya.
Kacha served the GURU, namely *Sukracharya for about a thousand years*, sincerely, and experienced many afflictions and at last was successful in learning about "Mruta Sanjeevini Vidya" from his Guru Sukracharya (*The fruit of "Guru sushroosha" is "Guru Prasadam"*)

44. ***One should not abandon a faultless, and an innocent dependent on any pretext.***

"SVAMISEVARATAM BHAKTAM NIRDOSHAM PARITYAJET
RAMASTYAKTVA SATEEM SEETAM SOKA SALYATURO BHAVAT"

One should not abandon a faultless, and an innocent dependent on any pretext;
Sri Rama sent *Sita*, his beloved and devoted wife, to a forest, bowing down to the pressure of public opinion and censure, although he knew, that Sita, was innocent and faultless later, because of this separation from his beloved wife Sita, Sri Rama, had to experience untold grief and sorrow.

45. ***One should strive to protect one's name and fame (RENOWN) on the earth and make it (RENOWN) endure on the earth for as long as possible, since enduring renown here ensures a longer stay for the soul, in the heaven;***

"RAKSHET KHYATIM PUNAH SMRUTYA YASAHA KAYASYA JEEVANEEM,
CHUTAHA SMRUTO JANIHE SVARGA MINDRA DUMNAHA PUNARGATAHA"

One should strive to protect ones name and fame (Renown) on the earth and make it endure for as long as possible, since enduring renown here ensures a longer stay for the soul, in the heaven;
Once upon a time, *King Indradumna* acquired spiritual merit, by performing many deeds of virtue, as a result of which, he entered *SVARGALOKA* (*Heaven*) and stayed

there for a long time. However, King Indradumna returned to BHOOLOKA (THE EARTH), when his spiritual merit was exhausted.
An *ancient tortoise* named '*AKOOPARUNDU*' advised king Indradumna to perform many more deeds of merit. King INDRADUMNA performed many more deeds of merit and as a result of which he reentered Heaven and stayed there for a longer duration.

46. ***Laxmi (The Goddess of Wealth), by her very nature is fickle (inconstant, changeable) and fleeting (transitory)*;**

One should not allow timidity to come in the way of protecting one's wealth;
"NA KADARYA TAYA RASHE LAKSHMEEM KSHIPRA PALAYENEEM
YUKTYA VYĀDEENDRA DATTA BHYAM HRUTA SREER-NANDA BHOO BRUTAHA"
Laxmi The Goddess of Wealth), by her very nature is fickle (in constant, changeable) and fleeting (transitory);
One should not allow timidity to come in the way of protecting one's wealth;
Once upon a time, *two Brahmanas* named *Vyadi* and *Indradutta* respectively, snatched away the wealth of *King Nanda* by the use of a cleaver strategy namely '*PARAKAYA PRAVESAM*' (*The art and science of reanimating a corpse*)

47. 1.***When one's strength is on the wane (decline) one should cultivate forbearance (Patience)*;**
2.***One should not fight with an enemy stronger than oneself.***

"SAKTI KSHAYE KSHAMAM KURYANNASAKTAHA SAKTA MAKSHIPET
KARTA VEERYAHA SASAMRAMBHAM BABANDHA DASAKANDHARAM".

1.When one's strength is on the wane (decline) one should cultivate forbearance (Patience);
2.One should not fight with an enemy stronger than oneself;
RAVANA fought with *KARTA VEERYARJUNA, an enemy stronger than himself, was defeated and imprisoned by the latter.*

48. ***Do not trust and yield to the charm of a harlot (prostitute), as deception is a part and parcel of her daily routine*;**

"VESYA VACHASI VISVASEE NA BHAVENNITYA KITAVE
RUSYA SRUNGO PE NISSANGAHA SRUNGAREE VESYAYA KRUTAHA"

Do not trust and yield to the charm of a harlot (prostitute), as deception is a part and parcel of her daily routine;
Once upon a time, there was a *King* named '*Romapada*', who was the ruler of *Angadesa.* At that juncture, *Angadesa* was overtaken by a *severe famine. Vebhandaka Maharishi*, had a son named '*Rushya Srunga*' (*he had a horn on the head*). Rushyasrunga was renowned for his Tapas. The king Romapada was informed if

"Rushyasrunga" was persuaded to leave his Ashramam in the forest and enter Angadesa famine would abate in Angadesa. *A harlot volunteered to do this task. Rushyasrunga* was captivated by the charm of the dancing girl. He left the Ashramam and entered Angadesa, along with the dancing girl. *He gave up his Tapas and became engrossed in sensual pleasures.*

49. ***One should not insult an enemy, because he is younger than self and also assuming that he is weaker than self;***

"ALPAMAPYAVAMANYETA NA SATRUM BALADARPITAHA
RAMENA RAMAHA SISUNA BRAHMANYA DAYAYOJEGHA TAHA"

One should not insult an enemy, because he is younger than self and also assuming that he is weaker than self;
Parasurama, the son of Jamadagni, was a *renowned Brahmana warrior,* and also an *implacable enemy of all Kshatriya Kings.* Parasurama's Guru was *Siva,* and as Sri Rama lifted and tried to string up the "*SIVA DHANUSSU*" at the "*SVAYAMVARAM*" (the election of a husband by a princess at a public assembly of suitors held for the purpose) held at *Mithilanagara, Parasurama* felt that *Sri Rama* had insulted and offended *his Guru "Siva".*
Parasurama confronted Sri Rama, and insulted and abused him in many ways. Sri Rama patiently answered him and tried to pacify him. Finally Sri Rama touched *the "VISHNAVADHANUSSU"* of Parasurama and withdrew the extra ordinary power that was in it. From that moment Parasurama, became an *ordinary Bhahmana.* Parasurama humbly begged Sri Rama to pardon his for his insolent behaviour. *Sri Rama pardoned him and let him go.*

50. ***One should never trust a cruel murderer***

"NRUSAMSAM KROORAKARMANAM VISVASENNA KADACHANA,
JAGADVIREE JARASANDHAHA PANDA VENA DVIDHA KRUTAHA

One should never trust a cruel murderer
Once upon a time, there was a *King* named *JARASANDHA.* He was the ruler of *Magadha* city. *Jarasandha was a cruel murderer.* He *killed many kings;*
Bheemasena, under the guidance of Sri Krishna engaged Jarasandha in a pugilistic encounter and finally tore him apart.

51. 1.***One's conduct should always be governed by the bounds of propriety and*** 2.***One should not try to achieve one's purpose by any means (i.e.) without paying attention to the means, whether it is proper or improper,***

"OUCHITYA PRACHUTACHARO YUKTYA SVARDHAM NA SADHAYET
VYAJA VALI VADHENIVA RAMAKEERT EHE KALANKITA"

One's conduct should always be governed by the bounds of propriety and
One should not try to achieve one's purpose by any means (i.e.) without paying attention to the means, whether it is proper or improper

Sri Rama killed Vali by stealth. Sri Rama hid himself behind a big tree and shot the fatal arrow at *Vali, the brother of Sugreeva,* and thus killed him.
Sri Rama's good reputation was sullied forever by this killing of Vali by stealth.
To rely on deception, secrecy and stealth to achieve one's goal is to be avoided.

52. ***Even for a man, who has acquired complete control over his sense organs, it is better for him if he avoids to be alone even with his own mother.***

"VARJAYE DINDRIYA JAYEE VIJANE JANANEEMAPI
PUTREE KRUTOPE PRADUMNAHA KAMITAHA SAMBARA STEERYA"

Even for a man, who has acquired complete control over his sense organs, it is better for him if he avoids to be alone even with his own mother.
Once upon time, there was *RAKSHASA* named "*Sambarudu*". He had a wife named "*Mayavati*". *Pradumna, (son on Sri Krishna and Rukmini), was brought up by Mayavati.* PRADUMNA grew up to become a handsome youth. Mayavati was captivated by the youth and beauty of Pradumna and fell in love with him even *forgetting that he was deemed to be a son to her by relationship.*

53. ***Do not meddle with the intense tapas (deep and absorbing religious meditation attended with austerity) of great men, either to test their courage or their forbearance.***

"NA TEEVRA TAPASAM KURYAD DHIRYA VIPLAVA CHAPALAM
NETRAGNI SALABHEE BHAVAM BHAVO NISHEENMANOBHAVAM"

Do not meddle with the intense tapas (deep and absorbing religious meditation attended with austerity) of great men, either to test their courage or their forbearance;
Once upon a time, *Manmadha* repeatedly tried to disrupt the *Tapas of Siva.* Siva was enraged at the impudence of Manmadha. *Siva* opened his *Trinetra* (*or the third eye*). A fierce flame issued forth from the Trinetra and destroyed Manhadha. *Thus Manhadha was burnt down to a heap of ashes.*

54. 1.***Keep away from gambling;***
2.***The evil habit of gambling leads to daily internecine (destructive to one another mutually) quarrels;***

"NA NITYA KALAHA KRANTE SAKTIM KURVEETA KITAVE
ANYADHA KRUDVI PANNO BHOODDHARMARAJO YUDHISTIRAHA"

Keep away from gambling;
The evil habit of gambling leads to daily internecine (destructive to one another mutually) quarrels;
YUDHISTIRA not only lost his entire kingdom in gambling but also (and) experienced many afflictions on account of it.

55. ***A ruler may show kindness towards a servant and may even bestow many favours on him yet, the servant should not be carried away by the display of kindness and favours, as they are all motivated by expedience, and they are all as temporary and***

evanescent (quickly fading) as the scenes in a dream.

"PRABHU PRASADE SATYASAM NA KURYAT SVAPNA SANNIBHE
NANDENA MANTREE NIHITAHA SAKATALO HE BANDHANE".

A ruler may show kindness towards a servant and may even bestow many favours on him yet, the servant should not be carried away by the display of kindness and favours, as they are all motivated by expedience, and they are all as temporary and evanescent (quickly fading) as the scenes in a dream;

Once upon a time, *King Nanda,* did not hesitate to imprison his favourite minister and his family, namely *Minister Sakatala and his family, on the grounds of a trivial suspicion.*

(*RAJANEETI* (*Statesmanship*): A king or a ruler never depends solely on any servant, however loyal and trustworthy he might be, for the fulfilment of his various plans.

A ruler displays kindness, and gives many gifts to a servant, whose services are most useful and necessary for the successful completion of his various plans.

If the ruler finds the servant to be not so useful or necessary for the successful completion of his various plans, he will not hesitate to dismiss, imprison or if necessary even to kill him. Such is the essence of RAJAEETI (Statesmanship).

56. ***Do not become an atheist.***

"NA LOKAYATA VADENA NASTIKATVERPAYED DHIYAM
HARIRHARANYA KASEPUM JAGHANA STAMBHA NIRGATAHA

Do not become an atheist.

Once upon a time there was a great Rakshasa King named "*Hiranyakasipu*". *Bhakra Prahlada* was his son. Bhakta Prahlada was great devotee of *Maha Vishnu*;

On one occasion Hiranyakasipu demanded Prahlada to tell him the whereabouts of "Maha Vishnu" Prahlada replied that if one, (seeks) Mahavishnu with all sincerity and devotion, "HE" could be found everywhere and in everything. Enraged at Prahladas reply. Hiranyakasipu questioned him if "Maha Vishnu" could be found in a pillar of the king's mansion. Bhakta Prahlada said "yes".

Hiranyakasipu struck forcibly at a pillar with his club ("GADA"). The pillar cracked and fell apart. *Mahavishnu* materialized out of that pillar in the form of "*NARASIMHA*" (*Half a lion and half a man*) *and tore up Hiranyakasipu into pieces.*

57. ***Do not insult those who are worthy to be honoured and worshipped, even when you occupy and eminent post.***

"ATUNNATA PADAROODHAHA POOJYANINNA VĀVAMANA YET
NAHOOSHAHA SAKRATAMETYA CHUTO GASTYAVA MANA NAT"

Do not insult those who are worthy to be honoured and worshipped, even when you occupy an eminent post.

Once upon a time, there was king named *Nahoosha.* He performed many deeds of virtue, and acquired a lot of spiritual merit and as a result of which, he was able to enter "*SVARGALOKA*" (or the heaven) and occupy the highest position, in the heaven *namely that of* "*Indra*"

Nahoosha's arrogance and conceit knew no bounds. He even dared to insult, the great sage *Agastya. Maharshi Agastya* was enraged at the insolent behaviour of *Nahoosha*, and he not only banished *Nahoosha* from "*Svargaloka*" (or the heaven), but also cursed him to become a *snake* (*a python* = A large kind of serpent) and live in that form for many years on the earth.

58. ***One should never trust, and take an enemy for granted, even when he seeks reconciliation and agrees to maintain peace;***

"SANDHIM VIDHAYA RIPUNA NA NIHESANKAHA SUKHEE BHAVET
SANDHIM KRUTVA VADHEE DINDRO VRUTRAM NIHESANKA MANASAM"

One should never trust, and take an enemy for granted, even when he seeks reconciliation and agrees to maintain peace;

Once upon time, there was a "*Rakshasa*", named "*Vrutrudu*". Vrutrudu performed Tapas for many years and acquired many boons and became very powerful "*Devatas*" were defeated many times by *Vrutrudu. Indra* sought reconciliation with Vrutrudu and made a peace treaty with him. *However Indra killed "Vrutrudu", when the latter was not wary and not on guard*

(Never trust an enemy totally even when he seeks reconciliation and agrees to maintain peace. *After all a friend is a friend and an enemy is an enemy.* An enemy will only be on friendly terms, as long as it suits his purpose and will be constantly waiting and watching for an opportunity to strike down his opponent)

59. ***One should carefully listen to the counsels of wise men, and endeavour to put their advice into practice in a suitable manner;***

"HITOPADESAM SRUTVA TU KURVEETA CHA YADHOCHITAM
VIDUROKTAMA KRUTVA TU SOCHYO BHOOT KOURAVESVA RAHA"

One should carefully listen to the counsels of wise men, and endeavour to put their advice into practice in a suitable manner;

King Dhrutarastra listened many times to the counsels of "*wise Vidura*", *but he failed to put them into practice*

Atrocities of *Duryodhana* and his brothers, *aided* and *abetted* by *Drutarastra* eventually led to a great war between *Kouravas and Pandavas* (*Kurukshetra War*), in which all *Kouravas*, were killed.

60. 1.***Moderation in eating is the best;***
2.***Immoderate eating by a sickman leads to further suppression of his appetite and makes him a prey to many more diseases;***

"BAHVANNASANA LOBHENE ROGEE MANDARUCHIR BHAVET
PRABHOOTAJYA BHUJO JADYAM DAHANASYAPYA JAYATA"

Moderating in eating is the best;
Immoderate eating by a sickman leads to further suppression of his appetite and make him a prey to many more diseases.
Even *Agnideva* had to suffer from indigestion because of drinking "*GHRUTAM*" (GHEE) immoderately for *12 years in 'Yagna'* performed by *King Svetake.*

61. ***One should try to get rid off evil qualities, which are inherent in one's own mind (such as 1. KAMA 2. LOBHA 3. MOHA 4. MADA 5. KRODHA and 6. MATSARYAS) by effort and exertion, and not by undertaking intense Tapas and austereties;***

"YATNENA SHOSHAYEDDOSHANNA TU TEEVRA VRATIS TANUM
TAPASA KUMBHAKARNO BHOONNITYA NIDRA VICHETANAHA"

One should try to get rid off evil qualities, which are inherent in one's own mind (such as 1. KAMA 2. LOBHA 3. MOHA 4. MADA 5. KRODHA and 6. MATSARYAS) by effort and exertion, and not by undertaking intense Tapas and austereties;
Once upon a time, there was a Rakshasa named '*Sumali*'. "*Kikase*" *was the daughter of Sumali.* Her husband's name was "*Visravasudu*". (1) *Dasakantha*, (2) *Kumbhakarna*, (3) *Sooparnakha and* (4) *Vebheeshana* were the off spring of *Visravasudu and Kikase.*
Kumbhakarna did intense Tapas for *ten thousand years.* At last *Brahma* was pleased with the Tapas of Kumbhakarana and wanted to grant him a boon. *Kumbhakarana* requested the boon of prolonged sleep from *Brahma.* From then onwards, Kumbhakarana went on sleeping. *Alas! the end result of Kumbakarna's ten thousand years of intense Tapas was futile prolonged sleep only.*

62. ***One should not expect the continuation of existing state of affairs or circumstances either in the present time or in the future in this world.***

"STHIRATASAM NA BADHNEE YAAD BHUVI BHAVESHHU BHAVISHU
RAMO RAGHUHU SIBIHE PANDUHU KVA GATASTE NARADHIPAHA"

One should not expect the continuation of existing state of affairs or circumstances either in the present time or in the future in this world.
All creatures in this world are subject to change and disintegration in the course of time; Great kings and emperors like *Rama, Raghuvu, Sibi, Pandu* and many others lived, ruled and have departed long ago. *Where did they go? Ponder deeply on this question.*

63. 1.***Do not jeer or jest at the elderly and the wise;***
2.***One should not make fun of their speech, defects in their bodies or their deeds;***
"VIDAMBAYENNA VRUDDHANAM VAKYA KARMA VAPUHU KRIYAHA

SREE SUTAHA PRAPA VIROOPYAM VIDAMBITA TANUR MUNEHA"

Do not jeer or jest at the elderly and the wise;

One should not make fun of their speech, defects in their bodies or their deeds;

Once upon a time there was a *great Rushe* named "*Astavakrudu*", in whose body there were eight deformities. *Astavakrudu* was renowned for his wisdom *Sreesuta, son of Laxmi* (Manmadha), was extremely proud of his own handsome features. Sreesuta jeered at the disfigured body of the great Rushi 'Astavakrudu' and *as a consequence lost his own handsome features.*

64. ***To teach or train unworthy and undeserving students is futile***;

"NOPADESE PYABHAVYANAM MIDHYAM KURYAT PRAVADITAM
SUKRA SHADGUNYA GUPTAPE PRAKSHEENA DITYA SANTATI HE"

To teach or train unworthy and undeserving students is futile;

Once upon a time, there was a renowned teacher of *RAJANEETI* (Politics of Statesmanship), named *Sukracharya.* All the Rakshasas were his students. *Sukracharya taught them "Rajneeti", which consisted of six branches namely*

1. *SANDHI* (Treaty with an enemy)
2. *VIGRAHAMU* (Declaring war with an enemy)
3. *YANAMU* (Attacking the enemy (1) when one is strong and powerful, or (2) when the enemy has become weaker than before

   (*Again YANAMU IS subdivided into five types* 1. *Sandhaya Yanamu* 2. *Prasanga Yanamu* 3. *Vigruhya Yanamu* 4. *Sambhooya Yanamu* and 5. *Vupekshya Yanamu*)
4. *ASANAMU* (To stand still)

   Again Asanamu is subdivided into five types. These five types are just similar to the five types of yanamu, mentioned above.
5. *DVIDHAMU*—when there are two enemies on either side:
   1. To give the impression that he is on the side of one enemy
   2. To make a peace treaty with one enemy
   3. To declare war on one enemy
6. *ASRAYAMU*—To join the army of an enemy

   Rakshasas won many wars and defeated *Devatas* many times, as they had the benefit of excellent teachings of *Sukracharya.*

   Yet Rakshasas were destroyed in the end as they were *inherently evil minded, unworthy and undeserving pupils.*

65. ***Do not antagonise and cause displeasure to a man who has an inherent tendency to bear enmity for a long time***;

"NA TEEVRADEERGA VIRANAM MANUM MANASE ROPAYET

KOPENA PATA YANNANDAM CHANAKYAHA SAPTABHER DINIHE"

Do not antagonise and cause displeasure to a man who has an inherent tendency to bear enmity for a long time.

Once upon a time, *King Nanda* performed a "Shraddha" ceremony in his palace. "*Chanakya*" was also invited by the minister *Sakatlal* to the "Shraddha" ceremony. However *King NANDA* chose *one BRAHMANA named "Subandhudu" as the "Agrabhokta"* (as the first Brahmana who is fed as the representative of the Devas or the Pitrus in a Shraddha ceremony). *Chanakya was ignored and thus felt insulted.* Chanakya was enraged at King Nanda's impudence and *took a vow to destroy him within seven days.*

King Nanda died seven days after this incident.

66. ***Do not insult and cause displeasure to a chaste and virtuous woman engaged in intense Tapas (Deep and absorbing religious meditation attended with austerity)***

"NA SATEENAM TAPODEEPTAM KO PAYED KRODHA PAVAKAM
VADHAYA DASAKANTHASYA VEDAVATYA TYAJATTANUM"

Do not insult and cause displeasure to a chaste and virtuous woman engaged in intense Tapas (Deep and absorbing religious meditation attended with austerity)

Once upon a time "*Vedavati*", daughter, of "*Kushadvajudu*", renowned for her beauty and virtue, was engaged in intense Tapas in *the Himalayas*, with the sole intention of marrying "*Vishnu*".

Ravana was captivated by *Vedavati's* beauty and asked her *to marry him instead of Vishnu. Vedavati* refused. Then *Ravana* caught hold of her hair. Vedavati was enraged at Ravana's impudence and created a fire by her "*TAPASSAKTI*" and performed *self immolation.*

"*Vedavati*" was born as "*Sita Devi*" in her next birth. *Ravana* kidnapped her. This event led to a war with *Sri Rama* (*Rama Ravana Sangrama*) in which *Ravana* and all *his descendants were destroyed.*

67. ***Serve, honour and worship the "Guru" with humility, diligence and devotion to acquire VIDYA (Knowledge) from him;***

"GURUMARADHAYED BHAKTYA VIDYAVINAYASADHANAM,
RAMAYA PRADADOU TUSHTO VISVAMITRO STRA MANDALAM"

Serve, honour and worship the "Guru" with humility, diligence and devotion to acquire VIDYA (Knowledge) from him;

Sri Rama, son of *King Dasaratha*, served honoured and worshipped "*Visvamitra*" with humility, diligence and devotion.

Visvamitra was extremely pleased with the "*GURUSUSROSHA*" of Sri Rama and taught him a *number of powerful ASTRAS* (ASTRAMU an arrow discharged with a magic formula and hence working miraculously)

68. ***A gift which you have promised to give to another give it before a third person***

compells you to give it;

"VASUDEYAM SVAYAM DADYAD BALAD YAD DAPIAYET PARAHA DRUPADO PAHNAVEE RAJYAM DRONENA KRAMYA DAPITAHA"

A gift which you have promised to give to another give it before a third person compells you to give it.

Once upon a time, *Drupada*, the prince of *Panchala* Kingdom and *Drona*, the *son of "Bhardvaja"*, studied under a Guru named "*Agnivesa*".

Drupada, on one occasion, promised to give half of Panchala Kingdom to this childhood friend and fellow student, namely "Dronacharya", when he was crowned as a King. After a few years Drupada was crowned as a King of Panchala Desa;

Dronacharya and his family were destitute and surviving somehow under extreme poverty. Dronacharya approached King Durupada and reminded him about their early days of friendship and requested him to help him *King Durupada brushed aside the claim of friendship of Dronacharya and refused to help him*;

After a few years, *Arjuna*, trained by *Dronacharya* fought a war with *King Drupada* and defeated him. *Arjuna* offered *Durupada* and his Kingdom as a "*Gurudakshina*" to his *Guru Dronacharya.*

Thus *Durupada's Panchala Kingdom* was given to *Dronacharya* at the *behest* (command) of *Arjuna.*

69. ***Try to achieve Purushardhas, namely DHARMA, ARTHA and KAMA, in a mutually harmonious and complimentary manner;***

"SADHAYE DDHARAMA KAMARDHAN PARASPARAMA BADHAKAN TRIVARGA SADKANA BHOOPA BABHO VU HU SAGARA DAYAHA"

Try to achieve Purushardhas, namely DHARMA, ARTHA and KAMA, in a mutually harmonious and complimentary manner;

Pursuit of *Dharma (duty)* depends on the acquisition of *Artha* (Wealth), and *Artha* enables one to fulfil *KAMA* (*Desires*), but none of them should be pursued singly with a exclusion of the other two; one should always try of pursue "TRIVARGAS", namely *DHARMA, ARTHA* and *KAMA* in a *moderate, harmonious and complementary manner.*

"*Sagarudu*", a Sooryavansa King, and a renowned ancestor of *Sri Rama*, many other Kings and many great Rushis (Sages) followed this mode of achieving "*TRIVARGAS*".

70. 1. ***One should always try to safeguard the honour and prestige of one's ancestors.*** 2. ***It is better at least to come up to their standards, but it is the best to enhance further the honour and prestige of one's ancestors.***

"SVA KULANNONYATAM NECCHET TULYAHA SYADADHA VADHIKAHA

SOTKARSHEPE RAGHO RYAMSE RAMO BHOOT SVAKULADHI KAHA"

One should always try to safeguard the honour and prestige of one's ancestors. It is better at least to come up to their standards, but it is the best to enhance further the honour and prestige of one's ancestors.

Sri Rama, sone of *King Dasaradha* was born in the renowned and illustrious *Raghuvansa*. Sri Rama enhanced further its honour and prestige by his *exemplary conduct* and *many deeds of valour*.

71. ***Try to keep your body and soul pure and unsullied (hence bright) by bathing in all "PUNYA TEERTHAS";*** **(Holy water of a river, tank or lake or particular places in the ocean)**

"KURYATTE RTHAOMBUBHEHE POOTAMATMANAM SATATOJJVALAM
LOMASADISTA TEERDEBYAHA PRAPUHU PARDHAHA KRUTARDHATAM"

Try to keep your body and soul pure and unsullied (hence bright) by bathing in all "PUNYA TEERTHAS"; (Holy water of a river, tank or lake or particular places in the ocean)

On the advice of *Lomasa Maharshi*, *Pandavas* bathed in all *Punyateerthas*, and because of spiritual merit so acquired, were able to come out victoriously in the *Kurukshetra War.*

72. ***Try to learn an art or a craft with zeal and diligence, which may help you, when you are overtaken by an adversity or calamity*****; (Zeal = Enthusiasm or ardour)**

"APATKALOPA YUKTASU KALASU SYAT KRUTA SRAMAHA
NRUTYA VRUTTI RVIRATASYA KIREETEE BHAVANE BHAVAT"

Try to learn an art or a craft with zeal and diligence, which may help you, when you are overtaken by an adversity or calamity; (Zeal = Enthusiasm or ardour)

Arjuna, when he was in *INDRALOKA* (Heaven) learnt many powerful "Astras" from Indra and other Devatas; over a period of five years. Finally on the advice of Indra, *Arjuna*, studied and learnt "*NRUTYASASTRA*" (The art of Dance and Music) under the guidance of *Gandharva* named *Chitrasena*.

"*NRUTYASASTRA*" which *Arjuna* had learnt during his stay in "Indraloka", helped him during his "*AGNATHAVASA*" period, when he had to eke out his livelihood, by teaching dancing and music to princesses in the "ANTHAHPURAM" (Inner apartments in a Royal palace set apart of King Virata or women) under the guise of "*Bruhannala*", in the court of *King Virata*.

73. ***Free yourself from undue attachment to worldly pleasures and objects.***

"ARAGABHOGA SUBHAGAHA SYAT PRASAKTA VIRAKTA DHEEHA
RAJYE JANAKA RAJO BHOONNIRLE POMBHASI PADMAVAT"

Free yourself from undue attachment to worldly pleasures and objects;

Once upon a time, there was a King of 'Mithila' named '*Janaka*' he was renowned as a *great JNANI* (A wise man). *King Janaka*, lived and ruled his kingdom in a mentally detached state called "*BHOGA VILASA NIRLIPTITA*", just as a *lotus* remains untouched by water although, there is always water around it.

74. ***A Guru should never forego his respectability by volunteering his services, with an ulterior motive for gain, to an undeserving and unworthy disciple (ASISHYA);***

"ASISHYA SEVAYA LABHA LOBHENA SYAD GURUR LAGHUHU
SAMVARTA YAGNA YACHABHERLLAJJAM LEBHE BRUHASPATIHE"

A Guru should never forego his respectability by volunteering his services, with an ulterior motive for gain, to an *undeserving* and *unworthy disciple (ASISHYA);*

Once upon time, a *King* named '*Samvartaka*' was conducting an '*Yagna*' (an act of worship, a sacrifice any offering or oblation). '*Bruhaspati*' was renowned as the "*Devaguru*" at that time. *Bruhaspati volunteered* his *services* as an "*Acharya*" (Head Priest) for *the yagna of King Samvartaka.* However *King Samvartaka* flatly refused the request of *Devaguru Bruhaspati.* From then onwards *Bruhaspati was laden* (painfully burdened with) *with shame.*

75. ***It is better to give up any association with an unchaste (or fallen) woman, as she is sure to entangle one in undue attachment (RAGAMU) and infatuation; (MOHAMU)***

"NASTASEELAM TYAJENNAREEM RAGAVRUDDHE VIDHAYENEEM
CHANDROCCHISTADHIKA PREETYI PATNEE NINDYA PYA BHOOD GUROHA"

It is better to give up any association with an unchaste (or fallen) woman, as she is sure to entangle one in undue attachment (RAGAMU) and infatuation (MOHAMU); Once upon a time there was *Guru* for all *Devatas*, named '*Bruhaspati*'. Bruhaspati had a very beautiful wife named '*Tara*'.

'*Chandrudu*' was a young and handsome student of *Devaguru Brahaspati.* Tara, the wife of Brahaspati fell in love with the young and handsome "*Chandrudu*". *Tara left her husband and went away with CHANDRUDU. TARA bore a son named "Budhudu" by Chandrudu.*

Bruhaspati brought back his wife 'Tara' from Chandradu, overlooking all her transgressions, because of his undue attachment and infatuation towards her *Bruhaspati*, from then onwards, had to face ridicule and contempt from all, because of this lapse in propriety in his conduct.

76. ***One should not be inordinately addicted to past times such as singing or playing on musical instruments such as a lute (Veena), as they may endanger ones safety;***

"NA GEETA VADYABHIRATER VILASA VYASANEE BHAVET

VEENA VINODA VYASANEE VATSESAHA SATRUNA HRUTAHA"

One should not be inordinately addicted to past times such as singing or playing on musical instruments such as a lute (Veena), as they may endanger ones safety.

Once upon a time there was a *king named "Udayanudu*". He was the ruler of *Kousambee City. Udayanudu was a renowned Lute player of his time.*

The *King* of *Ujjain*, named "*Chanda Mohana Pradyotudu* was an enemy of *King Udayanudu.* He was fully aware of the latter's addiction to Lute playing. *The King of Ujjaine* devised a clever plan to capture the *King of Kousambee*, namely 'Udayanudu'.

Udayanudu was enticed out of the limits of his Kingdom by a "*mechanical elephant*" (made of wood and containing a mechanical device, which enabled it to walk, and in its vast interior, *armed soldiers* were hidden (concealed).

King Udayanudu went on playing on his Lute, and followed the *mechanical elephant unwarily.* At an opportune time, armed soldiers came out of the "*elephant*" captured *King Udayanudu, and took him as a prisoner to Ujjain City.*

77. ***One should not cause distress to a woman known for her delicacy and tenderness by his sharp and pungent remarks.***

"VUDVEJAYENNA TIKSHYENA RAMAHA KUSUMA KOMA LAHA
SOORYO BHRAYA BHAYO CCHITYI TEJO NIJAMA SATA YAT"

One should not cause distress to a woman known for her delicacy and tenderness by his sharp and pungent remarks.

Soorya's (The Sun) wife was named Sangna. *Sangna was the daughter of Visvakarma. Sangna* was terribly scared of the lustre and brightness of 'Soorya'.

To pacify his wife Sangna, Soorya consented to reduce his brilliance by 1/8th fraction of his original brilliance. Out of this 1/8th fraction of Soorrya's brilliance, *Vishnu Chakara, Siva*'s *Trisoolamu Kubera*'s *Pushpakamu* and *Kumara's Saktyaudhamu* came into existense.

78. ***Protect your wealth from evil grabbers otherwise you will become as bankrupt as a lotus whose honey has been robbed off by bumble bees (BOMBINATRIX GLABRA)***

"PADMAVANNA NAYET KOSAM DHOORTA BHRAMARA BHOJYATAM
SURI HE KRAMENA NEETARDAHA SREE HEENO BHOOT PURAM BUDHE HE"

Protect your wealth from evil grabbers otherwise you will become as bankrupt as a lotus whose honey has been robbed off by bumble bees (BOMBINATRIX GLABRA).

Once upon a time, *the ocean (PALAKADALI)* was churned by *Devas* and *Danvas. The ocean* yielded to them many precious things such as 1. *AMRUTAMU* 2. *KALPA VRUKSHAMU* 3. *KAMADHENUVU* 4. *CHANDRUDU* 5. *LAXMI* 6. *VUCCHI*

SRAVAMU 7. *IRAVATAMU* 8. *CHINTAMANI* 9. *KOUSTUBHAMU* 10. *APSARAS*, etc. *and in the end, the ocean became bankrupt.*

79. ***One should cherish reverently, and keep in memory the teachings of great men, otherwise their teachings will fade out of memory, just as water seeps out of a leaky pot*:**

"NOPADESAMRUTAM PRAPTAM BHAGNA KUMBHA NIBHA STYA JET

PARTHO VESMRUTA GEETARDHAHA SASOOYAHA KALAHE BHAVAT"

One should cherish reverently, and keep in memory the teachings of great men, otherwise their teachings will fade out of memory, just as water seeps out of a leaky pot.

Sri Krishna himself gave '*UPADESAMRUTAM*' (namely *Bhagvad Geeta*) to *Arjuna* before the commencement of *Kurukshetra War*. Yet *Arjuna* did not cherish reverently and keep in memory the immortal teachings of *Sri Krishna* contained in "*Bhagvad Geeta*".

During Kurukshetra war, ARJUNA was overcome by anger, jealousy and contentiousness (prone to quarrelsome behaviour) and behaved as if he had never heard "BHAGAVADGEETA"

(The ideal sequence to cherish reverently and to keep in memory the teachings of a great man is as follows:

(1) *MANANAMU* (Retention); (2) *SMARANAMU* (Repeated Recall); (3) *DHARANAMU* (Keeping for ever in the memory); (4) *ACHARANAMU* (finally following the precept in the day to day life)

80. ***A wise parent should never handover his wealth and property to his sons prematurely; if he does so, his value and status will be reduced (i.e.) to less than that of a grass blade***

"NA PUTRAYATTA MISVARYAM KARYAMARTIYAHA KADACHANA

PUTRARPITA PRABHUTVO BHOOD DRHUTARATRA TRUNO PAMAHA"

A wise parent should never hand over his wealth and property to his sons prematurely; if he does so, his value and status will be reduced (i.e.) to less than that of a grass blade.

King Drhutarastra cherished inordinate affection towards his son *Duryodhana* and he handed over the reins of power to *Duryodhana* and his brothers, *rather prematurely. After the transfer of power, Duryodhana and his brothers did not pay any attention to Drutarastra and treated him with scant respect and regard.*

81. ***One should not entrust any work to a man who is enmical or hostile towards self; if one does so, one will be courting ones own ruin.***

"NA SATRUSHESHA DOOSHYANAM SKANDE KARYAM SAMARPAYET

NISHPRATA PO BHAVAT KARNAHA SALYA TEJO VADHARDITAHA"

One should not entrust any work to a man who is enmical or hostile towards self; if one does so, one will be courting one's own ruin.

During *Kurukshetra war, Duryodhana* persuaded *King Salya* to be *the Charioter (SARADHI) of Karna. King Salya had a poor opinion about Karana's lineage and also about his valour and skill in the warfare;*

King Slaya openly insulted and reviled Karna on the battle field many times. *King Salya thus succeeded in undermining the courage and confidence of Karana during the Kurukshetra war.*

82. ***One should not accept hazardous tasks allotted to self even by one's own King, although the latter may tempt you with flattery, attention and rewards.***

"NA LABDHE PRABHU SAMANE PHALA KLESAM SAMASRAYET
ESVARENA DHRUTO MOORDHNE KSHEENA AVA KSHAPA PATEHE"

One should not accept hazardous tasks allotted to self even by one's own King, although the latter may tempt you with flattery, attention and rewards;

Moon is carried on the head by *Siva*, and *inspite of such promixity with Siva, moon is still subject to waxing and waning;*

(*The powerful and the rich men, be friend a poor, weak and a lowly person for various ulterior reasons. One should not be carried away by such flattery, attention and rewards and accept hazardous tasks allotted by them and for them. One's own safety, security and good reputation should never be sacrificed to please them.*

Finally one's own status in the society is determined only by one's own skill, ability and tasks successfully completed by him only and not by the expedient (advantageous; advisable on practical rather than moral grounds) patronage of the powerful and the rich.

83. ***One should never forsake the path of Sadachar (Good Conduct)***

"SRUTI SMRUTUKTA MACHARAM NATYAJET SADHU SEVITAM
DITYANAM SREE VEYOGO BHOOT SATYA DHARMA CHUTA ATMANĀM"

One should never forsake the path of SADACHARA (GOOD CONDUCT), as laid down in the VEDAS, SMRUTIS and as practiced by SAJJANAS (Men of Virtue);

DANAVAS (RAKSHASAS) forsake *Satyam* (Truth) and *Dharma* (Virtue) and *Sadachara* (Good Conduct), and thereby *forfeited* (were deprived of) the chance of possessing wealth and enjoying prosperity.

Vedas and *Dharma Sastras* have laid down the principles of *SADACHARA* (Good Conduct) SAJJANAS always try to follow the path of *SADACHARA* (Good Conduct) *Satyam (Truth) is the foundation of Sadachara. One should never forsake Satyam (Truth). Those who have forsaken Truth are bound to be evil; where Truth is enshrined, there you will find prosperity, renown and victory.*

84. ***Goddess of wealth and prosperity (Laxmi) always seeks the company of a Sajjana(***

a man of virtue).

"SRIYAHA KURYAT PALAYENYA BANDHAYA GUNA SANGRAHAM
DITYAM STAYAKTVA SRETA DEVA NIRGUNA SSAGUNAHA SREYAHA"

Goddess of wealth and prosperity (*Laxmi*) always seeks the company of a Sajjana(a man of virtue). "*Laxmi*" *inherently is very fickle and tends to flee from one to another*; If one wants to prevent this fleeing of Laxmi from one to another, one should equip oneself with *ropes* called "*SUGUNAS*" (Virtues), *to tie up Laxmi and thus make her stay in that place for a longer duration*;
Laxmi forsook the company of Danavas (Rakshasas) who had abandoned their Virtues (Sugunas) and sought the company of *Devatas*, who were renowned for their virtues (Sugunas).
Laxmi is inherently fickle and tends to flee from one to another. However *Laxmi always seeks the company of those who are renowned for virtue, Courage and mercy, and when these exemplary qualities are neglected or abandoned by them, Laxmi moves on to another, who has the above mentioned exemplary qualities namely virtue, courage and mercy. This is the primary reason for the fleeting nature of Laxmi.*

85. ***One should not touch with one's feet and defile (spoil the purity of) the following 1. FIRE 2. COW 3. GURU AND 4. DEVATAS.***
One should not touch with hands contaminated by spittle or Salivā and thereby defile it GHRUTAM (or Ghee),

"PADAGNIM GAM GURUM DEVAM NA CHOCCHISTAHA SPRUSED GMRUTAM
DANA VANAM VINASTA SREE RUCCHISTA SPRUSTA SARPISHAM

One should not touch with one's feet and defile (spoil the purity of) the following 1. *FIRE* 2. *COW* 3. *GURU* and 4. *DEVATAS*.
One should not touch with hands contaminated by spittle or Saliva GHRUTAM (or Ghee) and there by defile it;
Once upon a time *Danavas* (Rakshasas) defiled (polluted) *Ghrutam* (or Ghee) by touching it with hands contaminated by spittle or saliva;
Laxmi (The goddess of wealth and prosperity), because of the above mentioned act of defilement, forsook the company of *Danavas (Rakshasas)*
Uncleanness or impurity of the body paves the way for impure and improper conduct and impure and improper conduct entangles one in wickedness, and hence uncleanness and impurity of the body and mind should at all times be eschewed (avoided).

86. 1.***The marriage of a bride from a higher social status (or caste) with a bridegroom from a lower social status (or caste), is not advisable (such marriages are called Pratiloma Vivahas) although, one may hope to facilitate a rise in the social status of the bridge groom from a lower social status;***

2."PARTILOMA VIVAHAS" are fraught (attended with) with many undesirable consequences.

"PRATILOMA VIVAHESHU NA KURYADUNNATE SPRUHAM
YAYATEHE SUKRA KANYAYAM SASPRUHO MLECCHA TAMGATAHA"

1.The marriage of a bride from a higher social status (or caste) with a bridegroom from a lower social status (or caste), is not advisable (such marriages are called PRATILOMA VIVAHAS) although, one may hope to facilitate a rise in the social status of the bridegroom from a lower social status.

2."PARTILOMA VIVAHAS" are fraught (attended with) with many undesirable consequences.

Sukracharya was the renowned Guru for all *Danavas (Rakshashas).* He had a daughter named *DEVAYANI. Devayani was married to king YAYATI by the consent of Sukracharya.* However, as a consequence of this *PRATILOMA VIVAHA, King yayati* later became a "*MLECCHA*" (A beef eating barbarian or a foreigner) most probably because of a curse of Sukracharya.

(*A bride from a higher social status or caste is not likely to forego her pride in her lineage and is sure to consider the bridegroom from a lower social status or caste as an inferior person; she will try her level best to have complete control over him, and in case she fails in her objective she is likely to be enraged with him and will not even hesitate to harm him in one way or the other; Hence "Pratiloma Vivahas" are fraught with many undesirable consequences and are better avoided*)

87. ***Do not jeer or jest at people who have no handsome personality (or deformed) wealth, lineage or learning.***

"ROOPARDHA KULA VIDYADE HEENAM NOPA HASE NNARAM
HASANTAMA SAPANNANDEE RAVANAM VANARA NANAHA"

Do not jeer scoft (joke in words) or jest at people who have no handsome personality (or deformed) wealth, lineage or learning;

Once upon a time, *Ravana* met *Nandi* at the *Kailas Mountain,* during his travels in the "*Pushpaka Vimanamu*". *Nandi* was standing guard at the entrance to *Siva's abode.*

Ravana jeered at Nandi as the latter's face resembled that of a monkey. Nandi was enraged by the insolent behaviour of Ravana, and cursed him and his descendants to be destroyed *by hordes of monkeys.*

88. 1.***It is better to try to dispel any cause of enmity or hatred among relations.***
2.***One should not take sides in a conflict among relations, and thus escalate it further.***

"BANDHOONAM VARAYED VIRAM NIKA PAKSHASRAYO BHAVET
KURU PANDAVA SANGRAME YUYUDHE NA HALA YUDHA HA"

It is better to try to dispel any cause of enmity or hatred among relations;
One should not take sides in a conflict among relations, and thus escalate it further;
During *the Kurukshetra War, Balarama (Elder brother of Sri Krishna), refused to take sides, and remained neutral throughout the war.*

89. ***To be kind, and to help others is the quintessence of mundane (worldly) existence;***

"PAROPAKARAM SAMSARASARAM KURVEETA SATVAVAN
NIDADHE BHAGAVAN BUDDAHA SARVASATVO DHRUTOU DHIYAM"

To be kind, and to help others is the quintessence of mundane (worldly) existence;
Bhagavan Buddha endeavoured to help and better the lot of all living creatures.

90. 1.***One should try to help and aid, one's poverty stricken relations;***
2.***One should try to succour (come to the rescue of) endangered friends;***

"BEBHRUYAD BANDHU MADHANAM MITRAM TRAYETA DURGATAM
BANDHU MITROPA JEEVYO BHOO DARDHI KALPA DRUMO BALIHE"

One should try to help and aid, one's poverty stricken relations;
One should try to succour (come to the rescue of) endangered friends;
Emperor Bali acquired everlasting renown as a "*KALPAVRUKSHA*" for all his relations friends and the needy in the world because of his *unstinting* (lavish, ungrudging) generosity.
(Kalpavruksha = metaphorically a very generous donor)

91. ***It is forbidden to use deceptive methods such as Mantras or Tantras (Magical ceremonies performed to kill somebody) to kill an enemy.***

"NA KURYADABHICHARO GRA VADHADE KUHAKAHA KRIYAHA
LAXMANENDRAJIT KRUTYADYABHE CHARA MAYO HATAHA"

It is forbidden to use deceptive methods such as Mantras or Tantras (Magical ceremonies performed to kill somebody) to kill an enemy.

INDRAJIT used many deceptive tactics such as *Marana Homas, Mantras,* and *Tantras* (Magical ceremonies performed to kill somebody) while fighting with *Lakshmana* during *Rama Ravana Sangrama.*

However *Lakshmana* fought with *Indrajit* in an *open battle and killed him relying only his valour and weapons.*

92. ***Follow the natural sequence of periods of life (namely Asramas : Life in a religious point of view being divided into four such periods They are 1. Brahmacharya (5-25 years) 2. Garhasthyamu (25-50 years) 3. Vanaprasthamu (From 50 years) (preparatory stage for the Sanyasa Asrama) 4. Sanyasa Asramamu : (The final***

Asramam).

"BRAHMACHAREE GRUHASTHAHA SYAD VANAPRASTHO YATEHE KRAMAT
ASRAMADA SRAMAM YATA YAYATE PRAMUKHA NRUPAHA"

Follow the natural sequence of periods of life (namely Asramas : Life in a religious point of view being divided into four such periods They are 1. *Brahmacharya* (5-25 years) 2. *Garhasthyamu* (25-50 years) 3. *Vanaprasthamu* (From 50 years) (preparatory stage for the Sanyasa Asrama) 4. *Sanyasa Asramamu* : (The final Asramam). One renounces the world completely, becomes an ascetic and strives to achieve Moksha (Liberation)

Greats King like Yayate, Yagnavalaka, Ekshvaku etc. followed this natural sequence of Asramas, and achieved renown in the pursuit of Dharma.

93. ***Give away your surplus wealth to the deserving and needy, otherwise your wealth will be taken away and spent by others.***

"KURYAD VYAYAM SVAHASTENA PRABHOOTA DHANA SAMPADAM
AGASTYA BHUKTE VATAPOU KOSASYANNIU HA KRUTO VYAYAHA"

Give away your surplus wealth to the deserving and needy, otherwise your wealth will be taken away and spent by others;

Once upon a time, there was a *Rakshasa* named '*Vatape*'. *Vatape acquired enoromous wealth, by hoarding up all the wealth of his numerous victims.*

Finally *Vatape* himself was eaten up by *Maharshe Agastya. Later all the wealth hoarded up by Vatape was taken away and spent by others.*

94. ***Do not do an evil deed for which you will have to grieve and repent till to the end of your life.***

"JANMAVADHE NA TAT KURYADANTE SANTĀPAKARI YAT
SASMARIKA SIRAHA SESHAHA SEETA KLESAM DASANANAHA"

Do not do an evil deed for which you will have to grieve and repent till to the end of your life.

Ravana was grief stricken and filled with remorse for the evil deed of kidnapping *Sita* (*the wife of Sri Rama*), even unto the last moment of his life (i.e.) even when he had only one head, which was about to be finally severed by the arrows of Sri Rama.

95. ***When a man has grown old, and when the hair on his head has changed to white colour it is wiser to renounce the world and live in a TAPOVANA (A penance grove or wood) for the rest of his days.***

"JARASUBRESHU KESESHU TAPOVANA RUCHIRBHA VET

ANTE VANAM YAYURDHEERAHA KURU POORVA MAHEEBHUJAHA"

When a man has grown old, and when the hair on his head has changed to white colour it is wiser to renounce the world and live in a TAPOVANA (A penance grove or wood) for the rest of his days.
Great Kings such as *Kuru* and *his renowned ancestors*, when they were over taken by old age, renounced the world, and lived in Tapovanas for the rest of their days.

96. ***Endeavour to achieve Moksha (or Liberation), when you are overtaken by old age.*** **Moksha is the remedy for the travails of old age and it prevents rebirth.**

"PUNARJANMA JARACCHEDA KOVIDAHA SYAD VAYA HA KSHAYE
VIDURENA PUNARJANMA BEEJAM JNANAANALE HUTAM"

Endeavour to achieve Moksha (or Liberation), when you are over taken by old age. Moksha is the remedy for the travails of old age and it prevents rebirth.
Vidura pursued "*Jnana*" from his childhood; he burnt (or burned) all the 'seeds' of good and evil deeds (Karmas) done by him in a fire called "*Jnana*" and *thus released* himself from *Rebirth.*

97. ***When your earthly existence is about to end, try to visualize "ATMAJYOTI" (The eternal light in the soul) in your own heart.***

"PARAMATMANAMANTE NANTAR JYOTEHE PASYET SANATANAM
TAT PRAPTYA YOGINO JATAHA SUKA SANTANA VADAYAHA"

When your earthly existence is about to end, try to visualize "ATMAJYOTI" (The eternal light in the soul) in your own heart.
Sukayogi, Bheesma and *others were able to realize* "ATMAJYOTI" (The eternal light in the soul) *in their own hearts, and thus attained 'Moksha'*

98. ***Try to perform deeds of virtue throughout your life, even when you are not able to live to the end of a normal life span.***

"PRAPTAVADHERA JEEVEPE JEEVET SUKRUTA SANTATEHE
JEEVANTYADYAPE MANDHTRU MUKHAHA KAYIRYASO MAYAHA"

Try to perform deeds of virtue throughout your life, even when you are not able to live to the end of a normal life span.

Great men like Mandhata and others performed many good deeds during their life time. They achieved everlasting renown, though their lives ended ages ago.

99. ***When your earthly existence is about to end, pray to and worship "VISHNU", who is the embodiment of all bliss and who will destroy all your afflictions.***

"ANTE SANTOSHADAM VISHNUM SMARE DDHANTARA MAPADAM
SARATALPAGATO BHEESMAHA SASMARA GARUDA DHVAJAM"

When your earthly existence is about to end, pray to, and worship "Vishnu", who is the embodiment of all bliss and who will destroy all your afflictions.

BHEESMACHARYA, lying on a bed of arrows, and when his earthly existence was about to end, prayed to and worshipped "*Garuda Vahana* (or Vishnu), and *thus attained "Moksha"* (*or Liberation*). (GARUDA = A mythological bird, which is the vehicle of Vishnu)

100. *KSHEMENDRA, a disciple of Vyasa wrote "Charu Charya" (Exemplary Conduct) which is approved and appreciated by Sajjanas (Men of Virtue), in a concise form, after thorough deliberation and reflection.*

"SRAVYA SREE VYASADASENA SAMA SENA SATAM MATA
KSHEMENDRENA VICHARYEYAM CHARUCHARYA PRAKASITA"

KSHEMENDRA, a disciple of Vyasa wrote 'Charu Charya' (Exemplary Conduct) which is approved and appreciated by Sajjanas (Men of Virtue), in a concise form, after thorough deliberation and reflection.

Sources

1. Charu Charya —Kshemendra, Telugu translation by P. V. Ramana Reddy, 1979
2. Charu Charya — Kshemendra, Telugu translation by Eluripati Anantharamaiah, 1980.

❑❑❑